Teachers, Schools, and Society

fifth edition

Teachers, Schools, and Society

Myra Pollack Sadker
Late Professor, The American University

David Miller Sadker
The American University

Boston   Burr Ridge, IL   Dubuque, IA   Madison, WI   New York   San Francisco   St. Louis
Bangkok   Bogotá   Caracas   Lisbon   London   Madrid   Mexico City   Milan
New Delhi   Seoul   Singapore   Sydney   Taipei   Toronto

McGraw-Hill Higher Education

A Division of The McGraw-Hill Companies

TEACHERS, SCHOOLS, AND SOCIETY, FIFTH EDITION

Copyright © 2000, 1997, 1994, 1991, 1988 by The McGraw-Hill Companies, Inc. All rights reserved.
Printed in the United States of America. Except as permitted under the United States Copyright Act of
1976, no part of this publication may be reproduced or distributed in any form or by any means, or stored
in a data base or retrieval system, without the prior written permission of the publisher.

This book is printed on acid-free paper.

2 3 4 5 6 7 8 9 0 QPH/QPH 0 9 8 7 6 5 4 3 2 1 0

ISBN 0–07–228795–0

Editorial director: *Jane E. Vaicunas*
Sponsoring editor: *Beth Kaufman*
Developmental editor: *Cara Harvey*
Marketing manager: *Daniel M. Loch*
Project manager: *Renee C. Russian*
Senior production supervisor: *Sandra Hahn*
Coordinator of freelance design: *Michelle D. Whitaker*
Photo research coordinator: *John C. Leland*
Supplement coordinator: *Stacy A. Patch*
Compositor: *GAC–Indianapolis*
Typeface: *9/12 Stone Serif*
Printer: *Quebecor Printing Book Group/Hawkins, TN*

Freelance cover/interior designer: *Christopher Reese*
Cover image: © *Diana Ong/SuperStock*
Photo research: *Feldman and Associates, Inc.*

Photo credits section for this book appear on page 593 and is considered an extension of the copyright page.

Library of Congress Cataloging-in-Publication Data

Sadker, Myra.
  Teachers, schools, and society / Myra Pollack Sadker, David Miller
Sadker. — 5th ed.
    p.   cm.
  Includes bibliographical references and index.
  ISBN 0–07–228795–0
  1. Teaching.   2. Education—United States—History.
3. Educational sociology—United States.   4. Education—Study and
teaching—United States.   5. Teachers—Training of—United States.
I. Sadker, David Miller, 1942– . II. Title.
LB1775.S24 2000
371.102—dc21   99–27512
                                                              CIP

www.mhhe.com

About the Authors

Dr. Myra Sadker was professor of Education and Dean of the School of Education until 1995. Dr. Sadker wrote the first book on gender bias in America's schools in 1973, and became a leading advocate for equal educational opportunities. She died while undergoing treatment for breast cancer in 1995. In her name, *Myra Sadker Advocates* was established to continue her efforts and create more equitable and effective schools. You are invited to learn more about Myra's contributions and the work of Myra Sadker Advocates by visiting the website established in her name: www.sadker.org

Dr. David Sadker is a professor at The American University (Washington, DC) and has taught at the elementary, middle school and high school levels. David Sadker has been a teacher educator for three decades, conducting teacher preparation programs both in the United States and overseas. Dr. Sadker and his late wife gained a national reputation for their work in confronting gender bias and sexual harassment. He has directed more than a dozen federal education grants, authored five books and more than seventy-five articles in journals such as *Phi Delta Kappan, Harvard Educational Review,* and *Psychology Today.* His research and writing document sex bias from the classroom to the boardroom. He has published and trained in areas ranging from bias in professional communications to sexual harassment, from effective strategies in management to effective strategies in the classroom.

The Sadkers' work has been reported in hundreds of newspapers and magazines, including *USA Today, USA Weekend, Parade Magazine, Business Week, The Washington Post, The London Times, The New York Times, Time,* and *Newsweek.* They appeared on local and national television and radio shows, such as *The Today Show, Good Morning America, The Oprah Winfrey Show,* Phil Donahue's *The Human Animal,* National Public Radio's *All Things Considered,* and twice on *Dateline: NBC* with Jane Pauley. The Sadkers received the American Educational Research Association's award for the best review of research published in the United States in 1991, professional service award in 1995, and the Eleanor Roosevelt Award from The American Association of University Women in 1995. The Sadkers' book, *Failing at Fairness: How Our Schools Cheat Girls,* was published by Touchstone Press in 1995.

Contents In Brief

Contents

3 Teacher Effectiveness   49

4 Student Diversity   82

8 Controversy over Who Controls the Curriculum   234

intermission: **Part 2 Schools and Curriculum**

part three Foundations

9 The History of American Education   280

14 Technology in Education   460

15 Your First Classroom   491

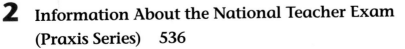

inter**mission:** **Part 4 Tomorrow**   **525**

Appendices

Preface

We want you to enjoy reading this textbook and to learn a great deal. We have written this book to share with you the excitement we feel about teaching.

Teachers, Schools, and Society is designed for introductory courses in teacher education variously labeled Introduction to Education; Introduction to Teaching, Schools, and Society; or Foundations of Education. The primary intent of such a course, whatever its label, is to provide you with sufficiently broad yet detailed exposure to the realities of teaching. The text should help you answer those all-important questions: Do I want to become a teacher? What do I need to become the best teacher possible? What should a professional in the field of education know? To help you answer these questions, we offer a panoramic and stimulating view of education.

Content Coverage

We have elected to view the field from several vantage points. In Part One, you will see the world of teachers and students from a new perspective—the teacher's side of the desk. In Part Two, your field of vision will be widened, so that you can examine the structure, culture, and curriculum of that complex place called school. Part Three then examines the broad forces (historical, legal, financial, organizational, and philosophical) that provide an educational foundation. In Part Four, you will have a chance to examine, debate, and speculate about issues and trends. Following each of the four parts are *Inter-missions,* based on the *INTASC* principles. The *Inter-missions* offer you the opportunity to develop crucial skills related to the teaching profession and to start your teaching portfolio. The *Appendix* contains information about teacher licensing, including relevant addresses; National Teacher Examination Information; and an *Observation Manual* with guidelines and strategies for collecting important information about teaching as you observe in schools.

Style of Presentation

The trouble with panoramic views is that the observer is often at such a distance from what is being viewed that all richness of detail is lost. Vague outlines devoid of human interaction dominate the scene. To clear this haze, at various points throughout the text we have replaced our wide-angle lens with a more intimate view that captures the human drama as well. For example, in many chapters, we introduce traditionally dry, abstract topics with illustrative scenarios that help personalize and dramatize the topic at hand. The *In the News* feature offers insightful, humorous, and poignant educational news items taken from newspapers, the Internet, and the popular press. *Class Acts* offer personal insights into teaching and schooling. Several "pop" quizzes probe your prior knowledge and beliefs and introduce, even personalize, governance, law, and philosophy. We hope that these stylistic elements, along with a writing style that is deliberately informal rather than academic, will add spice and human interest to the text.

Changes in This Edition

This fifth edition of *Teachers, Schools, and Society* is designed to improve an already comprehensive text through the following changes:

- *New features* include
  Class Acts is a collection of personal stories by exceptional students and teachers.
  Inter-missions include activities to help you reflect on teaching, build a portfolio, and enhance your understanding of the concepts in this text. (The *Inter-missions* are based on the *INTASC* standards.)
  In the News provides recent, relevant, humorous, and poignant stories taken from the pages of today's newspapers and the Internet.
  Our Textbook Web site: www.mhhe.com/sadker
  Photos in Contrast offers visual evidence of how education is shaped by time, economics, and culture.
  Focus Questions and *Chapter Previews* offer an initial overview of chapter highlights.
  Key Terms and People and chapter *Summaries* pull together the main ideas discussed in each chapter.
- *New/expanded topics and issues.* Topics receiving increased attention in this edition include induction, technology, ethics, student diversity, multiple and emotional intelligences, national standards and testing, and the emergence of EMOs (Educational Maintenance Organizations).
- *New chapters.* A chapter on the induction period, "Your First Classroom," has been added, exploring the issues and resources that are a part of that first teaching experience. "Technology in Education" also is new, offering insights into the fast pace of computer technology in schools. To make room for these additions, we have combined former Chapters 10 and 12 into "Financing and Governing America's Schools" (Chapter 10). Also, ethics was included as the "Law and Ethics" chapter was reshaped (Chapter 11), as was "The Struggle for Educational Opportunity," which pulls together issues on student diversity and contemporary social challenges. The chapter "Schools, and Beyond" now includes a great deal more on the choice and options issues involved in schools. The four major parts of the text have also been modified and retitled.
- *Multicultural focus.* Special attention is given to the topic of student diversity, which may be the single most critical issue facing our schools and society in the decades ahead. Accordingly, we have updated "Student Diversity" (Chap-ter 4). History, curricular issues, relevant laws, and instructional strategies that impact diversity have been infused throughout the book. We have also reorganized our important discussion of women's struggle for educational equality.
- *Technology* has been greatly expanded throughout the text, as well as the "Technology in Schools" chapter. Technological insights are infused throughout the book.
- *Web site.* The web site that accompanies this book offers additional learning resources, review questions to help you prepare for examinations, addresses and links to supporting web sites and information, and the opportunities to

speak with students in other institutions using this text and to chat with the author at prescheduled times. You can also visit the Virtual High School at www.concord.org! Visit our web site at www.mhhe.com/sadker

- ***Accompanying instructional and learning resources.*** This new edition of *Teachers, Schools, and Society* is accompanied by
  1. *Instructor's manual and test bank.* For each chapter, the instructor is provided with a brief overview, a list of learning objectives, and a variety of in-class and field activities. The test bank includes hundreds of matching, true-false, multiple-choice, short-answer, and essay questions in written or electronic format.
  2. *Overhead transparencies.* A set of color overhead transparencies is available free to users of this text. These transparencies include figures from the book, as well as outside material prepared especially for this text. Many also available on *PowerPoint.*
  3. *Web site support.* Student projects, activities, resources, links to relevant sights and even practice questions can be assigned to support instructional opportunities.
  4. *Videotape.* Created especially for this text, the videotape explores several of the book's key concepts. More than passive viewing, the tape is designed to encourage student analysis of classroom scenes and to spark discussions of relevant issues. This videotape brings elementary and secondary school realities to the college classroom.

Acknowledgments

In March 1995, Myra died undergoing treatment for breast cancer. She worked on this textbook even while undergoing chemotherapy, and she was always the major force behind providing a student-friendly introduction to teaching. She will always be the primary author of this book.

In the fall of 1995, two graduate assistants, Christine Cozadd and Jane Lonnquist, helped conceptualize, research, draft ideas, and critique drafts with incredible professionalism and insight. They were and are gifts, and I am deeply in their debt. Myra would have been proud of Jane and Chris, both as colleagues and as teachers.

In this fifth edition, veteran of the classroom and new parent Chris was enlisted once again and edited every word of this text. She edits with precision and tact, a rare combination. But, more important, she reads with intelligence and insight, and the structure of the book is more logically organized and more coherent, thanks to her talents. If she ever moves from this area, I will consider relocating.

When Phyllis Lerner and I were married, she had no idea how stressful this literary pregnancy would be. Little sleep, meals at strange hours of the day, personal disputes that erupted from nowhere—but, nine months later, there you are, parents of a wonderful book. And you look back and wonder: was it worth it? Yup. This book is stronger, more interesting, and more relevant because of her efforts. Her twenty-nine years of working with educators is reflected on the book's pages. She has become a major contributor to this text. While the Inter-missions bear her name and her practical wisdom, all the chapters reflect her comments and contributions. She has made this book more student-friendly and multicultural. I was lucky to have her participate. She is lucky that this year is over.

Jackie Sadker, one of two extraordinary daughters, did major revisions on Chapter 7, "What Students Are Taught in Schools." The first draft of this book was written before Jackie started school. Now she is a contributor. It shows you that even bright and gifted children can wander from the straight and narrow and become involved in all sorts of unpredictable behavior. Thanks, Jackie.

Jen Engle, my new graduate assistant, worked on this edition of the textbook and has grown from researcher to idea woman. She tracked down references, checked and updated charts, and began suggesting ideas and approaches. She has helped enormously. Thanks, Jen.

In previous editions, others have contributed to this text, and their efforts are included in this latest edition. Sarah Irvine-Belson, my colleague at American University, became the textbook's tech-expert. She reviewed the technology chapter, contributed ideas and materials, and drafted some of the computer and Internet applications. I am indebted to her. We would like to thank Daniel Spiro, Lynette Long, and Elizabeth Ihle for their work on the Philosophy of Education chapter. Nancy Gorenberg researched several topics and was particularly helpful in presenting legal issues. Elsie Lindemuth, Mary Donald, June Winter, Kirstin Hill, Kate Volker, Ward Davis, Pat Silverthorn, Jacqueline Sadker, Julia Masterson, and Amy Monaghan were researchers, uncovering critical and contemporary resources. Jacqueline Sadker prepared the index for both the third and fourth editions of this text. Kathryn McNerney researched and updated sections about future developments, as well as the *Observation Manual*.

Our editor, Beth Kaufman, was a constant source of ideas and encouragement, a partner and friend in shaping and revising this text. Her support made this venture much sweeter. Cara Harvey, developmental editor, took charge of the production and whipped the manuscript into shape (us too!). Our thanks to Renee Russian, our project manager, for transforming manuscript into book in record-breaking fashion. Thanks and kudos to Shirley Pollack and Robin Carter for their patience and skill in typing early versions of the manuscript. We also want to thank the following users of *Teachers, Schools, and Society* for generously sharing with us their experiences in teaching the book:

Larry Julian, *Brewton Parker College;* Robert Hewitt, *Edison Community College;* Alvin Futrell, *Henderson State University;* Marianne Reynolds, *Mercer County Community College;* Nancy Estes, *Broward Community College;* Thomas O'Keefe, *Bucks Community College;* Philip Matlock, *Columbia State Community College;* Leslie Swetnam, *Metropolitan State College of Denver;* Kaye Abight, *Missouri State Southern College;* Jerry Long, *Emporia State University;* Pat Novak, *Florida International University;* Marie Roos, *Jackson State University;* Allan Ten Eyck, *Grand Valley State;* Norris D. Fox, *University of Northern Texas;* Richard Simmons, *College of DuPage;* Robert Marsh, *University of Texas at Tyler;* Robert A. Levin, *Youngstown State University*

Finally, proving that one's physical size is not a measure of one's contributions, I would like to thank my daughters, Robin and Jackie, for their tolerance, insight, and love. When they were in elementary school (during the first edition of this book), they endured the piles of paper, research notes, and drafts that made our house literally a version of the paper chase. At the time of this fifth edition, Jackie is working in the United States Senate, and Robin, now Dr. Sadker, is beginning her career in internal medicine. The editions that preceded this one all benefited from their ideas and critiques and their growing pains. They are the two most special people in my life, and Myra and I continue to dedicate this book to them.

David Miller Sadker

Teachers, Schools, and Society

One

chers and Students

Class Act

TO: Mary, Music Department
AT: Northville High School
RE: Your students
FROM: Gideon Sanders, ComedySportz

Dear Mary and Student Group,

Many times after students have attended a show, they write letters to thank the performers. Well, I had to write you first and thank you for attending the show on your trip to Washington, DC. My gratitude is extended to you on many levels, and I will explain.

I have been with ComedySportz for two years now, and this is the first time I have experienced a school group as large and as well tuned in as yours. The enthusiasm of the students, especially in such a close setting, was infectious. As the energy of the crowd increased, my level of performing energy/intensity rose to match. The room turned electric, the performance was enjoyed by all, including those on stage, and everyone went home a winner.

You'll recall that, following my training at Clown College, I worked for one year with the international touring company of Barnum and Bailey Circus. I just finished a graduate program in International Affairs, and since January I have been searching for the right employment. I have come across things that interest me, but nothing that really sparked my fire to ignite the passion I seek from a job.

Thursday night's show for me was an epiphany (sorry, no beam of light leading my way or glowing flames surrounding the kids). While I was driving home, I reveled in the feeling that we had entertained, and people had left happy. Then I realized, it is just as important that I walk away happy. Sure, I have had shows that have left me with a good feeling, and thinking that people would be warm all over for the rest of the evening. However, teenagers and young ones to me are worth my best work. They appreciate it, they enjoy it, they can't get enough of it, and they can learn from it. And what really struck me was that I cannot get enough of them.

I have found the employment path that will bring me the happiness I seek—education. And in no small part the students from Northville High School Chorus–Spring Trip 1998 are responsible for this. I wanted to express a great deal of gratitude and wish each individually, by name if I could remember them all, much success.

Northville, and I say this jokingly to many loyal fans at the end of a show, but for the first time I can say it with absolute honesty, YOU WERE THE BEST AUDIENCE I EVER HAD.

Sincerely and gratefully,

Your friend and future teacher,

H. Gideon Sanders

Fall 1998
Social Studies Methods
American University

1

Becoming a Teacher

Focus Questions

- What are the advantages and disadvantages of being a teacher?
- How has teacher preparation changed over the years?
- Should teaching be considered a "profession"?
- What are the satisfactions—and complaints—of today's teachers?
- How do educators and the public differ on how teachers should be educated?

Chapter Preview

You have watched teachers in action for most of your life, but, as students, you have had a unique view of their world (and they of yours!). This chapter offers you a glimpse of classroom life, but this time through the teacher's eyes. To get a sense of what teachers think and feel, "balance sheets" shed light on multiple perspectives of life in the classroom, both the pros and cons.

In the past, teachers' second-class citizenship was evident by their meager wages, the pressures they felt to conform to strict moral and social codes, and their lack of legal rights and political tools to change these conditions. Times have changed. With schools now the center of a sometimes stormy national debate on educational reform and renewal, teachers are also experiencing the winds of change. Teachers' salaries have gone up, and so have the public's expectations of what teachers should accomplish. Your study of education comes at a propitious time, a period of ferment and change as teachers move toward a more professional, more influential role in U.S. society. Many economists, journalists, and politicians believe that the future economic health of the nation will be determined in our classrooms. This chapter will offer you an insight into the fascinating interplay between the public's perception of what our schools should be about and the ways in which educators shape those schools.

Welcome to our classroom.

What Are You Doing for the Rest of Your Life?

In a "Peanuts" cartoon, Linus comments that "no problem is so big or complicated that it can't be run away from." As usual, Charles Schulz succinctly highlights a human frailty shared by most of us—the tendency to put aside our problems or critical questions in favor of day-to-day routine. In fact, it is amazing how little care and consideration many of us give to choosing a career. It is always easier to go to the movies or study for the next exam than it is to reflect on and plan for the future. This is probably one reason the question "What are you going to be when you grow up?" is so frequently asked but so infrequently answered with any conviction.

A careful analysis of who you are and where you are going can help you determine the extent of your commitment to teaching. For some of you, teaching may become a forty-year career filled with joy and satisfaction. For others, teaching may be limited to only a few years spent in the classroom, one of several careers you explore during your working years. And, for others, this course will help you reach an equally useful and important decision: teaching is definitely not a good match for your interests or skills.

To help you analyze your commitment to and compatibility with teaching, the following series of Teaching Balance Sheets summarize many of the advantages and disadvantages of teaching. Read and reflect on them by yourself first, and then you may want to discuss them with a friend or classmate. This should help you gain greater awareness of the realities of teaching and whether it is the right profession for you.

TEACHING BALANCE SHEET 1   WORKING WITH PEOPLE

The Good News
Among the Very Young at Heart . . .
If you enjoy being in contact with others, particularly young people, teaching could be the right job for you. Almost the entire working day is spent in human interaction. Your discussions will include an amazing array of topics—from rules for adding fractions to procedures for feeding pet snakes, from an analysis of *The Catcher in the Rye* to advice on applying to colleges. If you truly enjoy children, the pleasure of these interactions will be heightened, because young people are so often funny, fresh, and spontaneous. They will make you laugh and they will make you cry, but always they will make you feel needed. As America's students become increasingly diverse, you will find yourself learning about different cultures and different life experiences. Your life will be enriched, by the varied worlds of different children—black, white, Hispanic, Asian, blended—all kinds of children, who will broaden your horizons.

As one Denver high school teacher says, "I think that for the first time in my life, I feel useful. I didn't feel that way at the insurance company when I was pushing buttons and managing people. . . . They were machines, the whole outfit

was a machine. But [in teaching] you're working with exciting people. I find high school kids exciting. They're doing things, and they're looking for people to help them do things."[1]

When you have free time away from the classroom, you can join friends and colleagues in the faculty room and discuss anything from the movie you saw last night to the effectiveness of the new curricular materials your school has just purchased. Of course, if you want some quiet time to grade papers, plan lessons, or simply rest, you can usually get that in the faculty room too.

The Bad News
Stop the Crowd—I Want to Get Away
There is so much involvement with others that sometimes, perhaps right in the middle of a language arts lesson when fifteen kids have their hands in the air, you may feel like saying, "Stop, everybody. I feel like being alone for the next fifteen minutes. I'm going out for a cup of coffee." However, given the hectic pace of classroom interaction, such announcements are virtually impossible. For the major part of each day, your job demands that you be involved with

(Balance Sheet 1 continues on next page)

people in a fast-paced and intense way—whether you feel like it or not. In fact, according to researchers, you will be involved in as many as one thousand verbal exchanges in a single day.

Equally as important as the degree of involvement is whom you are involved with—in this case, children. Even if you love young people, there undoubtedly will be times when they will get on your nerves, as when there is one Internet terminal and twelve kids want it.

Being surrounded by children all day can have strange effects on adult behavior. One 33-year-old teacher said, "I knew something was wrong when I began to skip out of school."[2] Another woman who taught in a kindergarten tells of the time she warned her 40-year-old brother "to be sure and put on his galoshes. Wow! Did he give me a strange look."[3]

And teaching children from very diverse backgrounds, children with varied racial, linguistic, and cultural origins, can be particularly challenging. As America's classrooms become more multicultural, teachers will increasingly find themselves stretching beyond their own background, pushing to learn how best to teach children whose lives may differ radically from their own.

For most teachers, it is just them and a crowd of kids, sometimes kids very different from the ones they grew up with. Funny, but you can feel very alone under those circumstances.

TEACHING BALANCE SHEET 2   RECOGNITION OF YOUR EFFORT AND COMPETENCE

The Good News
The Smell of the Chalkboard, the Roar of the Crowd . . .

You have spent several days researching and planning your lesson on social protest literature for your eleventh-grade English class. You have collected many fine poems and statements to share; you have brought your favorite compact discs and videotapes of social protest songs into the classroom; you have prepared an excellent Power-Point presentation to highlight the key labor figures and issues of the time; and your lesson is punctuated with thoughtful discussion questions and creative follow-up activities. Beautifully organized, you carry the lesson off with dashing style. Wow, what a lesson!

The students are spellbound. They ask many questions and make plans for doing their own research on social protest. One group even decides to meet after school to write a social protest song about the destruction of the natural environment. Their animated discussion continues as the bell signals their passage to the next classroom.

When you have taught well, your students will let you know it. On special occasions, they will come up to you after class or at the end of the year to tell you they appreciate your effort and ability. At younger grade levels, they may write you notes (often anonymous), thanking you for a good class or a good year.

Usually, students are not this direct in expressing their appreciation, but you can tell from their expressions when you are doing a good job. Perhaps it is in the excited way they respond to questions or share personal experiences. Or it comes through in their intense efforts to do their very best work for you. If you are a sensitive listener and observer, your students will send you nonverbal messages that translate into "I'm very happy to be in your classroom."

The Bad News
Is Anybody There?

After teaching your fantastic lesson on social protest literature, you want to share your elation with your colleagues, so you head for the teachers' room and begin to talk about the lesson. But it is hard to capture the spirit of what went on in the classroom for those magical forty-five minutes. You can sense that your description is falling flat. Besides, people are beginning to give you that "What kind of superstar do you think you are?" look. You decide you had better cut your description short and talk about CDF (Casual Dress Friday) instead.

Positive recognition is infrequent in teaching. It is rare to have another adult spend even ten minutes observing you at work in your classroom. Once you have obtained tenure, classroom observation becomes rare, and, in many school districts, years go by before a tenured teacher is "officially" observed. Often, the evaluation is little more than perfunctory. As one teacher said, "I live in my own little world in my classroom. Sometimes I think that my children and I share a secret life that is off-limits to anybody else." Consequently, most of your teaching and administrative colleagues will have only a general impression of your teaching competence. (Of course, if you cannot get your students to settle down, everyone will know about it: Excitement is its own advertisement.)

In short, the word may leak out—through students, parents, or even the custodian—if you are doing a really fine job; however, on the whole, when you call out, "Hello, I'm here, I'm a teacher. How am I doing?" there will be little cheering from anyone outside your classroom.

TEACHING BALANCE SHEET 3   INTELLECTUAL STIMULATION

The Good News
As a Teacher, You Are Constantly Involved in Intellectual Matters

You may have become very interested in a particular subject. Perhaps you love a foreign language or mathematics, or maybe you are intrigued by contemporary social issues. Whatever content excites you, if you decide you want to share this excitement and stimulation with others, then teaching offers a natural channel for doing so.

As a teacher, particularly at the secondary level, you will have the opportunity for continued involvement in the subject area of your choice. In the classroom, your interest and enthusiasm can be contagious, in some cases instilling in others your love of the subject. When this happens, the whole process becomes self-rejuvenating, as students offer you new ideas and fresh interpretations. Listen to what high school teachers say about the intellectual stimulation of their subject matter:

> I went into high school teaching because I was excited about science. Even if they never use science in their lives, these kids should know some of what science offers them. They live in a technological age, and I want them to be equipped to understand that age.[4]

> I guess at some level I want them to be exposed to what I love and what I teach. I want them to know somebody, even if they think I'm crazy, who's genuinely excited about history.[5]

This process of intellectual stimulation and growth can be further advanced by using your extended vacation times for travel and other activities that continue your education. Or you may want to use the Internet to communicate with other teachers in your field. The Internet is a great source for finding creative teaching ideas, discussing new books, sharing curricular insights, and joining teacher chat groups; all this and more can add to your intellectual growth. And don't forget the non-"techie" sources of information. Professional journals, weekly educational newspapers, and conferences and meetings (sponsored by school districts and professional education associations) can fill your professional life with ideas and excitement. In short, you will have ready access to the intellectual community, if you want it.

The Bad News
The Same Matters Year After Year After Year

Although it is true that you will be continually involved in academic subject matter, the word *continually* is a double-edged sword. Teaching, like most other jobs, entails a lot of repetition. After a while, you may get tired of teaching the same subject matter to a new crop of students every September. If this happens, excitement and interest may be replaced by boredom and a feeling that you are getting intellectually stale.

Also, if you truly love the particular subject you teach, it can be frustrating and disillusioning to work with students who seem unmoved by the ideas that excite you. If this happens, you may turn to your colleagues for intellectual stimulation, only to find that they are more concerned about weed killer and TV shows than the latest genetic breakthrough or the intricacies of current government policy.

Since you are just embarking on your teaching career, you may find it difficult to imagine yourself becoming bored with the world of education. However, as you teach class after class on the same subject, interest can wane.

Or perhaps a different scenario will emerge, as you are pressed into teaching one or more subjects that don't interest you. Staffing decisions and enrollment changes can transform you from a science teacher into a science AND a history teacher. Perhaps your "other" teaching assignment doesn't interest you at all. If you are not motivated, it is more challenging to motivate students.

TEACHING BALANCE SHEET 4   CREATIVITY

The Good News
Portrait of the Teacher as an Artist

For countless years, there has been an ongoing debate as to whether teaching is a science or an art, and so far no one has come up with a definitive answer. Some writers, however, draw clear parallels between teachers and artists and highlight the creativity that is essential to both:

> I love to teach as a painter loves to paint, as a musician loves to play, as a singer loves to sing, as a strong man rejoices to run a race. Teaching is an art—an art so great and so difficult to master that a man or woman can spend a long life at it without realizing much more than his [or her] limitations and mistakes, and his [or her] distance from the ideal. But the main aim of my happy days has been to become a good teacher. Just as every architect wishes to be a good architect and every professional poet strives toward perfection.[6]

Unless you are a slavish follower of instructor's guides and mass-produced lesson plans, you will determine and develop

(Balance Sheet 4 continues on next page)

what will be taught in the classroom each day and how this instruction will be carried out. You can construct everything from original simulation games to videotapes, from multimedia programs to educational software. Even the development of a superb lesson plan is an exercise in creativity, as you strive to meet the needs of the various children who come into your classroom each day. This truly demands creativity.

The Bad News
The Bog of Mindless Routine

Much has been said about the creativity of teaching, but, under close inspection, the job breaks down into a lot of mindless routine as well. A large percentage of the day is consumed by clerical work, child control, housekeeping, announcements, and participation in ceremonies. Although there is opportunity for ingenuity and inventiveness, most of the day is spent in the three *R*s of ritual, repetition, and routine. As one disgruntled sixth-grade teacher in Los Angeles said,

> Paper work, paper work. The nurse wants the health cards, so you have to stop and get them. Another teacher wants one of your report cards. The principal wants to know how many social science books you have. Somebody else wants to know if you can come to a meeting on such and such a day. Forms to fill out, those crazy forms: Would you please give a breakdown of boys and girls in the class; would you please say how many children you have in reading grade such and such. Forms, messengers—all day long.[7]

TEACHING BALANCE SHEET 5   SOCIAL CONCERN

The Good News
To Touch a Life and Make a Difference

Teaching is not an insignificant, an irrelevant, a paper-shuffling kind of a job. It has meaning, worth, and value. It gives you the opportunity to touch a young and impressionable life and make it better.

> We were the luckiest class in the school. We had a homeroom teacher who knew the core truth of education: Self-hate destroys, self-esteem saves. This principle guided all her efforts on our behalf. She always minimized our deficiencies, neutralized our rage, and enhanced our natural gifts. She never, so to speak, forced a dancer to sing or a singer to dance. She allowed each of us to light his own lamp. We loved her.[8]

> Mr. Jacobs won our hearts, because he treated us as though we were already what we could only hope to become. Through his eyes we saw ourselves as capable and decent and destined for greatness. . . . Mr. Jacobs introduced us to ourselves. We learned who we were and what we wanted to be. No longer strangers to ourselves, we felt at home in the world.[9]

As a teacher, you will have a rare privilege and responsibility: you can affect and change the lives of children. It is the basic nature of the job to guide academic learning, to help a puzzled and frustrated child finally crack the phonic code or discover pattern and meaning in what were once the lifeless and unrelated facts of history. But the teaching of reading, history, and other content areas does not take place in an emotional vacuum.

Each classroom is a composite of the anguish and joy of all its students. Students occupy psychological as well as physical space. There is the child in the fourth seat who seldom volunteers but who always knows the answer. You can feel the pain of the child's shyness. There is the rambunctious one who spills all over the classroom in a million random ways but is unable to focus on any one task or project. There is the "victim," who inspires taunts and even physical abuse from usually well-mannered classmates. There is the child who barely acknowledges your presence and pencil-taps on the desk in a disturbing and incomprehensible rhythm.

All of these children are struggling for self-esteem and for the discovery of who they are and what they can become. You can become an important part of their sometimes painful and sometimes joyful quest for growth and self-discovery.

If you are drawn to teaching because you want to work with children and in some way make a difference in their lives, you have plenty of company. In fact, most teachers choose their career because it is a helping profession; some people even call it a secular ministry. All other reasons given for becoming a teacher are minor, compared with this commitment to making a difference in children's lives. Christa McAuliffe, the teacher who touched all our lives before her tragic death in space, put it well: "I touch the future. I teach."

The Bad News
The Tarnished Idealist

We all hope to be that special teacher, the one students remember and talk about long after they have left Farrington Elementary School or Monroe High, the one who has reached them in such a personal and intense way that their lives are forever enriched.

In reality, it is not so easy to be this kind of teacher. Too often, idealistic goals give way to survival—simply making it through from one day to the next. Teachers are especially vulnerable to feelings of frustration during their first year or two in the classroom. Some find their situations so intolerable that they leave teaching.

One of the key factors leading to depression and dropping out is the importance placed on discipline. All too often, new teachers find themselves judged on their ability to maintain a quiet, orderly room rather than on their ability to reach their students or to achieve instructional objectives. Idealistic young teachers find the worship of control incompatible with their humanistic goals. Likewise, they feel betrayed if a student naively mistakes their offer of friendship as a sign of weakness or vulnerability. They feel hurt and disillusioned when experiments in student self-control result in wild, out-of-control classrooms. As a result, many learn the trade secret—"don't smile until the holidays"—and adopt it quickly.

It is not only the newly initiated who find themselves caught in the unfortunate war of teacher against student. Long-time veterans also throw up their hands in despair and sometimes throw out their teaching credentials as well.

Teacher-student conflict is not the only source of teachers' lost idealism. Some teachers feel a lack of support from school administrators who do not do enough to help them with discipline problems or even to help them secure basic supplies. How can teachers stay inspired when their classrooms seem to be falling apart around them?

Sometimes teaching means confronting student apathy, tangling with bureaucratic red tape, or doing without the basic tools of the job. Then trying to make a difference may result in more frustration than satisfaction. Knowing this, can you still say to yourself, "I want to be a teacher"?

TEACHING BALANCE SHEET 6   MONEY MATTERS AND OTHER BENEFITS

The Good News
You've Come a Long Way, Teacher
Between 1981 and 1997, salaries, adjusted for inflation, rose about 20 percent. At the end of the 1980s, the average teacher's salary was approaching $30,000. By 1997, it had risen to $38,500 a year.

Salaries vary from state to state and from community to community, often reflecting different costs of living and different levels of support for education. For example, if you decide to teach in Connecticut, you will earn a good deal more than if you teach in West Virginia or North Dakota. In most areas, though, salary increases are tied to years of service and academic training. Additional salary comes from work in the summer or work as a coach or other extra faculty responsibilities. And occupational benefits, such as health and retirement, are generally excellent. (The "rule of 85," used in many districts, enables a teacher who is 55 years old and has taught for thirty years to retire; 30 plus 55 equals 85.)

Besides an improved salary picture, you will enjoy long vacation periods, both during the academic year and during longer-than-typical vacations. You can use your vacation time for much-needed rest and leisure, for professional and academic study, or for time with friends and family. A few school districts provide teachers with an opportunity to study, travel, or engage in other forms of professional improvement through an extended leave or sabbatical program. All of these considerations make for a more relaxed and varied lifestyle, one that gives you time for yourself as well as your family.

If you feel the need for more money, you can turn your vacation time into an opportunity for a second income. Some teachers run summer camps; others teach in summer school; still others write and publish curricular materials. Some schools offer merit pay or other salary incentives for

additional work, as well as extra pay for club advisors and coaches. Some teachers work on grants or special school projects to earn extra money. Whether you use your "free time" to be with your family, to travel, or to make extra money, time flexibility is a definite plus.

The Bad News
But Not Far Enough
Although teachers' salaries have improved, they still lag behind what most people would call a good income. Anyone trying to support a family on a teacher's salary will tell you that it is a far cry from wealth and prosperity. Just listen to some teachers talk about trying to make ends meet. A history teacher with a master's degree says, "It's really difficult to maintain a family. . . . I've struggled by doing odd things. I operated the football stadium. I operate the gymnasium for the basketball games, to pick up a few extra dollars. I'm not sure I could have done it then except for a wife who's not demanding or pushy. She's completely comfortable with the things we have, and we don't have a great deal."[10] A Missouri school teacher who supplements his income by working as a service station attendant says, "You know, it's degrading to serve customers who are the parents of the kids you teach."[11] And the following comment was overheard in a school that services a well-to-do suburban community: "You can always tell the difference between the teachers' and the students' parking lots. The students' lot is the one with all the new cars in it."[12]

The long periods of vacation are nice—but they are also long periods without income. When a factory worker is put on two months' leave with no pay, it is called a layoff, not a vacation! The fact is that teachers are among the most active moonlighters, and many hold down two or more jobs in order to make ends meet. In short, your vacations cost you money.

TEACHING BALANCE SHEET 7   THE PRESTIGE FACTOR

The Good News
I'm Proud to Be a Teacher

Fortunately, most people recognize the critical importance of teachers. President John F. Kennedy said, "A child miseducated is a child lost." On the lighter side, Mark Twain wryly commented, "To be good is noble, but to teach others how to be good is nobler—and less trouble."

In the past, public opinion polls have confirmed the importance of teachers in our society. A 1967 Louis Harris poll ranked teaching fifth out of a possible seventeen professions. Teachers were ranked higher than such professionals as corporate executives, psychiatrists, United States Supreme Court justices, the clergy, reporters and publishers, and members of Congress. Teacher status took a battering from public criticism during the 1970s and early 1980s, but the public is once again acknowledging the importance of teachers. In a 1984 Gallup poll, the public rated the value of teachers' services to society just below those of the clergy and medical doctors and ahead of school principals, judges, lawyers, business executives, and bankers. While, in 1981, only 46 percent of parents said they wanted their children to go into teaching, in 1996 more than a third of students expressed an interest in becoming a teacher, and two-thirds gave their teachers a grade of A or B.[13] In short when you become a teacher, society will accord you respect, because it values the worth of what you do. You will be someone whose specialized training and skills are used to benefit others.

The Bad News
I Don't Get No Respect

When you join the ranks of a particular occupation, you are personally measured and valued according to how society regards that group as a whole. You have done this yourself. Suppose you walk into a room and are introduced to five people: an assembly-line worker, a college president, a doctor, a garbage collector, and an accountant. Before getting to know these people as individuals, you would probably form some distinct impressions about their intelligence, character, and general worth, based on their occupation. Whether we like it or not, people play status games and value us according to the kind of job we have.

Right now when you meet new people, you are probably introduced as a student from a particular university. How will you feel about meeting the world as a teacher? Will that make you feel proud or apologetic?

Ironically, the importance of educating our children is widely recognized, but the key people in this process—teachers—are not always highly valued. There are several reasons for this paradox, one of which is the sexist nature of our society. Almost all occupations with large numbers of women seem to have prestige problems, and teaching is no exception. There may come a day when we will not have to mention this issue, but, for the time being, prejudice still exists.

Another reason has to do with the materialistic nature of our society. People's work is frequently measured by the size of the paycheck they bring home, and, as already discussed, the wallets of most teachers are modestly endowed.

Some people question whether teachers should even be considered professionals. In dismissing teachers from the professional ranks, these critics call attention to teachers' relatively short training period (compared with that of doctors or lawyers, for example), and they note that teacher preparation programs are not particularly selective in their admissions procedures. Further, unlike most other professionals, teachers do not choose their clients (students), nor do they have much choice in what they will teach. Their professional autonomy is further limited by school administrators, who hire and fire them and determine their salaries.

Although there has been a resurgence of support for teachers, when it comes to the game of impressing people, teachers are still not collecting a large pile of status chips.

PROFILES IN TEACHING: JAIME ESCALANTE

Jaime Escalante may be best known for an incident in 1982 involving the Educational Testing Service (ETS) and fourteen of his students at Garfield High in East Los Angeles. For four years, Escalante had been struggling to build a strong advanced placement (AP) calculus program at Garfield, a troubled inner-city school with a poor academic history and an uncertain future. It had been difficult going, but the program finally blossomed that year. Escalante had eighteen students in his class, almost double the number from the year before, and they worked so hard that every one of them passed the difficult and prestigious AP examination.

During the summer, however, an unpleasant controversy developed. The ETS, which administers the AP exam, told fourteen of the students that a high correspondence in their answers suggested that they may have cheated. They would either have to retake the test or have their scores nullified. Escalante, the students, and others protested. There had been no cheating, they argued. It seemed to be just another example of the experts' underestimating the potential of students who are poor and Latino. But the ETS would not budge, so a retest was arranged. Even after a summer away from the theorems and formulas, all of the students passed the test again, many with higher scores than the first time.

After then, Escalante's calculus program took off, involving hundreds of students every year and during the summer. And his success encouraged other Garfield teachers to add and expand AP classes in history, English, biology, and other subjects. By 1987, Garfield had become known as one of the best public schools in the country.[a]

How does Escalante account for his achievements? He sums up much of his teaching as the pursuit of *ganas,* a Spanish word meaning "the will to succeed."

> Really it's not just the knowledge of math. Because to have knowledge is one thing, and to use that knowledge is another, and to know how to teach or how to motivate these kids is the combination of both. My skills are really to motivate these kids, to make them learn, to give them *ganas*—desire to do something—to make them believe they can learn.[b]

Escalante's own life story demonstrates much of the persistence and love of hard work that he inspires in his students. When he immigrated to the United States from Bolivia in 1963, he had already been teaching for 11 years, ever since he was 22 years old, gaining a reputation as one of the finest teachers in La Paz. In Bolivia, he was used to teaching without textbooks or other materials, and the low salary required him to teach three sets of classes a day in order to get by.

> Anybody, any kid can learn if he or she has the desire to do it. That's what *ganas* is about. The teacher plays an important role in education—we all remember the first teacher who really touched our lives, or gave us some encouragement, or at least appreciated our best. The teacher gives us the desire to learn, the desire to be Somebody.[c]

In class, Escalante is an unpredictable showman as well as a stern father. To get his students' attention and understanding, he will do almost anything, from starting a class with a group cheer to translating a complex question into a play from a basketball game. But while "Kimo," as he is nicknamed, can be a charming, colorful character to those who show sincere effort, latecomers and those with incomplete assignments find themselves interrogated, hounded by calls to parents, and threatened with a transfer to a less effective school a very long bus ride away. Whether he has to resort to rewards, taunts, afternoon study sessions, or even mild bribery, Escalante refuses to allow students to give up.

> I use the team approach, I make them believe that we have a team which is going to prepare for the Olympics. And our Olympics is the advanced placement calculus exam. I always talk to them and tell them, "Look, we prepared two years for this competition, and you have to play strong defense. Don't let the test put you down. You're the best." And every time the kids go to take the advanced placement calculus exam, they wear the jacket with a bulldog, which is the school mascot, and the kids go to the testing room yelling "Defense! Defense! Defense!"[d]

Although he has been the subject of the movie *Stand and Deliver,* a biography, and numerous articles, the reasons behind much of Jaime Escalante's success remain a mystery. Many have discussed and argued over whether to view great teaching as an art or a skill, something innate or something learned, but it may be better to just let Escalante be Escalante. In his own words,

> The teacher has to have the energy of the hottest volcano, the memory of an elephant, and the diplomacy of an ambassador. . . . Really, a teacher has to possess love and knowledge and then has to use this combined passion to be able to accomplish something.[e]

[a]Jay Mathews, *Escalante: The Best Teacher in America* (New York: Henry Holt, 1988).
[b]Quoted in Anne Meek, "On Creating Ganas: A Conversation with Jaime Escalante," *Educational Leadership* 46, no. 5 (February 1989): pp. 46–47.
[c]Ibid.
[d]Ibid.
[e]Ibid.

Source: This Profiles in Teaching was written by Rafael Heller.

From Passivity to a Profession

So you are interested in a teaching position? If you will just agree to the following stipulations and sign the following contract (which dates from the 1920s, when only women needed to apply), we may be able to use you.

Teaching Contract

Miss _____ agrees:

1. Not to get married. This contract becomes null and void immediately if the teacher marries.
2. Not to keep company with men.
3. To be home between the hours of 8 P.M. and 6 A.M. unless in attendance at a school function.
4. Not to loiter downtown in ice-cream parlors.
5. Not to leave town at any time without the permission of the Chairman of the Trustees.
6. Not to smoke cigarettes. This contract becomes null and void immediately if the teacher is found smoking.
7. Not to drink beer, wine, or whiskey. This contract becomes null and void immediately if the teacher is found drinking beer, wine, or whiskey.
8. Not to ride in a carriage or automobile with any man except her brother or father.
9. Not to dress in bright colors.
10. Not to dye her hair.
11. Not to wear less than two petticoats.
12. Not to wear dresses shorter than two inches above the ankles.
13. To keep the schoolroom clean:
    a. To sweep the classroom floor at least once daily.
    b. To scrub the classroom floor at least once weekly with soap and hot water.
    c. To clean the blackboard at least once daily.
    d. To start the fire at 7 A.M. so that the room will be warm by 8 A.M. when the children arrive.
14. Not to wear face powder, mascara, or to paint the lips.

(Reprinted courtesy of the *Chicago Tribune*, September 28, 1975, Section 1.)

Interested? Probably not. But, not so long ago, teaching contracts rigidly dictated both the personal and the professional lives of teachers. The reward for this austere dedication was an unimpressive $75 a month.

Despite this pathetic position description, insightful people have been quick to recognize and write about the importance of a life spent in the classroom. Consider the following:

"What noble employment is more valuable to the state than that of the man who instructs the rising generation?" (*Cicero*)

"Education makes a people easy to lead, but difficult to drive; easy to govern but impossible to enslave." (*Lord Brougham*)

"I shou'd think it as glorius [sic] employment to instruct poor children as to teach the children of the greatest monarch." (*Elizabeth Elstob*)

"The man who can make hard things easy is the educator." (*Ralph Waldo Emerson*)

In his preface to *Goodbye, Mr. Chips,* James Hilton writes that his portrait of the lovable school master is a "tribute to a great profession." But is teaching really a profession? Some experts in the business of defining professions say that it is difficult to determine whether teaching qualifies.

What is a profession, anyway? *Educating a Profession,* a publication of the American Association of Colleges for Teacher Education (AACTE), lists twelve characteristics of a profession. Read these carefully and try to determine which criteria the occupation of teaching meets, marking your reactions in the appropriate column. You may find it interesting to compare your reactions with those of your classmates.

	Yes	No	Don't Know
1. Professions are occupationally related social institutions established and maintained as a means of providing essential services to the individual and society.	____	____	____
2. Each profession is concerned with an identified area of need or function (for example, maintenance of physical and emotional health, preservation of rights and freedom, enhancing the opportunity to learn).	____	____	____
3. The profession collectively, and the professional individually, possesses a body of knowledge and a repertoire of behaviors and skills (professional culture) needed in the practice of the profession; such knowledge, behavior, and skills normally are not possessed by the nonprofessional.	____	____	____
4. Members of the profession are involved in decision making in the service of the client, the decisions being made in accordance with the most valid knowledge available, against a background of principles and theories, and within the context of possible impact on other related conditions or decisions.	____	____	____
5. The profession is based on one or more undergirding disciplines from which it builds its own applied knowledge and skills.	____	____	____
6. The profession is organized into one or more professional associations which, within broad limits of social accountability, are granted autonomy in control of the actual work of the profession and the conditions which surround it (admissions, educational standards, examination and licensing, career line, ethical and performance standards).	____	____	____
7. The profession has agreed-upon performance standards for admission to the profession and for continuance within it.	____	____	____

8. Preparation for and induction into the profession is provided through a protracted preparation program, usually in a professional school on a college or university campus.

9. There is a high level of public trust and confidence in the profession and in individual practitioners, based upon the profession's demonstrated capacity to provide service markedly beyond that which would otherwise be available.

10. Individual practitioners are characterized by a strong service motivation and lifetime commitment to competence.

11. Authority to practice in any individual case derives from the client or the employing organization; accountability for the competence of professional practice within the particular case is to the profession itself.

12. There is relative freedom from direct on-the-job supervision and from direct public evaluation of the individual practitioner. The professional accepts responsibility in the name of his or her profession and is accountable through his or her profession to the society.[14]

Do not be surprised if you find some criteria that do not apply to teaching. In fact, even the occupations that spring to mind when you hear the word *professional*—doctor, lawyer, clergy, college professor—do not completely measure up to all these criteria.

Those who developed these twelve criteria for a profession also listed another twelve criteria that would describe a **semiprofession.** Read these items carefully, and compare them with the characteristics that define a profession. Consider each item separately. Does it accurately describe teaching, or does it sell teaching short? After you have considered all the items and have marked your reactions in the appropriate column, decide whether you think teaching is actually a profession, or whether it would more accurately be termed a semiprofession.

	Yes	No	Don't Know
1. Lower in occupational status	___	___	___
2. Shorter training periods	___	___	___
3. Lack of societal acceptance that the nature of the service and/or the level of expertise justifies the autonomy which is granted to the professions	___	___	___
4. A less specialized and less highly developed body of knowledge and skills	___	___	___
5. Markedly less emphasis on theoretical and conceptual bases for practice	___	___	___
6. A tendency for the individual to identify with the employment institution more and with the profession less	___	___	___
7. More subject to administrative and supervisory surveillance and control	___	___	___

8. Less autonomy in professional decision making, with accountability to superiors rather than to the profession   _____ _____ _____
9. Management of organizations within which semiprofessionals are employed by persons who have themselves been prepared and served in that semiprofession   _____ _____ _____
10. A preponderance of women   _____ _____ _____
11. Absence of the right of privileged communication between client and professional   _____ _____ _____
12. Little or no involvement in matters of life and death[15]   _____ _____ _____

Many people feel that teaching falls somewhere between professional and semi-professional in status. For them, it might best be thought of as an emerging profession. Where do you place teaching?

Why does all this "profession talk" matter? You may be more concerned with such questions as "Do I want to work with children?" "What age level is best for me?" "Will I be good at teaching?" "Will the salary be enough to give me the quality of life that I want for myself and my family?" "Why," you may be thinking, "should I split hairs over whether I belong to a profession? Who cares?"

Although the issue of professionalism may not matter to you now or even during your first year or two of teaching, when classroom survival and performance have top priority, it will eventually become one of the most important issues you face during your career in education. Why?

Here's what Ellen Hogan Steele, a teacher who cares passionately about the privilege, responsibility, and dignity of belonging to a profession, says:

> I recall a carpenter—he visited my home to discuss a renovation—talking about a school strike in a neighboring town. Unaware of my occupation he called teachers ignorant, lazy, and lucky to be employed.
>
> "Can you imagine thinking they should make as much as me?" he fumed.
>
> I can imagine that. I presume my work to be as demanding and skilled as that of the carpenters I employ. . . . What do teachers want? This teacher wants to make a reasonable living, to be recognized as a person who performs an essential service, to be considered an expert in my small area of experience, to be occasionally praised when I do well and to be helped to improve when I don't. . . . In short, I want someone to know that I'm alive, and unless they do, I'll keep on kicking.[16]

Listen to another teacher, Patricia Dombart:

> Take a look at the working world of the insider. You will find that it is not an atmosphere that nourishes vision. Though we teachers are numerous, we are virtually powerless. We affect none of the key elements in our working lives. For example, we have no control over class size or the length of the school day and class periods.
>
> We have almost no input into the form and content of report cards. We do not select our schedules, grade levels or the buildings in which we teach. Indeed, we do not even control the time within our own classrooms, for we are slaves to the P.A., to notes from the nurse, from guidance, the librarian,

the main office. We are often without the essentials, like paper and pencils and desks. In many buildings, janitors and secretaries control these. Acquiring a new pencil sharpener may involve stroking three separate egos and forgetting everything you ever read about reporting sexual harassment. Often, obtaining the basics interferes with teaching the basics.[17]

These two teachers speak for most of their colleagues when they call for an adequate salary and the sense of pride and self-worth that comes from doing an important job well and knowing that others respect your competence. Financial well-being and community respect usually go hand-in-hand with professional status.

Professional status also requires self-determination, power, and the ability to make important decisions about the nature of one's work. Historically, teachers have been relatively powerless. Outside their classrooms, they have little say about school policies, procedures, schedules, curriculum, and other matters that have a direct bearing on the quality and effectiveness of their work. But times are changing. You are about to enter a field undergoing significant upheaval.

Tension Point: Professionalism at the Crossroads

"Are You Treated Like a Professional? Or a Tall Child?" This provocative title from *NEA Today* raises questions that often confront educators. When education reform stresses the need for a national curriculum, or for decisions made at the district central office or by state governments, a clear pattern emerges: the lack of direct teacher involvement in shaping their own professional world. Many teachers resent this kind of deprofessionalization. Says English teacher Carol Davis, "We're told when to get here, when to leave, what to teach, what to want, what not to want, and how to think. . . . I'm trained in how to teach English, but I'm rarely asked for my opinion. If I were to be 'promoted out of my classroom' my opinion would be more respected immediately. The irony would be that I'd no longer be teaching children."[18]

This tendency toward infantalization of teaching is now being radically challenged. The new pride in professionalism takes the perspective that teachers are not slaves to rules and routines established in state education departments and textbook publishing houses. Rather, they are reflective decision makers, selecting objectives and teaching procedures to meet the needs of different learners. They must know

Collectively, teachers struggle to empower their profession; individually, they struggle to empower their students.

their subject matter, learning theory, research on various teaching methodologies, and techniques for curriculum development. This view provides the rationale for transforming teaching into a true profession.[19]

Despite this new vision of professionalism, the United States remains ambivalent about its teachers. Even as interest in teacher empowerment mounts, policies are in effect that threaten to derail teaching's bid for full professional status. For example, many states have alternative certification programs, which allow people with limited training to go into classrooms and teach children. One such controversial program is **Teach for America,** in which highly motivated volunteers undergo very brief teacher training programs and enter some of America's most difficult classrooms. Many educators see such programs as the height of irresponsibility and the opposite of profession building.[20] Can you imagine lawyers or doctors preparing for their professions in this manner? How can teaching be a profession, critics point out, if it grants substandard licenses?

While entrance into teaching often includes competency tests (a move toward professionalism), the tests are too simple. As educational researcher Linda Darling-Hammond points out: "Rather than 'legitimizing complexity' as professions must do when they seek bars to entry, these assessment instruments reinforce conceptions of teaching as simple cookbook-driven work."[21]

In the 1990s, the Carnegie Forum was influential in creating the **National Board for Professional Teaching Standards (NBPTS).** The goal of the NBPTS is to recognize extraordinary teachers, those whose skills and knowledge indicate their high level of achievement. This is a significant departure from simply licensing new teachers who reach minimal standards. During its first years of operation, the NBPTS developed assessment procedures to identify highly competent teachers, teachers who would be designated "board-certified." Like medicine, teaching now had not just an entry license—a standard teaching license—but advanced recognition of a higher level of skills and competencies. By 1998, over one thousand teachers were compiling professional portfolios (including videotaped examples of their teaching), taking a battery of assessment tests, and undergoing interviews and other tests en route to becoming board-certified teachers. As you might imagine, the board assessment is not inexpensive (a cost sometimes, but not always, paid for by sponsoring school districts). All this effort is invested in recognizing superior teachers, a concept that was not even considered just a few years ago.

Is teaching a full profession? Or is it doomed to semiprofessional status? The case is at a crossroads.

Teacher Education: From Normal Schools to Board-Certified Teachers

Basic to any discussion of a profession is the issue of how its members are prepared. As you read this brief history of teacher preparation, think about whether teachers are prepared in a way commensurate with belonging to a profession.

From colonial America into the twentieth century, the burning question about teacher education was "Why have it?" More often than not, teachers in colonial America received no formal preparation at all. In fact, most elementary teachers never even attended a secondary school. Some learned their craft by serving as apprentices to master teachers, a continuation of the medieval guild system. Others were indentured servants paying for their passage to the New World by teaching for

CHRISTA McAULIFFE AND HER TESTAMENT

A few weeks ago I wrote a piece about school teachers going up in space. I speculated as to what kinds of candidates my own teachers at P.S. 35 would have made if they had applied for the trip. It was a light piece because, like most Americans, I never dreamed anything could happen to the flight of the shuttle *Challenger.*

During the last numbing week, as I watched the television screen, I got to thinking about teachers. Although Christa McAuliffe wasn't a professional astronaut, she did leave behind a wonderful legacy.

Consider this.

For the past 15 or 20 years, America's teachers could not have been held in lower esteem. They were underpaid, underrated and blamed for anything that went wrong with our schools.

It appeared the only time we saw teachers on TV was when they were on strike or arrested for child abuse. The perception was that teachers were people who taught because they couldn't make it in the real world.

Except for covering vandalism and crime in schools, the media ignored what was going on in the classroom. And with reason: If teachers were teaching, and students were learning, it wasn't news—that is, until the destruction of *Challenger.*

Suddenly our schools received more attention than they have ever been given before. Seven brave people died that morning, but it was the death of a school teacher that made our children cry.

When the TV cameras entered the nation's classrooms to record their grief, we saw principals and teachers fighting back their own tears as they tried to comfort the students.

The cameras not only focused on teachers but also panned to the agonized faces of students. They showed teacher to pupil and pupil to teacher—and in that moment of sadness we witnessed the educational process at its best.

When these pictures came into our homes we were reminded of something we tend to take for granted: the role teachers quietly play in the lives of children.

The lesson was not just for grown-ups. You had the feeling that the students had gained a new respect for teachers as well. It went something like this. "Christa was a teacher,

and Christa died in space, but it could have been anybody's teacher—including mine."

So what was Christa McAuliffe's legacy?

When *Sputnik* went up and we realized the Russians were ahead there was a great clamor to educate American children and make our schools second to none. Then after the successes of our own space program, the clamor died down. Education was dropped as our No. 1 priority.

At least it was until last week. After that one horrifying moment in Florida, things changed again. The parent-teacher-pupil bond that had been fraying for a generation seemed to be joined again.

Christa McAuliffe's gift to us is not in the skies but here on earth. From everything you can read, she was a teacher before she went up and she intended to be a teacher when she returned. In death her legacy is to give her fellow professionals new dignity and honor. Thanks to Christa, each one of them can say with pride, "I'm a teacher, too."

Source: Art Buchwald, *Washington Post,* 6 February 1986.

a fixed number of years. Many belonged to the "sink-or-swim" school of teaching, and the education of an untold number of students undoubtedly sank with them.

The smaller number of teachers working at the secondary level—in academies or Latin grammar schools and as private tutors—had usually received some college education, more often in Europe than in America. Some knowledge of the subject matter was considered desirable, but no particular aptitude for teaching or knowledge of teaching skills was considered necessary.

Teaching was viewed not as a career but as temporary employment. Many of those who entered teaching were teenagers who taught for only a year or two. Others were of dubious character, and early records reveal a number of teachers fired for drinking or stealing.

From this humble beginning there slowly emerged a more professional program for teacher education. In 1823, the Reverend Samuel Hall established a **normal school** (named for its European counterpart) in Concord, Vermont. This private school provided elementary school graduates with formal training in teaching skills. This modest normal school marked the beginning of teacher education in America. Sixteen years later, in 1839, **Horace Mann** was instrumental in establishing the first state-supported normal school in Lexington, Massachusetts. Normal schools typically provided a two-year teacher training program, consisting of academic subjects as well as teaching methodology. Some students came directly from elementary school; others had completed a secondary education. The normal school was the backbone of teacher education well into the twentieth century.

As enrollments in elementary schools climbed and as secondary education became widely accepted, the demand increased for more and better-trained teachers. Many private colleges and universities initiated teacher education programs early in the 1900s. The normal schools expanded to three- and four-year programs and gradually evolved into state teachers' colleges. Interestingly, as attendance grew, these teachers' colleges expanded their programs and began offering courses and career preparation in fields other than teaching. By the 1950s, many of the state teachers' colleges had evolved into state colleges. In fact, some of today's leading universities were originally chartered as normal schools.

The 1980s marked the beginning of the modern effort to reshape education. A number of education reform reports fanned the flames of controversy regarding professionalism and teacher preparation, including one written by a group of prominent education deans. The **Holmes Group,** as the deans were called, debated the teacher preparation issue for several years before releasing its report, entitled ***Tomorrow's Teachers*** (1986).[22] The same year, the Carnegie Forum also issued a highly publicized report, ***A Nation Prepared.***[23] Both reports called for higher standards and increased professionalism for the nation's teachers. The Carnegie report also called for an end to the undergraduate teaching major, to be replaced by master's-level degrees in teaching. While some universities followed this recommendation and created five-year teacher education programs (bachelor's and master's degrees required for teacher education candidates), other colleges continued their undergraduate education programs. Teacher education remains a hodgepodge of approaches. Some critics, such as John Goodlad, place much of the blame on universities themselves, for failing to adequately fund and support schools of education.[24]

But not all of the attention has been on initial teacher education. As teachers move toward board certification, how will states and communities recognize, reward, and use these talented teachers? Some states and communities help teachers reach board certification; others do not. (See Figure 1.1.) Will board-certified teachers be paid higher salaries or be given more release time to develop curricula or to work with new teachers? Will these board-certified teachers become leaders—or will the movement become simply another failed attempt to transform what some view as a semi-profession into a true profession?[25]

These and other pivotal questions will likely be answered during your time as a classroom teacher.

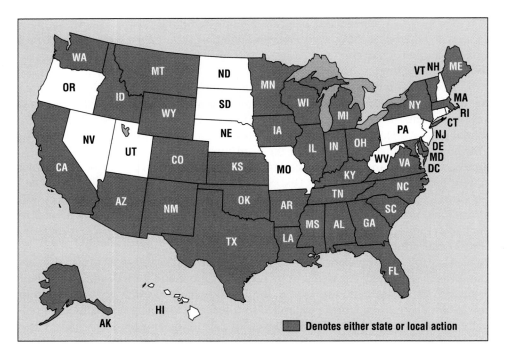

FIGURE 1.1

Support for teachers pursuing national board certification. Incentives for National Board Certification are provided in more than ninety school districts in thirty-five states.

Source: National Board for Professional Teaching Standards, State and Local Action Report, October 1998.

Do Teachers Like Teaching?

We designed the balance sheets in this chapter to help you focus on the pros and cons of becoming a teacher. The National Education Association (NEA) and the National Center for Educational Statistics (NCES), part of the U.S. Department of Education, have created their own balance sheet.[26] They surveyed teachers from around the nation, asking them why they decided to become teachers and why they decided to stay in teaching. People choose a career in the classroom for very positive reasons, including a desire to work with young people, the significance of education generally, and even the love of a particular subject—not a bad bunch to have as colleagues. While these reasons draw people to teaching, what keeps them in teaching?

In the NEA and NCES survey, the vast majority of the teachers, about 80 percent, reported that they were satisfied with their jobs and with their working conditions. Almost 90 percent were satisfied with the intellectual challenge of their work, their job security, and their autonomy in the classroom. The teachers also gave high scores to supervisors, with solid majorities viewing their school principals as supportive and encouraging, leaders who were able to communicate their expectations and to enforce school rules. When asked about the adequacy of resources, such as textbooks, supplies, and copying machines, over 70 percent of the teachers agreed that the materials were available as needed. But not everything surveyed was rosy.

High on the teachers' "Top Ten List of Things I'd Like to Change About My Job" was salary, with 55 percent registering their dissatisfaction. Salaries, although better today than they have been historically, are still inadequate for many teachers. But it is not salaries alone that concerns teachers. Incremental obstacles pile up and wear down a teacher. Teachers focus their complaints on heavy workloads and extra

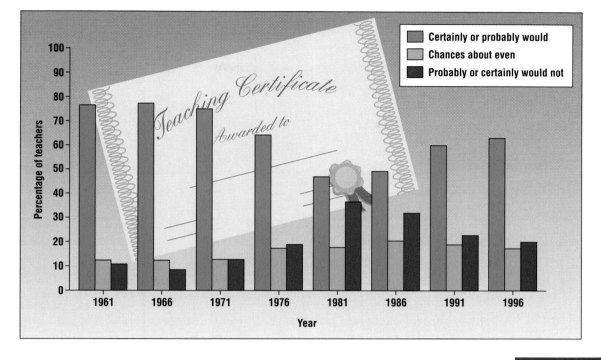

FIGURE 1.2

Teachers' willingness to enter teaching again, by year, 1961–1996. Teaching conditions seem to be improving, with an increase in teachers reporting that they would become teachers again during the past twenty years.

Source: National Education Association status of the American public school teacher, 1995–1996 © 1997.

responsibilities, discipline issues, negative attitudes expressed by students, unresponsive school administrators, and lack of support from parents. Parental support, like most of these factors, varies dramatically from school to school. If you were seeking the schools with the highest levels of parental support, you would be well advised to begin your search in private schools and at the elementary level.

On the whole, teaching conditions do seem to be improving. Fewer teachers today register complaints than did teachers in the 1980s, and the percentage of teachers considering another career has dropped as well. Asked whether they would enter teaching again, only 17 percent of today's teachers report they probably or certainly would not; fully 66 percent report that they certainly or probably would become teachers again (see Figure 1.2).

What Should Teachers Learn?

Which is more important for new teachers to learn—how to motivate students or how to manage them?

What should teachers do if they discover that a student is cheating?

Should teachers promote competitions, such as a class honor roll?

In 1997, Public Agenda, a nonpartisan, nonprofit organization, surveyed 900 education professors from around the nation about just these issues and compared their responses not only with those of the public but also with those of practicing classroom teachers. Public Agenda's poll found fundamental differences of opinion on how best to train teachers. Considering these differences of opinion early in your program gives you an opportunity to think about what you value in an effective teacher and to identify what skills you would like to acquire in your own teacher education program.

IN THE NEWS . . . HOUSING TEACHERS

Baltimore Public Schools offers a $5,000 home-buying grant to assist new teachers to buy homes in the city. In an aggressive strategy to recruit 500 new teachers, Baltimore also raised starting salaries by $3,000 and pays $1,200 to help offset relocation expenses.

Source: *Education Week on the Web,* 3 June 1998.

On Discipline . . .

Are discipline problems a sign of student boredom, or are they an indication that teachers lack the firm standards needed to control a classroom?

The Public Agenda survey indicates that education professors believe students arrive at school wanting to learn and that student misbehavior is a sign of bad teaching.[27] They shy away from punitive measures, and only 30 percent of the professors report that their teacher education programs stress skills such as managing a difficult classroom. On the other hand, the public believes that schools need to focus more on control and discipline. Teachers are even more intense on these issues. Classroom teachers are zealous in their belief that students caught with drugs or weapons should be permanently removed from school.

On Competition . . .

Should teachers create a more rigorous and competitive learning environment?

"My kid is an honor student at Tara Lipinski High School" is not the kind of bumper sticker that the typical education professor would affix to the rear of his or her Saturn. Professors report a general aversion to academic competition and external rewards. Ask the public, on the other hand, and you will hear vivid memories of *their* schooling, replete with rigorous tests, enormous amounts of homework, and incredibly demanding teachers. (Okay, maybe their memories have been colored by time, and their schooling experiences were not as challenging as they recall, and they didn't have to walk three miles uphill, in the snow, to AND from school when they were children. Nevertheless, they remember tougher, more demanding schools.) It's not surprising that 70 percent of the public believes that schools need to raise standards and not promote students who do poorly.

On Honesty and Dependability . . .

How much emphasis should teachers place on traditional values, such as punctuality, politeness, and even honesty?

Eighty-eight percent of the public in the Public Agenda survey opined that, if students were to arrive at school on time and were generally more dependable, academic achievement would improve significantly. An even higher percentage of classroom teachers agree (93 percent). While a smaller majority of professors concur

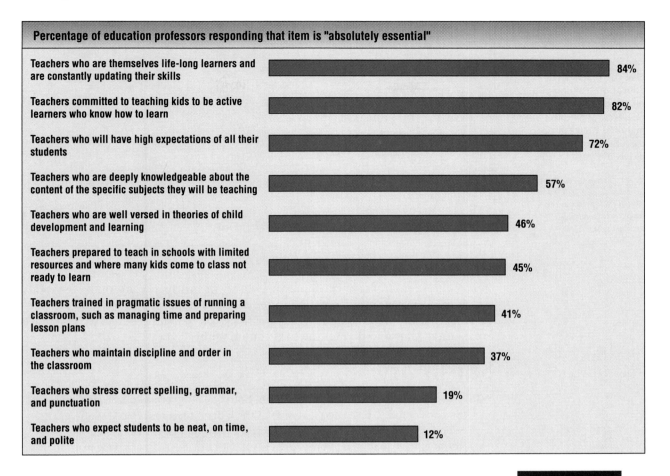

Percentage of education professors responding that item is "absolutely essential"

Teachers who are themselves life-long learners and are constantly updating their skills	84%
Teachers committed to teaching kids to be active learners who know how to learn	82%
Teachers who will have high expectations of all their students	72%
Teachers who are deeply knowledgeable about the content of the specific subjects they will be teaching	57%
Teachers who are well versed in theories of child development and learning	46%
Teachers prepared to teach in schools with limited resources and where many kids come to class not ready to learn	45%
Teachers trained in pragmatic issues of running a classroom, such as managing time and preparing lesson plans	41%
Teachers who maintain discipline and order in the classroom	37%
Teachers who stress correct spelling, grammar, and punctuation	19%
Teachers who expect students to be neat, on time, and polite	12%

FIGURE 1.3

"What's Worth Teaching Teachers"
These are the qualities education professors believe teacher education programs should impart to their students.

Source: Different Drummers: How Teachers of Teachers View Public Education, Public Agenda, 1997.

(78 percent), few professors consider it "absolutely essential" for teachers to expect students to be on time or to be neat or polite (only 12 percent). Only 8 percent of the professors reported that their programs prepare teachers to handle problems such as cheating. Eighty-five percent of the professors felt that schools are already expected to deal with too many problems (see Figure 1.3).

Although the poll illustrates that teacher education programs do not meet everyone's expectations, they do many things well. Today's teachers give higher marks to their college teacher education programs than did their predecessors. From 1984 to 1997, the percentage ranking their own teacher preparation *A* or *B* jumped from 49 percent to 64 percent.[28] (See Figure 1.4.) That's a remarkable—and encouraging—increase.

Why the improvement? Today's teacher preparation programs typically emphasize current research as well as practical classroom skills, often working in close collaboration with local schools. Many teacher education students are studying at the graduate level, bringing more of life's experiences to the classroom than did their predecessors, all signs of positive changes in teacher preparation.

Education is a dynamic field, surrounded by controversies, misperceptions, and surprises. This text will immerse you in that excitement. We want this book to tweak your interest, to be fun as well as informative. (Okay, so it's not a Stephen King *Fright Night at the School Prom* novel for that rainy day at the beach. But we do want this text to be more exciting and interesting than most, to mirror the enthusiasm that we feel

FIGURE 1.4

What grade would you give the teacher education training you received? Today's teachers give higher marks to their college training than teachers did in the past.

Source: Carol Langdon, The Fourth Phi Delta Kappa Poll of Teachers' Attitudes Toward the Public Schools, *Phi Delta Kappan,* Volume 79, Issue 3, November 1997.

What grade would you give the teacher education training you received?

Report card

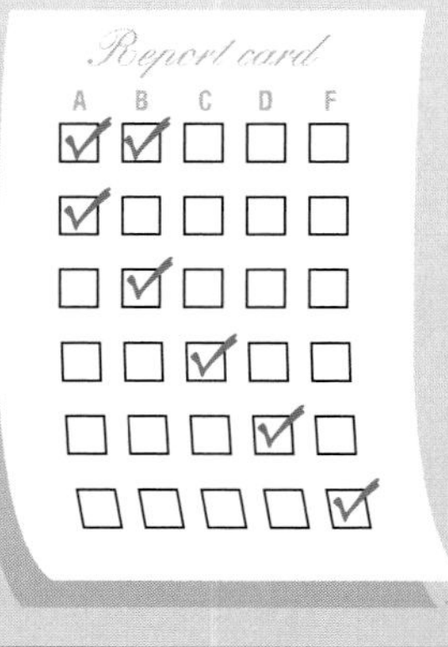

	1997 %	1989 %	1984 %
A and B	64	57	49
A	23	17	14
B	41	40	35
C	25	32	33
D	8	7	10
Fail	2	3	6
Don't know	1	1	2

about education.) In the next chapter, we will try to anticipate some of the questions that may be on your mind, questions often asked by students new to teaching. If we miss any that you would like answered, we invite you to write or e-mail us, so that we can consider your question for the next edition of this text.

Summary

1. When weighing the merits of teaching, both advantages and disadvantages must be considered. On the negative side of the ledger, teachers typically earn less than wonderful salaries, lack professional respect from others, get bogged down by routine, have inadequate time for contact with other adults, and face frustration when idealistic goals collide with student apathy, parent hostility, and the demands of old-fashioned bureaucratic red tape.

2. On the positive side of the ledger are rising salaries, the growing pride in the profession, the joy of working with children and caring colleagues, and the intellectual stimulation that are so often a part of classroom life, as well as the opportunity to affect the lives of the nation's youth. As teacher Christa McAuliffe said, "I touch the future. I teach."

3. In colonial times, teachers were treated as meek and docile servants of the public. Their conduct both in and out of school was scrutinized closely, and their income was so meager that many had to board with different families to make ends meet. From these beginnings, those in the field of teaching have struggled for greater income, respect, and professionalism.

4. There is an ongoing debate as to whether teaching is a field that has reached true professional status. Some claim it has not and is, at best, a semiprofession. To support their point of view, these critics note the short preparation time needed for becoming a teacher and the employment of teachers with little or no training, in programs such as Teach for America. Critics also cite the lack of teacher influence over certification and curricular standards. Teachers are not even central in determining who is permitted into the field or who should be forced out of teaching due to incompetence.

5. Those who claim that teaching has earned full professional status assert that it is one of the most noble of occupations. Its knowledge and research base is growing, and a number of colleges and universities now require more study (five

years) to meet minimum teacher education requirements. In addition, most states now administer qualifying exams, another indication that the entrance standards to teaching are being raised. The development of a National Board for Professional Teaching Standards to identify "board-certified" teachers, teachers who excel in their professional skills and competencies, represents a new level of professional development.

6. Initially, teaching was considered only temporary employment. In 1823, a private normal school was established to provide future teachers with formal training. In the 1900s, many private universities established teacher education programs. Today, reform reports, including *Tomorrow's Teachers* and *A Nation Prepared,* urge higher standards, increased professionalism for teacher preparation, and recognition of superior performance through board certification.

7. The vast majority of teachers surveyed indicate that they are satisfied with their jobs, but there are problems. While teachers' salaries have improved, many teachers believe that their pay is still inadequate. Local conditions have a major impact on teacher satisfaction. On the teacher's wish list for job improvement is lighter workloads, more parental backing, fewer discipline problems, and greater administration support.

8. Public opinion research indicates that, on a number of key points, teachers, education professors, and the general public differ on what schools should value and emphasize. On discipline, for example, professors view management problems as a sign that teachers are not effectively motivating students, while the public and classroom teachers believe that tough classroom standards and rules are a prerequisite to learning. Classroom teachers and the general public are also more likely than the professors to support ensuring that new teachers instill traditional values, including punctuality, neatness, competition, and tougher promotion standards.

9. What are the important skills for new teachers to master? It is unrealistic to believe that any teacher education program can meet everyone's needs or expectations in this area. Teacher candidates must become active participants in their own professional development, refining their own approach to teaching and exploring resources in addition to those offered by their "official" teacher education program.

Key Terms and People

A Nation Prepared
board-certified teachers
Holmes Group
Horace Mann

National Board for Professional Teaching Standards (NBPTS)
normal school
professionalism

semiprofession
Teach for America
Tomorrow's Teachers

www.mhhe.com/sadker

Discussion Questions and Activities

1. The Teaching Balance Sheets presented both the positive and negative sides of teaching. Seek out books that will increase your awareness of the pros and cons of teaching, such as the following:

   • *Up the Down Staircase,* by Bel Kaufman

   • *Teacher,* by Sylvia Ashton-Warner

   • *The Water Is Wide,* by Patrick Conroy

   • *900 Shows a Year,* by Stuart Palonsky

- *Goodbye, Mr. Chips,* by James Hilton
- *Among Schoolchildren,* by Tracy Kidder
- *Amazing Grace,* by Jonathan Kozol
- *Horace's Compromise* or *Horace's School,* by Theodore Sizer
- *Tales Out of School: A Teacher's Account from the Front Lines of the American High School Today,* by Patrick Welsh (editor)
- *Mentors, Masters and Mrs. MacGregor: Stories of Teachers Making a Difference* by Jane Bluestein (Editor)

As you read these personal accounts, you may want to keep your own balance sheet of the aspects of teaching to which you react positively and those to which you react negatively. You may also wish to share your reading as well as your balance sheet with your classmates and your instructor.

2. This chapter emphasized the importance of well-thought-out career decision making. You may want to read one of the many career books now available to help you with this process. (For example, Richard N. Bolles' *What Color Is Your Parachute?* contains many exercises that should help you clarify your commitment to teaching.) These books, or a visit to your career center, can help you determine what other careers present viable options for you.

3. Interview teachers at different grade levels to determine what they think are the positive and negative aspects of teaching. Share those interview responses with your classmates.

4. Interview students at various grade levels to determine their perceptions of teachers. Ask them to describe a teacher who has been influential in their lives. Share these interview responses with your classmates.

5. Suppose you could write an open letter to students, telling them about yourself and why you want to teach. What would you want them to know? When you attempt to explain yourself to others, you often gain greater self-knowledge. You might want to share your letter with classmates and to hear what they have to say in their letters. Perhaps your instructor could also try this exercise and share his or her open letter with you.

6. Watch the movie *Stand and Deliver.* What factors make Jaime Escalante a great teacher? How can his teaching be improved?

7. Check out teacher-related web sites on the Internet. Schools and school districts, professional teacher organizations, and all sorts of interest groups sponsor not only web sites but also listservs, chat groups, and other Internet activities. This may present an opportunity to interact with practicing classroom teachers about their own classroom experiences. (Check out our web site at www.mhhe.com/sadker)

8. Interview some practicing teachers to determine their opinions of how teaching is—or is not—a profession. Summarize your findings.

9. In your opinion, is teaching a profession? Give reasons for your answer.

10. Imagine that you are taking part in a career fair. Someone asks why you are exploring teaching. Briefly frame your answer.

A Question-and-Answer Guide to Entering the Teaching Profession

Focus Questions

- What does the teaching job market look like? (Put another way, Will you get the job of your dreams?)
- How do teacher salaries and working conditions in public schools compare with those found in private schools?
- What steps can I take now to prepare to enter teaching?
- How do I get a teaching license, and is the process as difficult and bureaucratic as people say?
- What exactly is tenure, and is it a good idea for the profession? Is it a good idea for me?
- What education jobs exist beyond the classroom?

Chapter Preview

As you read through this book, you will detect a common thread linking most of the chapters: a specific topic, such as professionalism or the pros and cons of teaching, provides the chapter with a theme or focus. Then the topic is explored with stunning clarity, and, whenever possible, interesting anecdotes and interactive techniques are included in order to keep you, the reader, spellbound. You undoubtedly noticed that the first chapter followed this format; in fact, so do most of the chapters. Not here. The structure of this chapter is different. (However, we trust it will still keep you spellbound.)

Beyond questions concerning the content of any subject, students often have more personal and practical questions about teaching, the kind of questions that are more likely to be asked after class or during office hours. Students considering an education career want to know everything from how teachers are licensed to where the jobs are, from how to land a teaching position to what kinds of education careers are available beyond the classroom. We trust that this chapter will answer some of the questions you are beginning to ask, and even some you never thought to raise.

```
┌─────────────────────────────────────────────────────────┐
│                    YOU'VE GOT MAIL                      │
├─────────────────────────────────────────────────────────┤
│  TO:   Steve@AU.edu,                                    │
│        Anna@State.edu                                    │
├─────────────────────────────────────────────────────────┤
│  SUBJ:   New Major??!!                                   │
│                                                         │
│  OK, I am going to do it! I am thinking about changing  │
│  my major. I enjoy the courses that I am taking, but the│
│  truth is that I just can't see any future for this when│
│  I finish school.                                       │
│                                                         │
│  Yup, you guessed it, I was always interested in        │
│  teaching, so I think I'll try it. I've been asking     │
│  around, but I am getting so many different answers      │
│  about what I need to do. Even James and Alicia, who are│
│  majoring in teacher education, are giving me different  │
│  answers. I want to know about the job market, how I get │
│  a license, even salary information, so I am going to    │
│  the Teacher Ed orientation meeting to get some answers. │
│                                                         │
│  Can you imagine . . . me, a teacher!!!?                 │
└─────────────────────────────────────────────────────────┘
```

Q **What Are My Chances of Finding a Teaching Position?**

A This is a practical and quite natural question for you to be asking right now. After all, you are thinking about investing time, energy, money, and talent in preparing yourself to become a teacher, so it makes sense to ask whether you will be able to land a position when you graduate. Here is a shortcut to sorting out your employment possibilities, the **"four Ws"**: *when, what, where,* and *who.* Let's begin with *when* first.

Although you may not have controlled *when* you would enter teaching, the good news is that this is a terrific time to be looking for a position in education. While there are few guarantees when it comes to predicting national labor needs, several factors suggest that there will be a significant number of teaching positions available into the next decade. Perhaps we can appreciate the current situation better if we take a look at "the bad old days."

Historically, the demand for new teachers has resembled a roller coaster ride. In the 1950s and 1960s, a teaching shortage meant virtually anyone would be hired as a teacher, with or without the proper credentials. Back then, new graduates of teacher education programs enjoyed the view from the roller coaster as it soared. By the 1970s, the teacher employment roller coaster had begun to descend. Shrinking school budgets and the end of the baby boom had led to far more teachers than there were positions; as more teachers were licensed than positions existed, **teacher oversupply** became part of the educational lexicon, and teacher unemployment was common. By the 1980s and 1990s, the roller coaster was back on the ascent, as teacher retirements increased and student enrollments began to climb.

Strong demand for new teachers continues into the twenty-first century.[1] An increasing student population, calls for smaller class sizes, ongoing teacher retirements, and the relative attractiveness of a teaching career have increased the demand for teachers. Let's consider the second *W: what* subject and grade level you plan to teach. Teachers of certain subjects, such as science and math, are in short supply, and many school districts are being forced to hire science and math teachers who have not taken enough courses to qualify for a teacher's license in these fields. Science, computer science, and math are "hot" fields; in many districts, so are bilingual and special education, as well as speech pathology. One way to make yourself more marketable is to consider course work and school experiences in subjects and skills that are in demand.

Population shifts and political actions affect teacher demand, and they contribute to the third *w, where.* Recently, teacher shortages were felt in western and southwestern states (Arizona, California, Alaska, and Hawaii), while the need for new teachers was generally lower in the Northeast, Great Lakes, and Middle Atlantic areas. But, despite these general trends, there are notable exceptions; for example, population increases in some communities in New Jersey and New Hampshire created local teacher shortages. Large cities, one of the more challenging classroom environs, also continue to experience a shortage of new teachers. For instance, over half of the administrators in Washington, DC, report difficulty in attracting qualified teacher applicants.[2]

States and local communities also differ in their resources and priorities. Wealthier districts are more likely to sponsor a greater variety of programs and course offerings and to establish smaller average class sizes, actions that translate into a need for more teachers, while many urban areas struggle to find qualified teachers and adequate resources. Some districts and states are more responsive than others in providing students with special services. In the early 1990s, for example, over 15 percent of the school-age children in Massachusetts were receiving special education assistance for disabilities, while Louisiana was serving fewer than 8 percent of its students with such services.[3]

As if all this were not confusing enough, many school districts are committed to hiring a diverse teaching staff providing students of all racial and ethnic backgrounds with role models in order to send a clear message that the school district is practicing the lessons of democracy, as well as teaching them. This is the last *w,* the *who.* Thus far, this effort has had only a limited impact, as most faculties continue to be populated mainly by monolingual white teachers of European ancestry, a fact of life likely to continue into the foreseeable future. Relatively few people of color enter teaching. School personnel officers are also intrigued with the need to correct the gender imbalance in elementary school teachers. Because approximately 90 percent of elementary teachers are women, schools often hire newly qualified male elementary teachers as soon as they graduate. (School districts appear less motivated to correct the gender imbalance in administration, where about 90 percent of school principals and superintendents are males.)

Local and state governments are experimenting with new methods of school organization, changes that may impact the job market and go beyond the traditional four *Ws.* **Privatization** (the movement to turn over school management to private companies) as well as vouchers and even charter schools are challenging the traditional employment practices by introducing productivity measures, individual school decision making, and the participation of parents and others in personnel actions. These changes may affect teacher supply and demand in the years ahead.

With student enrollments climbing, a sizable number of teachers moving into their retirement years, and an ever greater focus being placed on improving schools, education is now a growth industry. In fact, given the role schools play in preparing workers for an increasingly competitive world economic market, it is likely that improving schools will remain high on the national agenda. In terms of employment opportunities, teaching remains a good career choice into the foreseeable future.

Q **Who Are My Teaching Colleagues? What Are the Demographics of Today's Teachers?**

A In the late 1990s, there are more than 3 million full-time teachers, an increase of over half a million from the early 1980s. More than 2½ million of these teachers are in public schools, with fewer than half a million working in private schools. About 75 percent of all teachers, and approximately 90 percent of elementary teachers, are women. Only in vocational education and the social sciences do male teachers outnumber females. The average teacher's age is 43, a number that has been rising, suggesting that, over the next few years, teacher retirements will be increasing as well. Despite the desire to moderate the domination of the teacher ranks by those of European background, this is not happening. In the mid-1990s, although 16 percent of students were African American, only 9 percent of their teachers were African American. While 12 percent of students were Hispanic, only 4 percent of their teachers were Hispanic. Eighty-seven percent of the nation's teachers are white and non-Hispanic, yet about one-third of the nation's students come from other backgrounds, a cultural and racial difference likely to grow in the years ahead.[4]

Q **What Are My Chances for Earning a Decent Salary?**

A People are generally drawn to teaching for the personal gratification that comes from working with children and enhancing the quality of life in their communities. Still, most teachers have more than a passing interest in the salary they will earn. While teachers have been underpaid historically, the good news is that teachers' salaries have been steadily improving. When asked if teaching offers a decent salary, only 37 percent of the teachers surveyed in the mid-1980s said yes; by the mid-1990s, this had risen to 63 percent.[5] (See Figure 2.1.) Consider the following:

- Between 1981 and 1997, after adjusting for inflation, the average public school teacher salary increased from $31,100 to $38,500 (in 1997 constant dollars). Elementary and secondary school teacher salaries increased approximately 20 percent.
- The average beginning public school teacher salary increased 23 percent between 1980 and 1997, from $20,800 to $25,500 (in 1997 constant dollars).
- Increases in teacher salaries are greatly influenced by geography and the size of the school district. Teachers in the Northeast receive the highest pay and those in the South the least. The smallest school districts tend to pay the least (top salary reaching about $36,500), while the next larger district pays $43,800. As school districts increase in size, salary levels also increase.[6]

Figure 2.2 offers insights into average teacher salaries and regional differences. But even these ranges don't tell the whole story. Within each state, school districts' salaries vary, often dramatically. (We don't have enough pages to illustrate those numerous differences.) You may want to contact specific school districts that you are interested in to request a copy of their teaching salaries, often referred to as the teaching **salary scale.**

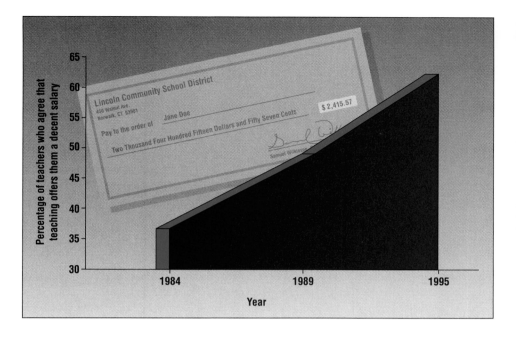

FIGURE 2.1

Teacher satisfaction with teaching salaries. Teachers have increasingly come to believe that their occupation provides them with the opportunity to earn a decent salary.

Source: Louis Harris & Associates (NY) 1995. Metropolitan Life Survey of the Am. Teacher, 1984–1995: Old Problems, New Challenges.

Q **Do Private Schools Pay Less Than Public Schools?**

A Yes. Private or independent schools generally pay teachers lower salaries. Although many private school teachers are fine teachers, they often have less schooling, have less experience, and participate less in professional development than do public school teachers, differences that are used to explain their lower salaries. But, while the average teacher salary is lower, private schools may offer teachers a different set of benefits—smaller classes, more motivated students, more supportive parents, a greater sense of community, a greater sense of teacher autonomy, a shorter school year, a more challenging curriculum, or even housing and meals—so each school needs to be contacted in order to determine the entire employment picture. Individual private schools, like their public counterparts, vary significantly in their academic standing, salaries, and employment practices, and each school needs to be evaluated individually. While some are quite competitive with local public school employment benefits and are academically demanding, most do not fare as well. Figure 2.3, which provides regional public school salaries, also compares average public and private school salaries by region.[7]

Q **What Steps Can I Take Between Now and Graduation to Make Myself an Attractive Teaching Candidate?**

A **Become Informed About the Job Market.**
Begin gathering current information about the job market and search out those particular content areas and skills that will increase your marketability. This information will help you select appropriate courses and extracurricular activities. There are many sources for obtaining this information, including the major professional associations and state departments of education, listed in the appendix of this text. Want more information? You can write the NEA at 1201 Sixteenth Street, N.W., Washington, DC 20036, or www.nea.org, and the AFT at 555 New Jersey Avenue, N.W., Washington, DC 20001, or www.aft.org.

District or school characteristics	Districts/schools with salary schedules					Districts/schools without salary schedules		
	Percentage with salary schedules	Bachelor's, no experience	Master's, no experience	Master's, 20 years experience	Highest step on schedule	Percentage without salary schedules	Salary range	
							Average lowest	Average highest
Public school districts	93.9	$24,080	$26,312	$40,874	$44,503	6.1	$22,164	$32,401
Region								
Northeast	91.9	28,098	30,455	51,177	56,313	8.1	26,541	49,817
Midwest	91.4	22,932	25,277	39,231	42,193	8.6	19,940	24,927
South	99.5	22,415	23,850	34,000	37,177	0.5	(*)	(*)
West	94.5	24,068	26,916	41,519	45,382	5.5	(*)	(*)
Private schools	63.4	17,836	19,354	27,667	29,957	36.6	14,553	23,978
Region								
Northeast	63.8	18,084	19,434	28,692	31,153	36.2	13,901	27,009
Midwest	68.1	17,408	18,879	27,782	29,926	31.9	15,008	22,395
South	57.7	16,555	17,916	24,330	26,662	42.3	14,520	22,485
West	63.7	20,044	22,086	30,752	33,010	36.3	14,892	24,208

* Too few observations for reliable estimates.

FIGURE 2.2

Average teacher salary of schools with published pay scales. Teacher salary schedules are determined by several factors, including geographic region, school characteristics, and level of teachers' experience.

Source: U.S. Department of Education, National Center for Education Statistics, Condition of Education, 1998.

For additional sources of information, check with your university's placement office. You may want to begin reading professional education journals that include information about the employment picture. Web sites are often the best source of up-to-date information, so you may want to visit sites sponsored by school districts, professional associations, placement services, or your university. You can also visit real sites, such as job fairs sponsored by school districts. Knowledge about the employment picture and the kind of candidate that is in demand can give you a powerful start on your teaching career.

Many studies emphasize the importance of the interview in obtaining a teaching position.

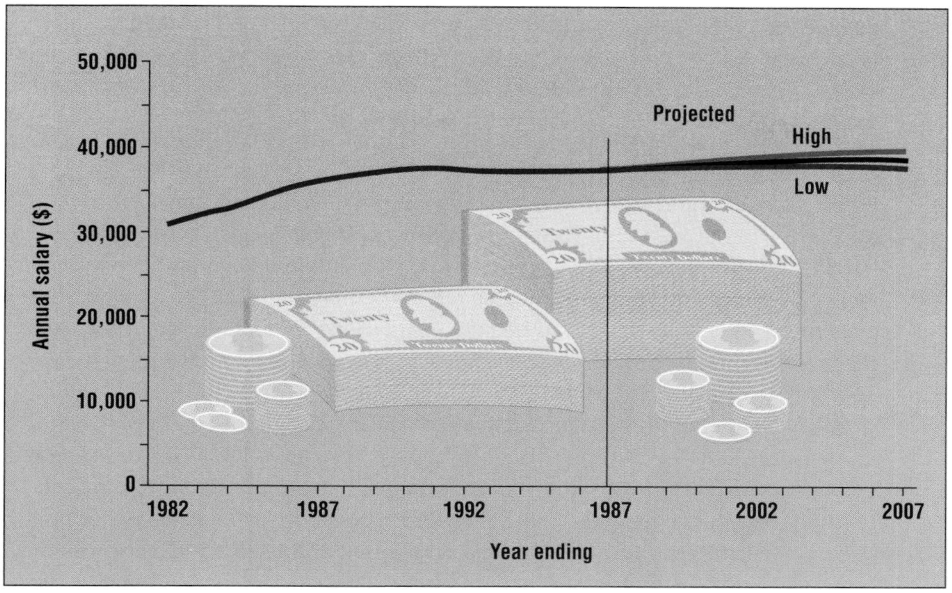

FIGURE 2.3

Average annual salaries of public school teachers with projections to 2008. Teacher salaries are expected to continue to increase into the twenty-first century.

Source: National Center for Education Statistics, Projections of Education Statistics to 2007. Washington, DC: U.S. Department of Education, 1998.

A **Make Sure Your Coursework Is Planned Carefully.**

Your first concern should be to enroll in courses that fulfill your certification and licensure requirements. We will explore certification and licensure in some depth in the next few pages, but for now it is worth remembering that, in addition to earning your degree, you want to leave your program licensed to teach. A second consideration is to make yourself more marketable by going beyond minimum course requirements. For example, technology skills are often in demand by schools, as are elementary teachers with special competence in math or any teacher with a proficiency in a second language. Plan to develop a transcript of courses that will reflect a unique, competent, and relevant academic background. Your transcript will be an important part of your overall candidacy for a teaching position.

A **Do Not Underestimate the Importance of Extracurricular Activities.**

Employers are likely looking for candidates whose background reflects interest and experience in working with children. A day care center or summer camp job may pay less than the local car wash, bank, or restaurant, but these career-related jobs may offer bigger dividends later on. Think about offering your services to a local public school or community youth group. Try to make your volunteer situation parallel the future job you would like to have. You want to build an inventory of relevant skills and experiences as well as personal contacts, efforts that can translate into winning that desired teaching job.

A **Begin Networking.**

Through both your coursework and your extracurricular activities, you will come into contact with teachers, administrators, and other school personnel. You should be aware that these people can function as an informal **network** for information about the local employment picture, as can your professors and even your classmates. Go out of your way to let these people know of your interests, your special skills, and your commitment to teaching. This does not mean that you should become such a nuisance that people will duck behind their desks when they see you coming. It does mean that, at the right times and in the right places, you can let them know what jobs you are looking for and the skills and experiences you have that qualify you for those jobs. Most professionals like to see new jobs filled by competent people. If they know about you and are impressed with what they know, they will want to help you.

A Begin Collecting Recommendations Now.

Studies reveal that letters of recommendation greatly influence employment decisions. Do not wait until you are student teaching to begin gathering these letters. Extracurricular activities, coursework, part-time employment, and volunteer work can all provide you with valuable recommendations. Your university placement office may be able to begin a **placement folder** for you, maintaining these recommendations and forwarding copies to potential employers at the appropriate time.

Ask for letters of recommendation while you are in a job or course or immediately after leaving it. (While this may not endear you to all, letters can be a powerful persuader in your quest for that perfect teaching position.) Professors, teachers, and past employers may move to new locations, and, believe it or not, they may even forget you and just how competent and talented you are. You may be asked to help by drafting key points you would like to stress. Anything you can do to lighten the burden would be appreciated, so collecting letters of recommendation should be a continual process, not one that begins in the last semester of your teacher education program.

A Develop a Résumé and Portfolio.

Traditionally, a **résumé** has been a central document considered during job applications, typically including a specific career objective and summarizing education, work experience, memberships, awards, and special skills. For example, a résumé might target a social studies teaching position in a particular area as your career objective, and it might report membership in the student NEA, an office held in school government, fluency in Spanish, experience with a student newspaper, honors you have won, and any relevant jobs, such as summer camp counselor or work in a day care center. If you would like to explore the possible ways of constructing résumés, many computer programs have résumé templates, there are scores of books devoted to résumé writing, and advisors and counselors at your school should be able to assist.

Today, many colleges and school districts are moving beyond résumés and toward **portfolios,** a more comprehensive reflection of a candidate's skills. If you would like to do something a bit more innovative than simply preparing a dynamite résumé and providing sparkling letters of recommendation, or if your teacher education program is promoting more authentic and creative assessment strategies, then you might want to consider developing a portfolio. This text will help you in that process. You will find, cleverly placed between the major sections of this book, a special feature called "Inter-mission." The "Inter-mission" will encourage you to reflect on your reading, undertake some interesting observations and activities, and begin collecting relevant materials for your portfolio. Even if you decide not to develop a portfolio, these "Inter-mission" activities will be useful for developing professional materials that you can use in many different ways.

A Make Good First, Second, Third, and Fourth Impressions.

In many education courses, you will be asked to participate in local school activities. This participation may take the form of observing or of being a teacher's aide or student teacher. (You may find the Observation Handbook in the appendix of this book particularly useful for school visits.) Recording and thinking about your impressions can be a useful step in deciding on the kind of position you want. In each case, you will be making an impression on the school faculty and administration. Good impressions can lead to future job offers. Poor impressions can result in your name being filed in the *persona non grata* drawer of people's needs.

Consider every visit to a school as an informal interview. Dress and act accordingly. Demonstrate your commitment and enthusiasm in ways that are helpful to school personnel. If you are viewed as a valuable and useful prospective member of the school community, you immediately become a candidate for a current or future teaching position. Remember, known quantities are nearly always preferred to unknown quantities.

Q What Do I Need in Order to Teach—a License or Certification? By the Way, What's the Difference?

Project yourself a few years into the future. You have just graduated from college. After you return home, you stop by your local public school office and make a belated inquiry into teacher openings. The school secretary looks up from a cluttered desk, smiles kindly, and says, "We may have an opening this fall. Are you certified? Do you have a license?"

Oops! Certified? License? Now I remember. It's that paperwork thing. . . . I should have filled out that application back at college. I should have gone to that teacher licensure meeting. And I definitely should have read that Sadker textbook more carefully. I knew I forgot something. Now I'm in trouble. All that work and I will not be allowed to teach. What a nightmare!

And then you wake up.

A Many people use the terms *teacher certification* and *teaching license* interchangeably (as in "She has her teacher certification" while really meaning "She has her teaching license"). But it is important for you to be able to distinguish between a professional certification and a legal license, so we make the distinction in this book. **Teacher certification** confers professional standing; a **teacher's license** is a legal document. Teacher certification indicates that a professional group recognizes (certifies) that a teacher is competent and has met certain standards. A teacher's license, issued by the state government, grants the legal right to teach, not unlike a driver's license grants the legal right to drive. Both licenses mean that the "minimum" state requirements have been met. If you have been out on the roads recently, you know that meeting these minimum requirements to drive is not an indication that a person can, in fact, drive very well. It is the same with a teacher's license: not all holders can teach well, especially if they are teaching a subject without adequate training in that field, a sad but not uncommon practice.

Q Who Awards Licenses, and How Do I Get One?

A Teaching licenses are not awarded by your college but by each of the fifty states and the District of Columbia. In a similar way, states are involved with the licensure of doctors, lawyers, and other professionals and nonprofessionals. When you meet the state's requirements, you can apply for and receive your teacher's license.

As you may already have detected, there are drawbacks to this process. Perhaps the most significant problem is that each state has its own requirements for teacher licensure. States have different policies concerning what courses teachers should take, what kinds of teacher's licenses should be offered, and even the length of time for which a teacher's license is valid. You may meet the standards in one state, but, if you decide to teach in another, you may find yourself unqualified for its license.

Since the courses and experiences you need vary from state to state, it is useful to understand the major areas of preparation relevant to certification and licensure. Joseph Cronin, writing in the *Handbook of Teaching and Policy,* suggests three categories: knowledge of subject matter, knowledge of pedagogy, and practice teaching.[8] Chances are that your course work will fit within these three.

A few final notes on licenses are in order. Do not assume that your teacher certification or state license will automatically be issued to you when you graduate. Remember, state departments of education, not colleges and universities, issue teacher's licenses; professional associations grant certification. Some colleges will apply to a designated state department in your name and request a license; others will not. In most states, filling out an application and passing the required national or state tests are all that is needed if you have graduated from an approved program. But not all teacher education programs are accredited. Either way, remember that *you* will probably need to apply to the state for a teacher's license.

When you have questions about obtaining a license, consult immediately with your college instructor, adviser, or teacher education placement office, or write directly to the appropriate state department of education. Do not depend on friends, whose advice may not be accurate.

Although the licensure process is sound in principle, it is no guarantee of competency. Unfortunately, we have all been taught by individuals who managed to obtain a license but were not particularly talented or competent as teachers. Conversely, competent teachers are sometimes denied the right to teach because they have not met all the technical requirements of licensure. Nevertheless, the intent of certification and licensure is to maintain high standards for teachers, and you should be aware of the necessary steps to get your teacher's license on schedule.

Teachers who are certified often receive their licenses rather quickly. But, when there are teacher shortages, or alternative paths to a teacher's license are used, unqualified individuals who have not met certification standards may be granted a license to teach. In fact, states issue various levels of license, depending on an individual's qualifications.

A Most states issue more than one kind of license in order to differentiate among the applicants' qualifications and career goals. Although the specific names of these licenses (sometimes called certificates, now how's that for confusing!) vary from state to state, there are four common types:

1. An **initial,** or **provisional, license**—also called a *probationary certificate*—is the type frequently issued to beginning teachers and is generally nonrenewable. If you are awarded a provisional license, it means that you have completed most, but not all, of the state's legal requirements to teach. It may also mean that you need to complete some additional course work or that you need to teach for several years before you qualify for a higher or more permanent license. You may find yourself first getting a provisional license, giving you some breathing room as you work to complete all of the state's requirements for a standard, or professional, license.

2. The **standard,** or **professional, license** is issued by the state after you have completed all the requirements to teach in that state. These requirements may include a specified number of courses beyond the bachelor's degree or one or more years of teaching experience.

IN THE NEWS . . . FROM VIENNA TO THE BRONX

New York City, while short of math and science teachers, is not short on creative ways to recruit them. The city distributed flyers in Vienna, Austria: *If you can read this, have we got a deal for you.* New York City was able to recruit 30 new English speaking Austrians to teach science and math.

Source: *The American School Board Journal,* October 1998.

3. A **special license** is a nonteaching license designed for specialized educational careers, including those in administration, counseling, library science, school social work, and school psychology. If after teaching for several years you decide that you want a career in school counseling (or administration, library science, and so forth), you will have to meet the requirements for this license.

4. A **conditional,** or **emergency, license** is a substandard license that is issued on a temporary basis to meet the needs of communities that do not have licensed teachers available. For example, a small high school in a rural community may not be able to attract a qualified teacher in physics. Faced with the unattractive prospect of not offering its students physics courses, the community may petition the state to award an emergency license to someone who does not meet current licensure standards.

Conditional licenses become commonplace when a shortage of teachers forces states to hire uncertified teachers. Historically, this has even included people who had never completed college. It is an unfortunate fact of life that, even today, when shortages in certain fields or geographic areas arise, substandard teaching licenses are issued.

Q   **What Is an Endorsement?**

A   In some cases, a candidate may be certified to teach in an additional area through what is termed an **endorsement.** For many teachers, especially those teaching in areas that have a large supply of candidates, endorsements can give you the edge over other applicants. You may want to give some consideration to this opportunity. Carefully planning your courses can help you get a second teaching area. So can practical experience. For instance, a teacher may have a standard or professional license in U.S. history but finds herself teaching biology courses as well. Or perhaps she has taken a number of college courses in biology and decides she wants to be recognized as a biology teacher as well as a history teacher. Since she already has a standard or professional license (in history), she need not apply for a new license. Instead, she applies to the state for an *endorsement* in biology. Although she did not take biology methods or student teach in biology, her teaching experience and background are considered for her endorsement in biology. The endorsement means that the state has approved her teaching both history and biology. Sometimes the subjects are more closely related than these. A teacher licensed in bilingual education, for example, with a number of courses in English as a Second Language (ESL), may

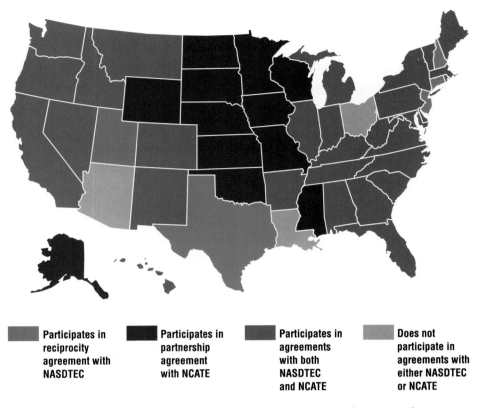

FIGURE 2.4

State participation with accrediting agencies. Accreditation of teacher education programs by an outside agency helps facilitate the certification process across states.

Source: National Council for the Accreditation of Teacher Education (NCATE) and National Association of State Directors of Teacher Education and Certification (NASDTEC), November 1998.

Participates in reciprocity agreement with NASDTEC

Participates in partnership agreement with NCATE

Participates in agreements with both NASDTEC and NCATE

Does not participate in agreements with either NASDTEC or NCATE

seek an endorsement in ESL as well. How common are endorsements? In many school districts, they are fairly common.

Q What Is Accreditation, and What Does It Mean for Me?

A Some teacher preparation programs receive **accreditation** by an outside agency that ensures the institution meets accepted standards. Two such accrediting agencies are the **National Council for the Accreditation of Teacher Education (NCATE)** and the **National Association of State Directors of Teacher Education and Certification (NASDTEC).** If your teacher preparation program has been accredited, you will find that the process of becoming licensed in a number of states is facilitated. (See Figure 2.4.)

   If your teacher education program has not been accredited by either NCATE or NASDTEC, your program may still be recognized in your state. State accreditation is fine if you plan to teach only in that state, but it is less than fine if you are considering other locations. You might want to check to see whether your state has made any **reciprocity agreements** with other states. A number of states have entered such agreements (sometimes referred to as *interstate reciprocity agreements*), in which one state agrees to recognize and license teachers from another state. Your state might have such an agreement or pact with other states, especially neighboring states; if so, this will increase your professional mobility. You should keep up-to-date with licensure requirements in states where you would like to teach. (See Appendix 1 for the addresses of the departments of education in every state.)

Q What Are "Alternative Routes" to Getting a Teacher's License?

A Alternative licensing programs are gaining in popularity. Many of these programs enable college graduates to become teachers with less education training than required in traditional teacher education programs. While teacher shortages represent one reason alternative licensure programs are popular, it is not the only reason. Some critics of teacher education have promoted these alternative paths, because they believe that traditional education courses and programs are not effective in preparing classroom teachers. Only eight states offered alternative routes to licensure in 1984, a movement that began in New Jersey. By the mid-1990s, 41 states had implemented some form of alternative licensure option.[9]

How does alternative licensure work? It all depends on the state. Some states permit selective alternative licensing only, such as at the secondary but not the elementary level, or only in fields in which there are teacher shortages, such as math or science. Some states only allow alternate routes that are designed by higher education institutions. Most alternative programs require a bachelor's degree, and some education course work, but usually far fewer education courses than are typically required. One of the best known of these alternative approaches is **Teach for America.**

Teach for America recruits applicants who have little if any education background but who are motivated to make a positive contribution by teaching in areas that suffer a teacher shortage, particularly inner-city and rural areas. This program has attracted individuals whose altruistic response is reminiscent of Peace Corps volunteers, and Teach for America has also drawn to teaching a higher percentage of mathematics and science applicants than have traditional programs. Moreover, alternative approaches have an impressive track record in recruiting applicants of color. Studies indicate that the alternative program has produced almost five times as many teachers of color as the "regular" program. For example, in Texas, 43 percent of the teachers entering the profession through the alternative teacher licensure program are from non-European ancestry, compared with only 9 percent of all the teachers in the state. Advocates of alternative approaches point to these statistics as proof that there is more than one way to prepare teachers.[10]

Not everyone views alternative routes to teacher preparation as terrific innovations. For one, the attrition rate for these programs is quite high: many who volunteer to join also volunteer to leave, and no wonder. With limited preparation, these rookies wade into challenging teaching situations in some of the nation's most troubled and impoverished communities. Many teacher educators are concerned that this approach is a step back to times past, when "anyone" who wanted to teach was hired. They fear that the alternative preparation of teachers signals a retreat from efforts toward full teacher professionalism. Some also worry about the elementary and secondary students who will be in classrooms with these new and not well-prepared teachers.

Studies of alternative licensure preparation have indicated that graduates of alternative programs represent more of an attempt at a "quick fix" for teacher shortages than a permanent solution. In many cases, their not-yet-honed teaching skills are unlikely to be improved, since graduates of alternative programs are less committed to staying in teaching or to pursuing graduate studies than are students from traditional teacher education programs. (In fact, about 2 percent of the alternative teachers report that they did not graduate from college.) Although alternative preparation programs try to attract older Americans to a teaching career, more than half of those enrolled are fresh out of college.

It is interesting to note that, despite the attention that alternative licensure programs have received in the press, relatively few teachers have moved through these programs and into the classroom. Since 1985, only 50,000 of the nation's teachers have been licensed through alternative programs. That's 50,000 out of 2.6

IN THE NEWS . . . PROMISING PORTRAIT OF TODAY'S TEACHERS

According to a study released by the National Education Association, today's teachers have more academic training and classroom experience than their predecessors. The majority of teachers (54%) have a master's degree or comparable course work, a rate twice as high as teachers in the 1970s. The typical teacher has been in the classroom for 16 years, compared to an average of 10 years in the 1970s.

Source: *Washington Post,* 3 July 1997.

million, less than 2 percent. There are several reasons for this. Alternative programs prepare relatively few teachers; their graduates typically stay in teaching for only a brief period of time; and, when competing for a position, alternative candidates seem to be at a disadvantage. As one dean of a school of education pointed out, very few alternatively prepared teachers get hired when there are well-qualified traditionally prepared teachers available.[11] Because these programs are relatively new, studies of their effectiveness will undoubtedly continue in the years ahead.

Q **What Are Teacher Competency Tests?**

A Most states require teacher competency tests, and others are experimenting with additional forms of evaluation, such as supervised internships. Why are teachers facing new hurdles and higher standards? One reason is that, during the past few decades, the public became outraged about reports of student achievement decline in standardized tests and high school graduates who could not read or write. Between the 1960s and the 1980s, average SAT scores tumbled 42 points on the verbal and 26 points on the mathematical sections of the test. In 1983, the U.S. Department of Education published *A Nation at Risk,* highlighting these depressing test scores and calling for significant school changes, including fewer electives, an increase in core course requirements, more student testing, and better paid and more qualified teachers. In response, many states required elementary and secondary students, as well as teachers, to pass **minimum competency tests.** The movement for state-required competency tests spread— or raced—from a few states in the Southeast to the overwhelming majority of states across the nation. By the early 1990s, all but a handful of states had begun to use standardized tests for admission into teaching programs, for certification, and for licensure.[12] Chances are strong that you will be tested, perhaps more than once, if you decide to enter teaching. Some of these tests are sponsored by states, and applicants have been required to write essays on topics related to education, as well as to pass basic skills tests of spelling, grammar, and punctuation. Some states also test mathematical skills. In other cases, states or local districts have developed more complex, competency-based evaluation systems. But many states now use a national exam.

The **National Teacher Examination (NTE),** initiated in 1940 under the auspices of the American Council on Education (ACE), came about when a group of superintendents asked for help in teacher selection. With a grant from the

Carnegie Foundation, ACE and others formed the Educational Testing Services (ETS), and the exam became its responsibility. By the early 1990s, ETS determined that a new test was needed.

That new test is the **Praxis Assessment for Beginning Teachers,** a three-part teacher assessment. (See Appendix 2.) The first level, *Praxis I: Preprofessional Skills Test* consists of hour-long academic skills tests in reading, writing, and mathematics. These basic tests apply to prospective teachers in all fields and all grades; by the mid-1990s, a number of states required that these academic skills tests such as *Praxis I* be taken by applicants for teacher licensure. *Praxis I* can be taken in the standard paper-and-pencil format on specified dates around the country or by means of a more costly computer version, with far more flexible timing, widespread availability, and immediate scoring.

The *NTE Specialty Tests* and *Praxis II* assess subject area, pedagogy, and professional education knowledge; they comprise more than 100 exams in subjects ranging from accounting to U.S. history. *Praxis II* exams are required in approximately half the states. *Praxis III,* which is a classroom performance assessment of teaching skills, covers classroom management, instructional and planning skills, and assessment of student learning. While this third level comes closest to a realistic assessment of instructional performance, it is also the most challenging and costly test to implement, and it has not gained the widespread popularity of *Praxis I* and *II.*

Educators differ sharply as to whether the Praxis series or other competency tests are necessary. Those who support competency exams maintain that the exams lend greater credibility and professionalism to the process of becoming a teacher. They claim that such tests identify well-educated applicants who can apply their knowledge in the classroom. They cite examples of teachers who cannot spell, write, or perform basic mathematical computations, and they plead persuasively that students must be protected from such teachers.

Some critics of the teacher exams argue that they are incredibly easy and not a real measure of competence. Other critics believe that such tests are more a political gesture than a way of improving education.[13] Part of the problem is the lack of evidence supporting the idea that teacher testing predicts teacher performance. Some believe that the tests are unnecessary and that the current process of state licensure and period of assessment prior to tenure are sufficient vehicles to weed out incompetent teachers. Still others worry that we do not really know what makes good teachers, and we know even less about how to create tests to separate the good from the bad. We don't have tests that can measure enthusiasm, dedication, caring, and sensitivity—qualities that students associate with great teachers. But the *Praxis* and other test makers are constantly working to respond to these charges, and to create more effective tests.

Another provocative and controversial problem is the impact of standardized competency tests on teaching candidates of color. Earlier, when African American teachers were systematically paid less, the NTE was used as a vehicle for teachers of color to attain salary equity with whites. More recently, however, competency exams appear to inhibit candidates from the nondominant culture from gaining teaching positions. Test results in states across the nation document the problems African American and Hispanic teacher candidates are having in passing such exams, problems that have been attributed to reasons ranging from test bias to social and educational differences. Nevertheless, the courts have ruled that the NTE is an acceptable means of screening teacher candidates.[14]

The problem is that such exams may worsen an already serious situation. The pipeline of nonwhite candidates for teaching careers, which was only a trickle to begin with, continues to get smaller and is in danger of drying up. Approximately 91 percent of all teachers are white, 7 percent are black, and only 2 percent are Hispanic. This is happening at a time when more than a third of K–12 enrollment and most urban students are children of color.[15]

Most people—educators and the public alike—agree that testing teachers is hardly the whole answer to raising student achievement. However, with strong public sentiment in favor of testing teachers and with the myriad of competency tests and other evaluation procedures being implemented at state and local levels, you had better be prepared to face competency testing when you graduate. The best way to do this is to take all aspects of your education seriously—both the liberal arts and the professional components. If doctors and lawyers have to pass examinations, perhaps you should also.

Q   How Do Teaching Contracts Work?

A   Congratulations; you have been hired by the school system of your choice, and a contract is placed before you. Before you sign it, there are a few things you should know about teacher contracts. This contract represents a binding agreement between you and the school district. It will be signed by you as the teacher being hired and by an agent of the board of education, often the superintendent. The contract usually sets the conditions of your work, perhaps including specific language detailing your instructional duties, and, of course, your salary.

If you do not have tenure, you will receive a new yearly contract. Once you earn tenure, you will be working under a continuing contract and will probably be asked to notify the school district each year as to whether you plan to teach for the district the following year.

Q   What Are Some Advantages of Tenure?

A   A teacher was once asked to leave his teaching position in Kentucky because he was leading an "un-Christian" personal life. He was Jewish.

A second-grade teacher was dismissed from her teaching assignment in Utah because of her dress. She wore miniskirts.

In Massachusetts, a teacher was fired because of his physical appearance. He had grown a beard.

Fortunately, these teachers all had one thing in common: **tenure.** And tenure prevented their school districts from following through on dismissal proceedings.

A vast majority of states currently have tenure laws. A newly hired teacher is considered to be in a probationary period. The **probationary teaching period** can be two, three, or even five years for public school teachers and about six years for college professors. After demonstrating teaching competence for the specific period, the teacher is awarded tenure, which provides a substantial degree of job security. Generally, a tenured teacher can be fired only for gross incompetence, insubordination, or immoral acts or because of budget cuts stemming from declining enrollments. In practice, public schools rarely fire a tenured teacher.

Since teachers have enjoyed the protection of tenure for many years, it is easy to forget how important this protection is. To get a fresh perspective on tenure, consider what life in schools might be like without it.

Without tenure, hundreds, perhaps thousands, of financially pressed school systems could respond to pressure from taxpayers by firing their experienced teachers and replacing them with lower-paid, less experienced teachers. This would significantly reduce school budgets, usually the largest cost item in the local tax structure. After two or three more years, these teachers would also face the financial ax. In short, teachers would once again become an itinerant, poorly paid profession. Would anyone really benefit?

Without tenure, the fear of dismissal would cause thousands of teachers to avoid controversial topics, large and small. Many teachers would simply become a mirror of their communities, fearing to stir intellectual debate or to teach unsettling ideas because job security had become their prime objective. Classrooms would become quiet and mundane places, devoid of the excitement that comes from open discussion of controversial ideas.

Without tenure, many teachers would have to modify their personal lifestyles. In some communities, they would have to avoid places where liquor is served; in others, their clothing or hairstyles would have to be altered. Any behavior that differed from the norms of the community would be potentially dangerous, for such behavior could provide the spark that would trigger public clamor for dismissal. A conformist philosophy would spread from the classroom to teachers' personal lives.

In short, without some protection such as tenure, teaching would take a giant step backward. Tenure provides teachers with the fundamental security that allows them to develop and practice their profession without fear of undue pressure or intimidation. Unfortunately, not all teachers have respected the academic freedom provided by tenure, as we shall see in the next section.

Q What Are Some Disadvantages of Tenure?

A Over the years, it has become apparent that the protection of academic freedom through the tenure process has entailed serious drawbacks. One such drawback is the reality that ineffective teachers are protected from dismissal. Many of these ineffective teachers view tenure as a right to job security without acknowledging a corresponding responsibility to continue professional growth. Feeling that they are no longer subject to serious scrutiny, such teachers fail to keep up with new developments in their field, and each year they drag out old lesson plans and fading lecture notes for yet another outdated performance. Who pays the price for such ineffective teaching? The students, of course. Think back a moment. How many ineffective, tenure-protected teachers were you subjected to during your total school experience? How many do you face at present?

During the past few years, attempts to "reform" or "dismantle" tenure have gained momentum. Some school districts have extended the amount of time it takes to be awarded tenure, while some states have gone even further. In Florida, a recent law reduced the time that poor-performing teachers are given to improve from one year to ninety days. New Hampshire's Republican lawmakers failed in their attempt to require teachers to pass tests and renew their licenses every three years, while a special Colorado task force has been formed to explore ways to limit tenure. One reason for these attempts is the cost involved in dismissing a tenured teacher. A New York School Boards Association Study showed that, in that state in the mid-1990s, it took an average of 455 days and $177,000 to dismiss a teacher. If the teacher appealed, the average price rose to $317,000.[16]

As you can see, tenure is a double-edged sword. It serves the extremely important function of preserving academic freedom and protecting teachers from arbitrary and unjust dismissal. But it also provides job security for ineffective teachers, not good news for the students of these teachers or for the new and more competent teachers trying to enter the profession.

You may find your education niche beyond the traditional classroom. Here are some authentic employment opportunities printed in the "want ads" of newspapers.

CAN YOU TEACH?

The largest computer software and network training company in the world is looking for additional full-time instructors to teach classes. Candidates must possess excellent presentation skills. Computer experience is helpful but not necessary; we will train you.

EDUCATIONAL CONSULTANT

We are seeking an experienced Education Consultant with classroom teaching background for per diem contracted and long-term assignments, with expertise in one or more of the following: dimensions of learning, performance assessments, state learning standards, early literacy, cooperative learning, differentiated instruction.

PRIVATE GIRLS' HIGH SCHOOL

seeks Director of Technology/ Computer Teacher, Classroom Experience Necessary.

ELEMENTARY ZOO INSTRUCTOR

The Education Department of the Zoo, one of the country's foremost institutions of informal science teaching, is seeking a dynamic instructor for its elementary-level programs. A highly interactive teaching approach, creativity, and a theatrical background will be helpful. This position involves program development for parents and teachers in addition to direct instruction of children ages 4–12. Excellent oral and written communication skills required.

EDITOR/WRITER

Familiar with higher edu. issues needed for Publications Dept. Will work with campus colleagues and assoc. staff to develop a natl. quarterly newsletter for faculty & administrators. Must know curriculum development, have solid editorial and publications mgmt. skills, research aptitude, & good writing skills.

Major nonprofit YOUTH SERVICE AGENCY seeks to fill the following positions (Bilingual, Spanish/English preferred): YOUTH COUNSELOR: B.A. 2 years experience in social service setting, PROGRAM COORDINATOR: B.A. 3–5 years experience, strong supervisory/communication skills necessary.

EDUCATIONAL RESEARCHER

Research and develop abstracts for www-based project about science and math education. Writing skills, attention to detail, ability to synthesize information quickly, and confident phone skills. Background in education helpful.

EDUCATIONAL COORDINATOR

The Historical Society seeks a creative, self-motivated team player to plan, implement, & promote educational programs for schools, families, & adults. Responsibilities incl.: organizing public programs & tours: coordinating National History Day, providing services for schools.

CHILD CARE DIRECTOR

Join our management team! Nonprofit corporate-sponsored child care management co., looking for a talented director to manage our state-of-the-art center. Must have ECE experience and have been through NAEYC accred. process.

LEARNING CENTERS offering individualized diagnostic and prescriptive programs are looking for dynamic PT cert. teachers to instruct students of all ages in reading, writing, math, and algebra.

SUBSTANCE ABUSE PREVENTION INTERVENTION SPECIALISTS

Seeking experienced professionals to provide services to students in substance abuse prevention and intervention. Will provide both group and individual counseling and conduct peer leadership groups for students at risk at various schools.

AMERICAN INTERNATIONAL SCHOOLS

Seeking excellent candidates. June interview in major cities. Two years of experience reqd.

WORKSITE TEACHER

Conduct worksite visits & act as liaison between worksite & classroom instruction, BA plus 2 yrs. teaching experience with adults req'd.

LOVE TO TEACH?

Are you considering a career change where you can continue to use your teaching ability? Call.

PROGRAM ASSISTANT

New vision in schools seeks a program assistant to provide support to a major school reform initiative. Must be meticulous with details & be able to write well, handle multiple projects, & and meet deadlines. Interest in public schools is preferred.

EDITOR

One of the most progressive and respected names in children's publishing is currently seeking an editor for a supplement in early childhood. In addition to a degree, editorial/publishing experience, and early childhood classroom experience, you must be highly creative and possess a strong knowledge of early childhood issues.

COLLEGE GRAD

Prestigious sports program for children sks highly motivated coaches. Sports background & a love for children a must. Education majors a +.

EDUCATIONAL SALES REPS

See our ad in the SALES section under "Education."

VIOLENCE PREVENTION PROGRAM

(Peace Games) seeks F/T director to create curricula & resources for students, parents, & teachers.

TEACH ENGLISH ABROAD

BA/BS required. Interested in education. No exp nec.

SPECIAL EDUCATION

The Learning Center, a place for emotionally disturbed children, has the following possible positions: Resource Counselor, Cert. Teacher, Music Teacher, Level III Secretary, Therapist Assistant.

Q Are Untenured Teachers Protected?

FIGURE 2.5

Education want ads.

A Many believe that, until tenure is granted, they are extremely vulnerable, virtually without security. This is not true. During the 1970s, in *Goldberg v. Kelly, Board of Regents v. Roth,* and *Perry v. Sinderman,* the United States Supreme Court outlined several of the rights that are enjoyed by nontenured teachers. In many circumstances, these rights include advance notice of the intention to dismiss a teacher, clearly stated reasons for termination, and a fair and open hearing. In addition, teacher organizations, such as the National Education Association (NEA) and the American Federation of Teachers (AFT), provide legal assistance for teachers who might be subjected to the arbitrary and unjust action of a school system. If the AFT and the NEA ever merge, one result may be even greater legal protection for teachers.

If, during your probationary years, you feel that you have been unfairly victimized by the school administration, you should seek legal advice. Even nontenured teachers possess rights, but these rights are effective only if they are exercised.

Q Can Principals Be Tenured?

A Although about a dozen states still grant tenure or equivalent rights to principals, this protection has all but disappeared. Georgia, Massachusetts, North Carolina, and Oregon recently joined the movement to remove tenure protection for principals. Historically, a satisfactory probationary period of one to five years would result in principals earning tenure, as teachers do. Not anymore. Many of the same arguments used against granting teachers tenure (a shield for mediocrity or even incompetence, a lengthy process to remove poor performers, and so on) have been successfully used to rescind tenure for principals. The crux of the argument seems to be how one views principals. Those who see them as managers believe that, if they are not managing well, they should be fired. Others view principals as master teachers (from the term "principal teacher"), who should be afforded the same protections from arbitrary political pressures and inappropriate personnel decisions as other teachers. The management view is clearly winning out.[17]

Q What Kinds of Educational Careers Are Available Beyond Classroom Teaching?

A The assumption that your education degree has prepared you only for a teaching career is a widespread myth. Actually, there are dozens of education-related careers, although tunnel vision often keeps them from view. (See Figure 2.5.) Obviously, if you are interested in school administration or a counseling career, starting as a classroom teacher makes a lot of sense and gives you an important perspective that will serve you well in these other school careers. But beyond administration and counseling lie many other options. The following list is intended to give you some idea of the less typical but potentially quite rewarding **nontraditional educational careers** available to you.[18]

Early Childhood Education. If you want to stay in touch with teaching but prefer a climate other than the typical classroom, you may want to explore such options as **day care centers.** Early childhood education is a vital component of the nation's educational system. Working parents seek quality options, not only for child care but for child education and development as well.

Although day care rarely offers much pay or status, a number of talented educators find early childhood education incredibly satisfying. If you are creative and flexible, you might even be able to develop your own facility. For example, some department stores advertise a day care service for shopping parents. You might consider opening a similar early childhood program and marketing your "children's center" to other stores, shopping malls, or businesses. (Check out your state's laws regarding operating standards, building restrictions, number of children permitted, and so on.) If you enjoy working with young children, you will find opportunities galore in this growing field.

Adult Education. If you prefer to work with a mature population, you might be attracted to **continuing** and **adult education** programs. These are offered through city and county governments, local school systems, and nearby colleges and universities. In addition, some private businesses now sponsor courses that are related to their products—recreation, crafts, cooking, technical training, and so forth. As the ranks of the retired swell with baby boomers, you can expect this field to grow rapidly. Older Americans often have the time, interest, and income to pursue education in topics, skills, and hobbies that have long eluded them. Elder hostels around the world are responding to the educational demand created by retirees. Researching available programs may take time, but you are apt to discover a variety of adult learning programs that can provide nontraditional teaching opportunities.

Pupil Service Professionals. Service professionals—school social workers, counselors, and psychologists—typically work as a team, assisting teachers in creating more effective learning environments. These professionals receive special training and education to meet the unique needs that frequently emerge in schools. Social workers, for example, work to improve the relationship between home and school. School psychologists, prepared in education and mental health, are responsible for coordinating and evaluating special learning and behavior problems.

Colleges and Universities. You will find many nonteaching, yet education-related, jobs in colleges and universities. To name a few, academic advisers work primarily on a one-to-one basis with students, discussing courses of study; admissions officers respond to the needs of students; alumni relations personnel conduct fund-raising campaigns, organize alumni events, and maintain job placement services; and student services personnel do psychological and vocational counseling, advise international students, and administer residential programs. Most colleges offer their employees tuition benefits, so, if you want to pursue graduate studies, this may be a good way to gain both experience and an advanced degree.

Community Organizations. Think of a community group. Chances are, that group has an educational mission. Churches, synagogues, and nursing homes can use creative instructors and program planners. For example, a former English teacher, disturbed by the demeaning, artsy-craftsy programs in a local nursing home, inspired the residents to write their life histories, an experience they found very stimulating. Recreation and community centers hire instructors, program planners, and directors for their numerous programs. Hospitals and health clinics need people to plan and deliver training to their professional and administrative staffs. Some of the large municipal zoos conduct programs to protect endangered animal species and to interact with school groups. Libraries and media centers require personnel to maintain and catalog resources and equipment, as well as to train others in their use. Art galleries and museums hire staff to coordinate educational programs for school and civic groups and to conduct tours of their facilities.

The Media. The publishing and broadcasting industries hire people with education backgrounds to help write and promote their educational products. For example, large newspapers, such as *The Washington Post,* maintain staff writers whose job is to cover education, just as other reporters cover crime, politics, and finance. Some newspapers even publish a special edition of their paper for use in schools. Likewise, textbook publishers, educational journals, the Internet service providers, and television talk shows need people familiar with educational principles to help develop their programs.

Private Industry and Public Utilities. Large public and private corporations often rely on education graduates in their programs to train their staffs in areas such as organizational effectiveness, new technology training, civil rights and safety laws, and basic company policies and practices. Sometimes client needs come into play, as many of these firms need people with well-developed instructional skills to demonstrate the use of their sophisticated equipment or products to potential customers. Some education-related companies maintain permanent learning centers and seek persons with education backgrounds to plan and run them. If you like writing, you may want to work on pamphlets, brochures, curricula, and other materials describing a company's services and products, often written by education graduates.

Computer Software Development. With the dramatic increase in the use of educational software in the classroom, many companies are soliciting people with experience in education as consultants to help develop new programs. Creativity, familiarity with child psychology, and knowledge of the principles of learning are important resources for developing software that will appeal to a diverse and competitive market.

Technology. The blossoming of the computer age, with its software, e-mail, web sites, and Internet resources, has divided the population into those who are computer literate and those who are computer challenged (sometimes called technophobic). Those who are not yet citizens of cyberworld represent a ready population of potential students. If you enjoy programming, surfing the Net, or designing web sites, you may want to become a tech-teacher, teaching these skills in either formal or informal settings. You may consider a position as a technology consultant for schools, helping design web sites, create networks, or select software.

You may choose to work outside a school organization, as a company representative providing educational services and equipment.

Educational Associations. National, state, and regional educational associations hire writers, editors, research specialists, administrators, lobbyists, and educators for a host of education-related jobs, from research and writing to public relations. There are hundreds of these associations, from the NEA to the American Association of Teachers of French. Check the *National Trade and Professional Associations of the United States and Canada* (Columbia Books, Inc.) for listings and descriptions of positions, or use the *Encyclopedia of Associations* (Gale Research) to contact the associations directly.

Government Agencies. A host of local, state, and federal government agencies hire education graduates for training, policy planning, management, research, and so on. Various directories can help you through the maze of the federal bureaucracy. Among these is the *United States Government Manual* (Office of the Federal Register, National Archives and Records Service), which describes the various programs within the federal government, including their purposes and top-level staffs. The Internet is another useful source for exploring career opportunities in government-related education programs.

Global Opportunities. Want an international experience? Consider Department of Defense schools, private international schools, religious and international organizations, military bases offering high school and college courses to armed forces personnel, and the Peace Corps. A number of foreign companies now hire American college graduates to teach English to their workers, positions that are sometimes very well paid. No matter the wages, high or low, the excitement of teaching in another culture (while learning about that culture) is hard to match.

We've tried to supply answers to some of your questions about entering the teaching profession. But now, let's turn our attention to teaching itself. What does research teach us about effective instructional behaviors? That's a great question and, by an amazing coincidence, the focus of our next chapter.

Key Terms and People

www.mhhe.com/sadker

accreditation

adult education

conditional (emergency) license

continuing education

day care centers

endorsement

four *W*s

initial (provisional) license

minimum competency tests

National Association of State Directors of Teacher Education and Certification (NASDTEC)

National Council for the Accreditation of Teacher Education (NCATE)

National Teacher Examination (NTE)

networking

nontraditional educational careers

placement folder

portfolios

Praxis Assessment for Beginning Teachers

privatization

probationary teaching period

provisional teaching

reciprocity agreements

résumé

salary scale

special license

standard (professional) license

Teach for America

teacher certification

teacher oversupply

teacher's license

tenure

Teacher Effectiveness

Focus Questions

- Is teaching an art or a skill?
- What memories and impressions of good teaching endure, and why?
- What are some of the key research findings concerning effective teaching?
- Why is classroom management such a central issue in successful teaching?
- What are some of the current models of effective teaching?
- What are some of the new directions in effective teaching?

Chapter Preview

Albert Einstein believed that they awakened the "joy in creative expression and knowledge." Elbert Hubbard saw them as those who could make "two ideas grow where only one grew before." Gail Godwin surmised that they are "one-fourth preparation and three-fourths theater." Ralph Waldo Emerson believed that they could "make hard things easy." About whom are these talented geniuses talking? You guessed it: teachers. Although these intellectual leaders shared an insight into the importance of teaching, even these artists and scientists could not decide if teaching was an art or a science, a gift or a learned skill. Perhaps it is both.

Some individuals seem to take to teaching quite naturally. With little or no preparation, they come to school with a talent to teach and touch the lives of students. Others bring fewer "natural" talents to the classroom yet, with preparation and practice, become master teachers, models others try to emulate. Most of us fall in the middle, bringing some skills to teaching but also ready to benefit and grow from teacher preparation and practice teaching.

Historically, there have been little solid data about the skills that comprise good teaching, but, over the past few decades, research findings have provided insights into effective teaching. This chapter provides you with many of those insights, with a core set of skills and strategies associated with effective teaching. Also included are several distinct models of instruction, from cooperative learning to project-based instruction, classroom approaches that have become particularly popular in recent years. You may draw on these skills and models in your own classroom, selecting those that best fit your subject, students, and purpose.

Is Teaching an Art or a Skill?

Think about the best teacher you ever had: try to evoke a clear mental image of what this teacher was like. Here is what some of today's teachers say about their favorite teachers from the past:

> The teacher I remember was charismatic. Going to his class was like attending a Broadway show. But it wasn't just entertainment. He made me understand things. We went step-by-step in such a clear way that I never seemed to get confused—even when we discussed the most difficult subject matter.

> I never watched the clock in my English teacher's class. I never counted how many times she said *uh-huh* or *okay* or paused—as I did in some other classes. She made literature come alive—I was always surprised—and sorry—when the bell rang.

> When I had a problem, I felt like I could talk about it with Mrs. Garcia. She was my fifth-grade teacher, and she never made me feel dumb or stupid—even when I had so much trouble with math. After I finished talking to her, I felt as if I could do anything.

> For most of my life, I hated history—endlessly memorizing those facts, figures, dates. I forgot them as soon as the test was over. One year I even threw my history book in the river. But Mr. Cohen taught history in such a way that I could understand the big picture. He asked such interesting, provocative questions—about our past and the lessons it gave for our future.

The debate has been raging for decades: is teaching an art or a science? What do you think?

If you think it is a combination of both, you are in agreement with most people who have seriously considered this question. Some individuals—a rare few—are naturally gifted teachers. Their classrooms are dazzlingly alive. Students are motivated and excited, and their enthusiasm translates into academic achievement. For these truly talented educators, teaching seems to be pure art or magic.

But, behind even the most brilliant teaching performance, there is usually well-practiced skill at work. Look again at those brief descriptions of favorite teachers: each of them used proven skills—structure, motivation, clarity, high expectations, and questioning.

> "We went step-by-step in such a clear way that I never seemed to get confused—even when we discussed the most difficult subject matter." *(structure and clarity)*

> "She made literature come alive." *(motivation)*

> "After I finished talking to her, I felt as it I could do anything." *(high expectations)*

> "He asked such interesting, provocative questions—about our past and the lessons it gave for our future." *(questioning)*

Although there is ample room for the gift of artistry, most teaching is based on proven and practiced skills and models. See Figure 3.1 for a student view of teaching effectiveness. This chapter will introduce you to the research that you can put to work in your classroom.

FIGURE 3.1

Effective teaching through the eyes of students.

How To Be An Effective Teacher

Here is how to be an effective teacher. Start by making the students love you. You have to be funny and make the lessons interesting. Once the students love you and think your lessons are interesting, you will have their individual attention... ninety-nine percent of the time ... percent of th... they,

How To Become An Effective Teacher

The first thing you can do to become an effective teacher is to get your students to respect you. You need to make learning fun for your students and teaching fun for you. Be fair to all your students, giving attention to all of them. Make your lessons effective and not boring. Don't have too ...

To Be An Effective Teacher

If you want a child to listen, you should make sure the children are interested in what you are teaching otherwise it it dull. The class will stop listening to and paying attention to you. Make sure you are paying attention to them or notes will be flying across the room not ... lessons

From a students point of view a good teacher is a teacher who teaches a lot, is not strict, and teaches in a way that is fun. A teacher who teaches that way will make it more fun a teacher teach ... that will be re...

If you want to be a successful teacher you have to be able to teach your kids and have fun while you teach. You should get new things, like a computer game. You ... like ... t your ... h...

can't ... control of you and ... they do, punish ... they don't do it again. If you want your kids to like you, you have to have a sense of humor. If you do all of these things, you will earn the respect of your students and be successful.

Effective Teaching
(from a kid's point of view)

To become an effective teacher, it takes time and effort. You may want to try to have one day a week fun day. Don't have boring projects: have fun projects that your students enjoy doing. Instead of leaving all the work you give for homework, give a little class time. Instead of packing students down with homework, give them about ... homework ... ore study

The Mysterious Case of Teacher Effectiveness

This chapter describes teaching skills and models that have been shown to have a positive effect on student achievement. Some of these research findings may seem like common sense, part of the folk wisdom about teaching. However, common sense is sometimes taken for granted. In other cases, the research findings will seem surprisingly counterintuitive, exactly what you thought was *not* true. Research helps us distinguish between what we "think" will work and what really works. If you decide to teach, it will be your responsibility to keep up with the burgeoning and sometimes shifting **teacher effectiveness** research through conferences, course work, and education journals.[1] But, for now, let's begin with an introduction to the research on teacher effectiveness.

Academic Learning Time

Research shows that students who spend more time pursuing academic content achieve more. That's the commonsense part, and it's hardly surprising. What is startling is how differently teachers use their classroom time. For example, the Beginning Teacher Evaluation Study[2] showed that one teacher in the Los Angeles school system spent 68 minutes a day on reading, whereas another spent 137 minutes; one elementary school teacher spent only 16 minutes per day on mathematics, whereas another spent more than three times that amount. Similarly, John Goodlad's comprehensive research study, *A Place Called School,* found that some schools devote approximately 65 percent of their time to instruction, whereas others devote almost 90 percent.[3] The variation is enormous.

Although allocating adequate time to academic content is obviously important, making time on the schedule is not enough. How this allocated time is used in the classroom is the real key to student achievement. To analyze the use of classroom time, researchers have developed the following terms: allocated time, engaged time, and academic learning time.

Allocated time is the time a teacher schedules for a subject—for example, thirty minutes a day for math. The more time allocated for a subject, the higher student achievement in that subject is likely to be.

Engaged time is that part of allocated time in which students are actively involved with academic subject matter (intently listening to a lecture, participating in a class discussion, writing an essay, solving math problems). When students daydream, doodle, write notes to each other, talk with their peers about nonacademic topics, or simply wait for instructions, they are not involved in engaged time. When there is more engaged time within allocated time, student achievement increases. As with allocated time, the amount of time students are engaged with the subject matter varies enormously from teacher to teacher and school to school. In some classes, engaged time is 50 percent; in others, it is more than 90 percent.

Academic learning time is engaged time with a high success rate. Many researchers suggest that students should get 70 to 80 percent of the answers right when working with a teacher. When working independently, and without a teacher available to make corrections, the success rate should be even higher if students are to learn effectively. Some teachers are skeptical when they hear these percentages; they think that experiencing difficulty "stretches" students and helps them achieve. However, studies indicate that a high success rate is positively related to student achievement. How effectively teachers provide for and manage academic learning time in their classrooms is an important key in determining student achievement.[4]

In the following sections, you will learn about research-based teaching skills that you can use to increase academic learning time and student achievement. Since much time can be frittered away on organizational details and minor student disruptions, we will look first at effective strategies for classroom

Academic learning time is engaged learning time in which students have a high success rate. When working independently, as here, the success rate should be particularly high.

management. Then we will consider the instructional skills that seem consistently to produce higher academic achievement in students.

Classroom Management

As 10-year-old Lynette approached the room, she could hear the noise of her classmates. So this was going to be her fourth-grade class. Students were running everywhere. Some were drawing on the board; others were playing tag behind the library shelves. A fight seemed to be breaking out in the coat room. "Where is the teacher?" Lynette wondered. School was supposed to have started five minutes ago.

As Alicia headed to her fourth-grade classroom, she could see a smiling woman with glasses standing in the doorway and greeting students. "Hello, I'm Mrs. Michaelson," she said. "And you are?"

"Alicia Garza."

"I'm so glad you'll be in our class this year. Your seat is in the second row. Go to your desk right now and you'll find a paper you will need to fill out. It's a special interview form—everyone in the class has one—and it will give us a chance to get to know each other better. Be sure to look at the classroom rules posted on the board as you go in. These are very important for all of us, and I want us to discuss these rules this morning."

As Alicia entered the room, she stopped a minute to read the classroom rules:

1. Respect other people's rights and feelings. Avoid teasing and making fun of others.
2. Raise your hand to talk. Also, raise your hand if you need help. Share your time and efforts with others. Listening is as important as speaking.
3. Respect other people's property and places. Move around the room safely, and do not disturb others.
4. If you think of a rule that will help us all live and work together more effectively, please share it with us at any time.

Walking to her desk, Alicia noticed that many students, some unknown and some familiar, were already filling out their forms, and many were quietly laughing as they did so.

"I wonder what's on that form," thought Alicia as she slipped into her seat.

These are two different classrooms on the first day of school—in those first five minutes, it becomes obvious that the students will have two very different educational experiences.

Research shows that effective classroom managers are nearly always good planners.[5] They do not enter a room late, after noise and disruption have had a chance to build. They are waiting at the door when the children come in. Starting from the very first day of school, they teach rules about appropriate student behavior, actively and directly. Often they model procedures for getting assistance, leaving the room, going to the pencil sharpener, and the like. The more important rules of classroom behavior are posted, as are the consequences of not following them.[6]

Following are three basic principles for setting class rules: (1) rules should be few in number, (2) they should seem fair and reasonable to students, and (3) rules should fit the growth and maturation of the students. Not too long ago (perhaps when you were in school), rules meant obeying the teacher, being quiet, and not

IN THE NEWS . . . ISOLATION BOX

The classroom management approach used by the second grade teacher at Johnson Elementary School was not appreciated by parent Denise W. Her 7-year-old son was confined to a three foot high cardboard cubicle at the back of his class. While the cubicle met the teacher's need to reduce classroom distractions, it also reduced one student's ability to follow instruction. *Now I know why he hates school,* said Ms. W.

Source: *The American School Board Journal,* February 1998.

misbehaving. As schools have moved away from autocratic teaching styles, student responsibility and ownership of rules have become more central.

Student participation in rule formation can be handled in several ways. Some teachers like to develop the list of rules together with their students; other teachers prefer to present a list of established rules and ask students to give specific examples or to provide reasons for having such rules. When rules are easily understood and convey a sense of moral fairness, most students will comply.

Good managers also carefully arrange their classrooms to minimize disturbances, provide students with a sense of confidence and security, and make sure that instruction can proceed efficiently. They set up their rooms according to the following principles:

- *Teachers should be able to see all students at all times.* Student desks should be arranged so the teacher can see everybody from any instructional area. With all students in a direct line of sight, a teacher's nonverbal cues can often short-circuit off-task student behaviors.
- *Teaching materials and supplies should be readily available.* Arranging a "self-help" area so that students have direct access to supplies encourages individual responsibility while freeing up the teacher to focus on instructional activities.
- *High-traffic areas should be free of congestion.* Place student desks away from supply cabinets, pencil sharpeners, and so on. Minor disturbances ripple out, distracting other students from their tasks.
- *Students should be able to see instructional presentations.* Research shows that students who are seated far away from the teacher or the instructional activity are less likely to be involved in class discussions. Good teachers see the entire classroom as their stage, and they intentionally teach from different areas of the class. Placing instructional materials (video monitor, overhead projector, demonstration activity, flip chart, lab station, and the like) in various parts of the room gives each student "the best seat in the house" for at least part of the teaching day.
- *Procedures and routines should be actively taught in the same way that academic content is taught.* Initial planning and organization reduce time wasted on discipline problems and more quickly establish classroom routines and procedures.[7] For students who come from chaotic home environments, these routines offer a sense of stability. Once established, they allow teachers and students more time for academic learning.

The observer walked to the back of the room and sat down. It seemed to him that the classroom was a beehive of activity. A reading group was in progress in the front of the room, while the other children were working with partners on math examples. The classroom was filled with a hum of children working together, and in several languages—but the activity and the noise were organized and not chaotic.

The observer had been in enough schools over the past twenty years to know that this well-managed classroom did not result from magic but that carefully established and maintained procedures were at work. The observer scrutinized the classroom, searching for the procedures that allowed twenty-six students and one teacher to work together so industriously, harmoniously, and effectively.

First he examined the reading group, where the teacher was leading a discussion about the meaning of a story. "Why was Tony worried about the trip he was going to take?" the teacher asked (a few seconds' pause, all the children with eyes on the teacher, several hands raised). "Sean?"

As Sean began his response, the observer's eyes wandered around the rest of the room, where most of the children were busy at work. Two girls, however, were passing notes surreptitiously in the corner of the room.

During a quick sweep of the room, the teacher spotted the misbehavior. The two girls watched the teacher frown and put her finger over her lips. They quickly returned to their work. The exchange had been so rapid and so quiet that the reading group was not interrupted for even a second.

Another student in the math group had his hand raised. The teacher motioned Omar to come to her side.

"Look for the paragraph in your story that tells how Tony felt after his visit to his grandmother," the teacher instructed the reading group. "When you have found it, raise your hands."

While the reading group looked for the appropriate passage, the teacher quietly assisted Omar. In less than a minute, Omar was back at his seat, and the teacher was once again discussing the story with her reading group.

At 10:15, the teacher sent the reading group back to their seats and quietly counted down from ten to one. As she approached one, the room became quiet and

Modern classrooms are complex environments that require carefully planned rules and routines.

the students' attention was focused on her. "It is now time for social studies. Before you do anything, listen carefully to *all* my instructions. When I tap the bell on my desk, those working on math should put their papers in their cubbies for now. You may have a chance to finish them later. Then all students should take out their social studies books and turn to page 67. When you hear the sound of the bell, I want you to follow those instructions." After a second's pause, the teacher tapped the bell, and the class was once again a sea of motion, but it was motion that the teacher had organized while the students were now taking responsibility for their own learning.

The observer made some notes on his forms. There was nothing particularly flashy or dramatic about what he had seen. It was not the type of theatrical performance that teachers sometimes put on to dazzle him. But he was satisfied, because he knew he had been witnessing a well-managed classroom.

Can you remember from your childhood those activity books in which you had to find the five things wrong in a picture? Let us reverse the game: try rereading this classroom vignette and look for all the things that are *right* with the picture. What could the observer have noted about the teacher's behavior and her procedures that enabled her students to focus on academic content so effectively? Identify four or five observations.

In well-managed classes where teachers keep the momentum going, students are more likely to be on task. The teacher in this vignette used several strategies to avoid interruptions and to keep instruction proceeding smoothly.[8] Did you notice that

1. The teacher used a questioning technique known as **group alerting** to keep the reading group involved. By asking questions first and then naming the student to respond, she kept all the students awake and on their toes. If she had said, "Sean, why did Tony feel concerned about his trip?" the other students in the group would have been less concerned about paying attention and answering the question. Instead, she asked her question first and then called on a student to respond.

2. The teacher seemed to have "eyes in the back of her head." Termed **withitness** by researcher Jacob Kounin, this quality characterizes teachers who are aware of student behavior in all parts of the room at all times. While the teacher was conducting the reading group, she was aware of the students passing notes and the one who needed assistance.

3. The teacher was able to attend to interruptions or behavior problems while continuing the lesson. Kounin calls the ability to do several things at once **overlapping.** The teacher reprimanded the students passing notes and helped another child with a math problem without interrupting the flow of her reading lesson.

4. The teacher managed routine misbehavior using the principle of **least intervention.** Since research shows the time spent disciplining students is negatively related to achievement, teachers should use the simplest intervention that will work. In this case, the teacher did not make a mountain out of a molehill. She intervened quietly and quickly to stop students from passing notes. Her nonverbal cue was all that was necessary, and did not disrupt the students working on math and reading. The teacher might also have used some other effective strategies. She could have praised the students who were attending to their math ("I'm glad to see so many partners working well on their math assignments"). If it had been necessary to say more to the

Good classroom management requires constant monitoring of student behavior.

girls passing notes, she should have alerted them to what they *should* be doing, rather than emphasize their misbehavior ("Deanne and U-Mei, please attend to your own work," *not* "Deanne and U-Mei, stop passing notes").

5. The teacher managed the transition from one lesson to the next smoothly and effectively, avoiding a bumpy transition, which Kounin termed **fragmentation.** When students must move from one activity to another, a gap is created in the fabric of instruction. Chaos can result when transitions are not handled competently by the instructor. Did you notice that the teacher gave a clear transition signal, either the countdown or the bell; gave thorough instructions so her students would know exactly what to do next; and made the transition all at once for the entire class? These may seem simple, commonsense behaviors, but countless classes have come apart at the seams because transitions were not handled effectively.

This vignette illustrated routine classroom management and the handling of minor rule infractions. Sometimes teachers, of course, face more serious misbehavior, especially but not exclusively with older students. When students do not obey a simple reminder, the teacher should repeat the warning, clearly stating the appropriate behavior. If this fails, the teacher will need to apply stronger consequences, such as sending the student to the school office or calling the parents. When teachers must apply such consequences, these should immediately follow the inappropriate behavior, should be mildly but not severely unpleasant, and should be as brief as possible.[9] These episodes should communicate the message "I care about you, but I will not tolerate inappropriate behavior."

A child's rage can result from abuse, powerlessness, trauma, and even normal living, events beyond the teacher's power to alter. Nonetheless, teachers must understand and manage student anger and aggression. Several classroom strategies can help:

- *Choice.* Constantly taking away privileges and threatening punishment can cause students to feel intimidated and victimized. Teachers can provide appropriate options to give a student a sense of some control and freedom.

TIMES OF TRANSITION

Teachers must manage more than thirty major **transitions** every day, from one content area to another, through different instructional activities and through a myriad of routines, including having students line up, collecting papers, distributing texts, and the like. During these transitions, discipline problems occur twice as often as in regular classroom instruction. Classroom management expert **Jacob Kounin** identified five common patterns that can derail classroom management during times of transition:

- *Flip-flops.* In this negative pattern, the teacher terminates one activity, begins a new one, and then flops back to the original activity. For example, in making a transition from math to spelling, the teacher says, "Please open your spelling books to page 29. By the way, how many of you got all the math problems right?"
- *Overdwelling.* This bad habit includes preaching, nagging, and spending more time than necessary to correct an infraction of classroom rules. "Anna, I told you to stop talking. If I've told you once, I've told you 100 times. I told you yesterday and the day before that. The way

things are going, I'll be telling it to you all year, and, believe me, I'm getting pretty tired of it. And another thing, young lady . . . "
- *Fragmentation.* In this bumpy transition, the teacher breaks directions into several choppy steps instead of accomplishing the instructions in one fluid unit—for example, "Put away your reading books. You shouldn't have any spelling books on your desk, either. All notes should be off your desk," instead of the simpler and more effective "Clear your desk of all books and papers."
- *Thrusts.* Classroom momentum is interrupted by non-sequitors and random thoughts that just seem to pop into the teacher's head—for example, the class is busily engaged in independent reading, when their quiet concentration is broken by the teacher, who says, "Where's Roberto? Wasn't he here earlier this morning?"
- *Dangles.* Similar to the thrust, this move involves starting something, only to leave it hanging or dangling—for example, "Richard, would you please read the first paragraph on page 94. Oh, class, did I tell you about the guest speaker we're having today? How could I have forgotten about that?"

Source: Jacob Kounin, *Discipline and Group Management in Classrooms* (New York: Holt, Rinehart & Winston, 1970).

Encouraging a student to select a lunch mate or to choose a project topic offers a reasonable decision-making opportunity and can help avoid aggression and rage.

- *Voice.* Listening to young people is one of the most respectful skills a teacher can model. Students who feel they are not heard feel disrespected. Hearing and honoring students' words (and feelings) reduce the likelihood of misbehavior.
- *Responsibility.* Rechanneling student energy and interest into constructive activities and responsibilities can reduce misbehavior. When students are empowered, they are less likely to vent rage.[10]

Student misbehavior challenges most new teachers even more than leading instructional lessons. You will have students who will test your patience and others whose stories will tear at your heart. Being observant of student behaviors that might signal a problem is always a good idea. As newspaper stories too frequently remind us, student problems can sometimes explode into tragic violence.

While we can't always detect the signs of danger, we can be on the lookout and can create management plans to handle small distractions as well as major incidents. As researcher David Berliner says, "In short, from the opening bell to the end of the day, the better classroom managers are thinking ahead. While maintaining a pleasant classroom atmosphere, these teachers keep planning how to organize, manage, and control activities to facilitate instruction."[11] Berliner makes an important connection between management and instruction. Effective teachers, in addition to being good classroom managers, must also be good organizers of academic content and instruction.

The Pedagogical Cycle

How does one organize classroom life? Researcher **Arno Bellack** an-alyzed verbal exchanges between teachers and students and offers a fasci-nating insight into classroom organization, likening these interactions to a pedagogical game.[12] The game is so cyclical and occurs so frequently that many teachers and students do not even know that they are playing. There are four moves:

1. *Structure*. The teacher provides information, provides direction, and introduces the topics.
2. *Question*. The teacher asks a question.
3. *Respond*. The student answers the question, or tries to.
4. *React*. The teacher reacts to the student's answer and provides feedback.

These four steps make up a **pedagogical cycle,** diagrammed in Figure 3.2. Teachers initiate about 85 percent of the cycles, which are used over and over again in class-room interaction. When teachers learn to enhance and refine each of the moves of the pedagogical cycle, student achievement is increased.[13]

Clarity and Academic Structure

Have you ever been to a class where the teacher is bombarded with questions? "What are we supposed to do?" "Can you explain it again?" "What do you mean?" When such questions are constant, it is a sure sign that the teacher is not "setting the stage" for instruction. Students need a clear understanding of what they are expected to learn, and they need motivation to learn it.[14] Effective **academic structure** sets the stage for learning and occurs mainly at the beginning of the lesson. Although the spe-cific structure will vary depending on the students' backgrounds and the difficulty of the subject matter, an effective academic structure usually consists of

- *Objectives*. Let the students know the objectives of each lesson. Students, like the teacher, need a road map of where they are going and why.
- *Review*. Help students review prior learning before presenting new information. If there is confusion, reteach.
- **Motivation.** Create an "anticipatory set" that motivates students to attend to the lesson. Consider throwing out an intriguing question, an anecdote, a joke, or a challenging riddle.
- **Transition.** Provide connections to help students integrate old and new information.
- **Clarification.** Break down a large body of information. (This is sometimes called "chunking.") Do not inundate students with too much too fast. This is particularly true for young children and slower learners, although it also applies to older and faster learners.
- *Examples*. Give several examples and illustrations to explain main points and ideas.
- *Directions*. Give directions distinctly and slowly. If students are confused about what they are supposed to do, repeat or break information into small segments.
- *Enthusiasm*. Demonstrate personal enthusiasm for the academic content. Make it clear why the information is interesting and important.

FIGURE 3.2

Pedagogical cycle.

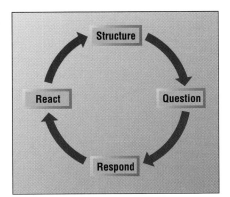

PEDAGOGICAL CYCLE: SAMPLE CLASSROOM DIALOGUE

Structure *(teacher)* **(Motivate)**	How many of you have ever stayed up late and felt terribly tired the next day? Being weary dulls your senses, so that you really don't feel much like talking with others. In some ways, nations are like people; they get weary as well.	**Respond** *(student)*	They began to expand, to take over the territory of other countries.
		React/Question *(teacher)*	Which countries?
(Review) (Transition)	Yesterday we discussed the horrible battles and terrible casualties of World War I. Today we are going to look at what happens to nations that get weary from war. Like people, nations don't see as clearly or react as quickly when they are war-weary. England and France after World War I were two such war-weary nations.	**Respond** *(student)*	Austria, Czechoslovakia.
		React *(teacher)*	Okay.
		Substructure *(teacher provides transition, clarification, examples)*	Now we indicated that Europe had undergone a terrible experience in World War I. Millions of lives were lost, property was destroyed, many careers and families were left in shambles, and many Europeans believed that they had seen the last of war. Many people thought that "The Great War," which we called World War I, was the war to end all wars. We described how the French and English were ignoring Germany's military moves because they wanted peace so badly, yet here were the Germans, gearing up for war.
	Although the signs of a new war were clear and growing, many of the British and French were still recovering from the casualties and physical destruction of World War I. That long and difficult struggle made them blind to new danger signs.		
(Objective)	Our objective today is to explore the pre-World War II mentality of the British and French.		
Question *(teacher)*	What are some of the signs that a new world war was coming?	**Question** *(teacher)*	Why were the Germans gearing up for another war after the pain and suffering they experienced in World War I?
Respond *(student)*	The growing military buildup in Germany.	**Respond** *(student)*	The Treaty of Versailles, the peace treaty, was pretty unfair to Germans. They had to pay reparations. They lost land. Their honor was tarnished. They were unhappy and wanted justice.
React *(teacher)*	Okay.		
Question *(teacher)*	Why was this military buildup of particular concern?	**React** *(teacher)*	Good points.
Respond *(student)*	Because it was prohibited by the Treaty of Versailles. The Germans were violating the treaty that prohibited them from building an army.	**Question** *(teacher)*	Any other reasons?
		Respond *(student)*	The depression really hurt Germany. Building industry helped their economy. Also, the Germans blamed the peace treaty for their economic problems. They blamed the Allies and wanted revenge.
React *(teacher)*	Good.		
Question *(teacher)*	Were the Germans involved in any other violations of the peace treaty?	**React** *(teacher)*	Those are terrific points.

- *Closure.* Close the lesson with a brief review or summary. If students are able to provide the summary, so much the better, for it shows that they have really understood the lesson.

The major activity in academic structuring takes place at the beginning of the lesson, but there may be several points throughout the lesson where substructuring or brief presentations of information are also necessary. Substructures initiate new pedagogical cycles and allow the discussion to continue. A clear summary or review is also important at the close of the lesson.

When teachers generate motivation and provide a clear introduction, all aspects of the lesson will proceed more smoothly.[15] Through effective and clear structure, as shown in Figure 3.2, the stage is set for the remaining steps of the pedagogical cycle.

Questioning

Good questioning is at the very core of good teaching. As John Dewey said,

To question well is to teach well. In the skillful use of the question more than anything else lies the fine art of teaching; for in it we have the guide to clear and vivid ideas, and the quick spur to imagination, the stimulus to thought, the incentive to action.[16]

Since questioning is key in guiding learning, all students should have equal access to classroom questions and academic interaction, yet sitting in the same classroom taught by the same teacher, students experience significant differences in the number of questions they are asked. Research shows that male students are asked more questions than female students, and white students are asked more questions than nonwhite students. One of the reasons boys get to answer questions as well as to talk more is that they are assertive in grabbing teacher attention. Boys are more likely than girls to call out the answers to the questions. However, when boys call out the answers to questions, teachers are likely to accept their responses. When girls call out the answers, teachers often remind them to raise their hands. Teacher expectations also play a role and are frequently cited as one of the reasons white students receive more questions and more active teacher attention than students who are members of other racial and ethnic groups.[17]

If you want all students, not just the quickest and most assertive, to answer questions, establish a protocol for participation. For example, make a rule that students must raise their hands and be called on before they may talk. Too many classes offer variations of the following scene:

TEACHER: How much is 60 + 4 + 12? (*Many students raise their hands—both girls and boys.*)

TONY: (*Shouts out*) 76!

TEACHER: Okay. How much is 50 + 9 + 8?
This scene, repeated again and again in classes across the country, is a typical example of the squeaky wheel—not necessarily the most needy or most deserving—getting the educational oil. Once you make the rule that students should raise their hands before participating, *hold to that rule.* Try to avoid the following:

TEACHER: Now it's time for Math Bowl. Remember to raise your hands and wait until I call on you. How much is 60 + 4 +12? (*Several students raise their hands.*)

TEACHER: Corena?

CORENA: 76.

TEACHER: How much is 50 + 9 + 8? (*Several students raise their hands.*)

TEACHER: Derrick?

DERRICK: 67.

TEACHER: How much is 17 + 14 + 5? (*Several students raise their hands.*)

TONY: (*Shouts out*) 36!

TEACHER: How much is 19 + 8 + 4?

Many teachers are well-intentioned about having students raise their hands, but, in the rapid pace of classroom interaction, they sometimes forget their own rule. If you hold to that "wait to be recognized" rule, you can make professional decisions

BLOOM'S TAXONOMY APPLIED TO QUESTIONING LEVELS

Level I: Knowledge

The student is required to recall or reorganize information. The student must rely on memory or senses to provide the answer.

Sample Questions

What is the meaning of "quixotic"?

List the first ten presidents of the United States.

Level II: Comprehension

The student is required to go beyond simple recall and demonstrate the ability to arrange and organize information mentally. The student must use previously learned information by putting it in his or her own words and rephrasing it.

Sample Question

In your chapter, the author discusses the causes of World War I. Can you summarize these in your own words?

Level III: Application

Students are required to apply previously learned information to answer a problem. At this level, students use a rule, a definition, a classification system, directions, or the like in solving a problem with a specific correct answer.

Sample Questions

Applying the law of supply and demand, solve the following problem. *(applying a rule)*

Identify the adjectives in the following sentences. *(applying a definition)*

Solve the quadratic equation. *(applying a rule)*

Level IV: Analysis

Students are required to use three kinds of cognitive processes:

1. To identify causes, reasons, or motives (when these have not been provided to the student previously).

Sample Question

Why do you think King Lear misjudged his daughter?

2. To analyze information to reach a generalization or conclusion.

Sample Question

What generalizations can you make about the climate of Europe on the eves of World War I and World War II?

3. To find evidence to support a specific opinion, event, or situation.

Sample Question

Many historians think that Abraham Lincoln was our finest president. What evidence can you find to support this statement?

Level V: Synthesis

Students are required to use original and creative thinking in (1) developing original communications, (2) making predictions, and (3) solving problems for which there is no single right answer.

Sample Questions

Write a short story about life on another planet. *(developing an original communication)*

What do you think life would be like if Germany had won World War II? *(making predictions)*

How can our class raise money for the graduation trip? *(solving problems for which there is no single right solution)*

Level VI: Evaluation

Students are required to judge the merits of an aesthetic work, an idea, or the solution to a problem.

Sample Questions

Which U.S. senator do you think is most effective?

Do you think that schools are too hard or not hard enough? Explain your answer.

about who should answer which questions and why. If you give away this key to classroom participation, you are abandoning an important part of your professional decision making in the classroom.

There is more to managing classroom questions than taking the role of a traffic cop. For instance, you might assign pairs of students to work together (sometimes called "Think-Pair-Share") to develop and record answers and then present them to the class as a whole. Or perhaps teams of four or five students can be established to tackle academic questions on a regular basis. When students are actively involved in either of these approaches, the teacher can move around the room as a facilitator, answering questions, motivating student groups, and assessing how the groups are doing. More important, the students take ownership of the questions, sincere questions reflecting their genuine interests.

While the distribution and ownership of questions are important, the type of question asked is also meaningful. This section provides more information about the different levels of classroom questions, as well as strategies for using them fairly and effectively.

Many educators differentiate between factual, lower-order questions and thought-provoking, higher-order questions. Perhaps the most widely used system for determining the intellectual level of questions is Benjamin **Bloom's taxonomy,** which proceeds from the lowest level of questions, knowledge, to the highest level, evaluation. [18]

A **lower-order question** can be answered through memory and recall. For example, "What is the name of the largest Native American nation?" is a lower-order question. Without consulting outside references, one could respond with the correct answer only by remembering previously learned information. Students either know the answer or they don't. Research indicates that 70 to 95 percent of a teacher's questions are lower-order.

A **higher-order question** demands more thought and usually more time before students reach a response. These questions may ask for evaluations, comparisons, causal relationships, problem solving, or divergent, open-ended thinking. Following are examples of higher-order questions:

1. Do you think that Ronald Reagan was an effective president? Why or why not?
2. What similarities in theme emerge in the three Coen movies: *The Big Lebowski, Raising Arizona,* and *Fargo*?
3. Considering changes that have taken place in the past decade, what is the impact of computer technology on campus life?
4. Considering what you have learned in this child care course, how would you go about solving the problem of an infant's persistent crying?
5. What would happen if our shadows were to come to life?

Although higher-order questions have been shown to produce increased student achievement, most teachers ask very few of them.[19]

Many educators think that different questioning levels stimulate different levels of thought. If you ask a fifth-grade student to define an adjective, you are working on lower-level basic skills. If you ask a fifth-grade student to write a short story, making effective use of adjectives, you are working on a higher level of student achievement. Both lower-order and higher-order questions are important and should be matched to appropriate instructional goals:

Ask lower-order questions when
- Students are being introduced to new information
- Students are working on drill and practice
- Students are reviewing previously learned information

Ask higher-order questions when
- You want students to manipulate already established information in more sophisticated ways
- Students are working on problem-solving skills
- Students are involved in a creative or affective discussion
- Students are asked to make judgments about quality, aesthetics, or ethics

Student Response

If you were to spend a few minutes in a high school English class, you might hear a classroom discussion go something like this:

TEACHER: Who wrote the poem "Stopping by Woods on a Snowy Evening"? Tom?

TOM: Robert Frost.

TEACHER: Good. What action takes place in the poem? Sally?

SALLY: A man stops his sleigh to watch the woods get filled with snow.

TEACHER: Yes. Emma, what thoughts go through the man's mind?

EMMA: He thinks how beautiful the woods are. *(Pauses for a second)*

TEACHER: What else does he think about? Joe?

JOE: He thinks how he would like to stay and watch. *(Pauses for a second)*

TEACHER: Yes—and what else? Rita? *(Waits half a second)* Come on, Rita, you can answer this. *(Waits half a second)* Well, why does he feel he can't stay there indefinitely and watch the woods and the snow?

RITA: He knows he's too busy. He's got too many things to do to stay there for so long.

TEACHER: Good. In the poem's last line, the man says that he has miles to go before he sleeps. What might sleep be a symbol for? Sarah?

SARAH: Well, I think it might be . . . *(Pauses for a second)*

TEACHER: Think, Sarah. *(Waits for half a second)* All right then—Mike? *(Waits again for half a second)* John? *(Waits half a second)* What's the matter with everyone today? Didn't you do the reading?[20]

Teacher questioning patterns have much to do with the learning climate in classrooms.

The teacher is using several instructional skills effectively. His is a well-managed classroom. The students are on task and engaged in a discussion appropriate to the academic content. By asking a series of lower-order questions ("Who wrote the poem?" "What action takes place in the poem?"), the teacher works with the students to establish an information base. Then the teacher builds to higher-order questions about the poem's theme and meaning.

If you were to give this teacher suggestions on how to improve his teaching skills, you might point out the difficulty students have in answering the more complex questions. You might also note the lightning pace at which this lesson proceeds. The teacher fires questions so rapidly that the students barely have time to think. This is not so troublesome when they are answering factual questions that require a brief memorized response. However, students begin to flounder when they are required to answer more complex questions with equal speed.

Although it is important to keep classroom discussion moving at a brisk pace, sometimes teachers push forward too rapidly. Slowing down at two key places during classroom discussion can usually improve the effectiveness and equity of classroom responses. In the research on classroom interaction, this slowing down is called **wait time**.[21]

Mary Budd Rowe's research shows that, after asking a question, teachers typically wait only one second or less for a student response (wait time 1). If the response is not forthcoming in that time, teachers rephrase the question, ask another student to answer it, or answer it themselves. If teachers can learn to increase their wait time from one second to three to five seconds, significant improvements in the quantity and quality of student response usually will take place.

There is another point in classroom discussion when wait time can be increased. After students complete an answer, teachers often begin their reaction or their next question before a second has passed (wait time 2). Once again, it is important for teachers to increase their wait time from one second to three to five seconds. Based on her research, Mary Budd Rowe has determined that increasing the pause after a student gives an answer is equally as important as increasing wait time 1, the pause after the teacher asks a question. When wait time 1 and wait time 2 are increased, classroom interaction is changed in several positive ways.

Changes in Student Behavior
- The length of student response increases dramatically.
- Students are more likely to support their statements with evidence.
- Speculative thinking increases.
- There are more student questions and fewer failures to respond.
- More students participate in discussion.
- Fewer discipline problems disrupt the class.
- Student achievement increases on written tests that measure more complex levels of thinking.

Changes in Teacher Behavior
- Teacher comments are less disjointed and more fluent. Classroom discussion becomes more logical, thoughtful, and coherent.
- Teachers ask more sophisticated, higher-order questions.
- Teachers begin to hold higher expectations for all students.

Research indicates that teachers give more wait time to students for whom they hold higher expectations. A high-achieving student is more likely to get time to think than is a low-achieving student. If we do not expect much from our students, we will not get much. High expectations and longer wait time are positively related to achievement. Researchers suggest that white male students, particularly high achievers, are more likely to be given adequate wait time than are females and students of color. Students who are quiet and reserved or who think more slowly may obtain special benefit from increased wait time. In fact, a key benefit of extended wait time is an increase in the quality of student participation, even from students who were previously silent.

Usually when teachers learn that they are giving students less than a second to think, they are surprised and have every intention of waiting longer, but that is easier said than done! In the hectic arena of the classroom, it is all too easy to slip into split-second question-and-answer patterns.

Sometimes teachers fall into a pattern of quickly repeating every answer that students give. Occasionally this repetition can be helpful—if some students may not have heard it or if an answer merits repetition for emphasis. In most cases, however, this "teacher echo" is counterproductive. Students learn they do not need to listen to one another, because the teacher will repeat the answer, anyway. The teacher echo also reduces valuable wait time and cuts down on the pause that allows students to think. Teachers who have worked on increasing wait time offer some useful tips.

Some teachers adopt self-monitoring cues to slow themselves down at the two key wait-time points. For example, one teacher says that he puts his hand behind his back and counts on his fingers for three seconds to slow himself down. Another teacher says that she covers her mouth with her hand (in a thoughtful pose) to keep herself from talking and thereby destroying "the pause that lets them think."

As mentioned previously, wait time is more important in some cases than in others. If you are asking students to repeat previously memorized math facts and you are interested in developing speed, a three- to five-second wait time may be counterproductive. However, if you have asked a higher-order question that calls for a complicated answer, be sure that wait times 1 and 2 are ample. Simply put, students, like the rest of us, need time to think, and some students may need more wait time than others. For example, when a student speaks English as a newly acquired language, additional wait time could help that student accurately translate and respond to the question. And many of us could profit by less impulsive, more thoughtful responses, the kind that can be engendered by a five-second wait time.

When teachers allow more wait time, the results can be surprising. As one teacher said, "I never thought Andrea had anything to say. She just used to sit there like a bump on a log. Then I tried calling on her and giving her time to answer. What a difference! She comes up with things that no one else has thought of."

Reaction or Productive Feedback

"Today," the student teacher said, "we are going to hear the story of *The Three Billy Goats Gruff*." A murmur of anticipation rippled through the kindergarten children comfortably seated on the carpet around the flannel board. This student teacher was a favorite, and the children were particularly happy when she told them flannel-board stories.

"Before we begin the story, I want to make sure we know what all the words mean. Who can tell me what a troll is?"

A tow-headed 5-year-old nicknamed B.J. raised his hand. "A troll is someone who walks you home from school."

"Okay," the teacher responded, a slightly puzzled look flickering over her face. "Who else can tell me what a troll is?"

Another student chimed in, "A troll is someone with white hair sticking out of his head."

"Okay," the teacher said.

Another student volunteered, "It hides under bridges and waits for you and scares you."

"Uh-huh," said the teacher.

Warming to the topic, another student gleefully described, "A troll has a long white beard. It loves to eat you up. It especially likes to eat children."

"Okay," the teacher said.

Wide-eyed, B.J. raised his hand again, "I'm sure glad we had this talk about trolls," he said. "I'm not going home with them from school anymore."

"Okay," the teacher said.

This is a classroom in which several good teaching strategies are in operation. The teacher uses effective academic structure, and the students are on task, interested, and involved in the learning activity. The teacher is asking lower-order questions appropriately, to make sure the students know key vocabulary words before the flannel-board story is told. The problem with this classroom lies in the fourth stage of the pedagogical cycle: this teacher does not provide specific reactions and adequate feedback. Did you notice that the teacher reacted with "uh-huh" or "okay," no matter what kind of answer the students gave? Because of this vague feedback and "okay" teaching style, B.J. was left confused about the difference between a troll and a patrol. This real-life incident may seem amusing, but there was nothing funny to B.J., who was genuinely afraid to leave school with the patrol.

Recently, attention has been directed not only at how teachers ask questions but also at how they respond to student answers. Sadker and Sadker, analyzing classroom interaction in more than 100 classrooms in five states, found that teachers generally use four types of reactions:

1. **Praise.** Positive comments about student work, such as "Excellent, good job."
2. **Acceptance.** Comments such as "Uh-huh" and "Okay," which acknowledge that student answers are acceptable. These are not as strong as praise.
3. **Remediation.** Comments that encourage a more accurate student response or encourage students to think more clearly, creatively, or logically. Sample remediation comments include "Try again," "Sharpen your answer," and "Check your addition."
4. **Criticism.** A clear statement that an answer is inaccurate or a behavior is inappropriate. This category includes harsh criticism ("This is a terrible paper"), as well as milder comments that simply indicate an answer is not correct ("Your answer to the third question is wrong.")[22]

Which of these reactions do you think teachers use most frequently? Did you notice that the kindergarten teacher relied heavily on the acceptance, or "okay," reaction? So do most teachers from grade school through graduate school. The study found that acceptance was the most frequent response, accounting for more than half of all teacher reactions. The second most frequent teacher response was remediation, accounting for one-third of teacher reactions. Used infrequently, praise comprised only 11 percent of reactions. The rarest response was criticism. In two-thirds of the classrooms observed, teachers never told a student that an answer was incorrect. In the classrooms where criticism did occur, it accounted for only 5 percent of interaction. (See Figure 3.3.)

In *A Place Called School,* John Goodlad writes that "learning is enhanced when students understand what is expected of them, get recognition for their work, learn about their errors, and receive guidance in improving their performances."[23] But many

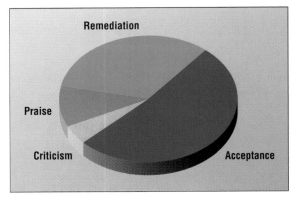

FIGURE 3.3

Teacher reactions.

students claim that they are not informed or corrected when they make mistakes. Perhaps this is caused by overreliance on the acceptance response, which is the vaguest kind of feedback that teachers can offer. Since there is more acceptance than praise, criticism, and remediation combined, some educators are beginning to wonder: "Is the 'okay' classroom okay?"

Although the acceptance response is legitimate and often appropriate, it is overused. Since achievement is likely to increase when students get clear, specific **productive feedback** about their answers, it is important for teachers to reduce the "okay" reaction and to be more varied and specific in the feedback they provide. Researcher **Jere Brophy** has done an analysis of praise and student achievement. He found that praise may be particularly important for low-achieving students and those from low socioeconomic backgrounds. Brophy found that it is best when

1. *Praise is* contingent *upon student performance.* Praise should closely follow student behavior the teacher wants to recognize.
2. *Praise is* specific. When teachers praise, they should clearly indicate what aspect of the student behavior is noteworthy (for instance, creative problem solving or good use of evidence to support an argument).
3. *Praise is* sincere. Praise should reflect the experiences, growth, and development of the individual student. Otherwise, it may be dismissed as being disingenuous.
4. *Praise lets students know about their* competence *and the importance of their* accomplishments—for instance, "The connection you made between French history and Victor Hugo's work shows your ability to connect this year's work with your reading from last semester."
5. *Praise attributes success to* ability or effort—for example, "Your analysis of the paintings of the Impressionists is excellent. I'll bet you spent a long time studying their work in the museum" *(attribution to effort).* Or "This story is fantastic. You've got a real flair for creative writing" *(attribution to ability).* When praise is attributed to abilities or effort, students know that successful performance is under their own control.
6. *Praise uses* past performance as a context *for describing present performance*—for example, "Last week you were really having trouble with your breast stroke. Now you've got it together—you've learned to push the water behind you and increase your speed."[24]

Just as students need to know when they are performing well, they need to know when their efforts are inadequate or incorrect. If students do not have information about their weak areas, they will find it difficult to improve.

1. *Corrective feedback is specific and contingent upon student performance.* The teacher's comments should closely follow the student behavior the teacher wants to improve.
2. *Critical comments focus on student* performance *and are not of a personal nature.* All of us find it easier to accept constructive criticism when it is

detached from our worth as a person, when it is not personal, hostile, or sarcastic.

3. *Feedback provides a clear blueprint for improvement.* If you tell a student that an answer is wrong and nothing more, the student has clear feedback on level of performance but no strategies for improvement. Effective feedback suggests an approach for attaining success, such as "Check your addition," "Use the bold headings as a reading guide when you study for the exams," "Check the periodic table for the correct abbreviation of this element," or "Let's conjugate this verb in both French and English, to see where the error is."

4. *An environment is established that lets the student know it is acceptable to make mistakes.* "We learn from our errors."

5. *Corrective feedback relates eventual success to effort.* "I know you can do it if you give yourself some more time. Give yourself a solid hour tonight working on this, and I bet that you will get most of it correct. I'll check with you tomorrow."

6. *Corrective feedback recognizes when students have made improvements in their performance.* "Last week you were having trouble identifying which of Newton's Laws are applicable in each of the problems. Now you've mastered that skill. You've done a good job."

An "okay classroom" allows student error and misunderstanding to go uncorrected; it lets B.J. think that the patrol will eat him up after school. In classrooms where there is appropriate use of remediation and constructive criticism, students know not only when they have made mistakes but also how to correct them. They also recognize that this process leads to growth and achievement.

Variety in Process and Content

Variety is the spice of life, the saying goes—the spice of lessons also, because variety can enhance both teaching effectiveness and student achievement.[25]

Have you ever listened to a lecture for an hour and found your initial interest lapsing into daydreams? Have you ever watched a class begin a seatwork assignment with active concentration and found, after thirty minutes, that involvement had turned into passing notes and throwing paper airplanes? When the teacher fails to provide sufficient variety, lessons become monotonous and students get off task.

Effective teachers provide **variety** in both content and process. In elementary school, variety in content can involve moving from one subject area to another. In secondary instruction, the move might be in the same subject area, such as the switch from memorizing vocabulary to analyzing symbols in a short story.

As any smart teacher knows, student interest can be maintained by moving from one activity to another during a single lesson. For example, a 60-minute lesson on the French Revolution might

A positive classroom atmosphere that includes precise, encouraging feedback helps motivate and guide student effort.

begin with a 10-minute overview providing the structure for the class, then move into a 15-minute question-and-answer session, then change to a 25-minute video, and conclude with a 10-minute discussion and closure. Following is a sampler of activities teachers can use to maintain student interest by varying the pattern of the lesson.

discussions	games
lectures	contests
movies, videotapes, and other audiovisual presentations	creative writing
	plays
role plays	field trips
simulations	boardwork
small-group activities	participation in learning centers
software for individuals and groups	music activities
	art activities
guest speakers	tutoring
independent seatwork	spot quizzes
guided practice	panel discussions
student presentations	brainstorming sessions
tests	students tutoring one another
visits to web sites	cooperative learning activities
silent reading	debates

The preceding sections reviewed research on teaching skills that lead to increased student achievement. However, this provides only a beginning. You will be developing and refining skills in good teaching throughout your teacher preparation program. The next section of this chapter introduces four effective teaching models that you may see implemented in schools and classrooms where you do your field experiences.

Current Models for Effective Instruction

Part of the challenge for teachers is knowing which model of instruction to choose for particular educational purposes. Emphasizing high teacher visibility and on-task student behavior, the direct teaching model is particularly effective for subjects that are highly structured, such as mathematics, reading, grammar, and vocabulary. The cooperative learning model yields gains not only in achievement but also in interpersonal skills and relationships. The mastery learning model is based on the assumption that, given sufficient time and learning options, all students in a regular classroom can master academic objectives. Finally, project-based instruction provides students with the opportunity to go beyond academic questions and cross disciplines to explore "real" issues.

Direct Teaching

Also called *systematic, active,* or *explicit teaching,* the **direct teaching** model emphasizes the importance of a structured lesson in which presentation of new information is followed by student practice and teacher feedback. In this model, which has emerged

EVALUATION OF SOCRATES

Teacher Evaluation
Teacher: Socrates

A.   Personal Qualifications

		Rating (high to low) 1 2 3 4 5	Comments
1.	Personal appearance	X	Dresses in an old sheet draped about his body
2.	Self-confidence	X	Not sure of himself—always asking questions
3.	Use of English	X (4)	Speaks with a heavy Greek accent
4.	Adaptability	X (4)	Prone to suicide by poison when under duress

B.   Class Management

1.	Organization	X (5)	Does not keep a seating chart
2.	Room appearance	X (4)	Does not have eye-catching bulletin boards
3.	Utilization of supplies	X (1)	Does not use supplies

C.   Teacher-Pupil Relationships

1.	Tact and consideration	X (5)	Places student in embarrassing situation by asking questions
2.	Attitude of class	X (2)	Class is friendly

D.   Techniques of Teaching

1.	Daily preparation	X (5)	Does not keep daily lesson plans
2.	Attention to course of study	X (3)	Quite flexible—allows students to wander to different topics
3.	Knowledge of subject matter	X (5)	Does not know material—has to question pupils to gain knowledge

E.   Professional Attitude

1.	Professional ethics	X (5)	Does not belong to professional association or PTA
2.	In-service training	X (5)	Complete failure here—has not even bothered to attend college
3.	Parent relationships	X (5)	Needs to improve in this area—parents are trying to get rid of him

Recommendation: Does not have a place in education—should not be rehired.

Source: John Gauss, "Evaluation of Socrates as a Teacher," *Phi Delta Kappan* 63, no. 4 (January 1962), outside back cover. Reprinted by permission of author and publisher.

from extensive research, the role of the teacher is that of a strong leader, one who structures the classroom and sequences subject matter to reflect a clear academic focus.

Researchers put forward six principles of direct teaching. They say that effective teachers use these principles consistently and systematically:

1. *Daily review.* At the beginning of the lesson, prior learning is reviewed. Frequently, this review focuses on assigned homework, clarifies points of confusion, and provides extra practice for facts and skills that need more attention.

With direct teaching, teachers carefully explain what students must do to accomplish a task, then present a carefully structured lesson that is usually broken down into small, manageable steps.

2. *New material.* Effective teachers begin the presentation by letting students know the objectives to be attained. New information is broken down into smaller steps and is covered at a brisk pace. Main points are illustrated by the use of concrete examples. The teacher asks questions frequently to check for student understanding and to make sure that students are ready for independent work using new skills and knowledge.

3. *Guided practice.* Students use new skills and knowledge under direct teacher supervision. During guided practice, teachers ask many content questions ("What is the definition of a paragraph?") and many process questions ("How do you locate the topic sentence in a paragraph?"). Teachers check student responses for understanding, offering prompts and providing corrective feedback. Guided practice continues until students answer with approximately 70 to 80 percent accuracy.

4. *Specific feedback.* Correct answers to questions are acknowledged clearly, so that students will understand when their work is accurate. When student answers are hesitant, the teacher provides process feedback ("Yes, Juanita, that's correct because . . . "). Inaccurate responses are corrected immediately, before errors become habitual. Frequent errors are a sign that students are not ready for independent work, and guided practice should continue.

5. *Independent practice.* This stage is similar to guided practice, except that students work by themselves at their seats or at home. Independent practice continues until responses are assured, quick, and at a level of approximately 95 percent accuracy. Cooperative learning (see the next section) and student tutoring of one another are effective strategies during independent practice.

6. *Weekly and monthly reviews.* Regular reviews offer students the opportunity for more practice, a strategy related to high achievement. Barak Rosenshine, a pioneering researcher in developing the principles of direct teaching, recommends a weekly review every Monday, with a monthly review every fourth Monday.[26]

Direct teaching works well when you are teaching skill subjects, such as grammar or mathematics, or helping students master factual material. The direct teaching model is particularly helpful during the first stages of learning new and complex information, but it is less helpful when imaginative responses and student creativity is called for.

Cooperative Learning

In a classroom using **cooperative learning,** students work on activities in small, heterogeneous groups, and they often receive rewards or recognition based on the overall group performance. Although cooperative learning can be traced back to the 1920s, it seems startling or new because the typical classroom environment is frequently competitive. For example, when grading is done on a curve, one student's success is often detrimental to others. This competitive structure produces clear winners and losers, and only a limited number of *A*s are possible. Sometimes classrooms are set up to be less competitive, incorporating independent study or learning contracts. In these cases, students work by themselves to reach individual learning goals. But a cooperative learning structure differs from even these less competitive practices, because students depend on one another and work together to reach shared goals.

According to researchers, cooperative learning groups work best when they meet the following criteria.[27] Groups should be *heterogeneous* and, at least at the beginning, should be *small,* perhaps limited to two to six members. Since face-to-face interaction is important, the groups should be *circular* to permit easy conversation. Positive *interdependence* among group members can be fostered by a *shared group goal, shared division of labor,* and *shared materials,* all contributing to a sense that the group sinks or swims together.

Robert Slavin, a pioneer in cooperative learning techniques, developed student team learning methods in which a team's work is not completed until all students on the team understand the material being studied.[28] Rewards are earned only when the entire team achieves the goals set by the teacher. Students tutor one another, so that everyone can succeed on individual quizzes, and each member of the group is accountable for learning. Since students contribute to their teams by improving prior scores, it does not matter whether the student is a high, average, or low achiever. Increased achievement by an individual student at any level contributes to the overall performance of the group, resulting in equal opportunity for success.

In cooperative learning situations, students' individual goals and rewards are tied into group accomplishments.

Research shows that cooperative learning promotes both intellectual and emotional growth:

- Students make higher achievement gains; this is especially true for math in the elementary grades.
- Students have higher levels of self-esteem and greater motivation to learn.
- Students have a stronger sense that classmates have positive regard for one another.
- Understanding and cooperation among students from different racial and ethnic backgrounds are enhanced.[29]

As ability grouping becomes more controversial, educators are growing increasingly interested in cooperative learning as a strategy for working successfully with mixed-ability groups and diverse classroom populations.

Mastery Learning

Based on Benjamin Bloom's Learning for Mastery model developed in 1968, **mastery learning** programs are committed to the credo that, given the right tools, all children can learn. Stemming from an individualized reward structure, these programs are in use from early childhood to graduate school.

Mastery learning programs require specific and carefully sequenced learning objectives. The first step is to identify a **behavioral objective,** a specific skill or academic task to be mastered. Students are taught the skill or material in the objective; then they are tested to determine if the objective has been reached. Students who complete the test successfully go on for acceleration or enrichment, while the students who fail to demonstrate mastery of the objective receive corrective instruction and are retested. The success of mastery learning rests on the *instructional alignment,* which is a close match between what is taught and what is tested.[30]

In mastery learning, students typically work at their own pace, perhaps at a computer terminal or with individualized written materials. The teacher provides assistance and facilitates student efforts, but mastery still remains a student responsibility. Since studies have shown that many students, particularly younger ones, find it hard to take charge of their own instruction, mastery learning programs highlight the role of the teacher as instructional leader, motivator, and guide. Mastery learning is often geared for large groups, and it can benefit from technology, since computers and appropriate software can be particularly effective in self-paced mastery of skills and knowledge.

Studies suggest that mastery learning is a powerful tool:

- Students achieve more and remember what they have learned longer.
- Students at the elementary and junior high levels seem to benefit most.
- Students in language arts and social studies classes benefit more than those in math and science.
- In general, students have more positive attitudes about learning and their ability to learn.
- Teachers have more positive attitudes toward teaching and higher expectations for their students.[31]

Recently, a variation of mastery learning called **outcome-based education (OBE)** has received a good deal of attention. Outcome-based education was introduced in the 1980s and 1990s by policy-makers interested in focusing on educational results or outcomes, rather than on individual subjects and topics. These policy-makers were interested in moving away from the restrictions of a single subject field in order to include interdisciplinary subjects and broader ideas. They argued that learning is naturally interdisciplinary and that, to function effectively in the real world, students need to make connections across topics and use interrelated skills. For instance, a test on syntax and grammar would be less useful than a test on "communication skills," one that assesses how effectively a student can combine syntax and related skills into effective forms of communication. Moreover, in an effort to increase accountability, OBE advocates worked to identify more precisely what students were supposed to learn, and then how best to measure that learning.

OBE quickly became a political issue. Conservative groups spoke out against the movement, charging that OBE was an attempt to weaken basic subjects and fundamental skills while introducing "liberal values" and soft subjects. They believed that the outcomes were, in fact, "fuzzy," ill-defined, and political. Moreover, OBE reformers had included several other ideas in their proposals, such as recommendations for

HIGH SUCCESS RATE

Many teachers feel that students should be stretched to master challenging material, yet researchers find that such an approach may only frustrate students. Learners are most likely to achieve when they are working at a high level of success. How can you tell whether students are performing at a high success rate? Researchers offer the following guidelines:[a]

- During classroom discussions, at least 70 percent of teacher questions should result in accurate student answers. A high success rate is especially important

for younger students and for those who learn more slowly.

- During independent practice, such as homework or seatwork, the success rate should be almost 100 percent.

In theory, a high success rate results in achievement; in reality, students are often working at levels of failure. In one study, 14 percent of the time, student answers to teacher questions were 100 percent wrong.[b] Researcher Jere Brophy concludes that teachers have a tendency to assign tasks that are too difficult, rather than too easy.[c]

[a]Jere Brophy and Carolyn Evertson, *Learning from Teaching: A Developmental Perspective* (Boston: Allyn & Bacon, 1976). See also R. Marliave and J. Filby, "Success Rates: A Measure of Task Appropriateness," in C. W. Fisher and D. Berliner (eds.), *Perspectives on Instructional Time* (New York: Longman, 1986); Gary Borich, *Effective Teaching Methods* (Columbus, OH: Merrill, 1988); Richard Kindsvatter et al., *Dynamics of Effective Teaching* (New York: Longman, 1992).
[b]Gary Davis and Margaret Thomas, *Effective Schools and Effective Teachers* (Boston: Allyn & Bacon, 1989).
[c]Jere Brophy, "Classroom Organization and Management," *The Elementary School Journal* 83, no. 4 (1983).

a different report card system, which that did not find ready acceptance among the general public. The controversy surrounding OBE neutralized its impact, which is one reason today's efforts to improve educational standards remain focused on individual subject areas.[32]

Project-Based Instruction

Whereas outcome-based education has found limited acceptance, **project-based instruction (PBI)** has been more successful in going beyond traditional subject area boundaries. Focusing on real-life problems is at the heart of PBI, and, as you might imagine, real problems are not bound by a single subject field or even by the school building. This emphasis is apparent in the other terms used to describe PBI: *experience-based education, problem-based instruction,* and *anchored instruction* (because it is "anchored" in the real world). In this instructional model, a crucial aspect of the teacher's role is to identify activities that fuel students' interest, such as

- Design a plan for protecting a specific endangered species.
- Formulate solutions that might have kept the United States from plunging into a Civil War.
- How can we stop violence in this school?
- How can pollution in a local river or bay or the ocean be checked, or even reversed?
- Develop a set of urban policies to halt the deterioration of a central city.
- How can the racism and sexism in this community be eliminated?

Finding scintillating questions and projects to excite and motivate students is critical, but it is only one aspect of PBI. Other characteristics include

- *Learner cooperation.* Similar to cooperative learning, PBI depends on small groups or pairs of students collaborating as they explore and investigate various issues. This approach de-emphasizes competition. For teachers, the goal is to guide and challenge a dozen such small groups simultaneously.

IN THE NEWS . . . GOOD TEACHERS MAKE A DIFFERENCE

Although it is popular to believe that teachers and schools make little or any difference in the lives of the nation's poorest children, a series of studies indicate quite the opposite: children with bright, well trained and effective teachers scored much higher on achievement exams. While the least effective teachers produced student gains of 14 percentile points over the school year, students taught by more effective teachers posted gains of 53 percentile points. In Boston, the top one-third of the teachers produced six times the learning. Teacher background and test scores were good predictors of teacher performance.

Source: *Washington Post,* 11 August 1998.

- *Higher-order thinking.* Exploring real and complex issues requires students to analyze, synthesize, and evaluate material.
- *Cross-disciplinary work.* PBI encourages students to investigate how different academic subjects shed light on each other. In exploring ecological issues, for example, students touch not only on biology and chemistry but also on economics, history, sociology, and political science.
- *Artifacts and exhibits.* Students involved in PBI demonstrate what they learn in a very tangible way. Students may produce a traditional report, or may create a video, a physical model, a computer program, a portfolio of artifacts, or even a presentation, such as a play or a debate. Teachers might organize a class or schoolwide exhibit to share the progress made by PBI students.
- *Authentic learning.* Students pursue an actual unresolved issue. They are expected to define the problem, develop a hypothesis, collect information, analyze that information, and suggest a conclusion, one that might work in the real world. The learning is authentic, not academic, artificial, or hypothetical.

While features of PBI have been around for a long time, in its current form it is both a comprehensive and demanding approach that develops real intellectual skills in students. Moreover, students function as adults in that they explore authentic contemporary issues. Working together, they attempt to solve these problems—in effect, getting a jump on the adult world, even before they are adults.[33]

New Directions for Effective Teaching

Research conducted in the 1980s sought to determine specific teaching behaviors that would result in greater student achievement. The goal was to establish a scientifically based blueprint for effective instruction. However, research in the 1990s was more closely grounded in the principles of how students learn—not as passively receiving information but, rather, as intentionally constructing their own meaning. This represents a substantial shift, offering the potential for future instructional reformation. Four constructs are fundamental to this shift in focus: the structure of knowledge, the significance of "deep" rather than "shallow" teaching, the importance of prior knowledge, and the social nature of learning.

TEACHING THAT WORKS

Good teachers . . .

- Know their *subject matter*
- Are enthusiastic about teaching and their subject area
- Develop deep rather than shallow knowledge
- Connect new learning to prior knowledge
- Spend the major part of class time on academic activities
- Teach content at a level that ensures a high rate of success
- Are *organized*
- Structure learning experiences carefully
- Ensure that students have sufficient time to practice skills
- Clearly present both directions and content information

- Maintain high *student interest and engagement*
- Actively monitor student progress
- Involve all students (not just volunteers) in discussions
- Ask both higher- and lower-order questions as appropriate to the objectives of the lesson
- Use adequate wait time
- Provide clear academic feedback
- Vary student activities and procedures
- Hold high expectations for students
- Have high regard for students and treat them with respect
- Build classroom learning communities

The **structure of knowledge** varies across the content areas. Each subject—history, literature, science, math—has its own patterns, facts, ideas, notations, and structure. "A map is not like a musical score, which is not like the equation of a function, which in turn differs from an evolutionary tree."[34] The actions a chemistry student goes through to gain knowledge do not look or feel like what a literature student goes through to write a creative story. Given these essential differences, content-specific teaching skills are needed. Effective teaching research of the 1990s asks the question "What teaching skills are most relevant to each of the different academic disciplines?" How does the organization of the French language, for example, lend itself to teaching and learning French? What instructional skills should be taught to French teachers, based on the unique organization of the French language? These questions and answers are not often guiding the development of current teacher education programs—but perhaps they should.

The idea of the classroom as a "learning community" conceives of the teacher as someone who helps students activate their prior knowledge of some subject and thereby become intellectually engaged with one another.

WHY IS IT SO HARD TO CHANGE THE WAY TEACHERS TEACH?

After reading about intriguing approaches to teaching, different ways of organizing classes, and the latest research on effective teaching, two questions often pop up in people's minds: Where are all the changes? Why does teaching look so similar year in and year out? **Larry Cuban** tried to answer these questions in *How Teachers Taught: Constancy and Change in American Classrooms, 1890–1980*. Despite the efforts of waves of educational reformers working hard to increase student-centered instruction, most classrooms have remained teacher-centered over the past century. Why?

Cuban uncovered several reasons that change had been thwarted, including simple physical reality. Schools were built around teachers, not students, especially in the early part of the century. Classrooms featured desks all facing front, bolted to the floor, physically reinforcing the notion of the teacher as the center of instruction. As if nuts and bolts were not enough, curriculum demands also placed the teacher center stage. To survive instructing eight or ten subjects to very large classes, teachers became dependent on reading and dictating assignments directly from the text. This approach also strengthened the idea of the teacher as the focal point of learning, one who molds students into vessels to be filled with information. Uniformity and standardization became important in the twentieth century, as principals told teachers

what to do and teachers told students what to do. The organizational climate did not nurture new teaching techniques, nor did it encourage giving more responsibility to students.

As if all these in-school barriers were not enough to defeat change, teacher training all but guaranteed that the status quo would be maintained. New teachers were brought into the profession through a modeling or an apprenticeship program, doing their student teaching under the tutelage of veteran, often conventional, older teachers. It was a system geared to the passing down of traditional approaches and conservative attitudes from one generation of teachers to the next.

Cuban believes that the suppression of student-based instruction was no accident. Schools were designed to mold a compliant workforce; student-centered instruction was viewed as rebellious, dangerous, and threatening to educational and economic stability.

While Cuban recognizes that classrooms have undergone a few relatively minor changes—experiments with open classrooms, greater informality between teacher and student, and even movable chairs—instruction at the close of the century looks strikingly similar to classroom instruction when the twentieth century was new. Do you agree?

Source: Larry Cuban, *How Teachers Taught Constancy and Change in American Classrooms, 1890–1980* (White Plains, NY: Longman, 1984).

"Less is more," an aphorism attributed to education reformer Ted Sizer, applies directly to this new approach to teaching and learning. According to Sizer, today's schools are mistaken when they emphasize "covering" material. The goal seems to be teaching and learning a vast body of information, albeit superficially, in order to have a sense of accomplishment. In textbooks, this is called the "mentioning phenomenon," the tendency to include as many potential topics as possible, even if the topic is only "mentioned." But international tests in science, for example, show that, although U.S. students have studied more science topics than have students in other countries, they have not studied them in depth, and their lower test scores reflect this superficiality. In Sizer's vision of effective instruction, good teachers limit the amount of content they introduce but develop it sufficiently for students to gain in-depth understanding. Some have termed this **deep teaching.** Teachers work to organize their content around a limited set of key principles and powerful ideas and then engage students in discussing these concepts. The emphasis is on problem solving and critical thinking, rather than on memory.[35]

Through discussion and higher-order inquiry, the teacher's challenge is to elicit the **prior knowledge** students bring to the classroom. For example, the headline "Vikings Cream Dolphins" has a different meaning, depending on whether the student is "thinking about eating habits of ancient seafarers or about U.S. football teams."[36] The approach of many teachers today is to simply plan a structure for a lesson that assumes all students enter the class with precisely the same level of information and the same kind of experiences. Such an assumption rarely holds true. When prior knowledge is made explicit, teachers can help students connect new information to this existing knowledge base or enable them to confront and revise prior knowledge that is inaccurate.

Finally, this new vision of effective teaching highlights the social nature of learning and of the classroom. As the builder of a classroom learning community, the teacher is called on to be a guide or facilitator, skillful in conducting discussions, group work, debates, and dialogues. In this way, the teacher empowers the students to talk with one another and to rehearse the terminology and concepts involved in each discipline.[37]

Whether you are methodically working to hone individual skills, such as questioning, structuring, and giving critical feedback, or are embracing new and different models of instruction, perhaps the most important thing you can do is practice **reflective teaching.** Good teachers continually and intensely analyze their own practices, and they use their analysis to improve performance. "In order to tap the rich potential of our past to inform our judgment, we must move backward, reflect on our experiences, then face each new encounter with a broader repertoire of content-specific information, skills, and techniques."[38] When teachers engage in this active and systematic reflection, they ask themselves such questions as

- What teaching strategies did I use today? How effective were they? What might have been even more effective?
- Were my students engaged with the material? What seemed to motivate them the most? If I were to reteach today's class, how could I get even more students involved?
- How did I assess my students' learning today? Would there have been a better way to measure their learning? How well did the students grasp the main points of today's lesson? Do I need to reteach some of these concepts?
- Can I fine-tune tomorrow's or next week's lessons to capitalize on the gains made today?

Going far beyond the rhetorical, these questions are designed to raise consciousness, engender self-scrutiny, and result in effective teaching.[39]

Summary

1. The way in which the teacher allocates time spent on academic content affects student achievement. Allocated time is the amount of time a teacher schedules for a particular subject. Engaged time is the amount of allocated time during which the students are actually involved with the subject matter. Academic learning time is engaged time with a high success rate.
2. Good classroom management is a skill that can lead to high student achievement. It involves planning effectively, establishing rules that are reasonable and not excessive in number, and arranging the classroom so that instruction goes smoothly.
3. Skills that are necessary for maintaining a well-managed classroom include group alerting, withitness, overlapping, use of the principle of least intervention, and the creation of smooth transitions.
4. The pedagogical cycle describes the interaction between the teacher and students. The four steps of the cycle are (1) structure, (2) question, (3) respond, and (4) react. The structure must give students a clear understanding of what they are expected to learn. The teacher should ask both higher-order and lower-order

questions. Teachers need to remember to wait three to five seconds after asking a question (wait time 1) and before reacting to a student answer (wait time 2). Teachers also need to be thoughtful in the way in which they react to student comments. Generally, teachers react by using either praise, acceptance, remediation, or criticism in responding to the student. Research indicates that teachers use acceptance more than all the other reactions combined, a sign that their reactions may lack precision, and perhaps their questions may not be challenging students.

5. Four models of instruction that can lead to high student achievement include (1) direct teaching, (2) cooperative learning, (3) mastery learning, and (4) project-based instruction.

6. The principles of direct teaching include daily review, presentation of new material in a clear manner, guided practice, teacher feedback, independent practice, and weekly and monthly reviews.

7. In a cooperative learning classroom, students work in small groups, and appraisals often reflect the entire group's performance.

8. Mastery learning programs involve specific objectives that must be met, as indicated by assessment. Typically, students work at their own pace, going on to new material only when mastery of previous work has been demonstrated. Teachers often play a central role in content and skill mastery.

9. Project-based instruction stimulates students to explore authentic issues. Individually and in small groups, students cross traditional subject boundaries as they investigate real-life problems and demonstrate what they have learned.

10. New research in effective teaching emphasizes the structure of knowledge, deep rather than shallow teaching, the importance of prior knowledge, and the social nature of learning.

Key Terms and People

www.mhhe.com/sadker

A Place Called School
academic learning time
academic structure
acceptance
allocated time
behavioral objective
Arno Bellack
Bloom's taxonomy
Jere Brophy
clarification
cooperative learning
criticism
Larry Cuban
dangles
deep teaching
direct teaching

engaged time
flip-flops
fragmentation
John Goodlad
group alerting
higher-order questions
Jacob Kounin
least intervention
lower-order questions
mastery learning
motivation
outcome-based education (OBE)
overdwelling
overlapping
pedagogical cycle

praise
prior knowledge
productive feedback
project-based instruction (PBI)
reflective teaching
remediation
Mary Budd Rowe
Robert Slavin
structure of knowledge
teacher effectiveness
thrusts
transition
variety
wait time
withitness

Discussion Questions and Activities

1. Do you think education is a science or an art? Debate a classmate who holds the opposite point of view. Interview elementary and secondary teachers and ask them what they think about this question. Do some of them say that it is a combination of both? If so, why? Which part is art, which part science?

2. Observe social studies, literature, science, and math teachers. What teaching skills seem to be most relevant to each of these academic disciplines?

3. Why do you think there is so much variation in how different teachers and schools use time for learning? Observe in your own college classrooms to determine how much time is wasted. For each class observed, keep a fairly detailed record of how time is lost (students six minutes late, class ends fifteen minutes early, and so on).

4. Research suggests that, in order to achieve, students should be functioning at a very high success rate. Do you agree that this is likely to lead to higher achievement? Or do you think that students need to cope with failure and be "stretched" in order to achieve? Defend your position.

5. Interview teachers at the elementary, secondary, and postsecondary levels, and ask them for strategies they use to involve quieter students in classroom discussion. Share the list of strategies with your classmates.

6. Research suggests that less than 10 percent of classroom questions are higher-order, or thought-provoking, questions. Why do you think this is so? How can increasing wait time help teachers ask more higher-order questions?

7. Why do you think classroom discussion at the elementary and secondary levels proceeds at such a rapid pace? Using a watch with a second hand, calculate wait time 1 and wait time 2 in your college classrooms. Is the time split-second, or do your professors provide three to five seconds of time for thinking?

8. Analyze teacher reactions to student answers in elementary and secondary classrooms where you are an observer and in the college classrooms where you are a student. Are most of these classrooms "okay" classrooms? Why do you think some teacher reactions are vague and diffuse?

9. Think back to your own experiences as an elementary and secondary student. Can you remember a time when you received specific praise concerning an aspect of your performance? How did this make you feel? Describe the incident to your classmates and compare it with their memories. What conclusions can you make about the use of praise in school?

10. Do you think that criticism always has a negative impact? Can you remember any incidents in your own career as a student when criticism was helpful? harmful? Discuss these incidents with your classmates and listen to their descriptions. What generalizations can you make about criticism and its impact on students?

11. Observe in a classroom that is using direct teaching, cooperative learning, mastery learning, or project-based instruction. Discuss these approaches with your classmates. What are their respective benefits? Do there seem to be disadvantages?

4

Student Diversity

Focus Questions

- How should teachers respond to different student learning styles?
- What are the most effective ways to organize classrooms to meet students' different cognitive and emotional intelligences?
- How is the increasingly multicultural nature of America's students reshaping instruction?
- What are the salient issues in the bilingual education controversy?
- How do the needs of exceptional learners impact life in today's classrooms?

Chapter Preview

At the dawn of the twenty-first century, basic educational concepts are being redefined, re-examined, and expanded. What does "intelligence" really mean? How many kinds of intelligences are there? What is E.Q. (emotional intelligence quotient), and is it a better predictor of success than IQ (intelligence quotient)? How should classrooms best be organized to meet the needs of different learning styles?

Not only are our basic concepts and assumptions changing; today's students are changing as well. An increasing number of students have their family roots not in Europe or Africa but in Asia and Latin America. As a result of an extraordinary increase in immigration to this country, the native language of well over 30 million Americans is a language other than English, creating a remarkable and formidable challenge for the nation's schools.[1] In many schools, the terms *minority* and *majority* are gaining new meanings as student demographics change.

Another educational transformation is the increasing numbers of school children now identified as exceptional learners—learning and physically disabled, mentally retarded, and emotionally disturbed—all of whom deserve appropriate educational strategies and materials. Gifted and talented students represent a student population whose special abilities are too often lost in the current educational system.

This chapter will describe the demographic and conceptual changes reshaping America's schools, as well as provide you with insights into and strategies for successful teaching in tomorrow's classrooms.

```
┌─────────────────────────────────────────────────────────┐
│░░░░░░░░░░░░░░░░░░░░ YOU'VE GOT MAIL ░░░░░░░░░░░░░░░░░░░░░░│
│┌───────────────────────────────────────────────────────┐│
││ TO:   Steve@AU.edu,                                   ││
││       Anna@State.edu                                  ││
││ SUBJ:   Committee Assignment                          ││
│├───────────────────────────────────────────────────────┤│
││▽                                                      ││
││                                                       ││
││ Guess what? Lucky me! The principal told me last week ││
││ that I was assigned to the Teachers' Committee for a  ││
││ More Effective Learning Climate. It is part of the    ││
││ school district's plan to give teachers a bigger role ││
││ in governing our school. The good part is that I will ││
││ get to know some of the other teachers much better.   ││
││ But, as a school volunteer, I am concerned that I     ││
││ really can't contribute that much, so I am reviewing my││
││ college notes. Problem is, the teachers' ideas for    ││
││ creating an effective learning climate do not agree   ││
││ with my notes. At first, I thought that this would be ││
││ easy, just common sense. Now I don't know. I am going ││
││ to fax a copy of the survey to you. How would you     ││
││ respond?                                              ││
│└───────────────────────────────────────────────────────┘│
└─────────────────────────────────────────────────────────┘
```

Different Ways of Learning

The committee's responsibility is to offer recommendations to the school board regarding academic climates to increase the academic performance of the district's students. It is an awesome responsibility. Here is the first draft of an eight point proposal. Take a moment and indicate your reaction to each of the points.[2]

	Strongly Agree	Agree	Disagree
1. Schools and classrooms should be quiet places to promote thinking and learning.	____	____	____
2. All classrooms and libraries should be well lighted to reduce eye strain.	____	____	____
3. Difficult subjects, such as math, should be offered in the morning, when students are fresh and alert.	____	____	____
4. School thermostats should be set at 68 to 72 degrees Fahrenheit to establish a comfortable learning environment.	____	____	____
5. Eating and drinking in classrooms should be prohibited.	____	____	____
6. Classroom periods should run between forty-five and fifty-five minutes to ensure adequate time to investigate significant issues and practice important skills.	____	____	____
7. Students must be provided with adequate work areas, including chairs and desks, where they can sit quietly for the major part of their learning and study.	____	____	____

8. Emphasis should be placed on reading
   textbooks and listening to lectures, for this is
   how students learn best.   ____   ____   ____

These points seem to make a lot of sense. And, for many students, they may lead to
higher academic achievement—for many, but not all. Ironically, for a significant
number of students, these recommendations can lead to poorer performance, even
academic failure. The reason is that students have different **learning styles**—diverse
ways of learning, comprehending, knowing.

Did you notice these different learning styles in your own elementary and secondary school experience? Perhaps you see them now in college or graduate school.
Some students do their best work late at night, while others set an early alarm because
they are most alert in the morning. Many students seek a quiet place in the library to
prepare for finals; others learn best in a crowd of people with a radio blaring; still others study most effectively in a state of perpetual motion, constantly walking in circles
to help their concentration. Some students seem unable to study without eating and
drinking; simultaneously imbibing calories and knowledge, they all but move into
the refrigerator when preparing for tests, (These differences really strike home if you
and your roommate clash because of conflicting learning styles.)

We are a population of incredibly diverse learners, and intriguing new research
has focused on the ways students learn. These studies suggest that learning styles may
be as unique as handwriting. The challenge for educators is to diagnose these styles
and to shape instruction to meet individual student needs.

At least three types of factors—as diagrammed in Figure 4.1—contribute to each
student's individual learning style:

1. *Cognitive (information processing).* Individuals have different ways of perceiving,
   organizing, and retaining information, all components of the **cognitive
   domain.** Some students prefer to learn by reading and looking at material,
   while others need to listen and hear information spoken aloud. Still others
   learn best kinesthetically, by whole body movement and participation. Some
   learners focus attention narrowly and with great intensity; others pay
   attention to many things at once. While some learners are quick to respond,
   others rely on a slower approach.

2. *Affective (attitudes).* Individuals bring different levels of motivation to learning,
   and the intensity level of this motivation is a critical determiner of learning
   style. Other aspects of the **affective domain** include curiosity, the ability to
   tolerate and overcome frustration, and the willingness to take risks. A
   fascinating aspect of the affective domain is a concept termed **locus of
   control.** Some learners attribute success or failure to external factors ("Those
   problems were confusing," "The teacher didn't review the material well," or
   "My score was high because I made some lucky guesses"). This is called an
   "external" locus of control. Simply stated, they do not take responsibility for
   their behavior. Others attribute performance to internal factors ("I didn't
   study enough" or "I didn't read the directions carefully"). These students have
   an "internal" locus of control because they have the sense that they control
   their fate, that they can improve their performance.

3. *Physiology (biology).* Clearly, a student who is hungry and tired will not learn as
   effectively as a well-nourished and rested child. Other physiological factors are
   less obvious. Different body rhythms cause some students to learn better in
   the day, while others are night owls. Some students can sit still for long
   periods of time, while others need to get up and move around. Light, sound,

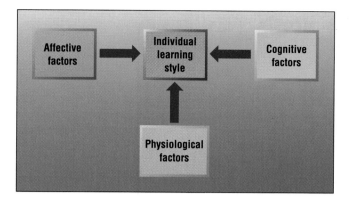

FIGURE 4.1

Factors contributing to
learning styles.

and temperature are yet other factors to which students respond differently based on their physiological development.[3]

With this introduction to learning styles, you now know that the committee's eight recommendations will not create a productive learning climate for all students. The following section paraphrases the original recommendations, explodes myths, and provides research concerning diverse learning styles.[4]

Myth	Fact
Students learn best in quiet surroundings.	Many students learn best when studying to music or other background noise. Others need so much silence that only ear plugs will suffice, but there is no simple sound rule that applies to all.
Students learn best in well-lighted areas.	Some students are actually disturbed by bright light and become hyperactive and less focused in their thinking. For them, dimmer light is more effective.
Difficult subjects are best taught in the morning, when students are most alert.	Peak learning times differ. Some students are at their best in the morning, while others function most effectively in the afternoon or evening.

Myth	Fact
Room temperature should be maintained at a comfortable 68 to 72 degrees Fahrenheit to promote learning.	Room temperature preferences vary greatly from individual to individual, and no single range pleases all. What chills one learner may provide the perfect climate for another.
Eating or drinking while learning should be prohibited.	Some students learn better and score higher on tests if they are allowed to eat or drink during these times. Banning such activities may penalize these individuals unfairly.
The most appropriate length of time for a class is forty-five to fifty-five minutes.	This period of time may be too long for some and too brief for others. The comfort time zone of the student rather than a predetermined block of hours or

TEACHING TIPS FOR DIFFERENT LEARNING STYLES

Many educators believe that students have preferred learning styles and that teaching to these preferred styles will increase educational success. Following are three learning styles frequently mentioned in the literature. (Do you recognize yourself in any of these categories?) Since all of these students are typically in class at the same time, as a teacher you will be called on to use a variety of instructional approaches to reach all of them.

Visual Learners

About half of the student population learns best by *seeing* information. They are termed visual learners.

Teaching Tips

Textbooks, charts, course outlines, and graphs are useful instructional aids.

Ask these students to write down information, even rewriting or highlighting key points.

Ask students to "preview" chapters by looking at subheadings and illustrations before they read each chapter.

Seat these students up front, away from windows and doors (to avoid distractions).

Encourage them to ask for comments or directions to be repeated if they did not understand directions the first time.

Use overheads and flip charts.

Kinesthetic Learners

This is another popular learning style, which is also called *haptic* (Greek for "moving and doing") or *tactile*. These are "hands on" learners, students who learn best by doing.

Teaching Tips

Try to plan for student movement in class presentation, as well as independent study time.

Movement should be planned to avoid distracting others. Memorizing information can be enhanced if these learners are encouraged to physically move about the room.

Providing students with a colored desk blotter or a colored transparency to read a book is called "color grounding" and can help focus their attention.

Ask them to take notes and encourage them to underline key points as they read.

Encourage them to take frequent but short breaks.

Try to use skits and role plays to help make instructional points.

Auditory Learners

This is a style used less frequently than the previous two. These students learn best by hearing; they can remember the details of conversations and lectures and many have strong language skills.

Teaching Tips

Provide the opportunity for auditory learners to recite the main points of a book or lecture.

Encourage these students to study with a friend, so they can talk through the main points.

Audiotapes of classroom activities can be helpful.

Suggest that they read class notes into a tape.

Encourage them to read the textbook out loud.

It can be helpful for these students to say out loud the meaning of the illustrations and main subject headings, as well as reciting any new vocabulary words.

Group work can be a useful class activity for auditory learners.

Students should be provided with appropriate work areas, including chairs and desks, where they spend most of their classroom time.

Reading a textbook or listening to a lecture is the best way to learn.

minutes is the factor critical to effective learning.

A substantial number of students need to move about to learn. For these learners, sitting at a desk or a computer terminal for long periods of time can actually hinder academic performance.

Diverse students learn through a variety of modes, not only through reading or listening. While many students rely on these two perceptual modes, they are less effective for others. Some learn best through touch (for example, learning to read by tracing sandpaper letters), while others rely on kinesthetic movement, including creative drama, role-play, and field-based experiences.

Learning style is not the only area undergoing demystification: our understanding of **intelligence** is also being reconstructed. The IQ score, developed early in the twentieth century, is supposed to be a measure of a person's innate intelligence, with a score of 100 defined as "normal," or average. The higher the score, the "brighter" the person. Some of us grew up in communities where IQ was barely mentioned. In many cases this lack of knowledge might have been a blessing. Others of us grew up with "IQ envy," in communities where IQ scores were a big part of our culture. Since the score is considered a "fixed, permanent measure" of intellect, like a person's physical height, the scores engendered strong feelings. Friends who scored 150 or 160 or higher on an IQ test had a secret weapon, a mysteriously wonderful brain. We were impressed. But then our friend, the "genius," was stumped trying to unpack and plug in a toaster oven or got hopelessly lost trying to follow the simplest driving directions. How could this person have such a high IQ? We may have been equally puzzled when another friend, who scored horribly low on an IQ test, went on to fame and riches (and promptly forgot that we were ever their friends). What is this IQ score supposed to mean?

Multiple Intelligences and Emotional Intelligence

Also puzzled by these contradictions was Harvard professor **Howard Gardner.** Concerned about the traditional assessment of intelligence, with such a heavy emphasis on language and mathematical-logical skills, he broadened the concept to define *intelligence* as "the capacity to solve problems or to fashion products that are valued in one or more cultural settings."[5]

Some students learn best in cooperative learning situations.

Recent research indicates that the ability to perform intricate and extended physical maneuvers is a distinct form of intelligence.

Gardner identified eight kinds of intelligence, not all of which are commonly recognized in school settings, yet Gardner believes that his "theory of **multiple intelligences**" more accurately captures the diverse nature of human capability. Consider Gardner's eight intelligences:

1. *Logical-mathematical.* Skills related to mathematical manipulations and discerning and solving logical problems (*related careers:* scientist, mathematician)
2. *Linguistic.* Sensitivity to the meanings, sounds, and rhythms of words, as well as to the function of language as a whole (*related careers:* poet, journalist, author)
3. *Bodily-kinesthetic.* Ability to excel physically and to handle objects skillfully (*related careers:* athlete, dancer, surgeon)
4. *Musical.* Ability to produce pitch and rhythm, as well as to appreciate various forms of musical expression (*related careers:* musician, composer)
5. *Spatial.* Ability to form a mental model of the spatial world and to maneuver and operate using that model (*related careers:* sculptor, navigator, engineer, painter)
6. *Interpersonal.* Ability to analyze and respond to the motivations, moods, and desires of other people (*related careers:* psychology, sales, teaching)
7. *Intrapersonal.* Knowledge of one's feelings, needs, strengths, and weaknesses; ability to use this knowledge to guide behavior (*related benefit:* accurate self-awareness)
8. *Naturalist.* (Gardner's most recently defined intelligence) Ability to discriminate among living things, to classify plants, animals, and minerals; a sensitivity to the natural world (*related careers:* botanist, environmentalist, chef, other science- and even consumer-related careers.)[6]

Gardner and his colleagues continue to conduct research, and this list is still growing. A possible ninth intelligence being explored by Gardner concerns an *existential intelligence,* the human inclination to formulate fundamental questions about who we are, where we come from, why we die, and the like. Gardner believes that we have yet to discover many more intelligences. (Can you can think of some?)

The theory of multiple intelligences goes a long way in explaining why the quality of an individual's performance may vary greatly in different activities, rather than reflect a single standard of performance as indicated by an IQ score. Gardner also points out that what is termed *intelligence* may differ, depending on cultural values. Thus, in the Pacific Islands, intelligence is the ability to navigate among the islands. For many Muslims, the ability to memorize the Koran is a mark of intelligence. Intelligence in Balinese social life is demonstrated by physical grace.

Gardner's theory has sparked the imaginations of many educators, some of whom are redesigning their curricula to respond to differing student intelligences. Teachers are refining their approaches in response to such questions as[7]

- How can I use music to emphasize key points?
- How can I promote hand and bodily movements and experiences to enhance learning?

WHERE DO THE MERMAIDS STAND?

Giants, Wizards, and Dwarfs was the game to play.

Being left in charge of about eighty children seven to ten years old, while their parents were off doing parents things, I mustered my troops in the church social hall and explained the game. It's a large-scale version of Rock, Paper, and Scissors, and involves some intellectual decision making. But the real purpose of the game is to make a lot of noise and run around chasing people until nobody knows which side you are on or who won.

Organizing a roomful of wired-up grade schoolers into two teams, explaining the rudiments of the game, achieving consensus on group identity—all of this is no mean accomplishment, but we did it with a right good will and were ready to go.

The excitement of the chase had reached a critical mass. I yelled out: "You have to decide *now* which you are—a GIANT, a WIZARD, or a DWARF!"

While the groups huddled in frenzied, whispered consultation, a tug came at my pants leg. A small child stands there looking up, and asks in a small concerned voice, "Where do the Mermaids stand?"

A long pause: A *very* long pause. "Where do the Mermaids stand?" says I.

"Yes. You see, I am a Mermaid."

"There are no such things as Mermaids."

"Oh, yes, I am one!"

She did not relate to being a Giant, a Wizard, or a Dwarf. She knew her category, Mermaid, and was not about to leave the game and go over and stand against the wall where a loser would stand. She intended to participate, wherever Mermaids fit into the scheme of things. Without giving up dignity or identity. She took it for granted that there was a place for Mermaids and that I would know just where.

Well, where DO the Mermaids stand? All the "Mermaids"—all those who are different, who do not fit the norm and who do not accept the available boxes and pigeonholes?

Answer that question and you can build a school, a nation, or a world on it.

What was my answer at the moment? Every once in a while I say the right thing. "The Mermaid stands right here by the King of the Sea!" (Yes, right here by the King's Fool, I thought to myself.)

So we stood there hand in hand, reviewing the troops of Wizards and Giants and Dwarfs as they rolled by in wild disarray.

It is not true, by the way, that Mermaids do not exist. I know at least one personally. I have held her hand.

Source: Robert Fulghum, *All I Really Need to Know I Learned in Kindergarten* (New York: Villard Books, 1989), pp. 81–83.

- How can I incorporate sharing and interpersonal interactions into my lessons?
- How can I encourage students to think more deeply about their feelings and memories?
- How can I use visual organizers and visual aids to promote understanding?
- How can I encourage students to classify and appreciate the world around them?

As instruction undergoes re-examination, so does evaluation. The old pencil-and-paper tests used to assess linguistic, math, and logical intelligences seem much less appropriate for measuring these new areas identified by Gardner.[8] The **portfolio** approach, used in this text, is an example of a more comprehensive assessment, which includes student artifacts (papers, projects, videotapes, exhibits) that offer tangible examples of student learning. Some schools ask students to assemble portfolios that reflect progress in Gardner's various intelligences. In other cases, rather than *A*s and *B*s or 80s and 90s, schools are using descriptions to report student competence. In music, for example, such descriptions might include "The student often listens to music," "She plays the piano with technical competence," "She is able to compose scores that other students and faculty enjoy," and so on. Whether the school is exploring portfolios, descriptive assessment, or another evaluation method, Gardner's multiple intelligences theory is reshaping many current assessment practices.[9]

While the theory of multiple intelligences raises fundamental questions about instruction and assessment, EQ may be even more revolutionary. **EQ,** or the **emotional**

IN THE NEWS . . . CLASS ACT

The Stuttgart, Arkansas Junior High School varsity football team all shaved their heads so they could look more like teammate Stuart H., who lost most of his hair while undergoing chemotherapy. The coach explained: *They got together so he wouldn't feel weird, so they would all look weird together.*

Source: *The American School Board Journal,* December 1997.

intelligence quotient, is described by **Daniel Goleman** in his book *Emotional Intelligence.* Goleman argues that, when it comes to predicting success in life, EQ may be a better predictor than IQ. How does EQ work? The "marshmallow story" may help you understand:

> A researcher explains to a 4-year-old that he/she needs to run off to do an errand, but there is a marshmallow for the youngster to enjoy. The youngster can choose to eat the marshmallow immediately. But, if the 4-year-old can wait and *not* eat the marshmallow right away, then an extra marshmallow will be given when the researcher returns. Eat one now, or hold off and get twice the reward.

What do you think you would have done as a 4-year-old? According to the social scientists who conducted the marshmallow experiment, decisions even at this age foreshadow an emotional disposition characteristic of a successful (or less successful) adult. By the time the children in the study reached high school, the now 14-year-olds were described by teachers and parents in a way that suggested their marshmallow behaviors predicted some significant differences. Students who ten years earlier were able to delay their gratification, to wait a while and garner a second marshmallow, were reported to be better adjusted, more popular, more adventurous, and more confident in adolescence than the group who ten years earlier had gobbled down their marshmallows. The children who gave in to temptation, ate the marshmallow and abandoned their chances for a second one, were more likely to be described as stubborn, easily frustrated, and lonely teenagers. In addition to the differences between the gobblers and waiters as described by parents and teachers, there was also a significant SAT scoring gap. The students who, ten years earlier, could wait for the second marshmallow scored 210 points higher than did the gobblers. Reasoning and control, "the regulation of emotion in a way that enhances living,"[10] might be new, and perhaps better, measures of what we call "smart," or "intelligent."

Emotional intelligence "is a type of social intelligence that involves the ability to monitor one's own and others' emotions, to discriminate among them, and to use the information to guide one's thinking and actions."[11] Goleman suggests that EQ taps into the heart, as well as the head, and introduces a new gateway for measuring intelligence, for children and adults.[12] By the way, how would you rate your EQ?

SO WHAT'S YOUR EQ?

Like Daniel Goleman, Yale psychologist Peter Salovey works with emotional intelligence issues, and he identifies five elements of emotional intelligence. How would you rate yourself on each of these dimensions?

Knowing Emotions

The foundation of one's emotional intelligence is self-awareness. A person's ability to recognize a feeling as it happens is the essential first step in understanding the place and power of emotions. People who do not know when they are angry, jealous, or in love are at the mercy of their emotions.

Self-Rating on Knowing My Emotions
Always aware of my emotions__ Usually aware__ Sometimes aware__ Out of touch, clueless.__

Managing Emotions

A person who can control and manage emotions can handle bad times as well as the good, shake off depression, bounce back from life's setbacks, and avoid irritability. In one study, up to half of the youngsters who at age 6 were disruptive and unable to get along with others were classified as delinquents by the time they were teenagers.

Self-Rating on Managing My Emotions
Always manage my emotions__ Usually manage__ Sometimes manage__ My emotions manage me.__

Motivating Oneself

Productive individuals are able to focus energy, confidence, and concentration on achieving a goal and avoid anxiety, anger, and depression. One study of 36,000 people found that "worriers" have poorer academic performance than nonworriers. (A load off your mind, no doubt!)

Self-Rating on Motivation and Focus
Always self-motivated/focused__ Usually self-motivated/focused__ Sometimes self-motivated/focused__ I can't focus on when I was last focused (and I don't care).__

Recognizing Emotions in Others

This skill is the core of empathy, the ability to pick up subtle signs of what other people need or want. Such a person always seems to "get it," even before the words are spoken.

Self-Rating on Empathy
Always empathetic__ Usually empathetic__ Sometimes empathetic__ I rarely "get it."__

Handling Relationships

People whose EQ is high are the kind of people you want to be around. They are popular, are good leaders, and make you feel comfortable and connected. Children who lack social skills are often distracted from learning, and the dropout rate for children who are rejected by their peers can be two to eight times higher than for children who have friends.

Self-Rating on Relationships
I am rich in friendship and am often asked to lead activities and events.__ I have many friends.__ I have a few friends.__ Actually, I'm pretty desperate for friends.__

Ratings

Give 4 points for each time you selected the first choice, 3 points for the "usual" or "many" second option, 2 points for the "sometimes" selection, and 1 point for the last choice.

18–20 points: A grade—WOW! Impressive!
14–17 points: B grade—You have considerable skills and talents.
10–13 points: C grade—Feel free to read further on this topic.
5–9 points: D grade—This may be a perfect subject to investigate in greater detail. Do you have a topic for your term project yet?

Goleman and Gardner are toppling educational traditions, stretching our understanding of what schools are about. In a sense, they are increasing the range and diversity of educational ideas. This chapter is all about diversity. The students you will teach will learn in diverse ways, and a single IQ or even EQ score is unlikely to capture the range of their abilities and skills. But these are not the only differences students bring to school. Let's turn our attention to how cultural, ethnic, and racial diversity is transforming life in the classroom.

Cultural Diversity

America has just experienced the greatest immigration surge in its history. In the past few decades, more immigrants have come to this country than came at the beginning of the twentieth century, a time often thought of as the great era of immigration and Americanization. These new Americans have arrived mainly from Latin America and Asia, but also from the Caribbean, the Middle East, Africa, and Eastern Europe. Today, about one in ten Americans is foreign born.

Consider the following:

- By 2012 the west (the geographic area expected to witness the greatest changes) will become "minority majority," with no single racial or ethnic group having a majority.
- The nation has approximately 2 million Native Americans and Inuit belonging to over 300 federally recognized tribes speaking more than 200 languages.
- By 2020, the number of U.S. residents who are nonwhite or Latino will be 120 million, nearly double what it was in the 1990s.
- The number of Southeast Asians in the United States skyrocketed from 20,000 in 1960 to more than 1 million by 1990, while the number of Indian Asians reached 570,000 in 1990.[13]

Demographic forecasting, the study of people and their vital statistics, provides a fascinating insight into tomorrow's schools. Demographers indicate that at the dawn of the twenty-first century, one out of three Americans will be of color. Some forecast that by 2020 almost half the school population will be from non-European ethnic groups. Demographers draw a portrait of a new generation of students far more diverse—by race, ethnicity, culture, and language—than our country has ever known. You will teach in a nation more diverse and less Eurocentric than the one you grew up in. How will this affect your life in the classroom?

Although the national demographics are powerful, you will not be a national teacher. You will be a local teacher, and the demographic realities you experience will be shaped by where you teach. If you teach in a large, urban school system, you will likely encounter classrooms where the majority of students are of color. In many cities today, students of color already constitute 70 to more than 90 percent of the students. Lower standardized test scores achieved by students of color indicate a continuing educational challenge (see Figure 4.2). If you decide to start your career in the tony suburbs outside the nation's capital, in Fairfax, Virginia, or Montgomery County, Maryland, for example, you may very well find third- and fourth-generation American children from wealthy homes attending your school, along with students recently arrived in this country—thousands of students speaking more than a hundred different languages. Of course, not every American community is experiencing dynamic population changes. You may find yourself teaching in a very stable school district, one where student demographics have remained basically unchanged for decades. But, even in these communities, changing national demographics will not go unnoticed. As the nation's population changes, so will the nation's culture, politics, and economy. To a degree, we are all part of the national fabric. The challenge for educators is how to prepare all of the nation's students for this more diverse America.

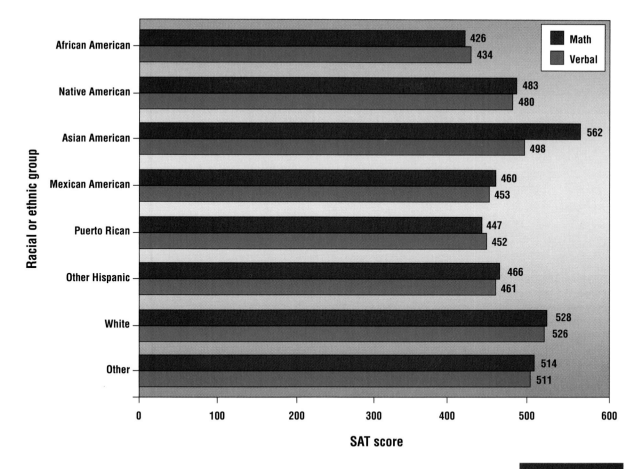

Teaching Them All

Imagine this. You have graduated from your teacher preparation program and have signed the contract for your first teaching job, and now you stand before your very first class. As you survey your sixth-grade students, you see fifteen boys and fourteen girls. As you look at your class, you realize that you will be teaching a wonderfully diverse group. Off to the right, near the windows, are half a dozen students eagerly talking in Spanish. Some African American children, comparing their schedules, look to you with curiosity. In the front of the room, several Asian American children are in their seats, looking up to you, awaiting your comments. (You do have a good opening, right?) Several white children and a few students whose backgrounds may reflect more than one racial or ethnic group are looking at the motivational posters you hung just last night. You know from reading student records that six of your students have learning disabilities, and the child in the wheelchair has muscular dystrophy. One of the children has been identified as gifted. About half of your students are from single-parent homes. A third come from middle-class backgrounds, and the remaining children are from working-class or poor families. Whew! The proverbial American melting pot looks more like a tossed salad in your class.

You know from your training, reading, and experience that each of these young lives has been shaped, in part, by geography, ethnicity, exceptionality, social class,

FIGURE 4.2

1998 SAT scores by racial and ethnic group. Students' educational achievement is influenced by many social factors, including race and ethnicity.

Source: College Board, 1998 Profile of SAT Program Test Takers, New York: College Board, 1998.

race, and gender. You understand that these characteristics will influence how these children perceive the world—and how the world views them. You also know that each one is likely to have a learning style as unique as his or her appearance.

How will you meet the needs of these twenty-nine different learners? What strategies and approaches will you use to foster equity and excellence in your classroom?

Culture and Education 101

Before teaching your first class, you may be required, or you may elect, to take courses in special education, gender equity, and multicultural education. Here we offer an introduction, some suggested topics that might be found in a course designed to help you teach diverse learners. We'll call our course "Culture and Education 101." Additional information and strategies for dealing with diversity will be described later in this book.

Generalize, Don't Stereotype

Although you are the teacher and your students are the "learners," be prepared to do quite a bit of learning yourself. As you assimilate information about your students, their culture, and their experiences, you will need to distinguish between stereotypes and generalizations. While the dangers of stereotyping are common knowledge these days, the usefulness of generalizations is less well known.

Stereotypes are absolute statements applied to all members of a group, statements that ignore individual differences. Stereotypes tend to close off discussion by providing simplistic characterizations. Generalizations offer information about groups that can help you teach more effectively. For instance, a generalization that members of a certain group avoid direct eye contact, while not applying to every group member (that would be a stereotype), is a generalization that teaches us what to expect from many if not most group members. **Generalizations** are flexible insights that provide us with clues about groups, useful information for instructional planning. Generalizations are discussion openers, recognizing that we are all members of many groups: religious, gender, geographic, class, interest, skills, and the like. Look for generalizations about your students' backgrounds that will help you plan for teaching. Avoid stereotypes.

Model Skills and Behaviors That Reflect Sensitivity

Looking for the first time at ethnically diverse names on a class list, a teacher might blurt out, "I'll never be able to pronounce that one!" or "That's the first time I heard that name." Such comments reflect a lack of cultural understanding and sensitivity, hardly endearing a teacher to a student. Some teachers dig a deeper hole, converting the "unusual" name to an easier to pronounce "nickname" or unilaterally deciding to Americanize the name, as in "Miguel, do you mind if I call you Mike?" Such names as Tomàs, Twanda, Chu, Ngyuen, or Kenji may take an extra effort to learn to pronounce correctly, but it is an effort that demonstrates cultural and personal respect.

Once you have learned about your students and their cultural background, you will have to take the next big giant step: ensure that your knowledge is reflected in your behavior. Being responsive to cultural norms is yet another way to demonstrate cultural sensitivity. For instance, one Native American and Asian cultural norm is to shun competition. As their teacher, you may want to minimize the practice of publicly praising one student's work in front of others, or even providing the stage for such comparisons. You could choose to review student performance through quiet, individual conferences, rather than announcing or posting such grades. Such steps go a long way in promoting effective relationships in and beyond the classroom.

Being a good teacher in the years ahead will almost surely mean dealing with a culturally diverse population.

Use Classroom Strategies That Build on Student Learning Styles

As was discussed earlier in this chapter, individuals, and even groups, have different, preferred learning styles. If your students are similar to the ones in the class described earlier, they are likely to bring with them an incredible assortment of educational styles and experiences. To get a sense of each student's unique approach to learning, observe each of them doing their work and analyze how each approaches the curriculum. Some schools assist you in this effort by providing learning style assessments that you can administer to your students. Use this information and plan a variety of instructional options and teaching strategies that appeal to the different intelligences described by Gardner and others. Give all your students the chance to succeed.

Give Equal Instructional Attention

The research on classroom interaction, described in greater detail in Chapter 3, reflects subtle and not so subtle teacher biases. Male students tend to call out more than female students, and, even when males do not call out, teachers tend to call on them more than females. White students also garner more instructional time than students of color. The result is that white males receive more of the most precious items in the teacher's repertoire, time and attention. Even silence is not distributed equally. Teachers give males and perceived high achievers more wait time—more quiet time to respond to questions and to think about their answers. These patterns of bias are usually so subtle that teachers are not aware of them.

To avoid elusive interaction bias, you may want to ask a colleague, friend, or student to carefully and objectively tally the interactions you have with different students. Whom do you talk to the most? Who gets helped or praised the most? How is your wait time distributed?

Similar patterns of bias exist in instructional materials, as some groups receive more attention than others in textbooks. Students in your class will naturally look for themselves in the curricular materials, to see how they are presented. Will they find themselves in the materials that you use, or will they be invisible? Are the instructional

THE SONG IN HIS HEART

As I look back over a lifetime of teaching, one special student stands out. Kou was the most memorable student I've ever taught. Short, bandy-legged, and incredibly strong for a 13-year-old, he had come from a rural mountain village deep within Laos to my special-education class in the Santa Barbara suburbs. Although he was no bigger than an American nine-year-old, the hormones of puberty had thrown a dark fuzz over his lip. His voice was deep, a shock coming from that small a body. Often, he wore a bemused expression, compounded of amazement and tolerance for the Americans who were so different from his countrymen in pastoral Laos.

On the playground, Kou was king. He could throw farther, higher, and harder than any other child in school. He was unsurpassed at *hack,* a Laotian game played with the head and feet that seemed like a cross between volleyball and soccer. And in soccer, he was the best. He also carved wonderful wooden tops, which served as trade goods for the American treasures the other boys had.

In the classroom, however, Kou had a problem. The letters, numbers, and words that he painfully memorized one week seemed to vanish during the next.

Although I tried every trick in my teaching bag, nothing seemed to work. With my help, Kou attempted all sorts of experiments designed to help him learn: writing in colored chalk, making clay letters, drawing on the playground. Throughout every effort, he remained cheerful and willing. His attitude seemed to be, "Well, this is how it is in America." But his skills did not improve.

Over time, I noticed that Kou often sang to himself as he worked. "Kou, tell me about your song," I said one day. In his halting English, he told me that the song was about a woman whose man had left her all alone.

"Write it down, Mrs. Nolan," demanded La, his friend. And so our song translation project began. As the class chimed in and squabbled over the meaning of different words, Kou sang, thought, then said the words in his fractured English. I wrote the song down on a sheet of paper. When I was finished, the children all read the song aloud, then sang it with Kou. The next day, my students brought tapes of their native music to school. Suddenly, we had a full-fledged language-experience project underway! As we listened, hummed, and made illustrated booklets about the songs and read them back, the legends and stories of Laos and the Hmong people began to tumble from Kou. For the first time, he had a reason to communicate.

Brief, primitive, and loaded with mistakes, Kou's stories became the foundation for his reading, writing, and language instruction. Never a fan of basal readers, I used this experience as an opportunity to leave the textbooks behind. Kou's quickly improving skills were a source of pride for both of us. When Kou was 15, he left us for junior high. By then he could read at a third-grade level and do survival math. He still had that sweet smile and he still sang softly as he worked. He still longed for the hills of Laos and his old job of herding ducks beside a lake, but he spoke and wrote much better English.

And me? How much I had learned from Kou. Not only did he open the door into a rich and mysterious realm where ghosts walked and crocodiles roamed, but he taught me something about how to be a teacher. From him I learned about the value of starting with a student's interests—and about how powerful a learning tool sharing a culture can be.

Source: Virginia Nolan, "The Song in His Heart," *Instructor* 101, no. 8 (1992): p. 94.

materials free of stereotypes? Are the views and information presented solely through Eurocentric eyes, or are diverse perspectives included?

Because students spend an enormous amount of time working with textbooks and related materials, curricular choices are central to classroom learning. If you were, in fact, enrolled in our fictitious course, "Culture and Education 101," you would undoubtedly invest a fair amount of time studying curriculum. One of the best-known writers in this area is James Banks, whose useful framework for incorporating multicultural concepts in the curriculum is described in the next section.

Multicultural Education

According to **James Banks,** the primary goal of **multicultural education** is to transform the school so that male and female students, exceptional students, and students from diverse cultural, social-class, racial, and ethnic groups experience an equal opportunity to learn.[14] A key assumption of multicultural education is that students are more likely to achieve when the total **classroom climate** is more consistent with their diverse cultures and learning styles.

We have already discussed individual learning styles but have yet to focus on cultural learning styles. Some educators posit that, through **enculturation,** particular groups are likely to exhibit characteristic approaches to learning. For example, based on the groundbreaking work of **Carol Gilligan,** some studies show that women are more likely than men to personalize knowledge; in general, they prefer learning through experience and first-hand observation.[15] Other research suggests that the African American culture emphasizes learning that is aural and participatory. When African American children are required to translate their participatory style onto a written test, they are likely to concentrate on the unaccustomed form of expression, to the detriment of their knowledge of the content.[16] Multicultural educators say that, if we can identify and understand cultural learning styles, we can target curriculum and instruction more appropriately. Further research in cultural and gender learning styles holds the promise of transforming tomorrow's schools.

Multicultural education also seeks to help all students develop more positive attitudes toward different racial, ethnic, cultural, and religious groups. According to a 1990s survey of more than one thousand young people between 15 and 24 conducted by People for the American Way, about half of the students described the state of race relations in the United States as generally bad. Fifty-five percent of the African Americans and whites said they were "uneasy" rather than "comfortable" in dealing with members of the other racial group. However, most respondents felt their attitudes toward race relations were healthier than those of their parents.[17]

James Banks notes that one way to achieve more positive attitudes toward different groups is to integrate the curriculum, to make it more inclusive. He describes four approaches, described below and illustrated in Figure 4.3.[18] (Do you remember any of these approaches in your own schooling?)

1. Multicultural education often begins with the *contributions approach,* in which the study of ethnic heroes (for example, Sacajawea, Rosa Parks, or Booker T. Washington) is included in the curriculum. At this superficial contributions level, one might also find "food and festivals" being featured or such holidays as cinco de mayo being described or celebrated.

2. In the *additive approach,* a unit or course is incorporated, often but not always during a "special" week or month. February has become the month to study African Americans, while March has been designated "Women's History Month." Although these dedicated weeks and months offer a respite from the typical curricular material, no substantial change is made to the curriculum as a whole.

3. In the *transformation approach,* the entire Eurocentric nature of the curriculum is changed. Students are taught to view events and issues from diverse ethnic and cultural perspectives. For instance, the westward expansion of Europeans can be seen as "manifest destiny" through the eyes of European descendants, or as an invasion from the east, through the eyes of Native Americans.

4. The fourth level, *social action,* goes beyond the transformation approach. Students not only learn to view issues from multiple perspectives but also become directly involved in solving related problems. Rather than political passivity, the typical by-product of many curricular programs, this approach promotes decision making and social action in order to achieve multicultural goals and a more vibrant democracy. (See Chapter 8 for additional multicultural strategies and for a discussion of the current debate concerning the place of multiculturalism in the curriculum.)

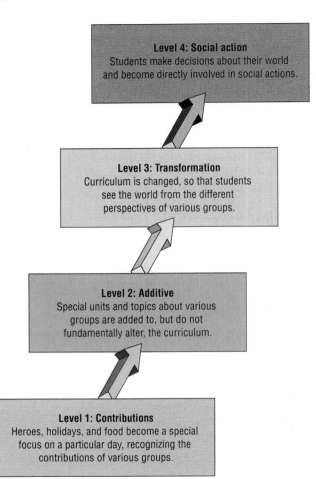

Level 4: Social action
Students make decisions about their world and become directly involved in social actions.

Level 3: Transformation
Curriculum is changed, so that students see the world from the different perspectives of various groups.

Level 2: Additive
Special units and topics about various groups are added to, but do not fundamentally alter, the curriculum.

Level 1: Contributions
Heroes, holidays, and food become a special focus on a particular day, recognizing the contributions of various groups.

FIGURE 4.3

Banks's approach to multicultural education.

Cooperative Learning

No discussion of diversity would be complete without exploring **cooperative learning,** a prevalent instructional strategy in diverse classrooms. We examined cooperative learning in Chapter 3 and showed how it promotes cooperation over competition and builds self-esteem. If you were to use cooperative learning in your class, you might create groups to include boys and girls, high- and low-ability students, and children from different races and ethnic backgrounds. These small groups would work together for an extended period of time, from several days to several months. These students might be part of other groups as well, learning to work with different classmates on other projects. At the elementary school level, for example, you might begin by distributing the week's vocabulary words on Monday. From Tuesday through Thursday, a period of time could be set aside, so that the students can work together to plan and create a game that would show mastery of the vocabulary words, a game they can use with all their classmates at the end of the week. On Friday, the entire class would "play" the games, demonstrating their understanding of the week's new words. At the high school level, an in-depth research project or class presentation might be assigned to cooperative learning groups in which each student receives both an individual and a group grade. In fact, there are many different methods for organizing cooperative learning, including Jigsaw, Student Teams Achievement Division (STAD), and Group Inquiry, terms likely to become more familiar to you during your teacher education program.

Research shows that cooperative learning enhances not only achievement but relationships as well.[19] When students of diverse ethnic and racial backgrounds work cooperatively, they learn to like and respect one another, as well as to focus on higher academic goals. Cooperative learning also helps mainstreamed students with disabilities gain social acceptance. But do not expect the magic of cooperative learning without your active participation: teachers need to monitor the groups, directly teaching social skills.[20]

The following steps offer some helpful ways to create cooperative learning in your classroom:

1. Start with cooperative learning projects that are short and simple.
2. Make sure students understand how important it is to work cooperatively with other people—not only in the classroom but throughout life.
3. Don't assume that students automatically know how to work in groups in the classroom. Teach and model social skills, such as how to talk quietly in groups.
4. Praise students when they use skillful social behaviors.

School learning environments in the future must accommodate a wide variety of individual and cultural learning styles.

5. Use group roles to help students develop social skills. For example, if you have a student who dominates group discussions, assign that person the role of observer.

6. Have enrichment or extension activities available for groups who finish first. Also, those who complete their work early might observe or help other groups.[21]

Bilingual Education

What is going on in America? It is amazing, and disturbing, to ride on a road and see street signs that are printed not only in English but in other languages as well. What's more, even legal documents are now being written in foreign languages. How unnerving to walk down an American street and not understand what people are talking about. Maybe this isn't America. I feel like a stranger in my own land. Why don't they learn to speak English?

Sound like a stroll through today's Miami, or San Diego, or perhaps San Antonio? Good try, but you not only have the wrong city, you are also in the wrong century. Benjamin Franklin expressed this view in the 1750s.[22] He was disgruntled that Philadelphia had printed so many things, including street signs, in another language (German, in this case). Even the *Articles of Confederation* were published in German as well as English, and children were taught in Dutch, Italian, and Polish.

Bilingual education in America is hundreds of years old, hardly a "new" issue. In 1837, Pennsylvania law required that school instruction be given on an equal basis in German as well as English. In fact, that example provides us with a fairly concise definition of **bilingual education,** the use of two languages for instruction. But, almost a century later, as America was being pulled into World War I,

In some bilingual education programs, English is learned as a second language, while the student takes other academic work in his or her native language.

foreign languages were seen as unpatriotic. Public pressure routed the German language from the curriculum, although nearly one in four high school students was studying the language at the time. Individual states went even further. Committed to a rapid assimilation of new immigrants, and suspicious of much that was foreign, these states prohibited the teaching of *any* foreign language during the first eight years of schooling. (The Supreme Court found this policy not only xenophobic but unconstitutional as well, in *Meyer v. State of Nebraska,* 1923.)[23]

Despite the long history of bilingual education in this country, many school districts never really bought into the concept. In districts without bilingual education, students with a poor command of English had to sink or swim (or perhaps, more accurately, "speak or sink"). Students either learned to speak English as they sat in class—or they failed school, an approach sometimes referred to as **language submersion.** If submersion was not to their liking, they could choose to leave school. Many did.

Bilingual education had a rebirth in the 1960s, as the Civil Rights movement brought new attention to the struggles of many disenfranchised Americans, including non-English speakers trying to learn in a language they did not understand. And, unlike the 1800s, by the 1960s and 1970s education had become less an option and more a necessity, the threshold to economic success. To respond to this need, Congress passed the **Bilingual Education Act** in 1968. This act provided federal financial incentives, using what some people call "a carrot approach," to encourage schools to initiate bilingual education programs. Not all districts chased the carrot.

From the start, the Bilingual Education Act was fraught with problems. The act lacked concrete recommendations for implementation and did not specify standards. Individual school districts and, in some cases, even individual schools, experimented with different approaches. The result was a patchwork of programs of varying quality, threadbare in spots and peppered with holes where no programs existed at all. In too many cases, the act simply failed to serve the students it was meant to serve.

During the early 1970s, disillusioned parents initiated lawsuits. In 1974, the Supreme Court heard the case of ***Lau v. Nichols.*** This class action lawsuit centered around Kinney Lau and 1,800 other Chinese students from the San Francisco area who were failing their courses because they could not understand English. The Court unanimously affirmed that federally funded schools must "rectify the language deficiency" of these students. Teaching students in a language they did not understand was not an appropriate education. The Court's decision in *Lau v. Nichols* prompted

BILINGUAL AMNESIA

"My grandparents picked up English like everyone else back then, in school, where children learned their lessons in English, not in Spanish or Vietnamese."

"If people want to remain immersed in their old culture and old language, they should stay in their old country."

"Bilingual education had given us illiterate youngsters who can do little more than work at Taco Bell."

Sound familiar? After all, many of our ancestors came to America with few resources or funds, but they were able to learn English, pick up American ways, get through school, and succeed against great odds, so why can't today's immigrants do the same? According to Richard Rothstein—author of *The Way We Were?*—we suffer a bad case of national amnesia, and our recollection of history differs significantly from actual events. The author believes that some bilingual programs work well, and some do not. The key is to find out which are the effective ones and to move the issue of bilingual education out of the political arena and into objective evaluation. Rothstein reminds us that

- *Bilingual education is an American tradition.* In 1837, New York City established bilingual programs for German children, and, throughout the 1800s, Maryland, Colorado, Oregon, Kentucky, Indiana, and Iowa, to name but a few, established their own bilingual programs.
- *Opinions back then were also divided.* Some believed that the programs were essential for academic success, while others thought that they slowed down mastery of English. Then as now, individuals who were being taught in bilingual classrooms—Italian, German, Polish, French, Spanish, and so on—differed as to whether or not bilingual education was a good idea.

- *School performance for immigrants in English immersion programs was horrific.* From 1880 through the 1930s, immigrants were far more likely to drop out of school than to graduate, and they dropped out at much higher percentages than today's students.

- *Non-English-speaking students in New York City early in the twentieth century were 60 percent more likely than English speakers to be labeled "retarded,"* including more than a third of the Italian students.

- In most cases, immigrants to this country never mastered English. In fact, *it was not until the third generation that most immigrant groups became fluent enough in English to excel in school.*

- *As World War I pulled America into the conflict, communities across the nation reacted by eliminating not only bilingual education programs but even the teaching of foreign languages,* the most popular of which was German. It was not until the Supreme Court decision in the 1970s that bilingual education re-emerged as an issue in the nation's schools. And, by then, most Americans had not only forgotten the bilingual education programs of the past, but they had also forgotten what happened to students without them.

Adapted from Richard Rothstein, "Bilingual Education: The Controversy," *Phi Delta Kappan 79,* no. 9 (May 1998): pp. 672–78.

Congress to pass the **Equal Educational Opportunities Act (EEOA).** Under this law, school districts must take positive steps to provide equal education for language-minority students by eliminating language barriers.

Typically in the bilingual approach, **limited English proficiency (LEP)** students learn English as a second language while taking other academic subjects in their native language. The **transitional approach** begins by using the native language as a bridge to English-language instruction. Academic subjects are first taught using the native language, but progressively the students transition to English, to their new language. This is the most widely used approach. The **maintenance,** or **developmental, approach** emphasizes the importance of maintaining both languages. The goal is to create a truly bilingual student, one who acquires English while maintaining competence in the native language. Students are instructed in both languages. **English as a Second Language (ESL)** supplements either the maintenance or transitional programs by providing special ESL classes for additional instruction in reading and writing English.

Two approaches which cannot truly be considered bilingual, language submersion and immersion, remind us of the "sink or swim" mentality but are used with LEP children nonetheless. Language submersion places students in classes where only English is spoken, and the student either learns English as the academic work progresses, or doesn't. **Immersion** is somewhat less rigid than submersion, because the teacher usually understands the native language and responds in English, sometimes using a "sheltered" or simplified English vocabulary.

Even in schools using one or more of these approaches, problems persist. Consider the following:

> . . . last week I saw an elementary school teacher who was teaching a class of 31 children in the third grade, and the 31 children spoke six languages, *none* of which was English. The teacher had one year of Spanish in her collegiate training.[24]

As schools struggle to meet the needs of LEP students, bilingual education continues to spark political controversy. Approximately 3 million students speak hundreds of languages and dialects, including not only Spanish but Hmong, Urdu, Russian, Chinese, Polish, Korean, Tagalog, and Swahili. Misunderstandings are multiplied when language barriers are accompanied by racial and ethnic differences, leading to even greater isolation and segregation for many LEP students. And, while some struggle to make bilingual education work, others believe that it never will.

Opponents of bilingual education point to studies showing that first- and second-generation Hispanic students who attended bilingual programs from the 1970s to the 1990s earned considerably less money than Hispanics who attended "English only" classes. Moreover, Hispanic students who dropped out of bilingual programs were less likely to return and complete high school than were Hispanics who attended English-only programs.[25] LEP parents despair over their children's lack of progress in learning English and graduating from school. The dropout rates for Hispanic students, the largest group of LEP students, hovers around 50 percent.[26] Many parents of students in bilingual programs now oppose these programs, an ironic turnabout, since it was parent protests in the 1960s and 1970s that forced reluctant schools and the federal government to initiate bilingual education. In 1998, more than 60 percent of the voters in California, including a sizable minority of Hispanic voters, supported an initiative to replace most bilingual maintenance programs with a fast-track transition to English. Proposition 227 required that LEP students be provided a year of English immersion instruction and then be shifted into regular classrooms where only English is spoken, unless their parents obtain a waiver. The legality of this proposition is in the courts as of this writing.[27]

Many people worry that bilingual education threatens the status of English as the nation's primary vehicle of communication. As a result, an **English-only movement** has emerged (see Figure 4.4). Those who support this movement feel that English is a unifying national bond that preserves our common culture. They believe that English should be the only language used or spoken in public and that the purpose of bilingual education should be to quickly teach English to LEP students. In fact, they assert that bilingual education hurts LEP students, by making them dependent on their native language and discouraging them from learning English.

Bilingual education advocates argue that America is a mosaic of diverse cultures and that diversity should be honored and nurtured. One problem, they point out, is that we simply do not have enough competent bilingual teachers who can respond to the large numbers of LEP children now in our schools. Bilingual advocates oppose the English-only movement, and they feel that it promotes intolerance, will turn back the clock, and may very well be unconstitutional. Education writer James Crawford points out, "It is certainly more respectable to discriminate by language than by

States with official English rule and year enacted		States without official English rule
Alabama	1990	Arizona
Alaska	1998	Connecticut
Arkansas	1987	Delaware
California	1986	D.C.
Colorado	1988	Idaho
Florida	1988	Iowa
Georgia	1986 & 1996	Kansas
Hawaii*	1978	Maine
Illinois	1969	Maryland
Indiana	1984	Michigan
Kentucky	1984	Minnesota
Louisiana*	1811	Nevada
Massachusetts*	1975	New Jersey
Mississippi	1987	New Mexico
Missouri	1998	New York
Montana	1995	Ohio
Nebraska	1920	Oklahoma
New Hampshire	1995	Oregon
North Carolina	1987	Pennsylvania
North Dakota	1987	Rhode Island
South Carolina	1987	Texas
South Dakota	1995	Utah
Tennessee	1984	Vermont
Virginia	1981 & 1996	Washington
Wyoming	1996	West Virginia
		Wisconsin

*NOTES: Hawaii has recognized English and Hawaiian as official languages. An 1811 "enabling act" requires Louisiana to keep records in English. A 1975 state Supreme Court ruling said English is the official language of Massachusetts.

FIGURE 4.4

The State of 'English-Only'
Twenty-two states have passed referendums or laws that declare English the sole official language of the state. Most of these declarations are largely symbolic.

Adapted from: Washington Post, February 6, 1999: p. 4.

race. . . . Most people are not sensitive to language discrimination in this nation, so it is easy to argue that you're doing someone a favor by making them speak English."[28]

Through the 1990s, the opponents of bilingual education gained ground as Congress sharply reduced funding for bilingual education. Moreover, a score of "English-only" bills made their way through various state legislatures and Congress. The future of bilingual education is still being defined.

What does the research say about these opposing views and the effectiveness of bilingual education? Unfortunately, the research is not clear. Educators are just now beginning to analyze long-term data, and they are uncovering some useful findings. In one case, the researchers found that, when language-minority students spend more time learning in their native language, they more likely to achieve at comparable and even higher levels in English.[29] Another study found that, the earlier a student starts learning a new language, the more effective that language becomes in an academic setting.[30] Yet another study showed that no single approach holds a monopoly on success, and different approaches to bilingual education can each be effective, suggesting that local school systems should carefully select the programs most appropriate for their communities.[31]

One major bilingual study directed by Virginia Collier and Wayne Thomas evaluated the experiences by 42,000 students over a thirteen-year period. Early findings suggested that the students enrolled in well-implemented bilingual programs actually *outperform* the students in monolingual programs. One successful approach assumed bilingual education to be a two-way street, one in which English speakers and LEP students would learn from each other. In this model, during the Spanish part of the day, the Spanish-speaking students explained the lessons to native-English peers, while, during English instruction, the reverse took place. Collier and Thomas report that, by fourth grade, the students in these two-way classes had actually outperformed the native English speakers who attended English-only classes.[32]

More than two centuries ago, Ben Franklin expressed his fears about the multiple languages heard on America's streets. His concerns have echoed through the centuries, despite a world in which national borders seem to be blurring or even disappearing. In today's global community, Russians and Americans are working together in space, such international organizations as the United Nations and NATO are expanding their membership, and corporations are crossing national boundaries to create global mergers in an international marketplace. Moreover, technological breakthroughs, such as the Internet, have made international communications not only possible but commonplace. However, for most Americans, these international conversations are viable only if the other side speaks English. In this new international era, Americans find themselves locked in a monolingual society. How strange that, instead of viewing those who speak other languages as welcome assets to our nation, some seem eager to erase linguistic diversity.

Exceptional Learners

In a typical classroom, a teacher faces students with a great range of abilities, from students reading years behind grade level to students reading years ahead. Both these groups of students are described by the same broad term: **exceptional learners.** Integrating exceptional learners into the regular classroom adds further challenge to the job of teaching diverse students.

Typically, exceptional learners are categorized as follows:

- Students with mental retardation
- Students with learning disabilities
- Students with emotional disturbance or behavior disorders
- Students with hearing and language impairments
- Students with visual impairments
- Students with attention deficit hyperactivity disorder
- Students with other health and physical impairments
- Students with severe and multiple disabilities
- Gifted and talented students[33]

Today, children with disabilities constitute approximately 12 percent of the school-age population. Twice as many males as females are identified as disabled. Most of these students who attend public schools are learning disabled (46 percent), another 18 percent have speech and language impairments, and 10 percent are mentally retarded. Almost 90 percent of students receiving special education are considered "mildly handicapped."[34]

We will end this chapter with a close look at issues and developments in teaching exceptional learners, from students with disabilities to gifted and talented learners. Inclusion of each of these populations stretches not only the range of diversity in the classroom but also the range of skills you will need in order to meet the needs of all your students.[35]

PROFILES IN TEACHING: ANNE SULLIVAN

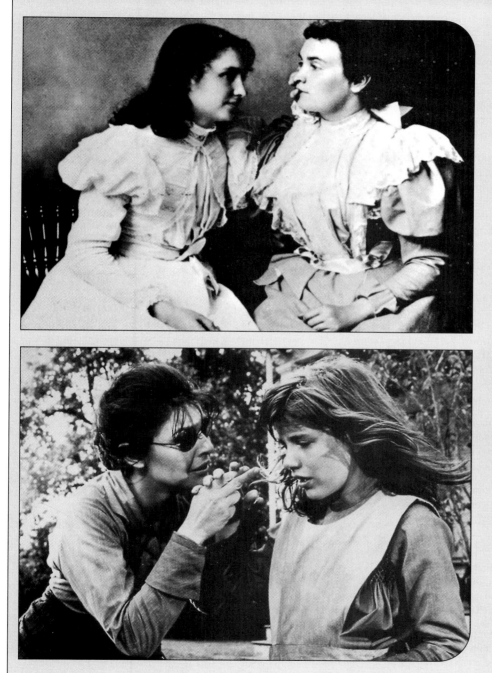

Anne Sullivan's work with Helen Keller is an inspiration for special education teachers.

This scene, from *The Miracle Worker,* tells the story of the brilliant and determined teacher, Anne Sullivan (played by Anne Bancroft) as she introduced the world to Helen Keller (played by Patty Duke).

Anne Sullivan taught a deaf and blind child to communicate with and inspire the world. Her difficult, trying, and soul-satisfying work with Helen Keller is one answer to the question "Why teach?"

When she was 19 months old, Helen Keller suffered a terrible illness. When her fever dropped, there was great rejoicing, for no one knew then that Helen would never see or hear again. In her autobiography, Helen Keller writes, "Gradually, I got used to

(Box concludes on next page)

the silence and darkness that surrounded me and forgot that it had ever been different, until she came—my teacher—who was to set my spirit free." It has been said that the genius of Helen's teacher, Anne Sullivan, was hardly less remarkable than that of her pupil. To have another Helen Keller, there would have to be another Anne Sullivan.

Anne Sullivan suffered a childhood of abuse, neglect, and illness, which left her half-blind. She studied at the Perkins Institute of the Blind, and she brought her own experience, the teaching methods of the Perkins Institute, and an indomitable will to the challenge of instructing a blind and deaf 7-year-old.

When she first arrived at the Kellers' home, Anne Sullivan found Helen to be a tireless, unmanageable force. It took time away from Helen's kind but indulgent family, with teacher and student living by themselves, before the child became tractable enough to learn. Day after day, Anne patiently fingerspelled words into Helen's hand while the little girl mimicked the motions of her teacher's fingers. Then came the breakthrough: Anne helped Helen unlock the secret of language. Helen describes it in her autobiography, *The Story of My Life:*

The morning after my teacher came she led me into her room and gave me a doll. The little blind children at the Perkins Institute had sent it and Laura Bridgman had dressed it; but I did not know this until afterward. When I had played with it a little while, Miss Sullivan slowly spelled into my hand the word "d-o-l-l." I was at once interested in this finger play and tried to imitate it. When I finally succeeded in making the letters correctly I was flushed with childish pleasure and pride. Running downstairs to my mother I held up my hand and made the letters for doll. I did not know that I was spelling a word or even that words existed; I was simply making my fingers go in monkey-like imitation. In the days that followed I learned to spell in this uncomprehending way a great many words, among them pin, hat, cup, and a few verbs like sit, stand, and walk. But my teacher had been with me several weeks before I understood that everything has a name. . . .

We walked down the path to the well-house, attracted by the fragrance of the honeysuckle with which it was covered. Someone was drawing water and my teacher placed my hand under the spout. As the cold stream gushed over one hand she spelled into the other the word water, first slowly, then rapidly. I stood still, my whole attention fixed upon the motions of her fingers. Suddenly I felt a misty consciousness as of something forgotten—a thrill of returning thought; and somehow the mystery of language was revealed to me. I knew then that "w-a-t-e-r" meant the wonderful cold something that was flowing over my hand. That living word awakened my soul, gave it light, hope, joy, set it free! There were barriers still, it is true, but barriers that could in time be swept away. I left the well-house eager to learn. Everything had a name, and each name gave birth to a new thought. As we returned to the house every object which I touched seemed to quiver with life. That was because I saw everything with the strange, new sight that had come to me. . . .

I learned a great many new words that day. I do not remember what they all were; but I do know that mother, father, sister, teacher were among them—words that were to make the world blossom for me, "like Aaron's rod, with flowers." It would have been difficult to find a happier child than I was as I lay in my crib at the close of that eventful day and lived over the joys it had brought me, and for the first time longed for a new day to come.[36]

Describing this incident in a letter, Anne Sullivan tells of the remarkable transformation in Helen. She also writes of her own joy as the teacher who worked a miracle:

April 5, 1887

We went out to the pump-house, and I made Helen hold her mug under the spout while I pumped. As the cold water gushed forth, filling the mug, I spelled "w-a-t-e-r" in Helen's free hand. The word coming so close upon the sensation of cold water rushing over her hand seemed to startle her. She dropped the mug and stood as one transfixed. A new light came into her face. She spelled "water" several times. Then she dropped on the ground and asked for its name and pointed to the pump and the trellis, and suddenly turning round she asked for my name. I spelled "Teacher."

P.S. I didn't finish my letter in time to get it posted last night; so I shall add a line. Helen got up this morning like a radiant fairy. She had flitted from object to object, asking the name of everything and kissing me for very gladness. Last night when I got in bed, she stole into my arms of her own accord and kissed me for the first time, and I thought my heart would burst, so full was it of joy.[37]

Exceptional Learners: An Exceptional Struggle for Educational Rights

Perhaps you have read the book *Karen.* It is the story of a child with cerebral palsy, a child who persevered despite devastating obstacles. A formidable obstacle was an educational system that had no room for children with disabilities. The book was written by Karen's mother, a woman who, like her daughter, refused the rejection of a hostile school and society. She wrote of her attempts to gain educational rights for her daughter and other children with disabilities:

> We constantly sought a remedy for this appalling situation which deprived so many of an education, and eventually we found a few doctors and educators who had made strides in developing valid testing methods for handicapped children. On one occasion, when I voiced a plea for the education of the handicapped, a leading state official retorted, "It would be a waste of the state's money. They'll never get jobs."
>
> We were frequently discouraged and not a little frightened as many of our "learned" men felt the same way.[38]

Such disparaging attitudes were common in our society for years and resulted in inadequate educational programs for millions of exceptional children. Today, the educational rights of these children have been mandated by courts of law and are being put into practice in classrooms across the nation.

Before the Revolutionary War, the most that was offered to exceptional children was protective care in asylums. The asylums made little effort to help these children develop their physical, intellectual, and social skills. Following the American Revolution, however, the ideals of democracy and the development of human potential swept the nation. Within this humanist social context, procedures were devised for teaching the blind and the deaf. Then, in the early 1800s, attempts were made to educate the "idiotic" and the "insane" children who today would be called "mentally retarded" or "emotionally disturbed."

For many years, the legal system mirrored society's judgment that the best policy toward the disabled was "out of sight, out of mind." The courts typically saw education as a privilege rather than a right, and they ruled that children with disabilities should be excluded from schools. The notion was that the majority of children needed to be protected from those with disabilities: from the disruptions they might precipitate, from the excessive demands they might make, and from the discomfort their presence in classrooms might cause.

The years following World War II brought renewed hope and promise. Such pioneers as Grace Fernald, Marianne Frostig, and Heinz Werner—to name but a few—conducted research, developed programs, and gave new impetus to the field of **special education.** Their work was aided by the emergence of new disciplines, such as psychology, sociology, and social work. Parents also continued their struggle, individually and collectively, to obtain educational opportunities for children with disabilities. They took their cause to both the schools and the courts. Special education has broken away from the isolation and institutionalization so common in the late nineteenth century and has moved to mainstream exceptional children, as much as possible, into typical school settings.

By the 1970s, court decisions and federal law had established five critical principles of special education:

1. **Zero reject.** The principle of zero reject asserts that no child with disabilities may be denied a free, appropriate public education. Representatives of the disabled have asserted that excluding children with disabilities from public schools violates the constitutional interpretation behind the Supreme Court's *Brown v. Board of Education* (1954) decision, which put an end to claims of "separate but equal" schooling. The courts have responded with landmark decisions in Pennsylvania (*Pennsylvania Association for Retarded Children v. Commonwealth*) and in Washington, DC, (*Mill v. D.C. Board of Education*) that mandate public schools in those jurisdictions to provide a free, appropriate education to all children with disabilities. Other federal and state decisions have followed suit.

2. **Nondiscriminatory education.** The principle of nondiscriminatory education, based on the Fifth and Fourteenth Amendments of the U.S. Constitution, mandates that children with disabilities be fairly assessed, so that they can be protected from inappropriate classification and tracking. Much of the court activity in this area has centered on the disproportionate number of children of color assigned to special education classes, a situation that some claim is the result of biased testing. In one case, a court ruled that IQ tests could not be used for placing or tracking students. Other courts have forbidden the use of tests that are culturally biased, and still others have ordered that testing take place in the children's native language.

3. **Appropriate education.** While the principle of zero reject assures that children with disabilities will receive an appropriate public education, it is important to recognize that this principle goes beyond simply allowing children with disabilities to pass through the schoolhouse door. The term "appropriate education" implies that these children have the right to an education involving the accurate diagnosis of individual needs, as well as responsive programs keyed to those needs.

4. **Least-restrictive environment.** The principle of least-restrictive environment protects children with disabilities from being inappropriately segregated from their age-group peers. Court decisions have urged that special classes and separate schools be avoided unless a child's disabilities are such that education in a regular classroom with the aid of special materials and supportive services cannot be achieved.

5. **Procedural due process.** The principle of procedural due process upholds the right of the disabled to protest a school's decisions about their education. Due process entails the right of children with disabilities and their parents to be notified of school actions and decisions; to challenge those decisions before an impartial tribunal, using counsel and expert witnesses; to examine the school records on which a decision is based; and to appeal whatever decision is reached.

These five principles of special education law are encompassed in landmark federal legislation passed in 1975 (**Public Law 94-142**), the Education for All Handicapped Children Act. This law offers states financial support to make a free and appropriate public education available to every child with disabilities. It was replaced and expanded in 1991 by the **Individuals with Disabilities Education Act (IDEA),** which not only provided a more sensitive description of the act's purpose but also extended the act's coverage to all disabled learners between the ages of 3 and 21, including individuals with autism or traumatic brain injuries. IDEA also provided for rehabilitation and social work services. IDEA requires that each disabled child "have access to the program best suited to that child's special needs which is as close as possible to a normal child's educational program."[39] Classroom teachers shoulder the responsibilities of monitoring the needs of each child with disabilities placed in their classrooms and of using constructive procedures to meet their needs. The law further states that an **individualized education program (IEP)** be developed to provide a written record of those needs and procedures. The law states that an IEP must be written for each child who receives special education services. The IEP must include:

A statement of the student's current performance, including long-term (annual) goals and short-term objectives

A description of the nature and duration of the instructional services designed to meet the prescribed goals

An overview of the methods of evaluation that will be used to monitor the child's progress and to determine whether the goals and objectives have been met

There is no specific IEP form that must be used, as long as goals, objectives, services, and evaluation are accurately reflected. In fact, hundreds of different IEP forms are currently in use; some run as long as twenty pages; others are only two or three pages. New teachers should learn about their school district's norms and procedures for writing

Public Law 94-142 placed students with disabilities into regular classrooms, so that they receive the "least-restrictive" education possible.

IEPs when they begin teaching. Remember, it is not the format that is important but, rather, whether or not the IEP accurately describes the educational needs and the related remedial plans. While writing these IEPs will undoubtedly consume a great deal of a teacher's time and energy, it often leads to better communication among the school staff, as well as between teachers and parents. Also, the practice of preparing IEPs will likely lead to more effective individualization of instruction for all children, not just those with disabilities.

IDEA has been one of the most thoroughly litigated federal laws in history. Parents whose children qualify for special education services can and do sue the school district if they believe their children's needs are not being met. Local courts agreeing with parents' views have ordered public schools to hire extra teachers or specialized personnel or to spend additional dollars to provide an appropriate education. When judges believe that a school is unable to meet the special needs of a child, even with these additional resources, they can and have ordered the public school to pay the tuition so that the student can attend a private school. The practice of judges ordering public schools to pay the private school tuition of some special needs children is currently being reviewed by the Supreme Court.[40]

There is considerable confusion in identifying learning-disabled (LD) students, in deciding who is entitled to additional resources. Educational literature reflects more than fifty terms to describe students with **learning disabilities.** Some believe that *learning disabled* has become a catchall term for many children whose achievement does not match their potential. Over the past decade, the number of children defined as needing special education services has multiplied, sharply driving up education costs as well.[41]

Some question the effectiveness of current practices. For instance, many students with mild disabilities attend regular classrooms for part of the day but leave for a period of time to receive special instruction in a resource room. Recently, these "pullout" programs have been charged with stigmatizing students while failing to improve their academic performance. Many who criticize pulling children out of mainstreamed classes for special education are proponents of what is known as the **regular education initiative.** This initiative endorses the placement of special needs children in a regular class from the start and emphasizes close collaboration between the regular classroom teacher and special educators in order to offer special services *within* the regular classroom. Debate over the best way to educate students with disabilities is certain to continue.[42]

Regular classroom teachers often express concerns about their ability to handle a mainstreamed classroom:

> They want us all to be super teachers, but I've got 33 kids in my class and it's really a job to take care of them without also having to deal with special needs kids too. I'm not complaining really—I wouldn't want to do anything other than what I'm doing—but it is demanding.[43]

Classroom teachers are expected to meet many of society's needs, including the education of special needs students, but are not always given adequate tools to meet those expectations. Frustration is often the result. To succeed with special education students, teachers could benefit from additional time to plan with other professionals, the availability of appropriate curricular materials, perhaps extra classroom assistance, and on-going staff development programs that provide up-to-date instructional strategies. In any case, for **mainstreaming** (also termed **inclusion**) to succeed, teachers must genuinely support the integration of students with disabilities into their classrooms. They must be committed to exploding stereotypes and must recognize the essential value of helping all children learn to understand and accept differences. Although we have emphasized the legal decisions that prompted the mainstreaming movement, inclusion is at its heart a moral issue, one that raises the timeless principles of equality, justice, and the need for all of us to learn to live and grow together—not apart.

The Gifted and Talented

Precocious children are among our most neglected students. They, too, have special needs:

> In Chicago, the school system turned down the request of a 5-year-old boy who wanted to enter school early. While he waits to be allowed to enter kindergarten, the boy spends his time in the public library doing independent research in astronomy and geography. His IQ has been measured at more than 180.
>
> In Westchester County, a suburb of New York City, a 2½-year-old boy already emulates the language abilities of his parents. He speaks and reads English, French, Hebrew, Spanish, and Yiddish, and he has mastered some Danish. He is studying music theory and is conducting scientific experiments. The parents, however, are unable to find any educational facility willing and able to educate their young, gifted child. A member of their local school board told them: "It is not the responsibility or function of public schools to deal with such children." As a result, the parents considered moving to Washington state, where there was an experimental preschool program for the gifted.[44]

If you are like most Americans, you may find it difficult to consider gifted and talented children to be in any way disadvantaged. After all, **gifted learners** are the lucky ones who master subject matter with ease. They are the ones who shout out the solution before most of us have a chance to write down the problem. Others may have perfect musical pitch, are athletic superstars, become the class leaders who inspire us, or demonstrate insights that amaze and inform us. Many exhibit endless curiosity, creativity, and energy. Small wonder that there is relatively little national support for extra funds or programs targeted at these gifted students, the ones who make the rest of us feel somewhat uncomfortable, inadequate, and sometimes just plain envious.

Defining *giftedness,* like defining *learning disabilities,* invites controversy. To some, the traditional definition of *giftedness* includes those with an IQ of 130 or higher; to others, the label *giftedness* is reserved for those with an IQ score of 160 or higher. Still others, such as Gardner and Goleman, have expanded the concept of gifted to include those with special creative or artistic abilities, athletic prowess, interpersonal gifts, or emotional insights.

Education experts Joseph Renzulli and C. H. Smith described the gifted in somewhat traditional terms, as those who demonstrate

1. High ability
2. High creativity
3. High motivation and persistence (the drive to initiate and complete a task)[45]

According to Renzulli and Smith, a child who is better than 85 percent of his or her peers in all three areas, and who exceeds 98 percent in at least one area, can be classified as gifted.

Another researcher, **Robert Sternberg,** has identified three major types of giftedness: analytic, synthetic, and practical. Students who are gifted analytically excel at dissecting problems and understanding their parts. Analytically gifted students usually do well on conventional tests of intelligence. Synthetic giftedness occurs in people who are creative, intuitive, or insightful. Individuals who are practically gifted can go into real-world situations, figure out what needs to be done, and negotiate and work with people to accomplish the task.[46]

While definitions of *giftedness* vary, only a small percentage of our population possesses this high degree of ability, creativity, motivation, or pragmatic talent, making for a very exclusive club. Exclusivity can invite hostility. Since most people are, by definition, excluded from this highly select group, few believe that the gifted merit any special educational attention. To many Americans, it seems downright undemocratic to provide special services to children who already enjoy an advantage. While many parents of gifted children are strong advocates for their children, even parents of the gifted have shown reluctance to request additional educational programs for their children.

Many gifted students do not make it on their own. Highly talented young people suffer boredom and negative peer pressure when kept in regular classroom settings.[47] Instead of thriving in school, they drop out. The result is that many of our nation's brightest and most competent students are lost to neglect and apathy, and some of our most talented youth have not always succeeded at school.

Even in school districts that recognize the special needs of gifted children, opposition to providing special programs and educational opportunities continues. In some cases, funds are lacking; in others, little interest and commitment to the gifted may be the problem. Some object to special programs for the gifted because they see it as a form of tracking, an undemocratic strategy that separates the gifted from the rest of the population.

Research shows that a significant number of gifted students contemplate suicide. Gifted students may be haunted by a sense of isolation and loneliness, pressure to achieve, and fear of failure.[48] Talent, giftedness, and creativity set adolescents apart

Until recently, schools did little to accommodate the special needs of the gifted and talented.

THE WAY THEY WERE IN SCHOOL

All of these people were considered poor learners in school:

Thomas Edison	Benjamin Franklin	Henry Ford
Paul Gauguin	Pablo Picasso	Abraham Lincoln
William Butler Yeats	Carl Jung	

The following individuals were expelled from school:

Albert Einstein	Edgar Allan Poe	Percy Bysshe Shelley
Salvador Dali	James Whistler	George Bernard Shaw

at a time when the push is for conformity, for being "normal" and "like everybody else." Gifted students most often talk about their feelings of isolation:

> I feel as though I'll never fit in any place, no matter how hard I try.

> Basically, the challenge in my schooling has not been academic, but having to conform—to be just like everyone else in order to be accepted.

> I hate it when people use you. For example, if you have an incredible vocabulary and someone wants your help writing a speech, and then later they tell you to get lost.[49]

The picture is especially dismal for females and children of color who are identified as "gifted," and once identified, are more likely to dropout than gifted white males. Many experts urge the use of multiple criteria for identifying and retaining gifted students, including teacher recommendations and assessments of special talents, so that such programs could be more equitable and inclusive.

Once identified, there is no guarantee that gifted students will find high-quality programs. The regular classroom remains a major instructional resource for gifted students. For instance, a gifted student might spend most of the day in a regular class and be pulled out for a part of the day, perhaps an hour or so, to receive special instruction. Another approach is to set up resource centers within the regular classroom, where gifted students are offered individualized tutoring.[50] At the secondary level, comprehensive high schools have augmented their offerings with challenging courses of study, such as the International Baccalaureate (IB) program, an internationally recognized degree program that includes rigorous science, math, and foreign language requirements. Special high schools, such as the Bronx High School of Science and the North Carolina School for Mathematics and Science, have long and distinguished histories of providing educational opportunities for intellectually gifted students. Other special schools have focused on programs in acting, music, and dance. Many communities now mirror this approach by creating their own special magnet or charter schools, which emphasize subjects ranging from science to communication skills, from theater to computer science.[51]

Some school districts go beyond their own resources in order to meet the needs of gifted students. For instance, one such program connects gifted high school students with the local college or community college. These students spend part of their day enrolled in college-level courses, being intellectually challenged and receiving college credit while still enrolled in high school. Still other gifted students receive additional instruction through summer camps or even special year-long programs that augment their regular courses. Johns Hopkins University, for example, has been sponsoring the Center for Talented Youth (CTY) in different parts of the nation for several decades.

Many of these college programs are termed **accelerated programs,** for they allow gifted students to skip grades or receive college credit early. Advanced

I TAUGHT THEM ALL

In "I Taught Them All," high school teacher Naomi White despaired over her failure to reach all the different kinds of students in her classroom. She wrote,

> I have taught in high school for 10 years. During that time, I have given assignments, among others, to a murderer, an evangelist, a pugilist, a thief, and an imbecile.
>
> The murderer was a quiet little boy who sat on the front seat and regarded me with pale blue eyes; the evangelist, easily the most popular boy in school, had the lead in the junior play; the pugilist lounged by the window and let loose at intervals a raucous laugh that startled even the geraniums; the thief was a gay-hearted Lothario with a song on his lips; and the imbecile, a soft-eyed little animal seeking the shadows.
>
> The murderer awaits death in the state penitentiary; the evangelist has lain a year now in the village churchyard; the pugilist lost an eye in a brawl in Hong Kong; the thief, by standing on tiptoe, can see the windows of my room from the county jail; and the once gentle-eyed little moron beats his head against a padded wall in the state asylum.
>
> All of these pupils once sat in my room, sat and looked at me gravely across worn brown desks. I must have been a great help to those pupils—I taught them the rhyming scheme of the Elizabethan sonnet and how to diagram a complex sentence.[a]

Naomi White wrote "I Taught Them All" in 1937. The frustration, challenges, and disappointments she experienced in the classroom are touching, and many similar situations continued into the next century. But, as you consider her words, consider also how things have changed. Notice which students pierce her consciousness—the active students, the males. What kinds of issues and problems may have confronted the girls in her class? Because the girls were quieter, were their problems invisible? Some of her boys became disappointments as adults, yet none of the girls were even traced and remembered into adulthood. Were their problems as women also seen as quieter, more private, of less concern to society?

[a]Naomi White, "I Taught Them All," *Progressive Education* 20 (November 1943): p. 321.

placement courses and exams (the APs), provide similar acceleration opportunities, permitting students to graduate before their chronological peers. While many Americans accept the notion of enrichment for the gifted, acceleration runs into stronger opposition. The common belief that the negative social consequences of acceleration outweigh the intellectual benefits represents an obstacle to implementing such programs for the gifted.

Whereas social maladjustment due to acceleration may indeed be a problem for some gifted children, others claim they feel just as comfortable, both academically and socially, with their intellectual peers as they do with their chronological peers. Moreover, the failure to accelerate gifted children may lead to boredom, apathy, frustration, and even ridicule. Although social trauma may result from acceleration, it may also result from no acceleration. Several studies confirm the value of acceleration, from early admission to elementary school to early admission to college. Grade-accelerated students surpass their classmates in academic achievement and complete higher levels of education. While research suggests that grade acceleration does not cause problems in social and emotional adjustment, cases of students who found acceleration to be a disaster are also plentiful.[52] No single program is likely to meet the needs of all gifted students.

Recognition of the special needs of the gifted has been slow in coming. It is estimated that most school systems provide special gifted services to between 7 and 12 percent of their students. However, with the current trend away from ability grouping, tracking, and special programs, it is possible that fewer resources will be available for the gifted in the years ahead.[53]

The qualities of effective gifted programs include a mastery dimension that allows students to move through the curriculum at their own pace; in-depth and independent learning; field study; and an interdisciplinary dimension that allows for the exploration of theories and issues across the curriculum. Moreover, an important but often overlooked advantage of these programs is the sense of community they offer, the opportunity for gifted students to connect with others like themselves. This is an important step in reducing student anxiety and alienation. When gifted students are placed in appropriate programs, they are often empowered to realize their full potential. One student was relieved to find that "there are lots of people like me and I'm not a weirdo after all." As one 12-year-old girl said,

> My heart is full of gratitude for my teacher who first wanted to have me tested for the gifted program. I'm not trying to brag, but I'm really glad there's a class for people like me. We may seem peculiar or odd, but at least we have fun and we respect each other's talents.[54]

In the final analysis, it is not only the gifted who have suffered from our national neglect and apathy; it is all of us. How many works of art will never be enjoyed? How many medical breakthroughs and how many inventions have been lost because of our insensitivity to the gifted?

These questions of opportunities lost can be broadened to include many of the different student populations discussed in this chapter. How many of these students—because of their race, language, or special needs—have slipped through the educational cracks? How many cultural breakthroughs, intellectual insights, and economic advances have been lost because of inadequate school programs or unresponsive teachers? We will never know the final cost of our neglect, but we can rededicate ourselves to uncovering and nurturing the talents in all our students.

Summary

1. Individuals exhibit diverse styles of learning, due to cognitive, affective, and physiological differences among people. Identifying a single optimal educational climate is not possible, since individuals differ so markedly in their learning styles.
2. While some educators challenge the concept of a single appropriate learning style, others challenge the notion of a single type of intelligence. Gardner's theory of multiple intelligences identifies at least eight kinds of intelligence, ranging from the traditional verbal and mathematical to musical, physical, and interpersonal abilities. New concepts such as emotional intelligence further broaden our traditional notions of IQ.
3. Changing patterns of immigration and birth rates are demographic trends that will result in very diverse classrooms in terms of race, ethnicity, and language.
4. Early in the twenty-first century, one-third of all students will be of color, both enriching and challenging our schools.
5. Moving LEP students into America's classrooms has been both an educational and a legal challenge. In *Lau v. Nichols* (1974), the Supreme Court ruled that schools were deficient in their treatment of students with limited English proficiency. Congress subsequently passed the Equal Educational Opportunities Act. Many districts have redoubled their efforts in bilingual education. Some teach students in their native language only until they learn English (the transitional approach), other schools use both languages in the classroom (the maintenance approach), some supplement with English as a Second Language (ESL) classes, while still others opt for nonbilingual means, such as immersion and submersion. Studies suggest that many bilingual programs fall short of their goals, and the future of bilingual education is in question.

6. Many of the strategies considered effective in working with students of color benefit *all* students as well. Effective multicultural practices that benefit all students include more equitable distribution of the teacher's attention, a greater representation of the contributions and experiences of diverse groups in curricular materials, and response to different learning styles.

7. Legislation and court decisions have required schools to provide students with disabilities with appropriate education in the least restrictive environment.

8. Students with disabilities are guaranteed access to public education under the Individuals with Disabilities Education Act (IDEA), which also requires that individualized education programs be developed to document the school's efforts in meeting the needs of these students.

9. Despite the Individuals with Disabilities Education Act, controversy exists about the identification of special needs children, the best ways to educate these learners, and the importance of providing teachers with training and resources.

10. Few resources are provided for gifted and talented students in many of the nation's school districts. When their needs are not met, these exceptional learners may become apathetic, bored, isolated, and alienated.

11. Gifted and talented programs usually promote one of two strategies: enrichment or acceleration. While many people worry that acceleration will lead to social maladjustment, research indicates that acceleration has a positive impact on gifted students.

Key Terms and People

www.mhhe.com/sadker

accelerated programs
advanced placement
affective domain
appropriate education
James Banks
bilingual education
Bilingual Education Act
classroom climate
cognitive domain
cooperative learning
demographic forecasting
demographic patterns
emotional intelligence quotient (EQ)
enculturation
English as a Second Language (ESL)
English-only movement
Equal Educational Opportunities Act (EEOA)

exceptional learners
Howard Gardner
generalizations
gifted learners
Carol Gilligan
Daniel Goleman
immersion
inclusion
Individuals with Disabilities Education Act (IDEA)
individualized education program (IEP)
intelligence
language submersion
Lau v. Nichols
learning disabilities
least-restrictive environment
limited English proficiency (LEP)
locus of control

mainstreaming (inclusion)
maintenance (developmental) approach
multicultural education
multiple intelligences
nondiscriminatory education
portfolio
procedural due process
Public Law 94-142
regular education initiative
special education
stereotypes
Robert Sternberg
student learning styles
transitional approach
zero reject

Discussion Questions and Activities

1. How would you characterize your own learning style? Interview other students in your class to determine how they characterize their learning styles. Based on these interviews, what recommendations could you offer your course instructor about how to meet the needs of different students in your class?

2. What is your opinion of Howard Gardner's theory of multiple intelligences? In which of the intelligences do you feel you are the strongest? the weakest?

3. Can you develop additional intelligences beyond the ones Gardner identifies? (This is often best accomplished in groups.)

4. Review Daniel Goleman's book *Emotional Intelligence* and present a summary of Goleman's findings to your classmates.

5. Write a research paper on the education and life experiences of at least one of the recent immigrant groups. If possible, interview students and family members who belong to that group about their experiences.

6. Do you believe that bilingual education should be saved or shelved? Why? If bilingual education is maintained, how can it be made more effective?

7. Given demographic trends, pick a region of the country and a particular community. Develop a scenario of a classroom in that community in the year 2020. Describe the students' characteristics and the teacher's role. Is that classroom likely to be impacted by changing demographics? How will learning styles and the new insights on intelligence be manifested in the way the teacher organizes and instructs the class?

8. Choose a school curriculum and suggest how it can be changed to reflect one of Banks's four approaches to multicultural education. Why did you choose the approach you did?

9. Investigate a special education program in a local school. Describe its strengths. What suggestions do you have for improving it?

10. Observe a mainstreamed classroom in a local school and interview the teacher. What is your assessment of the effectiveness of mainstreaming in this classroom?

11. Given budgetary limitations, do you think schools should provide special resources and programs for gifted students? Why or why not?

12. What is your opinion of ability grouping? If you had a gifted daughter or son, would you want your child in a special program? What kind of program?

inter-mission

by Phyllis Lerner

Intermissions during shows offer an opportunity to stretch your legs, think about the act you have just seen, and perhaps make some predictions about the rest of the performance.

Inter-missions in this book will give you a chance to explore your mission as an educator, stretch your teaching "legs," think about what you've already experienced, and make some preparations for your next steps as a teacher.

Welcome to the first inter-mission.

Inter-missions

The inter-missions are placed after each of the book's four major sections and are designed to help you reflect on and apply the main ideas found in the text. Each inter-mission will include

> *Applications,* which will allow you to actively apply your readings through observations, interviews, and action research
>
> *Reflections,* which will provide you introspective, developmental tasks to help you think deeply and realistically about education and your place in it
>
> *Portfolio artifacts,* which will challenge you to collect and manage the necessary items for finding and retaining a teaching position

Introduction to Portfolios

Our friend, Diane was retiring from education after twenty years, with regret but also with exciting plans to begin another career in the Northwest. By moving day, her garage was filled with her teaching career, all boxed up, neatly labeled, and ready for the journey. One box housed her college term papers, and another was marked "master's degree." There was a carton titled "Dinosaurs—grade 4" and another, just as intriguing, inscribed "Science Unit—Diseases." Diane wasn't quite ready to let go of her teaching career or her collection of materials. After all, what would happen if she missed the classroom too much and decided to apply for a teaching job? Still, how much boxed *stuff* could she afford (emotionally, financially, and professionally) to take with her? Diane had a garage filled with boxes—what she needed was a *portfolio*.

A portfolio is a purposeful collection of you as a teacher. In four places in this book, we have placed Inter-missions to help you work through the process of assembling yourself as a teacher by creating, collecting, researching, drafting, editing, organizing, and even borrowing the *stuff* that best represents you, your *portfolio*. Starting this procedure *now* will help you improve as a teacher and enhance the quality of your portfolio. (An added advantage may be more space in your garage!)

Building your portfolio can be thought of as a two-part process: creating an extensive *working* portfolio and then selecting just the right items for your *presentation* portfolio. As you visit schools, you'll become a hunter and gatherer of all things, front office paper (there is good stuff on the welcome counter, on bulletin boards, and even in dated and discarded materials), handouts from district workshops, student handbooks, and teacher rights and responsibilities manuals. Assembling your portfolio could also draw on the World Wide Web, library, telephone, and even regular snail mail. During the final inter-mission, you will analyze the content of your working portfolio, so that you can begin to refine what becomes part of your *presentation portfolio,* what gets boxed and saved, and what should be tossed in the trash! In the end, you want a portfolio that uniquely and accurately represents you as a growing and competent teacher.

Getting Started on Your Portfolio

Portfolios can serve many purposes. Today, they are being used by states for licensure renewal, by school districts for merit pay increases, and by individual schools for hiring new staff. The National Board for Professional Teaching Standards (NBPTS)[1] requires portfolios as part of the rigorous evaluation to reward and recognize high-achieving teachers with board certification. At the classroom level, students collect, build, and store their work portfolios in cubbies or lockers. Teachers are using portfolios as an alternative evaluation method. Parents and teachers may review student portfolios at parent-teacher conferences. Your portfolio will be a tool in your eventual search for a teaching position.

Consider making your portfolio

- Purposeful—based on a sound foundation, such as professional standards
- Selective—choosing only the appropriate materials for a specific purpose or circumstance, such as a job application
- Diverse—going beyond your transcript, student teaching critiques, and letters of recommendation to represent a broad array of teaching talent
- Ongoing—relaying your growth and development over time
- Reflective—both in process and product, demonstrating your thoughtfulness
- Collaborative—resulting from conversations and interaction with others (peers, students, parents, professors, teachers, administrators)[2]

Designate a storage place for your portfolio. A file section in a carton (remember the garage boxes) is the minimalist's marker. Eventually, you will want an actual presentation portfolio that is both professional and portable.

In the first section, you will want to have an introduction to you—your name and contact information, professional or present career objective, a brief résumé,

---

[1]National Board for Professional Teaching Standards, *Toward High and Rigorous Standards for the Teaching Profession,* (Washington, DC: National Board for Professional Teaching Standards, 1989).

[2]Kenneth Wolf and Mary Dietz, "Teaching Portfolios: Purposes and Possibilities," *Teacher Education Quarterly* (winter 1998): pp. 9–21.

INTASC STANDARDS FOR LICENSING BEGINNING TEACHERS

Principle 1   Knowledge of Subject Matter
The teacher understands the central concepts, tools of inquiry and structures of the discipline(s) he or she teaches and can create learning experiences that make these aspects of subject matter meaningful to students.

Principle 2   Human Development and Learning
The teacher understands how children learn and develop, and can provide learning opportunities that support their intellectual, social and personal development.

Principle 3   Diversity in Learning
The teacher understands how students differ in their approaches to learning and creates instructional opportunities that are adapted to diverse learners.

Principle 4   Variety of Instructional Strategies
The teacher understands and uses a variety of instructional strategies to encourage students' development of critical thinking, problem solving, and performance skills.

Principle 5   Motivation and Management
The teacher uses understanding of individual and group motivation and behavior to create a learning environment that encourages positive and social interaction, active engagement in learning, and self-motivation.

Principle 6   Communication Skills
The teacher uses knowledge of effective verbal, nonverbal, and media communication techniques to foster active inquiry, collaboration, and supportive interaction in the classroom.

Principle 7   Instructional Planning Skills
The teacher plans instruction based upon knowledge of subject matter, students, the community, and curriculum goals.

Principle 8   Assessment
The teacher understands and uses formal and informal assessment strategies to evaluate and ensure continuous intellectual, social, and physical development of the learner.

Principle 9   Reflection and Responsibility
The teacher is a reflective practitioner who continually evaluates the effects of her or his choices and actions of others (students, parents, and other professionals in the learning community) and who actively seeks out opportunities to grow professionally.

Principle 10   Relationships and Partnerships
The teacher fosters relationships with school colleagues, parents, and agencies in the larger community to support students' learning and well being.

Source: *Model Standards for Beginning Teacher Licensing and Development: A Resource for State Dialogue* developed by the Interstate New Teacher Assessment and Support Consortium (INTASC).

transcripts, letters of support, and a mission or philosophy statement. Don't panic. We will take you through much of this in the chapters, discussion questions, and activities and during the inter-missions.

A framework for your portfolio will keep you focused on becoming a teacher and presenting yourself in the job search. We recommend you organize your portfolio to highlight your competency and growth in each of ten areas identified by the Interstate New Teacher Assessment and Support Consortium (INTASC). The standards represent principles for preparing, licensing, and certifying educators.

Note: The Observation Manual in Appendix 4 describes general guidelines and data collection tools for various settings. Consult this appendix before you visit schools to observe or collect data.

Now, it's time for your first inter-mission.

inter-mission

Part 1 Teachers and Students

Applications and Reflections

1:1 Teacher Interview in Your Major or Favorite Subject Area

Purpose: Teachers are expected to have knowledge of both the subject(s) they teach and the students they are teaching. Deciding what to teach, and how best to teach it, is a constant responsibility. This activity gives you the opportunity to learn about how teachers go about these tasks and to begin thinking about how you might approach curricular decisions in your major subject area.

Activity: Interview a teacher in a subject area of special interest to you. Even if you plan to teach in an elementary program, still select the curricular area that you savor. Focus on how the teacher decides what content to teach and how best to teach this content to students. Following are some potential curricular questions to ask (but you are encouraged to develop your own questions as well):

- What factors contributed to your teaching this subject (at this grade level)?
- What do you enjoy most about teaching this curriculum? What do you enjoy least?
- How do you go about selecting what content and skills to teach?
- When do you do your planning? the year before, the night before, as the bell rings?
- Do you integrate other subject areas into your program?
- How do the school district's "official" curriculum and the textbook shape your decisions?
- Can you make your own decisions as to what topics to teach, or are you confined to the "official" school curriculum?
- Do professional associations influence your decisions?
- Do parents or students participate in deciding what is taught?
- Are selections made by you alone or with others in your department or grade-level team?
- Do you try to offer different perspectives (multidisciplinary? multifaceted?) on these topics?
- Are there areas of this subject that are controversial? How do you handle these "hot" topics?

Reflection: What advice given by the teacher do you believe may influence your own decisions? How does the teacher's view of the curriculum differ from your own? How will you decide what curriculum to select when you become a teacher? What roles will professional associations, parents, and students play in your decision making? How might you respond to input from others in your department or grade-level team? Why are you interested in this subject area, and how do you anticipate your interest will impact your students and teaching?

1:2 Interview Teachers at Three Adjacent Grade Levels

INTASC PRINCIPLE 2
Human Development and Learning

Purpose: One of the traditional ways we organize schools, by age level, requires teachers to understand the progressive patterns of children's growth, yet children are incredibly different, from day to day and from each other. Educators have been known to ask, "Who *is* the average 5-year-old? What's a tenth-grader really like?" Many future teachers have a particular age-level interest. They "love the little ones" or are fascinated by "puberty and the middle school mind." Spending time with students may confirm or redirect your plans. Your purposes are to observe students in a similar age group and to distinguish between or formulate concepts about age differences.

Activity: Visit three classrooms, at three adjacent grade levels (e.g., third, fourth, and fifth grades). Stay for at least twenty minutes. Whether roll is being taken, homework is being collected, or independent reading is proceeding, you will probably see distinctions between the younger and the older students. Look at their physical sizes and shapes too. Note how the entire group is treated, how small groups operate, and how individuals behave. Watch for evidence of teacher expectations that are especially high or extremely low. Observe the patterns and frequency of routines, instructional time, behavior management, and socialization.

Reflection: How alike were the students at each of the three grade levels? How different were they? Could you determine which students were the youngest or oldest, even at one grade level? What teacher behaviors were cued to the students' levels of development? Was the teacher's use of humor, warmth, or management related to the maturity of the class? Have you selected a particular grade level for your teaching? What growth and development realities are relevant for the grade level of your interest? Why might you be better at a higher grade? Why might you be better at a lower grade? Have you considered teaching a nongraded or combination class (such as a fourth/fifth combination), in a special education program (which could have students from 9 to 14 years old); or with adult vocational learners (from age 17 to 64)?

1:3 Multiple Intelligence Bingo

INTASC PRINCIPLE 3
Diversity in Learning

Purpose: Students approach learning in different ways. An effective teacher adapts instruction to these diverse learning styles. You have studied the concept of multiple intelligences (MI), and it is time to expand your awareness. While some teachers still tend to focus on the logical and linguistic abilities, others enthusiastically incorporate Gardner's theory into their classrooms. You may even find "MI Schools" that demonstrate MI in action. In this activity, you will be challenged to identify intelligences and to see the theory applied in lessons.

Classroom # _____ **Bingo Card**

Intelligence	Example During Instruction	Display or Material Example
Logical-mathematical		
Linguistic		
Bodily-kinesthetic		
Musical		
Spatial		
Interpersonal		
Intrapersonal		
Naturalist		
Others (your own)		

Activity: Visit two classrooms. Try to include one that your professor recommends as an MI model. Observe in each room for at least forty minutes. Use the following chart to record examples of multiple intelligences. Note both instruction and room displays or materials. Brainstorming with your peers before the observation will help you determine what might constitute evidence of a particular intelligence. See if your observation can fill every slot. Bingo!

Reflection: Review your chart and those of your peers. Were any of your classrooms filled with examples of the multiple approaches to learning (any Bingo winners? in how many minutes?)? After your observations, were there any slots that remained empty? What could you do to fill those spaces? Were some classes totally geared to only one or two intelligence areas? Do you suspect that some are easy and some are always tough to use? How did particular students respond when given an opportunity to explore different intelligences? Were some confident with certain challenges and others withdrawn? How did the class respond, in general, when the lessons involved intelligences other than the logical and linguistic?

1:4 Memories of a Teacher

INTASC PRINCIPLE 4
Variety of Instructional Strategies

Purpose: Many of us choose education because of a special teacher—someone who may have inspired us to bring a special "style" to the field. This individual was probably good because he or she modeled the best of effective instruction. You may not have been consciously aware of the skills and traits of a really effective teacher, but you knew the class was interesting, challenging, productive, and maybe even arduous. Perhaps you had friends in the class and you accomplished projects in meaningful ways. Possibly you were the star, the standout who could grasp the material and help others understand. You may have been the kid who didn't connect with others, but this teacher made your year better. Whatever the story, we suspect you have one and hope you have many.

Many teachers are purposely effective. They practice the skills and strategies discussed in Chapter 3. Connecting your memories with the research on effective teaching may help you be a more purposeful, and successful, educator.

Activity: Consider one terrific educator from your past. First, brainstorm (freely associate) memories from that class. On the left side of a piece of paper, list each item.

See what you can generate at this point without reading farther (it's tempting to peek but worth the effort to wait).

After your first and open response, use the following cues to generate even more memories. Think about the way lessons began, about the subject matter, and about the use of resources or even gimmicks.

- How was the room arranged?
- Where did the teacher "hang out"?
- Do you recall big field trips or perhaps small adventures?
- How were you engaged in academic learning?
- What management techniques or rules do you remember?
- Were transitions from one activity to another handled smoothly?
- What about questioning opportunities and teacher feedback? Did you raise your hand and were you called on? Were others?
- Can you recall anything about tests (their kind, frequency, and resultant anxiety level)?
- Were term papers, major projects, special event days, or assemblies part of the curriculum?
- What else made this teacher the one who made a difference for you?

Reflection: Now, take your brainstormed list of terrific teacher memories and meander back through Chapter 3, "Teacher Effectiveness." Consider each item on your list. What connections can you make between the research on instructional quality and your memorable teacher? What generalizations about effective instruction might you offer following this activity?

1:5 Why Teach?

INTASC PRINCIPLE 5
Motivation and
Management

Purpose: People may have already asked you why you are considering teaching. Sometimes they ask with reverent tones, other times with disbelief. (Remember, they are probably sharing something about their own perspective regarding a teaching career.) Analyze your reasons to teach, so that you can provide a good answer to the question and uncover a bit about your own thinking. Besides, in order to discern the various motivations your students bring to the classroom, it's best to understand your own. This examination will contribute to your mission or philosophy statement that belongs in your portfolio.

Activity: Consider the following list of reasons or motivations to teach. Rank them from the most significant to the least significant on the vertical scale at the right. Begin by identifying the one that is *most* important to you—your major reason for teaching—and write that in the first slot. Then select the one that is the *least* important or meaningful to you, and write that by number 12. It will be easiest to work through the list if you apply this strategy, as you will always look for the one that stands out as either the most or least important reason remaining.

Reflection: As you glance at your ranked list, are there any surprises? Are there any motivations missing from the list we presented? Where might you rank these items? What's your answer—why do you want to teach?

Motivating Forces	Rank
Really enjoy and value the subject	1.
Working with youngsters	2.
Salary and benefit package	3.
Job security	4.
Professional fulfillment	5.
Variety of activities	6.
Work and vacation schedules	7.
Collegial rapport	8.
Societal status of education	9.
Stepping stone for _____ (your call)	10.
Job autonomy and control	11.
It's tough and challenging.	12.

1:6 Principal Interview About the Job Market and Hiring Procedures

INTASC PRINCIPLE 6
Communication Skills

Purpose: It might be awkward if your first communication with a school adminis-trator was at your job interview. That's not the easiest circumstance for practicing ac-tive and effective communication. An informational interview, with a principal, is a great rehearsal for you and could provide timely information on the job market and hiring procedures. It's certainly advice you need and counsel he or she may have.

Activity: Arrange an interview with a local school administrator (principal, per-sonnel director). Consider going with a small group of peers (visitation team), so that your school leader is not inundated with too many requests. Review the material in the first two chapters that provides information on teacher supply and demand. De-velop questions as a visitation team. The following list of suggestions can also pro-vide a framework for your conversation. Don't overstay your welcome—twenty to thirty minutes should be adequate.

- How many and where are the job openings in this area? What are the openings like at particular grade levels or subject areas? What do you anticipate will happen to this pattern in two years? in five years?
- Are new schools being built or others planning to close?
- Are there teachers who move in and out of the system (family leave, special grant projects)?
- What is the diversity breakdown of teachers in the district? How does this compare with the students in this school and districtwide? How do these factors affect screening and hiring?
- In general, what is the application process for this district? Are other staff involved in the procedure and at what point? Do candidates face an individual or a panel interview? Do you require or recommend applicant portfolios?
- If you could describe a perfect candidate, what traits would that teacher possess?
- What other questions should we ask concerning the educational job market and hiring process?

Reflection: Meet with other visitation teams and compare your interviews. Are cer-tain trends evident in your locale? How do these realities influence your own decision making? What questions remain unanswered? Should you schedule a follow-up meeting, phone interview, or Internet conversation? Consider a similar interview during a trip home or while visiting another region of the country. How does all this information affect your teaching plans?

1:7 A Mini-Lesson with a Mini-Group

INTASC PRINCIPLE 7
Instructional Planning Skills

Purpose: Planning instruction takes a major portion of a teacher's time and talent. Creating a learning experience in the early part of your program is a chance to begin developing this critical skill. You have read information on effective instruction, and we hope you have observed it in action. The purpose, at this point, is to find your starting line for all the practice and teaching ahead. (Since we recommend working with your classmates, this mini-teaching session could also be a way to review this course's content. There's no better way to acquire new learning than to teach it.)

Activity: Develop and teach a mini-lesson (about five to eight minutes), using content from the text's first section. Work with a small group of peers (five to eight students). Use principles of direct teaching (see pp. 70–73 in Chapter 3) as you include a review or connecting thread for engagement, present material in a clear manner, offer guided practice, model teacher feedback, and set up for independent practice. Your greatest challenge is to make the content of your lesson small enough. Review the summary sections of the text chapters to identify possible lesson topics. Any techniques you use to promote variety in process and content will be appreciated by your "students."

Reflection: You did it. You taught a mini-lesson to your peers, something that many experienced faculty find frightening. What stages did you go through to create your lesson? Did the plan "come together"? What went well? What did not? Why? How did you adjust—or did you need to—during instruction? Were you working from notes? What evidence do you have that the climate of learning was comfortable and relaxed? (Recall nonverbal clues, such as sweaty palms and sleepy eyelids.) What else do you recall from the actual mini-lesson—or was it an out-of-body experience? Was the content clear? Did your students practice what they learned? Was your feedback effective? Did you spark their interest with independent practice? What's your evidence? If you were to replan this mini-lesson, what changes would you make?

1:8 Tutor Using Effective Feedback

INTASC PRINCIPLE 8
Assessment

Purpose: Assessment is a great deal more than testing and grading. Even the evaluative feedback you give students during one-on-one interactions is considered part of your assessment repertoire. The text covers four feedback reactions to student answers: praise, acceptance, remediation, and criticism (pp. 66–69). Using them effectively and fairly will be one of your toughest challenges.

Activity: If your program recommends working with a K–12 student, terrific! If not, commit yourself to a tutorial opportunity with a local youngster. Although a "one-shot deal" will accomplish the goals of this activity, an on-going relationship is an extraordinary chance for you (and a youngster) to learn. Audiotape your session (at least fifteen minutes) with the student. Remember to get permission from

Feedback (Sample Entries)	Number of Responses
Praise:	
Good job!	II
Acceptance:	
Okay.	IIII
Remediation:	
Now read all the word parts together.	I
Criticism:	
No, that's not the way to pronounce it.	I

the student and faculty coordinator by explaining the purpose of your taping. Listen to your session and code or note the category of your feedback. Review the criteria for each type of feedback and work with a partner if you are unsure about particular comments.

Reflection: What did you notice about yourself and the pattern or frequency of feedback? How did your tutorial session compare with the teacher reaction research (pp. 66–69)? What form did your acceptance comments take (*okay, ah ha,* silence)? Did your use of praise represent the attributes identified by Brophy on page 68? Was criticism clear when appropriate? Was remediation specific enough to allow the student to improve? How would you assess your use of these skills? What activity can you devise to help you practice and improve your feedback?

1:9 A Mini-Conference About Your Mini-Lesson

INTASC PRINCIPLE 9
Reflection and Responsibility

Purpose: Reflection and evaluation of one's *own* work are major responsibilities for good teachers. You won't always have colleagues who can attend your lessons, analyze your teaching, coach you through a crisis, and generate new challenges. There will be many times (almost all the time?) when you must do it yourself. That's the essence of this activity. You will have a chance to analyze your lesson (with a little help from your friends).

Activity: Earlier in this inter-mission (1:7 "A Mini-Lesson with a Mini-Group"), you had the opportunity to teach a brief lesson using content from the text. Gather two or three "students" from the lesson. As a framework for your conversation, discuss three questions: What, in terms of content, did you do? How, in terms of process, did you do it? What, in terms of reflection, were your afterthoughts? After your investigation, encourage your classmates to offer their concerns or compliments.

Reflection: Frequently, teachers are grateful for the end of a lesson and move quickly to the next one. A little pause for reflection, after a lesson, is a great habit to acquire. What of the content did you recall? What did you remember about the process of instruction? How might you and your peers improve the lesson? How did it feel to have others talking about your teaching? Were you able to "stay open" to the conversation? Were your "students" able to support their comments and compliments with evidence? What did you learn from others that went beyond your own self-assessment?

1:10 Visit a Staff Room

Purpose: A teacher's personal connection with colleagues represents a major dimension of school life. Friendships are often nurtured in small and informal ways: monitoring recess, attending conferences, developing special projects, serving on committees, working on curriculum, and the like. One of the most interesting places to learn about staff relationships and a school's power and social structure is the teachers' lounge. We are not asking you to be an undercover agent and sneak glances at places that are officially off-limits or unofficially verboten. We are suggesting that observing the faculty lounge, with and without teachers, is a chance to bring the anthropologist's skills to a world that is probably rather new for you.

Activity: With permission, visit a staff lounge during a quiet time of day. Make notes regarding the locale, size, and shape of the room; furniture decor, quality, and abundance; equipment access or absence; social atmosphere; and displays on the walls (both aesthetic and informational).

Be a guest in the room during a high use time: before or after school or during recess or faculty lunch.

- How many teachers visit the room compared with the number on staff?
- Are most departments represented or just certain teachers, grade levels, or curricular areas?
- Are there groups of faculty that congregate elsewhere?
- Is there free and open use of space, or do some teachers "possess" a particular chair or table space?
- Are the conversations "kid-" or other-centered? Is there a tone that you would classify as constructive or destructive, on or off task, fun or business?
- Are there categories you could use to describe groups in the room (the women sit around the table, the men at the sofa; the bilingual faculty stay together, the coaches never come in)?

Create a graphic design that illustrates the faculty lounge you visited. Your drawing will help you discuss the *who, what,* and *where* details. List additional observations and include both *factual comments* ("The entire grade-level team can sit comfortably in the lounge") and *color commentary* ("Two subject area cliques seemed visible at every break").

Reflection: Sit with a classmate who visited a different school's lounge. As you share and review your drawings, note similarities and differences. (Try to focus on accurate information rather than artistic talent.) What have you learned from your visit and your colleague's inquiry? What specific observations or inferences can you make about the social fabric and teaching climate of the schools?

Portfolio Artifact Collection

In addition to the activities and reflections (many of which belong in a beginner teacher's box of worthwhile *stuff*), the following collection of important artifacts will contribute to your career decision making. During the four inter-missions, you will be challenged to accumulate items for each of the ten principles.

1:P4 Tricks of the Trade

Purpose: Through trial and error or painstaking theoretical development, many successful instructional techniques already exist. Teaching methods on questioning strategies, deductive learning, "chunking" or grouping information in a lecture—all will become part of your knowledge base and routine. For the next few years, you may find descriptive handouts and materials everywhere. Many are well worth keeping.

Activity: Start collecting. Strategies are found in the text (e.g., cooperative learning or questioning using the levels of Bloom's Taxonomy in Chapter 3), a peer's graphic organizer during a classroom demonstration, your lesson notes from a method's class, or a conversation held on the Internet. These strategies are an important addition to your repertoire. Duplicate these excerpts (be sure to add the correct date and citation) and place them in your file box under Principle 4. As the years go by, you will upgrade and recreate your methods materials to meet your style and needs.

1:P7 My First Lesson

Purpose: A portfolio allows you to observe your teaching growth over time. When you save selected old lessons (not boxes full in the garage), you are reminded of your professional development and can draw energy from the lessons well learned.

Activity: Collect your lesson plan and the reflections from the earlier inter-mission sections (1:7, 1:9). Develop and date a cover page titled "My *First* Lesson." Briefly include *compliments* and *comments* in a chart. As you expand your knowledge and understanding of teaching, we predict that you'll enjoy looking back (under Principle 7) at your early lessons and assessments.

1:P9 State Licensure Requirements

Purpose: Don't wait until the end of your program to explore licensure requirements. While predicting exactly what's ahead may be impossible, planning for it is not.

Activity: Meet with your program adviser. Discuss where you are considering applying for a teaching position. Your school may have an arrangement with one or more of the states that will facilitate your receiving a license. For instance, if your school is NASDTEC or NCATE accredited, or if there is an interstate reciprocity agreement, obtaining a license may be greatly facilitated. If your college does not have a special relationship with a state that you are considering, you may want to contact the state directly. In any case, start a folder for all this teacher's license information. Include information about state license requirements, such as required teacher

My *First* Lesson*	Date: _____		
Action (*Sample Entries)		**Compliments**	**Comments**
Clear, stated objective		Organized, accurate plan	
Overreaction to a feisty student			Try the "look" sooner.

competency tests. Don't forget to keep all relevant information and correspondence from your teacher education program, as well as from the state departments of education (under Principle 9). It is important to remember to stay in touch with your teacher education program as you go through this process and to plan your course work accordingly. Your college or university can be a big help, but the responsibility for getting the license is yours.

1:P10 Special Education Services

Purpose: For many preservice-teachers, the laws and services for students with special needs can be complex and confusing. Gaining a professional understanding of these concerns will help anyone with career plans in education. It might even motivate you to teach children with disabilities. Begin by reviewing the information in the text that covers special education (Chapter 4, pp. 107–111).

Activity: Contact a local school district and identify the director of services for special education. Request a parent information packet that outlines the rights and responsibilities of the district regarding testing, resources, policy, practices, and all other information that would help you understand Public Law 94-142. Scan this material and highlight the key points to promote your understanding and file under Principle 10.

The lights have flickered. This inter-mission is over. It's time to open the next section: "Schools and Curriculum."

Part Two

Schools and Curriculum

Class Act

As an elementary school teacher, I was particularly eager to find good multicultural books. One day, I planned to read one of the many Juan Bobo stories. Juan Bobo (Simple John) depicts a "noodlehead" who does nothing right. This character is Puerto Rico's favorite fool and simpleton and has been the mainstay for generations.

Supposedly, Juan Bobo embodies the essence of Puerto Rico—the *jibaro*—a product of three cultures: Taino Indian, African, and Spaniard. The character stands for the honest and uncorrupted life of the country folks against the pomposity and falsehood of those in the city (i.e., the aristocratic Spaniards and those imitating them). But too often Juan Bobo is instead a mockery of the *jibaros*—equated with the poor and uneducated country folks. Additionally, Juan Bobo is frequently portrayed as either a person of apparent Black and/or Indian heritage. Among Puerto Ricans, it is highly insulting to be called either *jibaro* or Juan Bobo.

As I prepared to read to them, I looked into the face of one of my students— a Latino boy of African heritage. I was transported back to my childhood and saw myself—a little girl of African heritage, also waiting for the teacher to read a story to the class. I recalled painful memories.

Growing up biracial in Puerto Rico made me aware at a very young age of the deep racism in Latino culture. Although family and friends called me *triguena* (wheat colored), I recall classmates' and even teachers' crueler taunts.

I glanced at the cover of the book I was about to read. It clearly pictured Juan Bobo as a poor country boy of African heritage. I looked back at the faces of my students— innocent faces reflecting their African and Indian heritage. What was I doing? Persons of African and Indian ancestry are the majority in most Latino countries. Yet the folklore and literature, adults' and children's alike, predominantly present characters of Spanish ancestry. Country folks and Latinos of color disappear or are presented as ignorant and superstitious, as criminals, servants, and buffoons. Those in power are White Latinos.

Over the years, I have come to an important understanding. Just because a book is "multicultural" doesn't mean it is free of bias. Juan Bobo and other culturally authentic stories have been translated into English and other languages—they can now take their biases across cultures.

I placed the book down on my lap and told the class: "Today, we are going to do something really special. Books are stories that have been written by authors so others can read and hear them. Today, I am going to tell you a story from my childhood and then, we will tell each other our stories. We are going to write our stories down and publish them so others can read them later." I proceeded: "Once I climbed a tall mountain and thought I had reached the top of the world where the Taino Indian god Yukiyu lives . . . "

Marta I. Cruz-Janzen, Ph.D.
1998
Assistant Professor of Secondary Education
The Metropolitan State College of Denver

Source: Cruz-Janzen, M.I. (1998, Fall). "Culturally Authentic Bias." *Rethinking Schools.* Vol 13, No 1, p. 5.

5

Schools and Beyond

Focus Questions

- What are the various expectations Americans hold for their schools?
- Should schools transmit the American culture or change it?
- What are common criticisms leveled at schools?
- What different school purposes have been emphasized by the three waves of educational reform?
- How are magnet and charter schools, open enrollment, and vouchers reshaping our concept of the neighborhood public school?
- Will the business community's for-profit approach to education create more efficient schools?
- Why are so many families choosing home schooling?

Chapter Preview

Although most of us take school for granted, the proper role of this institution continues to evoke heated debate. Is a school's role to prepare students to adjust to society or to equip them to change society? Not only do people hold widely divergent views regarding both the goals and the effectiveness of America's schools, but these views seem to vary depending on the times.

In this chapter, you will have the opportunity to examine some of the major purposes assigned to schools and some of the major criticisms that have been leveled at them. Reform efforts have encouraged educators, politicians, and business executives to explore school innovations and models. The traditional link between a community and its neighborhood school is being strained, if not ruptured. In fact, the right to choose a school is quickly becoming a major national issue. Competition among schools is being fueled by the business community, which views schools as potential profit centers. And concerned parents, in ever greater numbers, are choosing to remove their children from school and are converting their homes into classrooms, so what are schools for?

```
                      YOU'VE GOT MAIL
  TO:   Steve@AU.edu,
        Anna@State.edu
  SUBJ:   You would think I knew already!!!
```

```
The professor asks, "What's a school for?" Easy, right?
Let's face it, I'm close to an expert on that one. I
can't remember life without school. Except . . . when I
heard the question, I froze!

Is a school . . .

     to teach everyone
     how to read?          Of course.

     to get a job?         I guess so, gotta eat.

     to get along better
     with others?          Can't we just get along?

     to change society?    Sure, we all want to improve.

     to make a big
     business profit?      I'm not so sure.

     to keep unemployment low by keeping kids out of the
     workforce?

Whoa there! The professor suggested that we ought to
figure out which purposes we believe in, and which
schools we would like to work in. (With vouchers and
charter schools popping up all around the country, and
parents deciding to teach their kids at home, the old
neighborhood public school may evaporate before I get
there to teach!)
```

A Meeting Here Tonight

Sam Newman has been principal of Monroe High School for just under five years. Becoming principal seemed a natural step to take after teaching and coaching for eight years.

Sam's plans to improve school morale and community relations, as well as to increase faculty involvement in key decisions, pleased the school board enough to give him the principalship over two, more senior candidates. He got off to a good start. He organized rallies, proclaiming, "Monroe is tops!"; he met with parents and teachers in endless meetings; and he created teacher management teams. But all that seems long ago.

Sam now spends his time rushing from one emergency to another. He spends two nights a week trying to complete federal, state, and school district paperwork and one or two more nights attending meetings. During the day, there is an endless parade of students in trouble, teachers with complaints, outraged parents, and, of

Today's large, comprehensive high schools reflect the diversity and the conflicting interests of the larger society.

course, more meetings. Between budgets to balance and supplies to order, Sam rarely has time to think about how to significantly improve education at Monroe.

And now, to top it all off, statewide results show that Monroe students have fallen almost a year behind the norm in math and reading. He must have received a hundred calls from angry parents, complaining about higher taxes and inefficient schools, so a meeting has been called to explore solutions to the problem of declining test scores.

On his way to the meeting, Sam detours to the bathroom. As he stares into the mirror to comb his thin, graying hair, he notes sadly the almost complete disappearance of his belt beneath his belly. He once prided himself on staying in shape. Now his shape is mostly round.

He allows himself a brief reminiscence of that naive "I can do anything" time when he first became principal, when he was full of plans. But being a principal is not the same as being a coach, and a school is very different from a team. Each passing year has taught him how precious little he knows about schools. He schedules. He budgets. He writes plans. He calms parents. He disciplines students. But, all the while, he realizes that he has little time to shape and direct the school. He is not really leading the school—he is not even sure where to lead it; he is simply trying very hard to keep it afloat. Although he knows more about flowcharts than about philosophy, a line from his college philosophy course sticks in his mind. The line is Santayana's, and it seems to have a lot of meaning for him and for Monroe High School: "Fanaticism consists of redoubling one's efforts after having forgotten one's aim."

A quick glance at his watch brings an abrupt end to philosophical speculation. He is already late. He hurries down the hallway to the meeting.

George Elbright unconsciously tugs at his tie as he mounts the long stairway to Monroe High School. He glances up at the motto, chiseled in stone for generations to enjoy: "Knowledge Is Power." He thinks back to the first time he read those words, as a 15-year-old freshman. Fear raced through his heart then; now, thirty years later, the memory still makes him perspire and pull at his tie. Funny how schools do that to you.

For George Elbright, Monroe High conjures up memories of hard work, homework assignments that were graded, and midterms so tough that kids sometimes broke down and cried, unable to go on. And finals! The whole year's work riding on one exam. Tests were rough then, but kids learned. Not like today. Not at all.

And that is why George is back at Monroe High. For years, he has watched schools disintegrate, and he has complained bitterly about the lack of discipline, the growing permissiveness, the new teaching methods that sound as if the teachers do not have to teach at all, and courses in sex education, drug education, environmental education—everything but real education. No wonder the kids can't read or write. No wonder George, Jr., is doing so poorly. No wonder George Elbright, Sr., is about to attend his first parent-teacher meeting in six years.

George reaches into his pocket and pulls out his wrinkled, handwritten list. He has to be clear and forceful. He slowly rehearses his list:

1. Teachers must reassume their responsibility. Skills development, homework, and tests should be the main activities of the classroom. Free-for-all discussion, with the teacher acting as a television talk show host instead of a teacher, has to end. Children have to learn that learning is serious.
2. Students must learn the importance of discipline and respect. Students should speak to adults with respect. We should consider a new dress code or even school uniforms. Sloppy dress and poor manners lead to lazy attitudes and poor work.
3. The notion that all students must be promoted—no matter what—has to end. Kids who do not pass tests should be left back until they do pass them. Too many high school graduates can't read or write well.
4. I am tired of trying to decipher "progress reports" about my child's "social adjustment" and "satisfactory efforts." I want to see report cards with grades and without educational jargon.
5. A school is supposed to teach fundamental skills, and not sex education, human relations, or other frills and electives. It is time that schools get back to the basics.
6. And it is high time that teachers and kids stop bad-mouthing this country. Schools should instill patriotism. It is time once again to raise Old Glory to the top of the flagpole!

George allows a smile to cross his lips as he tucks the list safely back into his pocket. Perhaps it will work; perhaps he can get the school back on the right track. The newspapers are filled with reports that seem to support his point of view. Why, he even read a report that said schools are so weak they jeopardize America's future. At any rate, he has to try for George, Jr.'s sake. All the family's hopes are pinned on him. George, Jr., would be the first Elbright to make it to college. This is no time for the school to let him down.

Shirley Weiss sits alone in her classroom, sipping lukewarm coffee from a commuter cup. The evening meeting gives her a chance to stay after school and catch up on her paperwork. She finished grading 15 minutes ago but is determined to wait until the last minute before going down to the auditorium for the meeting. Although anxious to make her position known, she is not anxious to get into one-to-one encounters with angry parents, so she waits.

She is amazed at public reaction to the declining test scores. It is, of course, unfortunate that students at Monroe are not doing as well as they should, but, given the teacher cuts and the large size of today's classes, it really isn't all that surprising.

Everyone seems to be missing the point entirely. Teenagers today simply aren't contemporary versions of the kids who attended Monroe High ten or twenty years ago. Violence, alienation, racism, sexism, drugs, teen pregnancy—the world is so much more complex. Kids should find out who they are and where they are going. President Jackson's 1830s fight over the National Bank does not exactly speak to them.

That is why Shirley Weiss has restructured her American history course into a contemporary social problems course. Students have to *want* to learn and grow, and that's what her course is all about.

And the students do well in her course. They are genuinely interested. They study and they learn. As a matter of fact, if those test makers ever were to leave their air-conditioned, swanky offices and rejoin the real world, they would revise their tests to parallel her authentic assessments, and her kids would soar! The problem is not really with the school or the kids at all! It is with the test makers and the parents who are stuck in the past!

Shirley is good and angry as she pushes back her chair and makes her way down to the auditorium.

ᴛᴛᴛ

Phil Lambert begins to fidget as he waits for the meeting to begin. His business suit and the twenty-five-year-old wooden seat are less than perfect fits.

He has not been back to Monroe since his youngest daughter graduated, almost ten years ago. And he is not overjoyed at being here now. But declining test scores represent a serious problem, not just for Phil but for the entire community.

Phil Lambert, owner of Lambert's Department Store, is also president of the chamber of commerce. Every week, he is involved with enticing professionals, even high-tech firms, and developers to relocate in Monroe. Sooner or later, these discussions always turn to the quality of the school system. In a sense, the success of the schools is a barometer of the town's future growth and development. And now the barometer is falling; stormy days are ahead. Declining test scores could cost the town plenty.

But Phil is particularly upset because he has warned people about this problem for years. High school kids are getting into more and more trouble. He has recently been to court three times to deal with teenage shoplifters. And, when kids today apply for work, it is so sad it is almost funny! Wearing baggy jeans and fouling up the application form, they just come off as irresponsible and stupid. For years, Phil has been asking rhetorically, "Didn't you learn *anything* in school?" Now his question is no longer rhetorical.

The schools simply have to get down to business, literally, and begin preparing kids for the real world. Our whole nation is in economic trouble because of weak schools. More courses should be offered, stressing not only the basics but also how to get a job and the importance of the work ethic. Students have to understand that school is not a place where they can come late, dress sloppily, and goof off. Once they understand how serious the real world is, how important getting a job is, they will get serious about their schoolwork.

Lambert checks his pager for messages and makes a mental note that the meeting is starting sixteen minutes late. If he were to run the store the way they run the schools, he'd have been bankrupt years ago.

ㄱㄱㄱ

The late start of the meeting gives Mary Jackson a chance to unwind. She has rushed from her job to make the meeting and is beginning to feel the consequences of her long day.

As she gauges the audience, she sees that once again the "haves" outnumber the "have-nots." The middle-class, white, well-dressed parents don't look half as tired as Mary Jackson feels. But they sure do seem worried. For the first time, they are getting a small taste of the problem Mary has been fighting for years. Lower achievement scores are shaking them up.

But they could never know the problem as well as Mary does. Even with the drop in scores for white kids, they are still scoring almost two years ahead of the African American students.

Mary has two daughters enrolled in Monroe High. Both are working hard, yet they cannot seem to catch up to the top students. The teachers may mean well, but they just do not understand the realities of the black experience. Her kids have never had a nonwhite teacher. And her kids have never gotten into the honors track. Somehow it seems that only white students end up there.

She has tried to make the school aware of the special problems faced by students of color and females by organizing the Parents' Multicultural Task Force. Everyone at Monroe seems sympathetic, from Mr. Newman on down. But nothing has changed, and that makes her feel tired and discouraged—but not tired and discouraged enough to give up.

Mary looks around at the almost completely filled auditorium. The mainly white, middle-class parents overwhelm the few black faces in the audience. But Mary would speak for those who could not come, and for those who have given up all hope of changing things. Monroe High should be their stepping-stone up, not an obstacle. Mary would tell them. The past few frustrating years have worn her patience thin.

ㄱㄱㄱ

Sam Newman twists the microphone stand to within a few inches of his mouth and prepares to open the meeting. He looks out at the packed auditorium and begins to assess the crowd:

There is Pat Viola, the art teacher. What is she doing here? Art is never assessed on those tests.

Oh, there's Mrs. Jackson, the chair of the Multicultural Task Force. She's not going to pull any punches about those test scores. The black students are two years behind the white students on achievement tests.

And Dr. Sweig, the humanities professor from the university, is here. He's probably going to make his pitch about requiring all students to study the classics. He must have given that "cultural literacy for all" speech a dozen times.

Mrs. Benoit, president of the school board, looks distressed. As long as I can find a solution that pleases everyone and doesn't increase the budget, she'll be satisfied. She needs a magician, not a principal, to run this meeting.

Phil Lambert is here and Shirley Weiss. Isn't that the Elbright kid's father? Wonder what's on their minds?

Sam Newman begins to perspire. He feels certain that he knows how the Christians must have felt as they entered the Colosseum to face the lions. He leans forward and announces, "Okay, let's begin."

Good schools depend on strong community support.

The Purposes of School

Sam Newman in the vignette that opened this chapter has a dilemma on his hands. Parents and teachers are pulling him—and trying to pull Monroe High—in different directions. If it is any comfort to Sam—and it probably is not—he is confronting an old question: what is the purpose of a school?

Having spent much of your life as a student, you may find this question too basic, even obvious. Answers come quickly to mind. We go to school to learn things, to earn good grades, to qualify for better jobs, to become a better person—or to please our parents (or even ourselves). But these divergent reasons represent the view only from a student's side of the desk. There are other perspectives, broader views, and more fundamental definitions of the purposes of schools. Although brainstorming all the possible reasons for schools could lead to some creative insights, it may be more practical at this point to focus on two fundamental, yet somewhat antithetical, purposes of schools.

Purpose 1: To Transmit Society's Knowledge and Values (Passing the Cultural Baton)

Society has a vital interest in what schools do and how they do it. Schools reflect and promote society's values. Consider all the options. There is a world of knowledge out there, more than any school can possibly hope to teach, so one of the first tasks confronting the school is to *select* what to teach. This selection creates a cultural message. Each country chooses the curriculum to match and advance its own view of history, its own values, its self-interests, and its own culture. In the United States, we learn about U.S. history, often in elementary, middle, and high school, but we learn little about the history, geography, and culture of other countries—or of America's own cultural diversity, for that matter. Even individual states and communities require schools to teach their own state or local history, to advance the dominant "culture" of Illinois or of New York City. By selecting what to teach—and what to omit— schools are making clear decisions as to what is valued, what is worth preserving and passing on.

Literature is a good example of this selection process. American children read works mainly by U.S. and British writers, and only occasionally works by Asian, Latin American, and African authors. This is not because literary genius is confined to the British and U.S. populations; it is because of a selection process, a decision by the keepers of the culture and creators of the curriculum that certain authors are to be taught, talked about, and emulated and others omitted. Similar decisions are made concerning which music should be played, which art viewed, which dances performed, and which world events studied, as well as which historical figures are worth learning about and which are of lesser stature. As each nation makes these cultural value decisions, it is the role of the school to transmit these decisions to the next generation.

As society transmits its culture, it also transmits a view of the world. Being American means valuing certain things and judging countries and cultures from that set of values. Democratic countries that practice religious tolerance and respect individual rights are generally viewed more positively by Americans than are societies characterized by opposing norms, standards, and actions—that is, characteristics that do not fit our "American values." Afghani women being denied access to schools, hospitals, and jobs by the Taliban conflicts with our cultural and political standards and is repulsive to most Americans. Repression of religious, racial, and ethnic groups usually engenders similar negative feelings. By transmitting culture, schools breathe the breath of cultural eternity into a new generation and mold its view of the world.

But this process is limiting as well. In transmitting culture, schools are teaching students to view the world from the wrong end of a telescope, yielding a constricted view that does not allow much deviation or perspective. Cultural transmission may contribute to feelings of cultural superiority, a belief that "we are the best, number one!" Such nationalistic views may decrease tolerance and respect for other cultures and peoples.

Purpose 2: Reconstructing Society (Schools as Tools for Change)

If society were perfect, transmitting the culture from one generation to the next would be all that is required of schools. But our world, our nation, and our communities are far from ideal. Poverty, hunger, injustice, terrorism, pollution, overpopulation, racism, sexism, and ethical challenges—and, of course, the dark clouds of nuclear, chemical, and biological weapons—are societal problems on a depressingly long list. **Reconstructionism** views schools as instruments of change, a way that society can address and correct these economic and social ills. There is a saying, "If it ain't broke, don't fix it." To reconstructionists, society is broken, it needs to be fixed, and the school is a perfect tool for making the needed repairs.

Reconstructionists hold a wide spectrum of beliefs. As you might anticipate, there are both liberal and conservative reconstructionists, each pushing schools in different directions. It is not only values that differ; strategies differ as well. At one end are those who believe that students should be made aware of the ills of society; study these critical, if controversial, areas; and equip themselves to confront these issues as they become adults.[1] Other reconstructionists are more action-oriented and believe that schools and students shouldn't wait until the students reach adulthood. They call for a **social action curriculum,** in which students actively involve themselves in eliminating social ills. For example, if a poor neighborhood lacks a day care facility for young children of working parents, the students could establish such a center. Students could petition government officials and private corporations for

Is the business of schools just academic learning, or might the goals include fostering an awareness of the benefits of community service, such as volunteering to tutor others?

funds, or they could work to build equipment for the center, or they could even serve as teaching assistants.

This idea of students contributing to society is not unique. The Carnegie Foundation for the Advancement of Teaching recommends that every student be required to earn a **service credit,** which might include volunteer work with the poor, elderly, or homeless. The idea behind a service credit includes not only an effort to reduce social ills but also the idea of providing students with a connection to the larger community and of encouraging them to develop a sense of their personal responsibility for improving the social condition.[2] During the 1980s and 1990s, several states and communities supported the concept of social reconstructionism as described by the Carnegie Foundation, and they incorporated service learning activities, credits, and even graduation requirements as part of their curricula.

While social democratic reconstructionists are reform-minded, *economic reconstructionists* hold a darker view of society's ills and advocate more drastic, even revolutionary, action. They believe that schools generally teach the poorer classes to accept their lowly stations in life, to be subservient to authority, to unquestioningly follow rules while laboring for the economic benefit of the rich. To economic reconstructionists, schools are currently tools of oppression, not institutions of learning. They believe that students must be introduced to curricula that analyze and reform economic realities. For example, one such curriculum project targets a popular and highly visible athletic company, one that produces incredibly expensive sport shoes. This company manufactures their products in developing nations, maintaining horrid working conditions. Children in these third world countries are sold into labor bondage by their impoverished families. As young as 6, they work twelve or more hours a day, enduring cruelty and even beatings as they earn only pennies an hour. While the companies defend themselves by saying that they cannot change local conditions, economic reconstructionists believe that companies intentionally select locations because of their cheap labor costs. Economic reconstructionists point out that American children "play" with products made through the agonizing toil of other children. All the while, the companies profit. Educators who focus on economic

IN THE NEWS . . . HELP WANTED: VOLUNTEERS AGAINST VOLUNTEERING

Not everyone thinks that volunteerism is a good idea. Author Ayn Rand believed that the world should be ruled by self-interest, that the pursuit of one's self-interest is the highest moral principle. In fact, her philosophy portrays altruism as immoral. It is not surprising, therefore, that the Ayn Rand Institute in Marina del Ray, California, was displeased when service credits and community volunteering became a requirement in several high schools. The institute decided to fight fire with fire: They recruited high school volunteers to work against service requirements. The high school volunteers fighting volunteerism can get service credit for their volunteer work. According to the director, volunteering to help others might be problematic, but volunteering in one's self-interest is fine.

Source: *Washington Post Magazine,* 4 October 1998.

reform have developed materials, web sites, and social action projects that not only teach children about such exploitation but also provide them with strategies to pressure companies into creating more humane and equitable working conditions.[3]

Perhaps the most noted economic reconstructionist was **Paulo Freire,** author of **_The Pedagogy of the Oppressed,_** a book about his efforts to educate and liberate poor, illiterate peasants in Brazil.[4] In his book, Freire describes how he taught these workers to read in order to identify problems that were keeping them poor and powerless. From this new awareness, they began to analyze their problems—such as how the lack of sanitation causes illness—and what they could do to solve specific problems and liberate themselves from their oppressive conditions. Freire highlighted the distinction between schools and education. Schools can either educate and liberate or miseducate and oppress. But true education liberates. Through education, the dispossessed learned to read, to act collectively, to improve their living conditions, and to reconstruct their lives. (See The Education Hall of Fame in Chapter 9 for more about Freire.)

Public Demands for Schools

While preserving the status quo and promoting social change represent two fundamental directions available to schools, they are not the only possible expectations. When you think about it, the public holds our schools to a bewildering assortment of tasks and expectations.

John Goodlad, in his massive study **_A Place Called School,_** examined a wide range of documents that tried to define the purposes of schooling over 300 years of history. He and his colleague found four broad goals:

1. *Academic,* including a broad array of knowledge and intellectual skills
2. *Vocational,* aimed at readiness for the world of work and economic responsibilities
3. *Social and civic,* including skills and behavior for participating in a complex democratic society
4. *Personal,* including the development of individual talent and self-expression[5]

FIGURE 5.1

Goals of schools.

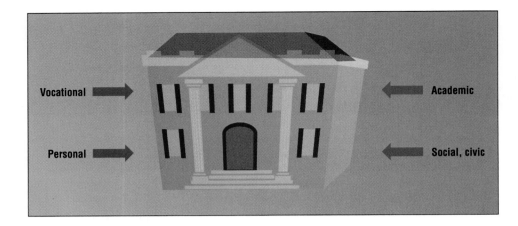

Goodlad included these four goal areas in questionnaires distributed to parents, and he asked them to rate their importance. (See Figure 5.1.) Parents gave "very important" ratings to all four. When Goodlad asked students and teachers to rate the four goal areas, they rated all of them as "very important." When pushed to select one of these four as having top priority, approximately half the teachers and parents selected the intellectual area, while students spread their preferences fairly evenly among all four categories, with high school students giving a slight edge to vocational goals. When it comes to selecting the purpose of schools, both those who are its clients and those who provide its services resist interpreting the purpose of schools narrowly.

What do Americans want from their schools? Evidently, they want it all! As early as 1953, Arthur Bestor wrote, "The idea that the school must undertake to meet every need that some other agency is failing to meet, regardless of the suitability of the schoolroom to the task, is a preposterous delusion that in the end can wreck the educational system."[6]

Then, in the 1980s, **Ernest Boyer** conducted a major study of secondary education and concluded,

> Since the English classical school was founded over 150 years ago, high schools have accumulated purposes like barnacles on a weathered ship. As school population expanded from a tiny urban minority to almost all youth, a coherent purpose was hard to find. The nation piled social policy upon educational policy and all of them on top of the delusion that a single institution can do it all.[7]

Where Do You Stand?

Identifying school goals seems to be everyone's business—parents, teachers, all levels of government, and various professional groups. Over the years, dozens of lists have been published in different reform reports, each enumerating goals for schools. What could be simpler? The problem arises when schools cannot fulfill all of these goals, either because there are too many goals or because the purposes actually conflict with one another. Then schools must establish priorities and decide which goals to pursue. The two primary, and sometimes conflicting, purposes of schools—to preserve the culture and to reconstruct society—are often broken down into more distinct and immediate goals. It is these smaller pieces that often dominate discussion. Should schools focus on preparing students for college? Should they try to inhibit drug use, or lessen the threat of AIDS? Perhaps schools ought to focus on the economy and train students to become members of a more efficient workforce, one that can successfully compete in the world marketplace.

Over the years, you also have had ideas about the purpose of schools. To help you clarify your thoughts—and raise options you may have not yet explored—look at the following list of school goals. These goals come from a variety of sources and are sometimes contradictory. But they have been advocated singly and in combination by different groups at different times and have been adopted by different schools. In each case, you register your own judgment on the values and worth of each goal. When you have completed your responses, we shall discuss the significance of these goals, and you can see how your responses fit into the bigger picture.

Circle the number that best reflects how important you think each school goal is.

1 Very unimportant

2 Unimportant

3 Moderately important

4 Important

5 Very important

	Very Unimportant				Very Important
1. To prepare workers to compete successfully in a technological world economy	1	2	3	4	5
2. To transmit the nation's cultural heritage, preserving past accomplishments and insights	1	2	3	4	5
3. To encourage students to question current practices and institutions; to promote social change	1	2	3	4	5
4. To develop healthy citizens aware of nutrition, exercise, and good health habits	1	2	3	4	5
5. To lead the world in creating a peaceful global society, including an understanding of other cultures and languages	1	2	3	4	5
6. To provide a challenging education for America's brightest students	1	2	3	4	5
7. To develop strong self-concept and self-esteem in students	1	2	3	4	5
8. To nurture creative students in developing art, music, and writing; to encourage creative cultural achievement	1	2	3	4	5
9. To educate students in avoiding social pitfalls: unwanted pregnancy, AIDS, drugs, alcoholism	1	2	3	4	5
10. To unite citizens from diverse backgrounds (national origin, race, ethnicity) as a single nation with a unified culture	1	2	3	4	5

		Very Unimportant			Very Important	
11.	To provide support to families through after-school child care, nutritional supplements, medical treatment, and so on	1	2	3	4	5
12.	To encourage loyal students committed to the United States; to instill patriotism	1	2	3	4	5
13.	To teach students our nation's work ethic: punctuality, responsibility, cooperation, self-control, neatness, and so on	1	2	3	4	5
14.	To develop academic skills in reading, writing, mathematics, and science	1	2	3	4	5
15.	To provide a dynamic vehicle for social and economic mobility, a way for the poor to reach their full potential	1	2	3	4	5
16.	To prepare educated citizens who can undertake actions that spark change	1	2	3	4	5
17.	To ensure the cultural richness and diversity of the United States	1	2	3	4	5
18.	To help eliminate racism, sexism, anti-Semitism, and all forms of discrimination from society	1	2	3	4	5
19.	To prepare as many students as possible for college and/or well-paid careers	1	2	3	4	5
20.	To provide child care for the nation's children and to free parents to work and/or pursue their interests and activities	1	2	3	4	5

You may also want to consider whether you lean more toward a view of schools as transmitters of culture or as change agents for restructuring society. To help you determine this, record your scores on the following selected items.

PURPOSE OF SCHOOLS

Transmitting Culture		Reconstructing Society	
Focused Item		*Focused Item*	
1	_____	3	_____
2	_____	5	_____
10	_____	9	_____
12	_____	15	_____
13	_____	16	_____
19	_____	18	_____
Total	_____	*Total*	_____

Does your total score suggest that you favor one view of the purpose of schools over another? Are you more likely to be a preserver of the culture or a reformer committed to change? If no clear philosophical leaning is apparent, read on. Actually, read on either way.

You may be wondering about the items not included on these two lists. Although they may not clearly fit into one or the other camp, they can tell you quite a bit about your own values and priorities. Take a moment and select three goals that you consider most important:

Feel free to write your valued goals here.

Three valued goals: _____, _____, _____.

Let's investigate how your choices reflect your values. Did you select item 3, 17, or 18? These items indicate a commitment to civil rights and student empowerment, hallmarks of the 1960s and 1970s.

In more recent years, improving school performance has been high on the national agenda. Statements reflecting this view are clear in items 1, 13, and 14. Are you "in sync" with this educational emphasis?

Other goals also rise and fall with the historical tide. For instance, item 17, ensuring cultural diversity, is once again important in schools as new waves of immigrants from Asia, Latin America, the Caribbean, and Eastern Europe join the many ethnic and racial groups already in the United States. If you scored high on this goal, you reflect a sensitivity to our nation's cultural diversity.

While diversity is often valued, so is the need to bind different cultures into a single nation. If you scored high on items 2 and 10, then you value the role schools serve in preparing Americans to adhere to a common set of principles and values. There have been times in our history when this has been a central role of schools— during the early forging of the nation and the beginning and end of the twentieth century, as large numbers of immigrants arrived. Various terms have been used to describe this effect of schools, from *melting pot* to *tossed salad,* from **acculturation** to **Americanization,** depending on whether the "old" culture was to be retained or replaced.

One goal that cast a long shadow over U.S. schools during most of the twentieth century is a commitment to national defense. During more than four decades of the Cold War, the focus of education was on national defense, on preparing soldiers to fight, engineers and scientists to build better weapons, and citizens to patriotically support the war effort. If you rated high on item 12, you are responding to this education-defense connection.

How did you rate items 15 and 19? Seeing schools as a step up, a route to social and economic advancement is part of our Horatio Alger folklore. Many Americans have been transformed—poor to wealthy, unknown to famous, "rags to riches"— because their intellect and talent blossomed in public schools. However, in reality, many students who enter school in poverty leave the same way. A high score here suggests your idealism is untarnished.

The goal of developing healthy citizens (item 4) was made popular by the ancient Greeks, who believed that a sound mind and a sound body are necessarily linked. Our current interests in healthful foods, lifestyles, and exercise indicate the endurance of this goal.

Item 20 addresses the fact that the schools give parents time to pursue work and other interests beyond child care. Few people see schools as baby-sitters, but, without this service, most parents would be overwhelmed. And consider the impact that millions of adolescents would have on the job market. Unemployment would skyrocket

WHAT'S IN A NAME?

Ever wonder how schools get their names—and which names are the most popular? The National Education Resource Center researched the most popular proper names for U.S. high schools: Washington, Lincoln, Kennedy, Jefferson, Roosevelt (both Franklin and Teddy), and Wilson. (Presidents do well.) Lee, Edison, and Madison round out the top ten names. (To date, no school has chosen Richard M. Nixon as a namesake.) But proper names are not the most common high school names. Directions dominate: Northeastern, South, and Central High School are right up there. While creativity obviously is not a criterion, politics is. Citizens fight over whether schools should be named after George Washington—who, after all, was a slave holder—and over why so few African Americans, Hispanics, and people of non-European ancestry are honored by having a school named after them. And, considering how many women are educators, it is amazing that so few schools are named to honor women—Eleanor Roosevelt, Amelia Earhart, Christa McAuliffe, and Jacqueline Kennedy are exceptions. Some schools have honored writers (Bret Harte, Walt Whitman, and Mark Twain) or reflect local leaders and culture. (In Las Vegas, you will find schools named Durango, Silverado, and Bonanza, which some complain sound more like casinos than western culture.) What choices do you think educators might make if they were responsible for school names? If students were in charge, would schools be named after sports figures or music and media stars?

- How do our school names reflect the power and culture in a society?
- What's in a name?

and wages would tumble. By minding the children, schools provide parents with time and keep our workforce down to a manageable size.

Some education goals have never enjoyed great popularity. Goals that emphasize the needs of gifted students (item 6) and the development of creative and artistic talents (item 8) have rarely won widespread support. However, many people do respond to what they see as urgent social needs (item 9). Today, teenage violence and AIDS are two such concerns.

Seeing the United States as a member of a community of nations (item 5) may be more relevant in the years ahead than it has been in the past. The same could be said for item 11, viewing the school as a social services center, a recent trend in school reform. Citizenship education (item 16) has traditionally been an important goal for our schools.

Not all of these goals are easy to define. For example, self-esteem (item 7) is a relatively new addition to the school goal arena, one that is surrounded by controversy. Should this be a goal central to a student's psychological well-being? Or is it merely an end product of an effective education, not part of the "official goals" of a school at all? How do you see it?

What did your ratings teach you about your values and your view of schools? Were your goals popular during particular periods of our past, or are you more future-oriented? In a later chapter, you will have the opportunity to gain insight into your philosophy of education. You may want to compare your goals for education here with your philosophical preferences as described in Chapter 12.

Education Reform

Our Nation is at risk. Our once unchallenged prominence in commerce, industry, science, and technological innovation is being overtaken by competitors throughout the world. . . . If an unfriendly foreign power had attempted to impose on America the mediocre educational performance that exists today, we might well have viewed it as an act of war. As it stands, we have allowed this to happen to ourselves. We have even squandered the gains in student achievement made in the wake of the *Sputnik* challenge. Moreover, we have dismantled essential support systems which helped make those gains possible. We have, in effect, been committing an act of unthinking, unilateral educational disarmament.[8]

So began the report of the **National Commission on Excellence in Education,** *A Nation at Risk: The Imperative for Educational Reform,* released in 1983. The report cited declining test scores, the weak performance of U.S. students in comparison with those of other industrialized nations, and the number of functionally illiterate adults. *A Nation at Risk* condemned the "cafeteria-style curriculum." The report called for a more thorough grounding in the "five new basics" of English, mathematics, science, social science, and computer science. It called for greater academic rigor, higher expectations for students, and better-qualified and better-paid teachers.

This report galvanized Americans, touched a vital nerve, and moved education to center stage. Remember, in 1983, we were in two wars: the Cold War with the Soviet Union and an economic war with Japan. Our national security was at stake, and poor school performance was putting the nation at risk. With the battle cry sounded, governors, state legislators, and foundations issued a wave of reports (see Appendix 3 for a summary of the salient reform reports). Within the next two years,

- Nearly 300 local and state panels were formed.
- More than 40 states increased course requirements for graduation.
- Thirty-three states instituted testing for student promotion or graduation.
- More than 700 state statutes were passed stipulating what should be taught, when it should be taught, how it should be taught, and who should do the teaching.
- Almost half the states passed legislation to increase qualification standards and pay for teachers.
- Most states increased the length of the school day and/or school year.
- Most states passed laws that required teachers and students to demonstrate computer literacy.[9]

Although state legislatures passed laws, many critics remained skeptical that such changes would truly improve education. They pointed out that these were top-down approaches, dictates from above and far removed from the real world of the classroom.[10] Teachers felt dumped on (*teacher bashing* was the phrase used to protest this), controlled, and regulated by new rules and requirements. Other critics worried that these new regulations might do more harm than good. Increasing student graduation requirements without providing for special programs could hurt racial and ethnic minorities, non-English speakers, females, special education students, and other groups not testing well. Different groups struggled to claim their place on the new list of educational priorities. To be left out of the goals for education reform could be costly, indeed.[11]

The reform reports—and there were many—came in three waves (see Figure 5.2). These **three waves of reform** continue to influence American education today. The first wave of reports came immediately after *A Nation at Risk* and, as previously described, viewed school reform in terms of national defense and economic competition. Corporations complained about the need to teach employees basic reading and math skills, and the military struggled to recruit technically skilled personnel for increasingly sophisticated equipment. Education critics pointed to low scores by American students on international tests, especially in math and science, as they made their case that schools were not meeting the nation's economic and technical needs.

FIGURE 5.2

**Waves of reform:
1982–present.**

Source: Adapted from Joseph
Murphy, "The Educational
Movement of the 1980s: A
Comprehensive Analysis," in Joseph
Murphy (ed.), *The Educational
Reform Movement of the 1980s*
(Berkeley: McCutchan, 1990).

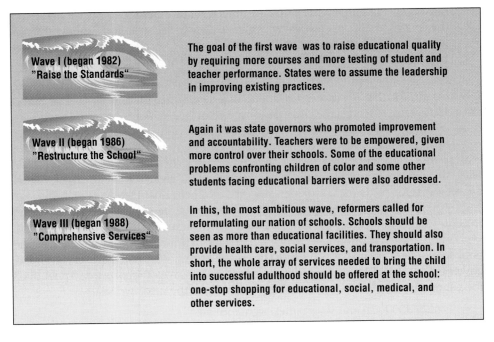

**Wave I (began 1982)
"Raise the Standards"**

The goal of the first wave was to raise educational quality by requiring more courses and more testing of student and teacher performance. States were to assume the leadership in improving existing practices.

**Wave II (began 1986)
"Restructure the School"**

Again it was state governors who promoted improvement and accountability. Teachers were to be empowered, given more control over their schools. Some of the educational problems confronting children of color and some other students facing educational barriers were also addressed.

**Wave III (began 1988)
"Comprehensive Services"**

In this, the most ambitious wave, reformers called for reformulating our nation of schools. Schools should be seen as more than educational facilities. They should also provide health care, social services, and transportation. In short, the whole array of services needed to bring the child into successful adulthood should be offered at the school: one-stop shopping for educational, social, medical, and other services.

Although these criticisms have been widely accepted, some point out that American industry has itself to blame for some of its problems, including many inefficient production practices. Educator Clinton Boutwell, author of *Shell Game: Corporate America's Agenda for Schools,* asserts that, contrary to popular belief, technical and scientific education in America's schools is stronger than ever. Boutwell believes that sinister motives might be at play. Many business leaders complaining about the lack of scientists and engineers are the same executives who fire tens of thousands of scientists and engineers as they "downsize" the workforce in an effort to increase profits.[12] In fact, the vast majority of new jobs are service-oriented and do not require large numbers of highly educated employees at all.

The second wave of reform, which began in the mid- and late 1980s, was led by educators such as **Theodore Sizer,** John Goodlad, and Ernest Boyer, rather than by politicians and business leaders. Based on research and school observations, these educators stressed the need for basic reform of school practices. Gerald Grant, for example, in his "schoolography" of Hamilton High, calls for teachers to be given more responsibility to reshape their schools, a process called **empowering teachers.** Theodore Sizer and others see the superficial nature of the curriculum as a central weakness, recommending that students "cover" fewer topics but study them in greater depth. The second wave of reformers are alarmed at the loss of teacher autonomy in oppressive school climates, bland teaching, and poor academic performance. They emphasize thoughtful changes: reducing bureaucracy; creating a more professionally trained, treated, and salaried corps of teachers; implementing local decision making; strengthening the role of the school principal; and studying subjects in greater depth.

The third wave of reform recognizes that struggling families are unlikely to possess the time and resources required to ensure high-quality education. Underway since the late 1980s and early 1990s, the third wave advocates **full service schools,** providing a network of social services, nutrition, health care, transportation, counseling, and parent education. School boards would be replaced by **children's boards,** made up of professionals and community members who work on the

A byproduct of recent calls for educational reform has been an explosion of student (and teacher) testing to ensure that revised school goals are being met.

comprehensive needs of children. School policy, focused only on education, would be replaced by **children's policy,** responding to the multiple needs of children. In the late 1990s, full service schools in Florida, New York, and California were operating long hours and providing an array of community services.

At Intermediate School 218, in the Washington Heights section of New York City, school is open by 7 a.m. for breakfast, sports activities, dance or Latin band practice, all before school "officially" opens. At the school's Family Resource Center, parents receive social services, including immigration, housing, and employment consultations. Social workers, mental health counselors, a health and dental clinic are all on site. After classes end, the building remains open until 10 p.m. for sports, computer lab, music, art, mentoring, English classes, parenting skills, and cultural classes. Intermediate School 218 is a full service school.[13]

Falling Short of Our National Goals

Presidents Reagan, Bush, and Clinton all promoted plans to reform and improve the nation's schools. Working with the nation's governors, President Bush developed six national education goals that he called **America 2000,** and President Clinton added two new goals for teacher development and parental involvement to these original six, calling his plan **Goals 2000.**

America 2000/Goals 2000
- All children in the United States will start school ready to learn.
- The high school graduation rate will increase to at least 90 percent.
- U.S. students will leave grades 4, 8, and 12 having demonstrated competency in a range of challenging subject matter that includes English, mathematics, science, history, and geography; and every school in the United States will ensure that all students learn to use their minds well, so that they may be prepared for responsible citizenship, further learning, and productive employment in our modern economy.

- U.S. students will be first in the world in science and mathematics achievement.
- Every adult American will be literate and will possess the knowledge and skills necessary to compete in a global economy and exercise the rights and responsibilities of citizenship.
- Every U.S. school will be free of drugs, unauthorized firearms, alcohol, and violence and will offer a disciplined environment conducive to learning.
- The nation's teaching force will have access to programs for the continued improvement of their professional skills and will be given the opportunity to acquire the knowledge and instructional skills needed for the next century.*
- Every school will foster partnerships that will increase parental involvement and participation in promoting social, emotional, and academic growth of children.*[14]

*Added by President Clinton under Goals 2000

America 2000 and Goals 2000 provided Americans with a national educational target. The problem was that, when the millennium arrived, it was clear that we had missed the target, and the millennium promise had not been kept. But the experience taught us an important lesson: national goals do not necessarily translate into performance, but they can be a catalyst for improvement and reform.

Beyond the Neighborhood Public School

Many teachers, parents, and political and business leaders, discouraged by the slow pace of educational change, have been experimenting with their own reform ideas.[15] Throughout the 1990s, in communities across the United States, dynamic school structures and new ways to organize and manage schools challenged the very concept of the neighborhood public school.

The Choice Concept

In the 1950s, economist **Milton Friedman** suggested that public schools would be more effective if they functioned as a free market, much as private schools do. Friedman believed that public schools were not working well, even back then, because there was no competition, no incentive for them to do their best. Parents were forced to send their children to the neighborhood school, and the neighborhood school had no incentive to compete with other schools or improve. It had a "trapped" clientele. But not everyone was trapped. Because they could afford private school tuition, wealthy parents were able to bail out if the public school was performing poorly. Friedman believed that everyone needed the same freedom to choose what the wealthy enjoyed.

In a 1981 study, **James Coleman** found that private schools were doing a better job of educating students than were the neighborhood public schools. Not only were the students attending independent, often religiously affiliated, private schools better behaved, but they also scored higher on tests. Coleman noted that the private schools enforced more rigorous academic standards and gave teachers and administrators more autonomy. In 1993, another study found that Catholic schools not only were providing particularly effective education for inner-city students of color but also were providing this education at a lower per student cost and in less segregated classrooms than were neighboring public schools.[16] The call for **school choice** was getting louder.

Magnet Schools

Over a quarter century ago, a number of public schools actually began a choice program, although few called it that. In the 1970s, as schools struggled to desegregate, "forced" busing became quite unpopular. But, with neighborhoods so racially segregated, desegregating schools required that students and teachers attend schools outside their local communities. **Magnet schools** were created to "draw" students, much like a magnet, beyond their neighborhoods. The magnet school "draw" was offering high-quality educational programs, unique programs unavailable in local schools, programs well worth the bus ride.

Today, more than a million students attend several thousand magnet schools. Magnet schools offer unique educational programs in such areas as science and technology, communication skills, career specialties, mathematics and computer science, theater, music, and art. How effective have magnet schools been? After a quarter of a century, the results are mixed. About half of these schools have helped desegregation efforts, but, in hypersegregated cities and other areas, they have had little or no impact on desegregation. In terms of educational quality, some studies suggest that students in magnet schools outperform students in other public schools and in Catholic schools. Research also indicates that those attending career magnet schools that prepare students for the world of work are less likely to be involved in fighting and drinking, and they earn more college credits than their contemporaries in public schools. Although magnet schools cost more than neighborhood public schools, these studies suggest that they may also be more effective.[17]

Open Enrollment

In 1988, Minnesota instituted **open enrollment,** which eliminated the requirement that students must attend the closest public school. Like the magnet schools, open enrollment encouraged parents to choose a school, but it greatly increased the number of schools to choose from. Any public school with available space became eligible. Arkansas, Iowa, Nebraska, and other states soon followed Minnesota's lead and introduced open enrollment legislation. However, even more radical proposals were being launched, proposals threatening to redefine, if not eliminate, the neighborhood school.

Vouchers

The approach that Milton Friedman favored was neither open enrollment nor magnet schools: Friedman proposed that **educational vouchers** be given to parents. The vouchers would function like admission tickets. Parents would "shop" for a school, make their choice, and give the voucher to the school. The school would turn over the voucher to the local or state government, and the government would pay the school a fixed sum for each voucher. Good schools would collect many vouchers and thrive, while poor schools would not attract "customers" and would go out of business. Some voucher plans would give parents the choice of selecting either a public or a private school, while other plans would limit the choice to public schools.

In 1990, Milwaukee became the site of the first publicly financed voucher program. Wisconsin lawmakers approved a plan for Milwaukee students to receive about $3,000 each to attend nonsectarian private schools, then, in 1995, amended the law to allow students to attend religious schools as well. And it is the inclusion of religious schools first in the Milwaukee voucher plan, then in a similar plan in

JONATHAN KOZOL: "I HAVE SOME PROBLEMS WITH THE IDEA OF

Jonathan Kozol, author of the best-selling *Savage Inequalities*, spoke at the University of Tennessee–Knoxville about the terrible disparities among public schools in this country. At the end of his speech, members of the audience were invited to ask questions. Here, reprinted with permission, is Jonathan Kozol's response to the question "What are your views on the proposed voucher system for public schools?"

The first time I ever heard vouchers proposed in the U.S. was by Milton Friedman, an economist respected among scholars for some of his pure economics work but better known to some people as the former economics advisor to Augusto Pinochet: the fascist dictator of Chile.

The first time I heard of schools of choice, it was after the Brown decision in the 1950s, when schools in many Southern states set up schools of choice—that was the word. They called them Freedom of Choice Schools as a ploy to avoid desegregation. That's the history.

What have I actually seen? Well, first of all, the idea behind choice (within the district), basically, is that if you let people choose, everybody will get the school they want. Everybody will have an equally free choice; everybody will have equal access. And, those I hear defend choice say it will not increase class or racial segregation. In fact, in virtually every case that I have seen, none of these conditions is met. People very seldom have equal choices, and even when they theoretically have equal choices, they rarely have equal access.

People can't choose things they've never heard of, for example. And lots of the poorest folks in our inner cities are functionally illiterate. I've written a book about that, as some of you know. In many of our inner cities, as many as 30 percent of our adults cannot read well enough to understand the booklets put out by school systems delineating their choices. That's one point.

Even if they can understand and even if the school system is sophisticated enough to print these things in five different languages for all the different ethnic groups in cities like New York or Chicago, there's a larger point that those who hear about new schools, good schools, first are almost always the well connected. They're almost always the people whose friends are in the school system, the people like myself who went to college with the principal or the superintendent or some of the people who run the system. Word of mouth always favors the children of the most wealthy or best educated.

And so, what often happens is that while everybody theoretically has the right to choose any school, the affluent, the savvy, the children of the academics, the children of the lawyers, the children of the doctors, the children of the school superintendent tend to end up in the same three little boutique elementary schools. And I call them boutique schools because they're always charming, and the press loves them, and they always have enough racial integration so it looks okay for the newspaper or the TV camera. But, in fact, they are separated by both race and class, and more and more by class.

What happens is that the poorest of the poor often do not get into these schools or get in in very small numbers. Large numbers of the kids who nobody wants end up concentrated in the schools that no one chooses except by default.

That's my profound reservation. I've been at it a long, long time. I've seen that happen. I'd add that there are some exceptions, as in an enlightened program in East Harlem. But there are unusual aspects of this program that are seldom found in choice plans elsewhere.

When you have choice *across* school districts, it gets even trickier. In Massachusetts, we now have a statewide plan

Cleveland, that sparked a heated controversy and a round of lawsuits. After all, the First Amendment of the Constitution ensures the separation of church and state, and paying for a religious education with taxpayer funds would violate the Constitution—or has all that changed?

In fact, the legal picture, once quite clear, is now somewhat cloudy. In 1971 in **Lemon v. Kurtzman** and in 1973 in the *Nyquist* case, the Supreme Court constructed clear walls limiting the use of public funds to support religious education. What became known as the *Lemon* test provided three criteria to determine the legality of government funds used in religious schools. According to Lemon, the funds (1) must have a secular purpose, (2) must not primarily advance or prohibit religion, and (3) must not result in excessive government entanglement with religion. However, over the past quarter of a century, an increasingly conservative Supreme Court has allowed more public funds to be used in religious settings, particularly when the funds first go to students or parents before being distributed to the religious school.

CHOICE, AND I WANT TO TELL YOU WHY."

called Massachusetts 2000. . . . What's happened? Eight hundred kids transferred to other districts within two months after the plan's initiation. Who were those kids? Ninety-three percent of them were white and middle class. Not one child transferred from a rich district to a poor district, which does tell us something about the value of money doesn't it?

Let me give you a simple case study. Two adjacent districts in Massachusetts: One is a small industrial town of 80 to 100,000 people, called Brockton, an old mill town. Half the people in Brockton are nonwhite, half are very poor—the same half largely. And the others are working class. There are few middle-class people in the town. About 1,000 kids in the school system are bilingual, that is, they are definitely not proficient in English. Of the kids who transferred from Brockton, only 5 percent were low-income and only one of these children was a bilingual student.

Brockton, last year, which already was in dire straits because of the recession, lost $850,000 to the neighboring, white affluent suburb of Avon, Massachusetts. $850,000! That's happening in every paired situation (where there are neighboring rich and poor schools) across our state. So what has choice done in Massachusetts? It has unleashed the flight of rich and middle class from poor; of white from black, Hispanic, and Asian. . . . What happens when you take choice to the ultimate, and let people take public money and go to a private school? It sounds wonderful, just like choice. It sounds so reasonable. Why shouldn't people have the right to do that? [Former] Secretary of Education Lamar Alexander says rich people already have the right to go to private school; why shouldn't we give poor children this right? Listening to his words, one might almost think he had undergone a conversion and was ready to give the poor black kids of Washington, D.C. a $15,000 voucher so they could go to Andover. But no, despite the disarming simplicity and the subtlety of his formula, that's

not what he intends at all. The choice plan he points to involves about $1,000 in vouchers. . . .

Class distinctions will remain unaltered. They will remain the same. I'm very much against voucher plans. . . .

Now the dark, terrifying prospect of vouchers or a choice agenda, of a so-called market basis for our public schools, is that rather than encourage a sense of common loyalties among people, choice will particularize loyalties. It will fragmentize ambition, so that the individual parent will be forced to claw and scramble for the good of her kid and her kid only, at whatever cost to everybody else. There will no longer be a sense of "What I choose for my child, I choose for everybody." There's a wonderful quote from John Dewey. He said "What the best and wisest parent wants for his own child, that must the community want for all its children. Any other ideal for our schools is narrow and unlovely. Acted upon, it destroys our democracy."

Just a tiny postscript: A lot of the people who are for vouchers don't know that much about vouchers. They're not right-wing or bigots or anything like that. They might be people who say, "Well, nothing else works. Why don't we try them?" That's a common mood in this country.

The best known voucher advocate, John Chubb, of the Brookings Institution, in Washington, says something—I'm paraphrasing him—like this: "Democratic governance of schools is what's wrong with schools. We need a voucher plan in order to break the bonds of democratic education, because it hasn't worked." That's what he says.

When I hear that, I think to myself, "Wait a minute. We've never tried democratic education." We haven't yet given equal, wonderful, innovative, humane schools—at the level of our finest schools—to all our children. I do not agree to "break the bonds" of democratic education. I think we should try it first, see how it might work.

Source: Reprinted with permission of *Educational Leadership* 50, no. 3 (November 1992): 90–92.

The courts have ruled, for example, that public funds can be used to provide a sign interpreter for a deaf student at a Catholic high school, that a state can give tax deductions to parents who send their children to religious schools, and that religious clubs can use public school facilities to hold their meetings. Future court challenges in this arena are likely.[18]

Charter Schools

Albert Shanker, the late president of the American Federation of Teachers, launched the **charter schools** movement in a 1988 speech, when he suggested that teachers be empowered in "charter schools," special schools that focus on student achievement.[19] In 1991, Minnesota was the first state to enact charter school legislation. California followed in 1992, and, by 1998, more than 800 charter schools had opened their doors.[20]

What are these charter schools? The concept is simple. The charter (or contract) represents legal permission from a local or state school board to operate the school, usually for a fixed period of time, perhaps five years, with the right to renew the charter if the school is successful. While charter schools must follow some of the same rules established for other publicly funded schools (for example, health and safety regulations, agreement not to discriminate), charter schools are exempt from many state and local laws and regulations. Charter schools, in effect, "swap" rules and regulations for greater freedom and the promise that they will achieve better results. A charter school typically

- Allows for the creation of a new or the conversion of an existing public school
- Prohibits admission tests
- Is nonsectarian
- Requires a demonstrable improvement in performance
- Can be closed if it does not meet expectations
- Does not need to conform to most state rules and regulations
- Receives funding based on the number of students enrolled

A charter school represents a break with the past, a new way to educate with tax dollars. A charter school might be established to improve academic performance or attendance, to explore a new organizational approach or teaching strategy, or to extend the hours of the school day or the length of the school year. Some charter schools are associated with national programs, such as the International Baccalaureate Degree, while others are independent, meeting local needs. In St. Paul, Minnesota, for example, the City Academy is a year-round charter school serving forty at-risk students. Metro Deaf serves deaf students, while the Teamsters Union and the Minnesota Business Partnership sponsor a vocational and technical school, called "Skills for Tomorrow," that uses internship placements to educate students interested in becoming skilled workers. The City on a Hill charter in Boston was created by two veteran teachers committed to providing a more effective education for poor inner-city children.[21] Although charter schools operate differently in different states, the increase in the number of charter schools across the country has been spectacular. Why?

Today, nineteen states, including New Jersey, have a law allowing public funding for charter schools, which operate outside normal public school channels to satisfy the specific educational goals of the founding group.

One reason is that charter schools are less controversial than voucher plans. They do not involve religious schools or competition between public and private schools. They appeal to people who support public schools but who have concerns about their quality. It is little wonder that charter schools find favor among both liberals and conservatives.

Who are the people who create such schools? Tom Watkins, director of the Detroit Center for Charter Schools, describes three types of charter advocates: reformers, zealots, and entrepreneurs.[22] *Reformers* are those who want to expand public school options and create more teacher- and student-centered institutions. These are the most mainstream advocates, the ones who often engender positive reports in the press. Watkins also describes *zealots,* those who prefer private to public schools, who view teacher unions as the obstacle to change and many of whom are themselves politically quite conservative. The final group consists of *entrepreneurs,* those who view schools as untapped profit centers and charter schools as vehicles for combining business and education. In the next section, we will take a closer look at these educational entrepreneurs. Figure 5.3 offers an insight into the "draw" of charter schools, who teaches there, and why parents choose them.

EMOs (Educational Maintenance Organizations): Schools for Profit

Wall Street calls them **EMOs,** paralleling the HMOs in the health maintenance industry. HMOs are big business, and many on Wall Street are predicting that EMOs will be too. During the past few years, for-profit businesses have contracted with local school districts to provide a wide range of services in an attempt to win a segment of the lucrative education market, a market that exceeds $300 billion a year, not that the entrance of private companies onto the public educational scene is completely new. For years, school districts have contracted with private businesses to provide school lunches and bus transportation. But, to provide education itself, to be responsible for academic performance, *is* new.

The largest for-profit venture in public schools, the **Edison Project,** took off after a chance encounter. In 1990, Benno Schmidt, the president of Yale University, was attending a party in the Hamptons, a posh section of Long Island. At that party, Schmidt met Chris Whittle, an entrepreneur who was involved with various education-related projects. Apparently, they hit it off. Whittle offered Schmidt a high salary, reported to be about $1 million a year, to leave Yale and assume leadership of the Edison Project. Chris Whittle's vision called for creating a model school, one based on proven educational programs, and then franchising the model nationally.

The Edison Project calls for lengthening the school day by one or two hours, while increasing the school year from 180 days to 210 days. In effect, these changes would add about two more years of study before graduation. Curricular changes include devoting more school time to math and science and using proven programs, such as the University of Chicago approach to math and a reading program developed at Johns Hopkins University. Learning contracts are used to increase student accountability. Edison's plan calls for linking each student to the school by a company-provided home computer. The computer would offer students a virtual library and would give both parents and students a dedicated communication link to teachers.

The project's start-up costs were enormous, and the franchise idea was not easy to implement. Whittle saw that opening charter schools would be an easier way to disseminate his plan.[23] By 1998, the Edison Project was operating fifty-one schools, including twelve charter schools in eight states. While the Edison schools multiply,

FIGURE 5.3

The Charter School Notebook.

The following information is from this year's "Charter Schools in Action," a two-year study by the Hudson Institute's Educational Excellence Network, which surveyed 16,000 students in 50 charter schools in 10 states, and from the 1997 U.S. Department of Education "A Study of Charter Schools: First Year Report."

Top reasons parents say they chose charter schools

Small school size	53.0%
Higher standards	29.0
Educational philosophy	44.0
Opportunities for parental involvement	43.0
Better teachers	41.9

Who teaches in charter schools?

Those...
with teacher certification	72.0%
working toward teacher certification	17.0
belonging to teacher's unions	23.6

Average amount of...
public school experience	5.6 years
private school experience	1.7 years
teaching in a university or elsewhere	1.4 years
home schooling	0.6 years

Student Demographics

Members of minorities	49.6%

broken down as follows:
Hispanic	25.0%
African American	15.7
Asian	4.1
Native American	3.7
Other	1.1

Students who
previously attended public schools	63.1%
previously attended private schools	10.7
previously attended another charter school	3.0
were not in school (e.g. prekindergarten)	16.8
had dropped out	5.0

Family Demographics

Parents with a college degree or higher	30.9%
Parents without a high school degree	12.0
Family income over $60,000	17.8
between $40,000 and $60,000	18.0
between $20,000 and $40,000	26.0
below $20,000	27.0

the key question is clear: are these schools effective? In Wichita, test scores in the Edison school increased; however, at the Boston Renaissance High School, one of the first Edison schools, inappropriate treatment of special education students, internal disputes, and high teacher turnover made the first years less than successful. While the schools may deserve more time before they are evaluated, there is some question as to how many more years will be available. Although public schools continue to buy into the Edison concept, questions about the financial stability of the Whittle educational empire persist.[24]

Other companies have harbored less grandiose plans than the Edison Project. Rather than redesigning schools and creating entirely new school programs, these companies have focused on improving school performance through greater efficiency. A pioneer in this effort, **Tesseract** (formerly **Educational Alternatives Incorporated,** or EAI), began contracting with schools as early as 1990. A contract with Miami schools was followed by contracts with schools in Baltimore, Maryland (1992), and Hartford, Connecticut (1994). Tesseract made national news by providing new school managers dedicated to efficiency. The costs of maintenance, supplies, security, transportation, food contracts, and even consultant salaries were scaled back, producing a leaner school budget overall. But student performance did not improve. Tesseract complained that it lacked the power to make real changes, and all of these contracts were eventually terminated. By the late 1990s, the company had changed its name and direction, focusing instead on operating charter schools, turning a profit in the process.[25]

The business community has not been timid about investing in public education. The Edison Project, for example, spent at least $40 million in just the start-up phase, and John Walton, son of Walmart founder Sam Walton, invested heavily in Tesseract, two strong signs indicating the size of the potential profits to be made in the **privatization** of public schools.[26] Private-sector education companies continue to multiply. Advantage Schools, a Boston-based company, focuses on urban school districts, hires nonunion teachers, and promotes "direct instruction," a program that relies on intense and frequent teacher-student interactions. Sylvan Learning Systems, known for its after-school learning centers, now provides services to several large school districts, including after-school instruction for students who are performing below expectations.[27]

Even Disney entered the school business. In a project called "Celebration," located near Disney World in Florida, Disney joined forces with the Osceola County school district and Stetson University to build and operate a state-of-the-art school. While the school is part of a new residential community "inspired by the main streets of small-town America and reminiscent of Norman Rockwell images,"[28] it was designed to meet the future's demands. Disney donated $11 million for the school itself and another $9 million for the creation of an adjacent academy, where teachers are trained in the techniques and strategies used at Celebration. The school district committed over $15 million to build this "school of tomorrow."

Not everyone is enamored by the growing business involvement in schools. Both the National Education Association (NEA) and the American Federation of Teachers (AFT) have criticized private sector initiatives, warning about "the merchants of greed" and cost-cutting measures that hurt teachers.[29] And while Wall Street sees the economic potential in the HMO-EMO analogy, others are less sanguine about that analogy. Educator Alex Molnar warns,

> The only reason that the health care industry can make a profit is that it has nothing to do with [social] equity. We've got 40 million Americans who on any given day don't have health insurance. Now that's a social catastrophe. The same thing would happen in education. If you cut the schools loose from any concern about equity, you could carve out schools that you could run for a profit. However, it would be at an enormous social cost.[30]

IN THE NEWS . . . THE NEW TREND IN PLANNED COMMUNITIES

Having a neighborhood school nestled among the freshly paved cul-de-sacs of a new housing development can be a real boost for home sales. Prospective buyers want to know about the neighborhood school before they purchase their new homes. But getting local governments to build such schools often takes years, and sometimes the neighborhood school is less than wonderful. Without a strong local school, houses are difficult to sell. Home builders in Arizona and Florida have come up with an answer: they want to build new schools along with their new houses. As a result, new housing developments would have their schools years earlier than expected, local governments would save millions of taxpayer dollars in construction costs, for-profit education companies, who would rent these schools, would have a brand new building to educate local children. Builders would benefit as well, earning additional profits by collecting rent on their schools. While the plan seems to offer something for everyone, not everyone is pleased. One critic noted, *There is a difference between a neighborhood school and a neighborhood country club subsidized by taxpayers. The larger question is: What is best for society as a whole?*

Source: *Education Week on the Web,* 16 April 1997.

Is Choice a Good Idea?

To many, introducing competition and choice to public education is inherently valuable. These people point out that wealthy families have always enjoyed educational options, the ability to exercise school choice. Studies have shown that as much as 88 percent of African Americans favor choice plans and that the highest support, 95 percent, comes from families earning less than $15,000 a year.[31] In impoverished neighborhoods—communities where numerous children of color attend some of the poorest public schools—vouchers and charter programs are applauded for offering choice to poorer parents. Although choice is widely popular in certain areas, it is not by itself a panacea. While parent satisfaction in choice programs is increased, there is precious little evidence that education itself is any better. Studies of student achievement in charter and voucher schools are contradictory at best, although magnet schools may fare better.

Critics fear the consequences of the new education-for-profit companies, as well as increasing competition among public schools for limited resources. They argue that all schools would improve if funding were increased. Other research suggests that the neediest students may, in fact, not be benefiting from these choices. The students most likely to participate in choice programs are the strongest ones, students with substantial academic records and with educated and involved parents. Many critics warn that, in choice plans, the hardest-to-educate students are left behind in underfunded public schools. With the exit of the best and brightest to other schools, the students left behind in the public schools face an even more dismal future, with less hope and fewer resources than before. And some worry about the societal fracture caused by charter and voucher schools, as children are channeled into different programs with different goals. They regret the loss of the "common" school envisioned by Horace Mann, a place where all Americans could learn together.[32]

PARENTS' REPORT CARD ON CHOICE

In 1993, 20 percent of children attended schools their families selected (11 percent chose a public school option, 9 percent a private school option). Most students, 80 percent, continued to attend the school "assigned" to them. Following are some interesting characteristics of the 20 percent of the parents who chose their children's school:

Race Differences
- Black students were more likely than white students to attend a school their parents chose.

Major Reason for Selection of School
- The most common reason for selecting a school was related to ensuring a better academic environment.

Reason for Selecting a Private School
- The second reason, after academics, for choosing a private school concerned moral or religious factors.

Reason for Selecting a Public School
- For those parents selecting a public school, the second reason, after academics, was convenience.

Satisfaction Rates
- Over 80 percent of the parents who selected their child's public school were positive about their choice.
- Over 90 percent of the parents who selected a private school for their child indicated that they were happy with their selection.

Source: M. C. Rubenstein, R. Hamar, and N. E. Adelman, *Minnesota's Open Enrollment Option* (Washington, DC: Policy Studies Associates, 1992); M. F. Williams, K. S. Hanscher, and A. Huner, *Parents and School Choice: A Household Survey* (Washington, DC: U.S. Department of Education, OERI, 1983).

SCHOOL BALANCE SHEET 1   THE SCHOOL CHOICE PLAN

Pro

Free to choose from different schools (guided by their parents), children will no longer be forced to attend their neighborhood school. Education will finally be democratic.

Choice will lead to competition. As schools compete, they will develop their unique strengths to attract students to their programs. Without students, they will be forced to close. Only good schools will survive and prosper.

The choice program will overcome the racism and classism of the neighborhood school and promote integrated schools open to all.

Teachers will enjoy the opportunity to leave the bureaucracy of the current system. Lifetime professionals, they will be free to create and manage their own schools.

For the first time, poor families will be given authority to choose a school that works instead of attending neighborhood schools they know don't work. Poor Americans will be given some control over their educational futures.

The choice system will increase national test scores. Schools will compete with each other academically, raising student achievement scores overall. In addition, unique types of schools will be more successful with different kinds of students.

Con

The neighborhood school is a community of neighbors learning to work together. This is the real meaning of democracy.

Transplanting businesslike competition into the education arena would be a disaster. False advertising, "special" promotions, a feel-good education—all the hucksterism of the marketplace will mislead students and their parents.

The choice program would deteriorate to the prejudice of private academies of the past, where race, religion, even disability factors would be used to keep certain students from attending.

Teachers would lose their tenure and work at the whim of the community. No professional should be forced to work from year to year without basic job security.

Poor families would be the most victimized under a choice plan. Without education or experience, poor families are more susceptible to false advertising and misleading claims.

The choice system would lower the nation's already low scores. All these different schools would teach and emphasize different topics. Without a central, accepted curricular core, fewer students would be prepared for national, standardized tests.

Home Schools, Home Teachers

Thirteen-year old Taylor is working at the kitchen table, sorting out mathematical exponents. At 10, Travis is absorbed in *The Story of Jackie Robinson,* while his brother Henry is practicing Beethoven's Minuet in G on his acoustical guitar. The week before, the brothers had attended a local performance of a musical comedy, attended a seminar on marine life and participated in a lively debate about news reports concerning corporal punishment in Singapore. These boys are part of a growing number of students being educated at home. What makes their story somewhat unusual is that their father is unable to participate in their education as much as he might like, because he must spend time at his own work: teaching English at a local public high school.[33]

Why would a schoolteacher choose to educate his own children outside of school? It is ironic that, while some educators view the world as a classroom, others see education as a cottage industry. Today between half a million and one and a half million children in the United States are believed to participate in **home schooling;** twenty years earlier, only 12,500 students were home schooled.[34] Why the huge increase? Most people credit the explosion in the number of home-schooled children to the growth of fundamentalist Christianity, many of whose adherents choose to educate their children at home. While religious motivation is the reason that most families choose home schooling, it is not the only reason.[35]

Some historical perspective might be helpful. Home schooling is not new; it predates schools and has always been around in one form or another. As recently as the 1970s, "romantic" critics—such as John Holt, Ivan Illich, and Jonathan Kozol—were advocating home schooling as a way to avoid the oppressive, dehumanizing public school practices. It is fascinating that home schooling appeals to liberals, who view schools as too conservative, as well as to conservatives, who view schools as too liberal. But conservatives, liberals, and middle-of-the-roaders can be drawn to home schooling for a number of reasons.

Researcher Van Galen divides home schoolers into two groups: ideologues and pedagogues. **Ideologues** are very focused on imparting their values and view the home as their school, a place where they choose the curricula, create the rules, and enforce the schedules. Van Galen classifies most religiously motivated home schoolers as ideologues. **Pedagogues** are motivated by more humanistic educational goals; they are interested in the process as much as the end product of learning. As a group, they are considered more open to various educational strategies. Pedagogues emphasize intrinsic motivation and experiential activities. While ideologues and pedagogues share a dissatisfaction with schools, they agree on little else.[36]

In urban areas, the lack of school safety may motivate some parents to educate their children in the security of their own homes, away from the dangers of guns and violence. Other parents are disenchanted with the quality and lack of responsiveness of schools, and home schooling provides them with a base from which to launch their ideas about education, and to test their own teaching skills, in an intimate and nurturing environment. Economics can play a role as well. In some two-parent working families, the income earned by one parent is consumed by the high cost of child care. In such cases, one parent can readily give up the "outside" job to become a home teacher—and the family may not lose any real income. But not all home schools are initiated for positive motivations. Sometimes racism, anti-Semitism, or another hateful reason can inspire an ideologue to withdraw his or her children from a public school and initiate home instruction.

IN THE NEWS . . . HOME-SCHOOL DIVORCE

Sixteen-year-old Jennifer S. and her parents are in court. While Jennifer's parents' traditional Christian beliefs led them to home school their seven children, Jennifer wants out. She's asked the courts to let her attend Virginia's Loudoun Valley High School. Jennifer says that she thrives in competition, appreciates the greater number of course options in school, and believes that her chances to eventually become a doctor will be enhanced if she is allowed to attend a regular high school. Her parents disagree. Their attorney argues that in America, parents have the right to make these kinds of decisions for their children. Jennifer believes that she is old enough to make these decisions herself. The courts have initially decided in Jennifer's favor, but the case is on appeal.

Source: *Washington Post,* 15 November 1998.

As home schools' philosophies vary, so does their quality. Some parents are incredibly talented and dedicated teachers, while others are less than competent. Even when parents fall short of teaching excellence, individualized instruction is powerful. This may be one reason home-schooled children generally score quite well on standardized tests, averaging between the sixty-fifth and eightieth percentiles.[37] A number of home-schooled children have even achieved national acclaim. Grant Colfax was taught by his parents, never attending elementary or secondary school. He won admission to Harvard, graduated *magna cum laude,* became a Fulbright scholar, and eventually graduated from Harvard Medical School. His home-schooled brothers enjoyed similar success—all endorsements of home schooling.

Home-schooling critics are more concerned with potential abuses than with success stories, such as that of the Colfax family. Do children educated in isolation from their peers suffer any negative consequences? What is lost by not working and learning with other children of diverse beliefs and backgrounds? Since Americans were originally motivated to build schools in order to promote Americanization, to meld a single nation, it is logical to wonder, will home schooling adversely affect our national cohesion?

Home-schooling families hold different views as to the importance of socialization. Some point out that much of what passes for socialization in school is negative, including everything from unhealthy competition to gang violence. They believe that, in the final analysis, their children come out ahead by remaining at home. Other home-school families believe that socialization is important and create their own social groups, such as book clubs, with like-minded others. Some forge a relationship with local school districts, so that their children, although instructed at home, can participate in district schools' sports and other extracurricular activities. School districts vary in their receptivity to such "dual" enrollments. In Virginia, for example, home schoolers are allowed to participate only "unofficially" in after-school sports. In Ames, Iowa, on the other hand, home schoolers participate in athletics equally, have access to school textbooks and standardized tests, and may take "enrichment" classes designed specifically for them. District policies on home schooling vary widely. Some school districts view home schoolers as educational partners; other

HOME-SCHOOLED—AND PROUD OF IT

Home schooling was more the norm than the exception in times past. Among wealthier British and U.S. families in the seventeenth and eighteenth centuries, parents and home tutors were the educators of choice. Home-schooling traditions exist in other cultures as well. In many Native American cultures, for example, the elders served—and often still serve— as teachers. Contemporary advocates often dip into the well of history to claim the success of home-schooled people, such as

- Woodrow Wilson
- Margaret Mead
- Florence Nightingale
- John Quincy Adams

- Franklin Roosevelt
- Thomas Edison
- The Wright Brothers
- Andrew Carnegie
- Abraham Lincoln
- Pearl Buck
- Agatha Christie
- Benjamin Franklin

These success stories indicate that home schooling can be effective. Then again, the student's needs and the teacher's talents—at home or at school—are more important than any list of home-schooled achievers.

Source: R. S. Moore and D. N. Moore, *Better Late Than Early: A New Approach to Your Child's Education* (New York: Reader's Digest Press, 1975); Gary Knowles, James A. Muchmore, and Holly W. Spaulding, "Home Education as an Alternative to Institutionalized Education," *The Education Forum* 58 (spring 1994): pp. 238–43; see also issues of *Growing Without Schooling* magazine.

A WORLD WITHOUT SCHOOLS

Even the decision to have schools reflects a value. In *Deschooling Society,* Ivan Illich likens schools to the church during medieval times.[a] He views schools as institutions that perform a political rather than an educational function. To Illich, the diplomas and degrees issued by schools reflect a certification role rather than an educational one. Schools provide society's "stamp of approval," announcing who shall succeed, who shall be awarded status, and who shall remain in poverty. In addition, by compelling students to attend, by judging and labeling them, by confining them, and by discriminating among them, Illich believes that schools are actually harming children. He would replace our traditional schools with a variety of learning "networks" that would be both lifelong and compulsory. To Illich, the notion of waking up to a world without schools is not an outlandish proposition. It would represent a dream fulfilled.

[a]Ivan Illich, *Deschooling Society* (New York: Harper & Row, 1973).

districts see them as competitors.[38] When seen as competitors, schools do not readily provide assistance. This has led to usually successful litigation by home schoolers to acquire selected school resources and support.[39]

Advances in technology have provided a catalyst for the home-schooling movement, particularly the proliferation of personal computers and increasing access to the Internet. America Online, for example, offers a home-schooling forum, complete with lesson plans, tutoring, legislative updates, and the capability for networking with others interested in group work. In Michigan, the Noah Webster charter school offers a "school-less school," one that connects children and parents to teachers and the curriculum through telephone lines and terminals. Technology is radically altering education, and the school of the future may be less a place than a password onto the information superhighway. In the future, home schooling may be far less exotic and far more prevalent.[40]

This chapter asks the deceptively simple question, What's a school for? This deceptively easy question invites many possible answers. Ivan Illich, for example, questions the role of **any** school. While the elimination of schools is both radical and unlikely, it is evident that schools are undergoing serious transition. The traditional neighborhood school is reshaping itself, moving from a public monopoly into the profit arena, from a single neighborhood institution into the wider community, from the cookie-cutter similarities of the past to different models and approaches. Today's teachers will have the opportunity to choose their future career settings from a greater variety of teaching options than ever existed before.

Summary

1. Since their inception, public schools have tried to meet many divergent needs. Parents, teachers, and students alike expect schools to meet academic, vocational, social, civic, and personal goals. The particulars of these goals are debated constantly, often resulting in bitter disputes. Perhaps nowhere else in our country do personal and societal values conflict so much as when communities examine their schools.

2. People have a myriad of goals and expectations for schools. These include, among others, protecting the national economy and defense, unifying a multicultural society, preparing students for the world of work, improving academic competence, encouraging tolerance for diversity, and providing social and economic mobility.

3. Two fundamental, often-opposing, purposes of schools are to *transmit* society's knowledge and values, passing on the cultural baton, and to *reconstruct* society, empowering students to engineer social change as adults—and, sometimes, as students.

4. The 1983 report *A Nation at Risk* triggered a renewed interest in the quality of public schooling. In response to declining test scores and poor student achievement, measured by worldwide standards, the report called for many back-to-basics measures. A deluge of reports and recommendations ensued, mostly supporting tighter regulation of schools. These "top down" reports—the "first wave"—emphasized using schools as tools to transmit rather than reconstruct the culture.

5. A second wave of reports, by Sizer, Goodlad, Boyer, and others, focused on strategies to strengthen the teaching profession and restructure education. These reports and books sprang from lengthy observations and research, and they stressed empowering educators at the school level, a bottom-up change.

6. The third wave of reform reports viewed the school as a comprehensive institution providing social, medical, and other services to children. Education would be linked to a broader array of student needs, and the child would be the focus of reform.

7. America 2000 and Goals 2000 are presidential plans to enhance the quality of instruction and the performance of U.S. students. The ambitiousness of the goals, budget-cutting, and a lack of commitment within many states have contributed to the nation's inability to attain these aims. Such efforts as goal setting serve as catalysts for other state and local school reforms.

8. Some critics believe that true reform can occur only at the local, school-district level. Such thinking has fueled the choice movement, represented by such innovations as open enrollment, voucher plans, and magnet and charter schools. Some educators and parents have reservations about these innovations as well and doubt that they will, in the long run, change schools for the better.

9. Charter schools, although only a decade old, are now operating in most states. Although they have sparked debates, charter schools have also attracted many

supporters: enthusiasts who prefer private over public education, reformers who intend to expand and improve public school options, and entrepreneurs, who see charter schools as a vehicle for combining business and educational goals.

10. In the past few years, Educational Maintenance Organizations (EMOs) have become increasingly involved in public education as they view schools for their profit potential. The Edison Project, Tesseract, Sylvan Learning Systems, and Advantage Schools are several of the better-known "for-profit" education businesses. While the long-term viability of this privatization is far from certain, EMOs are shaking up the educational landscape.

11. While home schooling is far from being a new phenomenon, the number of parents educating their children at home has grown dramatically in recent years. Home-schooling parents include the religiously motivated, as well as reform-minded parents who use experiential and individualized learning activities. Technological advances, including the use of the Internet, have opened the possibility of converting education into a "cottage enterprise."

Key Terms and People

www.mhhe.com/sadker

A Nation at Risk
A Place Called School
acculturation
America 2000
Americanization
Ernest Boyer
charter schools
children's boards
children's policy
James Coleman
Edison Project
educational vouchers

EMOs (Educational Maintenance Organizations)
empowering teachers
Paulo Freire
Milton Friedman
full service schools
Goals 2000
John Goodlad
home schooling
ideologues
Lemon v. Kurtzman
magnet schools
National Commission on Excellence in Education

open enrollment
pedagogues
privatization
reconstructionism
school choice
service credit
Theodore Sizer
social action curriculum
Tesseract (Educational Alternatives Incorporated)
The Pedagogy of the Oppressed
three waves of reform

Discussion Questions and Activities

1. Discuss your list of school goals that you recorded with your classmates. Which goals seem to be most important to your peers? to your instructor? Which do *you* consider most important? Give reasons for your priorities.

2. Do you believe schools should transmit society's knowledge and values, or do you think schools should prepare students to change society? Find someone of the opposing opinion and hold an informal debate.

3. Summarize the last decade of education reform. Predict what the next big reform report will propose. Consider both concerns and suggestions.

4. If you were charged with writing a national report on education reform, what would *you* advocate?

5. "More testing is good for American education" is a common theme in many reform reports. Do you believe that testing should be emphasized in these reports? Why or why not?

6. Which concerns do you agree with as expressed in *A Nation at Risk*?

7. Goals 2000 won both ardent support and harsh criticism. Identify three obstacles to achieving the goals. How might you advance similar goals today?

8. Imagine you are a school board member and your district is debating whether to move to an open enrollment or to a voucher system. Defend your opinion in a brief memo.

9. If you were to design a magnet school, what would it be like? What students would you recruit? What would you look for in your teaching faculty? Would you have a unique physical plan for your building?

10. Imagine you are a concerned parent and long-time neighborhood activist. As part of a committee petitioning for a charter school, what particular mission or vision would be your goal? Why should your charter be approved?

11. Collect newspaper, journal, and Internet articles concerning home schools. Decide whether the home schooling described in the articles falls into the "ideologue" or the "pedagogue" category. Are the stories generally objective, or can you detect a bias for or against home schooling?

12. Does your local public school district have an official (or unofficial) policy concerning home schooling? Do home-school students participate in any school activities or receive any school resources? How do you feel about these (un)official policies?

Life in Schools

Focus Questions

- How do classroom rules, rituals, and routines shape teachers and students?
- How does the teacher's "gatekeeping" function relegate students to passive and reactive roles?
- What are the consequences of school tracking?
- How does tracking become a "self-fulfilling prophecy"?
- In what ways do social relationships and the peer group status system impact students?
- How can educators create a more supportive school environment for adolescents?
- How do race, gender, and social class create difficult, even chaotic, student cultures?
- What are the characteristics of effective schools?

Chapter Preview

School is a culture. Like most cultures, it is filled with rituals and traditions, rewards and punishments, winners and losers. It can be an intense and even cruel culture, with only a few "winners," many "wanna-bes," and some "losers." After graduation, however, the losers and winners often change places, for the school and the real world are very different places.

From the moment you first entered school, you have been immersed in an informal and subtle network of interactions that forms a big part of school culture. Time plays a major role in this culture. The school world is divided into "chunks" of time, called periods or blocks, which are filled with "English" and "History" and other names. Typically energetic students are pinched into passive roles. For 50-minute blocks of time, children respond to questions from teachers but seldom ask any of their own. School tracking practices assign students to high and low achievement groups, and an academic caste system may emerge.

This chapter will take you beyond academics to the lesser-known three *R*s (rules, rituals, and routines). It also analyzes the subtle dynamics of classroom communication and the role of peer groups, especially within adolescent society. It asks you to assess some of the political realities of schools, such as tracking, and to consider what impact these may have on students. Finally, the chapter summarizes five factors traditionally associated with effective schools, offers examples of these factors, and explores new arenas of effective schools research.

Rules, Rituals, and Routines

Schools create their own cultures, replete with norms, rituals and routines. Even simple tasks, like distributing textbooks, are clothed with cultural cues, but they are cues that differ for students and teachers.

"Come Right Up and Get Your New Books": A Teacher's Perspective

Dick Thompson looked at the pile of poetry anthologies stacked on his desk and sighed. Getting texts distributed and starting a new unit always seemed like such a chaotic ordeal, particularly with seventh-graders. But worrying over possible mishaps wouldn't get this poetry unit launched. Besides, his students were getting restless, so he had better get things started.

"Okay, class, quiet down. As you can see, the poetry books we've been waiting for have finally arrived. All right, you can cut out the groans. Give the books a fair trial before you sentence them. I'd like the first person in each row to come up, count out enough books for his or her row, and hand them out."

Six students charged to the front and made a mad grab for the books. In the ensuing melee, one stack of books went crashing to the floor.

"Hey, kids, take it easy and stop the squabbling. There are plenty of books to go around. Since this procedure obviously isn't working, we'll just have to slow down and do things one row at a time. Bob, you hand out the books for row 1 first; then Sally will come up and get the books for row 2. It will take a little longer this way, but I think things will go more smoothly. When you get your texts, write your name and room number in the stamped box inside the cover."

Since the dispensing of books now seemed to be progressing in an orderly fashion, Mr. Thompson turned his attention to the several hands waving in the air.

"Yes, Jessica?"

"I can't fill in my name because my pencil just broke. Can I sharpen it?"

What is the hidden curriculum in this teacher-dominated classroom, where teachers actively talk and move about while students passively sit and listen?

"Go ahead. Jamie?"

"My pencil's broken too. Can I sharpen mine?"

"Yes, but wait until Jessica sits down. Let me remind you that you're supposed to come to class prepared. Now there will be no more at the pencil sharpener today. Scott?"

"Can I use the hall pass?"

"Is this absolutely necessary? All right then [responding to Scott's urgent nod]. Now I think we've had enough distraction for one morning. The period's half over and we still haven't gotten into today's lesson. After you get your book and fill in the appropriate information, turn to the poem on page 3. It's called 'Stopping by Woods on a Snowy Evening,' and it's by Robert Frost, one of America's most famous poets. Yes, Rosa?"

"I didn't get a book."

"Tomàs, didn't you hand out books to your row? Oh, I see. We're one short. Okay, Rosa, go down to the office and tell Mrs. Goldberg that we need one more of the new poetry anthologies. Now, as I was about to say, I'd like you to think about the questions that I've written on the board: How does the speaker in this poem feel as he looks at the snow filling up the deserted woods? Why does he wish to stop, and what makes him realize that he must go on? The speaker says, 'I have miles to go before I sleep.' He may be talking about more than going to bed for the night. What else may 'sleep' mean in this poem? Yes, Scott, do you have a comment on the poem already?"

"My glasses are being fixed and I can't read the board."

"All right. Take the seat by my desk. You'll see the board from there. April! Maxine! This is not a time for your private chat room. This is a silent reading activity— and I do mean silent. Okay, class, I think most of you have had enough time to read the poem. Who has an answer for the first question? Jordan?"

"Well, I think the guy in this poem really likes nature. He's all alone, and it's private, with no people around to interrupt him, and he thinks the woods and the snow are really beautiful. It's sort of spellbinding."

"Jordan, that's an excellent response. You've captured the mood of this poem. Now for the second question. Maxine?"

"I think he wants to stop because . . ."

Maxine's answer was cut short by the abrasive ring of the fourth-period bell.

"Class, sit down. I know the bell has rung, but it isn't signaling a fire. You'll have time to make your next class. Since we didn't get as far into our discussion as I had hoped, I want to give you an assignment. For homework, I'd like you to answer the remaining questions. Alice?"

"Is this to hand in?"

"Yes. Any other questions? Okay, you'd better get to your next-period class."

As the last student left, Dick Thompson slumped over his desk and wearily ran his fingers through his hair. As he looked down, he spotted the missing poetry anthology under his desk, a victim of the charge of the book brigade. The whole lesson was a victim of the book brigade. He had been so busy getting the books dispensed and fielding all the interruptions that he had forgotten to give his brief explanation on the differences between prose and poetry. He had even forgotten to give his motivating speech on how interesting the new poetry unit was going to be. Well, no time for a postmortem now. Stampedelike noises outside the door meant the fourth-period class was about to burst in.

"Come Right Up and Get Your New Books": A Student's Perspective

From her vantage point in the fourth seat, fifth row, Maxine eyed the stack of new books on the teacher's desk. She knew they were poetry books because she had flipped through one as she meandered into the room. She didn't care that it wasn't "in" to like poetry; she liked it anyway. At least it was better than the grammar unit they'd just been through. All those sentences to diagram—picking out nouns and pronouns—what a drag that was.

Maxine settled into her seat and began the long wait for her book; her thoughts wandered: "Mr. Thompson seems like he's in some kind of daze, just staring at the new books like he's zoned out. Wonder what's bugging him. Good enough, the first kids in each row are heading up to get the books. Oh, right, they're getting into a brawl over handing out the stupid books. What a bunch of jerks; they must think they're funny or something. Now it'll be one row at a time and will take forever. I suppose I can start my math homework or write some letters."

Maxine got several of her math problems solved by the time her poetry anthology arrived, along with instructions to read the poem on page 3. She skimmed through the poem and decided she liked it. She understood how Robert Frost felt, watching the snowy woods and wanting to get away from all the hassles. It sure would be nice to read this poem quietly somewhere without listening to kids going on about pencil sharpeners and hall passes and seat changes. All these interruptions made it hard to concentrate.

As she turned around to share her observation about hassles with April Marston, Mr. Thompson's sharp reprimand interrupted her. She fumed to herself, "Private chat room. What's with him? Half the class is talking, and old Eagle Eyes Thompson has to pick on me. And they're all talking about the football game Saturday. At least I was talking about the poem. Oh well, I'd better answer one of those questions on the board and show him that I really am paying attention."

Maxine waved her hand wildly, but Jordan got called for question 1. Maxine shot her hand in the air again for a chance at question 2. When Mr. Thompson called on her, she drew a deep breath and began her response. Once again, she was interrupted in midsentence, this time by the fourth-period bell. Disgruntled, she stuffed her poetry book under her arm and fell into step beside April Marston.

"I really knew the answer to that question," she muttered under her breath. "Now we have to write all the answers out. Boring. Well, next period is science and we're supposed to be giving reports. Maybe we'll have a chance to finish the English homework there."

Delay and Social Distraction

You have just read two capsular replays of a seventh-grade English lesson, one from the vantage point of the teacher, the other from the vantage point of a student. Mr. Thompson and Maxine play different roles, which cause them to have very different experiences in this class. In what ways is the same class experienced differently by teacher and student?

One difference you may have detected is that Mr. Thompson was continually leapfrogging from one minor crisis to the next, while Maxine was sitting and waiting. In his perceptive book **Life in Classrooms, Philip W. Jackson** describes how time is spent in elementary school.[1] He suggests that, whereas teachers are typically very busy, students are often caught in patterns of delay that force them to do nothing. Jackson notes that a great deal of teachers' time is spent in noninstructional busywork, such as keeping time and dispensing supplies. In the slice of classroom life you just read, Mr. Thompson spent a substantial part of the class time distributing new texts. Indeed, most teachers spend a good deal of time giving out things: paper, pencils, art materials, science equipment, floppy disks, exam booklets, erasers, happy faces, special privileges—the list goes on and on. Teachers also select those who will take roll, collect milk money, or take messages to the office. The classroom scene described also shows Mr. Thompson greatly involved in timekeeping activities. Within the limits set by school buzzers and bells, he determines when the texts will be distributed, when and for how long the reading activity will take place, and when the class discussion will begin.

What do students do while teachers are busy organizing, structuring, talking, questioning, handing out, collecting, timekeeping, and crisis hopping? According to Jackson's analysis, they do little more than sit and wait.[2] They wait for the materials to be handed out, for the assignment to be given, for the questions to be asked, for the teacher to call on them, for the teacher to react to their response, and for the slower class members to catch up so that the activity can change. They wait in lines to get drinks of water, to get pencils sharpened, to get their turn at the computer, to go to the playground, to get to the bathroom, and to be dismissed from class. If students are to succeed in school, they must be able to cope with continual delay as a standard operating procedure.

One plea that is rarely granted is that of talking to classmates beyond controlled learning activities. Like the character from Greek mythology, Tantalus, who was continually tempted with food and water but was not allowed to eat or drink, students are surrounded by peers and friends but are restrained from communicating with them. In other words, students in the classroom are in the very frustrating position of having to ignore social temptation, of acting as though they are isolated despite the crowd surrounding them. Furthermore, while trying to concentrate on work and to ignore social temptations, students are beset by frequent interruptions—the public address system blaring a message in the middle of an exam, the end-of-class bell interrupting a lively discussion, a teacher's reprimand or a student's question derailing a train of thought during silent reading.

Consider how Maxine in Mr. Thompson's English class had to cope with delay, denial of desire, social distraction, and interruptions. She waited for the delivery of her new text. She waited to be called on by the teacher. Her attempt to concentrate on reading the poem was disturbed by frequent interruptions. Her brief communication with a classmate was interrupted by a reprimand. Her head was filled with ideas and questions. In short, there was a lot she would like to have said, but there was almost no opportunity to say it.

The Teacher as Gatekeeper

Educators concerned about school improvement have called attention to the inefficient use of time in school, claiming that we lose between one-quarter and one-half of the time available for learning through attendance problems, noninstructional activities (such as class changes and assemblies), administrative and organizational activities, and disruptions caused by student misbehavior.[3]

In a major study of schools, **John Goodlad** found a fair degree of consistency in how time is spent in different activities as children go through the grades. As Figures 6.1 and 6.2 illustrate, about 2 percent of time is spent to social activities, 2 to

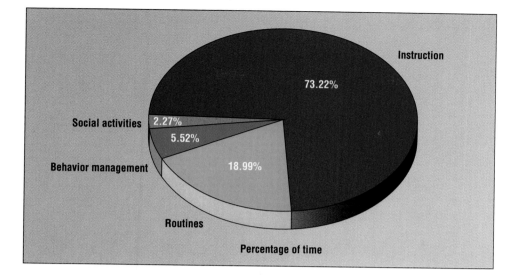

FIGURE 6.1

How do elementary children spend their class time.

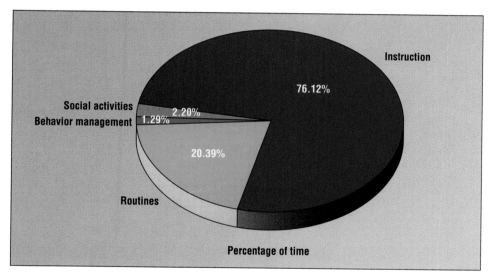

FIGURE 6.2

How do high school students spend their time?

5 percent to behavior management, 20 percent to routines, and 75 percent to instruction.

In Goodlad's study, although there was a general consistency in how time was spent at different levels of schooling, one of the most astonishing things Goodlad found was the enormous variation in the *efficiency* with which different schools used time. When examining the hours per week allocated to subject-matter learning, time ranged from a low of 18.5 hours in one school to a high of 27.5 hours in another. Goodlad was also surprised at the limited amount of time spent on the academic staples, such as reading and writing. He found that only 6 percent of time in elementary school was spent on reading. This dropped to a minuscule 2 percent at the high school level. In contrast, the amount of time students spent listening to teacher lectures and explanations increased from approximately 18 percent in elementary school to more than 25 percent in high school.[4] Some schools, equally surprised with Goodlad's studies, have incorporated alternative or block scheduling and special focus activities, such as sustained silent reading, to make better use of time in school.

Part of the hidden curriculum of schools is the "culture of waiting" that accompanies the many transition periods throughout the day. And often, waiting seems to be a gender segregated activity.

While the business world may suggest "time is money," for educators, time is learning. As one teacher points out,

> Time is the currency of teaching. We barter with time. Every day we make small concessions, small trade-offs, but, in the end, we know it's going to defeat us. After all, how many times are we actually able to cover World War I in our history courses before the year is out? We always laugh a little about that, but the truth is the sense of the clock ticking is one of the most oppressive features of teaching.[5]

There is a limited amount of time set aside for the school day. Research shows that, when more time is allocated to subject-matter learning, student achievement increases.[6] When this valuable resource is spent handing out supplies or reprimanding misbehavior, it is lost for learning. Looked at from this perspective, Mr. Thompson's class was not only frustrating, but it also deprived students of a precious and limited resource—the time to learn.

One of the functions that keeps Mr. Thompson and most other teachers busiest is what Philip Jackson terms **gatekeeping.** As gatekeepers, teachers must determine who will talk, when, and for how long, as well as the basic direction of the communication. Since classroom interaction is so critical to the teacher's role, let's take a closer look at this phenomenon.

Classroom Interaction

Philip Jackson reports that teachers are typically involved in more than one thousand verbal exchanges with their students every day.[7] Count the number of verbal exchanges Mr. Thompson had with his students during our abbreviated classroom scene and you will get some idea of how much and how often teachers talk.

As you may recall, (we *hope* you recall!) in Chapter 3 we reviewed some of the findings about classroom interaction, about just how much teachers dominate most classroom discussions. These studies tell us a lot about life in the classroom, but, just

THE PATTERNS OF THE CLASSROOM

After observing in more than one thousand classrooms, John Goodlad and his team of researchers found that the following patterns characterize most classrooms:

- Much of what happens in class is geared toward maintaining order among twenty to thirty students restrained in a relatively small space.
- Although the classroom is a group setting, each student typically works alone.
- The teacher is the key figure in setting the tone and determining the activities.
- Most of the time, the teacher is in front of the classroom, teaching a whole group of students.
- There is little praise or corrective feedback; classes are emotionally neutral or flat places.

- Students are involved in a limited range of activities—listening to lectures, writing answers to questions, and taking exams.
- A significant number of students are confused by teacher explanations and feel that they do not get enough guidance on how to improve.
- There is a decline in the attractiveness of the learning environment and the quality of instruction as students progress through the grades.

Goodlad concluded that "the emotional tone of the classroom is neither harsh and punitive nor warm and joyful; it might be described most accurately as flat."

Source: John Goodlad, *A Place Called School* (New York: McGraw-Hill, 1984).

in case you do not recall *all* those findings, following is a quick review, which provides a background for this chapter.

Researcher Ned Flanders uncovered "the rule of two-thirds." He found that someone is talking during two-thirds of the classroom time. Approximately two-thirds of that time, the person doing the talking is the teacher. Students are forced into a passive role, which eventually results in negative attitudes, lower achievement, and a general dependency on the teacher.[8]

Arno Bellack found that teachers structure (lecture and direct), question, and react to student comments, and they initiate about 85 percent of these verbal cycles.[9]

John Goodlad said that a snapshot of classrooms taken at random would, in all likelihood, show teachers talking and questioning and students listening and responding. Further, observations in one thousand classrooms showed that teachers interact less and less with students as they go through the grades. Not surprisingly, students say they are happiest when actively involved in their learning.[10]

While questioning signals curiosity, research indicates that it is the teachers, not the learners, who do the questioning, asking as many as 348 questions a day.[11] Further, research shows that most of these questions require that students use only rote memory.[12]

Ironically, while a major goal of education is to increase students' curiosity and quest for knowledge, it is the teachers, not the students, who dominate and manage classroom interaction. In fact, the typical student asks only one question per month.[13] Students are not given much time to ask, or even answer, questions. Teachers usually wait less than a second for student comments and answers.[14] In short, classroom interaction patterns do not train students to be active, inquiring, self-reliant learners. Rather, students learn to be quiet and passive, to think quickly (and perhaps superficially), to rely on memory, and to be dependent on the teacher.

The classroom language game, in which teachers talk and students listen, may encourage passivity and boredom.

Tracking

As students participate in both the formal and unofficial curricula of school life, they are continually being evaluated by teachers and administrators. These evaluations frequently get translated into an official and unofficial **tracking** system. Some students find themselves steered toward honors classes, others to remedial sections; some students are on their way to colleges, while others are preparing for vocations. One very crucial, political function of the school culture is that of screening and sorting students. Three decades ago, sociologist **Talcott Parsons** analyzed school as a social system and concluded that the college selection process begins in elementary school and is virtually sealed by the time students finish junior high.[15] Parsons's analysis has significant implications, for he is suggesting that future roles in adult life are determined by student achievement in elementary school. The labeling system, beginning at an early age, determines who will wear a stethoscope, who will carry a laptop computer, and who will become a low-wage laborer.

Several researchers consider students' social class a critical factor in this selection system. Back in 1929, Robert and Helen Lynd, in their extensive study of Middletown (a small midwestern city), concluded that schools are essentially middle-class institutions that discriminate against lower-class students.[16] Approximately fifteen years later, **W. Lloyd Warner** and his associates at the University of Chicago conducted a series of studies in New England, the deep South, and the Midwest and came to a conclusion similar to the Lynds':

> One group (the lower class) is almost immediately brushed off into a bin labeled "nonreaders, first grade repeaters," or "opportunity class," where they stay for eight or ten years and are then released through a chute to the outside world to become hewers of wood and drawers of water.[17]

In his classic analysis of class and school achievement, **August Hollingshead** discovered that approximately two-thirds of the students from the two upper social classes but fewer than 15 percent of those from the lower classes were in the college preparatory program.[18] In midwestern communities, **Robert Havinghurst** and associates reported that nearly 90 percent of school dropouts were from lower-class families.[19] The unfortunate tracking by class is one of the oldest of school traditions.

Parents and peers may influence academic choices even more than guidance counselors do.[20] When family and friends encourage children with similar backgrounds to stay together, students of the same race and class typically find themselves on the same school tracks. When school norms and children's culture clash, the result can also lead to racially segregated tracks. For example, some students of color devote time and attention to "stage setting." Stage setting may include checking pencils, rearranging sitting positions, and watching others—all part of a pattern of readiness before work can begin. To a teacher unfamiliar with this learning style, such behavior may be interpreted as inappropriate or as avoidance of work. Some racial and ethnic groups value cooperation and teamwork, yet school norms frequently stress individual, competitive modes of learning. Such cultural clashes work to the detriment of certain groups, dismissing them to lower-ability classes and tracks.[21]

Recently, there has been a great deal of debate over the morality and consequences of using schools as a sorting system. Many people claim that education is still a key avenue to class mobility and equality of opportunity. "True," they argue, "the school does track students, but it's for their own good. This occurs on the basis of individual ability, not race, class, ethnic background, or sex. It's unrealistic to think

THE ANTI-ACHIEVEMENT DILEMMA

Many students avoid academic excellence, because they fear their peers will label them nerds. According to B. Bradford Brown and Laurence Steinberg, who sampled eight thousand high school students in California and Wisconsin, this fear is warranted. Unlike athletes, who are offered adulation, high academic achievers often get resentment instead of respect.[a] To avoid the "nerd" label and the social rejection that comes with it, students learn that they should do well, but not *too* well. This brain-nerd connection causes students to put the brakes on academic achievement, cut corners, and do only what is necessary to get by. The anti-achievement climate is even stronger for African American students. Signithia Fordham and John Ogbu reported the results of a fascinating ethnographic study in a Washington, DC, high school, where the student population was 99 percent black.[b] They found that the students actively discouraged each other from working to achieve because attaining academic success was seen as "acting white." "Acting white" was understood to include speaking standard English, listening to white music and radio stations, being on time, studying in the library, working hard, and getting good grades. Students who did well in school were called "brainiacs," a term synonymous with *jerk*. The students who managed to achieve academic success and still avoid the "brainiac" label developed ingenious coping strategies. Some students camouflaged high achievement by "acting crazy," as class clowns or comedians. Others chose friends who would protect them in exchange for help with homework. Female achievers were more likely to hide out, keeping a low profile, so their peers would not know they were smart.

What can teachers do to break the brainiac-jerk association? How can the power of peer pressure be unleashed for success instead of mediocrity or failure? What do you think?

[a]B. Bradford Brown and Laurence Steinberg, "Academic Achievement and Social Acceptance," *The Education Digest* 55 (March 1990): pp. 57–60. Condensed from *National Center on Effective Secondary Schools Newsletter* 4 (fall 1989): pp. 2–4.
[b]Signithia Fordham, *Blacked Out: The Dilemmas of Race, Identity, and Success at Capital High* (Chicago: University of Chicago Press, 1996); Signithia Fordham and John Ogbu, "Black Students' School Success: Coping with the Burden of 'Acting White,'" *Urban Review* 18, no. 3 (1986): pp. 176–205.

everyone can master the same material or can cover it at the same pace. Intelligence testing, grouping, and tracking are necessary if we are to educate students according to their ability and future potential. Our best and brightest need to be identified as soon as possible. Who knows what they might achieve when given resources and opportunities. For the kids who are struggling, let's catch them up with special help and services."

Others counter, "No sorting system is consistent with equality of opportunity. Worse yet, the tracking system is not based on individual ability. It is badly biased in favor of white middle-class America. We must face the reality that poor children, often children of color, come to school far from being ready to learn. And the school, whose job it is to educate all our children, does little to help. The built-in bias in instruction, counseling, curricular materials, and testing must be overcome first. Students get shoveled into second-rate courses that prepare them for fourth-rate jobs. Their track becomes 'a great training robbery,' and the students who are robbed may be the ones with great abilities."

Several studies document differences in how students in the high-ability and low-ability tracks are treated. In a classic study done in the 1970s, **Ray Rist** observed a kindergarten class in an all-black urban school. By the eighth day of class, the kindergarten teacher, apparently using such criteria as physical appearance, socioeconomic status, and language usage, had separated her students into groups of "fast learners" and "slow learners." She spent more time with the "fast learners" and gave them more instruction and encouragement. The "slow learners" got more than their fair share of control and ridicule. The children soon began to mirror the teacher's behavior. As the "fast learners" belittled the "slow learners," the low-status children began to exhibit attitudes of self-degradation and hostility toward one another. This teacher's expectations, formed during eight days at the beginning of school, shaped the academic and social treatment of children in her classroom for the entire year and perhaps for years to come. Records of the grouping that had taken place during the first week in kindergarten were passed on to teachers in the upper grades, providing the basis for further differential treatment.[22]

In fact, more recent research on **ability grouping** continues to raise questions about its effectiveness. Studies indicate that tracking is detrimental to low-ability students. Low-ability groups have more classroom management problems, and students talk more about social rather than academic matters. Teachers hold lower expectations of, offer fewer constructive comments to, and make fewer demands of students in low-ability groups. Although small differences in ability do exist initially between children in upper and lower groups, these differences become greater over time. Over the course of a year, a child in the highest group may move ahead five times as quickly as a child in the lowest group. By the fourth grade, an achievement spread of a full four grades separates children at the top and the bottom of the class. These differences grow even greater as children go through school. Ability grouping seems to increase the achievement range, rather than reduce it.[23]

By high school, ability grouping has frequently turned into inflexible tracks. Studies of schooling and various advocacy groups have called for the elimination of this rigid division and implementation of a common core curriculum uniting all students. However, attempts to "detrack" schools are marked by controversy. Many proponents of ability grouping say these structures are beneficial to high-ability and especially to gifted students. At this point, research is not conclusive as to the effect of ability grouping on very bright students. Tracking is likely to remain an area of controversy in the years ahead, especially for educators who find it "the most professionally divisive issue" in the field.[24]

The Power of Peer Groups

GUEST COLUMN: Senior Haunted by Racist Attitudes

As graduation time approaches, I am supposed to get nostalgic about my community and my school. I should be thankful for how they have enriched my life, and I should expect to reminisce later on the "great things" about living here. Frankly, in my case, that will not be possible; I'll be trying to forget the bigotry here. Elementary school fostered my negative first impressions. One kid tried to insult me in the halls by calling me "African." My classmates told me to "go back where you came from." (Obviously they had no idea what country this was, but cultural education is another essay.) Often, I was used as an object in a "cooties" game. I was the contaminated one who had to touch all the other pure white-skinned kids. One day after school I was tied to a tree by some boys. The girls just stood around to laugh. They were the friendly ones because at least they did not inflict bodily pain. Wasn't I the naive buffoon to underestimate the burn of psychological humiliation?

Summer meant parks and recreation day camp, and that was hellish. Each day, I was de-pantsed by some fifth-grade boys in front of the amused campers. I was too embarrassed to tell my parents, and the counselors paid no attention to the foolish games all little boys play. Adult ignorance was by far the most agonizing injustice. In middle school, I sat in front of a boy who constantly whispered, "You f— nigger, black, disgusting" in my ear. Racism was intolerable. The teacher, I guess, disagreed. At least kids are honest. Isn't it amusing how they are little reflections of a community's attitudes? Today, the same people who tormented me as a child walk down the halls faceless. Once a racist reaches a certain age, he realizes that prejudice is not an outright verbal contract. It is subtle and "understood."

Just yesterday my five-year-old sister came home from her preschool and complained, "A girl said she didn't wanna play with me because I'm black." I said, "That's terrible! Did you tell the teacher?" My sister responded, "My teacher said, 'Just ignore her.'"

Yes, I'll have no trouble trying to forget this place.

Student letter to the school paper[25]

Sometimes the school's peer culture can produce overt racism; other times, the bias is more subtle and begins at an early age. Educational researcher Raphaela Best wanted to capture a portrait of life in school as a group of elementary school children experienced it. During a multiyear study, she played the role of participant observer, working with children during class time, playing with them at recess, eating lunch with them in the cafeteria, talking with them, observing them, and taking notes. She found that the children "organized their own intense, seething little world with its own frontiers, its own struggles, its own winners and losers. It was a world invisible to outsiders, not apparent to the casual observer,"[26] where the peer group became increasingly important in the children's lives—eventually competing with and even eclipsing parental influence.

In the first grade, when so much about school seems gigantic and fearful, children look to adults for safety: "What am I supposed to do in the classroom?" "Where do I get lunch?" "How do I find the bus to ride home from school?" Both girls and boys look to the teachers and to the principal for answers and for emotional support. In her study, Best found that the children ran to their first-grade teacher not only for this practical information but also for hugs, praise, and general warmth and affection. They climbed onto the teacher's lap and rested, secure and comforted.

Their relationship to the teacher was far more important than their interactions with one another. For example, when Anne and Matthew were fighting over how to put a puzzle together, the teacher encircled them in her arms and asked, "Can't we find another way to play?" The children nodded affirmatively. "Good! You're so good and I'm so happy with the way you've been playing, but you know that accidents can happen and someone might have to stay out of school. We wouldn't want that to happen, now would we?"[27] Both children solemnly shook their heads and indicated that they would comply with the teacher's request.

By the second grade, the boys had begun to break away from teacher dependence and to place more importance on their peer group. Though loosely structured, this group was largely sex-segregated, with its own leadership hierarchy. In the first grade, the boys and girls had sat side-by-side in the lunchroom, but, by the second grade, the boys had claimed one end of a lunchroom table for themselves. To ensure privacy from the female world, the group's meeting place became the boys' bathroom, where the boys talked about kids at school and decided what to play at recess.

By the third grade, the boys were openly challenging teacher authority. They banded together to organize an all-male club, complete with pecking order, assignments, secrets, and anti-establishment pranks, such as stuffing the locks with paper so the teachers could not get into the building in the morning. Also, by the third grade, the boys' territorial rights had increased, and they had staked out an entirely male lunchroom table for themselves. The playground also became increasingly sex-segregated, as blacktop and grassy areas were reserved for active boys' ball games, and the girls were relegated to the fringe areas, where they stood talking, played hop-scotch, and jumped rope. The girls used their time to chat, giggle, and re-create game rules to discourage cut-throat competition. Occasionally, an athletic girl breeched the cultural divide and played with the boys, yet her status as tomboy was always a limiting and noninclusive role. A powerful male culture had evolved, with the entitlement and rights of the privileged.

Excluded from this all-male society were not only the girls but also some boys who were considered sissies. For these rejected boys, the consequences of being left out of the **dominant male peer group** were painful and severe. As they progressed through their elementary school years, these excluded male students exhibited an increasing number of social, emotional, and academic problems. Afraid of being teased by the male club, they avoided playing with the girls, even though they might have been very happy doing so. Belonging nowhere, they banded together loosely, not out of liking but out of need.

The girls spent the first few years of school helping the teacher, not switching their allegiance to the peer group until the fourth grade. Throughout their school years, this allegiance was rewarded, in part with good report card grades. Then, instead of joining a club, they formed best-friend relationships, in which pairs of girls pledged devotion to one another. Sometimes fights broke out, when two girls argued over having a third as best friend. In the upper elementary grades, the girls also began to fantasize about the "cute" boys in their class and about what being married and having a family would be like. Being a good student and having a pleasing personality were seen as important, but, by the upper elementary grades, appearance had become the key to social status.

Social exclusion occurs in mixed sex or same sex peer groups. In either setting, rejection and isolation can be painful.

The **gender wall** blocking boys and girls from interacting is stronger than barriers to racial integration; there is more cross-race than cross-sex communication during the elementary school years. When Best asked students why there was not more friendship between boys and girls, they reacted with embarrassment. "Everyone would make fun of you," said one girl. Another commented,

> If you say you like someone, other kids spread it all over the school and that's embarrassing. . . . If you even sit beside a boy in class, other kids say you like him. And they come to you in the bathroom and tease you about liking the boy. Once some of the girls put J. S. and B. B. on the bathroom walls. That was embarrassing.[28]

How children relate to one another is crucial, spilling over into every nuance of school life. For you, as the teacher, a negative peer group dynamic can mean a problem-filled year. For children, the power of the peer group is even more devastating.

> "If you hate Graham, sign here." The petition was making the rounds in one fourth-grade classroom not long ago. Fortunately, the teacher intercepted the paper just before it reached Graham's desk. This time, at least, Graham was spared.[29]

In one sense, Graham is not alone. Many children share his predicament. When students respond to questions designed to measure their friendship patterns, 10 percent of them emerge as not being anybody's friend. About half of these are just ignored. The other half become the victims of active peer group rejection and hostility. These social preferences can be graphically presented in **sociograms** (see Figure 6.3).

Most friendless children are aware of their problem and report feeling lonely and unsuccessful in relating to others. Children without friends are more likely to experience adjustment problems in later life. Rejection by the child's peer group is a

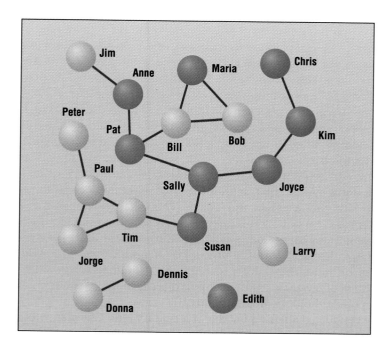

FIGURE 6.3

Sociogram of friendship relations.

sensitive indicator of future problems, ranging from juvenile delinquency to mental breakdown. In fact, elementary school sociometric measures predict social adjustment better than most other personality and educational tests do.[30]

The elementary school culture is driven by blatant and subtle peer group dynamics. An insightful teacher can structure a classroom to minimize negative and hurtful interaction and maximize the positive power of peer group relations. For instance, eliminating social cliques and race- and gender-based segregation is a precursor to successful cooperative groups. An "intentional" teacher often assigns students to seats or to group work to counter pupil favoritism and bias. A teacher's perceptiveness and skill in influencing the social side of school can mean a world of difference in the student's environment. For youngsters approaching an adolescent society, the pressures for popularity become increasingly extreme.

High School's Adolescent Society

Rock singer Frank Zappa said, "High school isn't a time and a place. It's a state of mind." Sociologist James Coleman says that high school is "the closest thing to a real social system that exists in our society, the closest thing to a **closed social system.**" Sociologist Edgar Friedenberg points out that most high schools are so insular that they have their own mechanism for telling time—not by the clock but by periods, as in "I'll meet you for lunch after fourth period." Author Kurt Vonnegut says that "high school is closer to the core of the American experience than anything else I can think of." In his inaugural speech before Congress, President Gerald Ford confided, "I'm here to confess that in my first campaign for president—at my senior class at South High School—I headed the Progressive party ticket and I lost. Maybe that's why I became a Republican." More than forty years later, Gerald Ford still remembered high school. No matter where we go or who we become, we can never entirely run away from high school. It is an experience indelibly imprinted on our mind.[31]

More than 13 million students arrive at twenty thousand public high schools every day. These schools run the gamut from decaying buildings plagued by vandalism and drugs to orderly, congenial places with educators who hold positive expectations and high standards for their students. They vary in size from fifty to five thousand students, who spend days divided into either six or seven 50-minute periods or perhaps fewer, longer blocks of time.

In his book *Is There Life After High School?* Ralph Keyes stirs up the pot of high school memories and draws a very lively picture of what life was like during that time and in that place and state of mind. In researching his book, he asked many people, both the famous and the obscure, about their high school experiences. He was amazed at the vividness and detail with which their memories came pouring out—particularly about the status system, that pattern of social reward and recognition that can be so intensely painful or exhilarating. High school was remembered as a caste system of "innies" and "outies," a minutely detailed social register in which one's popularity or lack of it was continually analyzed and contemplated. Using sociological language, James Coleman documents this status phenomenon in ***The Adolescent Society,*** when he states that a high school "has little material reward to dispense, so that its system of reward is reflected almost directly in the distribution of status. Those who are popular hold the highest status."[32]

In a major study conducted almost a quarter of a century after Coleman wrote *The Adolescent Society,* John Goodlad reached a similar conclusion; the junior and senior high school students he researched were preoccupied not with academics but,

IN THE NEWS . . . HONORS BATHROOM

At Northgate High School near Pittsburgh, integrity and honesty pay off in unusual ways. Students who pledge not to smoke or damage the fixtures will be issued magnetized cards that admit them to an *honors bathroom*. Smoke free lavatories are predicted to be the *in* thing, according to senior Rob S. *Most kids will want to be there, he says. I don't think the honors bathroom kids will be nerds.*

Source: *Newsweek,* 19 October 1998.

rather, with athletics, popularity, and physical appearance. Only 14 percent of the junior high and 7 percent of the senior high students said that "smart students were the most popular." Thirty-seven percent of the junior high students said that the "good-looking" students and 23 percent said the "athletes" were the most popular. In senior high, 74 percent of the students said that the most popular kids were "good-looking" and "athletes."[33]

When junior and senior high school students were asked to identify the one best thing about their school, they usually said, "My friends." "Sports activities" ranked second. "Nothing" ranked higher than "classes I'm taking" and "teachers." In some secondary schools, peer group interests bubbled so close to the surface that they actually pushed attention to academic subjects aside and almost took over the classroom. When asked to describe her school, one high school junior said,

> The classes are okay, I guess. Most of the time I find them pretty boring, but then I suppose that's the way school classes are supposed to be. What I like most about the place is the chance to be with my friends. It's nice to be a part of a group. I don't mean one of the clubs or groups the school runs. They're for the grinds. But an informal group of your own friends is great.[34]

These informal groups are rigidly homogeneous, as becomes apparent in the seating arrangements of the secondary school cafeteria. A student in one high school described the cafeteria's social geography like this: "Behind you are the jocks; over on the side of the room are the greasers, and in front of you are the preppies—white preppies, black preppies, Chinese preppies, preppies of all kinds. The preppies are the in group this year; jocks of course are always in and greasers are always out."[35]

In some cases, entire sections of the school are staked out by special groups. In a suburban high school near Chicago, the vice principal easily identified the school's different cliques. The "scums" were the group of students who partied all the time and were rebelling against their parents. Next to the cafeteria was "Jock Hall," where the male athletes and their popular girlfriends could be found. Close to the library was the book foyer, where the bright kids got together.[36]

Perhaps high school students flock to others most like themselves because making their way in the adolescent society is so difficult. David Owen is an author who wanted to find out what life in high school was like in the 1980s. Although he had attended high school from 1969 to 1973, he returned undercover, almost a decade later. Posing as a student who had just moved into the area, he enrolled in what he calls a typical American high school, approximately two hours out of New York City.

Peer groups appear to be homogeneous and, more than anything else, tend to define the quality of students' school life.

During his experience, he was struck by the power of the peer group and how socially ill at ease most adolescents are. He likened adolescents to adults who are visiting a foreign country and a strange culture. Experimenting with new behavior, they are terrified of being noticed doing something stupid:

> Relationships among teenagers are founded on awkwardness more than most of them realize. When a typical high school student looks around at his classmates, he sees little but coolness and confidence, people who fit in better than he does. That was certainly the way I thought of my old high school classmates much of the time; no matter how well adjusted I happened to feel at any particular moment, other people seemed to be doing better. At Bingham, though, I saw another picture. Everyone seemed so shy. The kids hadn't learned the nearly unconscious social habits that adults use constantly to ease their way through the world. When kids bumped into each other in the halls, they almost never uttered the little automatic apologies—"Oops," "Sorry"—that adults use all the time. They just kept plowing right ahead, pretending they hadn't noticed. One day, when I was hurrying to my history class, I realized I was on a direct collision course with a girl coming the other way. Each of us made a little sidestep, but in the same direction. Just before we bumped, an expression of absolute horror spread across the girl's face. She looked as though she were staring down the barrel of a gun. The bubble of coolness had been burst. She probably brooded about it for the rest of the day. . . . Being an adolescent is a full-time job, an all-out war against the appearance of awkwardness. No one is more attentive to nuance than a seventeen-year-old. . . . When a kid in my class came to school one day in a funny-looking pair of shoes that one of his friends eventually laughed at, I could see by his face that he was thinking, "Well, that does it, there goes the rest of my life."[37]

IN THE NEWS . . . CLASS ACT

He was the captain of the school baseball, basketball, and football teams, and he was as good-hearted as he was athletic. When the McMinnville, Oregon senior found out that seven girls did not have dates to the prom, he worked afterschool to raise $500 so that they could all go together.

Source: *The American School Board Journal,* July 1998.

The memory of high school rejection is powerful, even for generations of the rich and famous. Actress Mia Farrow recalls a high school dance at which every girl was on the dance floor except her. Cartoonist Charles Schulz has not forgotten the day the yearbook staff rejected his cartoon, and actress Eva Marie Saint recalls the time she did not get a part in the class play. No matter where we were in the high school system, few of us have egos so strong or skins so tough that we fail to get a psychological lift when we learn that beautiful actress Ali McGraw never had a date during high school, that actor Gregory Peck was regarded as least likely to succeed, that singer John Denver was called "four-eyes," or that former Secretary of State Henry Kissinger is recalled as a little fatso with whom nobody would eat lunch.[38]

For those who remember jockeying unsuccessfully for a place within the inner circle of the high school social register, it may be comforting to learn that the tables do turn. No study shows any correlation between high status in high school and later achievement as an adult. Those who are voted king and queen of the prom or most likely to succeed do not appear to do any better or any worse in adult life than those whose yearbook description is less illustrious. What works in that very insular adolescent environment is not necessarily what works in the outside world. One researcher speculates that it is those on the "second tier," those who group just below the top, who are most likely to succeed after high school. He says, "I think the rest of our lives are spent making up for what we did or did not do in high school."[39]

Most students know the feeling of being judged and found wanting by high school peers, and some spend the rest of their lives trying to compensate or get even. Comedian Mel Brooks sums it up well:

> Thank God for the athletes and their rejection. Without them there would have been no emotional need and . . . I'd be a crackerjack salesman in the garment district.[40]

For some students, the impact of rejection does not lead to such positive outcomes. These students struggle to break through clique walls that are invisible but impervious. As one student stated: "I've never really been part of any group. I suppose I don't have anything to offer."[41] Without the support of friends and peers, they remain on the periphery of high school, where feelings of loneliness can become overwhelming.

The Affective Side of School Reform

By the 1980s and 1990s, teachers were sounding an alarm bell about unmet psychological, emotional, and social needs of the nation's children, concerns about **affective student needs** that continue today. By the mid-1990s, 76 percent of teachers were concerned about student drinking, 64 percent were concerned about drug use, 59 percent were worried about teen pregnancy, 50 percent were concerned about apathy, 41 percent were troubled by violence, and 34 percent worried about absenteeism.[42] In the 1980s, a kindergarten teacher from an urban school system said,

> The difficult part of teaching is not the academics. The difficult part is dealing with the great numbers of kids who come from emotionally, physically, socially, and financially stressed homes. Nearly all of my kindergarten kids come from single parent families. Most of the moms really care for their kids but are young, uneducated, and financially strained. Children who have had no breakfast, or who are fearful of what their mom's boyfriend will do to them—or their moms—are not very good listeners or cooperative partners with their teachers or their peers. We are raising a generation of emotionally stunted and troubled youth who will in turn raise a generation of the same. What is the future of this country when we have so many needy youngsters?[43]

Those who teach in urban settings warn us that the future of poor and minority children is at risk. But all is not well in suburbia, either. Consider this comment from a teacher in suburban New Jersey: "In the large, efficient suburb where I teach the pressure is on kids from kindergarten to high school to get good grades, bring up the test scores, and be the best on the test."[44] Another teacher says that there is such pressure to get high test scores that students are rushed from one workbook to another. There is no time for anything not directly related to cognitive achievement. "We feel guilty," she says, "doing an art lesson or having a wonderful discussion."[45]

In another study, **Frances Ianni** describes the affluent lifestyle in the suburb of Sheffield (name fictitious), a place where families keep well-manicured lawns and push their children to succeed. Students are groomed to be good at everything—athletics, social skills, academic achievement. "People in Sheffield will tell you," Ianni says, "that the two things you never ask at a cocktail party are a family's income and the Scholastic Assessment Test scores of their children."[46] English teacher Patrick Welsh tells of teenagers who take the SATs four or five times, pushed on by their parents' promises of new cars if they score well:

> I've had kids in class with their fingernails bitten to the quick and looking miserable, feeling they have to get As, and their parents going to the point of rewriting their papers for them. Every fall T.C. is gripped by "Ivy League Fever." Sweatshirts marked "Harvard" or "Princeton" start appearing. . . . I got so fed up, that one day in class I horrified everybody by saying I have yet to see anybody wearing an Ivy League sweatshirt get into an Ivy League school. The sweatshirts went back to the drawer after that.[47]

Pushed beyond their abilities and alienated from family, friends, and community, some teenagers develop a "delusion of uniqueness," a sense that "no one knows how I feel, no one else faces these problems, no one cares about me." When children are cut off from what Urie Bronfenbrenner calls "the four worlds of childhood"—family, friends, school, and work—the situation can become serious and even life-threatening.[48] Sara Lawrence Lightfoot describes the following incident that took place in an elite school in a wealthy suburb in the Midwest:

> A student with a history of depression . . . had been seeing a local psychiatrist for several years. For the last few months, however, she had discontinued her psychotherapy and seemed to be showing steady improvement. Since September, her life had been invigorated by her work on *Godspell*—a student production that consumed her energies and provided her with an instant group of friends. After *Godspell,* her spirits and enthusiasm declined noticeably. In her distress, she reached out to a teacher who had given her special tutorial support in the past, and the school machinery was set in motion. A meeting was scheduled for the following day to review her case. That night, after a visit to her psychiatrist, she killed herself.
>
> The day after, the school buzzed with rumors as students passed on the gruesome news—their faces showing fear and intrigue. . . . But I heard only one teacher speak of it openly and explicitly in class—the drama teacher who had produced *Godspell*. Her words brought tears and looks of terror in the eyes of her students.
>
> "We've lost a student today who was with us yesterday. We've got to decide where our priorities are. How important are your gold chains, your pretty clothes, your cars? . . . Where were we when she needed us? Foolish old woman that I am, I ask you this because I respect you. . . . While you still feel, damn it, feel . . . reach out to each other."[49]

This "reaching out" is what Ianni recommends in her **youth charter** network. "Communities," she says, "can create youth charters that encourage youngsters to move from dependence to independence, from the ethnocentrism of early adolescence to the social competence of young adulthood." She urges the community to move from benign neglect or outrage at the young to an organized system of positive involvement and guidance.[50] Many other child advocates are calling for a coordinated system of school-based social services to replace the existing maze of bureaucratic agencies.[51]

Alfie Kohn is one educator who claims that the social and affective sides of school must become an explicit part of the formal curriculum: "It is possible to integrate prosocial lessons into the regular curriculum. . . . Indeed to study literature or history by grappling with moral or social dilemmas is to invite a deeper engagement with these subjects." According to Kohn, such schools as the California-based Child Development Project, a long-term effort in prosocial education, teach children to take responsibility and care for one another.[52]

While most reform reports emphasize increased academic achievement, only a few recognize the social and emotional needs of children. The Carnegie Council on Adolescent Development report, ***Turning Points: Preparing American Youth for the 21st Century,*** warns that one in four adolescents are in serious jeopardy. Their basic human needs—caring relationships with adults, guidance in facing sometimes overwhelming biological and psychological changes, the security of belonging to constructive peer groups, and the perception of future opportunity—go unmet at this critical stage of life. Millions of these young adolescents will never reach their full potential.[53] Pointing to a society dangerous to adolescent health—one of drug abuse, poor school performance, alienation, and sexual promiscuity—the report calls for comprehensive middle school reform to help protect these youngsters.

Middle-grade schools—junior high, intermediate or middle schools—are potentially society's most powerful force to recapture millions of youth adrift. Yet all too often they exacerbate the problems youth face. A volatile mismatch exists between the organization and curriculum of middle-grade schools and the intellectual, emotional, and interpersonal needs of young adolescents.[54]

Describing the trauma students face when they shift from a neighborhood elementary school, where they spent most of the school day with one or two teachers who knew them well, to a larger, colder institution, where they move through six or seven different classes daily, the Carnegie report makes the following recommendations:

- Divide large schools into smaller "communities" for learning.
- Create a core curriculum.
- Eliminate tracking.
- Emphasize cooperative learning.
- Develop stronger partnerships between schools and communities.
- Assign teams of teachers and students, with an adult adviser for each student.
- Emphasize the link between education and good health.
- Strengthen teacher preparation for dealing with the adolescent age group.

Imagine life in a school that implements these recommendations. You would see a smaller middle school or high school, one emphasizing community activities and moving away from an atmosphere that produces "large-school alienation." Health issues would become more central, linking diet and exercise more directly to education, enhancing the longevity and quality of students' lives well into adulthood. But, to create such a caring and healthful school, teacher education itself would need to be changed. As you examine your own teacher education program, can you identify ways that these recommendations are being promoted? How does your teacher education program prepare you to develop school-community partnerships, promote cooperative learning, and respond more effectively to the needs of adolescents? Significant changes in many teacher education programs across the nation will need to be made if the recommendations of the Carnegie report are to be implemented.

What Makes a School Effective?

While the Carnegie Council's *Turning Points* recommendations are designed to create more sensitive and humane school climates, other studies have offered suggestions for creating more academically demanding schools. Although the major focus of this chapter is on the social and interpersonal side of schools, it is important that academic life not be forgotten. For example, consider the following situation: Two schools are located in the same neighborhood. They are approximately the same size, and the student populations they serve are similar in all characteristics, including socioeconomic level, racial and gender composition, achievement scores on school entry, and parental education and occupation. However, in one school, the students have high dropout rates and low scores on national achievement tests. In the other school, the students' test scores are at or above the national average, and the students are more likely to stay in school. Why should such differences emerge?

Puzzled by situations such as this, researchers attempted to determine what factors have made some schools more effective in encouraging student achievement. As early as 1971, George Weber studied four schools that seemed successful in teaching reading.[55] Through research such as his, the more effective schools have been identified as those in which achievement, especially for students of color and of poverty, is at a uniformly successful level of mastery. One of the best-known studies, conducted by Ronald Edmonds and his colleagues, concluded that, in an effective school, students with a working-class background score as high as middle-class students on tests of basic skills.[56] Other groups around the country, from the Connecticut School Effectiveness Project to the Alaska Effective Schooling program, have conducted research to figure out what makes good schools work. In study after study, researchers have found a common set of characteristics, which has resulted in a **five-factor theory of effective schools.**[57] Researchers say that effective schools are able, by means of the five characteristics, to reduce the harmful effects of poor socioeconomic background. The values and norms embedded in these five school characteristics create a culture of achievement. Following is a discussion of these five factors and how they contribute to strong school performance.

Factor 1: Strong Leadership

In her book ***The Good High School,*** Sara Lawrence Lightfoot drew portraits of six effective schools.[58] Two, George Washington Carver High School in Atlanta and John F. Kennedy High School in the Bronx, were inner-city schools. Highland Park High School near Chicago and Brookline High School in Brookline, Massachusetts, were upper middle-class and suburban. St. Paul's High School in Concord, New Hampshire, and Milton Academy near Boston were elite preparatory schools. Despite the tremendous difference in the styles and textures of these six schools, ranging from the pastoral setting of St. Paul's to inner-city Atlanta, they all were characterized by strong, inspired leaders, such as Robert Mastruzzi, principal of John F. Kennedy High School.

When Robert Mastruzzi started working at Kennedy, the building was not yet completed. Walls were being built around him as he sat in his unfinished office and contemplated the challenge of not only his first principalship but also the opening of a new school. During his years as principal of John F. Kennedy, his leadership style has been collaborative, actively seeking faculty participation. Not only does he want his staff to participate in decision making, but he gives them the opportunity to try new things—and even the right to fail. For example, one teacher made an error about the precautions necessary for holding a rock concert (800 adolescents had shown up, many high or inebriated). Mastruzzi realized that the teacher had learned a great deal from the experience, and he let her try again. The second concert was a great success. "He sees failure as an opportunity for change," the teacher said. Still other teachers describe him with superlatives, such as "he is the lifeblood of this organism" and "the greatest human being I have ever known."[59]

Mastruzzi seems to embody the characteristics of effective leaders in good schools. Researchers say that students make significant achievement gains in schools in which principals

- Articulate a clear school mission
- Are a visible presence in classrooms and hallways
- Hold high expectations for teachers and students
- Spend a major portion of the day working with teachers to improve instruction
- Are actively involved in diagnosing instructional problems
- Create a positive school climate[60]

Successful principals provide instructional leadership. They spend more of their time working with students and less time in the office. They observe what is going on in the classrooms, hold high expectations for teacher performance and student achievement, and provide necessary resources, including their own skills and knowledge. They are active and involved. As a result, they create schools that make a positive difference in the lives of students.

Factor 2: A Clear School Mission

When researchers study principals at work, they typically find them in a state of perpetual motion:

> Generally I am working on four things at a time, but I know my priorities. I may have two students in my office to reinstate. I get a call, telling me there is a fight on the third floor. I send the students out of my office and lock the door. As I move upstairs, a teacher confronts me, holding a student by the collar, upset about his behavior. I must ignore her to get up to the fight. By the time I reach the third floor, that teacher informs me the situation is under control. All this effort, and what have I accomplished?[61]

A day in the life of a principal can be spent trying to keep small incidents from becoming major crises. But the research is clear; in effective schools, good principals somehow find time to develop a vision of what that school should be and to share that vision with all members of the educational community. Successful principals can articulate a specific school mission, and they stress innovation and improvement. In contrast, less effective principals are vague about their goals and focus on maintaining the status quo. They make such comments as "We have a good school and a good faculty, and I want to keep it that way."[62]

It is essential that the principal share his or her vision, so that teachers understand the school's goals and all work together for achievement. Unfortunately, when teachers are polled, more than 75 percent say that they have either no contact or infrequent contact with one another during the school day. In less effective schools, teachers lack a common understanding of the school's mission, and they function as individuals charting their own separate courses. Pyne Poynt Middle School in Camden, New Jersey, is one example of the power of teachers and administrators working together:

A positive, energizing school atmosphere characterized by accepting relationships between students and faculty often begins with the principal.

IN THE NEWS . . . SOCIAL SECURITY PACKAGE

In response to the mass shootings of teachers and students in Arkansas, Kentucky, and Mississippi by boys as young as 11, Senator Jeff Bingaman of New Mexico received unanimous Senate approval for a 10 million dollar appropriation to develop custom security packages for schools. Congress already passed the Gun Free School Act, requiring school districts to expel for at least one year any student determined to have brought firearms to school.

Source: *Education Week on the Web,* 1 April 1998.

Not long ago at Pyne Poynt Middle School teachers regularly confiscated weapons. Parents feared visiting Pyne Poynt after dark. Student achievement was low. Staff morale was lower.

Today Pyne Poynt is a deeply proud school, with abundant reason for pride: Attendance is up, truancy is down. Discipline has returned. Reading and math scores have soared. . . . How to explain this metamorphosis? . . . The entire school staff recognized that in their efforts to turn Pyne Poynt around, they were neglecting their most valuable resource: each other. The school staff—teachers and administrators together—then began revamping established schedules and procedures to ensure the regular exchange of ideas and insights.

"We became a team," says Pyne Poynt principal Vernon Dover, "and Pyne Poynt became a different place."[63]

The need for the principal to share his or her vision extends not only to teachers but to parents as well. When teachers work cooperatively and parents are connected with the school's mission, the children are more likely to achieve academic success.

Factor 3: Preventing School Violence: A Safe and Orderly Climate

- For more than two decades, opinion polls have shown that the public considers lack of discipline to be among the most serious problems facing schools.[64]
- The National Institute of Education's Safe School study found that, in the late 1990s only one in every fifty-eight school crimes was reported to the police.[65]
- The National Parent-Teacher Association has reported that the annual cost of vandalism, probably in excess of $600 million, is greater than the nation's total budget for textbooks.
- More than 3 million crimes occur on school grounds each year. That's sixteen thousand crimes a day.
- Each year, scores of students and teachers are killed by gun fire, hundreds are wounded, and hundreds more are held hostage.

Welcome to School

What do you suspect these students (and their teachers) feel as they enter their school? How might those feelings influence learning?

- Almost one in six students report being victimized on school property during any six-month period.
- Approximately one in ten high school students report that they carried a weapon at least once during the past month.[66]

To understand how such statistics can emerge, we can begin by looking at what works—how safe and orderly schools function. In these schools, there is a focus on academic achievement, families and communities are involved in a meaningful way in school activities, students and staff treat each other with respect, and student concerns and interests are supported. Student problems are identified and attended to before they deteriorate into violence. How are these student problems detected? Following are several warning signs, indicators of impending violence:

- Many students at times display social withdrawal, feelings of excessive isolation, or even rejection, not unique feelings for adolescents. But these feelings can be carried to extreme, and their presence should be noted as possible precursors to violence.
- Children who are victims of sexual or physical abuse, or are "picked on" and bullied by others, may themselves resort to violence.
- The reasons for poor academic performance need to be assessed. Weak academics can be a result of emotional or psychological turmoil.

- Impulsivity, anger, and a history of disciplinary problems are clear examples of a troubled past and indicators for potential future problems.
- Affiliation with gangs; prejudice and bigotry toward racial, ethnic, gay, and lesbian groups; drug or alcohol use; and inappropriate access to firearms are all harbingers of impending trouble.[67]

Safe schools implement a variety of programs and social services. School psychologists, special education programs, family social workers, and schoolwide programs instituted to increase communication and reduce tension are all components of preventing school violence. In some of America's most distressed neighborhoods, achieving a safe climate can be a challenge for educators, but it provides a needed refuge for students. For example, Sara Lawrence Lightfoot tells of the long distances that urban students travel to reach John F. Kennedy High School in the Bronx. One girl, who did not have money to buy a winter coat or glasses to see the chalkboard, rode the subway 1 hour and 40 minutes each way to get to school. She never missed a day, because for her school was a refuge—a place of hope where she could learn in safety.[68]

Good schools have safe environments.

Factor 4: Monitoring Student Progress

As the researcher walked through the halls of a school we will call Clearview Elementary School, she noted attractive displays of student work mounted on bulletin boards and walls. Also posted were profiles clearly documenting class and school progress toward meeting academic goals. Students had a clear sense of how they were doing in their studies; they kept progress charts in their notebooks. During teacher interviews, the faculty talked about the individual strengths and weaknesses of their students. Teachers referred to student folders that contained thorough records of student scores on standardized tests, as well as samples of classwork, homework, and performance on weekly tests.

A visit to Foggy Bottom Elementary, another fictitious school with a revealing name, disclosed striking differences. Bulletin boards and walls were attractive, but few student papers were posted, and there was no charting of progress toward academic goals. Interviews with students showed that they had only a vague idea of how they were doing and of ways to improve their academic performance. Teachers also seemed unclear about individual student progress. When pressed for more information, one teacher sent the researcher to the guidance office, saying, "I think he keeps some records like the California Achievement Tests. Maybe he can give you what you're looking for."

Following the visit, the researcher wrote her report: "A very likely reason that Clearview students achieve more than Foggy Bottom students is that one school carefully monitors student progress and communicates this information to students and parents. The other school does not." Effective schools carefully monitor and assess student progress in a variety of ways:

IN THE NEWS . . . SCHOOL UNIFORMS AND SCHOOL SAFETY

In 1994, Long Beach, California became the first school district to require school uniforms for elementary and secondary school students. Eagle Pass, Texas did them one better, requiring such uniforms for high schoolers as well. Baltimore, Chicago, Miami and Phoenix now allow individual schools to require uniforms. Why this growing popularity? Many parents and educators believe that a connection exists between safety and dress. Long Beach educators assert that gang clothing and designer sports clothes led to violence, fights, and overall delinquency. After the school uniform policy was initiated, school crime dropped by 76 percent, assaults dropped by 85 percent, and weapons offenses dropped by 83 percent. Meanwhile, attendance figures hit 94 percent, an all-time high. Parents supported the change, reporting that uniforms save them both money and time.

But not everyone agrees that uniforms are the reason for these encouraging figures. Critics indicate that dropping crime figures nationally are at least partially responsible for these positive changes. Educator Ray Rist believes that treating students in a special way affects their behavior. He believes it is not the uniforms, but the special attention that they are receiving that is responsible for the improved behavior. While some students like the uniform requirements, others do not. *I think it's stupid,* says ninth grader Jamie P., *What does school have to do with uniforms?*

Source: *Teacher Magazine on the Web,* March 1998.

- **Norm-referenced tests** are used to compare individual students with others in a nationwide norm group. Examples include the Metropolitan Achievement Test (MAT) and the Scholastic Assessment Test (SAT).
- **Objective-referenced tests** measure whether a student has mastered a designated body of knowledge. A school district or state may administer objective-referenced tests to identify which students are ready to move on to new tasks.
- Teacher-made tests, also objective-referenced, may be given far more frequently than assessments administered by the district or state. These tests should be given at least every two weeks to provide information to educators interested in improving curriculum and instruction.
- Recordkeeping counts too. Students should be responsible for keeping track of course objectives and their progress toward meeting those objectives.[69]

Assigning and monitoring homework can also be an important factor in promoting achievement. Researcher Herbert Walberg and colleagues indicate that, when homework is assigned without teacher feedback, it raises the scores of the typical student from the 50th to the 60th percentile. When it is graded and commented on, achievement is increased from the 50th to nearly the 80th percentile. Walberg and colleagues claim that the correlation between graded homework and student achievement is among the highest discovered in educational research.[70]

Photos in Contrast

School Uniforms

Many schools, public and private, have opted for official uniforms. Even when dress remains a student choice, peer pressure may create "unofficial" uniforms. Based on the appearance of these students, what assumptions might you make about their schools?

Factor 5: High Expectations

The teachers were excited. A group of their students had received extraordinary scores on a test that predicted intellectual achievement during the coming year. Just as the teachers had expected, these children attained outstanding academic gains that year.

Now for the rest of the story: the teachers had been duped. The students identified as gifted had been selected at random. However, eight months later, these randomly selected children did show significantly greater gains in total IQ than did another group of children, the control group.

In their highly influential 1969 publication, *Pygmalion in the Classroom,* researchers **Robert Rosenthal** and **Lenore Jacobson** discussed this experiment and the power of teacher expectations in shaping student achievement. They popularized the term **self-fulfilling prophecy** and revealed that students may learn as much—or as little—as teachers expect.[71] Although methodological criticisms of the original Rosenthal and Jacobson study abound, those who report on effective schools say that there is now extensive evidence showing that high teacher expectations do, in fact, produce high student achievement, and low expectations produce low achievement.[72]

Too often, teacher expectations have a negative impact. An inaccurate judgment about a student can be made because of error, unconscious prejudice, or stereotype. For example, good-looking, well-dressed students are frequently thought to be smarter than their less attractive peers. Often, male students are thought to be brighter than female students, particularly in math, science, and technology. Students of color are sometimes perceived as less capable or intelligent. A poor performance on a single standardized test (perhaps due to illness or an "off" day) can cause teachers to hold an inaccurate assessment of a student's ability for months and even years. Even a casual comment in the teachers' lounge can shape the expectations of other teachers.

When teachers hold low expectations for certain students, their treatment of these students often differs in unconscious and subtle ways. Typically, they offer such students

- Fewer opportunities to respond
- Less praise
- Less challenging work
- Fewer nonverbal signs (eye contact, smiles, positive regard)

In effective schools, teachers hold high expectations that students can learn, and they translate these expectations into teaching behavior. They set objectives, work toward mastery of those objectives, spend more time on instruction, and actively monitor student progress. They are convinced that students can succeed.

Finally, in effective schools, teachers hold high expectations for themselves. They believe that they can deliver high-quality instruction. In *The Good High School,* Sara Lawrence Lightfoot reported that this sense of teacher efficacy and power was prevalent at Brookline High, a school near Boston, where suburban and urban values met and often clashed. As Lightfoot listened in halls, classes, and the teachers' room, she heard faculty discussions about pedagogy, curriculum ideas, and the problems of individual students. "Star" teachers were respected as models to be emulated. Always striving for excellence, these teachers felt that, no matter how well a class went, next time it could be better.

A Note of Caution on Effective Schools Research

Although the research on what makes schools effective has had a direct impact on national reform movements, it has limitations.[73] First, there is disagreement over the definition of an effective school. Researchers use varying descriptions, ranging from "schools with high academic achievement" to schools that foster "personal growth, creativity, and positive self-concept." Although the five factors we have described are helpful, they do not really provide a prescription for developing successful schools.

Another problem is that much of the research has been conducted in the lower grades of elementary schools. Although some researchers suggest applicability to secondary and even higher education, caution must be used in carrying the effective-schools findings to higher levels of education. The generalizability of the research is also limited, since several of the studies were conducted in inner-city schools and tied closely to the achievement of lower-order skills in math and science. If one wanted to develop a school that nurtures creativity rather than basic skills, another set of characteristics might be more appropriate.

Beyond Five Factors

New effective-schools findings offer us insights beyond the five factors of effective schooling:

- *Early start.* The concept that there is a particular age for children to begin school needs to be rethought. The earlier schools start working with children, the better children do. High-quality programs during the first three years of life include parent training, special screening services, and appropriate learning opportunities for children. While such programs are rare, those that are in operation have significantly raised IQ points and have enhanced language skills. It is estimated that $1 spent in an early intervention program saves school districts $7 in special programs and services later in life.

- *Focus on reading and math.* Children not reading at grade level by the end of the first grade face a one-in-eight chance of ever catching up. In math, students who do not master basic concepts find themselves playing catch-up throughout their school years. Effective schools identify and correct such deficiencies early, before student performance deteriorates.

- *Smaller schools.* Students in small schools learn more, are more likely to pass their courses, are less prone to resort to violence, and are more likely to attend college than those attending large schools. Disadvantaged students in small schools outperform their peers in larger schools, as achievement differences for the rich and poor are less extreme. Many large schools have responded to these findings by reorganizing themselves into smaller units, into schools within schools. Research suggests that small schools are more effective at every educational level, but they may be most important for older students.

- *Smaller classes.* Although the research on class size is less powerful than the research on school size, studies indicate that smaller classes are associated with increased student learning, especially in the earlier grades. Children in classes of fifteen outperform students in classes of twenty-five, even when the larger classes have a teacher's aide present.

- *Increased learning time.* While not an amazing insight, research tells us what we already suspect: more study results in more learning. Longer school days, longer school years, more efficient use of school time, and more graded homework are all proven methods of enhancing academic learning time and student performance.

- *Assessment.* Investing time is useful, but assessing how effectively the time is spent is also important. Testing student performance has been tied to greater achievement, and some districts have gone so far as to pay teachers incentives for improvements in student test scores.

- *Teacher training.* Researcher Linda Darling-Hammond reports that the best way to improve school effectiveness is by investing in teacher training. Stronger teacher skills and qualifications lead to greater student learning. Conversely, students pay an academic price when they are taught by unqualified and uncertified teachers.

- *And What About Technology.* School districts that are hesitant to spend funds on teacher training, class size reductions, or early childhood education programs nevertheless are quick to invest significant sums in computers and upgraded technology. Research says very little about the impact of technology on school effectiveness and student performance. Studies are few, sometimes contradictory, and long-term results are still unknown. It is a sad commentary that the glamour of cyberspace is more persuasive than decades of research.[74]

Clearly, there are many exciting ways to view and measure school life.[75] The challenge facing teachers and school administrators in the years ahead may well be the thoughtful integration of the research on effective schools and effective teaching with the research on the social and psychological needs of children. How can we improve schools so that they enhance both psychological well-being and academic success?

Summary

1. Typically, teachers keep busy in class, while students spend their time sitting still and waiting. Most children respond by daydreaming or by training themselves to deny their desire to be active.
2. Teacher talk dominates classroom life. Flanders, Bellack, Goodlad, and others have found that teachers lecture a great deal and ask questions, while students are reduced to passive listening, active only when responding to the teacher. While we may envision a curious, inquiring, self-reliant learner, that is not the role our students are taught to play.
3. John Goodlad and others have documented startlingly inefficient use of time in schools. When teachers spend more time teaching, students learn more.
4. Being tracked into slower classes has a negative impact on students' self-esteem and achievement. Also, tracking discriminates against poor children and students of color, who are more likely to be labeled as slow learners.
5. Beginning in elementary school, peer pressure wields great power in children's lives. Young children's peer groups are rigidly segregated by sex, with boys tending to form hierarchic societies and girls usually forming pairs of best friends. Those left out may develop adjustment problems and emotional difficulties.
6. Educational reform efforts have focused on adolescents' social and personal needs. Many schools take on an increasing number of roles traditionally filled by parents, from sex education to drug and pregnancy counseling. Reports warn of the fragile condition of troubled adolescents, exhorting schools to do more to help the nation's youth.
7. Researchers have set forth a "five-factor theory" of effective schools. These factors can be summed up as (1) strong administrative leadership, (2) clear school goals shared by faculty and administration, (3) a safe and orderly school climate, (4) frequent monitoring and assessment of student progress, and (5) high expectations for student performance.
8. Some limitations on research findings on effective schools include the following: (1) definitions of an effective school vary; (2) research has focused on elementary schools; (3) findings are not specific enough to provide a blueprint for developing effective schools.

9. Beyond the five factors, research connects effective schools with early intervention programs, an emphasis on reading and math, smaller schools, smaller classes, increased learning time, assessment of student progress, and expanded teacher training. To date, there is little evidence connecting technology with school effectiveness.

Key Terms and People

ability grouping
affective student needs
closed social system
dominant male peer group
five factor theory of effective schools
gatekeeping
gender wall
John Goodlad
Robert Havinghurst
August Hollingshead

Frances Ianni
Philip W. Jackson
Lenore Jacobson
Life in Classrooms
Robert and Helen Lynd
norm-referenced tests
objective-referenced tests
Talcott Parsons
peer group power
Pygmalion in the Classroom
Ray Rist

Robert Rosenthal
self-fulfilling prophecy
sociograms
The Adolescent Society
The Good High School
tracking
Turning Points: Preparing American Youth for the 21st Century
W. Lloyd Warner
youth charter

www.mhhe.com/sadker

Discussion Questions and Activities

1. Observe in a local elementary school. What are the rules and regulations that students must follow? Do they seem reasonable or arbitrary? Do students seem to spend a large amount of time waiting? Observe one student over a 40-minute period and determine what portion of those 40 minutes she or he spends just waiting.

2. Visit several classrooms and calculate what percentage of the time is spent on noninstructional activity—administrative duties, student reprimands, and the like. Share what you find with your classmates.

3. Do you think that tracking is a valid method for enhancing student performance? Or do you think it is a mechanism for perpetuating inequality of opportunity based on social class, race, or sex? Debate someone in your class who holds an opposing point of view.

4. We have noted the vividness and detail with which many people recall their high school years. Try to answer the following:

   • Who was voted most likely to succeed in your high school class? (Do you know what he or she is doing today?)

   • What was your happiest moment in high school? your worst?

   • Name five people who were part of the "in crowd" in your class. What were the "innies" in your high school like?

   • Is there any academic experience in high school that you remember vividly? If so, what was it?

5. Visit a school and observe student interactions in informal settings. (A shopping mall might work as well.) Do you notice any cliques? Describe them.

6. Research the issue of adolescent alienation. Make some recommendations on how secondary schools could get students to become more involved in academic and extracurricular activities.

7. Read the 1989 report *Turning Points: Preparing American Youth for the 21st Century.* Compare this with the 1983 report *A Nation at Risk.*

8. Based on the characteristics of effective schools, would you consider your elementary, middle, and high schools effective? If not, why? Share your responses with your classmates.

What Students Are Taught in Schools

Focus Questions

- What is the difference between the formal and the hidden curriculum?
- What is the place of the extracurriculum in school life?
- How does the hidden curriculum affect students?
- What are contemporary subject matter trends and tension points?
- How can critical thinking be encouraged throughout the curriculum?
- How do social forces shape curriculum development?

Chapter Preview

What did you learn in school today? This is a time-honored question asked by parents, and avoided by children. What children learn varies, depending on whether they are more alert to the formal curriculum, made up of objectives and textbook assignments, or to the hidden curriculum, which emerges from the social side of school. What children learn in school also shifts with changing cultural and political values.

This chapter will provide a brief profile of what is taught in today's elementary and secondary schools. Using time capsules and sample student schedules, you will go back through time to gain historical perspective on the issues and controversies that have marked curriculum from the Puritans' two *R*s (reading and religion) to the current debate over national curriculum standards. The chapter also explores the curriculum pendulum, which swings between progressive and traditional educational approaches.

What Is a Curriculum?

As soon as she opened the door, Mary Jean knew she would like the teachers' room. There was the good smell of strong coffee, and, although it was early, groups of teachers were already clustered about the room, talking about their work and their lives.

As Mary Jean filled her mug and reluctantly turned away from the muffins, she scanned the room. There they were, Mr. Battersea and Mrs. Schwartz, sitting at a round table in the corner.

"I hope I'm not late," Mary Jean apologized as she slipped into the remaining seat at the table. "Is it after eight?"

"Oh no, you're right on time," said Mr. Battersea. "We've been here for a while. We get here early to plan for the day. As soon as you start teaching, those college days of sleeping late are over. So enjoy it while you can."

"He's so lively in the morning," Mrs. Schwartz grimaced. "Personally, I hate the morning. Maybe after I finish this cup of coffee I'll be more coherent." Then she gave Mary Jean a broad wink. "Just kidding. I gripe about the mornings as a matter of principle. I've gotten used to the early hours—well, almost used to them. You said that you needed to conduct an interview for your Introduction to Education class. How can we help you?"

Mary Jean pulled out the sheet her professor had distributed in class. "It says here I'm supposed to ask two teachers at the school where I'm observing to give me their definition of curriculum. So I guess that's the big question. What's a **curriculum?**"

"Kind of a big, broad topic, isn't it?" Mr. Battersea looked puzzled.

"I know. Our professor said you might feel that it was a very general question. But that was the idea. We are all supposed to get different reactions from the teachers in class and then compare them."

"I like that idea," said Mrs. Schwartz, looking a little more lively as she drained the mug. "In fact, I'd like to be a fly on the wall and listen in on your class discussion. I'll try to answer your question. A curriculum. . . . Hmm. . . . What is a curriculum? Well, . . . obviously, it's what kids learn in school. Its the goals and objectives our country sets for the different grade levels, and we certainly set an awful lot of them. We discuss those goals and objectives as a faculty here at Thomas Jefferson. Sometimes we add new objectives of our own, and we'll often decide, based on the needs of our own students, which to emphasize and what our priorities should be."

Carol Schwartz glanced at Mary Jean, who was scribbling furiously. "Got all that? Then, a curriculum is also the textbooks that are selected. Students are working with texts of one kind or another throughout the day, so what a text emphasizes becomes an important part of the curriculum. What we teachers do in class—our own interests and specialties—that becomes the curriculum too. For example, I love to travel. Every summer I go to a different country, and then all during the year I take some time to talk with the children about that place. Sometimes I'll bring in food or show them postcards and videos. I guess that becomes the curriculum too. A curriculum is simply what students learn from their teachers and textbooks in their classrooms."

Jim Battersea broke in, "Carol, I think you've made some great points for Mary Jean, but for me the curriculum is more than what is taught in classrooms. It's everything kids learn in school. For example, we have a drama group that's putting on a reggae version of Shakespeare's *A Midsummer Night's Dream.*" Mary Jean stopped writing and stared at Mr. Battersea. "Oh, I know it sounds weird," he grinned, "but the kids are doing a great job, and the drama teacher is very creative. Kids who are participating in that play are learning a tremendous amount—music, theater, Shakespeare. Other students participate in band, in chorus, in sports. There are several computer clubs. We even have a Special Friends Club that some students use for their service requirement. The students work with kids who have disabilities—take them bowling, play with them during lunch, tutor them. Children learn a lot through these experiences. I think extracurricular activities are an important part of what students learn in school."

"You're right, Jim. I was thinking about the formal academic curriculum. And what children learn in school is broader than that. I also remember one of my education professors talking about a hidden curriculum. I wasn't quite sure what he meant at the time, but, over the years I've been teaching, I've grown more and more aware of just how powerful this hidden curriculum is."

"I couldn't agree with you more." Jim Battersea leaned forward. "What Carol and I are talking about, Mary Jean, is all that subtle, incidental learning that occurs as children interact with each other, with the teacher, with all the different sides and angles of this thing we call school. For example, those kids in the drama club are learning so much more than Shakespeare. How does it feel to be on stage in front of 500 people? Are they nervous? How do they handle stage fright? What do they do if they forget their lines? Can they improvise? Do they help each other and cooperate, or do they compete? And think what a tremendous amount students learn about themselves and human nature when they work with kids with disabilities in the Special Friends Club. This hidden curriculum is an undercurrent of the formal class structure too. What do kids learn when they're playing a game in class and no one chooses them for the team? What do they take away if a teacher treats them unfairly or explodes in anger? Or think of all a youngster will learn from that teacher who sits down to talk with him or her about hobbies, goals, and problems."

"I know just what you're talking about." Mary Jean put down her pencil. "Like right now. I've learned a lot more than formal definitions of the curriculum. I know what the teachers' room is like early in the morning. I know how early you get here, and that you take time out of your busy schedules to talk with someone who wants to be a teacher. I've learned about curriculum and about teaching as well."

ㄱㄱㄱ

In 1962, highly regarded educator **Hilda Taba** said, "Learning in school differs from learning in life in that it is formally organized. It is the special function of the school to so arrange the experiences of children and youth that desirable learning takes place. If the curriculum is to be a plan for learning, its content and learning experiences need to be organized so that they serve the educational objectives."[1] Today, most educators regard the **formal curriculum** as the organization of intended outcomes for which the school takes responsibility.

In *A Place Called School,* one of the most important and influential studies of school life, **John Goodlad** refers to an explicit and an implicit curriculum.[2] The **explicit curriculum** is reflected in curriculum guides, courses offered, syllabi describing courses, tests given, materials used, and teachers' statements of what they want students to learn. When you study algebra or U.S. history, you are studying the explicit curriculum. But there are other curriculums as well. The **implicit,** or **hidden, curriculum** emerges incidentally from the interaction between the students and the physical, social, and interpersonal environments of the school. The third curriculum has been called the **extracurriculum** and includes student activities, such as sports, clubs, governance, and the student newspaper. Before we look at the formal, or explicit, curriculum of elementary and secondary schools, perhaps we should examine these powerful, less formal, curriculums first.

The Extracurriculum

"The Battle of Waterloo was won on the playing fields of Eton," said the Duke of Wellington, perhaps becoming the first to highlight the importance of extracurricular activities. Students seem to agree. In the early 1990s, 83 percent of all high school seniors participated in at least one extracurricular activity, with students from smaller schools and with stronger academic records most likely to be involved.[3] Varsity sports attracted the most students, with 44 percent of the high school boys and 28 percent of the high school girls participating. Students who participate in athletics typically learn leadership, teamwork, persistence, diligence, and fair play. Twenty-eight percent of students were involved with music and drama, developing their creativity and talents. Academic clubs were the third most popular activity, with about one-quarter of all students taking part by senior year, rates that have not changed since the early 1970s. Academic clubs— science, languages, computers, debate—enhance not only academic learning but social skills as well. Nationwide programs, such as Odyssey of the Mind and Future Bowl, promote cross-curricular interests and creative problem-solving skills. Advocates see these activities as so important that they refer to them not as the extracurriculum but as the *cocurriculum*.

Advocates proclaim the value of the extracurriculum to life both within and far beyond the high school years. Researchers Allyce Holland and Thomas Andre found that

- Extracurricular activities enhance student self-esteem and encourage civic participation.
- The extracurriculum, especially athletics, improves race relations.

Sports and varsity athletics comprise an important and influential part of school life.

FAIR PLAY

Female athletic participation has been associated with healthier lifestyles, including lower incidences of breast cancer,[a] reduced rates of teen pregnancy, lower usage of drugs, and higher graduation rates.[b] While the percentage of girls participating in sports grew dramatically after Congress passed Title IX (1972), a law prohibiting gender discrimination, this increase has slowed in recent years. If the current trend continues, it will take high schools until the year 2033 to achieve gender parity in their sports programs.[c]

[a]J. Raloff, "Exercising Reduces Breast Cancer Risk," *Science News* 149, no. 14 (1 October 1994): p. 215.
[b]Feminist Majority Foundation, *Empowering Women in Sports* (Washington, DC: 1995).
[c]Women's Sports Foundation. East Meadow, NY. Based on information in *Women's Sports Facts,* 1989, updated July 1995.

- Participating students have higher SAT scores and grades.
- Involvement in the extracurriculum is related to high career aspirations, especially for boys from poor backgrounds.[4]

Not everyone is so sanguine about the extracurriculum. The underrepresentation of low socioeconomic students is evident in many programs, as are gender differences in the performing arts, school government and literary activities, which are populated by significantly more females.[5] More skeptical than others about any real benefit to students, researcher B. Bradford Brown concludes that the best we can say "is that the effects of extracurricular participation on secondary school students' personal development and academic achievement are probably positive, but very modest, and are definitely different among students with different social or intellectual backgrounds."[6]

If you think back to your own high school days, you may remember both high- and low-profile students: the extracurricular superstar so involved in everything from the student council to the yearbook that she walked around with a little black calendar in her backpack to keep activities straight; the nominal participants, involved in a few activities (this is where most students fall); and the nonparticipants, those who were alienated and excluded from the extracurricular side of school.

Think about your own involvement in the extracurriculum. Were you a high-profile student? apathetic? alienated or uninvolved? What did you learn from the extracurricular side of school? Why did you choose to participate in some activities over others? Did you gain important skills and knowledge, or did you think the extracurriculum was a frill, diverting important resources and attention from formal academic coursework? If you were active in extracurricular activities, what were your motives?

High-profile students have a complex network of reasons for participating. For some, there is genuine interest and enjoyment. Others see the extracurriculum as a path to social success. One study found that only 16 percent of students surveyed said getting good grades increases status among peers. However, 56 percent of students said that extracurricular activities can lead to popularity.[7] Other calculating students base their choice of activities not on their own interests but, rather, with an eye to the interests of admissions officers, who select the chosen few for the nation's most prestigious colleges and universities.

Controversies about the extracurriculum often focus on its uneasy relationship with the academic side of school. For example, the current emphasis on a rigorous academic curriculum has spilled over in the form of policies that bar students from extracurricular participation if they fail a course. In Texas and other states, "no pass, no play" rules deny students in poor academic standing the right to participate in

CARING KIDS

Is the school's soccer team washing cars to raise money for a homeless shelter? Are the students in Spanish 3 tutoring children at the elementary school? Directing adolescent time and energy to benefit others can help students connect with each other and the real meaning of civic duty. Since many consider service such a worthy cause, it is frequently a requirement for graduation.

What works? When schools invest their resources to develop and schedule community service projects, student participation rates surge.

Who cares? About half of U.S. secondary students participate in service activities, and about half of those students are involved on a regular basis. Participants in extracurricular programs (student government and other school activities) and students who work for pay outside school are the most likely to contribute their time. The busiest young people are the most likely to be involved!

Source: *The Condition of Education 1998,* Indicator 25: Community Service Participation of Students in Grades 6–12. US Department of Education.

IN THE NEWS . . . LETTERING IN ACADEMICS

Michael K., a senior at Westchester High School in Los Angeles, has earned the right to wear a football letter on his school jacket. He chose instead to wear the academic letter. The school awards letters to students with a 3.5 or higher GPA. *I worked harder for the academic jacket than the one for football,* he explained.

Source: *The American School Board Journal,* August 1998.

varsity sports. In some communities, budget tightening has led to "pay to play" rules, in which a fee is required for sports participation, posing a serious problem for low-income families and students.

Such policies raise puzzling questions and issues. Should academic performance and financial constraints be factors in deciding who participates in extracurricular activities? If the extracurriculum is a vital part of the learning offered in school, should any students be denied access? According to data from the longitudinal study *High School and Beyond,* African American and Latino males are most likely to be affected by these policies, since one-third fail to maintain a 2.0 grade point average.[8] Since the top academic students, more likely to be wealthy and white, already dominate the extracurriculum, will "pay to play" regulations make this curriculum even more exclusive, driving deeper divisions between the haves and have-nots and further segregating racial and ethnic groups? As Figures 7.1 and 7.2 illustrate, both social class and gender influence extracurricular participation.

An ongoing concern is that, to many, the extracurriculum means only one thing—varsity sports. On any autumn Friday evening or Saturday afternoon in thousands of small towns across the United States, entire communities—accompanied by bands, parades, and pep rallies—cheer the hometown football team with a level of adulation that can only be dreamed of by academic stars. For small town or large city athletes, the media hype and possibility of multimillion-dollar contracts can lead

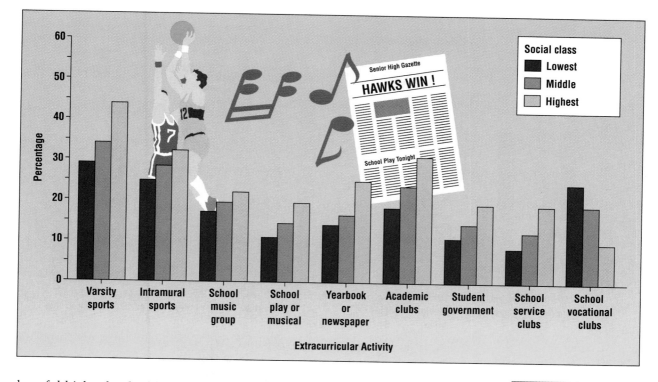

hopeful high school athletes down a treacherous road. While more than 5 million students across the nation play interscholastic varsity sports, 49 out of 50 will never make a college team. For every 100 male college athletes, only 1 will play professional sports. Many critics worry that the tail is wagging the dog in a system in which athletics get the resources, the hope, and the attention, while academics slide into the shadows.

FIGURE 7.1

Impact of social class on extracurricular participation of high school seniors.

Source: Condition of Education, 1995

The Hidden or Implicit Curriculum

While the relationship between the formal curriculum and the extracurriculum is occasionally controversial, they have one thing in common: both have goals and methods that are explicit and intentional. Although the hidden curriculum is absent from the official school catalog, it still teaches powerful lessons.

Jules Henry is an anthropologist who has analyzed the hidden curriculum of the elementary school and has studied the values and behavior it teaches. He concludes that students are capable of learning many things at one time and that the school teaches far more than academic content. The hidden curriculum consists of implicit learnings that are not always intended. For example, Henry described a fourth-grade classroom in which a spelling bee was taking place. Team members were chosen by two team captains. When a student spelled a word correctly on the board, a "hit" was scored. When three spelling errors were made, the team was "out." Students cheered or groaned, depending on the outcome for their team. According to Henry, these students were learning about more than spelling. They were learning about winning and losing, competition, and the feelings that accompany success and failure. If they were chosen early for a team, they learned about group support and

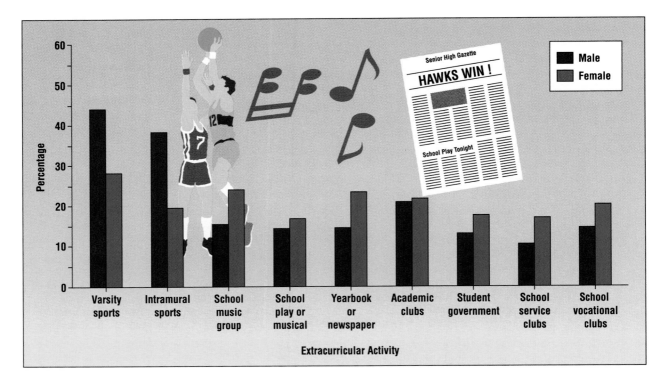

FIGURE 7.2

Impact of gender on
extracurricular
participation of high
school seniors.

Source: Condition of Education,
1995

recognition. If they were chosen late, they learned about embarrassment and rejection. Some of the more thoughtful students also learned about the absurdity of a spelling lesson being taught as a baseball game.[9]

Here is another example. The formal academic curriculum stresses the importance of preparing students to become active citizens in a democracy. Courses in government, civics, and history are offered to meet this goal. In the extracurriculum, elections to student government schoolwide and to offices in individual classes and clubs supposedly promote democratic participation. But the subtle and powerful message of the hidden curriculum may lead to some very different learning, learning entirely opposite to that which is intended. As they are run in most schools, elections may teach students that, rather than "selecting the best person for the job," they are merely casting a vote in a popularity contest or that the candidate with the best posters, rather than the best platform, is most likely to win. They may be learning that it does not matter if the winner has intelligent positions on issues, or the snazziest posters, or the most friends, because nothing changes, anyway. Perhaps the fact that a large segment of the adult electorate fails to vote in national elections is a testament to the power of the hidden curriculum.

The Formal or Explicit Curriculum

You will find striking similarities in the courses of study across the 50 states, in what is called the formal curriculum. National curriculum standards, already developed for math, science, social studies, geography, history, and the performing arts, will continue to make state curricula increasingly similar in the coming years. The following sections offer a synopsis of what is taught in the formal curriculum in today's schools. They also summarize current tension points and trends that may shape what is taught in the schools of tomorrow.

IN THE NEWS . . . COMMERCIALIZING SCHOOLS: A HIDDEN CURRICULUM

The Center for Commercial-Free Public Education is concerned about marketing products to captive student audiences. Here are some examples of their concern:

- Exxon teaches children that the *Valdez* oil spill was an example of environmental protection.
- In Colorado, Burger King and 7-Up advertise on school buses.
- A Texas school roof is painted with a Dr. Pepper logo to capture the attention of passengers flying overhead.
- McDonald's teaches about deforestation, but fails to include the negative impact of cattle ranching on the rain forest.
- Clairol distributes free shampoo to students leaving school, along with a survey asking if they had a bad hair day.

Source: *Educational Leadership,* October 1998.

Language Arts and English

Topics

Language arts programs emphasize multiple goals, including effective oral and written communication, comprehension and listening skills, problem solving, and language and literature appreciation. In elementary school, the language arts curriculum addresses the essentials of how to use language—reading, grammar, spelling, speaking, handwriting, composition, capitalization, punctuation, word processing, peer editing, and research skills. At the secondary level, language arts instruction (or simply, English class) shifts the focus to literature, which becomes the source for continued language development. Senior high school students usually read classics by such authors as Shakespeare, Poe, Whitman, and Austen.

Tension Points and Trends

Approximately one in five adults in the United States is functionally illiterate, a shocking statistic.[10] Adult illiteracy underscores the importance of the debate over whether to use the phonics or the whole language approach to reading instruction. **Phonics** consists of breaking down words into the smallest phonetic units—phonemes—and stringing them together to form words, independent of the words' meaning. **Basal readers,** which taught fundamental reading skills and dominated reading instruction in the 1950s and 1960s, relied on phonics. Some remember phonics as "sounding out the letters to build a word." The **whole language** movement condemned phonics as denying students the pleasure of reading for content and meaning. But some children who seemed slow or even unable to grasp the fundamentals of reading through the whole language approach soared to the top of their reading group when they became "Hooked on Phonics." Some teachers struggle to incorporate principles of both phonics and whole language into their language arts instruction.[11]

CONFLICTING CANONS

Typically, language arts programs use literature drawn from European and American white male authors as reflected in the first reading list below. But, as demonstrated by the selections required at Valley High School in Elk Grove, California, districts are revising these lists to be more representative of their students cultural backgrounds and interests.

Ten Most Commonly Assigned Books in High School English Classes

Romeo and Juliet	William Shakespeare
Macbeth	William Shakespeare
The Adventures of Huckleberry Finn	Mark Twain
Julius Caeser	William Shakespeare
To Kill a Mockingbird	Harper Lee
The Pearl	John Steinbeck
The Scarlet Letter	Nathaniel Hawthorne
Of Mice and Men	John Steinbeck
Lord of the Flies	William Golding
Diary of a Young Girl	Anne Frank

Required Reading for Valley High School in Elk Grove, California

Romeo and Juliet	William Shakespeare
I Know Why the Caged Bird Sings	Maya Angelou
The Grapes of Wrath	John Steinbeck
McTeague	Frank Norris
Their Eyes Were Watching God	Zora Neale Hurston
The Joy Luck Club	Amy Tan

Source: David Barton, "Classic Debate!" *Sacramento Bee*, 3 April 1998, p. SC-1.

Poor writing performance also remains a concern. According to the National Assessment of Educational Progress (NAEP), American students' reading skills have improved over the past three decades, while their writing skills have stagnated or declined.[12] The 1992 "snapshot of student writing" study collected the best writing samples of 2,200 fourth- and eighth-graders. Analysis showed that most students do not write at any length and do not write analytical or research papers, and that only 1 percent revise their work.[13]

The increased use of technology may reverse this trend. With the advent of computers and word processing, editing is simpler. Computer tools that facilitate spelling and grammar have also redefined the use of technical skills. As students become more involved with e-mail and Internet exchanges, time devoted to writing may increase, and perhaps their writing skills will improve as well.

Another trend worth noting is that, during the past century, the list of authors taught in English classes has become increasingly American. In 1907, nine of the forty most frequently assigned authors were American; by 1990, twenty-nine of the forty were American.[14] The inclusion of literature by women and non-Western writers is on the increase, and some argue that such changes will be at the expense of "classic" literature, sometimes referred to as the **canon.**

In San Francisco, two school board members proposed a curriculum that would mandate that seven authors of a ten-author syllabus must be people of color. This ambitious proposal was eventually tabled in favor of one that requires that four of the ten be minority authors. Some complain that political correctness is becoming a threat to academic excellence, while others argue that it is time to recognize that great writers come in all colors and both genders.[15]

Social Studies

Topics

Social studies curricula draw on the disciplines of history, government, geography, economics, sociology, anthropology, and psychology. History remains paramount, yet it has become the battleground for curriculum wars between multiculturalists and advocates of a **core curriculum** (see Chapter 8). While the curriculum battle still rages, history teaching has moved from a narrow emphasis on political and economic landmarks toward a broader perspective of social life and daily human struggles.[16]

The early elementary school social studies program emphasizes self, family, and community. Upper elementary school students begin the study of history, geography, and civics. At the high school level, the focus is on U.S. history and government, but a wide array of electives, such as economics, sociology, law, world history, anthropology, and current events, may be offered.

Tension Points and Trends

Civics is seen as a course to acquaint a diverse student population with the democratic tradition. The 1990 NAEP showed that more than 40 percent of high school seniors were not aware that the Declaration of Independence affirms the right to life, liberty, and the pursuit of happiness. Half of all twelfth-graders did not know that the amendments to the Constitution guarantee religious freedom and other basic rights.[17] As Figure 7.3 indicates, more than half of high school seniors fall below even a basic level of U.S. history achievement.

At all levels of instruction, there is insufficient attention to international topics, and today's students are shockingly ignorant of the history, politics, and geography of other nations. About half of all U.S. high school graduates have never studied world history; most of the other half have studied it for a year or less.[18] One out of three students cannot locate France on a map, and one out of five cannot even locate the United States.[19]

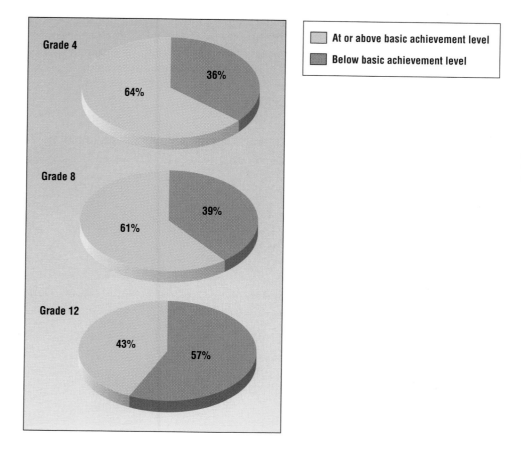

At or above basic achievement level

Below basic achievement level

Grade 4
36%
64%

Grade 8
39%
61%

Grade 12
43%
57%

FIGURE 7.3

Percentage of students at or above the basic achievement level in U.S. history.

Source: National Center for Education Statistics, National Assessment of Educational Progress (NAEP), 1994 U.S. History Assessment.

The 1990s revealed a promising trend in geography studies, particularly due to the efforts of the National Geographic Society. The number of college students choosing to major in geography rose 47 percent from 1986 to 1994. The Advanced Placement exams include geography, enabling students to obtain college credit for this content area.[20]

Mathematics

Topics

The National Council of Teachers of Mathematics (NCTM) issued groundbreaking curriculum and evaluation standards in 1989 that were widely accepted by teachers. These standards emphasized problem solving, reasoning, technology, communication, and the real-life application of mathematical concepts. Submitted year 2000 revisions stress increased attention to basic skills yet manage to reinforce the hands-on experiences that help students understand math facts.[21]

Mathematics instruction in elementary school focuses on basic skills and concepts: addition, subtraction, multiplication, division, fractions, decimals, percentages, graphing, calculator use and the rudiments of geometry. In secondary school, students are taught algebra, geometry, trigonometry, calculus, and computer programming.

Tension Points and Trends

According to the National Assessment of Educational Progress (NAEP), average mathematics performance improved between 1973 and 1990 for students at ages 9 and 13, while achievement recently increased for 17-year-olds.[22] International assessments suggest that Americans' mathematics skills do not compare favorably with those of students from other countries. A 1998 international study found that American seniors do not measure up to students in less developed nations in either general or advanced math knowledge (see Figure 7.4). Of twenty-four nations studied, American pupils turned in the worst performance.[23] In secondary school, females and students of color are scoring lower than white males.

A major focus of current curriculum reform is how to improve girls' mathematics test scores.

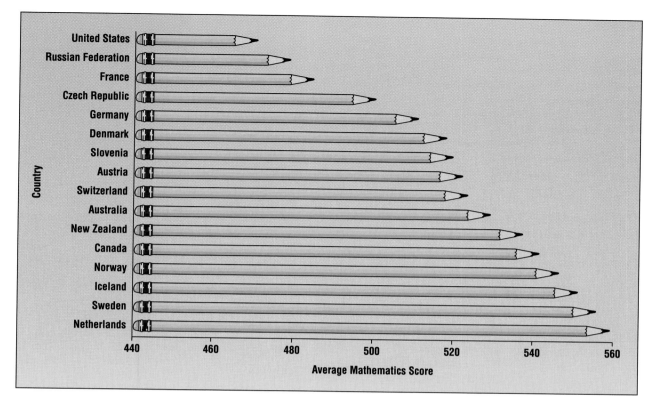

In 1992, the NCTM published *A Core Curriculum: Making Mathematics Count for Everyone*. The document suggested eliminating ability grouping and tracking and creating a core mathematics curriculum for all students. While algebra was previously taught only to eighth-grade students in the high-ability group, now all students should learn algebra. The report spoke to the need for students to see real-world applications of math and emphasized the use of computer and calculator graphics.[24]

Science

Topics

In the early elementary grades, science instruction emphasizes the child's orientation to the natural world—plants, animals, seasons, heat, sound, color, and light. The upper elementary grades typically study weather and climate, the solar system, electricity, and health. At the secondary level, the science curriculum includes biology, chemistry, physics, and earth and space sciences.

Tension Points and Trends

In international comparisons with students from other countries, U.S. students generally rank low in science achievement (see Figure 7.5). According to the 1990 NAEP, fourth- and eighth-grade science performance remained unchanged for twenty years, while twelfth-graders' performance dropped. Only 9 percent of the twelfth graders could demonstrate advanced scientific procedures. Fully 41 percent of the high school seniors reported never working on homework for their science classes.[25] Equally alarming was students' performance on a rigorous 1997 NAEP exam of basic science knowledge. Half of the fourth-graders proved unable to identify the Atlantic

FIGURE 7.4

Average mathematics score of twelfth-grade students, international mathematics and science test.

Source: Mullis et al. (1998). Mathematics and Science Achievement in the Final Year of Secondary School. Chestnut Hill, MA: Boston College.

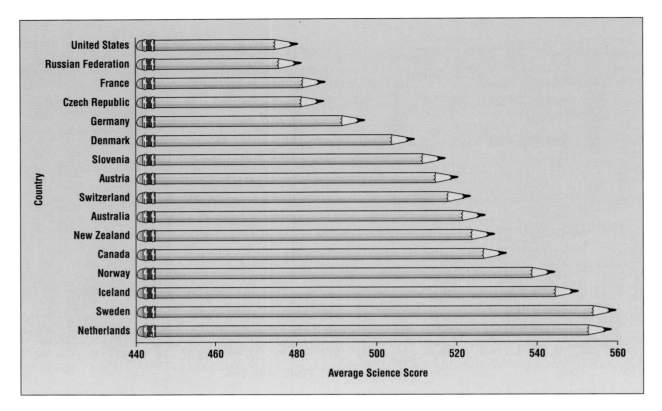

FIGURE 7.5

Average science score
of twelfth-grade
students, international
mathematics and
science test.

Source: Mullis et al. (1998).
Mathematics and Science
Achievement in the Final Year of
Secondary School. Chestnut Hill,
MA: Boston College.

and Pacific Oceans on a map, and many eighth-graders did not know how many days it takes the earth to circle the sun.[26] Try your hand at the sample problem in Figure 7.6.

In June 1998, the American Association for the Advancement of Science (AAAS) released the *Blueprints of Reform,* a study outlining necessary changes within schools, curricula, funding, and communities to enable American students to graduate from high school literate in math, science, and technology.[27] The AAAS standards emphasize learning through investigation and higher-order thinking, instead of rote memorization. The report urges that the number of concepts taught be reduced and deeper understanding of key scientific principles be encouraged. As did the mathematics standards, the science standards define a basic level of core knowledge for all students, regardless of background, ability level, or future aspirations. The proponents of "more is better" often come into conflict with those who believe "less can be more significant."[28]

Computers have the potential to significantly enhance science instruction. A challenge to the successful implementation of new science standards will be the schools' ability to provide students with costly technological resources and equipment.[29]

Foreign Languages

Topics

In 1915, 36 percent of all high school students studied a foreign language. By 1980, this percentage had been slashed by more than half, and only 5 percent of high school students continued their study of a foreign language for more than two years.

Today, the foreign language taught most often is Spanish, followed by French and German. The middle school curriculum includes grammar, vocabulary development, pronunciation, simple conversation, and appreciation of cultural diversity. In senior high school, the curriculum focus switches to conversational fluency, with expanded emphasis on the worldwide culture.

Tension Points and Trends

In a world where 2,700 languages are spoken, only 15 percent of its people are native English speakers. The language with the most speakers is Chinese, and Hindustani comes in second. The United States may be the most monolingual of all the developed countries. On the bright side, English has become the most common second language in the world—the language of business, science, and diplomacy.

This nation's geographic isolation has historically fueled our linguistic isolation, yet even that is changing as multilingual indicators appear at ATMs and telephone information services. As world travel and communication become commonplace, English language speakers will need to learn other languages to interact globally. Recently, many high schools and colleges have re-established foreign language requirements, and enrollment in these courses is climbing once again. Further, educators are calling for earlier emphasis on the study of foreign language—by the fourth grade and even before—and for blocks of time longer than forty or fifty minutes a day for the study of language.[30]

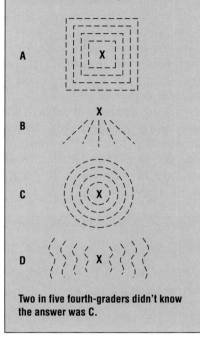

FIGURE 7.6

Sample problem on the NAEP test of basic science knowledge.

Source: National Assessment of Educational Progress

You stand on the end of a boat dock and toss a small stone out into a pond of still water. Ripples form on the surface of the water. Which drawing shows what you will see when you look down at the water? (X marks where the stone enters the water.)

Two in five fourth-graders didn't know the answer was C.

Technology

Topics

As computers flood American life, from the online trading of securities to cyber-dating, their use in the classroom continues its dramatic growth. Several states require computer literacy course work from kindergarten through twelfth grade. Often taught by teacher-specialists in computer labs, students learn sequenced skills, which may begin with technology games and keyboarding and move to web site development and software design. Other states integrate computers into subject area fields. Reading instruction, in the elementary grades, makes up the majority of technology time.[31] In high schools, computers are used primarily for word processing and computer literacy training. Schools continue to position themselves for the information age, as new equipment and school wiring run up budget costs. While solid research on academic effectiveness continues to evade most researchers, the "technological draw" of the computer age appears irresistible.

Tension Points and Trends

Despite the *e-rate,* which makes Internet connections available to schools at greatly reduced costs, today's classrooms still lack technological capabilities.[32] The National Center for Education Statistics (NCES) reports that, in 1996, over 50 percent of fourth-, eighth-, and twelfth-graders used a computer at school once a week or less. As disappointing as these statistics describing routine usage are, they represent a huge jump from 1984, when over half of students reported never using a computer at school at all. (See Figures 7.7 and 7.8 for computer use in selected subject areas.) In 1998, the NCES released *Technology at Your Fingertips,* a step-by-step guide for schools, detailing the process of acquiring computers, training users, obtaining technological support, and securing financial assistance. While providing each student with a computer is still far in the future, the federal government believes this goal is crucial to improving student performance.

Internet access in public schools has skyrocketed: in 1997, 78 percent of schools were online, compared with 35 percent just three years earlier. Although schools are going online, most classrooms are not. Also disturbing is the striking correlation between poverty and lack of Internet access. The NCES reports that schools serving students of color are far less likely to have access to either the World Wide Web or e-mail.[33]

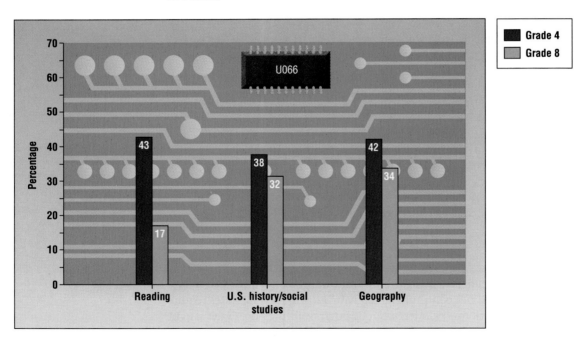

FIGURE 7.7

Percentage of students with teachers reporting the use of computers in teaching three subjects.

Source: NAEP Reading, History, Geography Assessment Electronic Data Almanacs, Teacher Questionnaire, National Assessment of Educational Progress, 1994.

While the focus is on providing students with access to computers and the Internet, few are asking what happens when schools finally do get hooked up electronically. While some studies suggest that student computer use is correlated to a rise in standardized test scores, that increase occurs only when teachers are well trained and comfortable with the technology.[34] All too often, teachers are unfamiliar with computer skills and have not received adequate training on how to integrate technology into the standard curriculum, seriously compromising the vast resources offered by computers.

		Percentage of students answering yes	
		Age 13	**Age 17**
Studied mathematics through computer instruction	1996	54 (1.8)*	42 (2.1)*
	1978	14 (0.9)	12 (1.1)
		Age 8	**Age 11**
Used a computer to write stories or papers	1996	91 (1.2)*	96 (1.1)*
	1984	15 (3.5)	19 (2.2)

Standard errors of the estimated percentages appear in parentheses.
* Indicates that the percentage in 1996 is significantly different than that in 1978 or 1984.

FIGURE 7.8

Computer comparisons in mathematics and writing.

Source: National Center for Education Statistics, National Assessment of Educational Progress (NAEP), 1996 Long-Term Trend Assessment.

The Arts

Topics

Visual arts, dance, theater, and music constitute the four comprehensive arts. The goals of the arts program include developing the ability to create art forms, understanding art as a cultural phenomenon, and developing aesthetic appreciation and perception. In elementary school, regular classroom teachers do most of the instruction in these areas. Children color, paint, and use materials to explore creatively and to use the elements of design (shading, size, and shape). In music, children learn sight reading and sing traditional childhood favorites, patriotic songs, and music from other lands. Drama and dance provide students with the opportunity to develop movement and related skills. In secondary school, the arts curriculum typically expands to include technical and graphic arts, design, crafts, theater, dance, film, photography, ceramics, sculpture, orchestra, band, chorus, and more specialized music courses.

Tension Points and Trends

Many educators consider the arts to be shamefully neglected—the last to be included and the first to be cut when the budget ax falls. The current emphasis on test score performance and core requirements has further diminished arts in schools. One study found that elementary schools commit only 4 percent of their school week to art instruction. Only 25 percent of that time is provided by trained art teachers. Further, some charge that there is too much emphasis on students' acquiring technical and performance skills, rather than gaining greater appreciation of aesthetics and human creativity.

In 1994, a panel of thirty-eight artists, educators, and business representatives approved new, voluntary standards for the arts curriculum that call for more ambitious and sequential instruction. The standards specify that, by high school graduation, students should have a basic level of competency in each of the four arts disciplines—dance, music, theater, and visual arts.[35] This Arts Education Consensus Project is the nation's most significant attempt to assess the arts with both qualitative and quantitative measures.[36]

Periodic curriculum reform efforts are nearly always motivated by competitive national goals, such as defense and economics. Should these goals always dominate the noncompetitive, humanistic concerns of the arts?

Physical Education

Topics

Research shows that physical education provides lifelong health dividends. High-quality programs emphasize not only physical competence and enjoyment but also social and psychological development, including leadership, teamwork, and cooperation. In the past few decades, there has been a shift away from competitive skill development to fitness and well-being through recreational and individual sports and well-rounded conditioning.

Elementary programs are structured around skill improvement, usually through games. Classes vary from little more than teacher-monitored recess to well-sequenced motor development instruction. Middle school programs are often the first time students have certified PE specialists, have a course of study, and "dress out" for class. By high school, the curriculum is governed by electives from aerobics to basketball.

Tension Points and Trends

According to the President's Council on Physical Fitness and Sports, our children are not physically fit. Fourteen percent of 6- to 11-year-olds and 12 percent of adolescents are overweight. Forty percent of boys cannot do more than one pull-up; 55 percent of girls cannot do any.[37] Forty percent of U.S. children between the ages of 5 and 8 exhibit obesity, hypertension, or high cholesterol.[38] The trends toward decreased childhood fitness and increased body fat are attributed primarily to high-fat diets and a lack of physical activity. Physical education classes account for less than 100 minutes of children's physical activity per week.[39] Illinois is the only state that retains daily physical education for all K–12 students, with Alabama and Wisconsin being lone partners in a K–8 daily requirement.[40]

Although in 1972 Title IX required physical education classes to be coeducational, many programs have remained silently gender-segregated.[41] Research shows that gender bias persists even in coed classes. By high school, boys are twice as likely as girls to be enrolled in physical education.[42]

IN THE NEWS . . . BACKPACKLESS

Public schools are getting serious about student backpacks. At North Carroll High School in Hampstead, Md., students may take backpacks to and from school but not to and from class. Teachers were having difficulty navigating the halls around the bulging packs, and administrators complained that food hidden in the packs was adding to the rodent problem. Other schools also were instituting backpack bans for fears ranging from transporting drugs or weapons to a concern that the weighty packs were contributing to back and neck problems.

Source: *The American School Board Journal,* November 1998.

Health

Topics

Years ago, health education meant little more than learning about the four basic food groups and routine dental care. A film on sex education at the high school level might "round out" the health program. However, we know that healthy children learn better across the curriculum. Today, many schools incorporate health education into both the elementary and secondary curricula. Areas for instruction include injury prevention and safety, consumer health services, nutrition and diet, substance abuse, disease prevention, and human growth and development.[43]

Tension Points and Trends

The same factors that put the health of our students at risk also create the public controversy that puts their health education classes at risk, especially in the areas of sex education, teen pregnancy, and AIDS and substance abuse prevention. Of adolescents aged 10–17, 25 percent are at high risk for premature illness or death, and another 25 percent are at moderate risk. When parents are unaware or incapable of dealing with these pressing health concerns, school programs may be the only valid source of information and understanding.[44]

Vocational and Career Education

Topics

Career education occurs informally in elementary school, with individual lessons on different occupations. At the secondary level, the **vocational education** curriculum is clearly targeted to specific types of work, and such course titles as "cosmetology," "auto body repair," "vocational printing," and "meal management" abound. "Tech prep" classes teach students word processing, systems administration, web page design, and even financial portfolio management. Computer-related vocational education also attracts many college-bound students seeking to gain that needed technical edge.

Despite the common belief that vocational education constitutes a discrete academic track for low-ability students who plan to work full-time after high school, a recent survey revealed that vocational education plays a much broader role. More than 97 percent of high school students take at least one vocational education course before graduation. Nearly half of all vocational education classes are taken by students who plan to attend a four-year or community college after high school.[45]

Tension Points and Trends

Critics point to statistics showing that students who graduate from vocational programs do not have an advantage in the job market, because vocational classes are often inadequate and irrelevant. Programs that lack modern equipment and well-trained staff cannot prepare students for high-tech fields. And the skills needed for low-paying jobs, such as work in fast-food restaurants, are better learned on the job than in school. Other opponents charge that a vocational curriculum tracks students into worthless nonacademic courses and should be abolished.

In 1990, Congress passed the **Carl D. Perkins Vocational and Applied Technology Act,** signaling a shift from the traditional job-skills orientation of vocational education to a broader integration with academic instruction. Proponents of this approach argue that higher-order thinking skills should be emphasized in all vocational courses in order to adequately prepare students for today's job market. The Perkins Act also channels federal funds to school districts with the highest proportions of poor students, promotes nonsexist career choices, assists displaced homemakers as they re-enter the job market, and offers support for post–high school vocational training programs.

The **School-to-Work Opportunities Act** (1994) directs federal funds to programs that contain three core elements: school-based learning, work-based learning, and connecting activities. In addition to the high school diploma, graduates receive an apprenticeship or a recognized skills certificate.

Toward Critical Thinking

Technological developments have shifted the focus of the U.S. economy from the production of goods (industrial) to information processing (postindustrial), as new careers in technology, computers, and communications emerge. This accelerated rate of change is also impacting the school curriculum. The tremendous knowledge explosion has produced more information than schools can teach, and many believe that schools need to turn away from the traditional curriculum and emphasize the thinking skills needed in the new information society.

What are these more relevant thinking skills? One of the pioneering works, *Teaching for Thinking: Theory and Application,* identified "thinking operations" that should be taught directly to students. These **critical thinking skills** include comparing, interpreting, observing, summarizing, classifying, decision making, creating, and criticizing. *Teaching for Thinking* incorporates these critical thinking skills into such subjects as mathematics and history, in which teachers ask higher-order questions that prompt students to analyze and evaluate data. Research indicates that not only do students learn critical thinking skills in such programs, but their knowledge of the content also increases when they apply these skills in the classroom.[46]

Teaching for Thinking is just one of several approaches. Following are some examples of other critical thinking programs.

- Edward de Bono attempts to teach thinking skills directly by helping students restate and diagram problems, break them into smaller parts, and compare them with similar problems that have already been solved.
- Arthur Whimby and J. Lochhead have developed procedures to help students be more systematic in their thinking. These exercises encourage students to work in pairs and externalize their thinking, or think aloud, so that errors and problems can be identified.
- Matthew Lipman's *philosophy for children* program offers classroom activities and a teacher education approach that emphasize reasoning by means of language skills and philosophy techniques.
- David Perkins of Harvard University's Project Zero emphasizes *thinking frames,* so that students develop a framework for acquiring information, internalizing practices, and transferring information.
- Reuven Feuerstein's *instrumental enrichment* curriculum stresses the development of such mental processes as comparing, classifying, and predicting. This Israeli psychologist has developed learning activities to help students adjust to and succeed in new environments.[47]

One of the best-known approaches, developed by Robert Marzano and his colleagues, identifies five dimensions of thinking:

1. **Metacognition** is awareness of one's own thinking while performing various tasks and operations. Metacognition enables students to monitor and control their commitment, attitudes, and attention during the learning process.
2. *Critical and creative thinking* are closely related. Critical thinking enables students to become objective and committed to accuracy and clarity, while creative thinking helps form new combinations of ideas that lead to original results.
3. *Thinking processes* are mental operations, such as comprehension, problem solving, decision making, research, concept and principle formation, composition, and oral discourse.
4. *Core thinking skills* are essential to the functioning of the broader dimensions of thinking. For example, the core thinking skill of goal setting can assist in the larger dimension of metacognition.
5. *Content-area knowledge and thinking skills* are connected in Marzano's program. Content specialists are encouraged to identify important models and modes of instruction in their academic disciplines and relate these to the dimensions of thinking.[48]

In addition to these five dimensions, Marzano has also explored personal characteristics that foster critical thinking. What personal traits and behaviors do you see as useful? As you might expect, Marzano found that open-mindedness and sensitivity to others allow in new information, so that it can be processed. People who value accuracy and clarity also possess fundamental traits related to critical thinking. Important traits for creative thinking include the ability to push one's own limits, the willingness to look at situations in new ways, and an ability to focus intensely on tasks. If these behaviors can be taught to students, they will become independent learners for the rest of their lives.[49]

The Curriculum Time Machine: A Historical Perspective

Like school itself, the curriculum serves a dual function. On the one hand, it preserves and transmits the culture and traditions of the past. On the other hand, it anticipates the knowledge, skills, and abilities that today's students will need in order to function effectively in tomorrow's society. Sometimes these two tasks—preserving and anticipating—come into conflict, and then some difficult curricular decisions must be made. When this clash occurs, it is important that the curriculum not be viewed as sacred and immutable, but as living and evolving, flexible enough to meet the emerging needs of a continually developing society.

Many of today's adults have witnessed a variety of curriculum changes in their lifetime. Men who went to junior high school in the 1950s and 1960s took a required course called "industrial arts," which was for boys only. Women who attended junior high school during this time took a required course called "home economics," which was only for girls. Today, some women can whip up a mean soufflé but are bewildered when confronted with even minor home repairs. Some men can fathom the intricacies of a house wiring system but work on one level when it comes to cooking—burned. There is nothing genetic about the ability to hammer a nail or measure a cup of flour: education and experience are needed to build skills.

Today, this gender split between industrial arts and home economics is disappearing as a result of the women's movement, federal law, and economic necessity. Girls now enroll in industrial arts, and boys study home economics. In many schools, these old courses now have more inclusive titles and activities, as girls and boys together learn to manipulate needles and wrenches, to change flat tires and to prepare meals.

Although most of you left high school just a few years ago, the curriculum you knew has changed even in that short span of time, responding to new needs and new perspectives. To see how social forces change the curriculum, we have created a curriculum time machine. Because Chapter 9, "The History of American Education," offers you a look at U.S. schooling from colonial times through the progressive era, this time machine will only briefly review this period, while emphasizing curricular issues from the 1950s to the present (see Figure 7.9). In fact, we will even begin to explore the future, setting the context for what and how you will teach.

Time Capsule 1: The Two *R*s in the Seventeenth Century

In the seventeenth century, religion underlay all human activity. Reading the Scriptures provided the route to salvation, and the "two *R*s" curriculum, a blend of reading and religion, prevailed. A white elementary student in those times would have acquired the rudiments of reading and religion from the **hornbook,** parchment attached to a paddle-shaped board and covered with a piece of transparent horn. If you were a white student toward the end of the century, you would be treated to a fear-inspiring dose of Puritan morality from America's first basal reader, **The New England Primer.** After elementary school, you would put away your hornbook if you were female. Secondary schooling was not offered to girls, while African Americans and Native Americans were routinely denied any formal education. If you were male and financially well off, you might go to the **Latin grammar school.** There

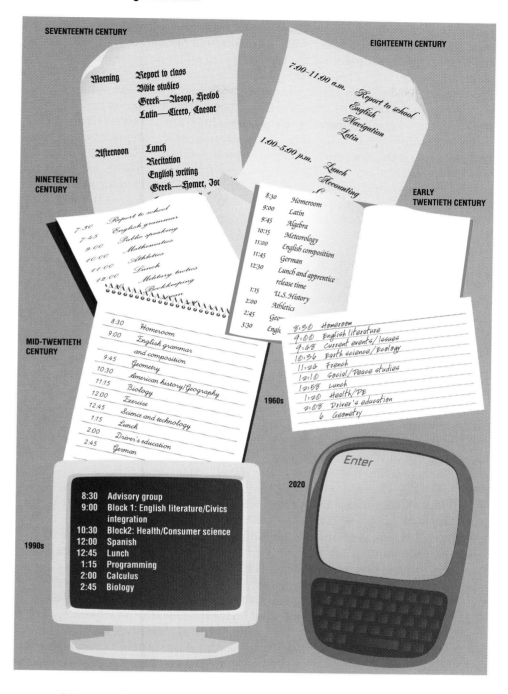

FIGURE 7.9

Student Class Schedules
Through Time.

you would learn Latin, Greek, and more Latin. If you grew weary of conjugating Latin verbs and translating Greek, you could always get a change of pace by reading the Bible and other religious texts.

Time Capsule 2: Curricula in the Eighteenth Century

New immigrants came to America, by choice or enslavement, and there was an upsurge in trade and commerce; the boundaries of the frontier stretched westward. These were optimistic times, with great faith in the progress and potential of humanity, dreams of fortunes to be made, and a growing commitment to life in the present instead of salvation after death. The shift from the spiritual to the secular began to free the curriculum from the tight bonds of religion. White elementary students still worked with *The New England Primer.* Studies focused on reading, religion, and morality, although writing and arithmetic were beginning to get more attention.

For secondary students, there were some new alternatives to the Latin grammar school. At the **English grammar school,** you could learn vocational skills, such as surveying, bookkeeping, accounting, and navigating. By the middle of the century, you could attend the **academy.** Academies were a blend of the Latin and the English schools, and they housed two different courses of study. You could choose either the traditional Latin curriculum or the English course of study, which included English grammar, some history, and foreign languages. The academy broke with tradition in another way, for its doors were open to women as well as men, though the color barriers remained.

Time Capsule 3: A Secularized Curriculum for More Students in the Nineteenth Century

The forces of nationalism, democratization, and industrial development spread across the land. As a result, universal literacy, vocational competence, and preparation for citizenship became curricular aims.

As an elementary school student, you would have traded in your *New England Primer* for McGuffey's readers. The course of study expanded to include writing, arithmetic, spelling, geography, and good behavior. As a secondary student, you would probably be enrolled in the academy, which by the middle of the century had become the dominant form of secondary school in America. You could choose either the Latin curriculum, which continued to focus on Latin, Greek, and arithmetic, or the expanding English curriculum, which included English grammar, public speaking, geography, history, and sometimes science, geometry, algebra, and a modern language—a long way from the two *R*s of the 1600s!

Time Capsule 4: Progressive Education in the First Half of the Twentieth Century

Migration changed our agrarian nation into a primarily urban one. New and diverse waves of immigrants (Irish, Polish, German, Jewish, Italian, Slovak, Greek, and Finnish) poured ashore; the schools were expected to Americanize them into a homogeneous and productive workforce. New educational philosophies, such as the progressive movement, were being explored, with John Dewey as its chief spokesperson.

As an elementary student, you would have time for creative expression in the form of drawing, painting, music, dance, and craftwork. Moreover, the rigid distinctions that had separated content fields were breaking down. Rather than studying history, geography, and civics, you would face an integrated course called *social studies.* *Language arts* encompassed reading, writing, speaking, and listening.

As a secondary student, you might attend the **junior high school,** which grew in popularity during the 1920s. Here a core curriculum stressed the integration of various subject areas, studying topics from "conservation in the development of American civilization" to "how I can use my spare time." During this period, high school changed from a college-oriented institution organized to meet the needs of the elite to a secondary school for most white Americans. By 1918, vocational courses, such as typing, stenography, bookkeeping, domestic science, and industrial arts, had joined the curriculum.

Immigrant children such as these were expected to be "Americanized" by the schools of the late nineteenth and early twentieth centuries.

Time Capsule 5: *Sputnik* in Space and Structure in Knowledge, 1940s–1960s

After World War II, the vocational and service-oriented courses of progressivism became known as **life-adjustment education.** As a student, you might have enrolled in such courses as "developing an effective personality" or "common learning," in which you would have studied your own social and personal problems. In the 1950s, the life-adjustment curriculum was ridiculed as anti-intellectual and undemocratic, and progressive education was under attack from many sides.

In 1957, the iciest of Cold War fears seemed to be realized, with the launching of the Soviet **Sputnik,** the first artificial satellite. The schools were made the scapegoat for the U.S. failure in the race for space. *Life* magazine urged an end to the "carnival" in the schools; Congress passed the National Defense Education Act (NDEA) and appropriated nearly a billion dollars for programs in science, math, modern languages, and guidance. Academicians and the lay public alike decried the schools' lack of intellectual rigor.

As a student after *Sputnik,* you and your classmates would have studied a foreign language and enrolled in rigorous math and science courses. Prestigious academicians became involved in curriculum development, particularly in math and science. One of these scholars was **Jerome Bruner,** a Harvard psychologist, who served as secretary of a conference of scholars, scientists, and educators at Woods Hole, Massachusetts. Bruner's report on this conference, ***The Process of Education*** (1960), had a major impact on curriculum. Translated into twenty languages and read by educators worldwide, this report put forward the premise that "any subject can be taught effectively in some intellectually honest form to any child at any stage of development."[50] Bruner conceptualized a discipline not as a collection of facts but, rather, in terms of its structure—the principles and methods of inquiry most central to its study. Bruner believed that, if students could learn these methods of inquiry, they could then study a field at different levels of sophistication. He envisioned the curriculum as a spiral in which students would return to the principles at the heart of the discipline and study them in progressively more complex and advanced forms. In terms of teacher training, Bruner advocated the **discovery method,** in which teachers would assist students in uncovering meanings for themselves.

Bruner's emphasis on the structure of the discipline intrigued scholars and curriculum developers, who then sought to categorize and sequence each body of knowledge. Thus, the students would grasp and build on basic principles and relationships, rather than memorize seemingly unrelated pieces of information. The result of this curriculum revolution was an array of discipline-oriented curricula, particularly in science and math.

Time Capsule 6: Social Concern and Relevance, 1960s–1970s

During the late 1960s and early 1970s, Cold War competition seemed less pressing, as racial strife and the war in Vietnam tore at the very fabric of our society. As a student of the times, you might have thought that the discipline-oriented curricula of the past decade were out of touch with the needs of disadvantaged children and alienated youth, the movement for civil rights, and the devastation of war overseas.

Once again, school curricula became the object of critical scrutiny, and once again they were found lacking—this time by critics who have been variously labeled the "radical," "compassionate," or **"romantic" critics.** Whatever their label, these critics were concerned about the irrelevance of curricula that emphasized academics at the expense of social reality.

New courses and topics burgeoned, spinning the curriculum into new areas. You would probably have found yourself studying an array of issues from multicultural curricula to your own attitudes and values. As you read about these curricular topics, consider how your own education may have been influenced by the social concerns of this era.

Women's Studies and Multiethnic Curricula

During the 1970s, curriculum developers began to design lessons, units, even entire programs, around the needs and contributions of women. These **women's studies** programs generally focused on patterns of sex bias and sought to compensate for the omissions of history and literature books, in which women and their contributions were systematically ignored. Educational institutions developed a **multiethnic approach** to the curriculum, particularly incorporated in social studies, language arts, and humanities.

Individualized Education Programs for Children with Disabilities

Public Law 94-142, the 1975 Education for All Handicapped Children Act, specified the components of the **individualized education program (IEP)** for each child who is eligible for special education: (1) assessment of the child's present achievement levels, (2) identification of goals and of the services needed to achieve those goals, and (3) systematic progress checks to see if the goals are being met or if they need to be revised. This act, renamed the Individuals with Disabilities Education Act (1990), remains controversial, as educators debate spiraling costs, accurate identification, and the impact of mainstreaming.

Social Issues: Death, War and Peace, the Environment

During the 1970s, some educators, psychologists, and parents opened up the curriculum to formerly taboo subjects, such as death and dying:

There is a need for guidance and knowledge about dying, grief, and bereavement [so that each child develops] an acceptance of death as a fact of life.[51]

Educators, also responding to the pervasive impact of violence and war, developed a peace curriculum through which students could analyze the conditions of peace, the causes of war, and the mechanisms for the nonviolent resolution of conflict. Courses in **peace studies** were first instituted in the 1960s, and, by 1974, twenty-nine colleges and universities had instituted either a certificate or an academic major in peace studies. In some cases, elements from these courses filtered down to secondary and elementary schools.

The 1970s ushered in an invigorated concern for the environment. Programs in ecology and **environmental education** stressed our planet's delicate environmental balance, and they continue to influence today's curricular materials.

The Open Classroom

In 1967, a Parliamentary commission in Great Britain encouraged English primary schools to adopt a child-centered approach called the **open classroom.** Based on the work of Swiss child psychologist Jean Piaget, the open classroom created **interest,** or **learning centers.** Children were encouraged to select activities they wished to pursue in these learning centers.

Today's recycling efforts have their roots in the environmental education programs that emerged in the 1970s.

Classrooms in the 1970s were exciting places, with students discussing topics ranging from war to changing sex roles; learning about the culture and heritage of various ethnic groups; studying sexuality, peace, drug, and consumer education; and moving freely from one interest center to another within the classroom. However, even as these innovations were occurring, newspaper editorials and articles in professional journals reflected a disenchantment with schools. The comments went something like this: "National tests show that our students are having trouble with reading, writing, and math. In view of this, what business do schools have dabbling in all these curricular frills? It's time to get back to the basics."

Time Capsule 7: Back to Basics and a Core Curriculum, 1980s–2000

There was no unifying manifesto for those who advocated **"back to basics."** The meaning of this movement varied from one individual and school to another. In the early 1980s, a composite of what many back-to-basics advocates wanted schools to do looked something like this:

1. Devote most of the elementary school day to reading, writing, and arithmetic.
2. Place heavy secondary school emphasis on English, science, math, and history.
3. Give teachers more disciplinary latitude, including the authority to use corporal punishment.

4. Use instructional procedures that stress drill, homework, and frequent testing.

5. Adopt textbooks that reflect patriotism and reject those that challenge traditional values.

6. Eliminate electives, frills, and innovations, such as peace education programs.

7. Test, test, and test. Tie student promotion from grade to grade and graduation from high school to demonstrated proficiency on specific examinations. Issue traditional report cards frequently to communicate and monitor student progress.[52]

The conservative *National Review* summed it up this way: "Clay modeling, weaving, doll construction, flute practice, volleyball, sex education, laments about racism, and other weighty matters should take place on private time." The public defined *back to basics* more succinctly as attention to the traditional subject areas of reading, writing, and arithmetic.[53]

The issue of declining test scores gave the movement its major impetus. Between 1952 and 1982, student scores dropped 50 points on the verbal part of the SAT and almost 30 points on the mathematics part. Parents and citizens were concerned about this negative trend. By 1977, the College Board had appointed a blue-ribbon panel to study the problem. The panel identified a number of issues needing resolution, including absenteeism, grade inflation, a lack of homework, and a profusion of watered-down electives.

Many researchers focused with alarm on this burgeoning number of electives as a cause for achievement decline. Philip Cusick found a mushrooming curriculum at the high schools he studied. For example, one high school had thirty-one separate courses in English; another had twenty-seven. There was a proliferation of easy electives, such as "girl talk," "what's happening?" "personal relations," and "trouble shooter." Also, activities that used to be extracurricular—yearbook, student council, newspaper, band, glee club—were often given academic credit.[54] Sara Lawrence Lightfoot, in her study *The Good High School,* also found a bewildering array of electives. One of the schools she visited had a 188-page catalog with more than 500 course descriptions. Career courses alone took up 23 pages.[55]

Even though the proliferation of electives may reflect academic richness, there is no doubt that students began to avoid the more rigorous courses. A U.S. Department of Education study showed that, between 1964 and 1980, students flocked from academic study to "personal service and social development" courses. In the 1960s, 12 percent of high school students were enrolled in these more open-ended electives. By the 1970s, enrollment had skyrocketed to 42 percent.

When faced with the question of whether to tilt in the direction of student choice or of a curricular core, most reform reports opted for the latter. For example, the National Commission on Excellence in Education report, *A Nation at Risk* (1983), called for new basics—four years of English, three years of mathematics, three years of science, three years of social studies, and one-half year of computer science.

In his book **High School** (1983), **Ernest Boyer** also called for a **core curriculum,** with the proportion of required courses increased from one-half to two-thirds of the total number of units necessary to graduate. He said that this core should include literature, history, math, science, foreign languages, the arts, civics, non-Western studies, technology, the meaning of work, and health. He advocated the abolition of the three traditional high school tracks (academic, general, and vocational), calling instead for the integration of all students into one track, with a

IN THE NEWS . . . BETTER LATE THAN EARLY

Minneapolis teenage students are sleeping about an hour later these days. Sleep authorities suggest that adolescent bodies can't manage early morning wake-up calls. The school district changed the 7:15 A.M. high school start time to 8:30 A.M. Middle schoolers don't start school until 9:40 A.M. What are the results of letting students sleep later? According to researchers at the University of Minnesota, these students are sleeping more, earning better grades, and experiencing less depression. And one more advantage: they are less likely to over sleep and miss school.

Source: *The Startribune.com,* November 1998.

pattern of electives radiating from the center of a common core of learning. Boyer also advocated a service requirement, which would involve students in volunteer work in their communities.[56]

Influential in the reform movement, John Goodlad's *A Place Called School* also recommended a core but stated that a common set of topics should not form the basis of the core. Rather, the core should comprise "a common set of concepts, principles, skills and ways of knowing."[57] Theodore Sizer's *Horace's Compromise* (1984) fueled the movement to reform public schools; it, too, emphasized the process of knowing. Arguing that less is more, Sizer believed that only certain essentials, such as literacy, numeric ability, and civic understanding, should be mandated.[58]

The reform report that placed the most stringent emphasis on core requirements was developed by philosopher and educator **Mortimer Adler,** in his controversial **The Paideia Proposal.** Adler advocated a required course of study that was the same for every child through the first twelve years of schooling. The only choice was the selection of which second language to study. Adler thought that electives only allow students "to voluntarily downgrade their own education."[59]

E. D. Hirsch, Jr., brought the issue of a core curriculum into the national spotlight with his best-selling **Cultural Literacy** (1987). According to Hirsch, the core cultural milestones can be identified. He extracted these markers and compiled them as lists of what literate Americans know.[60] "When the schools of the nation cease to transmit effectively the literate language and culture, the unity and effectiveness of the nation will necessarily decline."[61]

Time Capsule 8: New Directions for the Curriculum

While academic excellence and the core curriculum remain important, many educators are urging a widening of the core, an expansion to include more diversity and women. Others advocate a culturally specialized curriculum, such as Afrocentric education, to meet the unique needs of various ethnic and racial groups. This struggle to make the core more inclusive—or to change it—is complex and volatile, as demonstrated in the hotly contested debate over what should be included in national history standards (an issue explored in the next chapter).

Some reformers, frustrated by the dissected nature of the curriculum, its "egg carton" division of content into separated and disconnected academic disciplines, advocate an **integrated curriculum.** How, they ask, can you teach the Renaissance

The integrated curriculum uses activities that are innately interesting to create a variety of learning. Here, students performing in this play might incorporate literature and history lessons, artistic expression, and social learnings among others.

without connecting history, literature, music, and art? To slice knowledge into arbitrary and separated segments denies students a rich, textured, and coherent understanding of the past and present world.

Curricular integration faces many entrenched barriers, including class schedules, the physical structure of school buildings, and teachers themselves. A truly integrated curriculum makes enormous demands on the knowledge base of teachers, especially at the secondary level. Suppose, for example, you are a high school English teacher and your class is about to read *The Red Badge of Courage,* Stephen Crane's novel set during the Civil War. You have a B.A. in literature, with several credits toward your master's, and you have spent years developing and honing your academic specialty. However, you haven't had a history, math, or science course in years. How, you wonder, can you connect this novel to the history, music, and art of the Civil War? How can you possibly integrate scientific developments of the time—and work in some math as well? "You would integrate one step at a time," say curricular reformers, "and you wouldn't have to do it alone." There are many different models for helping students to connect their learning. Working more closely with teachers from other departments and grade levels is an important first step.

From these initial steps, the development of a connected curriculum can become a far more complex and sophisticated effort. As one advocate says, the connected curriculum would

> shun education which shortchanges insight, . . . which takes knowing a lot as a substitute for understanding, which tolerates the chocolate box model of learning—because learning like that will go stale the week after the test. It would emphasize connection-making performances within and across subject matter knowledge, performances that both build and show understanding. It would help to bring insight home to the classroom.[62]

As you have read how the curriculum has changed during the past decades, you may have felt a sense of déjà vu, with each innovation echoing past developments. There seems to be an ongoing struggle between educators who hold differing visions of what schools should/ought do. This debate between progressives and traditional-ists has yielded a history of curricular fads swinging with the motion of a pendulum. While other professions demonstrate steady, long-term progress, researcher Robert Slavin says that "education resembles such fields as fashion and design, in which change mirrors shifts in taste and social climate and is not usually thought of as true progress."[63] Many educators yearn for a more stable time when the radical curricular swing will be fine-tuned, so that innovation will depend more on research about what works than on the politics of who is in power. Only then can a reasonable and thoughtful compromise accommodate the legitimate concerns of various groups and best meet the needs of our students.

Summary

1. There are various forms of curricula in schools. One, the explicit curriculum, includes the courses offered, syllabi describing courses, tests given, materials used, and teachers' statements of what they want students to learn. The implicit, or hidden, curriculum, emerges incidentally from the interaction between the students and the physical, social, and interpersonal environments of the school. The extracurriculum, or cocurriculum, includes student activities, such as sports, clubs, student government, and school newspaper.

2. Extracurriculars have become fixed in the culture of American schooling, with 80 percent of all students participating in such activities as athletics, musical groups, and academic clubs. Proponents of the extracurriculum argue that it encourages student self-esteem and civic participation, improves race relations, and raises children's aspirations, as well as their SAT scores. Many remain skeptical, however, seeing extracurricular activities as having very little, if any, effect on achievement and personal development.

3. Controversies over the extracurriculum usually arise from conflict with the academic side of school. Some states have instituted "no pass, no play" rules, excluding low-achieving students from participating in varsity sports. Since these rules tend to affect minority students disproportionately, many people see these rules as making the extracurriculum exclusive and discriminatory. Others criticize the degree to which schools pour resources and attention into athletics, when that support could be going toward academics.

4. In addition to planned lessons, schools teach a hidden or implicit curriculum, subtle messages that students receive from teachers' and other students' behaviors.

5. School subjects are taught in the formal or explicit curriculum, which is currently undergoing scrutiny and revision. National standards have already been developed for math, science, geography, and other subject areas. The scope of these changes, as well as tension points, are reviewed in this chapter.

6. Curricula have two functions. One function is to preserve and transmit to students the culture and traditions of the past. The other is to anticipate the knowledge, skills, and abilities that today's students will need in order to function effectively in tomorrow's society. Sometimes these two functions of preserving and anticipating clash.

7. A significant curricular trend is the development of critical thinking skills. Educators believe that thinking must be taught directly and must be infused with the scope of subject matter content.

8. The seventeenth century witnessed the "two *Rs*" curriculum, emphasizing reading and religion. The only secondary schooling available was the Latin grammar school, which was open only to white male students who could afford the cost.

9. The eighteenth-century curriculum shifted toward the secular. The English grammar school and the academy became options for secondary schooling. White girls were allowed to attend the academy.

10. As a result of nationalism, democratization, and industrial development, the curriculum in the nineteenth century moved toward universal literacy, vocational competence, and preparation for citizenship. Elementary school studies included writing, arithmetic, spelling, geography, and good behavior. The academy was the dominant form of nineteenth-century secondary schooling until the last quarter of the century, when the academy gave way to tax-supported public high schools.

11. In the first half of the twentieth century, the curriculum was influenced by John Dewey and the progressive movement. Creative expression, social skills, and a more integrated study of subject areas were stressed. The junior high concept became popular during the 1920s. The mission of high schools was to meet the needs of all the students, not only the college-bound. By 1918, vocational course work had become an important part of the curriculum.

12. In 1957, the Soviets launched *Sputnik,* and weak American schools were viewed as the reason for the country's defeat in the race for space. As a result, the curriculum became discipline-oriented, particularly in math and science.

13. The curriculum in the late 1960s and the 1970s focused on social issues, with particular emphasis on the needs and contributions of women and minorities. Public Law 94-142, the Education for All Handicapped Children Act (later renamed the Individuals with Disabilities Education Act), required developing an individualized education program for each special needs child. Other issues emphasized in the curriculum were peace studies, ecology, and the secular presentation of topics relating to death.

14. Popular in the 1970s, open classrooms were divided into flexible areas called interest, or learning, centers. Children were encouraged to explore the classroom and choose activities they wished to pursue.

15. The curriculum of the 1980s was marked by the back-to-basics movement. Triggered by the problem of declining test scores, this movement stressed achievement in the traditional subject-matter areas. Today there is an ongoing debate over emphasizing a curricular core versus presenting the student with a variety of electives. Most reform reports urge a return to a core curriculum. There are also current movements toward an integrated or a connected curriculum and toward national standards as a way of unifying and improving schools (described in the next chapter).

Key Terms and People

www.mhhe.com/sadker

A Place Called School	critical thinking skills	Jules Henry
academy	*Cultural Literacy*	*High School*
Mortimer Adler	curriculum	E. D. Hirsch, Jr.
"back to basics"	discovery method	hornbook
basal readers	English grammar school	implicit (hidden) curriculum
Ernest Boyer	environmental education	individualized educational
Jerome Bruner	extracurriculum	program (IEP)
canon	formal or explicit curriculum	integrated curriculum
core curriculum	John Goodlad	interest (learning) centers

junior high school
Latin grammar school
life-adjustment education
metacognition
multiethnic approach
National Association of
  Educational Progress
  (NAEP)
open classroom

peace studies
Carl D. Perkins Vocational
  and Applied Technology
  Act
phonics
romantic critics
School-to-Work
  Opportunities Act
Sputnik

Hilda Taba
The New England Primer
The Paideia Proposal
The Process of Education
vocational and career
  education
whole language
women's studies

Discussion Questions and Activities

1. For some students, the hidden curriculum and the extracurriculum are most central to their high school experience. Define the roles of these unofficial curriculum experiences in your own high school education. If you were placed in charge of a high school today, how would you change these hidden and extracurricular experiences? Why?

2. Discuss your reactions to the current curriculum with your classmates. Were there any topics you studied that you now see as irrelevant? What subjects should be taught differently? Are there any subjects that are not included in the curriculum but that should be there?

3. If you were given the job of developing a core curriculum for elementary school, what would it look like? What would you include in a core curriculum for secondary school? for postsecondary education?

4. Reconsider your high school curriculum experience. Estimate the proportion of required courses versus electives. Did students perceive the electives as an opportunity to explore areas of interest or to avoid more rigorous courses? If you were in charge of a school's offerings, would you increase or decrease electives? Why? What particular electives would you want to design and teach?

5. "Critical thinking has always been a silent partner in the curriculum." Do you agree or disagree?

6. Consider past and present curricular developments and think about the changes in contemporary society. Then, with the help of your instructor and classmates, formulate what the school curriculum may be like in the year 2020.

Controversy over Who Controls the Curriculum

Focus Questions

- What forces shape the school curriculum?
- Why are school books so frequently the targets of censorship?
- Is a national curriculum a good idea?
- How do textbook publishers and state adoption committees "drive" the curriculum?
- What are the seven forms of bias in instructional materials?
- How does politics affect curricula decisions?
- Can the curriculum transmit our national heritage and still meet the demands of a changing world?
- Is the United States going test crazy?
- What is the teacher's role in curriculum development?

Chapter Preview

"We shape our buildings and afterwards our buildings shape us," said Winston Churchill. Had the noted statesman been a noted educator, he might have rephrased this epigram, substituting *curriculum* for *buildings,* for what children learn in school today will affect the kind of adults they will become and the kind of society they will eventually create. In fact, it is the power of curriculum to shape students and, ultimately, society that takes curriculum development out of the realms of philosophy and education and into the political arena.

In buildings from the little red schoolhouse to the White House, adults (and, occasionally, their charges) discuss what is supposed to be learned in school. How curriculum decisions are actually made and applied is the crux of this chapter.

```
┌─────────────────────────────────────────────────┐
│              YOU'VE GOT MAIL                     │
├─────────────────────────────────────────────────┤
│ TO: Steve@AU.edu                                │
│ FROM: Anna@State.edu                            │
│ SUBJ.: You had to be there!                     │
├─────────────────────────────────────────────────┤
```

After weeks of observing schools, students, and teachers, we are now looking at curriculum, so I watched three teachers do language arts. You wouldn't believe the differences.

One teacher grouped kids by reading level (no—they weren't called bluebirds). The teacher's aide went to each group and used questions from an instructor's guide to quiz the students about the story. The stories were all about kids, too, about the same age and ethnic background as the students in the class.

In another room, the whole class was reading one book (must have been a kid classic I missed) and they were going through it page-by-page. Some were struggling word-by-word while others were zooming through, then waiting for the rest to catch up.

Then there's the third class. They meet once a week in the library, to use the resources and computer lab. They were doing their "own thing." A few were online, finding out about spiders (they had all read *Charlotte's Web*), and others were setting up acting parts, as if they were turning it into a drama. A few students were meeting with the teacher, who was really focusing on reading skill development.

Me? I'm on pre-panic. I am supposed to assist in one of the classes, and I won't know which one until next week. Do I put the instructor's guide with prepared questions under my pillow, read the "kid classic," or learn about arachnids? Teachers have such totally different approaches!

Censorship and the Curriculum

Ruth Sherman lived just outside New York City, in a Long Island neighborhood known for its Italian community and easy commute to the city. Although she traveled only a short distance to P.S. 75, where she taught third grade, she might as well have been teaching in another country. P.S. 75 was in the Bushwick section of Brooklyn, a graffiti-filled neighborhood populated by poor black and Hispanic families living in the midst of a rampant drug culture. "Why there?" her friends asked her. "Because I want 'to turn things around,'" she responded. She was that kind of teacher. But, in just three months, it was Ruth Sherman, and not her students, who was turned around.

Her problems started in September, although she did not learn about it until later, when she assigned a book called *Nappy Hair,* by African American author Carolivia Herron. Her students loved the book, about a little black girl with "the nappiest, fuzziest, the most screwed up, squeezed up, knotted hair," and clamored for copies to take with them. By Thanksgiving, the parents in Ruth Sherman's class had also discovered the book, which they considered racially insulting. At a parents' meeting, she was confronted by fifty parents (most of them parents of children not in her class), who shouted racial epithets and eventually threatened her. The superintendent sent Ruth home, for her own protection. A review of the book followed. The review brought only praise for a book that promoted positive images for children and presented stories that appealed to them. Within a few days, the superintendent wrote her a letter, commending her performance, inviting her back to the school, and promising security escorts to protect her. But, by then, it was too late. Ruth Sherman, the teacher who wanted to make a difference, did not want to work in a climate that required "escorts" to ensure her safety. She transferred to another school.[1]

This incident occurred in 1998 in New York, but it could occur anywhere at anytime. Nearly everyone—teachers, parents, the general public, and various special interest groups—wants some say as to what is and is not in the school curriculum. No matter what content is found in a particular textbook or course of study, someone is likely to consider it too conservative or too liberal, too traditional or too avant-garde, racist, sexist, anti-Semitic, violent, un-Christian, or pornographic. When this happens, pressure to **censor** the offending materials soon follows. Religious conservatives are often a major source of censorship attempts; however, as the New York case illustrates, censorship can emanate from almost any quarter, liberal or conservative.[2]

There is no such thing as a totally safe, acceptable, uncontroversial book or curriculum. Each of the following has been subjected to censorship at one time or another:

- Mary Rodgers's *Freaky Friday:* "Makes fun of parents and parental responsibility"

In a multicultural society, to what extent should vocal community groups concerned about a particular issue (sex, religion, abortion, politics) be allowed to influence the school curriculum?

- George Eliot's *Silas Marner:* "You can't prove what that dirty old man is doing with that child between chapters"
- Plato's *Republic:* "This book is un-Christian"
- Jules Verne's *Around the World in Eighty Days:* "Very unfavorable to Mormons"
- William Shakespeare's *Macbeth:* "Too violent for children"
- Fyodor Dostoyevsky's *Crime and Punishment:* "Serves as a poor model for young people"
- Herman Melville's *Moby Dick:* "Contains homosexuality"
- Anne Frank's *Diary of a Young Girl:* "Obscene and blasphemous"
- E. B. White's *Charlotte's Web:* "Morbid picture of death"
- Robert Louis Stevenson's *Treasure Island:* "You know what men are like and what they do when they've been away from women that long"
- J. R. R. Tolkien's *The Hobbit:* "Subversive elements"
- Roald Dahl's *Charlie and the Chocolate Factory:* "Racist"
- William Steig's *Sylvester and the Magic Pebble:* "Anti-police" (one of the police officers is drawn as a pig)
- *Webster's Dictionary:* "Contains sexually explicit definitions"[3]

According to People for the American Way, during the 1995–1996 school year, there were 475 incidents of attempted censorship in forty-nine states.[4] In about half of the cases, censorship was imposed and the materials were either removed or placed on restricted-access shelves in libraries.[5] The most frequently challenged books between 1982 and 1996 were

- John Steinbeck's *Of Mice and Men*
- J. D. Salinger's *The Catcher in the Rye*
- Robert Cormier's *The Chocolate War*
- Mark Twain's *The Adventures of Huckleberry Finn*
- Maya Angelou's *I Know Why the Caged Bird Sings*
- Roald Dahl's *The Witches*
- Alvin Schwartz's *Scary Stories to Tell in the Dark*
- Alvin Schwartz's *More Scary Stories to Tell in the Dark*
- Anonymous, *Go Ask Alice*
- Katherine Paterson's *Bridge to Terabithia*[6]

At the heart of the case against censorship is the First Amendment, which guarantees freedom of speech and of the press. Those who oppose censorship say that our purpose as educators is not to indoctrinate children but to expose them to a variety of views and perspectives. The case for censorship (or, perhaps in a more politically correct phrase, "strict selection") is that adults have the right and obligation to protect children from harmful influences. For instance, challenges to books that include—critics say "promote"—homosexuality have become commonplace.[7] From the classroom to the courtroom, each side makes a compelling case for its own point of view.

The censorship controversy is symbolic of how politicized the curriculum debate has become. What knowledge is of most worth? Who decides? How is it transmitted? Who gets access to it? What information is left out? These questions are fundamentally political. Those who determine what should be known and who should know it have powerful influence over students, for they define how a society thinks and behaves.

IN THE NEWS . . . HOLLYWOOD CENSORED IN CASTLE ROCK

Castle Rock, Colorado has decided that *Schindler's List* should not be used in schools. Students will have to learn about the Holocaust without the Academy Award winning movie. The old school board required parental permission to show films rated "R" or "NC-17." Now, even with such permission, these films and videos are not permitted.

Source: *New York Times,* 28 January 1998.

Who and What Shape the Curriculum?

Parental and Community Groups

The scenario at the beginning of this chapter illustrates the power of parents to control classrooms, curricula, and instructional materials. Some citizens have pressured schools to provide courses as varied as drug education, student study skills, advanced technology, and changing gender roles. In more conservative communities, religious fundamentalists have objected to the absence of Christian values. Others who feel that job preparation is a key purpose of schools want a heavy emphasis on career and vocational education. Yet other parents see vocational preparation as a waste of time and want schools to emphasize the basics.

Students

Students are sometimes skeptical about the wisdom and honesty of people in high places; schools, being the institution students are most familiar with, have received a large share of their criticism. During the 1960s and 1970s, student protests covered all phases of the school curriculum. Demanding relevance, students tried to infuse more practical application into the formal curriculum and to liberalize the rules and rituals that constituted the hidden curriculum. Although students have not been particularly successful in influencing curriculum policy recently, they are able to influence individual lessons and units by selecting topics for independent projects, research papers, book reviews, and even authentic learning. Moreover, the Internet has substantially increased the amount of information available to students.

Administrators

The emphasis on the principal not only as a manager but also as an instructional leader has, in some cases, generated greater administrator involvement in curriculum development. For example, an elementary school principal may attend an in-service course on critical thinking skills and then urge teachers to include this topic in their instruction. Sometimes central-office personnel, such as language arts coordinators, play a major role in curriculum change in a system or district. Although administrators may involve teachers, community members, and students in curriculum planning, they usually retain the power to make many curricular decisions themselves.

The Federal Government

The federal government influences the curriculum by sponsoring school-related legislation and by promoting national education goals. For example, the National Defense Education Act (NDEA) of 1958 encouraged public schools to emphasize math, science, and foreign languages in order to train future scientists for the space race with the former Soviet Union. The Elementary and Secondary Education Act (ESEA) of 1965 influenced the curriculum in various ways, perhaps most notably in the development of special programs for children from low-income families. Federal programs, such as these, are usually updated and modified by different presidents and Congresses.

The federal government also flexes its educational muscle by identifying and promoting national goals. For example, to meet the economic challenges from abroad, several recent administrations have promoted the idea of national standards and national testing. While some states view the creation of national goals as a way to promote school quality, other states fear that this is the first step in creating a national curriculum, reducing the power and influence of the state government.

The State Government

States are now assuming a stronger leadership role in education, and their interest in curriculum matters has sharpened. While states have long exerted their influence over the curriculum, block grants from the federal government and court actions demanding financial reforms have moved state governments to center stage in educational reform. States issue curriculum guides and frameworks, which identify the topics and skills to be taught and the courses students must take in order to graduate.

Politics often play a big role in these state decisions. In more conservative states, the role of religion and the treatment of evolution versus creationism are hot button issues. In more liberal states, instructional materials are expected to include ethnic and racial diversity and to reflect the experiences and contributions of women.

Local Government

Local school boards, composed of elected or appointed citizens, make a variety of curriculum decisions, requiring courses from AIDS education to technology. Some educators and citizens feel that local school boards should have a strong voice in the curriculum, because they are closest to the needs of the local community and have a clear sense of the abilities and interests of the students. Others feel that school board members lack the training and broad perspective needed to maintain a flexible curriculum in touch with national issues. Although boards are intended to represent all groups within the community, in reality their membership is usually upper-middle-class and male.

Colleges and Universities

Institutions of higher learning influence curricula through their entrance requirements, which spell out courses students must have taken in order to gain admittance. Many secondary schools base their academic curricula on these college and university stipulations. During the 1990s, increased student enrollment in foreign language and advanced math and science courses reflected changes in college admissions requirements. As Bartlett Giamatti noted when he was president of Yale University,

> The high schools in this country are always at the mercy of the colleges. The colleges change their requirements and their admissions criteria and the high schools . . . are constantly trying to catch up with what the colleges are

thinking. When the colleges don't seem to know what they think over a period of time, it's no wonder that this oscillation takes place all the way through the system.[8]

National Tests

The results of national tests, such as the SATs or **National Assessment of Educational Progress (NAEP),** influence what is taught in the school. If students perform poorly in one or more areas of these countrywide tests, public pressure may push school officials to strengthen the curriculum in these weak spots.

Schools of education are not immune to the current focus on test performance. Because an increasing number of states are requiring new teachers to take qualifying tests, such as the National Teacher Exam (NTE, Praxis series), these tests have some influence on what is covered in teacher education programs. For example, if Benjamin Bloom's *Taxonomy of Educational Objectives* were emphasized on the NTE, teacher education programs across the nation would modify their curricula to make certain this high-stakes test topic is included in their programs.

National tests can have a positive influence in holding the school curriculum to high standards. However, their influence is less beneficial when teachers allow the tests to dictate their teaching styles and curricula.

Education Commissions and Committees

From time to time in the history of U.S. education, various committees, usually on a national level, have been called to study an aspect of education. Their reports often draw national attention and, subsequently, influence elementary and secondary curricula. The 1983 report by the National Commission on Excellence in Education called for new basics, with increased emphasis on academic subjects. In the 1990s, the National Commission on Teaching and America's Future declared that all children are entitled to "competent, caring and qualified teachers" by the year 2006.[9] While national goals are not always met, (we hope this one is!) such goals often move education in a positive direction. Added momentum for change is provided when educational commissions focus public attention on international comparisons, such as graduation rates. (See Figure 8.1.)

Professional Organizations

Many professional organizations—such as the National Education Association (NEA), the American Federation of Teachers (AFT), the National Association for the Education of Young Children (NAEYC), and numerous subject area associations (teacher groups in English, math, science, and the like)—publish journals and hold conferences that emphasize curriculum needs and developments. Their programs and materials may focus on teaching with technology, multicultural education, or authentic learning. Teachers inspired by these presentations might choose to modify their curriculum and implement new approaches and ideas.

Special Interest Groups

Major business and professional organizations—from labor unions to media conglomerates—have educational outreach programs, replete with curricular materials and instant lesson plans. These "how to" pieces range from using a daily newspaper for social studies to bringing the Olympics to your gymnasium. They are often so current and well framed that they are easily added to a teacher's agenda. Sometimes, these special interest packages become part of the formal curriculum. In addition, citizens' groups with wholesome names such as Citizens for Excellence in Education or

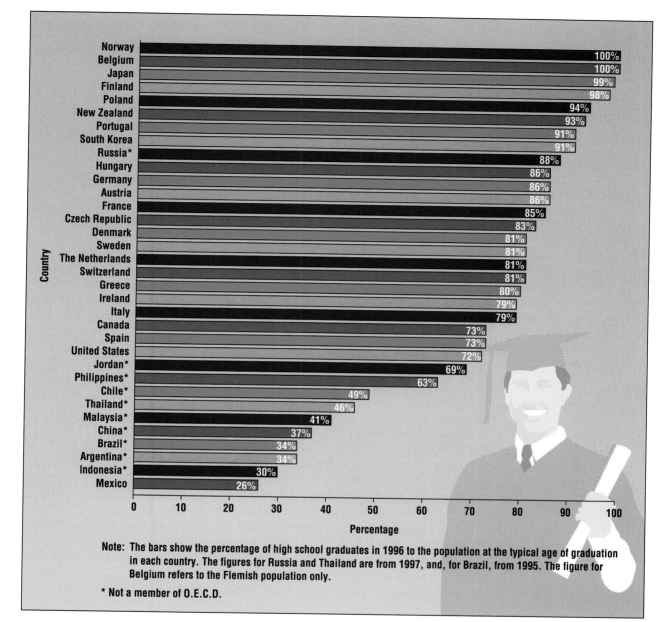

Note: The bars show the percentage of high school graduates in 1996 to the population at the typical age of graduation in each country. The figures for Russia and Thailand are from 1997, and, for Brazil, from 1995. The figure for Belgium refers to the Flemish population only.

* Not a member of O.E.C.D.

Family Friendly Libraries can exert strong pressures on such curricular issues as bilingual education, evolution, ebonics (black English), whole language instruction, and multiculturalism.

FIGURE 8.1

High school graduation rates in selected countries.

Source: *Education at a Glance*, OECD Indicators, 1998

Toward a National Curriculum

As you might expect, the collision of various interest groups has created curricula that are not particularly characterized by logic or planning. In fact, frustrated education reformers have often cited the haphazard, disorganized manner in which schools create their curriculum as an obstacle to improving education and have targeted this process for change. Into the 1990s, the United States was the only industrial nation without math and science standards. In

FIGURE 8.2

Groups shaping the
curriculum.

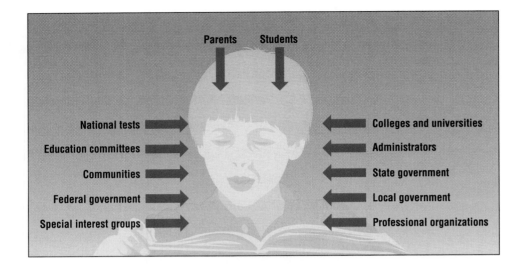

the early 1990s, the Bush administration began funding a project that harnessed the
efforts of experts in mathematics, history, English, physical education, and other
fields in a project aimed at giving some order and direction to the nation's curriculum
development. The National Education Standards and Improvement Council was
formed to oversee the project. Working with such organizations as the National
Council for Geographic Education, the National Council of Teachers of Mathematics,
and the National Academy of Sciences, educators and content area experts worked to
develop specific subject-matter guidelines, detailing precisely what students across
the United States should know at each grade level. The guidelines would serve as a
national yardstick, enabling one school district to compare its performance with that
of others.

More to the point, **national standards** were intended to improve school performance. With higher, uniform national curricular goals in place, educators in local
school districts would be motivated to implement more rigorous programs, and all
students would need to work harder. The end result of this effort would be "world-
class" students, as U.S. students moved from the bottom, or near-bottom, ranks in
international tests to the top. The popular Republican plan was also a popular Democratic plan, and President Clinton continued this effort with Goals 2000. Soon things
began to unravel, however, especially in history.

The publication of the proposed history standards prompted a storm of
criticism:

"Plan to Teach U.S. History Is Said to Slight White Males"
   (*New York Times* headline)

"History Hijacked"
   (Charles Krauthammer, *Washington Post*)

"The History Thieves"
   (*Wall Street Journal* headline)

The critics were led by Lynne Cheney, a former official in the Bush administration,
who argued that, in the new curriculum, white men were being slighted, business
leaders maligned, and heroes omitted. Lynne Cheney characterized the new standards as "a warped view of American history."[10] No such outburst had accompanied
the publication of the national standards for mathematics five years earlier. Forty-one

IN THE NEWS . . . STANDARDS

The Milwaukee school system placed an ad in a local newspaper entitled: *High Standards Start Here*. The ad explained that the system had *rigourous* standards and tough *proficiencey* exams.

Source: *The American School Board Journal,* June 1997.

states quickly adopted the mathematics standards, and math textbooks were modified accordingly. For mathematics, a national curriculum began to take shape.[11] Why was the process of adopting standards relatively easy for math but difficult for history? The basic reason is that mathematics raises few values questions, while other disciplines, such as history, live and breathe values. Here are just some of the values questions raised by history standards:

- Should traditional heroes, sometimes called "DWM" (*dead white males*)—such as Washington, Jefferson, and other revered Americans—be the focus of the curriculum, or should the experiences and contributions of other groups, women and people of color, be researched and included?
- Should history continue to emphasize European roots, or should Afrocentric issues be included? What about the views of other groups? For instance, should a penetrating view of European settlement of the Americas as seen through the eyes of Native Americans and Mexican Americans be taught to school children?
- Should U.S. history tell only a story of victors and triumphs, or should it also relate varied views of social, cultural, and economic issues?

The new history standards did not please those with traditional Eurocentric values, both because of what the standards omitted—for example, such familiar names as Daniel Webster, Paul Revere, and the Wright brothers—and because of what they included. Myra Colby Bradwell, for example, was included. Who was she? She was the first woman who took her bid to be admitted to the Illinois bar all the way to the Supreme Court. The Civil War received a different perspective as well, going beyond a chronology of battles to include an account of Northern riots by poor laborers who were being drafted for the deadliest war in American history, while rich men simply paid $300 and avoided the draft. It is clear that, whatever the standards, some Americans will be offended.[12]

So touchy is the issue of a national curricular movement that—like "Newspeak"—even the words used to designate it carry hidden meaning. If this effort had been termed a "standard, federal curriculum," rather than "national standards," it would have encountered even greater opposition. *Federal* suggests enforcement, a "strong arm" approach, but *national* indicates that everyone will be included—a far less offensive concept. *Standards* for a curriculum suggests that there may be multiple routes for meeting each standard, that schools can choose from different materials and a variety of approaches in order to accomplish these goals. But *standard curriculum* suggests inflexibility, a lock-step program that all must follow. Political criticisms

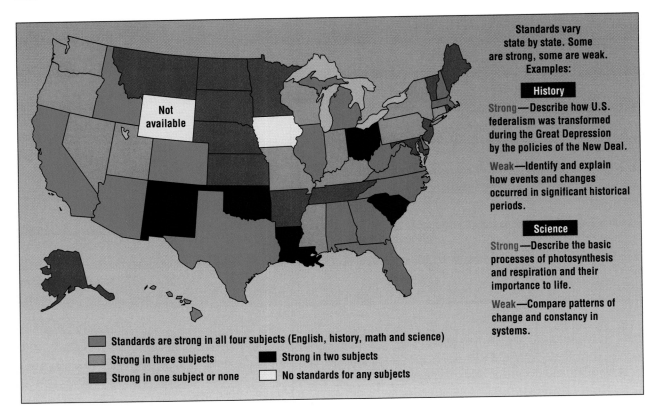

Standards vary state by state. Some are strong, some are weak. Examples:

History

Strong—Describe how U.S. federalism was transformed during the Great Depression by the policies of the New Deal.

Weak—Identify and explain how events and changes occurred in significant historical periods.

Science

Strong—Describe the basic processes of photosynthesis and respiration and their importance to life.

Weak—Compare patterns of change and constancy in systems.

☐ Standards are strong in all four subjects (English, history, math and science)
☐ Strong in three subjects   ■ Strong in two subjects
■ Strong in one subject or none   ☐ No standards for any subjects

---

FIGURE 8.3

State Views of National Standards. While standards are intended to have a national impact, their impact varies dramatically from state to state.

Source: *Time* Oct 27, 1997

and budget cuts directed at standards result in more sensitive and less offensive wording. Consequently, reformers suggest that not only will 50 to 70 percent of state standards be acceptable but, over time, they will be quite similar![13]

The Textbook Shapes the Curriculum

While national standards in *all* subjects continue to elude resolution, the textbook continues to dictate the curriculum in many of today's classrooms. Students spend from 70 to 95 percent of classroom time using textbooks, and teachers base more than 70 percent of their instructional decisions on them. Given this heavy reliance on texts, there is no doubt that they have a major daily influence on what is taught in schools. In fact, they are so pervasive and so frequently used that they constitute a curriculum of their own.

Before 1850, textbooks were made up of whatever educational materials children had in their homes. Students took these books to school, and instruction was based on them. Picture yourself trying to teach a class with the wide array of random materials children have in their homes. Although today we might use these personal resources to supplement instruction, back then it was difficult to teach with such disparate materials. In fact, despairing teachers appealed for common texts, so that all students could use the same materials. Local legislators responded by requiring schools to select appropriate books, and then parents were required to buy them. When families moved, they often had to buy new books. Concerned about the costly burden this lack of consistency placed on families, legislators mandated commonly used textbooks across larger geographic areas.

NATIONAL CURRICULUM BALANCE SHEET PERFORMANCE

The Good News
With Higher Standards, We Become More Economically Competitive

If we are going to succeed as a powerhouse in a highly competitive world economy, our workers must be well educated and able to acquire new information and technological skills in a rapidly changing world. The skills and talents of our workforce will be our real advantage—or our Achilles heel. See what is happening without these standards. Today, too many high school graduates must be retrained or brought to a level of basic literacy by the corporations that hire them. This sort of educational inefficiency has lowered our standard of living. With national standards, we can once again mobilize the nation's resources and successfully meet the economic challenges from abroad.

The Bad News
Performance: For Many Students and Schools, National Standards Are a Step Down

Any set of national standards must be viewed as a compromise, standards that can be met by the weakest as well as the strongest school districts. National standards would do nothing for strong school districts. And simply establishing higher standards would become little more than an exercise in frustration for the weaker schools that need resources, not merely reminders of how weak they have become. A set of national standards would provide neither incentive to the nation's best schools nor the funding needed by the weakest. Moreover, many believe that our educational system prepares very efficient workers. In fact, with frequent corporate downsizing of scientists and engineers, we may be overeducating our workforce. It seems that the workers most in demand are service personnel, who require a very limited formal education.

NATIONAL CURRICULUM BALANCE SHEET UNITY

The Good News
A National Curriculum Will Bind the Nation

If we are to survive as a united nation, we need a unifying experience. Schools provide that cohesive thread. As children, we all learn the same stirring stories of national leaders, of the development of our social institutions, and of our common heritage. This shared destiny and history tie our mainly immigrant nation together. So does a shared literary experience, as all students read and discuss the same great books and understand how our ideas and experiences have formed our culture. Without such a curriculum, we can become dangerously pluralistic and suffer the risk of becoming not one nation but several. There are already examples of countries that have lost this common thread and whose cultures have disintegrated.

The Bad News
The Effort to Create a National Curriculum Will Divide the Nation

While it is comforting to believe, as Hirsch and Bloom do, that cultural literacy can be defined, that we can all decide on what stirring stories to tell, which facts to remember (and which to forget), and which national leaders to study, we simply cannot agree on a single list of what is important, what is worth knowing. In fact, while learning popular facts and dates may be wonderful preparation for being a contestant on *Jeopardy,* or winning at "BLURT!", it does not create a common, national culture. What is important to one group of Americans may be unimportant to another. In fact, the effort to create such a national curriculum only highlights the obvious fact that there is no such consensus. The quest to find a national curriculum will divide our people.

Today, the process of textbook development and adoption has come under intense criticism. One of its chief critics, Harriet Tyson Bernstein, says,

Imagine a public policy system that is perfectly designed to produce textbooks that confuse, mislead, and profoundly bore students, while at the same time making all the adults in the process look good, not only in their own eyes, but in the eyes of others. Although there are some good textbooks on the market, publishers and editors are virtually compelled by public policies and practices to create textbooks that confuse students with non sequitors, that mislead

NATIONAL CURRICULUM BALANCE SHEET FROM LOCAL TO CENTRAL CONTROL

The Good News
Local Parochialism Will Be Eliminated
National standards will bring new insights and diverse points of view to the nation's children. Rather than being held hostage to the desires and views of local school boards, students will be able to consider broader perspectives. Children from liberal or conservative neighborhoods will be introduced to each other's point of view. The implementation of national standards can end debilitating local parochialism by broadening students' horizons, effectively countering the myopic views of so many communities.

The Bad News
Central Control of Our Lives Will Grow
The authors of the Constitution had it right—freedom and individual liberties are best protected without a "big brother" telling us what to believe, what is important. Every time there is an election, values change and new messages are sent. There is no central, federal wisdom. Local communities and individuals know their children best, and they hold the practical wisdom that made this nation great. All we need is faith in the common sense of Americans, because they do know what's best for their children.

NATIONAL CURRICULUM BALANCE SHEET TESTING

The Good News
Everyone Is Not Above Average
Garrison Keillor, in his *Lake Wobegon* radio show, always described the students in his town as "above average." Sometimes it seems that all of the nation's students are "above average," until you compare them with students from other countries—then it is obvious that they are well below average. Too many standardized achievement tests do not do the job needed, which is to objectively measure programs. The public and educators need to use national test scores to determine how well students are performing and whether programs are effective (that is, should the program be kept, modified, or discarded?). Because so many different tests are in use, no sense can be made of their scores. Even the SATs and ACTs are not taken by everyone. National standards would mean national assessments, honest numbers showing us how our schools, students, and teachers are doing. They would enable Americans to compare our educational efforts with those of past generations and in different geographic regions. They are long overdue.

The Bad News
Everyone Is Not the Same
Testing, testing, testing—it creates as many problems as it solves. Teachers and administrators do not want their schools to look bad, so they teach to the test. Test-driven instruction tends to deprofessionalize teaching. Many teachers will choose to leave the profession rather than teach to the test. Subjects not included on national tests will quickly be eliminated from the curriculum, because only "tested subjects" will affect a school's status or a student's future. Paper-and-pencil tests will dominate, but not all knowledge lends itself to paper-and-pencil exams. Higher-order skills and concepts will be replaced by simpler, discrete segments of information that are easier to assess. Test results often mislead the public because they reflect test-wise skills, not real learning. Moreover, some students "freeze" on such tests. In fact, tests rarely capture unique student talents, such as artistic skills. How many creative talents will be submerged and lost by national tests that reduce students to the lowest common denominator?[14]

them with misinformation, and that profoundly bore them with pointedly arid writing.

None of the adults in this very complex system intends this outcome. To the contrary, each of them wants to produce good effects, and each public policy regulation or conventional practice was intended to make some improvement or prevent some abuse. But the cumulative effects of well-intentioned and seemingly reasonable state and local regulations are textbooks that squander the intellectual capital of our youth.[15]

Here's how the system works and why Bernstein and other opponents are so angry. In 1900, when our current textbook system was designed, twenty-two states enacted laws that put in place a centralized adoption system. More than twenty states, located mainly in the South and the West, are **textbook adoption states.** (These states are indicated in Figure 8.4.)

Under a state adoption system, local school districts typically select their texts from an official, state-approved list. Those in favor of statewide adoption claim that this process results in the selection of higher-quality texts. This system creates a common, statewide curriculum, which unites educators and makes school life easier for students who move to different schools within the state. State adoptions also save time and work for educators at the local level, and, because of the large numbers of books purchased, the per book cost is kept low.

There is also criticism of statewide adoptions, much of it attacking the **Texas and California effect.** When these populous states buy textbooks for the students in their schools, the result is enormous income for the publishing companies. As you can well imagine, a publisher's dream is to be selected as one of very few "approved" sources of textbooks, especially in a populous state such as these. Critics charge that the huge revenues involved give these large states unfair influence over textbook development.

Criticism of the adoption does not stop with the influence of large states. Many textbook evaluators have limited training for their role, a problem that also filters down to the district and school levels. Often, severe time constraints hamper careful decision making. Reviewing large numbers of books in brief periods of time, harried committee members sometimes flip through a book to determine its merit. Publishers are well aware of this "flip phenomenon" and make sure that their books have "eye appeal." Teachers and site administrators asked to select a textbook, whether from a state-approved list or not, can be influenced by the cosmetics—the cover, the graphics, the headings, the design. While visual attractiveness can have a positive effect on learning, it is no substitute for well-written and accurate content.

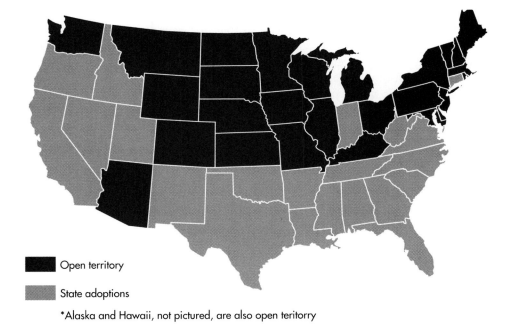

FIGURE 8.4

Textbook adoption states. While some school districts are free to choose any text, others are limited to state approved textbooks.

Source: Publishers Resource Group, Inc, Austin, Texas, 1998

■ Open territory

■ State adoptions

*Alaska and Hawaii, not pictured, are also open teritorry

IN THE NEWS . . . STRONGER GLUE NEEDED?

David B., a member of the Texas State Board of Education, objected to the content in an Algebra textbook. When his objection was considered inadequate, he pointed out that the book also had manufacturing defects, additional grounds for rejection. He demonstrated the manufacturing defects by ripping the book apart.

Source: *The American School Board Journal,* January 1998.

Frequently, adoption committees are given criteria sheets to assist them in determining textbook quality. Some criteria sheets are incredibly brief and general; others, in a well-intentioned attempt to be comprehensive, are long and unwieldy, too cumbersome to be used efficiently.[16]

Criteria sheets often include information on the books' readability, yet another problematic area. By sampling several passages, **readability formulas** assess word difficulty and sentence length to determine the reading skill level for the book. Initially, the use of readability formulas seemed a promising development. What could be more reasonable than making sure the books reading level was grade-appropriate? But readability formulas have created their own problems. Readability levels vary widely from passage to passage, so it is possible to find eleventh-, eighth-, seventh-, and fourth-grade passages in a single book designated as fifth-grade level. Worse yet, the different readability formulas give different results. For one text, the Spache readability formula indicated a 3.1 grade level, the Dale-Chall 4.2, and the Gunning 4.0, and the Fry put the text at the seventh-grade (7.0) level.[17]

Since some states will buy texts only if they have a specified reading level, publishers are under pressure to develop books that meet this criterion. Often, authors avoid difficult words and long sentences, so that, for example, *esophagus* becomes *food tube* and *protoplasm* becomes *stuff.* The result, according to former secretary of education Terrell Bell and other critics, is the **dumbing down** of the textbook. Ironically, readability formulas may make books harder, not easier, to read. When authors simplify vocabulary, they replace precise and clear terminology with simple, vague, even ambiguous words. When authors shorten sentences, they often leave out the connective issue—*and, but, therefore*—words that clarify the relationships between events and ideas. Shortening sentences to make reading simple can make understanding challenging ideas even more difficult.

Writing to the readability level not only hurts comprehension but "squeezes the juice out of some very fine tales."[18] For example, the following is one such distorted reading text version of "The Tortoise and the Hare":

Rabbit said, "I can run. I can run fast." "You can't run fast," Turtle said. "Look Rabbit. See the park. You and I will run. We'll run to the park."

Rabbit said, "I want to stop. I'll stop here. I can run, but Turtle can't. I can get to the park fast." Turtle said, "I can't run fast. But I will not stop. Rabbit can't see me. I'll get to the park."[19]

IN THE NEWS . . . TEXTBOOK OBITUARY?

University of Virginia professor Thomas Estes says that textbooks *cover more but uncover less* and are becoming peripheral to teaching. The textbook's curricular dominance is fading due to the increased use of technology and the Internet, the rapid growth of knowledge that makes texts quickly outdated, political disputes over textbook adoptions, the presence of various reading levels in the same class, and the desire of teachers to create their own learning activities.

Source: *Washington Post,* 20 March 1998.

In this textbook version, the characterization is gone. So is the moral. So is the meaning.

As textbooks skim over content, simply to *cover* it, the student loses sufficient information necessary for comprehension. Critics charge that texts typically include too many subjects and gloss over them to such a degree that students do not really understand what is going on. Students are as frustrated by this **mentioning phenomenon** as the adult critics; they say,

> Sometimes they just mention a person's name and then don't talk about them anymore in the whole book.

> They should talk more about each topic. For the War of 1812 there should be more information about the fighters and the treaties. What did the Treaty of Ghent contain? Who wrote it?[20]

One reason for the mentioning phenomenon is the knowledge explosion. But another cause can be traced to the adoption process. In their quest for higher scores on standardized tests, many states have called for aligning the curriculum in textbooks with what is on standardized tests. Adoption committees have delineated in minute detail all the names, dates, and places they want included. In many districts, textbooks are required to cover all the topics in a course syllabus; consequently, publishers, who must try to appeal to many districts and a variety of course syllabi, frequently trade off reasonable explanations and clarifying examples in favor of mentioning lots of names, places, and dates. When authors try to include everything, any sense of coherence is lost. The context essential for comprehension is deleted. So are vignettes that would give more flavor to the narrative.

Researchers have also found that basal readers and other texts, in attempting to be inoffensive to potential purchasers, include only a limited range of story types, often devoid of interpersonal and internal conflict.[21] In their efforts to satisfy local and regional groups, some companies even publish alternative versions of the same book. For example, in some texts, Thanksgiving is truly a "movable feast": if you grew up in Massachusetts, your social studies book may have told you that the first Thanksgiving took place in Plymouth; if you went to school in Virginia, you may have learned that this great celebration occurred in Jamestown.

Another problem is that texts, especially in social studies, still largely chronicle the events of white men. Although women and people of color are included more frequently than in the past, they still suffer from tokenism, and American society as a whole is presented in an unrealistic, even idealized manner. As one disgruntled critic concludes, "Adoption states, special interest groups, and readability formulas have all contributed to produce textbooks designed by a committee, written by a committee, and selected by a committee to please all and offend none."[22] Despite these efforts, textbooks often seem to please none and offend all.

Seven Forms of Bias

Many Americans are passionate about how various groups are portrayed in textbooks. In the 1970s and 1980s, textbook companies and professional associations, such as the American Psychological Association, issued guidelines for nonracist and nonsexist books; as a result, textbooks became more balanced in their description of underrepresented groups. Today, educators work to detect underrepresentation of those groups, not only in the texts but also in other resources, including the Internet, computer simulations, field trip experiences, guest lecturers, video and fine arts productions, and the extra handouts that so many use to compensate for less than satisfying resources. Moreover, today we have a better understanding of the various manifestations of bias.

Following is a description of **seven forms of bias,** which can be used to assess instructional materials.[23] Although this approach has been used to identify bias against females and various racial and ethnic groups, it can also help identify bias against the elderly, people with disabilities, non-English speakers, gays and lesbians, limited English speakers, and other groups.

Invisibility

Perhaps the most fundamental form of bias in instructional materials is the complete or relative exclusion of a particular group or groups from representation in text narrative and/or illustrations. Research suggests, for example, that textbooks published prior to the 1960s largely omitted any consideration of African Americans within contemporary society and, indeed, rendered them relatively invisible in accounts of or references to the United States after Reconstruction. Latinos, Asian Americans, and Native Americans were largely absent from most resources as well. Many studies indicate that women, who constitute more than 51 percent of the U.S. population, represented approximately 30 percent of the persons or characters referred to throughout the textbooks in most subject areas.

Stereotyping

By assigning rigid roles or characteristics to all members of a group, individual attributes and differences are denied. While stereotypes can be positive, they are more often negative. Some typical stereotypes include

- African Americans as servants, manual workers, professional athletes, troublemakers
- Asian Americans as laundry workers, cooks, or scientists
- Mexican Americans as non-English speakers or migrant workers
- Middle-class Americans in the dominant culture (white Anglo-Saxon-Protestant) as successful in their professional and personal lives

Teachers serving on textbook adoption committees apply specific criteria to determine text suitability for their curriculum.

- Native Americans as "blood-thirsty savages" or "noble sons and daughters of the earth"
- Men in traditional occupational roles (rarely as husbands and fathers) and as strong and assertive
- Women as passive and dependent and defined in terms of their home and family roles

Imbalance and Selectivity

Curriculum may perpetuate bias by presenting only one interpretation of an issue, a situation, or a group of people. These imbalanced accounts simplify and distort complex issues by omitting different perspectives. Examples include

- The origins of European settlers in the New World are emphasized, while the origins and heritage of other racial and ethnic groups are omitted.
- The history of the relations between Native Americans and the federal government is described in terms of treaties and "protection," omitting broken treaties and progressive government appropriation of Native American lands.
- Sources refer to the fact that women were "given" the vote but omit the physical abuse and sacrifices suffered by the leaders of the suffrage movement that "won" the vote.
- Literature is drawn primarily from Western male authors.
- Math and science courses reference only European discoveries and formulas.

Unreality

Many researchers have noted the tendency of instructional materials to ignore facts that are unpleasant or that indicate negative positions or actions by individual leaders, or the nation as a whole. By ignoring the existence of prejudice, racism, discrimination, exploitation, oppression, sexism, and intergroup conflict and bias, we deny children the information they need to recognize, understand, and perhaps some day conquer the problems that plague society. Examples of unreality may be found in programs that portray

- People of color and women as having economic and political equality with white males
- Technology as the resolution of all our persistent social problems

IN THE NEWS . . . HUCKLEBERRY FINN ALLOWED TO STAY IN SCHOOL

Tempe, Arizona high schools will continue using Mark Twain's *The Adventures of Huckleberry Finn* and William Faulkner's *A Rose for Emily,* according to a federal court judge's ruling. An African American parent had filed suit to remove these books from the required reading list because they contained the word "nigger." The parent complained that her daughter was made to feel uncomfortable reading the word and that the books created a racially hostile environment that increased the likelihood of harassment. The school had previously received complaints that white students were harassing blacks with racial slurs and graffiti. The court ruled that such books cannot be banned on the basis of content even if the intent was to reduce racism.

Source: *Washington Post,* 20 October 1998.

Fragmentation and Isolation

Bias through fragmentation or isolation primarily takes two forms. First, content regarding certain groups may be physically or visually fragmented and delivered separately (for example, a chapter on "Bootleggers, Suffragettes, and Other Diversions"), or even in boxes at the side of the page (for example, "Ten Black Achievers in Science"). Second, racial and ethnic group members may be depicted as interacting only with persons like themselves, isolated from other cultural communities. Fragmentation and isolation ignore dynamic group relationships and suggest that nondominant groups are peripheral members of society.

Linguistic Bias

Language is a powerful conveyor of bias in instructional materials, in both blatant and subtle forms. Written and verbal communication reflects the discriminatory nature of the dominant language. Linguistic bias issues include race/ethnicity, gender, accents, age, (dis)ability, and sexual orientation—for example,

- Native Americans are frequently referred to as "roaming," "wandering," or "roving" across the land. These terms might be used to apply to buffalo or wolves; they suggest a merely physical relationship to the land, rather than a social or purposeful relation. Such language implicitly justifies the seizure of native lands by "more goal-directed" white Americans, who "traveled" or "settled" their way westward.
- Such words as *forefathers, mankind,* and *businessman* deny the contributions and existence of females.

The insistence that we live in an English only, monolingual society creates bias against non-English speakers in this country and abroad. An imbalance of word order ("boys and girls") and a lack of parallel terms ("girls and young men") are also forms of linguistic bias.

Cosmetic Bias

Cosmetic bias offers the appearance of an up-to-date, well-balanced curriculum. The problem is that, beyond the superficial appearance, bias persists. Cosmetic bias emerges in a science textbook that features a glossy pullout of female scientists but includes precious little narrative of the scientific contributions of women. A music book with an eye-catching, multiethnic cover that projects a world of diverse songs and symphonies belies the traditional white male composers lurking behind the cover. This "illusion of equity" is really a marketing strategy directed at potential purchases who *flip* the pages and might be lured into purchasing books that appear to be current, diverse, and balanced.

Religious Fundamentalism

Some parents and educators argue that publishers have not gone far enough in producing nonsexist, multicultural books, but others believe that the publishers have gone much too far. While censorship attacks can originate from either liberals or conservatives, since the 1980s, they have been much more likely to come from conservative quarters. One such conservative group is Christian fundamentalists. **Christian Bible,** or **religious, fundamentalists** (sometimes called the **religious Right**), generally believe in a strict interpretation of the Bible and advocate a conservative social agenda. Such issues as abortion and evolution can spark a strong reaction from these groups.

> Pressures from the politically organized religious Right have made it risky for publishers to discuss evolution. If evolution is discussed at all, it is often confined to a chapter in the book. Students are conducted on a forced march through the phyla, and given no understanding of the overarching theory (evolution) that gives taxonomy life and meaning. Touchy subjects like dinosaurs, the fossil record, genetics, natural selection, or even the scientific meanings of the words "theory" and "belief" are treated skimpily or vaguely in order to avoid the ire of the Bible fundamentalists.[24]

Scenes like this one involving overt religious prayer have been banned from the school curriculum. Should the study of religion as a vital social force also be banned or watered down because it is politically dangerous?

The following two cases provide examples of the nature of these controversies.

Case 1. A 1986 case in eastern Tennessee made headlines when a group of fundamentalist Christian families objected to a series of Holt, Rinehart & Winston readers. They objected to an illustration in a first-grade reader showing a kitchen scene with a girl reading while a boy cooks (he is making toast). The plaintiffs argued that "the religion of John Dewey is planted in the first graders [sic] mind that there are no God-given roles for different sexes.[25] The plaintiffs also objected to *The Diary of Anne Frank,* which was cited as being antireligion in its acceptance of diversity in religious belief and practice. Consider the following passage:

ANNE: (Softly) I wish you had a religion, Peter.

PETER: No, thanks! Not me.

ANNE: Oh, I don't mean you have to be Orthodox . . . or believe in heaven and hell and purgatory and things . . . I just mean some religion . . . it doesn't matter what. Just to believe in something! When I think of all that's out there . . . the trees . . . the flowers . . . and seagulls . . . when I think of the dearness of you, Peter . . . and the goodness of the people we know . . . Mr. Kraler, Miep, Dirk, the vegetable man, all risking their lives for us everyday. . . . When I think of these good things, I'm not afraid anymore.[26]

Other categories called "offensive" included "futuristic supernaturalism, one-world government, situation ethics or values clarification, humanistic moral absolutes, pacifism, rebellion against parents or self-authority, role reversal, role elimination, animals are equal to humans, the skeptic's view of religion contrasting belief in the supernatural with science, false views of death and related themes, magic, other religions, evolution, godless supernaturalism . . . and specific humanistic themes."[27]

Case 2. During the spring of 1988, an assignment from Robert Marzano's *Tactics for Thinking* unleashed a storm of controversy in southern Indiana. Protesters charged that the following exercise could induce a self-hypnotic trance:

Have students focus their attention on some stimulus (e.g., a spot on the wall). Explain to them that you want them to focus all of their energy for about a minute and ask them to be aware of what it is like when they are really trying to attend to something.[28]

Many community members were persuaded that the book was brainwashing children into believing in a one-world government and religion. In Battle Ground, Washington, a group of citizens claimed that *Tactics for Thinking* was teaching the occult. Thomas McDaniel, dean of Converse College, reported that, in one county, *St. George and the Dragon, Puss in Boots,* and *Sylvester and the Magic Pebble* were dropped from the reading curriculum. Parents objected because they were about magic.[29] In at least a dozen other states, there were protests against these and other books connected with the New Age movement or secular humanism.

It is hard to define what is sometimes called the **New Age movement** and **secular humanism:** humanists might define these terms as living ethically without recourse to the supernatural or to organized religions. Opponents contend that "secular humanists" deny God, a creator, or any divinity by promoting global education, the occult, values clarification, Eastern mysticism, and a belief in a one-world government and religion. Termed *pseudoreligious beliefs,* critics charge that secular humanists promote "agnosticism, various forms of feminism, environmentalism, political liberalism and conservatism, various ethnic or sexual identities, and many more."[30]

Since his experience with textbook censorship in case 2 previously described, Marzano differentiates between Christian fundamentalists, a conservative religious group, and Christian reconstructionists. **Christian reconstructionism** is a grass-roots movement aimed at restoring Christianity to the public schools. Marzano says the group is growing at a geometric rate and is responsible for the increasing number of censorship attacks on books used in public schools.[31] Censorship can tie a school system into knots and pose a genuine threat to academic freedom.

While many people are perplexed by secular humanism, Christian reconstructionism, and New Ageism, fundamental Christian concerns have highlighted what could be an important educational issue: the invisibility of religion in our history textbooks. Three studies of public school textbooks, funded by the Department of Education, Americans United for the Separation of Church and State, and People for the American Way, have agreed that textbooks minimize the importance of religion in American life. Although 96 percent of Americans believe in God or a universal spirit and 58 percent go to a place of worship at least once a month, history texts do not reflect this reality.[32] For example, an analysis of forty social studies texts for grades 1 to 4 found that the majority of these books made no reference to any kind of religious activity. In one sixth-grade book, "Thank God" was changed to read "thank goodness" in an Isaac Bashevis Singer story. One history book told about the life of Joan of Arc without ever noting her religious beliefs, and other books described Thanksgiving without referring to the religious beliefs of the Puritans. In one book, the Pilgrims were defined as "people who make long trips"; in another, fundamentalists were described as rural people "who follow the values or traditions of an earlier period." The importance of religion in inspiring social movement such as the labor movement, prohibition, abolition, civil rights, and protests against the Vietnam War, is rarely noted.

There is an important difference between *teaching about* religion and *promoting* religion. Today's texts fail to discuss adequately many religious issues that are intellectually complex and socially controversial. Columnist Ellen Goodman suggests that as publishers retreat from controversy, they also retreat from many important lessons. Goodman points out that the strength of our nation, what children really need to learn, is that our history has not always had happy endings, and that we have not yet resolved all our differences. In fact, Americans may never resolve all of their differences. The lesson to be taught to children is that we can live together as a people and not agree on everything.[33]

Cultural Literacy or Cultural Imperialism?

Both George Orwell and Aldous Huxley were pessimists about the future. "What Orwell feared were those who would ban books," writes author Neil Postman. "What Huxley feared was that there would be no one who wanted to read one."[34] Perhaps neither of them imagined that the great debate would revolve around neither fear nor apathy but, rather, deciding which books are most worth reading.

Proponents of **core knowledge,** also called **cultural literacy,** argue for a common course of study for all students, one that ensures that an educated person knows the basics of our society. Novelist and teacher John Barth laments what ensues without core knowledge:

> In the same way you can't take for granted that a high school senior or a freshman in college really understands that the Vietnam War came after World War II, you can't take for granted that any one book is common knowledge even among a group of liberal arts or writing majors at a pretty good university.[35]

Allan Bloom's *The Closing of the American Mind* was one of several books that sounded the call for a curriculum canon. A canon is a term with religious roots, referring to a list of books officially accepted by the church or a religious hierarchy. A **curriculum canon** applies this notion to schools by defining the most useful and valued books in our culture. Those who support a curricular canon believe that all students should share a common knowledge of our history and the central figures of our culture, an appreciation of the great works of art and music and, particularly, the great works of literature. A shared understanding of our civilization is a way to bind our diverse people.

Allan Bloom, professor of social thought at the University of Chicago, took aim at the university curriculum as a series of often unrelated courses lacking a vision of what an educated individual should know, a canonless curriculum. He claimed that his university students were ignorant of music and literature, believing that too many students graduate with a degree but without an education.[36] One of the criticisms of Bloom's vision was that his canon consisted almost exclusively of white, male, European culture. Critics charged that the canons were loaded with "dead white males."

E. D. Hirsch, Jr., in his book *Cultural Literacy,* was more successful than Bloom in including the contributions of various ethnic and racial groups, as well as women. This is a rarity among core curriculum proponents. In fact, Hirsch believes that it is the poorer children and children of color who will most benefit from a cultural literacy curriculum. He points out that children from impoverished homes are less likely to become culturally literate. A core curriculum will teach them the names, dates, places, events, and quotes that every literate American needs to know in order to succeed. In 1991, Hirsch published the first volume of the core knowledge series, *What Your First Grader Needs to Know.* Other grades followed in these mass-marketed books directed not only at educators but at parents as well.[37] Try your hand at identifying some of Hirsch's core curriculum concepts:

Achilles

Homer

Uriah Heep

John Bull

je ne sais quoi

Pike's Peak

phylum

ukelele

Uncle Tom

Emile Zola[38]

Not everyone is enamored with the core curriculum idea. A number of educators wonder who gets included in this core, and, just as interesting, who gets to choose? Are Hirsch, Bloom, and others to be members of a very select committee, perhaps a blue-ribbon committee of "Very Smart People"? Why are so many of these curriculum canons so white, so male, so Eurocentric, and so exclusionary?

It is not surprising that many call for a more inclusive telling of the American story, one that weaves the contributions of many groups and of women as well as of white males into the textbook tapestry of the American experience. Those who support **multicultural education** say that students of color and females will achieve more, will like learning better, and will have higher self-esteem if they are reflected in the pages of their textbooks. And let's not forget white male students. When they read about people other than themselves in the curriculum, they are more likely to honor and appreciate their diverse peers. Educator and author James Banks calls for increased cultural pluralism:

> People of color, women, and other marginalized groups are demanding that their voices, visions, and perspectives be included in the curriculum. They ask that the debt Western civilization owes to Africa, Asia, and indigenous America be acknowledged. . . . However, these groups must acknowledge that they do not want to eliminate Aristotle and Shakespeare, or Western civilization, from the school curriculum. To reject the West would be to reject important aspects of their own cultural heritages, experiences, and identities.[39]

What balance should schools seek between teaching a common core curriculum that binds all Americans together and teaching a curriculum that celebrates the many cultures that have been brought to the United States?

Some opponents of cultural literacy take a more radical approach. They believe that an ethnocentric school curriculum is fine, as long as the focus for black children is Africa. **Afrocentrists** argue that African American children have been dislocated—first by their ancestors' removal from Africa and today by a school that devalues their history and culture. Their ideas have led to innovations, such as the African American immersion schools.

> A is for Armstrong, B is for Banneker, C is for Carver. For children at Victor Berger Elementary School, African American culture is the foundation of all instruction.
>
> The first graders are learning to count from 1 to 10 in Swahili as well as English. They know that the colors of the African American flag are red, black, and green just as surely as they know the American flag is red, white, and blue. And at art time, the children identify the pipe cleaner spiders they are making not as the itsy-bitsy spider in the well-known song but as the clever Anansi of African folk tales.[40]

Critics claim that an Afrocentric curriculum has no place in a public school, where common American values and culture should be taught. They worry about the disuniting of American school and society. Should there also be a curriculum that is centered on Asia or Latin America? Should these be further divided into separate strands for children from Vietnam or Nicaragua? As noted historian Arthur Schlesinger wonders,

> What good will it do young black Americans to take African names, wear African costumes, and replicate African rituals, to learn by music and mantras, rhythm and rapping? . . . Will such training help them understand democracy better? Help them fit better into American life? . . . The best way to keep a people down is to deny them the means of improvement or achievement and cut them off from the opportunities of the national life.[41]

Advocates of a core curriculum claim that it will empower the poor and the disadvantaged. Opponents say it will rob them of the chance to see their experiences reflected in history and literature. What some call *cultural literacy* others see as *cultural imperialism.* "Whose knowledge is of most worth?" is the question of the day. And, as America becomes a nation of growing diversity, the argument will continue to drive the debate about what is core, what is fair, and what should be in the curriculum.

Is the United States Going Test Crazy?

Those who support cultural literacy not only have a specific curricular content in mind but also have a clear idea of what a culturally literate test would look like. How would you rate on such a test? Assume that you have just applied to Cabin Cove Schools—a place where you have always wanted to teach. To ensure that teachers are "culturally literate," the school board requires that all teacher candidates take a knowledge exam—to be sure each has received an education in the basics, the things we all should know. Try your hand at the following questions and get a first-hand "feel" for the testing issue.

History
1. Thomas Jefferson authored
   a. The Bill of Rights.
   b. The Declaration of Independence.
   c. The U.S. Constitution.
   d. The Emancipation Proclamation.
2. The *Federalist Papers* were designed to
   a. win popular support for the American Revolution.
   b. establish freedom of speech.
   c. win support for the U.S. Constitution.
   d. free and enfranchise slaves.
3. Senator Joseph McCarthy was associated with
   a. government corruption.
   b. civil rights.
   c. education funding.
   d. Communist hunting.

4. The Cherokee syllabary was developed by
   a. Sitting Bull.
   b. Maria Tallchief.
   c. Geronimo.
   d. Sequoyah.

Literature
5. The novel *1984* concerns
   a. time travel.
   b. government-imposed conformity.
   c. a hoax about an invasion from Mars.
   d. World War III.
6. Stratford-on-Avon is associated with
   a. Shakespeare.
   b. Wollstonecraft.
   c. Chaucer.
   d. Shelley.
7. Jane Austen wrote about the Bennett family's five daughters in
   a. 10 Downing Street.
   b. Pride and Prejudice.
   c. Midliothian Tales.
   d. Clarissa.

Geography
8. List the states that touch on the Pacific Ocean.
9. List as many countries as you can that border the former Soviet Union.
10. Where is Mount St. Helens?

Science
11. Coal, gas, and oil shortages may result in an increased dependence on electricity. What is your evaluation of this idea?
    a. The economy cannot be changed that quickly.
    b. Electric automotive technology will simply not match gasoline engines.
    c. Electricity is generally produced from coal, gas, and oil, so it cannot replace them.
    d. The current cost of electricity is much higher than that of coal or gas and somewhat higher than that of gasoline, so it is a very expensive and unlikely eventuality.
12. What is the approximate distance between the earth and the sun?
    a. 90,000 miles
    b. 900,000 miles
    c. 9,000,000 miles
    d. 90,000,000 miles
13. What is the major cause of urban pollution?
    a. automobiles
    b. factories
    c. open incineration of garbage
    d. heat inversion causing smog

Cabin Cove Teacher Assessment Scale. Following are the answers to the quiz. Take a moment and see how you did:

1. b; 2. c; 3. d; 4. d; 5. b; 6. a; 7. b; 8. Hawaii, Alaska, Oregon, Washington, and California; 9. Afghanistan, China, Czechoslovakia, Finland, Hungary, Iran, Mongolia, North Korea, Norway, Rumania, and Turkey (if you identified at least seven of these countries, give yourself full credit); 10. Washington State; 11. c; 12. d; 13. a.

Add up your correct responses and compare your results with the following score card:

9–13 correct: You have demonstrated an adequate level of general knowledge. You are culturally literate. Welcome to the Cabin Cove School District.

6–8 correct: You have qualified for probationary status. If you agree to enroll in a number of courses at Cabin Cove College, you will be allowed to teach in the public schools.

Fewer than 6 correct: You have failed the teacher assessment test and will not be offered a position in this community.

How do you feel about the use of such a test to determine your future? Do you think that it is unfair to measure your teaching skills and abilities according to this single dimension, or do you feel that it is reasonable to assume all teachers should be expected to demonstrate a minimal level of general knowledge and cultural literacy? These questions and more have emerged in the past few years as the United States public has become concerned—some say obsessed—with testing.

The National Commission on Testing and Public Policy estimated that 127 million tests are given to elementary and secondary students each year.[42] In an extreme case, all students in Newark, New Jersey, including first-graders, were tested nine times a year.[43] Neither does the testing craze start only at the first grade. About half of all 4- and 5-year-olds will also be tested to determine kindergarten and prekindergarten placement.[44] In fact, by law, forty-two states require regularly scheduled **achievement tests,** starting in the first grade.

Tests are used to answer a growing list of educational questions: Who is "ready" to begin kindergarten? Who should be promoted or retained? Who should be given "special" education services? Who should be placed in the advanced track? Who should be allowed to graduate? Who should be admitted to prestigious schools or colleges?

More and more, it is not only students who are tested but educators and schools as well. Beginning teachers may be asked to take the Praxis series of tests (see Chapter 2 and Appendix 2) or a state test or local equivalent in order to obtain a position. Teachers, principals, and superintendents may have their job security determined by how well or poorly their students score on standardized tests. Poor test results may lead to reprimands or termination as communities rely more and more on test scores to determine the quality of their schools, and even their economic prosperity. Consider the following dialogues:

Real estate agent to prospective home owner: "Of course, this house costs more than similar houses in other neighborhoods. This is in the Whitmore School District. These are the best schools in the area, with the highest SAT scores. Houses here cost more."

Mayor to corporate executive: "If you move your corporate headquarters to our city, you will get more than special tax breaks. Your managers will be able to send their children to one of the finest school districts in the state, a school district with test scores in the top 10 percent nationally. I can't think of a more attractive enticement for relocating to our city. Your employees will love it here—and so will their spouses and children."

Testing, like the textbook industry, has become big business. The two largest firms producing and marketing the nation's standardized tests are Educational Testing Services (ETS) and American College Testing Program (ACT). Some firms that produce and market such tests, such as Harcourt Brace Jovanovich, also publish textbooks. Literally hundreds of millions of dollars are spent in testing, and these test companies have a great deal invested in maintaining, if not increasing, the level of test taking in the United States.[45]

Many argue that testing is far from perfect. Standardized tests are criticized for their assumption that a child's competence can be measured by his or her ability to recognize and choose correct responses from given lists. Such tests, critics insist, undermine the critical thinking, creative problem-solving, and cooperative skills that teachers are trying to build.[46] Furthermore, standardized tests limit a school's curriculum, since many teachers feel obligated to "teach to the test." However, the tests themselves yield little insight into individualizing or enriching instruction, since they give little feedback about student strengths and weaknesses. Edward B. Fiske speaks for many educators in his criticism of standardized tests: "They measure the wrong things in the wrong way for the wrong reasons."[47]

Standardized testing is also charged with bias against females and students of color. Researcher Phyllis Rosser found that girls receive lower scores than boys, in part because of bias in test construction. For example, 15 percent more males than females respond correctly to the following analogy item (and, as you might suspect, such a question may also be particularly challenging to less affluent students):

Dividends: Stockholders:

(A) investments: corporations

(B) purchase: customers

(C) royalties: authors

(D) tapes: workers

(E) mortgages: homeowners

If you are curious, the correct answer is (C).[48]

Test bias became a legal issue in New York in the early 1990s, when a group including the American Civil Liberties Union, the National Organization for Women, and the Girls Clubs of America, now called Girls, Inc., sued the Educational Testing Services, claiming that the Scholastic Assessment Test (SAT) and PSAT (a standardized test similar to the SAT) exams discriminated against females. Since New York State scholarship awards were based on these scores, the alleged sex bias had direct financial ramifications. In fact, males had regularly gotten higher PSAT and SAT scores and had received about twice as many scholarships as had females. The judge agreed with the plaintiffs, finding, among other problems, that these exams consistently underestimated female performance in school. New York State was ordered to find another means for awarding its college scholarships. This ruling, referred to as the *Walker* case (after Judge Walker) has implications for other state and national scholarship programs. The best known of these may be the National Merit Scholarships, distributed based on PSAT scores. Another similarity to the New York case is that here, too, boys score consistently higher than girls and receive about twice the number of scholar-ships. Legal challenges of this and other scholarship programs are sure to fill court-rooms in the years ahead.

The latest reform in testing is the creation of tests that are grounded more firmly in classroom performance. These are often referred to as forms of *alternative, performance-based,* or **authentic assessment**—implying that tests are truer when based on what students actually do in school. Authentic assessment represents actual performance, encourages students to reflect on their own work, and is integrated into the student's whole learning process. Such tests usually require students to synthesize knowledge from different areas and actively use that knowledge.[49] Teaching to an au-thentic test is encouraged, for in such a test the student must actually perform what he or she is expected to know. Comparisons are often made with sports, in which par-ticipants are expected to demonstrate in a game what they learned in practice. A ten-nis player works on her backhand, so that she can demonstrate mastery of it in a game; similarly, when students know that they will be called on to demonstrate and use their knowledge, they are more motivated to practice their academic skills.

Most states are exploring new (and more authentic) methods of assessment. The most popular method is the writing sample.[50] While this can be an effective means of judging children's writing, critics caution against evaluating a timed writing sample, since such a sample does not allow students time to demonstrate the mastery of the writing process, including revising and editing.

Some of the best examples of authentic assessment come from the Coalition of Essential Schools, led by prominent educator Theodore Sizer. The coalition encour-ages schools to define their own model for successful reform, guided by nine basic principles that emphasize the personalization of learning. These principles include the requirement that students complete "exhibitions," tasks that call on them to ex-hibit their knowledge concretely. The high school curriculum is structured around these demanding, creative tasks, which may include

- Completing a federal Internal Revenue Service Form 1040 for a family whose records you receive, working with other students in a group to ensure that everyone's IRS forms are correct, and auditing a return filed by a student in a different group
- Designing a nutritious and attractive lunch menu for the cafeteria within a specified budget and defending your definitions of *nutritious* and *attractive*
- Designing and building a wind instrument from metal pipes, then composing and performing a piece of music for that instrument
- Choosing one human emotion to define in an essay, through examples from literature and history, and in at least three other ways (through drawing, painting, or sculpture; through film, photographs, or video; through music; through pantomime or dance; or through a story or play that you create)[51]

The future of testing in the United States promises to shape education in many ways. If national tests become a reality, then a national curriculum may follow—such a curriculum has been heralded by some as vital to maintaining consistent quality across the nation and is dreaded by others as marking the end of individuality and autonomy in teaching. The persistence of traditional, standardized testing may prompt continued emphasis on the memorization of discrete facts. On the other hand, an increase in authentic testing may contribute to a greater classroom focus on critical thinking and personal development.

The Saber-Tooth Curriculum

How can the curriculum prepare for tomorrow while preserving the past? Here is how curriculum scholar Michael Apple puts it:

> The curriculum must simultaneously be both conservative and critical. It must preserve the ideals that have guided discourse in the U.S. for centuries: a faith in the American people, a commitment to expanding equality, and a commitment to diversity and liberty. Yet it must also empower individuals to question the ethics of their institutions and to criticize them when they fail to meet these ideals.[52]

Unless we carefully consider what a school is for and what kind of curriculum can meet those goals, we might end up with a "saber-tooth curriculum." Since many of you may never have read this classic satire on Paleolithic curriculum written by Abner Peddiwell, known in real life as Harold Benjamin, we will summarize the story of **The Saber-Tooth Curriculum** for you here. This clever parody reveals the flaws of a saber-tooth curriculum. Are there any positive aspects of this kind of curriculum?

New-Fist was a brilliant educator and thinker of prehistoric times. He watched the children of his tribe playing with bones, sticks, and brightly colored pebbles, and he speculated on what these youngsters might learn that would help the tribe derive more food, shelter, clothing, security, and, in short, a better life.

FIGURE 8.5

Saber-Tooth Curriculum. A satire on the slow pace of curricular change.

Eventually, he determined that in order to obtain food and shelter, the people of his tribe must learn to fish with their bare hands and to club and skin little woolly horses; and in order to live in safety, they must learn to drive away the saber-tooth tigers with fire. So New-Fist developed the first curriculum. It consisted of three basic subjects: (1) "Fish-Grabbing-with-the-Bare-Hands," (2) "Woolly-Horse-Clubbing," and (3) "Saber-Tooth-Tiger-Scaring-With-Fire."

New-Fist taught the children these subjects, and they enjoyed these purposeful activities more than playing with colored pebbles. The years went by, and by the time New-Fist was called by the Great Mystery to the Land of the Setting Sun, all the tribe's children had been systematically schooled in these three skills; the tribe was prosperous and secure.

All would have been well and the story might have ended here had it not been for an unforeseen change—the beginning of the New Ice Age, which sent a great glacier sliding down upon the tribe. The glacier so muddied the waters of the creeks that it was impossible for people to catch fish with their bare hands. Also, the melted water of the glacier made the ground marshy, and the little woolly horses left for higher and dryer land. They were replaced by shy and speedy antelopes with such a scent for danger that no one could get close enough to club them. And finally, as if these disruptions were not enough, the increasing dampness of the air caused the saber-tooth tigers to contract pneumonia and die. The tigers, however, were replaced by an even greater danger: ferocious glacial bears, who showed no fear of fire. Prosperity and security became distant memories for the suffering tribe.

Fortunately, a new breed of brilliant educators emerged. One tribesman, his stomach rumbling with hunger, grew frustrated with fruitless fish-grabbing in cloudy waters. He fashioned a crude net and in one hour caught more fish than the whole tribe could have caught had they fish-grabbed for an entire day. Another tribesman fashioned a snare with which he could trap the swift antelope, and a third dug a pit that captured and secured the ferocious bears.

As a result of these new inventions, the tribe again became happy and prosperous. Some radicals even began to criticize the school's curriculum and urged that net-making, snare-setting, and pit-digging were indispensable to modern life and should be taught in the schools. But the wise old men who controlled the schools objected:

> With all the intricate details of fish-grabbing, horse-clubbing, and tiger-scaring—the standard cultural subjects—the school curriculum is too crowded now. We can't add these fads and frills of net-making, antelope-snaring, and—of all things—bear-killing. Why, at the very thought, the body of the great New-Fist, founder of our Paleolithic educational system, would turn over in its burial cairn. What we need to do is to give our young people a more thorough grounding in the fundamentals. . . . The essence of true education is timelessness. It is something that endures through changing conditions like a solid rock standing squarely and firmly in the middle of a raging torrent. You must know that there are some eternal verities, and the saber-tooth curriculum is one of them.[53]

ᛙᛙᛙ

The Saber-Tooth Curriculum was written in 1939, but it has meaning today. Clearly, educators need to avoid a curriculum out of touch with the reality of today's students and thoughtlessly programmed for obsolescence. No educator worth his or her salt wants to be caught waving unnecessary firebrands at tigers long extinct. Today's debate over curricula for various ethnic groups versus a common, Eurocentric core is related to issues raised in *The Saber-Tooth Curriculum*. Is Latin a "saber-tooth" subject? What about the ancient history of the Romans and Greeks? Should these topics make way for subjects more relevant, useful, or culturally inclusive? If we omit these, do we lose an important part of the nation's cultural heritage? Is there room for everything? If not, how do we establish priorities? These are the kinds of questions thoughtful teachers face on a daily basis.

The Teacher as Curriculum Developer

In the midst of trends and tension points is the classroom teacher, a force in his or her own right in determining what and how children are taught in school. Listen in on some different perspectives from the teachers' room:

JO: Were you at yesterday's faculty meeting? The sales reps from the publishing company showed their new textbook series.

MAYA: No, I had an emergency dentist appointment—a root canal. That was painful enough! What's the new series like?

JO: Fabulous. It must be worth big money—superslick covers, beautiful photos and graphics. And talk about supplementary materials. They have everything! It's got a web site connection, which they promise to update regularly, that includes practical student projects. They went online for us yesterday, and it looks great. The objectives are totally spelled out, and there's a step-by-step teacher's guide saying exactly how to cover each objective. There are discussion questions after reading assignments and a student workbook with activities for the kids to do after we've finished the reading. They even have huge banks of test questions for weekly tests and unit exams on CD-ROM.

MAYA: What's got you so excited?

JO: Excited? You know how hard it is to get *into* a new series! The prep time alone is endless. Anything that saves me hours, I'm for. And these books look like a time-saving resource.

MAYA: Jo, we've been through so many TGIF afternoons—you know I need more "quality and quantity" time in my life. But some of these new comprehensive textbook systems make me nervous.

JO: What do you mean?

MAYA: I'm not so sure the people in slick offices (who do the slick covers) know what's best for our kids. What makes them so smart that they can determine what we should tell our students? I know my kids! What kind of expertise do they have to tell us how to teach? When was the last time those textbook writers were in a classroom, anyway? I'm not so sure that I want to relinquish my professional control over what and how I teach.

JO: Sounds like you.

MAYA: The other day I was talking with Jena, the new teacher who works across the hall from me. She just graduated from college a few years ago, and she has some terrific ideas. She's using an individualized reading program, and she's really got the kids into it. Instead of the basal reading selections, she's got the class reading everything from Judy Blume to Tolkien. And the kids are loving it. It's a tremendous success. But, instead of being psyched, she's in panic mode—afraid she's harming her students' reading development, because she's not following the *official* basal reader. The upcoming state reading test worries her, and a few parents are muttering she's not doing the *real* thing.

JO: You're kidding!

MAYA: I wish I were.

JO: So you're saying that some of us trust the textbooks more than we trust our own professional training, expertise, and experience. Or we just use the textbook packages without questioning or supplementing them.

MAYA: I think we walk a fine line between being technicians and being professionals. It's good to have books and supplemental materials that save us time, allow us to shift painlessly into new approaches, and give some teachers a concrete place to start. Me? I'd rather make decisions about how and when I'm using what. The way I figure it, that's a major part of my teaching job.

Teachers are formally and informally involved in **curriculum development.** In a formal way, teachers may be members of textbook selection committees that determine what texts the school will purchase, or they may actually work on writing a district's curriculum. In a less formal but no less powerful way, classroom teachers have the option to interpret and adapt whatever official text or curriculum guide has been assigned. As a teacher, you can stress certain points in a text and give scant attention to others; you can supplement or replace official texts with your own teacher-made materials; you can direct students to the Internet or even introduce lessons or units that are completely unrelated to the assigned text. This freedom to modify the official curriculum has led many to conclude that the real curriculum is whatever teachers actually choose to do in their classrooms.

Despite this freedom and influence, some critics warn that new directions in textbook production are a potential threat to the teacher's professional role in curriculum development. Today's trend is a comprehensive textbook package, with a

Although many groups attempt to influence the school curriculum, in the final analysis it is the classroom teacher who must plan the day-to-day instruction that matches the specific learning needs of his or her students.

highly sophisticated instructional design, student materials, classroom visuals, and even web site support. Obviously, there are positive elements in these comprehensive, commercially developed textbook systems. They can save overburdened teachers (especially new teachers) a great deal of time, which the teachers can then devote to individualized instruction, as well as a variety of classroom management duties. Some teachers enjoy this "freedom" from making curricular choices. Researcher Allan Odden has found that, the "more programs are ready made," the less teachers are worn out, reinforcing his belief that packages are more effective than teacher- or school-devised programs.[54]

For schools using these large-scale, often multiple-grade, curricular programs, critics fear that such programs could reduce teachers to mere technicians. When teachers execute someone else's instructional goals and ideas, teacher autonomy and creativity are lost.[55] "Instead of professional teachers who care about what they do and why they do it, we may have only alienated executors of someone else's plans."[56]

If teachers cease to practice curriculum development, other problems may also emerge. If teachers are seen as technicians rather than professionals, they become increasingly expendable. After all, anyone can administer "foolproof" materials, can't they? Eventually, the "technician" teacher may lose the ability to adapt these materials to the diagnosed needs, abilities, and interests of his or her own students.

"Knowledge is power," the saying goes, and in the final analysis the degree of power and talent you exert as an architect of the curriculum will depend on your own knowledge and skills. If you are supposed to teach a unit on the Civil War but you know little about it, it will be all you can do to implement commercially prepared materials. If you are to teach a unit on poetry but avoided literature classes in college, you will be at the mercy of whatever the publishers or the test makers tell you to do and say. If your knowledge of science is limited to that terrible memory of when you tried to dissect a frog, you may gratefully follow to the last dot on the *i* whatever instructions are in the teacher's manual (and beg for the science specialist to come in and do it for you). Your own knowledge about content and teaching skills is a classroom asset, giving you the power to put into action one of the most creative functions of teaching: shaping what your students learn in school.

Summary

1. The curriculum can be influenced by many different groups and data. These include students, parents, administrators, the federal government, the state government, the local government, colleges and universities, national test results, education commissions and committees, professional organizations, and special interest groups.

2. The effort to establish national curricular standards has moved forward for subjects such as mathematics, but it has encountered a vocal opposition in more value-laden disciplines, such as history, in which no national consensus exists as to what should be included. While some Americans believe that the institution of national standards will enhance the level of learning and national unity, critics argue that funding for additional resources, rather than national standards, is needed in order to improve America's schools.

3. More than twenty states, mainly located in the South and West, are textbook adoption states. Typically, in this centralized adoption system, local school districts select their texts from an official, state-approved list.

4. Those who are in favor of the state adoption system believe that this process leads to the selection of higher-quality texts and creates a common, statewide

curriculum. Those who criticize the state adoption system claim that large, populous states have unfair influence over textbook development.

5. Under pressure to publish books that have appropriate readability levels, publishers and authors "dumb down" textbooks or substitute simplified, shorter words and phrases for more complex ones. This may result in books in which sophisticated ideas are simplified into meaningless ones. Critics of textbooks cite the "mentioning phenomenon" as another problem. They claim that the books try to include too many subjects and gloss over them to such a degree that students fail to gain sufficient depth or context.

6. Seven forms of bias can characterize textbooks: invisibility, stereotyping, imbalance and selectivity, unreality, fragmentation and isolation, linguistic bias, and cosmetic bias.

7. Controversies over religious fundamentalism and secular humanism have characterized textbook adoption in recent years. In some communities, these controversies have led to book banning and censorship.

8. Debate continues over the impact of a core curriculum. Proponents of a core curriculum feel that it will benefit the disadvantaged and transmit the culture essential for well-educated citizens. Multiculturalists feel it will deny women and students of color the opportunity to see their experiences reflected in history and literature.

9. Testing has indicated that U.S. students are not scoring as well as students from other developed countries. These poor scores provided one catalyst for the reform movement. But, before long, the tests themselves became an issue. Critics voiced concern about the negative impact of teaching to the test, the excessive number of tests given to students, racism and sexism in standardized test questions, and the low level of thinking required by such examinations. Test advocates stress the need for objective measures of our students, programs, and schools.

10. The latest development in testing is authentic assessment, which calls for testing to represent real performance. An authentic assessment demands that students synthesize what they have learned in various areas to complete a challenging, creative task. Accomplishing something real is motivating for students, and teachers can learn a great deal about how to adjust instruction from student performances, which they seldom can with standardized tests. In *Horace's School,* Theodore Sizer presents many examples of authentic assessment tasks, which he refers to as "exhibitions."

11. When developing curricula, it is important to keep in mind the satire of *The Saber-Tooth Curriculum.* A curriculum must include objectives and activities that teach students how to preserve the past, function effectively in the present, and prepare for the future.

12. Although most classroom teachers cannot choose their own textbooks, they have the power to interpret the materials and emphasize or skim over content. While detailed guides and workbooks may save time and effort, they rob the teaching roles of autonomy and professionalism.

Key Terms and People

achievement tests
Afrocentrists
authentic assessment
Allan Bloom
censor

Christian Bible (religious) fundamentalists
Christian reconstructionism
core knowledge
cultural literacy

curriculum canon
curriculum development
dumbing down
E. D. Hirsch, Jr.
fundamentalist

mentioning phenomenon

multicultural education

National Assessment of Educational Progress (NAEP)

national standards

New Age movement

readability formulas

religious Right

The Saber-Tooth Curriculum

secular humanism

seven forms of bias

Texas and California effect

textbook adoption states

The Closing of the American Mind

Discussion Questions and Activities

1. This chapter has presented an overview of the various groups and forces that influence what children are taught in schools. In your opinion, which of these groups and forces have the most influence on curricula? Why?

2. What subject areas would spark the greatest debate and controversy over creating a single, national curriculum? Are there strategies to help reach a consensus on these issues? How might a national history curriculum written today differ from one written a century from now? a century ago? Why?

3. Do you believe that children's educational materials should be censored? Are there any benefits to censorship? any dangers? What kinds of materials would you refuse to let elementary school students read? secondary students? postsecondary students?

4. Are you in favor of a comprehensive textbook system, or do you think this inhibits teachers from pursuing one of the important professional aspects of their work?

5. Collect textbooks from your local elementary and secondary schools and analyze them according to the following criteria:

   - Do they include instructional objectives? Do these require students to use both recall of factual information and analytical and creative thinking skills?

   - Were readability formulas used in the preparation of the textbooks? If so, did this appear to have a negative or positive impact on the quality of the writing?

   - Are underrepresented group members included in the textbooks' narrative and illustrations? Are individuals with disabilities included?

   - When various individuals are included, are they portrayed in a balanced or a stereotyped manner?

6. Is American society best characterized as a melting pot? a salad? a stew? stir-fry in a sauce? Why? Is there another metaphor that better captures the nature of American society?

7. Consider the materials and textbooks used on your campus in your major courses. Do you think a traditional or a multicultural perspective is reflected?

8. Support the statement "More testing is good for U.S. education." Then refute it.

9. Do we have a saber-tooth curriculum today? Through satire, Abner Peddiwell made a persuasive case against the saber-tooth curriculum. Can you write a satire in its defense?

10. Your course instructor probably used this textbook as a framework for curriculum development in this course. How has this text served as a foundation for content, testing, discussion, and activities?

inter-mission

Part 2 Schools and Curriculum

It's been four chapters since your first inter-mission. To refresh your memory, here you will find a series of application and reflection tasks that parallels the INTASC (Interstate New Teacher Assessment and Support Consortium) principles. Tackling these tasks will lead to a firmer understanding of Part 2, and some of these efforts may become part of your growing portfolio collection.

Applications and Reflections

2:1 Curriculum and the Generation Gap

INTASC PRINCIPLE 1
Knowledge of Subject Matter

Purpose: The purpose of this activity is to informally acquire information regarding curriculum *changes* in your favorite subject or major field. Some teachers construct lessons that easily blend new content with time-tested approaches and strategies. Others are devastated when there is any change in the curriculum, such as a new textbook. Since curricular knowledge is ever changing and ever challenging, you will spend many of your teaching days in the *en garde* (or ready) position.

Activity: You're going to facilitate a *generation gap* conversation. Find two people (teachers or family or community members) who are from a different generation than you. Ask them about *your major* or *favorite subject* area during their years of schooling. Develop leading questions to see *what* they were taught and *how* it differed from your program.

Dig into your own experience to help generate questions. If you sang a song about the state capitals, in alphabetical order, when you took social studies, turn that into curriculum questions: "Did you have to memorize the states and their capitals? How did that assignment connect with other content in the class?"

Reflection: How have things changed? How are they the same? With the information explosion, has the coverage of subjects exploded as well? in what ways? What do you think is driving what we teach and how we include new concepts and content? Can you make any predictions about the curriculum you will be covering when you begin teaching?

2:2 Scoping School Culture

INTASC PRINCIPLE 2
Human Development and Learning

Purpose: Have you ever wanted to "stop the world" and, rather than get off, take the time to really observe people's behavior? Here's your chance. Your inherent curiosity, coupled with some directed observations, can offer a rich opportunity to study the growth and development of students.

Activity: Visit an elementary, middle, or high school campus, preferably one that you anticipate will be different from your own experience. Set yourself up to the side of the major thoroughfares with notepad, laptop, or sketchbook and make "notes." Consider three public and informal spaces: cafeteria, hallways, open space quad, blacktop/field, or "recess" areas.

- What does the "scene" look like? How are individuals and groups dressed? What else do you see?
- Focus on students and their body language. What's the composition of groups, pairs, or individuals? Who's talking, touching, or teasing? Describe the behavior.
- Focus on staff or faculty in the area. What are their roles? Are they detached, integrated, or "in charge"? Describe their actions.
- What noise is evident—music, varied languages, general chatter, or the "sounds of silence"?
- Compare and contrast these areas: cafeteria, hallways, open spaces. (Are various cliques entitled to special spots or activities? Is studying more evident in one section?
- What other behaviors, in general, do you observe?

Reflection: Check in with classmates who scoped out different schools and compare notes. Did the students' behavior appear to vary by such factors as gender, race, physical size, language fluency, and clothing? What insights did you have about this student body and individual pupils? How did their use of time and space in the halls, cafeteria, and open areas interest and inform you? What insights about student and teacher behavior might you draw from your observations? How might these observations help you understand human development?

2:3 Curriculum Bias Busters

INTASC PRINCIPLE 3
Diversity in Learning

Purpose: The way curricular materials portray different groups can promote either knowledge or stereotypes. In this activity, you will practice examining materials for bias. As a teacher, you must recognize bias, so that you can select good resources or adapt materials to serve multiple perspectives.

Activity: Review the seven forms of bias discussed in Chapter 8. Borrow a K–12 textbook (appropriate for your subject major or grade level) from your college's curriculum resource center, a local school, or a teaching friend. Look for an example of each form of bias, but here's the trick: your illustration can be either positive (for example, overcoming gender *invisibility*) or negative (for instance, reinforcing a racial *stereotype*).

Reflection: Selecting examples was intended to help you clarify your understanding of these forms of bias. Do several forms of bias appear in the same example? Why might this be the case? For each negative selection, how might you overcome this bias with your students?

BIAS BUSTERS

Book Title/Author/Reference Information:

Brief description of text:

Type of Bias	+ or −	Page #	Example
1. Invisibility			
2. Stereotyping			
3. Imbalance and selectivity			
4. Unreality			
5. Fragmentation and isolation			
6. Linguistic bias			
7. Cosmetic bias			

INTASC PRINCIPLE 4
Variety of Instructional Strategies

2:4 Time Capsule

Purpose: Good teachers want students to think critically, solve problems, and develop skills, and good teachers have purposeful ways of making this happen in classrooms. One strategy is to use a wide variety of materials (such as videotapes, comic strips, theater costumes) to promote instruction. A beginning teacher wrote, "I found that the path of least resistance was just to teach from books, notes—it took effort to use technology, hands-on artifacts, and so on, but it was very effective." Successfully incorporating teaching aids is indicative of a high-performing teacher.

Activity: Imagine you are creating a time capsule of the critical teaching aids for your classroom. Use a student backpack—a symbolic capsule of our times. What items would you pack inside to share with the generation of teachers one century from now? What symbols must be included that represent our curriculum? What educational minutia are a "must have"? Draw, video, list, or actually pack the items in your capsule.

Reflection: Spend "show-and-tell" time with classmates by sharing your backpack time capsule. What teaching aids are in your bag of tricks that are memorable? What items did you overlook or leave out?

2:5 Rules and Regulations: A Sampler

INTASC PRINCIPLE 5
Motivation and Management

Purpose: Most teachers struggle to balance motivating students with managing them. Sometimes, in an attempt to keep it "all together and in control" teachers overregulate a class. At other times, they wait too long to rein in exuberant students. Start to consider behavior techniques right along with your study of schools, because, as a prospective teacher, you need to begin figuring out how you will manage a classroom.

Activity: Gather at least four samples of school and class rules. You could use technology to collect regulations, policies, and practices. At a low-tech level, use a copying machine to duplicate examples from a local school, a peer's portfolio, or a management course. You might photograph or videotape posted class (or library, cafeteria, or office) rules. Surfing the Internet could connect you with teachers who would share their standards or rules. Students online might also add to your file. There are also web sites on student behavior and management that you will find useful.

Reflection: Consider your collection and what you might do during the first week of school to balance motivation and management. Which of these rules and approaches appeal to you? How will you implement your own management plan? Will you post rules or create them with your class? Will you avoid the topic until a need arises? Will you rely on the grade level or department rules, or will you distinguish yourself with personal policy and practice? How do you anticipate that you will manage management?

2:6 A Public Service Announcement for Your National Education Goals

INTASC PRINCIPLE 6
Communication Skills

Purpose: America 2000 and Goals 2000 provided a blueprint for educational reform. Your ability to formulate and express your own education goals may guide your formal application for a teaching position. Communicating your goals clearly and concisely will let you practice verbal language skills, a foundation of effective instruction.

Activity: Develop a public service announcement (PSA) supporting your own national goals, ones you feel strongly about. Think of it as a radio spot (thirty to forty-five seconds long) that tells the listening public just what *they* need to know. Write it, edit it, and practice it with a stop watch. Rewrite, edit again, and rehearse until it's right. You may not always be able to practice and tighten your lessons this thoroughly, but the strategies you use to develop and refine your PSA are a necessary part of your communication repertoire.

Deliver your PSAs in small groups during a class session, maybe as a series of "commercial breaks."

Reflection: How were your peers' messages similar or different? Which PSAs appealed to you the most? Why? If you were given a second chance, how would you redo your PSA? Sometimes, negative media attention surrounds education, and it is tough to let the public know about the positive things that occur. Developing PSAs is probably a useful device. What topic would you choose for your next one?

2:7 Story Starters

INTASC PRINCIPLE 7
Instructional Planning Skills

Purpose: Chapter 6, "Life in Schools," detailed five factors of effective schools: strong leadership, a clear school mission, a safe and orderly climate, the monitoring of student progress, and high expectations. These characteristics are also evident in successful classrooms. Your purpose is to do the good, conscious planning that can make instruction effective in five classroom scenarios.

Activity: To help you make this school-classroom connection, we have given you some *story starters.* It's your job to finish the following scenarios so they illustrate the connection between the five factors and student achievement. In keeping with Rosenthal and Jacobson's study, we hold high expectations for your ability to finish these stories with endings that promote student achievement. It's like making your own happy endings. Working in teaching teams or small groups might assist you in being both creative and on target.

1. The principal at your new school is an experienced educator and a true model of effective leadership. First-year teachers are required to submit sample lesson plans. You have a meeting with the principal this week, and you stack your old lesson plan file to take with you. What happens? (Remember—knowing what you've studied about the five factors, create a positive ending to our story starter, one that promotes student achievement.)

2. You have just accepted a job at a school that has revised and simplified its mission statement. One aspect of a school mission is a phrase that adorns the school's letterhead and is emblazoned across the cafeteria wall, such as *Every student's a winner.* At back-to-school night, in just two weeks, you are to share this mission with parents. What happens?

3. You join a high school faculty and hear that many of the teachers tend to avoid conflict with students by avoiding disciplining or managing them outside of the classroom. You are assigned to cover your department wing during nutrition break. Many kids start snacking near their lockers, a breach of policy. What happens?

4. You are trying to give your students meaningful homework and monitor it for accuracy. You know that you must provide feedback on their assignments that is informative and timely. In your first month of instruction, you sometimes grade papers, have partners edit assignments, and keep accurate records on all their efforts. What else do you do, and what happens? (Hey, it's your story. Make it a good one!)

5. You have a student in your class who is unlike anyone you've ever encountered. Thinking of the numerous possibilities, describe this student (in imaginative detail) and determine how your expectations will encourage this student's academic achievement. What will you think, say, and do? What happens? (Is there a movie script offer in your future?)

Reflection: Did you find some story starters easy to finish, others harder? Why? What did you learn about the connection between the five factors and student achievement? What factors do you suspect will carry over to your own teaching? Why?

2:8 Memoirs of a Time-Tested Student

INTASC PRINCIPLE 8
Assessment

Purpose: National, state, and district tests are a huge part of school culture, yet few teachers analyze their role in the current testing climate. This activity will help you define that role.

Activity: Think about the quizzes and tests you took as a student. Either through your own journal entry or a conversation with a partner (live, taped, or via an Internet chat room), consider the following questions as you review and ponder your experiences with test taking:

- What's an early memory of a "big deal" test? sharpening your number 2 pencil? unsealing special pamphlets in elementary school? being tucked in a

TESTING BALANCE SHEET

What Teachers SHOULD Do

1. Describe the purpose of the test*

2.

3.

etc.

What Teachers Should NOT Do

1. Leave the room*

2.

3.

etc.

*sample items

cardboard "cubby" for privacy? proctors milling through rows, looking for cheating? a just-for-you test dealing with special needs? gifted or disability issues? the President's Council on Physical Fitness twelve-minute run? taking a review course for the PSATs and SATs? Try to recall the good, the bad, and the ugly.

*   Consider thoughts from your classmates and see if more recollections are sparked.
*   On one side of a Testing Balance Sheet, brainstorm things that teachers can do to ensure a positive climate for student testing. On the other side, list actions teachers should definitely avoid.

Reflection: Looking back, would you rate your teachers as helpful, or not so helpful, when it comes to administering quizzes and tests? Are there any teacher actions you would replicate in terms of test-giving style?

2:9 Reflections of a High School Yearbook

INTASC PRINCIPLE 9
Reflection and Responsibility

Purpose: Part 2 of this text looked at all aspects of the school scene, from the student role to a teacher's reality. While you may have shifted perspective as you walked away from your high school graduation ceremony, the purpose of this activity is to look back and assess some of your choices and actions. Your high school yearbook symbolizes a snapshot of your school and a view of yourself in the social system. What does it show you about your school, yourself, and others?

Activity: Dig out your high school yearbook or see if it is posted on the Internet. Many schools now have their own web pages. Look at it carefully. Ponder the following points for later reflection:

*   Find yourself. How often and where are you? What is the caption under your senior photo? Did you get caught in candid shots? Are you with clubs, in activities, and in teams? Are you surrounded by your friends or often on your own? Which images shared with your college classmates recall emotions: pride, embarrassment, sadness? Did your school have an FTA (Future Teachers of America) organization? Were you pictured with them? How does being a future teacher or a member of that club look today? Were your curricular strengths evident by achievements, awards, and participation? (You were an officer for the Model UN and you're now a social studies major; you belonged to the Storyteller Society and you want to be an elementary teacher; you

lettered in many sports and plan to teach physical education.) In what ways are you the same or different today?

- Find your friends. In what ways were you similar or different from them? When and where do they appear?
- Find lesser-known faces. Stop and really stare at students you may have walked by for years. What of their stories do you suspect or know? What groups were they in? What labels described their lives?
- Who is invisible or missing? Are there students who appear only in their "mug shot" and never as part of the campus culture? Do female or male students, from varied racial and ethnic groups, dominate particular activities or campus locales?
- What about the faculty and administration? Are they a part of or apart from your yearbook? How and where do you imagine yourself in the *teaching* section of the annual?

Reflection: What do you notice, about your school and yourself, as you reflect on the yearbook? How does it compare with the student cultures described in your text? How would you write or edit it today? Would you want to teach there, at a similar, or at a very different site? What *stories* from your yearbook pages would be valuable to share with classmates?

2:10 Support Staff Interview

INTASC PRINCIPLE 10
Relationships and Partnerships

Purpose: When you have a teaching job, you become part of a learning community. Knowing about the roles and responsibilities of support personnel will enhance your understanding of the way schools work. Nonteaching employees contribute significantly to a well-functioning school. Bus drivers, clerical personnel, media and custodial staff, instructional aides, playground and lunch supervisors, resource specialists, medical and psychological professionals, and security and safety personnel all do their part. They befriend alienated kids, clean up after trashy nutrition breaks, reset chairs in an auditorium as many as eight times a day, frisk students with clothes baggy enough to cover goods and evils, know most students' names when they step up to the office counter, make lunchrooms smell like fresh cookies (maybe not quite often enough), find media materials with the leanest of hints from teachers and students, toss balls in one direction and *bench* students in another, and provide one-on-one practice for the most unique of tasks and talents. And these support personnel have their own unique view of students, schools, and teachers. Fostering relationships with these colleagues is a way to create a valuable extension of your classroom community.

Activity: Try to schedule a 20-minute interview with one of the nonteaching employees at a local school. Spend the time asking your interviewee about his or her job. What's a day in the life of _____ like? What are his or her reasons for working at a school? What are the benefits and drawbacks? How do students and teachers impact the employee's work? How do teachers *support* the support personnel?

Reflection: Exchange interview reflections with classmates. What information was confirmed by your interview? What new information have you gathered about the job and/or the personnel? How might this interview affect your rapport and behavior with support staff?

Portfolio Artifact Collection

2:P1 What's up to Standard?

INTASC PRINCIPLE 1
Knowledge of Subject Matter

Purpose: As you enter teaching, make sure you are knowledgeable about the current standards in your field. Many professional associations have developed national curriculum standards and program goals. Groups from AAHPERD (American Alliance for Health, Physical Education, Recreation and Dance) to NCTE (National Council of Teachers of English) have promoted their frameworks and subject-matter expertise.

Activity: Collect the most recent professional curriculum standards in your major or high interest field.

2:P3 Clippings File on Multiculturalism

INTASC PRINCIPLE 3
Diversity in Learning

Purpose: Education is "In the News"; just like the clippings you will find throughout this text, news accounts can grab our interests or reinforce our anxieties. Start a multicultural news file to expand your understanding of diversity.

Activity: Your clippings file on multicultural education may collect topics from Afrocentrism to Zen Buddhism. The coverage might provide stories of intolerance or inspiration. Read them and highlight comments that are significant. Be sure to log the source and date on each article.

This inter-mission is finished. Stretch your body a bit; then settle in for

Part 3: "Foundations."

Part Three

Foundations

There are certain things you remember from when you were 11 years old. You might remember the taste of some cookie your next door neighbor made for you, or the sight of your old room after you proudly cleaned it, or even the sound of the staircase that creaked every time you hit the fifth step. I remember the smell of my fifth grade teacher.

Ms. Gottlieb was very warm, fun-loving, and caring. You could never mistake her with any other teacher because she wore big golden-hooped earrings, a complete blanket of makeup, and she was enveloped in a cloud of perfume that I cannot forget.

Every Monday I had to give a brief report on a current event. I dreaded this. I hated facing the class, and worst of all, I was the first to go every time. The deal was that you could miss up to two current event reports, before you got a note sent home. Well two incompletes came and went. When I failed to do my third, she said nothing. I thought this was great. She really forgot. I am going to get away with this.

Two weeks later my mother received the note, and she became furious because I could not give her any reason for missing so many current events. She failed to grasp the fear an 11-year-old can have when put in front of his classmates.

The following week, I let another current event report come and go. I can still remember returning shoeless to the classroom (I was "feel" testing the school's new carpets) when Ms. Gottlieb stopped me in the hallway. She asked me why I wasn't doing a current event report each week. I was silent. Tears were forming in my eyes. I could think of no explanation that she would want to hear.

To be honest, I forget the words she said to this shoeless kid, but she recognized my fear, and helped me prepare for the next current event. She taught me how to conquer the unconquerable. I was a different person after that hallway encounter. A teacher's brief conversation filled with some simple strategies taught me how to face my classmates. Ms. Gottlieb noticed me, and she cared. She probably didn't even know that her class and her relationship changed my life.

Ever since then, I have wanted to be a teacher. In the fifth grade, I wanted to teach the fifth grade. In high school, I wanted to teach high-school. And in college, well, I still wanted to teach high-school. Ms. Gottlieb impacted my whole life.

Many years after that fifth grade class, I was walking in my town when I smelled that same perfume. I turned expecting to find Ms. Gottlieb, but found no one I knew. As that smell filled my head, all the memories and the images from her class came to me. I will always remember Ms. Gottlieb (and I can't forget her perfume).

Aidan O'Hara
10 March 1998
Foundations of Education,
American University

The History of
American Education

Focus Questions

- What major historical events have shaped American education?
- How have local, state, and federal governments shared in the creation of America's schools?
- How have elementary and secondary schools evolved?
- Who are some of the key individuals who have helped fashion today's schools?

Chapter Preview

Understanding the history of America's schools offers you perspective—a sense of your place in your new profession. Your classroom is a living tribute to past achievements and events.

This chapter will trace American education from colonial times to the present. Education during the colonial period was intended to further religious goals and was offered primarily to white males—typically, wealthy white males. For females and children of color, education was difficult to attain, and, even when available, the education was often inferior. Over time, educational exclusivity diminished, but, even today, wealth, race, and gender continue to impact educational quality. To a great extent, the story of American education is a battle to open the schoolhouse door to more and more of our citizens. In this chapter, we will continue the story of the struggle to have America honor its commitment to equality. Later in this book, in chapter 13 "The Struggle for Educational Opportunity," we will offer additional insights into the effort to open the schoolhouse door.

The complex network of expectations surrounding today's schools is the product of a society that has been evolving for over three centuries. Individuals, groups, and the government all have contributed to making public schools more accessible. Benjamin Franklin, Horace Mann, Emma Hart Willard, and Mary McLeod Bethune, for example, fought to free America from historical biases. New federal laws were designed to create more equitable and effective educational opportunities. In the colonial era, however, the goals were simple: to teach the Scriptures and to develop a religious community. We will begin by looking into the classroom of Christopher Lamb, a New England teacher in one of the earliest American schools, over three centuries ago.

Christopher Lamb's Colonial Classroom

The frigid wintry wind knifed through Christopher Lamb's coat, chilling him to the bone as he walked in the predawn darkness. The single bucket of firewood that he lugged, intended to keep his seventeenth-century New England schoolroom warm all day, would clearly not do the job. Once the fire was started, Christopher focused on his other teaching tasks: carrying in a bucket of water for the class, sweeping the floor, and mending the ever so fragile pen points for the students. More than an hour after Christopher's predawn activities had begun, Margaret, the first student, arrived. Although Margaret, like most girls, would stay in school for only a year or two, Christopher believed that she should learn to read the Bible, so that she could be a better wife and mother. With any luck, she might even learn to write her name before she left school. But that was really not all that important for girls. As other students trickled in, they were directed to either the boys' bench or the girls' bench, where, in turn, they read their Testament aloud.

Those who read the Scriptures without error took their place at the table and wrote on their slates. Christopher was amazed at how poorly some students read, tripping over every other word, whereas others read quite fluently. The last student to finish, Benjamin, slowly rose from the bench, cringing. Christopher called out, "Lazy pupil," and a chorus of children's voices chimed in: "Lazy pupil. Lazy pupil. Lazy pupil." Benjamin, if not totally inured to the taunts, was no longer crushed by them, either. He slowly made his way to the end of the student line.

After the recitation and writing lessons, all the children were lined up and examined, to make certain they had washed and combed. A psalm was sung, and Mr. Lamb exhorted the students to walk in God's footsteps. For ten minutes, the class and teacher knelt in prayer. Each student then recited the day's biblical lesson. Those who had memorized their lessons received an *O,* written on their hand, a mark of excellence. Those who failed to recite their lessons correctly after three attempts once again were called "lazy pupil" by the entire class, and this time their names were written down. If by the end of the day they had finally learned the lesson, their names were erased from the list, and all the children called out "Diligent!" to those students.

Christopher Lamb had been an apprentice teacher for five years before accepting this position. He rejected the rod approach used so frequently by his master teacher. Using the children to provide rewards and punishments was far more effective than welts and bruises, marks left by a teacher's rod. Yes, Christopher was somewhat unorthodox, perhaps even a bit revolutionary, but the challenges of contemporary seventeenth-century society demanded forward-thinking educators, such as Christopher Lamb.

Colonial New England Education: God's Classrooms

One of the striking differences between Christopher Lamb's colonial classroom and today's typical public school is the role of religion in education. The religious fervor that drove the Puritans to America also drove them to provide religious education for their young, making New England the cradle of American education. In Christopher Lamb's time, school was meant to save souls.

Recitation lesson in a colonial classroom.

Education provided a path to heaven, and reading, writing, and moral development all revolved around the Bible.

Early colonial education, both in New England and in other colonies, often began in the home. (Today's home schooling movement is not a *new* approach.) The family was the major educational resource for youngsters, and the first lessons typically focused on reading. Values, manners, social graces, and even vocational skills were taught by parents and grandparents. Home instruction eventually became more specialized, and some women began to devote their time to teaching, converting their homes into schools. These "dames" taught reading, writing, and computation, and their homes became known as **dame schools.** A "dame," or well-respected woman with an interest in education, became (for a fee) the community's teacher.

An **apprenticeship** program rounded out a child's colonial education. While boys, sometimes as young as 7 years of age, were sent to live with masters who taught them a trade, girls typically learned homemaking skills from their mothers. Apprenticeship programs for boys involved not only learning skilled crafts but also managing farms and shops. Many colonies required that masters teach reading and writing as well as vocational skills. The masters served *in loco parentis*—that is, in place of the child's parent. The competencies of the masters guiding apprentices varied greatly, as did the talents of family members, dames, ministers, and others fulfilling the teaching role. Not surprisingly, this educational hodgepodge did not always lead to a well-educated citizenry; a more formal structure was needed.

Twenty-two years after arriving in the New World, the Puritans living in the Commonwealth of Massachusetts passed a law requiring that parents and masters of apprentices be checked periodically to ensure that children were being taught properly. Five years later, in 1647, Massachusetts took even more rigorous measures to ensure the education of its children. The Massachusetts Law of 1647, more commonly known as the **Old Deluder Satan Law**—the Puritans' attempt to thwart Satan's trickery with Scripture-reading citizens—required that

- Every town of 50 households must appoint and pay a teacher of reading and writing.
- Every town of 100 households must provide a (Latin) grammar school to prepare youths for the university, under a penalty of £5 for failure to do so.[1]

By 1680, such laws had spread throughout most of New England. The settlement patterns of the Puritans, who lived in towns and communities rather than scattered throughout the countryside, made establishing schools relatively uncomplicated. After learning to read and write, most girls returned home to practice the art of housekeeping. Boys who could afford to pay for their education went on to a **Latin grammar school.** In 1635, only fifteen years after arriving in America's wilderness, the Puritans established their first Latin grammar school in Boston. The Boston Latin Grammar School was not unlike a "prep" school for boys and was similar to the classical schools of Europe. The Boston Latin Grammar School was a rather exclusive school for boys of wealth, charging tuition to teach boys between the ages of 7 and 14.

Many consider the Boston Latin Grammar School to be the first step on the road to creating the American high school, although the school's curriculum reflected European roots. Students were expected to read and recite (in Latin, of course) the works of Cicero, Ovid, and Erasmus. In Greek, they read the works of Socrates and Homer. (Back to basics in colonial times meant back to the glory of Rome and Greece.) By the eighteenth century, the grammar school had incorporated mathematics, science, and modern languages. Classes started at 7 A.M., recessed at 11 A.M., and picked up from 1 P.M. until 5 P.M. Graduates were expected to go on to college and become colonial leaders, especially ministers.

Within a year of the founding of the Boston Latin Grammar School, Harvard College was established specifically to prepare ministers. Founded in 1636, Harvard was the first college in America, the jewel in the Puritans' religious and educational crown.[2]

For attendance at exclusive schools, such as Boston Latin Grammar, or at college, wealth was critical. The least desirable educational and apprenticeship opportunities were left to the poor. Some civic-minded communities made basic education in reading and writing more available to the poor, but only to families who would publicly admit their poverty by signing a "Pauper's Oath." Broadcasting one's poverty was no less offensive in colonial times than today, and many chose to have their children remain illiterate rather than sign such a public admission. The result was that most poor children remained outside the educational system.

Blacks, in America since 1619, and Native Americans were typically denied educational opportunities. In rare cases, religious groups, such as the Quakers, created special schools for children of color.[3] But these were the exceptions. Racism and slavery not only denied formal schooling to most Native Americans and blacks, but it also eventually led to laws prohibiting their education. (See Chapter 13, "The Struggle for Educational Opportunity," for a more complete review of these issues.) Girls did not fare much better. After they had learned the rudiments of reading and

Old school buildings remind us of how much schools have changed— and how much they have not.

writing, girls were taught the tasks related to their future roles as mother and wife. They were taught various handicrafts. Girls memorized the alphabet and then learned to stitch and display their accomplishments. They also learned to reproduce and attractively display religious sayings, on the road to becoming good Christian wives and mothers. Those attractive old samplers that we see in antique stores symbolize the stunted education provided to females. As much as we value these beautiful samplers today, they are a sad reminder of a time when they marked the academic finish line for girls, the diploma of a second-rate education, a depressing denial of equal educational rights.

Location greatly influenced educational opportunities. The northern colonies were settled by Puritans who lived in towns and communities relatively close to one another. Their religious fervor and proximity made the creation of community schools dedicated to teaching the Bible a predictable development.

In the middle colonies, the range of European religious and ethnic groups (Puritans, Catholics, Mennonites, the Dutch, and Swedes) created, if not a melting pot, a limited tolerance for diversity.[4] Various religious groups established schools, and apprenticeships groomed youngsters for a variety of careers, including teaching. In the middle colonies, the development of commerce and mercantile demands promoted the formation of private schools devoted to job training. By the 1700s, private teachers and night schools were functioning in Philadelphia and New York, teaching accounting, navigation, French, and Spanish.

The first city in North America was St. Augustine, Florida, where there is evidence that the Spanish settlers established schools. In terms of education, the southern English colonies trailed behind. The rural, sparsely populated southern colonies developed an educational system that was responsive to plantation society. Wealthy plantation owners took tutors into their homes to teach their children not only basic academic skills but also the social graces appropriate to their station in life. Plantation owners' children learned the proper way to entertain guests and "manage" slaves, using such texts as *The Complete Gentleman*. Wealthy young men seeking higher education were sent to Europe. Girls made do with just an introduction to academics and a greater focus on their social responsibilities. Poor white children might have had rudimentary home instruction in reading, writing, and computation. Black children made do with little if any instruction and, as time went by, encountered laws that actually prohibited their education entirely.[5]

Education has come a long way from colonial days and from Christopher Lamb's class—or has it? Consider the following:

1. The colonial experience established many of today's educational norms:
   - Local control of schools
   - Compulsory education
   - Tax-supported schools
   - State standards for teaching and schools
2. The colonial experience highlighted many of the persistent tension points challenging schools today:
   - What is the role of religion in the classroom?
   - How can we equalize the quality of education in various communities?
   - How can the barriers of racism, sexism, religious intolerance, and classism be eliminated, so that all children receive equal educational opportunity?
   - How can we prepare the most competent teachers?

TABLE 9.1	THE DEVELOPMENT OF COLONIAL HIGHER EDUCATION

Many of today's colleges and universities began as small, religiously sponsored institutions founded to train the clergy. The first fifteen institutions of higher education established in the colonies were all affiliated with a religious denomination.

Year	Institution	Year	Institution
1636	Harvard University	1769	Dartmouth University
1693	College of William and Mary	1782	Washington College
1701	Yale University	1782	Washington and Lee University
1746	Princeton University	1783	Hampton-Sidney College
1754	King's College (Columbia University)	1783	Transylvania College
1755	University of Pennsylvania	1783	Dickinson College
1765	Brown University	1784	St. John's College
1766	Queen's College (Rutgers University)		

A New Nation Shapes Education

The ideas that led to the American Revolution revolutionized our schools. European beliefs and practices, which had pervaded America's schools, were gradually abandoned as the new national character was formed. None of these beliefs had been more firmly adhered to than the integration of the state and religion.

In sixteenth- and seventeenth-century England, the Puritans' desire to reform the Church of England was viewed as treason. The Puritans encountered both religious and political opposition, and they looked to the New World as an escape from persecution. However, they came to America *not* to establish religious freedom, as our history books sometimes suggest, but to establish their own church as supreme, both religiously and politically. The Puritans were neither tolerant of other religions nor interested in separating religion and politics. Nonconformers, such as the Quakers, were vigorously persecuted. The purpose of the Massachusetts colony was to establish the "true" religion of the Puritans, to create a "new Israel" in America. Schools were simply an extension of the religious state, designed to teach the young to read and understand the Bible and to do honorable battle with Satan.

During the 1700s, American education was reconstructed to meet broader, nonsectarian goals. Such leaders as **Thomas Jefferson** wanted to go beyond educating a small elite class or providing only religious instruction. Jefferson maintained that education should be more widely available to white children from all economic and social classes. Public citizens began to question the usefulness of rudimentary skills taught in a school year of just three or four months. They questioned the value of mastering Greek and Latin classics in the Latin grammar schools, when practical skills were in short supply in the New World.

In 1749, **Benjamin Franklin** penned *Proposals Relating to the Youth of Pennsylvania,* suggesting a new kind of secondary school to replace the Latin grammar school—the **academy.** Two years later, the **Franklin Academy** was established, free of religious influence and offering a variety of practical subjects, including mathematics, astronomy, athletics, navigation, dramatics, and bookkeeping. Students were

In addition to serving two terms as president, Thomas Jefferson was the colonial era's most eloquent spokesperson for education and was the founder of the University of Virginia.

EARLY TEXTBOOKS

A rich variety of textbooks, media, library books, and computer software provide today's teachers with curricular resources unimaginable just a few years ago. As a teacher, you will come across references to some of the limited but influential curriculum materials of the past. Here is a brief profile of the best-known instructional materials from yesterday's schools.

Hornbook

The most common teaching device in colonial schools, the **hornbook** consisted of an alphabet sheet covered by a thin, transparent sheet made from a cow's horn. The alphabet and the horn covering were tacked to a paddle-shaped piece of wood and often hung by a leather strap around the student's neck. Originating in medieval Europe, the hornbook provided colonial children with their introduction to the alphabet and reading.

New England Primer

The first real textbook, the **New England Primer** was a tiny 2½- by 4½-inch book containing 50 to 100 pages of alphabet, words, and small verses accompanied by woodcut illustrations. First published in 1690, it was virtually the only reading text used in colonial schools until about 1800. The *Primer* reflected the religious orientation of colonial schools. A typical verse was

> In Adam's Fall
> We sinned all.

Thy Life to mend,
This Book attend
The idle fool
Is whipt at School.

American Spelling Book

The task undertaken by Noah Webster was to define and nourish the new American culture. His **American Spelling Book** replaced the *New England Primer* as the most common elementary textbook. The book contained the alphabet, syllables, consonants, rules for speaking, readings, short stories, and moral advice. The bulk of the book was taken up by lists of words. Royalty income from the sale of millions of copies of this book supported Webster in his other efforts to standardize the American language, including his best-known work, which is still used today, the *American Dictionary.*

McGuffey Readers

William Holmes McGuffey was a minister, professor, and college president who believed that clean living, hard work, and literacy were the virtues to instill in children. He wrote a series of readers that emphasized the work ethic, patriotism, heroism, and morality. It is estimated that more than 100 million copies of McGuffey Readers educated several generations of Americans between 1836 and 1920. **McGuffey Readers** are noteworthy because they were geared for different grade levels and paved the way for graded elementary schools.

able to choose some of their courses, thus setting the precedent for elective courses and programs at the secondary level. In the late 1700s, it was the Franklin Academy and not the Boston Latin Grammar School that was considered the most important secondary school in America.[6]

The Franklin Academy accepted both girls and boys who could afford the tuition, and the practical curriculum became an attractive innovation. Franklin's Academy sparked the establishment of six thousand academies in the century that followed, including Phillips Academy at Andover, Massachusetts (1778), and Phillips Exeter Academy in Exeter, New Hampshire (1783). The original Franklin Academy eventually became the University of Pennsylvania.

Jefferson's commitment to educating all white Americans, rich and poor, at government expense, and Franklin's commitment to a practical program of nonsectarian study offering elective courses severed American educational thought from its European roots. Many years passed before these ideas became widely established practices, but the pattern for innovation and a truly American approach to education was taking shape.

The Common School Movement

During the early decades of the nineteenth century, education was often viewed as a luxury. However, even parents who could afford such a luxury had limited choices. The town schools still existed in Massachusetts, and some charity schools served the poor and orphans. Dame schools varied in quality. In some areas, religious schools of one denomination prevailed, while, in rural areas and the South, few schools existed at all. The United States was a patchwork quilt of schools, tied together by the reality that money was needed to attain a decent education.

During the early decades of the nineteenth century, the democratic ideal became popular as many "common people"—immigrants, small farmers, and urban laborers—demanded greater participation in the democracy. With the election of Andrew Jackson in 1828, the voices of many poor white people were heard, particularly their demands for educational access. Many more decades would pass before additional voices—particularly those of people of color—would also be heard.

Horace Mann became the nation's leading advocate for the establishment of what we know today as the public **elementary school,** a school open to all. Historians consider Horace Mann to be the outstanding proponent of education for the common person (the **common school** movement), and he is often referred to as "the father of the public school." (More about Mann appears in "The Education Hall of Fame," later in this chapter.) Mann helped create the Massachusetts State Board of Education and in 1837 became its secretary, a position similar to today's state superintendent of schools. In this role, Mann began an effort to reform education, believing that public education should serve both practical and idealistic goals. In practical terms, both business and industry would benefit from educated workers, resulting in a more productive economy. In idealistic terms, public schools should help us identify and nurture the talents in poor as well as wealthy children, and schools should ameliorate social disharmony.[7] Mann decried the rifts between rich and poor, Calvinists and religious reformers, new Irish immigrants and native workers. A common school instilling common and humane moral values could reduce such social disharmony (a popular belief today as well). Mann attempted to promote such values, but he encountered strong opposition when the values he selected revealed a distinct pro-Protestant tilt, one that offended Calvinists, atheists, Jews, Catholics, and others. His moral program to create a common set of beliefs had the opposite impact, igniting a dispute over the role of religion in school.

The idea of public education is so commonplace today that it seems difficult to imagine another system. But Horace Mann, along with such allies as Henry Barnard of Connecticut, fought a long and difficult battle to win the acceptance of public elementary schools. The opposition was powerful. Business interests predicted disaster if their labor pool of children were taken away. Concerned taxpayers protested the additional tax monies needed to support public education. There was also the competition. Private schools and religious groups sponsoring their own schools protested the establishment of free schools. Americans wondered what would become of a nation in which everyone received an elementary education. Would this not produce over-educated citizens, questioning authority and promoting self-interest? The opposition to public elementary schools was often fierce, but Horace Mann and his allies prevailed.

As he fought for public schools for all, Mann also waged a battle for high-quality schools. He continually attempted to build new and better schools, which was a problem, since so many Massachusetts schools were in deplorable condition. By

Contributing to the
school reforms of the
nineteenth century were
the poor physical
conditions that
characterized most
U.S. schools.

publicly disseminating information about which communities had well-built or
poorly built schools, he applied public pressure on districts to improve their school
buildings. He worked for effective teacher training programs as well and promoted
more stringent teacher licensing procedures. As a result of his efforts, several **normal
schools** were founded in Massachusetts, schools devoted to preparing teachers in
pedagogy, the best ways to teach children. He also championed newer teaching methods designed to improve and modernize classroom instruction. He opposed the routine practice of corporal punishment and sought ways to positively motivate students
to learn. Mann emphasized practical subjects useful to children and to adult society,
rather than the mastery of Greek and Latin. Mann saw education as a great investment, for individuals and for the country, and he worked for many years to make free
public education a reality. He worked for the abolition of slavery, promoted women's
educational and economic rights, and even fought alongside the temperance movement to limit the negative impact of alcohol. He was not only a committed educator
but a committed reformer as well.

By the time of the Civil War, this radical notion of the public elementary school
had become widespread and widely accepted. Educational historian Lawrence
Cremin summarized the advance of the common school movement in his book *The
Transformation of the School:*

> A majority of the states had established public school systems, and a good
> half of the nation's children were already getting some formal education.
> Elementary schools were becoming widely available; in some states, like
> Massachusetts, New York, and Pennsylvania, the notion of free public
> education was slowly expanding to include secondary schools; and in a few,
> like Michigan and Wisconsin, the public school system was already capped by
> a state university. There were, of course, significant variations from state to
> state and from region to region. New England, long a pioneer in public
> education, also had an established tradition of private education, and private
> schools continued to flourish there. The Midwest, on the other hand, sent a
> far greater proportion of its school children to public institutions. The

southern states, with the exception of North Carolina, tended to lag behind, and did not generally establish popular schooling until after the Civil War.[8]

The Secondary School Movement

With Mann's success in promoting public elementary schools, more and more citizens were given a basic education. In 1880, almost 10 million Americans were enrolled in elementary schools, and, at the upper levels of schooling, both private and public universities were established. But the gap between the elementary schools and the universities remained wide.

Massachusetts, the site of the first tax-supported elementary schools and the first college in America, was the site of the first free **secondary school.** Established in Boston in 1821, the **English Classical School** enrolled 176 students (all boys); shortly thereafter, 76 students dropped out. The notion of a public high school was slow to take root. It was not until 1852 that Boston was able to maintain a similar school for girls. The name of the boys' school was changed to The English High School and, even more simply, Boys' High School, to emphasize the more practical nature of the curriculum.

As secondary schools spread, they generally took the form of private, tuition-charging academies. Citizens did not view the secondary schools as we do today, as a free and natural extension of elementary education.[9] On the eve of the Civil War, over a quarter of a million secondary students were enrolled in six thousand tuition-charging private academies. The curricula of these academies varied widely, some focusing on college preparation and others providing a general curriculum for students who would not continue their studies. For those wanting to attend college, these academies were a critical link. In academies founded for females or in coeducational academies, "normal" courses were often popular. The normal course prepared academy graduates for teaching careers in the common schools. A few academies provided military programs of study.

A major stumbling block to the creation of free high schools was public resistance to paying additional school taxes (sound familiar?). But, in a series of court cases, especially the **Kalamazoo, Michigan, case** in 1874, the courts ruled that taxes could be used to support secondary schools. In Michigan, citizens already had access to free elementary schools and a state-supported university. The courts saw a lack of rationality in not providing a bridge between the two. The idea of public high school slowly took hold.

Almost from their inception, America's high schools have been viewed as a means of enculturating immigrant students into the mainstream of American life.

THE DEVELOPMENT OF AMERICAN SCHOOLS

Elementary Schools

Dame schools (1600s)

These private schools taught by women in their homes offered child care for working parents willing to pay a fee. The dames who taught here received meager wages, and the quality of instruction varied greatly.

Local schools (1600s–1800s)

First started in towns and later expanded to include larger districts, these schools were open to those who could afford to pay. Found generally in New England, these schools taught basic skills and religion.

Itinerant schools (1700s) and tutors (1600s–1900s)

Rural America could not support schools and full-time teachers. As a result, in sparsely populated New England, itinerant teachers carried schooling from village to village; they lived in people's homes and provided instruction. In the South, private tutors taught the rich. Traveling teachers and tutors, usually working for a fee and room and board, took varying levels of education to small towns and wealthy populations.

Private schools (1700s–1800s)

Private schools, often located in the middle colonies, offered a variety of special studies. These schools constituted a true free market, as parents paid for the kind of private school they desired. As you might imagine, both the curricula and the quality of these schools varied greatly.

Common schools (1830–present)

The common school was a radical departure from earlier ones in several ways. First, it was free. Parents did not have to pay tuition or fees. Second, it was open to all social classes. Previously, schools usually taught either middle-class or upper-class children. Horace Mann's common school was intended to bring democracy to the classroom. By the mid-nineteenth century, kindergarten was added. In the past few decades, many common schools, now called *elementary schools*, have added Head Start and other prekindergarten programs.

Secondary Schools

Latin grammar schools (1600s–1700s)

These schools prepared wealthy men for college and emphasized a classical curriculum, including Latin and some Greek. From European roots, the curriculum in these schools reflected the belief that the pinnacle of civilization was reached in the Roman Empire.

English grammar schools (1700s)

These private schools moved away from the classical Latin tradition to more practical studies. These schools were viewed not as preparation for college but as preparation for business careers and as a means of instilling social graces. Some of these schools set a precedent by admitting girls, thus paving the way for the widespread acceptance of females in other schools.

Academies (1700s–1800s)

The academies were a combination of the Latin and English grammar schools. These schools taught English, not Latin. Practical courses were taught, but history and the classics were also included. Some academies emphasized college preparation, while others prepared students to enter business and vocations.

High schools (1800s–present)

These secondary schools differed from their predecessors in that they were free; they were governed not by private boards but by the public. The high school can be viewed as an extension of the common school movement to the secondary level. High schools were open to all social classes and provided both precollege and career education.

Junior high schools (1909–present) and middle schools (1950s–present)

Junior high schools (grades 7–9) and middle schools (grades 6–8) were designed to meet the unique needs of preadolescents and to prepare them for the high school experience.

During the last half of the nineteenth century, the nation moved from agrarian to industrial, from mostly rural to urban, and people viewed the elementary school as inadequate to meet the needs of a more sophisticated and industrialized society. More parents viewed the high school as an important stepping-stone to better jobs. With the gradual decrease in demand for teenage workers, high school attendance grew. Half a century earlier, the public elementary school had reflected the growing dreams and aspirations of Americans and their changing economy. Now the public high school was the benchmark of these changes.

The high school developed in a uniquely American way. As a school for students with various social class, ethnic, and religious backgrounds, the American secondary school was a radical departure from the rigid tracking system of Europe. Relatively early in a European student's career, the limits of secondary education were set, with class status and wealth often primary factors. In the United States, although the high school served the dual purposes of vocational and college preparation, this rigid European tracking system was less pronounced, and early decisions did not predetermine a child's destiny. The high school became a continuation of elementary education, a path to public higher education, and an affirmation of democracy.

During the twentieth century, attendance at the secondary level grew significantly, and the demands on the high school increased. Organizational changes included the creation of **junior high schools** in 1909 and, more recently, **middle schools,** which typically consist of grades 6, 7, and 8.

School Reform Efforts

In 1890, the United States was a vibrant nation undergoing a profound transformation. Vast new industries were taking shape; giant corporations were formed; labor was restive; massive numbers of immigrants were arriving; population was on the upsurge; and traditional patterns of life were changing. In fact, these descriptions parallel changes much later, at the close of the twentieth century. How would education generally, and the new high schools specifically, respond to these changes?

In 1892, the National Education Association (NEA), one of the oldest teacher organizations, established the **Committee of Ten** to develop a national policy for high schools.[10] Chaired by Charles Eliot, president of Harvard University, the committee was composed, for the most part, of college presidents and professors who wanted to bring consistency and order to the high school curriculum. This committee of college professors viewed high schools in terms of preparing intellectually gifted students (typically, white males) for college. The Committee of Ten did not envision today's high school, one that serves all our youth. Nonetheless, many of the committee's recommendations have been influential in the development of secondary education. In 1893, the committee recommended the following:

- A series of traditional and classical courses should be taught sequentially.
- High schools should offer fewer electives.
- Each course lasting for one year and meeting four or five times weekly should be awarded a **Carnegie unit.** Carnegie units would be used in evaluating student progress.
- Students performing exceptionally well could begin college early.

A generation later, in 1918, the NEA once again convened a group to evaluate the high school. Unlike the Committee of Ten, this committee consisted of representatives from the newly emerging profession of education. Education professors, high school principals, the U.S. commissioner of education, and other educators focused concern not on the elite moving on to college but on the majority of students for whom high school would be the final level of education. This committee asked the question, What can high school do to improve the daily lives of citizens in an industrial democracy? This committee's report, ***Cardinal Principles of Secondary Education,*** identified seven goals for high school: (1) health, (2) worthy home membership, (3) command of fundamental academic skills, (4) vocation, (5) citizenship, (6) worthy use of leisure time, and (7) ethical character. The high school was seen as a socializing agency to improve all aspects of a citizen's life.

Since the publication of the *Cardinal Principles* in 1918, not a decade has passed without a committee or commission reporting on reforms needed to improve U.S. schools. During the 1930s, the Progressive Education Association (PEA) provided suggestions to promote social adjustment as well as individual growth. Similar findings reported in the 1940s and 1950s noticeably influenced the evolution of our high schools. More electives were added to the high school curriculum. Guidance counselors were added to the staff. Vocational programs were expanded. The result was the formation of a new, comprehensive institution.

In time, the United States has come full circle, echoing the original call for intellectual rigor first voiced by the Committee of Ten in 1893. In 1983, the federal government's National Commission on Educational Excellence issued *A Nation at Risk: The Imperative for Educational Reform,* maintaining that mediocrity, not excellence, characterized U.S. schools. The commission declared that the inadequate rigor of U.S. education had put the nation at risk, losing ground to other nations in commerce, industry, science, and technology. The commission called for fewer electives and a greater emphasis on academic subjects.

Reports on the status of education and recommendations for school reform have become a U.S. tradition. These reports have underscored a built-in schizophrenia in public education, a conflict between intellectual excellence and basic education for the masses, between college preparation and vocational training, between student-centered education and subject specialization. Some of the reports have called for more focus on the student, on programs to enhance the student's entrance into society and the workplace. Others have cited the need for more emphasis on academic and intellectual concerns, as well as for programs to enhance the student's preparation for college. This dichotomy has been and continues to be an integral feature of American education. Regardless of the particular reforms advocated, all the reports, from the 1890s to the present, have had a common theme: a faith in education. The reports have differed on solutions but have concurred on the central role of the school in maintaining a vibrant democracy.

John Dewey and Progressive Education

John Dewey was possibly the most influential educator of the twentieth century—and probably the most controversial one. Some saw him as a savior of U.S. schools; others accused him of nearly destroying them. Rather than become engrossed in the heated controversy surrounding Dewey, however, let us look at the roots of *progressivism,* the movement with which he is closely associated.

As early as 1875, Francis Parker, superintendent of schools in Quincy, Massachusetts, introduced the concepts of progressivism in his schools. By 1896, John Dewey, the most noted proponent of progressivism, had established his famous **laboratory school** at the University of Chicago. But it was not until the 1920s and 1930s that the progressive education movement became more widely known. During the 1920s and 1930s, the Dalton and Walden schools in New York, the Beaver Country Day School in Massachusetts, the Oak Lane Country Day School in Pennsylvania, and laboratory schools at Columbia and Ohio State universities began to challenge traditional practices. The progressive education approach soon spread to suburban and city public school systems across the country. Various school systems adapted or modified progressive education, but certain basic features remained constant, and elements of progressive education can still be found in many schools.

Progressive education included several components. First, it broadened the school program to include health concerns, family and community life issues, and a concern for vocational education. Second, progressivism applied new research in psychology and the social sciences to classroom practices. Third, progressivism emphasized a more democratic educational approach, accepting the interests and needs of an increasingly diverse student body.

Progressive educators, such as John Dewey, believed that participation in democratic decision making developed rational problem-solving abilities and social skills.

The focus of progressivism was to build on child-centered interests and needs, rather than traditional academic subjects presented by the teacher. Let's take a look at how progressivism might be adapted to today's classroom. Assume that, as a result of severe weather conditions in a community, a number of playgrounds, athletic fields, and social service agency offices have been damaged. During classroom discussions, the teacher and students might decide to do something about the damage caused by the storm. As a group, they volunteer hours helping in the cleanup of the playgrounds and the repair of the social service offices. Building on this interest, the teacher decides to modify the curriculum to include information about El Niño, global warming, and severe climatic conditions. Perhaps the teacher decides to incorporate possible human responses to these issues, including eco-planning, emergency services, the accuracy of weather predictions, and even the possibility that people might someday be able to influence or control climatic and weather conditions. The teacher's instructional decisions build on the natural interests of the students, lead to community service efforts, and modify the science and social science studies curriculum.

This model of education assumed that students learn best when their learning follows their interests. Passively listening to the teacher, according to the progressive movement, is not the most effective learning strategy. The role of the teacher is to identify student needs and interests and provide an educational environment that builds on them. In fact, progressive education shares some characteristics with project-based and authentic learning, popular innovations in some of today's schools.

Although not involved in all the progressive education programs, John Dewey, in many minds, is the personification of progressive education, as well as its most notable advocate. (See "The Education Hall of Fame" later in this chapter for a description of Dewey and his achievements.) In no small part, this is due to the tens of thousands of pages that Dewey wrote during his long life. (Dewey was born on the eve of the Civil War in 1859 and died during the Korean War in the early 1950s.) Toward the end of Dewey's life, both he and progressive education came under strong attack.

The criticism of Dewey and progressive education originated with far-right political groups, for it was the era of Senator Joseph McCarthy and his extremist campaign against communism. While McCarthy's hunt for communists was primarily directed at the government and the military, educators were not immune. Some viewed progressive education as an atheistic, un-American force that had all but destroyed the nation's schools. Because students were allowed to explore and question, many critics were able to cite examples of how traditional values were not being taught. Although these critics were generally ignorant of Dewey's ideas and progressive practices, a second group was more responsible in its critique.

This second wave of criticism came not from the radical right but from individuals who felt that the school curriculum was not academically sound. Hyman Rickover, a famous admiral and developer of the nuclear submarine, and Arthur Bestor, a liberal arts professor, were among the foremost critics decrying the ills of progressive education. They called for an end to "student-centered" and "life-adjustment" subjects and a return to a more rigorous study of traditional courses. While the arguments raged, the launching of *Sputnik* by the Soviet Union in 1957 put at least a temporary closure on the debate. The United States was involved in a space race with the Soviets, a race to educate scientists and engineers, a race toward the first moon landing. Those arguing for a more rigorous, science- and math-focused curriculum won the day. Although many still argued vociferously over the benefits and shortcomings of progressive education, the traditionalists were setting the direction for the nation's curriculum.

Before leaving progressive education, however, it will be beneficial to examine one of the most famous studies of the progressive movement. The Progressive Education Association, formed in 1919, initiated a study during the 1930s that compared almost three thousand graduates of progressive and of traditional schools as they made their way through college. The study, called the **Eight-Year Study,** was intended to determine which educational approach was more effective. The results indicated that graduates of progressive schools

1. Earned a slightly higher grade point average
2. Earned higher grades in all fields except foreign languages
3. Tended to specialize in the same fields as more traditional students
4. Received slightly more academic honors
5. Were judged to be more objective and more precise thinkers
6. Were judged to possess higher intellectual curiosity and greater drive

The Federal Government

As World War II drew to a close, the United States found itself the most powerful nation on earth. For the remainder of the twentieth century, the United States reconstructed a war-ravaged global economy while confronting world communism. In fact, the United States viewed education as an important tool in accomplishing these strategic goals. When the Soviets launched *Sputnik,* for example, the government enlisted the nation's schools in meeting this new challenge. Consequently, Congress passed the **National Defense Education Act (NDEA)** in 1958 to enhance "the security of the nation" and to develop "the mental resources and technical skills of its young men and women." The NDEA supported the improvement of instruction and curriculum development, funded teacher training programs, and provided loans and scholarships for college students that allowed them to major in subjects deemed important to the national defense (such as teaching). However, looking back in history, it is not at all clear how the federal government was legally able to do this. After all, the framers of the Constitution made their intentions clear: education was to be a state responsibility, and the federal government was not to be involved. How did the NDEA and other federal acts come to pass?

Many people are unaware that the responsibility for educating Americans is not even mentioned in the Constitution. Under the Tenth Amendment, any area not specifically stated in the Constitution as a federal responsibility is automatically assigned to the states. Why was education a nontopic? Some historians believe that, since the individual colonies had already established disparate educational systems, the framers of the Constitution did not want to create dissension by forcing the states to accept a single educational system. Other analysts believe that education was deliberately omitted from the Constitution because Americans feared control of the schools by a central government, any central government, as had been the case in Europe. They saw central control as a possible threat to their freedom. Still others suggest that the framers of the Constitution, in their haste, bartering, and bickering, simply forgot about education (what a depressing thought!). Whatever the reason, distinct colonial practices continued, as each state created its own educational structure—its own approach for preparing teachers and funding schools.

Over time, however, the federal government discovered ways to influence education. As early as the revolutionary period, the new nation passed the **Land Ordinance Act** of 1785 and the **Northwest Ordinance** of 1787. These acts required townships in the newly settled territories bounded by the Ohio and Mississippi rivers and the Great Lakes to reserve a section of land for educational purposes. The ordinances contained a much-quoted sentence underscoring the new nation's faith in education: "Religion, morality, and knowledge being necessary to good government and the happiness of mankind, schools and the means of education shall forever be encouraged."

The federal government also exerted its influence through targeted funding, or **categorical grants.** By using federal dollars on specific programs, the government was able to create new colleges and universities, to promote agricultural and

The Supreme Court decision in *Brown v. Board of Education of Topeka,* followed by the 1964 Civil Rights Act, made it possible for students of all races, cultures, and disabling conditions to receive a desegregated education.

IN THE NEWS . . . KKK WIZARD HONORED

School board member Roberta W. is trying to change the name of Nathan Bedford Forrest middle school in Gadsden, Alabama. Named for the Confederate general who went on to become the first grand wizard of the Ku Klux Klan, Ms. Roberta W. feels the time to change the name is long overdue. Her request to explore a new name was defeated when no one seconded her motion.

Source: *The American School Board Journal,* April 1998.

SELECTED FEDERAL LEGISLATION

Few educational issues are immune from federal influence. The following is a partial list of legislation indicating the long history of federal involvement in education.

1. *Land Ordinance Act* and *Northwest Ordinance* (1785 and 1787). These two ordinances provided for the establishment of public education in the territory between the Appalachian Mountains and the Mississippi River. In these new territories, 1 square mile out of every 36 was reserved for support of public education, and new states formed from these territories were encouraged to establish "schools and the means for education."

2. *Morrill Land Grant College Acts* (1862 and 1890). These acts established sixty-nine institutions of higher education in the various states, some of which are among today's great state universities. These acts were also called simply the *Land-Grant College Acts,* since public land was donated to establish these colleges.

3. *Smith-Hughes Act* (1917). This act provided funds for teacher training and program development in vocational education at the high school level.

4. *Servicemen's Readjustment Act* (G.I. Bill of Rights, 1944). This act paid veterans' tuition and living expenses for a specific number of months, depending on the length of their military service.

5. *National Defense Education Act* (1958). In response to the Soviet launching of *Sputnik,* the NDEA provided substantial funds for a variety of educational activities, including student loans, the education of school counselors, and the strengthening of instructional programs in science, mathematics, and foreign languages.

6. *Elementary and Secondary Education Act* (1965). In this omnibus piece of education legislation, the federal government attempted to remedy educational inequities between states and communities. This law provided for financial assistance to school districts with low-income families, provided for funding to improve libraries and

for instructional materials, promoted educational innovations and research, and provided for funds to improve the quality and services of state departments of education. In the 1970s, this legislation was expanded to include funding for bilingual education, drug education, and school lunch and breakfast programs, as well as for the education of Native Americans.

7. *Project Head Start* (1964–1965). This act provides medical, social, nutritional, and educational services for children 3 to 6 years of age who come from low-income families.

8. *Bilingual Education Act* (1968). In response to the needs of the significant number of non-English-speaking students, Congress authorized funds to provide relevant instruction to these students. The primary focus was on Spanish-speaking students with Mexican, Puerto Rican, and Cuban backgrounds, almost 70 percent of whom were failing to graduate from high school. Although many other languages besides Spanish are included in this act, a relatively limited percentage of non-English-speaking students participate in these programs, due to funding shortfalls.

9. *Title IX of the Education Amendments* (1972). This regulation prohibits discrimination on the basis of sex "under any education program or activity receiving federal funds." The regulation is comprehensive and protects the rights of both males and females from preschool through graduate school. Title IX prohibits sexual discrimination in sports, financial aid, employment, counseling, school regulations and policies, admissions, and other areas. Although Title IX has the potential for promoting sex equity, its enforcement has been lax and many schools are currently in violation of one or more aspects of the regulation.

10. *Individuals with Disabilities Education Act* (1975). This act provides financial assistance to local school districts to provide free and appropriate education for the nation's 8 million children with disabilities who are between 3 and 21 years of age.

Photos in Contrast

Twentieth Century Classrooms

How did classrooms change during the twentieth century? What do these rooms say about the roles of teachers and students? How would you describe the aesthetic of these rooms?

industrial research efforts, and to provide schools for Native Americans and other groups. During the Great Depression of the 1930s, the federal government became even more directly involved with education, constructing schools, providing free lunches for poor children, instituting part-time work programs for high school and college students, and offering educational programs to older Americans. With unemployment, hunger, and desperation rampant in the 1930s, states welcomed these federal efforts. More and more Americans were coming to realize that some educational challenges were beyond the resources of the states.

Court action also provided an avenue for federal involvement in schools, as in the landmark ***Brown v. Board of Education of Topeka*** (1954). In this case, the U.S. Supreme Court ruled that separating children "from others of similar age and qualifications solely because of their race generates a feeling of inferiority as to their status in the community that may affect their hearts and minds in a way unlikely to ever be undone." By the 1970s, courts had ruled that discrimination based on gender or directed at students with disabilities was a violation of the U.S. Constitution.

As the twentieth century drew to a close, more conservative administrations reduced federal financial support of education, but not federal influence. Through court action, presidential and congressional leadership, and selected legislation, the U.S. government continues to help shape the nation's schools.

The World We Created at Hamilton High: A Schoolography

In 1988, Gerald Grant published a fascinating book describing life at Hamilton High School (real school, fictitious name) from the 1950s to the 1980s. Like a biography that helps us understand the forces shaping and directing individual lives, *The World We Created at Hamilton High* may be thought of as a "schoolography," offering powerful insights into the forces that have shaped today's schools. The events at Hamilton probably mirror many of the developments in the life of the school you attended, or the one in which you will be teaching. The biography of Hamilton High offers a microcosm of the roots of and reasons behind the current demand for educational reform.[11]

A Super School (If You're on the Right Side of the Tracks), 1953–1965

In 1953, Hamilton High opened its doors to students growing up in one of the new suburban developments, a prototype of those that were sprouting up all across postwar America. Carefully coifed girls in sweaters and skirts and neatly dressed boys with crewcuts and baggy khakis relished their new school, with its tennis courts, modern design, and strong academic offerings. The social life of the Northern, all-white, middle-class school was driven by fraternities and sororities that prohibited or limited the membership of Catholics and Jews. The principal, a former coach, did not provide instructional leadership but certainly did run a tight ship. The purpose of the school was college preparation, and an evaluation of Hamilton written in 1960 reported that a "strong, almost pathological resistance to taking non-college preparation courses exists in this school community." While letters in the school paper debated whether school spirit was dwindling and what would happen if girls were allowed to wear miniskirts, the school board was approving a desegregation plan that would bring the "southern problem" to Hamilton and open a second, more volatile chapter of the school's history.

Social Unrest Comes to School, 1966–1971

Northern desegregation was as difficult as southern desegregation, with white teachers unprepared to teach black students and both black and white students encountering the reality of racism. SAT scores fell, racial incidents and conflicts rose, and white families began leaving the neighborhood. The proportion of African American students in the school system jumped from 15 to 33 percent. As racial confrontations grew, Hamilton was forced to close several times because of bomb threats and the cloud of threatened violence. Fear gripped the school, teachers became physically ill trying to survive the tension, and several principals, unable to control or eliminate the problems, came and went during this period. By the fall of 1971, more than 70 percent of the teachers who had taught at Hamilton in 1966 had left the school.

The Students' Turn, 1972–1979

The old world of fraternities, sororities, and a social structure that was discriminatingly clear disintegrated in the race riots of the 1960s and split the faculty: some were sympathetic to the curricular change and protest goals of the students; others opposed such changes. The administration used uneven standards of discipline, with white children penalized less harshly than black children. There was a lack of trust between the old and the young, parents and the school, and even between the students and administration at all levels as protests over the Vietnam War and the draft grew more intense. As America's social fabric unraveled, the Supreme Court handed down influential decisions awarding greater liberties to students, including grievance procedures and due process rights. Many teachers and administrators were unclear about what constituted legal or illegal discipline. As a result, they found it legally smarter not to discipline students. An abyss was created, with power unclear and the rules in limbo.

From this maelstrom, student leaders (with some faculty supporters) emerged, and student demands began to reshape the world at Hamilton. While teachers and the administration tolerated student infractions of the rules (for fear of being drowned in litigation), students suffered no such inhibitions. They flexed their legal muscles by bringing suits against parents, guardians, and teachers. In class, students felt free to play their radios—that is, when they attended; most students reported that they regularly skipped classes. Drinking and gambling became a part of the school parking-lot landscape, and the students even published an underground newspaper that kept them up-to-date on their legal rights, as well as strategies for cutting classes without being caught—not that the classes themselves were difficult or demanding. In fact, course requirements were reduced significantly. Electives were the choice of the day. Some students were revitalized by the new curriculum, but others took "gut" courses and graduated from Hamilton without much to show for their high school years.

In 1978, a new principal came to the high school, a veteran educator considered tough enough to handle the problems. A uniform discipline code for blacks and whites was established, administrators were taught to back up teachers in their discipline efforts, and the avalanche of easy courses was replaced by a more demanding curriculum. Student suspensions soared. That year, thirty seniors who had cut too many classes were prohibited from participating in graduation. Ever so slowly, adult authority was re-established, and Hamilton's experiment in rule by students came to an end.

New Students, Old School, 1980–1985

Racial desegregation and student protests radically changed Hamilton during the 1970s; the enrollment of students with disabilities sparked the school's second transformation. Although a new federal law (PL 94-142) required that special education students be mainstreamed and taught in regular classes, the teachers were unprepared to respond to their needs, and a number of Hamilton's students were hostile to the new arrivals. Students with disabilities were mainstreamed—and taunted. Mentally retarded, emotionally disturbed, and physically disabled students both experienced and caused frustration when placed in regular classrooms.

During these years, immigrants from Southeast Asia were introduced to Hamilton through the English as a second language (ESL) program. Tension between the newly arrived Vietnamese and Cambodian students and African Americans at Hamilton led to fights. While Hamilton searched for peace and consensus with its new student populations, some students escaped from reality through drug use. By 1984, a

EDUCATION MILESTONES

Seventeenth Century

Informal family education, apprenticeships, dame schools, tutors

1635

Boston Latin Grammar School

1636

Harvard College

1647

Old Deluder Satan Law

1687–1890

New England Primer published

Eighteenth Century

Development of a national interest in education, state responsibility for education, growth in secondary education

1740

South Carolina denies education to blacks.

1751

Opening of the Franklin Academy in Philadelphia

1783

Noah Webster's *American Spelling Book*

1785, 1787

Land Ordinance Act, Northwest Ordinance

Nineteenth Century

Increasing role of public secondary schools, increased but segregated education for women and minorities, attention to the field of education and teacher preparation

1821

Emma Willard's Troy Female Seminary opens, first endowed secondary school for girls.

1821

First public high school opens in Boston.

1823

First (private) normal school opens in Vermont.

1827

Massachusetts requires public high schools.

1837

Horace Mann becomes secretary of board of education in Massachusetts.

1839

First public normal school in Lexington, Massachusetts

1855

First kindergarten (German language) in United States

1862

Morrill Land Grant College Act

1874

Kalamazoo case (legalizes taxes for high schools)

1896

Plessy v. Ferguson Supreme Court decision supporting racially separate but equal schools

Twentieth Century

Increasing federal support for educational rights of under-achieving students; increased federal funding of specific (categorical) education programs

1909

First junior high school in Berkeley, California

1919

Progressive education programs

1932

New Deal education programs

1944

G.I. Bill of Rights

1954

Brown v. Board of Education of Topeka Supreme Court decision outlawing racial segregation in schools

1957

Sputnik leads to increased federal education funds.

1958

National Defense Education Act funds science, math, and foreign language programs.

1964–1965

Job Corps and Head Start are funded.

1972

Title IX prohibits sex discrimination in schools.

1975

Public Law 94-142, Education for All Handicapped Children Act (renamed Individuals with Disabilities Education Act, 1991), is passed.

1979

Cabinet-level Department of Education is established.

1990s

Increased public school diversity and competition through charter schools, for profit companies, open enrollment and technological options.

Source: Compiled from Edward King, *Salient Dates in American Education, 1635–1964* (New York: Harper & Row, 1966); National Center for Education Statistics, U.S. Department of Education, *Digest of Education Statistics, 1994.*

third of Hamilton's students were experimenting with drugs, typically marijuana. However, an increase in adult authority had checked the escalation of black-white tensions and had increased academic demands. The decline in national test scores at Hamilton had stabilized, and "white flight" had ceased. The school was settling down, but Hamilton was not a particularly inspiring or dynamic institution. The academic star of the 1950s had become an academic has-been of the 1980s. Many people were disappointed in their school.

The disappointment at Hamilton High has been felt in other communities. In 1983, *A Nation at Risk* was published, and it initiated a national evaluation of schools. Analysis and questioning of education goals and school quality continued throughout the 1980s and 1990s. How effective is our educational system? Is it accomplishing its goals? (These and other questions were considered in Chapter 5, "Schools, and Beyond.")

While Grant's account of Hamilton High ends in 1985, schoolographies continue. If you were to author the most recent period of school history, what title and description might you give to this latest, and as yet unwritten chapter, of *The World We Created at Hamilton High?*

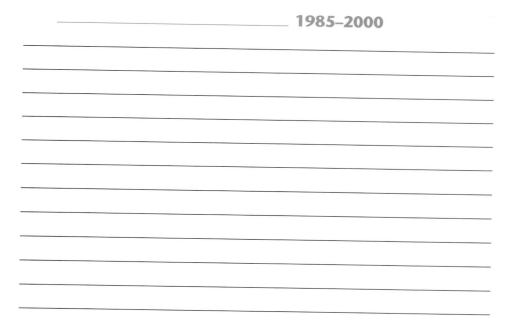

1985–2000

The Education Hall of Fame

A "hall of fame" recognizes individuals for significant contributions to a field. Football, baseball, rock and roll, and country music all have halls of fame to recognize outstanding individuals. We think education is no less important and merits its own forum for recognition. In fact, Emporia State University in Kansas is currently developing a Teacher's Hall of Fame. Building on this idea, in this section are the nominations we would offer to honor educators who we believe should be in a hall of fame.

Obviously, not all influential educators have been included in these brief profiles, but it is important to begin recognizing significant educational contributions. Indirectly or directly, these individuals have influenced your life as a student and will influence your career as a teacher.

For his pioneering work in identifying developmental stages of learning and his support of universal education—

Comenius, born Jan Komensky (1592–1670). A teacher and administrator in Poland and the Netherlands, Comenius's educational ideas were revolutionary for his day. Abandoning the notion that children were inherently bad and needed corporal punishment to encourage learning, Comenius attempted to identify the developmental stages of learners and to match instruction to these stages. He approached learning in a logical way and emphasized teaching general principles before details, using concrete examples before abstract ideas, sequencing ideas in a logical progression, and including practical applications of what is taught. He believed that education should be built on the natural laws of human development and that caring teachers should gently guide children's learning. Comenius supported universal education, and his ideas were later developed by Rousseau, by Pestalozzi, and, nearly 400 years later, by the progressive education movement in the United States.

For his work in distinguishing schooling from education and for his concern with the stages of development—

Jean-Jacques Rousseau (1712–1778). French philosopher Rousseau viewed humans as fundamentally good in their free and natural state but corrupted as a result of societal institutions, such as schools. Like Comenius, he saw children as developing through stages and believed that the child's interests and needs should be the focus of a curriculum. In *Emile,* a novel he wrote in 1762, Rousseau described his educational philosophy by telling the story of young Emile's education, from infancy to adulthood. Emile's education took place on a country estate, under the guidance of a tutor and away from the corrupt influences of society. The early learnings came through Emile's senses and not through books or the words of the teacher. The senses, which Rousseau referred to as the *first teachers,* are more efficient and desirable than learning in the schoolroom. Nature, geography, and the natural sciences were acquired through careful observation of the environment. Only after Emile reached age 15 was he introduced to the corrupt influences of society to learn about government, economics, business, and the arts. Rousseau emphasized the senses over formalized teaching found in books and classrooms, nature over society, and the natural instincts of the learner over the adult-developed curriculum of school. Rousseau's visionary education for Emile can be contrasted with the sexist education he prescribed for Sophie, the book's female character. Sophie's education amounted to little more than obedience school, because Rousseau expected women to be totally subservient to men. (This terribly restricted view of the role of women is an indication that even members of the Education Hall of Fame have their limitations.)

Rousseau was a pioneer of the contemporary deschooling movement, as he separated the institution of the school from the process of learning. His work led to the child study movement and served as a catalyst for progressive education. Rousseau's romantic view of education influenced many later reformers, including Pestalozzi.

For his recognition of the special needs of the disadvantaged and his work in curricular development—

Johann Heinrich Pestalozzi (1746–1827). Swiss educator Pestalozzi read, agreed with, and built on Rousseau's ideas. Rather than abandoning schools, Pestalozzi attempted to reform them. He established an educational institute at Burgdorf to educate children, as well as to train teachers in more effective instructional strategies.

He identified two levels of effective teaching. At the first level, teachers were taught to alleviate the special problems of poor students. Psychological, emotional, and physical needs should be remediated by caring teachers. In fact, the school environment should resemble a secure and loving home, contributing to the emotional health of the child. At the second level, teachers should focus on teaching students to learn through the senses, beginning with concrete items and moving to more abstract ideas, starting with the learner's most immediate surroundings and gradually moving to more complex and abstract topics.

Pestalozzi's ideas are seen today in programs focused on the special needs of the disadvantaged student. His curricular ideas emerge in today's expanding-horizons social studies curriculum, where children learn first about their family, then their community, their state, and eventually the national and world community. Pestalozzi's ideas influenced Horace Mann and other U.S. educators committed to developing more effective school practices.

For establishing the kindergarten as an integral part of a child's education—

Friedrich Froebel (1782–1852). Froebel frequently reflected on his own childhood. Froebel's mother died when he was only 9 months old. In his recollections, he developed a deep sense of the importance of early childhood and of the critical role played by teachers of the young. Although he worked as a forester, chemist's assistant, and museum curator, he eventually found his true vocation as an educator. He attended Pestalozzi's institute and extended Pestalozzi's ideas. He saw nature as a prime source of learning and believed that schools should provide a warm and supportive environment for children.

In 1837 Froebel founded the first **kindergarten** ("child's garden") to "cultivate" the child's development and socialization. Games provided cooperative activities for socialization and physical development, and such materials as sand and clay were used to stimulate the child's imagination. Like Pestalozzi, Froebel believed in the importance of establishing an emotionally secure environment for children. Going beyond Pestalozzi, Froebel saw the teacher as a moral and cultural model for children, a model worthy of emulation (how different from the earlier view of the teacher as disciplinarian).

In the nineteenth century, as German immigrants came to the United States, they brought with them the idea of kindergarten education. Margaretta Schurz established a German-language kindergarten in Wisconsin in 1855. The first English-language kindergarten and training school for kindergarten teachers were begun in Boston in 1860 by Elizabeth Peabody.

For his contributions to moral development in education and for his creation of a structured methodology of instruction—

Johann Herbart (1776–1841). German philosopher Herbart believed that the primary goal of education is moral education, the development of good people. He believed that through education, individuals can be taught such values as action based on personal conviction, concern for the social welfare of others, and the positive and negative consequences associated with one's behavior. Herbart believed that the development of cognitive powers and knowledge would lead naturally to moral and ethical behavior, the fundamental goal of education.

Herbart believed in the coordinated and logical development of all areas of the curriculum. He was concerned with relating history to geography and both of these to literature—in short, in clearly presenting to students the relationships among various subjects. Herbart's careful and organized approach to the curriculum led to the development of structured teaching. His methodology included preparing students for learning (readiness), helping students form connections by relating new material to previously learned information, using examples to increase understanding, and teaching students how to apply information.

Herbart's concern for moral education paved the way for contemporary educators to explore the relationship between values and knowledge, between a well-educated scientist or artist and a moral, ethical adult. His structured approach to curriculum encouraged careful lesson planning—that is, the development of a pre-arranged order of presenting information. Teachers who spend time classifying what they will be teaching and writing lesson plans are involved in the kinds of activities suggested by Herbart.

For opening the door of higher education to women and for promoting professional teacher preparation—

Emma Hart Willard (1787–1870). The sixteenth of seventeen children on a farm in Connecticut, Willard was fortunate enough to be born of well-educated and progressive parents who nurtured new ideas. At a time when it was believed that women could not learn complex subjects, Willard committed her life to opening higher education to women. In her own education, she pursued as rigorous an academic program as was permitted women at the time. She had mastered geometry on her own by the age of 12. At 17, she began her career in teaching. In 1814, she opened the Middlebury Female Seminary. In reality, the seminary offered a college-level program, but the term *college* was avoided and *seminary* was used so as not to offend the public. Although she herself was denied the right to attend classes at nearby Middlebury College, she learned college-level material on her own and incorporated this curriculum into the subjects she taught her female students at the seminary.

She put forth her views on opening higher education to women in a pamphlet entitled *An Address to the Public; Particularly to the Members of the Legislature of New-York, Proposing a Plan for Improving Female Education* (1819). The pamphlet, written and funded by Willard, won favorable responses from Thomas Jefferson, John Adams, and James Monroe, but not the money she sought from the New York State Legislature to open an institution of higher learning for women. Eventually, with local support, she opened the Troy Female Seminary, establishing a rigorous course of study for women, more rigorous than the curriculum found in many men's colleges. Moreover, the seminary was devoted to preparing professional teachers, thus providing a teacher education program years before the first normal (teacher training) school was founded. To disseminate her ideas and curriculum, Willard wrote a number of textbooks, especially in geography, history, and astronomy. In 1837, she formed the Willard Association for the Mutual Improvement of Female Teachers, the first organization to focus public attention on the need for well-prepared and trained teachers.

Emma Hart Willard was a pioneer in the struggle for women's intellectual and legal rights. She wrote and lectured in support of the property rights of married women and other financial reforms, and she dedicated her life to promoting the intellectual and educational freedom of women. Her efforts promoted the recognition of teaching as a profession and the creation of teacher education programs. In the years that followed, colleges, graduate schools, and the professions opened their doors to women. It was Emma Hart Willard's commitment to providing educational opportunities for women that has shaped the past two centuries of progress, not only for women but for all Americans.

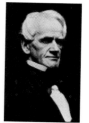

For establishing free public schools and expanding the opportunities of poor as well as wealthy Americans, and for his visions of the central role of education in improving the quality of American life—

Horace Mann (1796–1859). Perhaps the most critical factor in shaping the life of Horace Mann was not what he was given but what he was denied. Although he proved to be an able and gifted student, he was not afforded very much in the way of formal schooling. Forced to learn on his own, he acquired an education and was eventually admitted to Brown University. Before him was a career in law as well as a career in politics, but neither influenced his life as much as his struggle to gain an education. He worked to ensure that others would not be denied educational opportunities. That struggle directed his life and altered the history of U.S. education.

As an educator and a member of the Massachusetts House of Representatives, he worked to improve the quality of education. Corporal punishment, floggings, and unsafe and unsanitary school buildings were all denounced by Mann in speeches, letters, and his lobbying efforts before the state legislature and the U.S. Congress. Of the numerous challenges Mann confronted, he was probably most violently denounced for his efforts to remove religious instruction from schools. He also worked to lengthen the school term; to increase teacher salaries; and, by establishing the first public normal school in 1839, to prepare better teachers. He organized school libraries and encouraged the writing of textbooks that included practical social problems. Mann's efforts resulted in the establishment of the Massachusetts Board of Education, and he became the board's first secretary of education, a position equivalent to a state superintendent of schools.

Of the many achievements attributed to Mann, he is probably best remembered for his leadership in the common school movement, the movement to establish free, publicly supported schools for all Americans. He viewed ignorance as bondage and education as a passport to a promising future. Through education, the disadvantaged could lift themselves out of poverty, blacks could achieve freedom, and children with disabilities could learn to be productive members of society, Mann's credo was that social mobility and the improvement of society could be attained through a free education for all.

However, Mann's fervor was not confined to establishing quality public education. As a member of Congress, he denounced slavery, child labor, worker exploitation, workplace hazards, and the dangers of slum life. Later, as president of Antioch College, he provoked further controversy by admitting women and minority members as students. In the 1850s, this was not only a radical move; for many, it suggested the imminent collapse of higher education. Mann did more than verbalize the importance of freedom and education; his life and actions were a commitment to these principles. The fruits of Mann's efforts are found in our public school system; the education of minorities, the poor, and women; and efforts to provide well-trained teachers working in well-equipped classrooms.

For her integrity and bravery in bringing education to African American girls—

Prudence Crandall (1803–1889).[12] Born of Quaker parents, Prudence Crandall received her education at a school in Providence, Rhode Island, founded by an active abolitionist, Moses Brown. Her upbringing within Quaker circles, in which discussions of abolition were common, may have inspired her interest in racial equality, an interest that led her to acts of personal courage as she strove to promote education among people of all colors.

After graduating from the Brown Seminary around 1830, Crandall taught briefly in Plainfield, Connecticut, before founding her own school for girls in the neighboring town of Canterbury. However, her decision to admit a black girl, Sarah Harris, daughter of a neighboring farmer, caused outrage. While African Americans in Connecticut were free, a large segment of the white population within Canterbury supported the efforts of the American Colonization Society to deport all freed blacks to Africa, believing them to be inherently inferior. Many were adamant that anything but the most basic education for African Americans would lead to discontent and might encourage interracial marriage. The townspeople voiced fears that Crandall's school would lead to the devaluation of local property by attracting a large number of blacks to the area. Prudence Crandall was pressured by the local population to expel Sarah Harris. However, she was determined to defy their wishes. When the wife of a prominent local clergyman suggested that, if Harris remained, the school "could not be sustained," Crandall replied, "Then it might sink then, for I should not turn her out."

When other parents withdrew their children, Crandall advertised for pupils in *The Liberator,* the newspaper of abolitionist William Lloyd Garrison. A month later, the school reopened with a student body comprising fifteen black girls. However, the townspeople made life difficult for Crandall and her students. Supplies were hard to obtain, and Crandall and her pupils faced verbal harassment, as well as being pelted with chicken heads, manure, and other objects. Nonetheless, they persisted.

In 1833, only one month after Crandall had opened her doors to African American girls, the Connecticut legislature passed the notorious "Black Law." This law forbade the founding of schools for the education of African Americans from other states without the permission of local authorities. Crandall was arrested and tried. At her trial, her counsel advised the jury, "You may find that she has violated an act of the State Legislature, but if you also find her protected by higher power, it will be your duty to acquit." Her conviction was later overturned on appeal, but vandalism and arson continued. When a gang stormed the school building with clubs and iron bars, smashing windows and rendering the downstairs area uninhabitable, the school finally was forced to close.

Prudence Crandall's interest in education, racial equality, and women's rights continued throughout her life. Several of her students continued her work, including her first African American student, Sarah Harris, who taught black pupils in Louisiana for many years.

For her work in identifying the educational potential of young children and crafting an environment in which the young could learn—

Maria Montessori (1870–1952). Montessori was no follower of tradition, in her private life or in her professional activities. Shattering sex-role stereotypes, she attended a technical school and then a medical school, becoming the first female physician in Italy. Her work brought her in contact with children regarded as mentally handicapped and brain-damaged, but her educational activities with these children indicated that they were far more capable than many believed. By 1908, Montessori had established a children's school called the Casa dei Bambini, designed to provide an education for disadvantaged children from the slums of Rome.

Montessori's view of children differed from the views held by her contemporaries. Her observations led her to conclude that children have an inner need to work at tasks that interest them. Given the right materials and tasks, children need not be rewarded and punished by the teacher. In fact, she believed that children prefer work to play and are capable of sustained periods of concentration. Young children need a carefully prepared environment in order to learn.

Montessori's curriculum reflected this specially prepared environment. Children learned practical skills, including setting a table, washing dishes, buttoning clothing, and displaying basic manners. They learned formal skills, such as reading, writing, and arithmetic. Special materials included movable sandpaper letters to teach the alphabet and colored rods to teach counting. The children developed motor skills as well as intellectual skills in a carefully developed sequence. The Montessori teacher worked with each student individually, rather than with the class as a whole, to accomplish these goals.

The impact of Montessori's methods continues to this day. Throughout the United States, early childhood education programs use Montessori-like materials. A number of early childhood institutions are called **Montessori schools** and adhere to the approach she developed almost a century ago. Although originally intended for disadvantaged students, Montessori's concept of carefully preparing an environment and program to teach the very young is used today with children from all social classes.

For his work in developing progressive education, for incorporating democratic practices in the educational process—

John Dewey (1859–1952). John Dewey's long life began before the Civil War and ended during the Korean War. During his 93 years, he became quite possibly the most influential educator of the twentieth century. Dewey was a professor at both the University of Chicago and Columbia University, as well as a prolific writer whose ideas and approach to education created innovations and provoked controversies that continue to this day.

Dewey's educational philosophy has been referred to as *progressivism, pragmatism,* and *experimentalism.* Dewey believed that the purpose of education is to assist the growth of individuals, to help children understand and control their environment. Knowledge is not an inert body of facts to be committed to memory; rather, it consists of experiences that should be used to help solve present problems. Dewey believed that the school should be organized around the needs and interests of the child. The learner's interests serve as a springboard to understanding and mastering contemporary issues. For example, a school store might be used to teach mathematics. Students involved in the store operation would learn mathematics by working with money and making change. Dewey was committed to child-centered education, to learning by doing, and to the importance of experience. Classrooms became laboratories in which students could experiment with life and learn to work together.

Dewey's philosophy was founded on a commitment to democratic education. The student should be free to explore and test all ideas and values. Basic American beliefs and institutions should be investigated and restructured when necessary. Education consists of change and of reconstructing experiences. Children, like adults, should learn how to structure their lives and develop self-discipline. Autocratic governments and authoritarian schools are disservices to democracy, for students should participate in shaping their education. Not only should school be a preparation for democracy, but also it should be a democracy. Students should continue this process and shape their world as adults.

The disciples of Dewey's philosophy became a powerful force in education. They founded the Progressive Education Association, which influenced education well into the 1950s. Today, Dewey's writings and ideas continue to motivate and intrigue educators, and there still exist educational monuments to Dewey, both in a variety of school practices and in professional organizations, such as the John Dewey Society. Dewey's philosophy helped open schools to innovation and integrated education with the outside world.

For her contributions in moving a people from intellectual slavery to education—

Mary McLeod Bethune (1875–1955). The first child of her family not born in slavery, Bethune rose from a field hand, picking cotton, to an unofficial presidential adviser. The last of seventeen children born to South Carolina sharecroppers, she filled the breaks in her fieldwork with reading and studying. She was committed to meeting the critical need of providing education to the newly freed African Americans, and, when a Colorado seamstress offered to pay the cost of educating one black girl at Scotia Seminary in Concord, New Hampshire, she was selected. Bethune's plans to become an African missionary changed as she became more deeply involved in the need to educate newly liberated American blacks.

With $1.50, five students, and a rented cottage near the Daytona Beach city dump in Florida, Bethune founded a school that eventually became Bethune-Cookman College. As a national leader, she created a number of black civic and welfare organizations, serving as a member of the Hoover Commission on Child Welfare, and acting as an adviser to President Franklin D. Roosevelt.

Mary McLeod Bethune demonstrated commitment and effort in establishing a black college against overwhelming odds and by rising from poverty to become a national voice for African Americans.

For his creation of a theory of cognitive development—

Jean Piaget (1896–1980). As a student at the University of Paris, Swiss psychologist Piaget met and began working for Alfred Binet, who developed the first intelligence test (a version of which we know today as the Stanford-Binet IQ test). Binet was involved in standardizing children's answers to various questions on this new test, and he enlisted Jean Piaget to assist. Piaget not only followed Binet's instructions, but he went beyond them. He not only recorded children's answers but also probed students for the reasons behind their answers. From the children's responses, Piaget observed that children at different age levels see the world in different ways. From these initial observations, he conceptualized his theory of cognitive, or mental, development, which has influenced the way educators have viewed children ever since.

Piaget's theory outlines four stages of cognitive development. From infancy to 2 years of age, the child functions at the *sensorimotor stage.* At this initial level, infants explore and learn about their environment through their senses—using their eyes, hands, and even mouths. From 2 to 7 years of age, children enter the *preoperational stage* and begin to organize and understand their environment through language and concepts. At the third stage, *concrete operations,* occurring between the ages of 7 and 11, children learn to develop and use more sophisticated concepts and mental operations. Children at this stage can understand numbers and some processes and relationships. The final stage, *formal operations,* begins between 11 and 15 and continues through adulthood. This stage represents the highest level of mental development, the level of adult abstract thinking.

Piaget's theory suggests that teachers should recognize the abilities and limits at each stage and provide appropriate learning activities. Children should be encouraged to develop the skills and mental operations relevant to their mental stage and should be prepared to grow toward the next stage. Teachers, from early childhood through secondary school, need to develop appropriate educational environments and work with students individually according to their own levels of readiness.

Piaget revealed the interactive nature of the learning process and the importance of relating the learner's needs to educational activities. His work led to increased attention to early childhood education and the critical learning that occurs during these early years.

For his contributions in establishing a technology of teaching—

Burrhus Frederick (B. F.) Skinner (1904–1990). When poet Robert Frost received a copy of young B. F. Skinner's work, he encouraged the author to continue writing. But Skinner's years of serious writing in New York's Greenwich Village were unproductive. As Skinner explained, "I discovered the unhappy fact that I had nothing to say, and went to graduate study in psychology, hoping to remedy that short-coming."

Skinner received his doctorate from Harvard, where he eventually returned to teach. He found himself attracted to the work of John B. Watson, and Skinner's ideas became quite controversial. One critic described him as "the man you love to hate."

Skinner's notoriety stemmed from his belief that organisms, including humans, are entirely the products of their environment; engineer the environment, and you can engineer human behavior. Skinner's view of human behavior (called **behaviorism**) irked individuals who see it as a way of controlling people and enslaving the human spirit. Skinner's response was that he did not create these principles but simply discovered them and that a constructive environment can "push human achievement to its limits."

Skinner's early work included the training of animals. During World War II, in a secret project, Skinner trained, or conditioned, pigeons to pilot missiles and torpedoes. The pigeons were so highly trained that they were capable of guiding a missile right down the smokestack of an enemy ship.

Skinner believed that children could be conditioned to acquire desirable skills and behaviors. By breaking down learning into small, simple steps and rewarding children after the completion of each step, learning mastery is achieved. By combining many of these steps, complex behaviors can be learned efficiently. To advance his ideas, he developed the "teaching machine," a device that used these principles of step-by-step instruction requiring and rewarding student responses. This approach laid the foundation for the later development of behavior modification and computer-assisted instruction.

Skinner's creative productivity resulted in both inventions and numerous publications. The "Skinner box" enabled researchers to observe, analyze, and condition pigeons and other animals to master tasks, while teaching machines translated these learning principles into human education. Skinner's books, including *Walden Two, The Technology of Teaching,* and *Beyond Freedom and Dignity,* spread his ideas on the importance of environment and behaviorism to educators, psychologists, and the general public. He provided guiding principles about the technology of learning, principles that can be used to unleash or to shackle human potential.

For her creative approaches placing children at the center of the curriculum—

Sylvia Ashton-Warner (1908–1984). Sylvia Ashton-Warner began her school career in her mother's New Zealand classroom, where rote memorization constituted the main avenue for learning. The teaching strategies that Ashton-Warner later devised, with their emphasis on child-centered learning and creativity in the classroom, stand in opposition to this early experience.

Ashton-Warner was a flamboyant and eccentric personality; throughout her life, she considered herself to be an artist rather than a teacher. She focused on painting, music, and writing. Her fascination with creativity was apparent in the remote New Zealand classrooms, where she encouraged self-expression among the native Maori children. As a teacher, she infuriated authorities with her absenteeism and unpredictability, and in official ratings she was never estimated as above average in her abilities. However, during the peak years of her teaching career, between 1950 and 1952, she developed innovative teaching techniques that influenced teachers around the world and especially in the United States.

Realizing that certain words were especially significant to individual pupils because of their life experiences, Ashton-Warner developed her "key vocabulary" system for teaching reading to young children. Words drawn from children's conversations were written on cards. Using these words, children learned to read. Ashton-Warner asserted that the key to making this approach effective lay in choosing words that had personal meaning to the individual child: "Pleasant words won't do. Respectable words won't do. They must be words organically tied up, organically born from the dynamic life itself. They must be words that are already part of the child's being."

Bringing meaning to children was at the center of Ashton-Warner's philosophy. This belief provided the foundation of several reading approaches and teaching strategies used throughout the United States. Her work brought meaning to reading for millions of children. In her best-selling book, *Teacher,* she provided many future teachers with important and useful insights. Her emphasis on key vocabulary, individualized reading, and meaningful learning is evident in classrooms today in America and abroad.

For his work in identifying the crippling effects of racism on all American children and in formulating community action to overcome the educational, psychological, and economic impacts of racism—

Kenneth Clark (1914–   ). Born in the Panama Canal Zone, Clark was influenced by a forceful mother, who relocated the family to New York City when Clark was 5 years of age in order to provide better educational opportunities for her children. Working as a seamstress in a New York sweatshop, she helped organize the International Ladies' Garment Workers Union. Clark attributes the lessons he learned concerning the importance of "people doing things together to help themselves" to his mother.

Clark attended schools in Harlem, where he witnessed an integrated community become all black and felt the growing impact of racism. He attended Howard University and received his doctorate from Columbia University, but his concern with the educational plight of African Americans generally, and the Harlem community in particular, was always central in his professional efforts.

Clark participated in the landmark study of racial segregation undertaken by Gunnar Myrdal, which resulted in the publication of *An American Dilemma* in 1944. In his own work, he investigated the impact of segregated schools in New York City, concluding that black students receive an education inferior to that of whites. To counter this problem, he established several community self-help projects to assist children with psychological and educational problems. One of those programs, called HARYOU (Harlem Youth Opportunities Unlimited), was designed to prevent school dropouts, delinquency, and unemployment. His efforts served as a catalyst for government action, with both New York City and the federal government providing funds to enhance educational opportunities for minority students.

Kenneth Clark was the first African American appointed to a faculty position at the City College of New York. In books such as *Prejudice and Your Child,* he analyzed the impact of racism on both whites and blacks. The Supreme Court, in its 1954 *Brown* decision, cited Clark's work as psychological evidence for the need to desegregate U.S. schools. His psychological studies and community efforts represented pioneering achievements in desegregating U.S. schools and enhancing U.S. education. As Clark noted decades ago, "A racist system inevitably destroys and damages human beings; it brutalizes and dehumanizes blacks and whites alike."

For his contribution in establishing an American school of cognitive psychology and for his insights in shaping the school curriculum—

Jerome Bruner (1915—   ). As a graduate student in psychology at Harvard, Jerome Bruner found himself deeply involved in the study of animal perceptions and learning. Psychology was then a new field, and U.S. psychologists, heavily influenced by the behaviorist tradition, turned a deaf ear to studying anything as "unscientific" as human thinking and learning. But Bruner's involvement in World War II altered the direction of his efforts and helped initiate an American school of cognitive psychology, a movement to study human behavior.

During the war, Bruner worked in General Eisenhower's headquarters, studying psychological warfare. His doctoral dissertation concerned Nazi propaganda techniques. After the war, he published works showing how human needs affect perception. For example, poor children are more likely to overestimate the value of coins than are richer children. Adult values and needs affect the way they see the world as well, and realities that do not conform to these needs and beliefs are mentally altered. Bruner showed that human behavior can be observed, analyzed, and understood in an objective way. By 1960, he had helped found Harvard University's Center for Cognitive Studies. Bruner helped legitimize the systematic, objective, and scientific study of human learning and thinking.

Bruner's thoughtful and practical approach to issues was applied to the study of the school curriculum. He was a leader of the Woods Hole conference, a summit of scientists, educators, and scholars interested in reforming education. (The conference followed the Soviet success in launching *Sputnik.*) His report on the conference was published in ***The Process of Education*** (1960), hailed as a practical and readable analysis of curriculum needs. *The Process of Education* has been translated into twenty-two languages and is studied by teachers around the world. In his book, Bruner argued that schools should not focus on facts but should attempt to teach the "structure," the general nature, of a subject. He also stressed the need for developing intuition and insights as a legitimate problem-solving technique. Finally, in his best-known quotation from *The Process of Education,* Bruner stated, "Any subject can be taught effectively in some intellectually honest form to any child at any stage of development." Bruner has cogently argued for more problem solving and direct involvement in the process of education for all learners, from young children to adults.

For his global effort to mobilize education in the cause of social justice—

Paulo Reglus Neves Freire (1921–1997). Abandoning a career in the law, Brazilian-born Freire committed himself to the education of the poor and politically oppressed. His efforts moved literacy from an educational tool to a political instrument.

Freire denounced teacher-centered classrooms. He believed that instructor domination denied the legitimacy of student experiences and treated students as secondary objects in the learning process. He termed such instruction "banking" education, since the students become little more than passive targets of the teacher's comments. Freire championed a "critical pedagogy," one that places the student at the center of the learning process. In Freire's pedagogy, student dialogues, knowledge, and skills are shared cooperatively, legitimizing the experiences of the poor. Students are taught how to generate their own questions, focus on their own social problems, and develop strategies to live more fruitful and satisfying lives. Teachers are not passive bystanders or the only source of classroom wisdom. Freire believed that teachers should facilitate and inspire, that teachers should "live part of their dreams within their educational space." Rather than unhappy witnesses to social injustice, teachers should be advocates for the poor and agents for social change. Freire's best known work, ***Pedagogy of the Oppressed,*** illustrated how education could transform society.

Freire's approach obviously threatened the social order of many repressive governments, and he faced constant intimidation and threats. Following the military overthrow of the Brazilian government in 1964, Freire was jailed for "subversive" activities and later exiled. In the late 1960s, while studying in America, Freire witnessed racial unrest and the antiwar protests. These events convinced Freire that political oppression is present in "developed nations" as well as third world countries, that economic privilege does not guarantee political advantage, and that the pedagogy of the oppressed has worldwide significance.

Summary

1. In early colonial days, most education took place in the home, in the church, and through apprentice programs, with instruction dominated by religious teachings. While today's public school systems hardly resemble their colonial roots, many of our current controversies are rooted in the past. We continue to dispute the role of religion in schools, differences in state government education policies, and inequities in educational opportunities for women, people of color, and the poor.

2. In 1647, Massachusetts passed the "Old Deluder Satan Law," requiring that every town of 50 households appoint and pay a teacher of reading and writing, and every town of 100 households provide a Latin grammar school. This law offered a model for other communities and made the establishment of schools a practical reality.

3. Colonial Latin grammar schools prepared white boys for a university education. In the 1700s, academies were established; they were more secular and practical in their curriculum and were open to girls.

4. The Constitution has helped determine the shape of modern education in two ways. By omitting any mention of national education as a federal responsibility, the Constitution left the issue to the states as each state government set up its own policy, practice, and means of funding schools.

5. During the nineteenth century, the public began to feel that schools should serve the poor as well as the wealthy. As leader of the common school movement, Horace Mann is sometimes called the father of the public school. By the time of the Civil War, the concept of the elementary public school had become widely accepted.

6. Public high schools caught on much more slowly than elementary schools. But, as the country moved from agrarian to industrial and from rural to urban, resistance to public funding of high schools decreased. Eventually, high schools came to represent democratic ideals of equal opportunity; later, many believed that education could be a panacea for societal problems.

7. From the Committee of Ten in 1892 to the 1983 publication of *A Nation at Risk,* waves of educational reform have become part of the American landscape. While reform movements have not reached a consensus as to the best educational system for the nation, one idea remains key: schools should have a central role in maintaining a vibrant democracy.

8. Over the course of its development, the nation's educational system has been supported by a rich variety of instructional materials, including the colonial hornbook; the nation's first real textbook, *New England Primer;* Noah Webster's *American Spelling Book,* which replaced *The New England Primer* as the most widely used elementary textbook; and McGuffey Readers, emphasizing hard work, patriotism, and morality. McGuffey Readers sold more than 100 million copies between 1836 and 1920.

9. Progressivism, with John Dewey as its most notable advocate, had a significant impact on education in the twentieth century. Its emphasis on learning by doing and shaping curricula around children's interests has influenced many educators to this day. Dewey and others have come under frequent attack, however, first by conservative extremists of the 1950s, who saw progressivism as communistic and contrary to American values. Later, in the wake of the Soviet *Sputnik* launching, progressivism was blamed for causing U.S. students to lag behind in important subjects. While progressivism has ceased to be the organized educational movement it once was, many of its ideas continue to be debated and re-examined.

10. While the Constitution leaves most of the responsibility for schooling to the states, the federal government has played an increasing role in education over the past century. National programs have included targeted funds for such programs as the National Defense Education Act, as well as legislation and court action designed to fight segregation and other forms of discrimination in the schools. During the 1980s and 1990s, more conservative forces decreased federal funding, but not federal influence in education.

Key Terms and People

A Nation at Risk: The Imperative for Educational Reform
academy
American Spelling Book
apprenticeship
Sylvia Ashton-Warner

behaviorism
Mary McLeod Bethune
Brown v. Board of Education of Topeka
Jerome Bruner
Cardinal Principles of Secondary Education

Carnegie unit
categorical grants
Kenneth Clark
Comenius
Committee of Ten
common school

www.mhhe.com/sadker

In ***San Antonio v. Rodriguez*** (1973), the Supreme Court, in a hotly contested 5-to-4 decision, ruled against Rodriguez, claiming that education was not a "fundamental right" under the U.S. Constitution. The close Supreme Court vote may someday be reversed—a reversal that would have enormous impact. In *Rodriguez,* the justices made two important points: educational funding through the property tax was a seriously flawed system, and it was up to the states to change it. And that is precisely what happened. State courts, one after another, began a process of altering how the income from property taxes would be dispersed. But this took time.

It took sixteen more years before the Texas Supreme Court would act on the Rodriguez case. During that time, the gap between rich and poor only grew. By the mid-1980s, Edgewood had neither typewriters nor a playground, but affluent Alamo Heights had computers and a swimming pool. These inequities were mirrored throughout Texas, where per-pupil expenditures ranged from $2,112 in the poorest community to $19,333 in the wealthiest. On 2 October 1989, in ***Edgewood v. Kirby,*** the Texas Supreme Court justices agreed unanimously that such differences violated the Texas constitution. The court ordered Texas to devise a fairer plan, one that would avoid these gross inequities among communities.

The differences between Alamo Heights and Edgewood echo throughout the nation. In California, a similar case involved Baldwin Park and Beverly Hills. Almost thirty years ago, Beverly Hills, where the rich and famous pay very high property taxes on very valuable property, was spending $1,232 per student, while the much poorer Baldwin Park was paying only $577. In August 1971, the California Supreme Court, in a 6-to-1 decision, found that heavy reliance on the local property tax "makes the quality of a child's education a function of the wealth of his parents and neighbors. . . . Districts with small tax bases simply cannot levy taxes at a rate sufficient to produce the revenue that more affluent districts produce with a minimum effort." This landmark decision was known as ***Serrano v. Priest.***

INEQUALITIES: SAVAGE AND OTHERWISE

It is easy to forget that behind taxes and school budgets are people whose lives are shaped, and sometimes destroyed, by educational funding. **Jonathan Kozol** is not one to forget. In his best-selling book, *Savage Inequalities* (1991), Kozol describes the impact of funding differences through his eyewitness accounts of life in poor schools from East St. Louis to the Bronx.[a] Kozol writes of schools in poor neighborhoods that have no computers and would gladly settle for used typewriters. Schools report a chronic lack of textbooks. Some students go for part, most, or all of the year without a book. Others attend classes so overcrowded that students get desks only when enough other students are absent.

Despite this nation's wealth, about one in five students attend schools woefully lacking even the most basic facilities. For example, the science labs in East St. Louis schools are forty years out of date. The physics lab has six work areas, each with its own hole where pipes once carried water. The average temperature in the lab is 100 degrees, because the school's heating system tends to roast that side of the building—while the other half of the school freezes. At Morris High School in the South Bronx the chalkboards are so badly cracked that students are told not to use them for fear they will cut themselves. Plaster and paint chips fall from the ceiling with such regularity that students shower after school to wash the paint out of their hair. In the band room, chairs are positioned to avoid falling acoustical tiles. When it rains, water cascades down a staircase located just under a hole in the ceiling.

The heart of these savage inequalities, according to Kozol, is the economic gap between poor and rich communities in the United States. The nation's failure to fairly fund its schools goes beyond court cases and tax rates; it represents an ongoing human tragedy.

[a]Source: Jonathan Kozol, *Savage Inequalities: Children in American Schools* (New York: Crown, 1991).

LEGAL LANDMARKS IN EDUCATIONAL FINANCE

- *Serrano v. Priest* (California, 1971). Dependence on the property tax to fund education is unconstitutional in California, because it "invidiously discriminates against the poor." Similar rulings have been made by courts in other states.
- *San Antonio v. Rodriguez* (U.S. Supreme Court, 1973). By a 5-to-4 vote, the Supreme Court ruled that the property tax did not violate the U.S. Constitution but might violate state constitutions. The close vote moved the issue to the state level but did not rule out possible future decisions from the highest court as membership changed.
- *Serrano II* (California, 1976). Reaffirming the unconstitutionality of the property tax under the California constitution, the state court noted "a distinct relationship between cost and the quality of educational opportunities afforded."
- *Levittown v. Nyquist* (New York, 1982). In a setback for the school finance reform movement, the New York State Court of Appeals declared that the property tax approach had a "rational basis" and that any attempt to enforce a uniform property tax would undermine local control of schools.
- *Rose and Blandford v. Council for Better Education et al.* (Kentucky, 1989). In perhaps the most dramatic state ruling, the Kentucky supreme court declared the entire system of public education to be the cause of inequities. As a result, the legislature has radically reshaped education, replacing school boards with councils of parents, teachers, and administrators. More preschool opportunities for the disadvantaged have been mandated, and "ungraded" primary classes have been instituted.
- *Edgewood v. Kirby* (Texas, 1989). Taking the lead from the 1973 *Rodriguez* decision, the Texas supreme court declared that heavy reliance on property taxes led to major educational inequities and violated the Texas state constitution. As a result, funds have been redistributed from wealthier to poorer districts.
- *Abbott v. Burke* (New Jersey, 1990). The state court ordered that the funding of the 30 poorest school districts be raised to the average level of the state's 108 richest school districts. More state funds would go to these poorer districts, and fewer state monies would be given to wealthier districts. However, a number of middle-income and wealthy districts objected, and this delayed implementation.

Source: Adapted from Thomas Toch, "Separate but Not Equal," *Agenda* 1 (spring 1991): pp. 15–17.

TWO TYPICAL STATE PLANS TO LEVEL THE PLAYING FIELD

The **foundation program**, used by more than twenty states, establishes a minimal level, or "foundation," to be spent by each school district on each student. Regardless of the wealth or poverty of an individual community, the state provides funds to ensure that each student receives a minimal level of educational services. The problem is that the established minimum is frequently far below actual expenditures.

The **guaranteed tax base** adds state funds to the tax dollars raised at the local level. Since more funds are provided to poor districts than to wealthy ones, the guaranteed tax base helps reduce economic inequities.

There are states that use both of these programs as they strive for economic equity among wealthy and poor districts. Still, some courts have determined that even these efforts fall short of leveling the playing field.

The States to the Rescue

The *Serrano* decision in California, the *Edgewood* decision in Texas, and similar decisions in other state courts have assigned the responsibility for equalizing local educational expenditures to the states. By the mid-1990s, more than forty states were facing legal challenges to their school finance systems.[3] These legal cases led to **Robin Hood laws**—so named because courts have been redistributing wealth much as the hero of Sherwood Forest did, by taking from the rich and giving to the poor. In Camden, New Jersey, court action led to an $80-million increase in state aid. These funds were taken from more affluent districts, such as Cherry Hill. With these redistributed state funds, Camden established after-school homework centers, provided free tutoring, purchased computers, updated science labs, created parent education and teacher training programs, purchased new textbooks, and began to develop a new curriculum.[4] Still, Cherry Hill and other wealthy school districts were able to spend thousands of dollars more on each student's education than could Camden. Robin Hood was creating change, but not equality.

Some states are looking beyond **financial input** (per-pupil expenditures) to **educational outcome** (student performance) as a better gauge of educational equity. Believing that financial reform alone will not ensure satisfactory educational performance, these state courts are looking at how well schools, regardless of funding levels, are educating students. In Kentucky, for example, the court has adopted a more active role and has ruled that the state's "entire system of common schools was infirm." The court revamped the state's schools, defining an "efficient" educational system as one that provides students with oral and written communications skills; knowledge of economics, history, and social systems; and sufficient preparation for academic and career success. To meet these goals, the state legislature enacted the Kentucky Education Reform Act in 1990, launching a new curriculum, statewide performance tests, preschool programs for at-risk students, multiple grades in the same class, and economic incentives for educational progress.[5] Like Kentucky, other state courts may decide to go beyond economic reform and directly reshape school practices. Figures 10.1 and 10.2 indicate the increasing role of the state government, especially in poorer communities. Figure 10.3 reflects increasing per pupil expenditures in school.

States grapple with tough issues as they work to distribute funds fairly to wealthy and poor communities. But, even before they distribute these funds, they face the formidable obstacle of raising enough money to support schools and other state functions, no easy task. Let's look at how one governor searches for those much

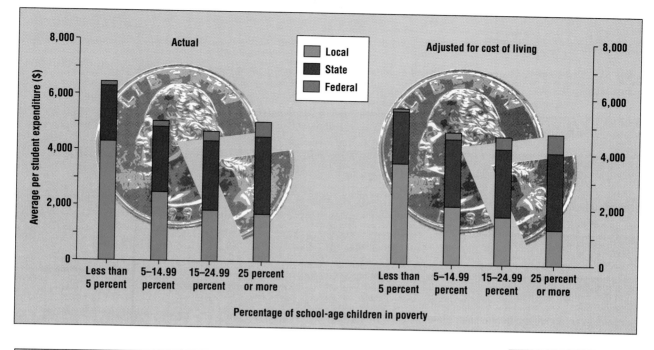

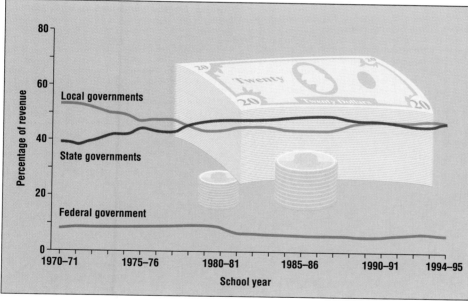

FIGURE 10.1

Source of revenue per student and school district wealth. Notice how state and federal funding increase in poorer communities.

Source: Condition of Education, 1998

FIGURE 10.2

Sources of revenue for public elementary and secondary schools: 1970–71 to 1994–95. Once primarily a local financial responsibility, state and local governments more evenly share today's educational expenses.

Source: U.S. Department of Education, National Center for Education Statistics, *Statistics of State School Systems; Revenues and Expenditures for Public Elementary and Secondary Education;* and Common Core of Data surveys.

needed education dollars. The following fictitious scenario presents a very real dilemma. Join our governor as she explores a problem that, if not resolved, could cost her the next election and, more important, could hurt our students as well.

The lights burned late in the governor's office as she tried again and again to fit the pieces together. There was no denying that the schools needed more money. From computers to vocational education to much needed repairs, significant increases in school funding could no longer be delayed. But where would these funds be found?

GOVERNANCE AND FINANCE BALANCE SHEET 1   EQUITABLE FINANCING

We Need to Redistribute Educational Funds Equitably Because . . .

As Kozol and others have poignantly documented, children born in poorer districts are denied an effective, even an adequate, education only because of the accident of geography. Their schools have fewer facilities and fewer programs, their teachers are paid less, and their graduation rates are lower. In many urban areas, dilapidated schools are downright dangerous, and high-quality education is all but impossible. In these schools, the scarcity of textbooks, the lack of computers, rats "sharing" the classrooms, health code violations, and the threat of violence are constant reminders of America's broken promise to the poor. We as a people are supposed to be committed to equality and fairness, yet paying twice as much to educate the children of the rich, while barely providing minimum education to the poor, makes a mockery of U.S. justice. Education is a basic right for all. And, when schools in poor areas do not do an effective job, society pays the bill. The decision is ours: we can pay for more effective, more successful schools today or get ready to spend far more on welfare, unemployment, and prisons tomorrow.

The idea that everyone enjoys equal political power regardless of race, gender, wealth, and geography, is fundamental to our democracy. Each child is entitled to equal educational opportunity. When students in one part of the state are given two, or even three, times more dollars for their education, that contradicts the idea of equal education for all. Educational dollars are fundamental to the survival of our democracy and must be shared equally.

The federal and state governments do not spend enough money on education in general, and poorer students suffer most. The United States ranks eleventh out of the top fourteen industrialized nations in the percentage of gross national product spent on elementary and secondary schools. While wealthier communities can and do make up the gap out of their personal wealth, poorer school districts do not have these resources. Ironically, it is the poorer students—whose educational needs are the greatest—who are most likely to suffer because of the relatively low level of public dollars spent on education.

(Balance Sheet 1 continues on next page)

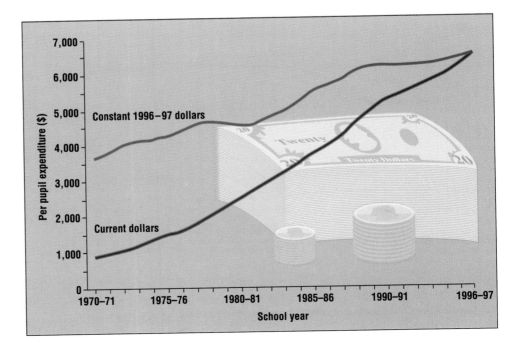

FIGURE 10.3

Current expenditure per pupil in average daily attendance in public elementary and secondary schools: 1970–71 to 1996–97.

Source: U.S. Department of Education, National Center for Education Statistics, *Statistics of State School Systems; Revenues and Expenditures for Public Elementary and Secondary Education;* and Common Core of Data surveys.

She turned to her veteran administrative assistant, Harriet Schukel. They had overcome numerous obstacles. Certainly, school finance could be mastered.

"Harriet," the governor said, "where will we find the money for our schools?"

LAW: THE ROBIN HOOD APPROACH

Forced Redistribution of Educational Funds is a Terrible Mistake Because . . .

While it may sound harsh, everyone is not equal. In our system, those who work hard and are talented are rewarded, while the less capable and less ambitious do less well. That reality motivates people, and it makes our system work. Government intervention disrupts this process and, by equalizing funding, deprives people of motivation. If less productive parents were simply "given" good schools, what would motivate them to do better? In fact, if we were to take money from successful parents and simply give it to less successful ones, we would negatively impact our most effective citizens. We would "demotivate" them. Our system of rewards is not always perfect, but it is better than the others available. The demise of the Soviet Union, the great equalizer and demotivator, is a classic example that the forced-equality approach is destined to fail.

The idea that the size of a school budget determines the quality of a school's education is not only simplistic, but it is inaccurate. Big school budgets create carpeted classes, well-paid teachers, and parking lots for students' expensive cars—nice accessories but not tied to education quality. There are too many examples of rich students doing poorly and poor students doing well for us to buy this "bigger budget, better school" argument.

Education is a state function, not a national democratic right. States can make some efforts to equalize spending among schools within the state (if they so choose), but what about differences among the states? Some states spend much more on education than do others, and there is no way of equalizing differences among the states, so attempts to equalize expenditures within a state, even if totally effective, would not change the funding differences in the United States. It is a futile effort.

Attempts to equalize education through funding are destined to fail. Many poorer districts are simply inefficient, even corrupt. There are too many examples of urban educators who use funds unwisely, if not illegally. Moreover, states trying to equalize educational efforts will discover that the weaker districts will never reach the level of the stronger ones. Should the best districts be given less money or told to lower their student achievement scores? There will always be differences, and throwing dollars at weaker schools will not eliminate these gaps.

The governor, working with the state legislature, is responsible for providing direction and financing for the state's schools.

"The simplest thing would be to hike the sales tax. Even a 1 percent hike would raise millions of dollars."

Sales Tax

If the governor were to increase the **sales tax,** the business community would simply add an extra 1 percent charge to all sales, and the state would receive the money.

Consumers would pay a few extra pennies for small purchases or a few extra dollars for large purchases, and the money would go from the sale directly to the state treasury. The state would not have to create any special fund-raising system or hire additional employees. There was a lot of appeal for the governor in this not too painful system. After all, more than forty states had a sales tax, usually between 2 percent and 8 percent, and these funds accounted for 30 percent of the typical state's income.[6]

"But, remember, Governor," Harriet said, "although the sales tax is simple, it could hurt business. The sales tax could kill your economic revitalization program."

The governor considered the problems posed by increasing the sales tax. The business community might lose sales to neighboring states, thus stifling the state's economic growth. Moreover, poor families would be particularly hard hit by a higher sales tax, and the governor's margin of victory in the last election had come from these poorer families. Over the past few years, the sales tax has been pulling in fewer dollars than expected. The drop in income has been a result of an increase in mail order sales and Internet purchases, both of which bring sales tax income to other states. Perhaps an additional sales tax was not as attractive after all. The governor turned to her aide.

"What are our other options?"

"The best is the personal income tax. It's probably the fairest."

Personal Income Tax

More than forty states use a personal income tax to raise funds totaling more than 25 percent of state revenues.[7] Like the federal income tax, the **personal income tax** is collected through payroll deductions, even before a worker receives his or her paycheck. Increasing the state income tax would simply increase the size of the deductions, and more money would be available for education. And Harriet was right: this approach would also be relatively fair. Individuals with a high income pay a higher amount, and those less able to pay, although taxed at the same percentage, are taxed on their lower income and pay fewer dollars in tax. In fact, the state income tax rules already made provisions for dependents, the disabled, and those with high medical bills and other special needs.

As usual, however, Harriet was quick to point out the problems: "Naturally, there is a downside to increasing the state income tax. Some of our wealthy citizens are not paying their fair share now; their accountants always manage to find tax loopholes. In fact, many manage to evade federal and state income tax completely. And, like the sales tax, if the economy sours and people's incomes drop, the increased income tax might result in no additional income."

"Harriet, let's look beyond the tried-and-true systems used by most states. Are there any other revenue sources that we can tap?"

"Well, Governor, we could institute a state lottery. That's popular all across the country."

State Lottery

Lotteries are definitely hot. Individuals buy a lottery ticket, usually for a dollar, and choose a series of numbers. If those numbers are selected, the lucky ticket holder wins an amount ranging from a few dollars to millions. Although some groups oppose lotteries as immoral gambling, there is a growing acceptance of this approach as a relatively painless method of raising funds for education. After the winners collect their millions in prize money, there are still enormous profits, profits which can be spent on education and other state needs.

Roughly two-thirds of the states now have lotteries, and nearly half of those claim to dedicate at least a portion of the revenues to education. In reality, however, most states use lottery revenues to supplement, not fund, parts of an established education budget.[8] Even if the lottery were structured to enhance educational resources, other social needs within the state would likely compete for the funding as well. The governor concluded that a lottery would be unlikely to provide significant additional long-range funding.

The governor was running out of options and began to review a potpourri of other tax sources.

Other Taxes

The governor considered imposing a series of small, targeted taxes in several areas. Raising the state tax on tobacco, gasoline, and liquor (generally called **excise taxes**) might work. The excise tax on gasoline alone accounted for approximately 9 percent of all state revenues (but these funds usually went for highway construction, not education). A tax on tobacco and alcohol (sometimes known as **sin tax**) could be implemented. At least one state has relied almost exclusively on the sin tax to support education. But its schools are critically underfinanced. A tax on the state's mineral wealth (**severance tax**) would help raise some funds. So would an increase in the motor vehicle license fee. Increasing estate or gift taxes was yet another possibility. But increasing many of these taxes would affect some citizens a lot more than others and might adversely affect business.

The governor glanced at her watch: 2:30 in the morning. She began to question Harriet again, but Harriet had closed her eyes five minutes earlier. The governor reviewed her options:

1. Sales tax
2. Personal income tax
3. State lottery
4. Tax package (excise, severance, sin tax, and so on)

If you were on her staff, which options would you recommend? Could you devise an entirely new scheme to raise funds for the state's underfinanced schools? It might be helpful to keep in mind, as Figures 10.4 and 10.5 indicate, that the public generally supports educational expenditures.

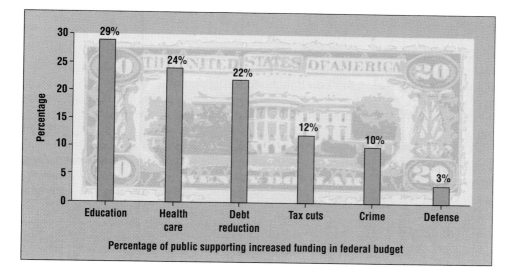

FIGURE 10.4

Percentage of public supporting more money for education in next year's federal budget. Public support for education continues to be strong.

Source: Greenberg-Quinlan Research, Inc./The Tarrance Group, January 1998

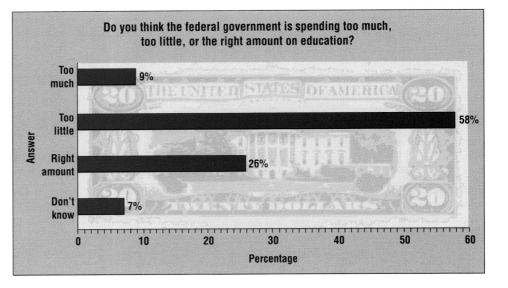

FIGURE 10.5

Opinion polls show
strong public support for
increased federal
educational spending.

Source: Greenberg-Quinlan
Research, Inc./The Tarrance Group,
January 1998

The Federal Government's Role in Financing Education

If states are focused on redressing educational funding imbalances among their wealthy and poor communities, why doesn't the federal government seek to eliminate funding inequities among the states? After all, the United States has wealthy states, poor states, and states in the middle, and the schools in one state can be funded at dramatically lower levels than schools in another state. The answer lies in the Constitution, which assigns educational responsibility to the states, not the federal government. In fact, the federal government typically pays only 6 to 8 percent of the nation's educational costs.

However, the federal government still manages to influence schools. How does it do this? One way has been through **categorical grants**—funds directed at specific categories and targeted educational needs. Categorical grants have provided funding for preschool programs for poor children, library construction, acquisition of new technology, educational opportunities for veterans, the training of teachers and administrators, educational research, lunches for low-income youth, and loans to college students. By targeting funds into these categories, federal aid, although limited, has had a significant impact on schools.

As you might suspect, the federal government has attached rules and regulations to its financial aid. These rules stipulate not only how the funds are to be used but also what kinds of federal reports must be filed and what federally sponsored legislation (for example, fair and nonbiased hiring practices) must be adhered to in order to qualify for the funds. Although the regulations and their attendant paperwork are sometimes demanding, most school districts seek and accept categorical federal aid.

The obligations, rules, and even competition associated with seeking federal dollars were greatly reduced in the 1980s and 1990s. States were awarded **block grants,** lump sums of money, and were given great latitude in how to spend this money. As a result, there were educational winners and losers in the quest for federal dollars:

Winners. Under the block grant system, more funds went to purchase instructional materials, including computers. Many rural communities that lacked the resources even to apply—much less compete—for federal dollars, received federal support. The paperwork for all districts was reduced.

Losers. Desegregation efforts were cut by two-thirds under the block grant approach. Disadvantaged and urban students, women's equity, and many other targeted programs were reduced or eliminated. Long-range programs lost support, and accountability for how the funds were spent was greatly weakened.[9]

Although the federal government's financial role is limited, it has exerted tremendous influence on our schools as a result of federal laws and court actions. For example, the 1954 *Brown* decision desegregated schools, and civil rights laws have increased educational opportunities for students of color, limited speakers of English, females, and others. In 1979, President Jimmy Carter established the **United States Department of Education,** raising federal involvement in education to cabinet status. The Department of Education influences schools through research, information, proposed legislation, and targeted, if limited, federal funds. Expenditures for the Department of Education are dwarfed by other federal priorities. (See Figure 10.6.)

What the Future May Hold for School Finance

What is likely to emerge from shifting governmental responsibility, concern for equity, and court actions? Following are some trends and issues likely to surface in the years ahead.

Accountability

The public wants to see academic progress for their tax dollars—in short, **accountability.** Students will be tested, and so will educators. Graduation will be based less on time spent in school and more on proven performance. Teachers may find tenure more difficult to obtain. Educational overhead likely will be reduced, perhaps by decreasing the number of administrators and supervisors. Schools will be required to identify specific goals, such as minimum achievement levels on standardized tests, and will then be held responsible for reaching these goals. As states increase their support of schools, it is reasonable to anticipate that they will develop new standards for school performance. Outcries for greater accountability may lead to organizational changes, merit pay, or even an increased number of teacher dismissals.

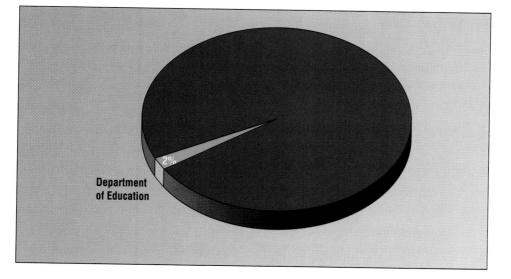

Department
of Education

2%

FIGURE 10.6

Federal budget. Within the federal budget, education expenditures remain quite small.

Source: NEA, based on the 1998 budget

Educational Foundations

As state courts continue their efforts to redistribute education dollars and to funnel additional state resources to poorer districts, parents choosing to keep their children in the public schools are developing creative strategies to ensure that the educational wealth and success of their schools are not endangered. One such strategy has prompted the formation of **educational foundations.**

About two thousand public high schools, or more than 10 percent of the high schools in the United States, have created their own foundations. Funded by private donations, these foundations provide schools with additional revenues for special projects, such as acquiring advanced science equipment, computers, or special devices for disabled students, as well as providing college scholarships. While the funds raised from such foundations amount to only a fraction of official school budgets, these foundations have a significant educational impact, because the dollars are spent directly on educational improvements and are not used for ongoing expenses, such as maintenance and salaries. Wealthy communities—such as La Jolla, California, Edgemont, New York, and Bellaire, Texas—have devoted time and dollars to creating foundations that support public schools with private resources. Supporters of such foundations believe that wealthy parents and their children "will flee to private school if they don't perceive the public education to be excellent."[10]

Choice Programs

A variety of alternative funding and choice options are being explored in communities across the nation. Educational vouchers, charter schools, and open enrollment give parents and students new educational options as they reshape how local schools are managed and funded. The neighborhood school, long a mainstay of public education, may be radically reshaped in the years ahead.

Decaying Infrastructure

Many of our schools are falling apart. We are now using schools in the twenty-first century that were built in the nineteenth. What time has not done, vandalism, poor management, and cost-cutting building programs have. Plumbing, electrical wiring, roofing, and even bricks are in desperate need of repair. Asbestos, a carcinogenic building material used in constructing many schools, has been a costly material to remove. Lead in paint represents yet another health risk. Widespread health, safety, and environmental violations plague these old buildings. Our school **infrastructure** is decaying.

As if that were not bad enough, technological advances are making demands that school buildings cannot meet. Installing adequate wiring for computers and sufficient phone lines for Internet connections entail major construction costs. The cost of repairing and rebuilding the nation's schools has been estimated at over $112 billion.[11]

Governing America's Schools

School Governance Quiz

The following quiz should help you focus on how schools are governed. If you are puzzled at some of these questions, fear not; the remainder of the chapter is organized around a discussion of these questions and their answers.

1. Most school board members are (*choose only one*)
   a. conservative, white, male, and middle or upper class.
   b. liberal, middle-class women, about half of whom have been or are teachers.

   c. middle of the road politically, about evenly divided between men and women, and representing all socioeconomic classes.

   d. so diverse politically, economically, and socially that it is impossible to make generalizations.

2. The chief state school officer is called
   a. superintendent.
   b. commissioner.
   c. secretary.
   d. All of the above.
   e. None of the above.

3. School boards and chief state school officers are
   a. elected by the people.
   b. elected by the people's representatives.
   c. appointed by the governor.
   d. appointed by officials other than the governor.
   e. All of the above.
   f. None of the above.

4. During the past two decades, control and influence over education have increased at the
   a. federal level.
   b. state level.
   c. local level.

5. The influence of the business community in U.S. schools can best be characterized as
   a. virtually nonexistent.
   b. felt only in vocational and commercial programs.
   c. extensive and growing.
   d. a recent phenomenon.

6. Your job security as a classroom teacher is considerably influenced by the *(you may choose more than one)*
   a. principal.
   b. state school superintendent.
   c. U.S. secretary of education.
   d. school secretary.
   e. parents.
   f. Teacher Arbitration and Labor Relations Board.

7. The major responsibilities of school district superintendents include all of the following *except*
   a. manage personnel.
   b. plan and administer budgets.
   c. effectively communicate with the public.
   d. win local elections.
   e. provide instructional and curricular leadership.

8. School superintendents can be characterized as
   a. mediating frequent conflicts.
   b. civil service–type administrators.
   c. female and minority, between the ages of 45 and 60.
   d. generally powerless figureheads.

9. The number of school districts in the nation is
   a. increasing.
   b. decreasing.
   c. remaining constant.
10. One current and growing organizational trend is the
   a. formation of educational partnerships.
   b. elimination of the superintendent position.
   c. increasing number of school districts.
   d. creation of "super" school boards, responsible for numerous school systems.
   e. replacement of the school principal with an educational manager.
11. In most schools, teachers are expected to
   a. design the policies guiding their schools.
   b. collaborate with principals and district officials to create policies to suit their schools.
   c. comply with policies made by principals and by district and state officials.
   d. comply with policies that seem appropriate and change those that do not.

School Governance Answer Key

1. a	3. e	5. c	7. d	9. b	11. c
2. d	4. b	6. a, d, e	8. a	10. a	

0 to 1 wrong: You receive the John Dewey Award.

2 to 3 wrong: You are a candidate for tenure.

4 to 5 wrong: Read the rest of the chapter carefully.

6 or more wrong: Take detailed notes on this chapter; find a friend to quiz you.

The Legal Control of Schools

The following sections review and discuss the quiz you have just taken, beginning with the first three questions:

1. *Most school board members are . . .* conservative, white, male, and middle or upper class.
2. *The chief state school officer is called . . .* superintendent, commissioner, or secretary.
3. *School boards and chief state school officers are . . .* elected by the people, elected by the people's representatives, appointed by the governor, or appointed by officials other than the governor.

As these responses indicate, there is great diversity in school governance. In some states, school boards and chief state school officials are elected; in others, they are appointed. Not only does the title of the chief state school officer change from state to state, but so do the responsibilities of the job. Although some say that "variety is the spice of life," you are probably thinking, "How did this strange system get started (and will I ever sort it out?)."

By the time the Constitution was written, control of schools by local communities had become well established. The Constitution did not assign education to the national government but recognized and reaffirmed the states' responsibilities in this area under the **Tenth Amendment:** "The powers not delegated to the United States by the Constitution, nor prohibited by it to the States, are reserved to the states, respectively, or to the people."

Today, the United States is unusual in this respect. Whereas most nations have a national ministry of education, which determines what and how children are taught in all parts of those nations, in the United States the legal responsibility for public education resides within each of the fifty states, the District of Columbia, and several U.S. territories. Since few governors or state legislators possess special expertise in education, state governments have delegated much of their authority to state boards of education, state superintendents and departments of education, and finally to local governments.

Probably the best way for you to learn how the different state educational agencies and offices actually function is for you to consider a specific example. Although this example is not representative of all states (no single example could be), it will provide you with an insight into the mechanics of state governance and how state actions can affect you.

State-level policy-making usually begins when someone suggests a new educational need or goal, such as the need to improve student writing skills or the need to limit the number of students in each class. For our example, let us assume that a new policy would require all candidates for a teaching license to complete at least three courses involving techniques for teaching students with learning, emotional, or physical disabilities.

Perhaps you're wondering, "Who thinks up those policies?" Policy suggestions originate from all kinds of sources: professional educators, school board members, state legislators, superintendents, state and federal court decisions, federal laws or initiatives, special interest groups, and the general public. In short, the role of the state school board is to consider recommendations for educational policy and to vote for or against their implementation.

Policy implementation is the responsibility of the chief state school officer and the state department of education. The **chief state school officer** is given different titles in different states (superintendent, director, commissioner, or secretary of education) and is usually the executive head of the state department of education. Together, the superintendent and the state department enforce state laws, evaluate teachers and schools, plan for future educational developments, and provide training and information to educators throughout the state. In our example, the superintendent would inform all school districts in the state of the new licensure requirement. If you were to apply for a teacher's license in the state, someone in the state department of education would review your transcript to make certain that you had successfully completed at least three special education courses. If this and other requirements were met, you would be issued your teacher's license.

What about a job? States issue teacher's licenses, but the hiring and firing of teachers is done by local education districts. The more than fourteen thousand school districts across the country are the most visible agency of educational governance—the ones you read about most often in your local newspaper. These districts are actually agencies of state rather than local governments, but they exercise control over such local matters as recruitment of school staff, curriculum formulation, and budgets—including teacher salaries and school building programs.

Most local school districts look something like the state government, but on a smaller scale. They have a school board, a superintendent, and an education office that, like the state department of education, helps administer the schools. Most local **school boards** are elected, although a few local communities appoint them. Each local board then hires a local **superintendent** to provide educational leadership within the community. Thus, in any given state, educational governance involves not only a state superintendent with a department of education and a statewide board

State government
(courts, governor, legislature)

State board of education

Chief state school officer
and
state department of education

Intermediate units
(regional service centers)

Local boards of
education

Local
superintendents
and local school
district central office

Principals,
teachers,
parents,
students

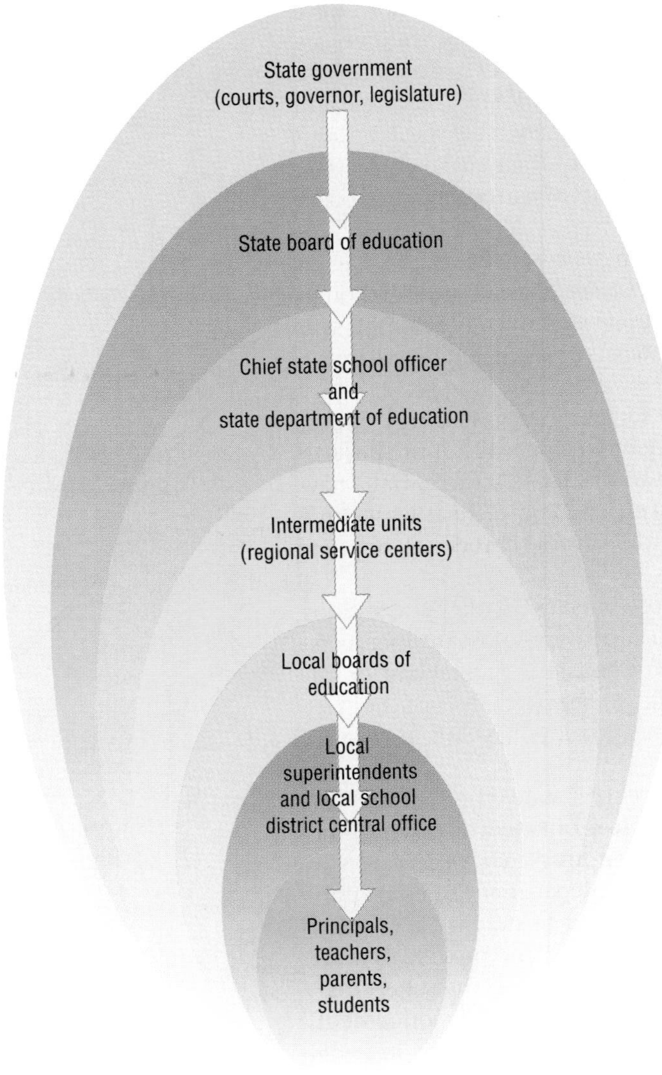

FIGURE 10.7

Structure of a typical
state school system.

but also local school boards and local superintendents. In many instances, local administrators and board members influence education more than do their counterparts at the state level. In practice, each state is unique in the way it delegates and administers its educational program. Figure 10.7 shows an example of a state school system's structure. And the main agents of school governance are described in the following paragraphs.

State Board of Education

The **state board of education** is responsible for formulating educational policy. The members are usually appointed by the governor, but sometimes they are chosen in a statewide election.

Chief State School Officer

Called *superintendent, commissioner, secretary of education,* or *director of instruction,* the **chief state school officer** is responsible for overseeing, regulating, and planning school activities, as well as implementing the policies of the board of education. The state superintendent is usually selected by the board of education but sometimes campaigns for the position in an election.

State Department of Education

The **state department of education** performs the administrative tasks needed to implement state policy. This includes licensing teachers, testing student progress, providing information and training to teachers, distributing state and federal funds, seeing that local school systems comply with state laws, and conducting educational research and development. The state superintendent usually manages state department of education activities.

School Districts—Local School Boards and Superintendents

All states except Hawaii have delegated much of the responsibility for local school operations to local school districts. (Hawaii treats the entire state as a single school district.) School districts vary in size from those serving only a few students to those with more than a million. Sometimes, local school districts are grouped into intermediate units as a way to simplify management. Most local school districts mirror the state organization, with a local school board, **superintendent,** and office of education. Local school districts may be responsible for school construction, taxing, budgeting, the hiring of school personnel, curriculum decisions, local school policy, and the education of students. Although school districts operate at the local level,

TABLE 10.1	**WHO CONTROLS WHAT? LEVELS OF EDUCATIONAL POWER**

State Governments

- Levy taxes

- License teachers and other educators

- Set standards for school attendance, safety, etc.

- Outline minimum curricular and graduation standards (sometimes including specific textbooks to be used and competency tests for student graduation and teacher certification)

- Regulate the nature and size of local school districts

Local School Districts

- Implement state regulations and policies

- Create and implement local policies and practices for effective school administration

- Hire school personnel

- Provide needed funds and build appropriate facilities

- Fix salaries and working conditions

- Translate community needs into educational practice

- Initiate additional curriculum, licensing, or other requirements beyond state requirements

- Create current and long-range plans for the school district

their authority derives from the state, and they must operate within the rules and regulations specified by the state. Table 10.1 summarizes the relationships between state and local control of schools.

State Government's Increasing Role

4. *During the past two decades, control and influence over education have increased at the . . .* state level.

State governments have been drawn into a more active role in education by a variety of circumstances. A series of government and private reports in the 1980s and 1990s detailed and decried the sorry state of American education, causing the media and the public, to demand reform. Although the federal government traditionally had responded to such calls for national reform, a changed political climate reduced federal involvement. The states were pressed into a leadership role. The courts required states to take a more active role in equalizing local funding disparities. State legislatures passed reform measures on everything from the financing of education to stiffened graduation and teacher licensure requirements.

While the states initiate reform, the impact is being felt at the local level. Across the United States, local school boards find themselves under a new barrage of criticism.

School Boards Under Fire

School boards have long been a sacred U.S. institution, representing the public's interest in shaping the policies and practices of their local schools. Forged in the hamlets of colonial New England, for centuries they have been a symbol of U.S.

Superintendents (mostly white males) along with members of state and local boards of education comprise the official governance system of schools.

small-town democracy. School board meetings represent the essence of Americana—the kind painted by Norman Rockwell and made into a Frank Capra movie starring Jimmy Stewart as the beleaguered, but triumphant, school board president. Therefore, it was a great shock to many when in 1992 America's school boards came under scrutiny. (See Table 10.2 for school board statistics.)

One of the most intensive studies of school boards in recent times was conducted by the Twentieth Century Fund and the Danforth Foundation. They recommended a total overhaul of the system. Their report, added to other criticisms of the U.S. educational system, has led to serious re-evaluation of the role of school boards. Following are some of the major criticisms:

- School boards have become *immersed in administrative details,* at the expense of more important and appropriate policy issues. One study of West Virginia school boards showed that only 3 percent of all decisions made concerned policy.
- School boards are *not representing local communities,* but only special interest groups. Elections to the school board receive little public support. In a New York City school board election, for instance, only 7 percent of the voters participated.
- The *politics of local school board elections* have a negative impact on attracting and retaining superintendents and lead to conflict with state education agencies.
- The composition of the boards is *not representative,* with individuals of color, women, the poor, and the young unrepresented or underrepresented.
- School boards have been in the *backseat when it comes to educational change and reform.* As a matter of fact, many school boards do not support current educational reform proposals, and members have lagged behind public opinion on such issues as school choice and educational vouchers.
- The education of children goes beyond school issues to include health, social, and nutritional concerns. School boards are *too limited in scope* to respond to all the contemporary concerns of children.

| TABLE 10.2 | EVERYTHING YOU ALWAYS WANTED TO KNOW ABOUT SCHOOL BOARDS BUT NEVER THOUGHT TO ASK |

- The first school board was established in 1721 in Boston.
- In the United States, there are almost 15,000 school boards in charge of 52 million students in 87,000 schools.
- Three-quarters of the school districts are small, with fewer than 2,500 students in each.
- Just 1 percent of the school districts in urban areas enroll 23 percent of all students in the United States.
- Eighty-five percent of local school boards are elected.
- School board members are typically white (86.9 percent), male (55.3 percent), financially secure (more than half earning above $50,000 and more than a third earning over $80,000), and middle-aged (85 percent being above 41 years of age).
- School boards hire superintendents who look much like themselves (96 percent of the superintendents are white, 89 percent are male, 95 percent are married).

Source: Data compiled from C. Emily Feistritzer, "A Profile of School Board Presidents," in Patricia First and Herbert Walberg (eds.), *School Boards: Changing Local Control* (Berkeley: McCutchan, 1992); Jesse L. Freeman, Kenneth E. Underwood, and Jim C. Fortune, "What Boards Value," *American School Board Journal* 178 (January 1991): pp. 32–37.
Digest of Education Statistics, 1997
Educational Vital Signs, 1997
Characteristics of the 100 Largest Public Elementary and Secondary School Districts in U.S.: 1993–94, May, 1996. NCES

- If schools continue to be *financed less from local funds and more from* state funds, local boards could become less influential.
- Many of the new reforms call for *new governance organizations*, site-based management, or choice programs that relegate the school board to a less important, perhaps even unnecessary, role.[12]

While these criticisms suggest a dismal future for school boards, preparing their obituary may be premature. School boards have endured a long time and may be around long after many of the reform recommendations are forgotten.

However, school board practices need to be improved. Board membership should be more representative of the communities they serve, including younger members, women, people of color, and less affluent individuals. Board responsibilities could be expanded to include nutrition, preschool programs, health care, welfare benefits, and other issues influencing the well-being of children. Perhaps school boards could benefit from a name change, such as Children's Education and Development Boards, to better reflect their broader responsibilities. Some educators suggest that we need to rethink how we currently select our boards, depending less on elections and more on appointments of nonpolitical educators. Too often, school board membership is seen as a political stepping-stone to higher office, or as a way of paying back political debts, instead of as an educational responsibility.

Finally, the relationship between school boards and superintendents needs to be improved. In regard to the official organization of a school district, the school board formulates policy and hires the superintendent to manage the day-to-day school district activities. So much for the official version. The unofficial version is quite different. Superintendents in many districts actually control their school boards. The increasing complexity of educational practice, law, and research makes the superintendent the expert and the school board members the amateurs. As a result, the superintendent often prepares the agenda for the school board members, and many important educational issues are never discussed. Most school board members do not have a research staff, and they rely on the superintendent for advice. In fact, board members rarely get paid. Clearly, change is needed if school boards are to regain their leadership in formulating policy and monitoring school district performance.[13]

The Business of America Is Business

5. *The influence of the business community in U.S. schools can best be characterized as . . . extensive and growing.*

Traditionally, children have been taught to work hard, to compete, to be punctual and neat, to follow rules and be loyal, and to "do as the others do"—in short, to conform,[14] all part of the business creed. But, according to many educators, "The most far-reaching initiative in education to emerge in recent years is the growing corporate interest in public schools."[15]

So intertwined have business values and school practices become that educators have adopted the business vocabulary. An education leader is called a *superintendent,* the same title originally given to a factory supervisor. A school building, like a factory, is called a *plant. Quality control, accountability, management design,* and *cost overruns* have also been expropriated from business and applied to education. Therefore, it is understandable that so many school superintendents are more involved in cost-effectiveness formulas than in educational innovation.

For some educators, business involvement in education might already be too intrusive, but trends indicate that it is still on the increase. In 1995, a *Business Week* survey of 408 senior executives at large corporations revealed that improving the educational system ranked second only to balancing the federal budget as the issue "most important to American business."[16]

Competition and other business-oriented values have become so familiar and pervasive in our schools that we have become inured to them.

IN THE NEWS . . . COLA WARS

Pepsi and Coke are fighting for the hearts and minds of America's students. In order to develop brand loyalty, as well as lucrative sales from schools, the cola companies are negotiating multimillion dollar contracts with school systems. Colorado Springs schools, for example, receive $8 million over ten years from the Coca-Cola company for the exclusive rights to sell Cokes on school property. In Evans, Georgia, a senior was suspended for wearing a Pepsi shirt at a time when school administrators were trying to persuade Coca-Cola officials to donate $10,000 for a contest. Critics of these contracts worry about commercializing schools and the health consequences of promoting colas. Supporters point out that these contracts respond to student tastes and bring much needed funds into the school budget.

Source: *Education Week on the Web,* 8 April 1998.

Covert Power in Schools

6. *Your job security as a classroom teacher is considerably influenced by the . . .* principal, parents, and perhaps the school secretary.

You think that the school principal is the only one responsible for school personnel decisions, including hiring and firing. Think again. Parents, vocal individuals, the school secretary, and community groups have **covert power** and can bring significant pressure to bear on which teachers stay in a school, and which leave. These unofficial but highly involved persons and groups constitute the **hidden government** of schools.

The concept of hidden government is not unique to schools. In fact, most of our institutions, including the White House, have developed their own unique forms of hidden government. There, decision making is often influenced more by old colleagues back home (the "kitchen cabinet") than by the president's official advisers and cabinet members.

How does hidden government operate in schools? Following are some examples.

Example 1

A first-year teacher in a New England junior high school spent long hours after school, preparing lessons and working with his students. Admirable as all this appeared, the school secretary, Ms. Hand, advised the teacher not to work with female students after school hours, because "You may get your fingers burned." The teacher smiled, ignored the secretary's advice, and continued providing students with after-school help.

Within a week, the principal called the teacher in for a conference and suggested that the teacher provide extra help to students only if both male and female students were present. The teacher objected to the advice and to the secretary's complaining to the principal. The principal responded, "You're new here, and I can understand your concern. But what you have to learn is that Ms. Hand is more than a secretary. She knows this school better than I do. Follow her advice and you'll do just fine."

GOVERNMENT AND FINANCE BALANCE SHEET 2   BUSINESS AND SCHOOLS

Business Involvement in Education Is Important Because . . .

Business values need to be taught in school. Initiative, punctuality, loyalty to organizations, competitiveness: these are bedrock values not only for the business community but also for all of society. Students must learn these values if they are to prosper in the real world beyond the classroom.

The generosity of the private sector adds immeasurably to the curricular resources in schools. For example, the National Association of Manufacturers (NAM) provides free teaching materials to schools, including videos and software. Many individual businesses and industries provide free or inexpensive instructional materials.

Corporate generosity has gone beyond curricular resources to embrace education funding. Companies provide large grants to assist impoverished schools, college scholarships to deserving students, equipment (such as computers), financial support for teacher training workshops, and funding for school building improvement projects.

Today, more than ever, the business community is leading the national reform effort. By creating charter schools, the business sector will set an example for the nation, demonstrating how to make schools both more efficient and more effective. What's more, it will open up a whole new industry, a whole new area of potential future profits.

Corporate America is filling in the gap for schools that fail. Although the education level of the U.S. workforce is generally increasing—one in four U.S. workers is now a college graduate—the lack of basic skills among entry-level workers has prompted corporations to teach reading, writing, and computing to their workers and to form partnerships with local school systems to educate the next generation of workers.

Although the United States has the world's largest technically educated workforce, other countries are working hard to catch up. The resources of business are necessary if our schools are to survive the international challenge and maintain an innovative advantage.[17]

In his Nobel Prize–winning research, Theodore Schultz reported that capital investment in education yields economic profits to business, to the nation, and to the individual. The involvement of the private sector in the nation's schools creates a more robust economy that benefits us all.[18]

Business Should Get Out of Education Because . . .

Business-oriented values, such as competition, have become so pervasive in our schools that we are oblivious to their negative influences. Competition, conformance to authority, and even greed, for example, may not be the best values to be promoting in democratic schools.

The "free" materials supplied by businesses may in the long run be incredibly expensive. "Free" materials distributed by the business community may promote a company's product or a lifestyle choice that results in business profits when students become adults.

For-profit schools may lead to some undesirable business practices. Misleading advertising could motivate unsuspecting, uninformed parents to enroll their children in weak schools. Slanted or biased reporting of test scores and other measures might make a school or an educational program look better than it really is. Or perhaps these schools will try to increase profits by cutting back on the costly resources required by the neediest students.

Despite what you hear in the news, reports that our schools are failing are greatly exaggerated. In fact, the problem with today's schools may be that they are doing too well. Consider the following:

- A RAND Corporation report concludes that we are educating 25 percent more graduates in engineering and science than we can employ.[19]
- High school enrollments in advanced math and science courses have increased dramatically in the past decade, as have college enrollments, yet individuals with more than twelve years of schooling experienced a 17 percent decline in real income between the 1970s and the 1990s.[20]
- Company downsizing is reducing the need for a full-time labor force while increasing the number of part-time and poorly paid workers. Eighty-six percent of American companies report that they "farm out" work that they used to do.[21] Corporate CEOs have been making millions of dollars in bonuses and salaries, not for their innovative management styles or technological breakthroughs, but simply for "downsizing," for firing thousands of people, and often those fired are the most educated and well trained.[22]
- The business community may be publicizing the need for more technical and scientific education in order to create a large, cheap—even overeducated—labor pool in order to keep labor costs low.[23]

The school secretary holds a position that can exert significant covert power in his or her pivotal role as the principal's "eyes and ears."

Lesson: You can't always tell which people hold the real power by their official position.

Lesson: The school secretary is often the eyes and ears of the principal. In some cases, the secretary manages the day-to-day operations of the school.

Example 2

A young teacher in an elementary school in the Midwest was called into the principal's office for a conference. The principal evaluated her teaching as above average but suggested that she maintain greater discipline. Her classroom was simply too noisy, and the students' chairs were too often left in disarray. The conference was over in ten minutes.

The teacher was offended. She did not feel her classroom was too noisy, and the chairs were always arranged in a neat circle. Moreover, the principal had visited her class for only five minutes, and during that time the students had said hardly a word.

The next day, in the teacher's lounge, all became clear when she discussed the conference with another teacher. The teacher nodded, smiled, and explained:

"Mr. Richards."

"The custodian?"

"Yup. He slowly sweeps the halls and listens for noisy classrooms. Then he tells the principal. He also hates it when the chairs are in a circle, since it makes sweeping harder. Nice straight rows are much easier. Just make sure your classroom is quiet when he's in the halls and have your students put the chairs in neat, straight rows at the end of the day. That's the ticket for getting a good evaluation!"

Lesson: School custodians are often a source of information for principals and of supplies for teachers. They make very helpful allies and powerful adversaries.

Example 3

An elementary school teacher in a rural southern community was put in charge of the class play. Rehearsals were under way when the teacher received a note to stop by the principal's office at 3:00 P.M.

The principal had received a call from a parent who was quite disappointed at the small part her daughter had received in the play. The principal wanted the teacher to consider giving the child a larger part. "After all," he explained, "her mother is influential in the PTA, and her father is one of the town's most successful businessmen. It's silly for you to alienate them. Give her a bigger part. Life will be easier for both of us, and we may be able to get her parents' support for the next school bond issue. That would mean a raise for all of us."

Lesson: Parents can also be influential in school decisions by applying pressure on principals, school boards, and community groups. When you decide to make a stand in the face of parental pressure, choose a significant issue and be able to substantiate your facts.

The School Superintendent's Role

7. *The major responsibilities of school district superintendents include all of the following except . . .* win local elections.
8. *School superintendents can be characterized as . . .* mediating frequent conflicts.

The first superintendents were hired to relieve school boards of their growing administrative obligations. The year was 1837, and these new superintendents worked in Buffalo and Louisville.[24] As the nineteenth century progressed, more communities followed this example. Superintendents were expected to supervise and hire teachers, examine students, and buy supplies, which had become too burdensome for the school boards themselves. Superintendents also kept school records, developed examinations, chose textbooks, and trained teachers.

By the twentieth century, the superintendent's role had changed from the board's administrative employee to its most knowledgeable educational expert—from helper to chief executive officer. Today, the superintendent is the most powerful education officer in the school district. The superintendent is responsible for budgets, buildings, new programs, daily operations, long-term goals, short-term results, and recruiting, hiring, demoting, and firing personnel. When things are going well, the superintendent enjoys great popularity. But, when things are going poorly, or school board members are not pleased, or local community groups are angry, or teacher organizations turn militant, or . . . you get the picture. When there is a problem, it is usually the head of the system, the superintendent, who gets fired. The superintendent lives and works in a fishbowl, trying to please various groups while managing the school district. It is a very insecure existence of sidestepping controversies, pleasing school board members, responding to critics, juggling many different roles and goals, and living with conflict.[25] In 1992, for example, twenty-five of forty-seven major urban school districts were looking for new superintendents, while almost 40 percent of the superintendents in medium-size school districts had been in their jobs for less than three years. In 1998, only three of forty superintendents in Westchester County, just north of New York City, had served more than eight years.[26]

One need not look hard for the reasons for this turnover. Successful superintendents must win and maintain public support and financing for their schools. This involves forming political coalitions to back their programs and to ward off attacks from those more concerned with rising taxes than with the school budget. In an era in which most citizens in many communities do not have children in schools, this becomes a real test of political acumen. Superintendents find themselves serving on a number of civic committees, speaking to community groups, and being the public relations spokesperson for the school district.

In addition to the role of politician, the superintendent must also be a manager. For large school districts that employ thousands of professionals and serve tens of thousands of students, management is a challenge. For instance, a superintendent in a large metropolitan school district was terminated when the textbooks were "lost" and could not be delivered to classrooms until Thanksgiving. In another case, a rural school superintendent was sent job hunting because the community did not agree with his choice of "snow days," days he canceled classes due to bad weather.

One of the promising trends for school superintendents is the increasing emphasis on being an instructional leader. Greater attention on student test performance has underscored the instructional accountability of the superintendent. Such school districts as Minneapolis, Philadelphia, and Los Angeles have adopted performance-based contracts that link superintendent compensation directly to student performance.[27] As the instructional leader of the community, it is the superintendent who is responsible for evaluating student progress, training teachers and administrators, and instructing school board members and the community about the educational needs and goals of the system.

Consolidation of School Districts

9. *The number of school districts in the nation is . . .* decreasing.

The shift to fewer, larger school districts is called **consolidation.** Consolidation has been going on since the early part of the twentieth century, thanks in part to the development of the intrepid yellow bus that could transport students to distant schools. The one-room schoolhouse began to fade into American folklore as small school districts merged, grew in size, built bigger schools, and were able to offer more courses and programs. (See Table 10.3.)

Consolidation raises an interesting question: what is the ideal size for a school district? If it is too small, course options and special electives are not offered. If it is too big, alienation and anonymity can become dilemmas. Some studies have suggested that a district with 10,000 to 12,000 students is ideal whereas others suggest that 50,000 and even 100,000 students is preferred.[28] Most school districts still have fewer than 2,000 students, and many have only a few hundred. The process of consolidation will likely continue into the future as these smaller school districts are combined and consolidated into larger ones in order to offer students a richer curriculum and to cut administrative costs. Ironically, very large districts, such as New York City, have moved in the opposite direction and have created subdistricts,

---

TABLE 10.3 CONSOLIDATION IN ACTION

The following numbers show the dramatic reduction in the number of school districts as smaller ones consolidate. Still, 75 percent of the remaining districts are fairly small, servicing fewer than 2,500 students each.

School Year	Number of Public School Districts
1929–1930	119,001
1939–1940	117,108
1949–1950	83,718
1959–1960	40,520
1970–1971	17,995
1980–1981	15,912
1989–1990	15,367
1995–1996	14,883

Source: *Digest of Education Statistics 1997,* U.S. Department of Education, National Center for Education Statistics.

smaller units to help avoid some of the problems of bigness, a process called **decentralization.** While "officially" a large school district, these smaller, more manageable, subdistricts accomplish day-to-day management. A federally sponsored study found that some decentralization of school districts into smaller and more responsive units might be a good idea. Larger school districts bear increased transportation and other costs, although the intent is to lower administration costs and save funds. Even more to the point, there is little evidence that student achievement increases as a result of consolidation.

Consolidation into larger school districts means that schools themselves become larger. As we consider the best size for a school district, we may want to ponder what is the most effective size for a school. Roger Barker and Paul Gump[29] indicate that students in smaller schools have more opportunities to participate in school activities. Alienation and apathy often afflict large schools, and a student lost in the crowd may not be reaping great benefits from plentiful curriculum offerings. While consolidation is a fact of life in U.S. education, its benefits are now being reconsidered.[30]

Trends in School Governance

10. *One current and growing organizational trend is the* . . . formation of educational partnerships.
11. *In most schools, teachers are expected to* . . . comply with policies made by principals and by district and state officials.

Parents, community organizations, and businesses are increasingly involved in local school activities, associations that have been termed **educational partnerships.** At the same time, school districts have been reshaping governance and increasing the decision-making responsibilities of teachers. The following sections will discuss both of these new trends. Since we have already talked about business participation in schools, here we highlight partnerships involving family and community groups.

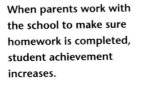

When parents work with the school to make sure homework is completed, student achievement increases.

IN THE NEWS . . . PARENT REPORT CARD

During parent-teacher conferences, parents in Stafford County, Virginia are getting something a little extra: a report card on how they are doing. In the form of a questionnaire, parents are asked to rate themselves in areas ranging from the nutritious meals served to children, volunteering to help in school field trips and other activities, and whether they discuss the importance of education with their children. Some parents even considered asking their children to grade them.

Source: *Washington Post,* 28 October 1998.

Educational Partnerships: Family

Education does not start and stop at the schoolhouse door. Although educators can exert enormous influence on children, children spend 87 percent of their time outside of school, mostly under the influence of their parents. According to public opinion polls, although parents want to become more actively involved in their children's education, they are not doing very well. A 1992 survey suggested that most parents earn less than a *C* grade: over 30 percent of the high school students who participated in the study agreed that their parents were rarely, if ever, involved in their schoolwork.[31] And 43 percent said their parents were only "somewhat" involved. In 1995, lack of parental support was the fourth most cited reason given by teachers considering leaving the profession.[32]

There is great disparity in how families invest their time in their children. Consider homework. Children who diligently complete their homework achieve higher scores than those who do not (not too surprising). In fact, whether a student regularly completes homework has three times as much impact on school performance as the family's socioeconomic background. Academic performance is enhanced when parents discuss and plan homework activities, check homework for accuracy, and actively assist their children in school assignments. Despite homework's importance, studies indicate that children spend far more time watching television than doing homework. Too many teachers take the course of least resistance and either do not assign or do not correct homework.[33]

School programs throughout the nation focus on improving home climates to ensure that schoolwork is done, and done well:

- Arizona teachers have organized a basic skills package, published in English, Spanish, and Navajo, to assist parents in working with children.
- Missouri funds an ambitious program called Parents as First Teachers. The program includes seminars about the language development of children, home visits by teachers, parental instruction on activities to promote hand-eye coordination, and the testing of children's vision, hearing, speech, and motor development. Missouri saw this funding as an investment in the future and a preventive measure to avoid the high cost of remedial programs for these children in later years.

- District hot lines for homework, family web sites, college information guides, practice tests and parent-teacher e-mail represent a growing technological link to enhance home-school partnerships.[34]

Educational Partnerships: Community Groups

While schools have reached out to community groups for many years, in recent days these partnerships have been growing. Most of these community resources can be grouped into nine major categories:

1. Professional associations (architects, doctors, lawyers, and engineers)
2. Environmental and conservation organizations
3. Museums, galleries, and other cultural attractions
4. Social and civic groups (League of Women Voters, Rotary and Lions clubs, fraternities and sororities)
5. Colleges and universities
6. Ethnic and cultural groups
7. Health agencies and hospitals
8. Senior citizens
9. Artists, musicians, and craftspeople

In Pittsburgh, the American Jewish Committee and the Urban League raise funds for schools. In Houston, architects teach students insights into the history and structure of the city's buildings. In Juneau, Alaska, the university provides teachers in the isolated Northern Arctic School District with workshops via television. In St. Louis, lawyers hold mock court in schools to teach students about the real workings of the legal system.

Obviously, wealthier and larger districts have the potential for greater variety in community partnerships. However, all schools have educational resources available in their community or in neighboring communities, and, more and more, they are reaching out to these groups.

Teacher Empowerment and School-Based Management

While parents, community groups, and the business sector carve out their roles in schools, teachers traditionally have been omitted from meaningful involvement in school governance. Imagine that you are the senior faculty member at Someplace High School. Having taught there for thirty years, you know the school like the back of your hand. You are regarded as an excellent teacher, an expert at judging the needs of your students. Should you participate in making decisions affecting the management of your school?

To get a sense of how little say teachers have once they leave their own classrooms, let's join the first faculty meeting of the fall at Someplace High. The principal, Mr. Will E. Tell, is discussing the new teacher assessment forms with the faculty:

MR. TELL: If you all look in your folders, you'll see the criteria on which you will be assessed when I observe in your classrooms. Look these forms over carefully, and let me know if you have any questions. I'll be scheduling my school observation visits with you shortly. Another issue I wanted to raise with you concerns our need to develop better relations with the community. I've passed around a sign-up sheet for a committee to turn around the low attendance at parent conferences. What I have in mind is a car wash or a bake sale or another fund-raising activity to bring the community together. Ms. Johnson, you have a question?

MS. JOHNSON: Yes, Mr. Tell. I thought that we were going to talk about setting up a better school web site, one that can pull parents into school conferences and activities, assist students with their homework, have links to resources, and address special interest topics for teachers and parents. We all indicated at last year's faculty meeting that this should be a top priority.

MR. TELL: You're absolutely right, Louise, and I'm glad you raised the topic. That was going to be our first order of business, but I'm happy to report that the district office called yesterday and has promised us web site support by the second semester. I'll be getting out my first newsletter to the faculty in a few weeks, and I'll be sure to include that information. I'll also be announcing the in-service training sessions for the fall semester. I heard some interesting speakers at the national convention I attended, and I think I'm going to be able to get some of them to come to our district. Before we end the meeting, I want to introduce our new faculty member. I hired Ms. Wetherby over the summer, and she'll join the teachers in our English department. I know you'll all do everything you can to make sure that Ms. Wetherby feels welcome. Now, if there are no further topics for discussion, let's all get back to our classrooms. Tomorrow the kids arrive. It's time for a new year.

From listening in on this faculty meeting, you can tell that many of the most crucial decisions were made by others. Whether a teacher will be assigned to advanced placement literature classes or remedial English is a decision usually made by the principal. Teachers, as a rule, do not participate in hiring new teachers, in developing criteria by which their teaching will be evaluated, in setting graduation requirements, or in scheduling classes.

Objection to top-down decision making by principals and school district authorities prompted a broad movement to give teachers a greater role in school governance.[35] You may hear such terms as *participatory management, shared leadership, teacher empowerment,* and *faculty-led renewal.* During the 1990s, two of the most widely adopted reforms were the related actions of moving decision-making authority to individual schools (known as **site-based,** or **school-based, management**)

Teachers, who know more than most people in the educational chain about the needs and interests of individual students, have often been excluded from school management and policy-making.

and dispersing the authority more broadly within schools (known as **collaborative decision making**). Large urban school systems, such as those in Chicago, Miami, Los Angeles, and San Diego, led the trend of adopting school-based management, while such states as Colorado, Kentucky, North Carolina, and Texas made collaborative decision making mandatory at every school.[36]

Today, all over the country, various visions and versions of school-based management and teacher empowerment are influencing how schools are governed. In Montgomery County, Maryland, for example, quality management councils composed of the principal, peer-elected teachers, and representatives appointed by the principal have jurisdiction over everything from ordering supplies and making curricular decisions to hiring new staff. Not all teachers are enamored with this, as one pointed out: "This may really help us. It may really hurt us. Especially if it turns out to be just another meeting you've got to go to."[37]

Caution is appropriate, since the success enjoyed by site-based approaches varies from community to community. In Dade County, Florida, site-based management was credited with decreasing teacher turnover and lowering student absences. But, in Los Angeles, a similar plan led to power struggles, conflict, and complaints of ineffectiveness. In Minneapolis, site teams have increased the sense of teacher professionalism and accountability, but measurable gains in student performance have been more elusive.

While there is a general consensus that teacher morale and parent involvement have increased at many schools that have made these changes, the impact on student achievement has been more difficult to discern. In order for school-based management to be truly effective, most experts suggest that it be part of a broader strategy for improving education. One parent involved in school governance summarized the situation this way: "Site-based management is an innovation, yet it is trying to fit into an administration and a school board that were made 92 years ago. It doesn't fit together . . . we need to look at a new system."[38]

Summary

1. States provide approximately half of the cost of education, with local communities providing most of the rest. Local communities generally fund their schools through a property tax, which many people consider outdated and unfair. Since some areas are wealthier than others, some school districts generate more than enough money, while others must struggle to keep schools open.

2. Local funding disparities have led to a series of state court decisions mandating new state formulas for funding schools. These decisions have been called Robin Hood laws, since they require that funding-level differences between wealthy and poor districts be reduced or eliminated. Some courts are even mandating changes based on differences in educational outcomes.

3. The adequate funding of education presents a yearly challenge for state and local officials. Each of the most common strategies to fund schools—property tax, sales tax, personal income tax, state lottery, and other taxes—has drawbacks. Funding is especially difficult for poorer communities and states, where even high tax rates do not provide enough money for the schools. Some states have experimented with new funding methods, such as foundation programs, a guaranteed tax base for all districts, and a combination of programs to help poorer communities fund schools, but none has proved very successful.

4. New challenges to school finance include techniques for tying school performance to funding levels (accountability), deteriorating school buildings and materials

(infrastructure), the role of the federal government in school funding, and the continuing effort to ensure the equal distribution of educational funds among wealthy and poor communities.

5. According to the U.S. Constitution, education is the responsibility of the states.

6. At the state level, the legislature, state board of education, state superintendent, and state department of education provide the policy and administration of schools. The state also delegates some of its power to local school boards and superintendents, who administer individual school districts.

7. The board of education at both the state and local levels is responsible for formulating educational policy. The chief state school officer, often called the superintendent, is responsible for implementing the policies of the board of education.

8. The state department of education's tasks are administrative and include licensing teachers and distributing state and federal funds.

9. On the local level, the responsibility of school operations rests with the local school districts, which generally have their own school boards and superintendents. They are responsible for school construction, the hiring of school personnel, and the formulation of school policy, all while operating within the rules and regulations of the state.

10. The business community has had a significant impact on schools. Certain business-oriented values, such as competitiveness and punctuality, have been adopted by schools. Moreover, many businesses are becoming directly involved in schools, donating products, dollars, and volunteers to work with students.

11. Parents, school secretaries, and custodians can be influential in a teacher's success. They are part of the hidden government of schools.

12. Consolidation has decreased the number of school districts while increasing the average size of schools. Those who oppose consolidation claim that it leads to higher costs for transportation and administration but does not increase student achievement. Supporters of consolidation believe that it increases educational opportunities and efficiency by absorbing small school districts with limited educational resources and electives into larger districts.

13. Although educational responsibility rests with the states, the federal government still plays an important role through targeted funds and the setting of national standards and goals.

14. Recently, educational partnerships involving parents, community groups, and the business sector have had a significant impact on local school systems.

15. Traditionally, teachers have not had a significant role in school governance. However, the recent trends of school-based management, also called site-based management and collaborative decision making, may provide teachers with a more influential position in school governance.

Key Terms and People

accountability

block grants

categorical grants

chief state school officer

collaborative decision making

consolidation

covert power

decentralization

Edgewood v. Kirby

educational foundations

educational outcome

educational partnerships

excise taxes

financial input

foundation program

guaranteed tax base

hidden government

infrastructure

Jonathan Kozol

lotteries

personal income tax

property tax

Robin Hood laws

www.mhhe.com/sadker

sales tax

San Antonio v. Rodriguez

Savage Inequalities

school boards

school bonds

Serrano v. Priest

severance tax

sin tax

site-based (school-based) management

state board of education

state department of education

superintendents

Tenth Amendment

United States Department of Education

Discussion Questions and Activities

1. Why has state support for local school systems grown?
2. Briefly describe the major sources of state and local funds for schools.
3. What are the typical programs for state distribution of education funds?
4. Create a plan for (a) raising funds for education and (b) distributing funds equitably to all school districts within a state.
5. How can the differences in state wealth be dealt with to ensure that all students, regardless of the state they live in, benefit from equal educational expenditures?
6. If you were a state judge, would you focus more on financial resources (input) or educational output?
7. Do you believe that educational expenditures and educational quality are directly related? Support your position.
8. If educational vouchers were applied only to public schools, what would be the result?
9. Contrast the *Serrano* and *Rodriguez* court decisions.
10. If you were a superintendent of schools, what steps would you take to avoid taxpayer opposition to increasing school funding levels?
11. Research the average costs of educating a student in a local district. Discuss with classmates as you compare district programs, tax base, facilities, and student achievement.
12. Why does a high property tax not always result in a well-funded school program?
13. You are the chief financial officer of a school district with a 3 percent increase on next year's budget. This amount will allow you to make some funding decisions. Determine what percentage of your monies will be spent on the following sample categories:

    teachers' raises

    new buildings and facilities

    expanding Internet access

    long-delayed capital expenses for a gymnasium and the heating/cooling system

    new hires to lower class size

    YOU DECIDE _____

    In what way would you divide (starting with 100 percent) your new monies? How would you defend your choices? (Use your imagination and the information in this chapter.)
14. Have you had any personal experience in an organization that had both a formal and a "hidden" government? Explain how these governments operated.
15. Identify both the advantages and the disadvantages of the unusual U.S. form of local control over schools.
16. Based on your own experiences in school, can you recall examples of how business values were taught to you? Do you feel that this is a positive or a negative aspect of public education? Why?

17. If you had the power to reorganize the governance structure of public education, what changes would you make?

18. Someone once said, "What is good for General Motors is good for the country." If we were to paraphrase this statement to apply to U.S. schools, would you agree or disagree? Why?

19. Have you ever had first-hand experience with the power of the hidden or the legal government of schools? Describe these experiences.

20. Support or refute the following statement: "The least critical expertise needed by school superintendents is knowledge about teaching, learning, and children."

21. Describe the advantages and disadvantages of (1) increasing state influence on education and (2) decreasing federal influence on education.

22. If you were responsible for creating school partnerships, what businesses, community groups, or other organizations would you seek out to contribute to the educational process? Why?

23. Why was the twentieth century marked by school consolidation? What problems did consolidation bring?

24. Identify at least five powers that states have to influence education.

25. Find a school that has implemented site-based management or collaborative decision making. Interview a teacher to find out what the effects have been for teachers.

School Law and Ethics

Focus Questions

- What are the legal rights and responsibilities of teachers?
- What legal protections are granted to students?
- How do court decisions and federal laws affect everyday life in school?
- What practical steps can teachers take to decrease their risk of being sued?
- What are the teacher's responsibilities in cases of suspected child abuse?
- How can teachers promote ethical behavior?

Chapter Preview

A teacher puts in extra time helping a student after school, and is accused of sexual harassment.

A single teacher in one community is fired for living with her boyfriend in a neighboring town.

A school puts the senior yearbook on its web page and finds that it has helped pedophiles identify potential targets.

A Kentucky parent sues a school for preventing her pregnant daughter from joining the National Honor Society.

A homosexual student sues a school district for discrimination.

Lawyers and judges are more and more becoming a part of school life. In this chapter, you will have the opportunity to respond to actual legal situations that have confronted teachers and students. (Get ready to determine your RQ—Rights Quotient.) Also included are some pragmatic steps for your legal self defense, steps that you can take to avoid potential problems. But, beyond the nitty-gritty of these legal case studies, we will ask more penetrating questions about right and wrong, questions that go beyond the law, such as: How should teachers deal with ethical issues that emerge in the classroom? Should teachers take positions on moral issues? Or should they play a more neutral role? We will offer some suggestions for ways teachers can organize their classrooms, and themselves, to handle these important but difficult ethical dilemmas.

```
┌─────────────────────────────────────────────────────┐
│═══════════════════ YOU'VE GOT MAIL ═══════════════════│
├─────────────────────────────────────────────────────┤
│ TO: Steve@AU.edu,                                     │
│     Anna@State.edu                                    │
│ SUBJ.: Law School??!!                                 │
├─────────────────────────────────────────────────────┤
│ Once I thought about law school, but I never liked the│
│ idea enough to actually take the LSATs and apply. Now │
│ I'm beginning to think it would have been a good move.│
│ I could have learned about "defensive teaching."      │
│                                                       │
│ Teachers need to know an awful lot of law these days, │
│ not only for their own protection, but for the        │
│ protection of their students as well. What if my      │
│ student asks to form a Christian Club? Can I copy      │
│ material for class, or do I have to worry about        │
│ copyright laws? According to the drama teacher, the law│
│ has disarmed the arts. She does Shakespeare without   │
│ swords. (Even her wooden swords would violate the     │
│ school's "no weapons" policy.) It's easy to make a BIG│
│ mistake.                                              │
│                                                       │
│ And did I tell you about this "role model" thing they │
│ keep stressing? How I lead my life becomes an ethical │
│ lesson for my students. It's not just what I say, it's│
│ what I do that teaches. Hey, I guess I am a walking    │
│ lesson plan! Now that's scary!                        │
└─────────────────────────────────────────────────────┘
```

Classroom Law: New Frontiers for Teachers

You have probably heard it before: the United States is a litigious society. "Take them to court," "I'll sue," and "Have your lawyer call my lawyer" are phrases that have worked their way into the American lexicon. And actions match words. People sue companies. Companies sue people. Governments sue companies. Companies and people sue governments. We tend to seek redress for all kinds of problems in the courts, from divorce to physical injury, from protecting our beliefs to complying (or not complying) with laws.

The story is told that, when the federal government ordered tougher antipollution standards in automobiles, U.S. and Japanese companies responded quite differently. Japanese automobile manufacturers increased the number of engineers working to solve the problem and design cars to meet the new antipollution standards. American corporations, on the other hand, increased the size of their legal budgets in order to fight the new requirements. Both strategies met with some success. The Japanese developed and sold cars that met the tougher standards, while the American companies won delays in implementing them.

This auto story has "wheels" for educators. Today, parents sue teachers. Students sue teachers. Despite the growing importance and influence of school-related law, many educators are still unaware of their basic legal rights and responsibilities. This can be a costly professional blind spot.[1]

What rights do you have in the classroom? Consider this exchange between a college professor and a former associate superintendent of public instruction for California:

SUPERINTENDENT: "Teaching is a privilege, not a right. If one wants this privilege, he or she has to give up some rights."

PROFESSOR: "Just what constitutional rights do people have to give up in order to enter teaching?"

SUPERINTENDENT: "Any right their community wants them to give up."[2]

Although such simplistic attitudes still exist, recent years have seen extraordinary changes in the legal rights of both teachers and students. Once the victims of arbitrary school rules and regulations, today's teachers and students can institute legal action if they believe that their constitutional rights are being threatened. In an increasing number of cases, the courts are finding school administrators guilty of violating the rights of both teachers and students.

As a classroom teacher, what can you legally say and do? Can you let your students log freely onto the Internet? What disciplinary methods are acceptable? How does your role as teacher limit your personal life? Knowing the answers to these questions *before* you step into a classroom can help you avoid costly mistakes.

While teachers would like to know definitively what is legal and what is not, courts often set forth standards with such terms as "reasonable care" or "appropriately under the circumstances." Courts try to balance legitimate concerns that can be raised on both sides of an issue and to keep their options open. Staying legally up-to-date is an ongoing professional task.

What Is Your Rights Quotient?

The following case studies focus on court cases or federal law.[3] The vignettes are divided into two parts: teachers' rights and students' rights. In each case, an issue is identified, a situation is described, and you are asked to select an appropriate (legal) response. After your selection, the correct response and relevant court decisions or laws are described. Keep track of your rights and wrongs; a scoring system at the conclusion will help you determine your RQ (rights quotient). Good luck!

I. Teachers' Rights and Responsibilities

Issue	Situation 1
Applying for a position	You did it! You finished student teaching (you were great!) and the school district you most want to teach in has called you for an interview. Mr. Thomas, from the personnel office, seems impressed with your credentials and the interview is going well. He explains that the school district is very committed to its teachers and invests a great deal of resources in training. He wants to make certain that this investment makes sense, so he asks you for your long-range plans with such questions as: "Do you see yourself teaching in this system for a long time?" and "Are you planning to get married or have children in the near future?"

_____ You answer the questions realizing that the district is entitled to know about your long-range plans.

_____ You avoid answering the questions. You think it's none of his business, but you are worried about getting the position.

Federal and State Laws, Court Decisions   Not too long ago, school districts regularly gave hiring and promotion consideration to marital status and parenthood. For women these were critical factors in being offered a job, and the "right" answer was: "No, I am not going to get married or have children." For male candidates, the question was less important and rarely asked. Now a variety of federal and state laws and court decisions make such inquiries illegal. Generally, interview questions must be related to the job requirements. Questions about race, creed, marital status, sex, religion, age, national origin, and physical or other disabilities and even a request for photographs along with an application are generally illegal. **Title IX of the Education Amendments (1972)** and **Title VII of the Civil Rights Act (1964)** are two federal laws that prohibit many of these practices. In situation 1, the questions are inappropriate and illegal, and you need not answer them. You may wish to notify the school district or even the Office for Civil Rights in order to stop the school district from asking such discriminatory questions in the future. The challenge, of course, is how you could answer such questions without ruining your chances for being offered a position—that is, if you still want the job.[4]

Issue Sexual harassment	**Situation 2** After surviving the gender discriminatory interview, you are offered a teaching position and decide to take it. After all, you like the community and the children, and with any luck you will never run into Mr. Thomas (the interviewer) again. You are very excited as you prepare for your first day. You are up an hour early, rehearsing your opening remarks. You enter the school, feeling hopeful and optimistic. Then it's your worst nightmare. You meet the new principal, Mr. Thomas, recently transferred from the personnel office. You spend the next year dodging his lewd comments, his unwanted touches, and his incessant propositions. At the end of the year, you find yourself in counseling and worried about your job. You decide that

_____ Your initial instincts were right. You should never have taken this job. Quit before things get worse.

_____ Enough is enough. You sue the district for damages.

Court Decision   Anita Hill's charges against Supreme Court nominee Clarence Thomas, as well as similar charges against President Clinton, a stream of Senators, and other officials have awakened millions of Americans to the issue of sexual harassment. The principal's behavior, both verbal and physical, is clearly an example of this problem. The Supreme Court ruled that victims of sexual harassment are also victims of sex discrimination and can recover monetary damages. Keeping a record of the principal's behavior and having witnesses will strengthen your case; however, you certainly can sue, and, if you are successful, you may be awarded significant monetary damages. You can also file a grievance with the Office for Civil Rights, without even having a lawyer. This grievance will launch an investigation of the school's practices. (When students are targets of sexual harassment, the court has created very high standards before a school district can be held financially accountable.[5])

Issue   **Situation 3**
Personal lifestyle   After your first few months, your reputation is established: you are known as a creative and effective teacher and are well liked by students and colleagues (isn't that wonderful!). But your life outside the classroom is not appreciated by school officials. You are single and living with your "significant other." Several school officials have strong feelings about this and believe that you are a poor role model for the students. The school system publicly announces that, because you are "cohabiting," your behavior is having a negative influence on your elementary-age students. The school board suspends you.

_____ You are the victim of an illegal action and should sue to be reinstated.

_____ The school board is within its rights in dismissing you and removing a bad role model from the classroom.

Court Decision   This case reflects various issues, all related to the degree of personal freedom an individual abandons when assuming the position of a teacher and becoming a role model for students. Although court decisions have varied, the following general standard should be kept in mind: Does your behavior significantly disrupt the educational process or erode your credibility with students, colleagues, or the community? If the school district can demonstrate that you have disrupted education or have lost credibility, then you may be fired.

In the case outlined here, the teacher sued the school district (*Thompson v. Southwest School District*). The court indicated that, until the school district took action to suspend the teacher on grounds of immorality, the public was generally unaware of the teacher's cohabitation with her boyfriend. The court decided that it was unfair of the board of education to make the issue public in order to gain community support for its position. Furthermore, the court ruled that the teacher's behavior had not interfered with her effectiveness in the classroom. With neither a loss of credibility nor a significant disruption of the educational process, the board lost its case and the teacher kept her job.

Issues concerning the personal lifestyles of teachers have emerged in a series of court cases on issues ranging from drinking problems to marijuana smoking, from church attendance (actually, a lack of church attendance) to personal appearance. Court decisions have differed from state to state. Driving while intoxicated or smoking marijuana was found to be grounds for dismissal in one state but not in another, depending on whether the behavior resulted in "substantial disruption" of the educational process. On the other hand, an attempt to dismiss a teacher because she did not attend church was not upheld by the court. In fact, the teacher in this case actually won financial damages against the school district.

What about your personal appearance? What can a school district legally require in terms of personal grooming and dress codes for teachers? Courts have not been consistent in their decisions, although, if the dress requirements are reasonable and related to legitimate educational concerns, the courts may uphold the legality of dress codes for teachers.[6]

Issue	**Situation 4**
Teachers' academic freedom	As a social studies teacher, you are concerned about your students' apparent insensitivity to racism in the United States. You have found a very effective simulation game that evokes strong student feelings on racial issues, but the school board is concerned by this activity and has asked you to stop using the game. The board expressed its concern over your discussion of controversial issues. Committed to your beliefs, you persist; at the end of the year, you find that your teaching contract is not renewed.

_____ Since you think your academic freedom has been violated, you decide to sue to get your job back.

_____ You realize that the school board is well within its rights to determine curriculum, that you were warned, and that now you must pay the price for your indiscretion.

Court Decision   The right to **academic freedom** (that is, to teach without coercion, censorship, or other restrictive interference) is not absolute, and the courts will balance your right to academic freedom with the school system's interests in its students' learning appropriate subject matter in an environment conducive to learning. Courts look at such factors as whether your learning activities and materials are inappropriate, irrelevant to the subjects to be covered under the syllabus, obscene, or substantially disruptive of school discipline. In the case of the simulation game

Academic freedom protects a teacher's right to teach about sensitive issues, such as AIDS or other sex education topics, as long as the topic is relevant to the course, is not treated in an obscene manner, and is not disruptive of school discipline.

involving racial issues, the activity appears to be appropriate, relevant, and neither obscene nor disruptive. If you were to sue on the grounds of academic freedom, you would probably get your job back.[7]

Issue   **Situation 5**
Legal liability   You are assigned to cafeteria duty. Things are pretty quiet, and
(negligence)   you take the opportunity to call a guest speaker and confirm a
                              visit to your class. While you are gone from the cafeteria, a
                              student slips on some spilled milk and breaks his arm. His
                              parents hold you liable for their son's injury and sue you for
                              damages.

_____ You will probably win, since you did not cause the fall and were on educational business when the accident occurred.

_____ The student's parents will win, since you left your assigned post.

_____ The student who spilled the milk is solely responsible for the accident.

_____ No one will win, because the courts long ago ruled that there is no use crying over spilled milk. (You knew that was coming, right?)

Court Decision   In recent years, litigation against teachers has increased dramatically. The public concern over the quality of education, the bureaucratic and impersonal nature of many school systems, and the generally litigious nature of our society have all contributed to this rising tide of lawsuits. Negligence suits against teachers are no longer uncommon. In the cafeteria example, you would be in considerable jeopardy in a legal action. A teacher who is not present at his or her assigned duty might be charged with negligence, unless the absence is "reasonable." The courts are very strict about what is "reasonable" (leaving your post to put out a fire is reasonable, but going to the telephone to make a call is unlikely to be viewed as reasonable). It is a good practice to stay in your classroom or assigned area of responsibility unless there is an emergency.

Teacher liability is an area of considerable concern to many teachers. Courts generally use two standards in determining negligence: (1) whether a reasonable person with similar training would act in the same way and (2) whether or not the teacher could have foreseen the possibility of an injury. Following are some common terms and typical situations related to teacher liability:

- *Misfeasance.* This is failure to conduct in an appropriate manner an act that might otherwise have been lawfully performed; for example, unintentionally using too much force in breaking up a fight is **misfeasance.**
- *Nonfeasance.* This applies to failure to perform an act that one has a duty to perform; for example, the cafeteria situation is **nonfeasance,** since the teacher did not supervise an assigned area of responsibility.
- *Malfeasance.* This is an act that cannot be done lawfully regardless of how it is performed; for example, starting a fistfight or bringing marijuana to school is **malfeasance.**
- *Educational malpractice.* Although liability litigation usually involves physical injury to students because of what a teacher did or failed to do, a new line of litigation, called **educational malpractice,** is concerned with

"academic damage." Some students and parents have sued school districts for failing to provide an adequate education. Many courts have rejected these cases, pointing out that many factors affect learning and that failure to learn cannot be blamed solely on the school system.

Issue
Teachers' freedom of speech

Situation 6

As a teacher in a small school district in Illinois, you are quite upset with the way the school board and the superintendent are spending school funds. You are particularly troubled with all the money being spent on high school athletics, since these expenditures have cut into your proposed salary raise. To protest the expenditures, you write a lengthy letter to the local newspaper, criticizing the superintendent and the school board. After the letter is published, you find that the figures you cited in the letter were inaccurate.

The following week, you are called into the superintendent's office and fired for breaking several school rules. You have failed to communicate your complaints to your superiors and you have caused harm to the school system by spreading false and malicious statements. In addition, the superintendent points out that your acceptance of a teaching position obligated you to refrain from publicizing critical statements about the school. The superintendent says although no one can stop you from making public statements, the school systems certainly does not "have to pay you for the privilege." You decide to

‾‾‾‾‾ Go to court to win back your position.

‾‾‾‾‾ Chalk it up to experience, look for a new position, and make certain that you do not publish false statements and break school rules in the future.

Court Decision   This situation is based on a suit instigated by a teacher named Marvin Pickering. After balancing the teacher's interests, as a citizen, in commenting on issues of public concern against the school's interests in efficiently providing public services, the Supreme Court ruled in favor of the teacher. It found that the disciplined operation of the school system was not seriously damaged by Pickering's letter and that the misstatements in the letter were not made knowingly or recklessly. Moreover, there was no special need for confidentiality on the issue of school budgets. Hence, concluded the Court, prohibiting Pickering from making his statements was an infringement of his First Amendment right to freedom of speech. You, too, would probably win in court if you were to issue public statements on matters of public concern, unless your statements were intentionally or recklessly inaccurate, disclosed confidential material, or hampered either school discipline or your performance of duties.[8]

Issue
Copying published material

Situation 7

You read a fascinating two-page article in a national magazine, and, since the article concerns an issue your class is discussing, you duplicate the article and distribute it to your students.

This is the only article you have distributed in class, and you do not bother to ask either the author or the magazine for permission to reprint it. You have

_____ Violated the copyright law, and you are liable to legal action.

_____ Not violated any copyright law.

Federal Law   Initially, as the copier machine became commonplace in staff rooms, teachers could reproduce articles, poems, book excerpts, or whatever they pleased with virtually no fear of legal repercussions. But, in January 1976, PL 94-553 was passed, and teachers' rights to freely reproduce and distribute published works were greatly curtailed. Under this law, in order to use a published work in class, teachers must write to the publisher or author of the work and obtain written permission. This sometimes requires the payment of a permission fee, something that teachers on a limited budget are usually unwilling to do. Under certain circumstances, however, teachers may still reproduce published material without written permission or payment. This is called **fair use,** a legal principle that allows the limited use of copyrighted materials. To use copyrighted materials, teachers must observe three criteria in selecting the material: brevity, spontaneity, and cumulative effect. As we review these criteria, you can apply them to the example outlined in the vignette to determine if, in this case, you stayed within the limits of the new copyright law.

1. *Brevity* means that a work can be reproduced if it is not overly long. Publishers do not all agree on the meaning of brevity, so it is always wise to contact them directly, but typical limits might include the following criteria. Poems or excerpts from poems must be no longer than 250 words. Articles, stories, and essays of less than 2,500 words may be reproduced in complete form. Excerpts of any prose work (such as a book or an article) may be reproduced only up to 1,000 words or 10 percent of the work, whichever is less. Only one illustration (photo, drawing, diagram) may be reproduced from the same book or journal. The brevity criterion limits the length of the material that a teacher can reproduce and distribute from a single work. If you were the teacher in this example and you reproduced only a two-page article, you probably would not have violated the criterion of brevity.
2. The second criterion, *spontaneity,* allows a teacher to reproduce material if there is not enough time to secure written permission. If a teacher has an inspiration to use a published work and there is simply not enough time to write for and receive written permission, then the teacher may reproduce and distribute the work. The teacher in our vignette has met this criterion and, consequently, is acting within the law. If the teacher wishes to distribute the same article to a class during the next semester or the next year, written permission would be required, since ample time exists to request such permission.
3. The final criterion, *cumulative effect,* limits the number of published works that may be used in a course. The total number of works reproduced without permission for class distribution must not exceed nine instances per class per semester. Within this limit, only one complete piece or two excerpts from the same author may be reproduced, and only three pieces from the same book or magazine. Cumulative effect limits the number of articles, poems, excerpts,

and so on that can be reproduced, even if the criteria of spontaneity and brevity are met. From the description in the vignette, the teacher has not reproduced other works and therefore has met this criterion also.

Under the fair use principle, single copies of printed material may be copied for your personal use. Thus, if you want a single copy for planning a lesson, that is not a problem. Whenever multiple copies are made for classroom use, each copy must include a notice of copyright.

Three new areas should also be considered: videotapes, computer software, and mixed media. Without a license or permission, educational institutions may not keep copyrighted videotapes (for example, from a television show) for more than forty-five days. The tape should not be shown more than once to students during this period, and then it must be erased. The growing use of computers prompted the amendment of the Federal Copyright Act in 1990 to prohibit the copying of software for commercial gain. Teachers should observe all copyright restrictions when using software. For other materials, including mixed-media products that combine text, graphics, and film images, it is always advisable to check with your local school district officials to determine school policy and procedures.[9]

Issue
Labor rights

Situation 8

Salary negotiations have been going badly in your school district, and at a mass meeting teachers finally vote to strike. You honor the strike and stay home, refusing to teach until an adequate salary increase is provided. During the first week of the strike, you receive a letter from the school board, stating that you will be suspended for fifteen days without pay at the end of the school year, owing to your participation in the strike. You decide

_____ To fight this illegal, unjust, and costly suspension.

_____ To accept the suspension as a legal action of the school board.

Although many states have laws prohibiting teachers from striking, most communities choose not to penalize striking teachers.

Court Decision   In a number of cases, courts have recognized the right of teachers to organize; to join professional organizations, such as the NEA (National Education Association) and the AFT (American Federation of Teachers); and to bargain collectively for improved working conditions. You cannot legally be penalized for these activities. On the other hand, courts have upheld teachers' right to strike in only about half the states. (In some states, the courts have determined that teachers provide a vital public service and cannot strike.) You need to know your state laws to know if you are breaking the law by honoring the strike. The school board may be within its rights to suspend, fine, or even fire you for striking.

Although about half of the states have laws that prohibit strikes, many communities choose not to prosecute striking teachers. If they do prosecute, the teachers may be penalized. Conversely, even though membership in teacher organizations and the right to collective bargaining have been upheld by the courts, some communities and school boards are adamantly opposed to such organizations and refuse to hire or to renew contracts of teachers who are active in them. Such bias is clearly illegal; nevertheless, it is very difficult to prove in court and, consequently, it is very difficult to stop.

In summary, law and reality do not always coincide. Legally speaking, teachers may be prohibited from striking by state law but are rarely prosecuted or penalized. In some communities, however, active involvement in teacher organizations may result in discriminatory school board actions. Finally, if you choose to strike, do so with the realization that such activity makes you liable to legal sanctions.[10]

II. Students' Rights and Responsibilities

Issue

Student records

Situation 9

You are a high school teacher who has decided to stay after school and review your students' personnel folders. You believe that learning more about your students will make you a more effective teacher. As you finish reviewing some the folders, Phyllis, a 16-year-old student of yours, walks in and asks to see her folder. Since you have several sensitive comments recorded in the folder, you refuse. Within the hour, the student's parents call and ask if they can see the folder. At this point, you

_____   Explain that the information is confidential and sensitive and cannot be shared with nonprofessional personnel.

_____   Explain that the parents can see the folder and describe the procedure for doing so.

Federal Law   The *Family Rights and Privacy Act,* commonly referred to as the **Buckley Amendment** (1974), allows parents and guardians access to their children's educational records. The amendment also requires that school districts inform parents of this right and establish a procedure for providing educational records on request. Moreover, written parental permission is needed before these records can be shared with anyone other than professionals connected with either the school the student attends or another school in which the student seeks to enroll, health or safety officials, or persons reviewing the student's financial aid applications. If the student has reached 18 years of age, he or she must be allowed to see the folder and is responsible for granting permission for others to review the folder.

Under this law, you should have chosen the second option, for it is the parents' right to see this information.[11]

Issue

Distribution of scholarships

Situation 10

As a secondary teacher, you are concerned with the manner in which scholarships and other financial awards (donated by the local booster club and neighborhood businesses) are distributed at graduation. You notice that nearly all the awards are going to boys. You mention this to the principal, who explains that this has been the case for as long as anyone can remember. The groups donating the scholarship funds use such categories as leadership skills and sports abilities in choosing the recipients. The principal says that, although this is not exactly equitable, it is realistic, because future financial burdens hit males more than females. You decide that

_____ It is an unfortunate but realistic policy.

_____ It is unfair, unreasonable, and unrealistic. You file a complaint with the Office for Civil Rights.

Federal Law   Using sex as a criterion by which to grant awards, scholarships, or financial aid is one of the many areas of sex discrimination prohibited under Title IX. Objective criteria fairly applied without regard to sex should be the appropriate policy in awarding these funds. If it turns out that the most qualified students in a given year are predominantly or entirely of one sex, that is acceptable, as long as the procedures and criteria have been fairly applied. But sex itself should not be a criterion; this example is a violation of Title IX and should be corrected.[12]

Issue

Suspension and discipline

Situation 11

You are teaching a difficult class, and one student is the primary source of trouble. After a string of disorderly episodes on this student's part, the floppy disks for the entire class mysteriously disappear. You have put up with more than enough, and you send the student to the principal's office to be suspended. The principal backs you up, and the student is told not to return to school for a week. This action is

_____ Legal and appropriate (and probably long overdue!).

_____ Illegal.

Court Decision   Although troublesome and disorderly students can be disciplined, suspension from school represents a serious penalty, one that should not be taken lightly. In such cases, the Supreme Court has ruled (*Goss v. Lopez*) that teachers and administrators are required to follow certain procedures in order to guarantee the student's **due process** rights. In this case, the student must be informed of the rule that has been broken and of the evidence. The student is also entitled to tell his or her side

IS CORPORAL PUNISHMENT LEGAL?

Corporal punishment, the physical discipline of students, is deplored by most educators, yet it remains legal in twenty-three states. Such punishment is restricted in six states and it is outlawed in twenty-one states. Knowing whether it is legal in your school is only part of the issue; sorting out your ethics on physical retribution is a more penetrating question.

Illegal	Restricted	Legal
California	Alaska	Alabama
Connecticut	New Hampshire	Arizona
Hawaii	New York	Arkansas
Illinois	Rhode Island	Colorado
Iowa	South Dakota	Delaware
Maine	Utah	Florida
Maryland		Georgia
Massachusetts		Idaho
Michigan		Indiana
Minnesota		Kansas
Montana		Kentucky
Nebraska		Louisiana
Nevada		Mississippi
New Jersey		Missouri
North Dakota		New Mexico
Oregon		North Carolina
Vermont		Ohio
Virginia		Oklahoma
Washington		Pennsylvania
West Virginia		South Carolina
Wisconsin		Tennessee
		Texas
		Wyoming

Source: *Child,* September 1997.

of the story in self-defense. For suspensions in excess of ten days, the school must initiate more formal procedures. School officials can be held personally liable for damages if they violate a student's clearly established constitutional rights (*Wood v. Strickland*).

If you look back at this vignette, you will notice that you do not know for sure that this student is responsible for the missing floppy disks, nor is the student given the opportunity for self-defense. If you selected "illegal," you chose the correct response.

While looking at discipline, let us look at the legality of **corporal punishment.** In *Ingraham v. Wright* (1977), the Supreme Court ruled that physical punishment may be authorized by the states. The Court ruled that the corporal punishment should be "reasonable and not excessive," and such factors as the seriousness of the student offense, the age and physical condition of the student, and the force and attitude of the person administering the punishment should be considered. Although the courts have legalized corporal punishment, many states and school districts do not believe in it and have prohibited the physical punishment of students; other districts and states provide very specific guidelines for its practice. You should be familiar with the procedures and norms in your district before you even consider this disciplinary strategy.[13]

Issue

Freedom of speech

Situation 12

During your homeroom period, you notice that several of your more politically active students are wearing t-shirts with a red line drawn through "www." You call them to your desk and ask them about it. They explain that they are protesting censorship, the new school board policy that limits student access on the Internet. You tell them that you share their concern but that wearing the t-shirts is specifically forbidden by school rules. You explain that you will let it go this time, since they are not disturbing the class routine but that, if they wear them again, they will be suspended.

Sure enough, the next day the same students arrive at school still wearing the t-shirts, and you send them to the principal's office. The students tell the principal that, although they understand the rule, they refuse to obey it. The principal, explaining that school rules are made to be followed, suspends them. The principal's action is

_____ Legally justified, since the students were given every opportunity to understand and obey the school rule.

_____ Illegal, since the students have the right to wear t-shirts if they so desire.

Court Decision   In December 1965, three students in Des Moines, Iowa, demonstrated their opposition to the Vietnam War by wearing black arm bands to school. The principal informed them that they were breaking a school rule and asked that they remove the arm bands. They refused and were suspended.

The students' parents sued the school system, and the case finally reached the Supreme Court. In the landmark **Tinker case,** the Court ruled that the students were entitled to wear the arm bands, as long as the students did not substantially disrupt the operation of the school or deny other students the opportunity to learn. Since there was no disruption, the Court ruled that the school system could not prohibit students from wearing the arm bands or engaging in other forms of free speech. The school system in this vignette acted illegally; it could not prevent students from wearing the protest t-shirts.[14]

Courts have upheld students' freedom of speech in a number of cases, so long as the protests were not disruptive of other students' right to learn and were not obscene.

The issue of allegedly "obscene" speech has been more recently considered by the Supreme Court. In a 1986 decision (*Bethel School District v. Fraser*), the Court evaluated the First Amendment rights of a high school senior, Matthew Fraser. Fraser presented a speech at a school assembly that contained numerous sexual innuendoes, though no explicit, profane language. After Fraser was suspended for his speech and told that he was no longer eligible to speak at his class's graduation, his father sued the school district. The Court upheld the suspension on the grounds that the language in the speech was indecent and offensive and that minors should not be exposed to such language.[15]

Issue	**Situation 13**
School prayer	A student on your team objects to the daily prayer recitation. You are sensitive to the student's feelings, and you make certain that the prayer is nondenominational. Moreover, you tell the student that he may stand or sit silently without reciting the prayer. If the student likes, he may even leave the gym while the prayer is being recited. As a teacher, you have

_____ Broken the law.

_____ Demonstrated sensitivity to individual needs and not violated the law.

Court Decision   You were sensitive but not sensitive enough, because you violated the law. The Court has ruled that educators must be completely neutral with regard to religion and may neither encourage nor discourage prayer. Educators should not allot time for any kind of religious observance, even for a moment of silence. As a result of leaving the gym, the student might be subjected to embarrassment, ostracism, or some other form of social stigma. The Court has ruled that the separation of church and state prevents educators, but not necessarily students, from promoting religious activities. In recent years the Supreme Court has allowed students to form religious clubs on school property if other, nonreligious clubs are given space in school. While "official" prayers are not permitted, including at graduation ceremonies (where they frequently occur despite the law), it is not clear if it is legal for a student giving a graduation speech to use that speech as a platform for prayer. The students' right to free speech, even religious speech, as compared with the school's role in promoting such prayer, seems to be a growing legal distinction. While students may make some religious choices in schools, teachers cannot make such choices for them.[16]

Issue	**Situation 14**
Search and seizure	The drug problem in your school is spreading, and it is clear that strong action is needed. School authorities order a search of all student lockers, which lasts for several hours. Trained police dogs are brought in, and each classroom is searched for drugs. The dogs sniff suspiciously at several students, who are taken to the locker rooms and strip-searched.

_____ School authorities are well within their rights to conduct these searches.

_____ Searching the lockers is legal, but strip-searching is inappropriate and illegal.

Student locker searches for contraband items are permissible since schools have parentlike responsibility for the safety of their students.

_____ No searches are called for, and all of these activities present illegal and unconstitutional violation of student rights.

Court Decision   Courts have ruled that school authorities have fewer restrictions than do the police in search-and-seizure activities. Courts have indicated that school property (such as lockers or cars parked in the school lot) are actually the responsibility of the school. Moreover, the school has a parentlike responsibility (termed **in loco parentis**) to protect children and to respond to reasonable concerns about their health and safety.

In situation 14, the search of lockers is legal. However, using police dogs to sniff students (rather than things) is allowable only if the dogs are reliable and the student is a reasonable suspect. The strip-search is illegal.

The second choice is the correct response. Although school personnel have great latitude in conducting school search and seizures, educators should be familiar with proper legal procedures and should think carefully about the related ethical issues.[17]

Issue	**Situation 15**
Freedom of the press	_The Argus_ is the official student newspaper, written by students as part of a journalism course, but it has run afoul of school administrators. First the student newspaper printed a story critical of the school administration. In the next edition, the paper included a supplement on contraception and abortion. With their patience worn thin, school administrators closed the publication for the remainder of the school year.

_____ Closing the student newspaper is a legal action.

_____ Closing the student newspaper is an illegal action.

Court Decision   In 1988, a relatively conservative Supreme Court ruled in the *Hazelwood* case that student newspapers may be censored under certain circumstances. The Court held that student newspapers written as part of a school journalism course should be viewed as part of the official school curriculum. School administrators, according to the Court, can readily censor such a paper. Since, in situation 15, the publication is part of a journalism course, closing the school newspaper would be legal.

If, on the other hand, the newspaper were financed by the students and not associated with an official school course, the students would enjoy a greater degree of freedom. Additional grounds for censoring a school newspaper include obscenity, psychological harm, and disruption of school activities.[18]

Issue HIV-infected students	**Situation 16** As you enter school one morning, you are met by a group of angry parents. They have found out that Randy, one of your students, is HIV positive, and hence can transmit the AIDS-related virus to others. There is no cure for AIDS, and there is no compromise in the voices of the parents confronting you. Either Randy goes, or they will keep their children at home. You listen sympathetically, but find your mind wandering to your own contact with Randy. You worry that you, too, may be at risk. In this case, you decide

_____   It's better to be safe than sorry, so you ask Randy to return home while you arrange a meeting with the principal to discuss Randy's case. There is no cure for AIDS and no reason to put every child's life in jeopardy.

_____   It's probably okay for Randy to attend school, so you check with your principal and try to calm the parents down.

Court Decision   In a case very similar to this situation, Randy, a hemophiliac, and his brothers were denied access to De Soto County Schools in Florida when they tested positive for the HIV virus. The court determined that the boys' loss of their education was more harmful than the remote chance of other students' contracting AIDS. In fact, in this 1987 case, Randy's parents won an out-of-court settlement in excess of $1 million for the pain the school system inflicted on the family. In another case, the court determined that HIV-infected students are protected under PL 94-142, the Individuals with Disabilities Education Act. Clearly, medical guidelines direct the court. If some AIDS children present more of a public risk (for example, because of biting behavior, open sores, fighting, and so on), more restrictive school environments may be required. To date, however, HIV-infected students and teachers are not viewed as a significant risk to the health of the rest of the population and cannot be denied their educational rights.[19]

Issue Internet censorship	**Situation 17** You have found a terrific web site, one that really communicates recent changes and unique insights about the economics topic your class is studying. You give out the URL address, and some students log on in class, while several others tell you that they will follow up at home. The next day, the principal calls you into her office to tell you that she has gotten several

parent complaints about the web site. It seems that a number of the items on the site are controversial, and some of the topics discussed have upset them. You thank her, go back to your classroom, and recheck the site. Now you see the problem. There is slick advertising, directing site visitors to free games and prizes. There are links to information forms with personal questions about beliefs and finances. And, you find a story about money management and family decision-making ideas that probably conflicts with the more traditional views of your students' parents. While none of the sites are pornographic, vulgar, or age-inappropriate, some of the positions taken are well out of the mainstream.

_____ You decide that the principal is right and that students should not have unfettered access to the Internet. You take responsibility for inappropriately directing your students to this controversial site, offer an apology, and eliminate it from the curriculum.

_____ You decide to resist, believing that the web site has good information and that your students should have access.

Court Decision   In 1997, the Supreme Court struck down the federal Communications Decency Act, an attempt by Congress to make it a crime to transmit on the Internet indecent material to anyone under 18. The high court found such a law a clear violation of the First Amendment. But what can *legally* be put on the Internet and what schools *choose* to allow into their buildings and curricular assignments are entirely different issues. Many schools have implemented technological measures to ensure that vulgar or pornographic materials are not accessible in school, a position that seems entirely within their legal rights. While few laws have been written about the new technology, general guidelines for the curriculum may be instructive.

The courts have ruled that educators can restrict vulgar, age-inappropriate, and educationally unsuitable materials from the school. Thus, if the web site that you assigned reflects any of these characteristics, an apology and withdrawal is called for. The courts have also ruled that controversial materials expressing unpopular ideas are not grounds for censoring material, so merely upsetting parents, as the principal explained, is not grounds for removing site access. Future court cases may extend decisions about the print curriculum to the Internet.

In this instance, the school would be wise to formulate appropriate Internet guidelines for all teachers. The guidelines should allow teachers to assign unpopular and "controversial" ideas. While legitimate educational concerns may be given as a reason for censoring the Internet, disagreeing with ideas is not reason enough.[20]

Issue
Sexual harassment

Situation 18

One of your favorite students appears particularly upset. You are concerned, so you go over to Pat and put your arm around him. Pat stiffens his shoulder and pushes you away. He is obviously distressed about something. The next day, you offer to take Pat to a local fast-food restaurant after school, to cheer him up with a hot fudge sundae. He refuses to go but thanks you for the gesture. A few weeks later, the principal calls you into her office to explain that you have been charged with sexual harassment.

_____ You feel bewildered and betrayed that your gestures of kindness have been misconstrued.

_____ You decide to fight the charges, believing that you have been victimized.

_____ You decide to apologize, realizing that you have overstepped the boundaries of propriety.

Court Decision   In _Franklin v. Gwinnett_ (1992), the Supreme Court extended the reach of Title IX, allowing students to sue a school district for monetary damages in cases of sexual harassment. The Gwinnett County case involved a Georgia high school in which a student was sexually harassed and abused by a teacher, a case much more serious than the pat on the back and offer of a hot fudge sundae described in the vignette. In Georgia, the teacher's behavior was extreme and the school district's response inadequate. The school district was instructed to pay damages to the student—establishing a precedent.

However, just a few years later, in 1998, the Court made collecting personal damages from school districts more difficult. The Court ruled that the school district had to show "deliberate indifference" to complaints about sexual harassment before the district would be forced to pay damages (_Gebsner v. Lago Independent School District_). In fact, just notifying the principal when sexual harassment occurred was insufficient, according to the Court. More powerful officials would need to know and not act on this information before damages could be collected—clearly, an extremely difficult standard. The school district could suffer Title IX penalties (lose federal funds), and the individual accused of harassment could be forced to pay personal damages, but the school district, the place where large funds are available, could not be sued.[21]

Sexual harassment complaints against teachers have been increasing. Teachers need to realize that **sexual harassment** laws protect individuals not only from extreme actions, as in the Georgia case, but from offensive words and inappropriate touching. The mild scenario of comforting words, touching, and an offer of ice cream can indeed lead to problems. While the teacher's intention might have been pure and caring, the student's perception might have been quite different. The threat of the legal broadside that can result from this gap between teacher intentions and student perceptions has sent a chill through many school faculties. Teachers now openly express their fears about the dangers of reaching out to students, and some teachers are vowing never to touch a student or be alone in a room with a student, no matter how honorable the intention. Many teachers lament the current situation, recalling earlier times, when a teacher's kindness and closeness fostered a caring educational climate, rather than a legal case.[22]

Scoring

To determine your RQ (Rights Quotient), the following scoring guide may be useful:

15 to 18 correct: Legal eagle

13 or 14 correct: Lawyer-in-training

HOW PRIVATE IS YOUR PERSONAL LIFE?

The courts are constantly asked to draw the line between a teacher's personal freedom and the community's right to establish teacher behavior standards. Historically, the scales have tilted toward the community, and teachers have been fired for wearing lipstick, joining a certain church, or getting married. Today's courts make more deliberate efforts to balance personal liberty and community standards. Although each case must be judged on its own merits, some trends do emerge. The courts have ruled that the community has the right to fire a teacher for

- Making public homosexual advances to nonstudents
- Incorporating sexual issues into lessons and ignoring the approved syllabus
- Inciting violent protest among students
- Engaging in sex with students
- Encouraging students to attend certain religious meetings
- Allowing students to drink alcohol
- Drinking excessively
- Using profanity and abusive language toward students
- Having a sex-change operation
- Stealing school property (even if it is returned later)
- Not living within his or her district if that is listed as a condition of employment

On the other hand, courts have ruled that teachers should not be fired for

- Smoking of marijuana
- Private homosexual behavior
- Obesity (unless it inhibits teaching performance)
- Adultery
- Use of vulgar language outside of school

Why are teachers dismissed in some cases and not in others? Often, the standard the courts use is whether the behavior under question reduces teacher effectiveness. Public behavior, or behavior that becomes public, may compromise a teacher's effectiveness. In such cases, the courts find it reasonable and legal to terminate the teacher. If the behavior remains private, if the teacher shows discretion, the teacher's "right to privacy" often prevails. What lies ahead? Courts continue to draw the line between the private and public lives of teachers. Courts have disagreed on whether the following three situations constitute grounds for dismissal of a teacher. If you were the judge, how would you rule on the following issues?

- Unwed cohabitation
- Unwed parenthood
- Conviction for shoplifting

Source: These examples have been adapted from Louis Fischer, David Schimmel, and Cynthia Kelly, *Teachers and the Law* (New York: Longman, 1991).

11 or 12 correct:	Paralegal
9 or 10 correct:	Law student
8 or fewer correct:	Could benefit from an LSAT prep course

This brief review of the legal realities that surround today's classroom is not meant to be definitive. These situations are merely intended to highlight the rapid growth and changing nature of school law and the importance of this law to teachers.

However, this sample of teacher and student rights underscores the legal side of the classroom. Ignorance of the law, to paraphrase a popular saying, is no defense. More positively, knowledge of fundamental legal principles allows you to practice "preventive law"—that is, to avoid or resolve potential legal conflicts so that you can attend to your major responsibility: teaching.

TEACHERS' AND STUDENTS' RIGHTS

What rights do students and teachers have when they enter school? What rights do school authorities have? The judicial system has frequently been called on to resolve these conflicting viewpoints. The following brief summaries highlight the critical cases that have defined the boundaries of civil rights and liberties in American schools. You may not agree with all the decisions, and the current, more conservative Supreme Court may modify some of these rulings. But, for now, they are the law of the land.

Teachers' Rights
Freedom of Association

Shelton v. Tucker, 364 U.S. 479 (1960)

A statute required all teachers in public schools to list all of the organizations they had belonged to or had contributed to during the preceding five years. The Court held that, under the First Amendment, teachers could *not* be required, as a condition of employment, to comply. The state has a right to request information relevant only to teachers' fitness and competence.

Keyishian v. Board of Regents, 385 U.S. 589 (1967)

A state law required all teachers to sign a *loyalty* oath, to declare openly whether they were members of the Communist Party or any other "subversive" group. Teachers who did not sign were fired from their positions as teachers. The Court struck down the New York loyalty laws and declared that political association alone could not constitute an adequate ground for denying employment.

Freedom of Speech

Pickering v. Board of Education, 391 U.S. 563 (1968)

A teacher's letter to the newspaper, a letter that criticized the school board, contained some false statements made because of incomplete research. The teacher was fired. The Court determined that the teacher's letter neither seriously damaged the disciplined operation of the school, disclosed confidential information, nor contained any misstatements that were made knowingly or recklessly. Under the First Amendment, a teacher has the same rights as all other citizens to comment on issues of legitimate public concern, such as a school board's decisions in allocating funds. (See situation 6.)

Separation of Church and State

Engel v. Vitale, 370 U.S. 421 (1962)

A local school board instructed that a prayer composed by the New York Board of Regents be recited aloud every day by each class. The prayer was nondenominational and voluntary. Students who did not want to recite the prayer were permitted to remain silent or leave the classroom while the prayer was said. The Supreme Court held that the New York statute authorizing the prayer in school violated the First Amendment, particularly the **establishment clause,** and that official, organized prayer in school is not permitted. (See situation 13.)

Wallace v. Jaffree, 472 U.S. 38 (1985)

Alabama enacted a law that authorized a 1-minute period of silence in all public schools for meditation or voluntary prayer. The Supreme Court held that the Alabama law violated the establishment clause. To determine whether the Alabama law was constitutional, the Court applied the three-part test established in 1971 in *Lemon v. Kurtzman,* 403 U.S. 602 (1971): did the policy (1) have a secular purpose, (2) have a primarily secular effect, and (3) avoid excessive government entanglement with religion? In *Wallace,* the statute was found to have a religious rather than a secular purpose and was thus ruled unconstitutional, even though prayer was not required during the moment of silence.

McCollum v. Board of Education, 333 U.S. 203 (1948); Board of Education of the Westside Community Schools v. Mergens, 496 U.S. 226 (1990)

An Illinois school district allowed privately employed religious teachers to hold weekly religious classes on public premises. The students who chose not to attend these classes in religious instruction pursued their secular studies in other classrooms in the building. In this 1948 case, the Court ruled that a program allowing religious instruction inside public schools during the school day was unconstitutional, because it violated the establishment clause. However, in 1990, the Court modified this somewhat by allowing the use of school facilities by student organizations after school hours if other student clubs had similar access. The issue of the use of school facilities during school hours has not been resolved.

Stone v. Graham, 449 U.S. 39 (1980)

A Kentucky statute required the posting of a copy of the Ten Commandments, purchased with private contributions, on the wall of each public classroom in the state. On the bottom of each of these posters, there was a statement in fine print explaining that the Ten Commandments are secular and are fundamental to the legal code of Western civilization and the common law of the United States. Despite the fact that the copies of the Ten Commandments were purchased with private funds and had a notation describing them as secular, the statute requiring that they be posted in every public school classroom was declared unconstitutional. Under the three-part *Lemon* test, the Court concluded that the statute requiring posting of the Ten Commandments failed under part 1 of the test in that it lacked a secular purpose. Merely stating that the Ten Commandments are secular does not make them so.

Students' Rights
Freedom of Speech (Symbolic)

Tinker v. Des Moines Independent Community School District, 393 U.S. 503 (1969)

Unless there is substantial disruption in the school caused by student protest, the school board cannot deprive the students of their First Amendment right to freedom of speech. Students do not shed their constitutional rights at the school door. (See situation 12.)

West Virginia State Board of Education v. Barnette, 319 U.S. 624 (1943)

A compulsory flag-salute statute in the public school regulations required all students and teachers to salute the U.S. flag every day. Two Jehovah's Witness students refused to salute the flag, because doing so would be contrary to their religious beliefs, and they were not permitted to attend the public schools. The courts determined that students cannot be compelled to pledge allegiance to the flag in public schools, a right protected by the First Amendment.

Freedom of Speech (Verbal)

Bethel School District v. Fraser, 478 U.S. (1986)

The Supreme Court, balancing the student's freedom to advocate controversial ideas with the school's interests in setting the boundaries of socially appropriate behavior, found that the First Amendment does not prevent school authorities from disciplining students for speech that is lewd and offensive. (See situation 12.)

Freedom of the Press

Hazelwood School District v. Kuhlmeir, 108 S.Ct. 562 (1988)

Two articles about divorce and teenage pregnancy that were written in the student paper were deleted by the principal.

The Supreme Court held that, since the student paper was school-sponsored and school-funded and was part of the school's journalism class, the school principal had the right to control its content. (See situation 15.) On the other hand, the courts have ruled that school authorities may not censor student newspapers produced at the students' own expense and those produced off school property, papers not part of any school's curriculum.

Freedom of Access to the Printed Word

Board of Education, Island Trees Union Free School District No. 26 v. Pico, 457 U.S. 853 (1982)

A school board decided to remove nine books from the school library because the board members felt the books were objectionable and improper for students. The court ruled that school boards may not suppress ideas by removing books from a school library based on their feelings that the material contains bad or unpopular viewpoints.

Right to Due Process

Goss v. Lopez, 419 U.S. 565 (1975)

Several high school students were disciplined by being suspended from school for ten days. The Supreme Court held that before a principal can suspend a student, he or she must present the student with the charges and provide the student with a hearing or an opportunity to present a defense against the charges. The procedures mandated as a result of this decision can be compared to the "Miranda rights" mandated in criminal cases. The *Goss* decision set forth the due process requirements for students suspended for up to ten days. Schools may be required to establish even greater due process procedures than those mandated in *Goss* before suspending students for more than ten days. (See situation 11.)

Ingraham v. Wright, 430 U.S. 651 (1977)

Florida statute allowed corporal punishment. Two students were punished by being hit with a flat wooden paddle and later sued the schools. The Supreme Court held that corporal punishment, such as the paddling, is not cruel and unusual punishment and does not necessarily deprive the student of his or her rights. (See the description following situation 11.)

Note: The section on legal landmarks was originally written by Nancy Gorenberg.

Teaching and Ethics

Sam, the new student, seems so awkward in school, and he is often late. You have asked him more than once why he can't get to class on time, but he is barely audible as he mumbles, "I dunno." What's more, his behavior is strange. He seems to have an aversion to chairs, and, whenever possible, he prefers to stand in the back of the room alone. His clothes are not the neatest or cleanest, which is unusual in your class, where most of the children come from middle-class homes and dress fairly well. You have never seen Sam laugh or even smile. Every day, even on the hot ones, he wears a long-sleeve shirt. What is that all about? What a puzzle.

Then, one day, Sam arrives in class with some bruises on his face, and you begin to suspect that there is more to this story. You ask Sam, who shrugs it off and says that he fell and bruised his face. But you are not so sure. You begin to put the puzzle pieces together: quiet . . . standing rather than sitting . . . wearing long-sleeve shirts all the time . . . late . . . no smiles . . . no real friends . . . and now bruises. You arrive at a frightening thought: could Sam be an abused child? How horrible! Now, what do you do?

In this case, you are confronting both an ethical dilemma and a legal challenge. Maybe you should speak to Sam's parents, just to make certain. Or should you press Sam for more information? Checking with other teachers makes sense, to see how they would handle the problem. Or perhaps it is time to go to the administration and let them find out what is going on.

Wait a second. What if you are wrong? Sam says he fell down and bruised himself. Maybe that is all it is. You should not go around accusing people without real evidence. Are you responsible for Sam's family situation? Is that a private concern rather than your business? Maybe the prudent course of action would be to monitor the situation for now and keep your suspicions to yourself. What would you do?

The ethical issue is pressing. If Sam is being injured, if his safety is in jeopardy, then waiting could be costly. Many would find that the most ethical course to follow would be to share your concerns with an appropriate person in your school, perhaps a school psychologist, counselor, or administrator. The potential for injury is simply too great to remain silent. Sharing your concern is not the same as making an accusation of child abuse, which may be false. You have every right to be suspicious, but you do not have the right to make unsupported accusations. By bringing the situation to the school's attention, you start the wheels in motion to uncover facts.

It is not possible for teachers to always know when child abuse has occurred. In fact, many teachers avoid difficult ethical issues. The American Humane Institute reports that only 13 percent of all child abuse reports come from educators, yet it is the ethical responsibility of teachers to report the abusive treatment of children. Fortunately, as far as suspicion of child abuse is concerned, this ethical responsibility is reinforced by the law. Every state requires that teachers report "suspected" cases of abuse, and failure to report such cases can result in the loss of a teacher's license. Most laws also protect teachers from any legal liability for reporting such cases.

As a teacher, you may well encounter child abuse. From the late 1970s to the early 1990s, reports of child maltreatment grew from 416,033 to 1,700,000 a year[23] and most experts believe that at least 2 million more cases annually are not reported. Because teachers are often the only adults aside from family members who regularly see the children, they may be society's best opportunity to recognize and prevent child abuse. However, recognizing such abuse is not always easy, and stepping in to prevent it may be difficult for many teachers.

Child abuse and neglect include a range of behaviors and effects, such as the following:

- Physical abuse, evidenced by cuts, welts, burns, and bruises
- Sexual molestation and exploitation
- Neglect: medical, educational, or physical
- Emotional abuse

It is not possible for teachers who identify one or more of these problems to know for sure that child abuse and/or neglect is the cause, but these signs suggest that something serious and harmful may be happening. It may be helpful to remember that child abuse and neglect often originate with adults who were themselves abused as children. Parents who hold unrealistic expectations for their children or who are under a great deal of financial or psychological stress are also more likely to become abusers. It is important to remember that abuse and neglect rarely occur as a result of intentional actions. Rather, they usually represent moments of misplaced outrage or a lack of resources or knowledge about how to care for children.

Child abuse affects not only this generation but the next as well. As abused children grow to adulthood, they are more likely to perpetuate crime and violence. Adults who were abused as children constitute 90 percent of all violent criminals, 97 percent of hard-core juvenile offenders, 65 percent of runaways, half of female drug abusers, and 80 percent of prostitutes.[24] Preventing child abuse during the school years pays dividends for both this and the next generation.

In *Cry Out!* P. E. Quinn recounts the horror of his abused childhood. His story stands as a plea to teachers to become involved:

> As an adult survivor of six years of severe child abuse—both physical and emotional—I often wonder why the church did nothing to help me, my brothers, and my parents. Was it that they could not see the bruises, the cuts, scratches and abrasions covering my body? Could they not see the desperation out of which my parents lived? Or the need? Surely as I attended church school classes someone must have noticed the pain and terror in my eyes, the hopelessness with which I moved, my withdrawal into isolation, or, at least, the swelling in my hands and feet. Surely some must have noticed me.[25]

While we hope that doing what is legal and doing what is ethical will always be the same, this is not always the case. Before there was a Supreme Court, a Constitution, or a Bill of Rights, there were great ethical teachers whose lessons did not always conform with local laws and sometimes even violated those laws. Moses, Socrates, Confucius, Jesus, Buddha, and Mohammed were all great teachers who sometimes ran afoul of the law. The ethical content of their lessons spoke to higher principles than did the laws of their time.

Some citizens believe that the most important issue that will face U.S. schools in the near future will be the ethical ones. They believe that, beyond adhering to the law, teachers will need to teach more enduring and pervasive moral lessons. Surveys in the 1990s found that 95 percent of Americans want schools to teach basic values, such as honesty and respect, and that six out of ten students support teaching values in school (with students of color and females being the strongest supporters of values instruction). But values can also include religious beliefs and ideas that are not

CHILD ABUSE: WARNING SIGNS

Children who suffer physical abuse may

- Exhibit signs of frequent injury—burns, black eyes, and other bruises
- Refuse to change into gym clothes; wear long-sleeves even in very warm weather
- Not want to sit down
- Show unusually aggressive or unusually withdrawn behavior
- Not show emotion—no joy, pain, or anger
- Be frequently absent or tardy for no good reason
- Be unusually eager to please
- Complain about pain, beating, or other abusive treatment
- Show a significant change in school attitude, behavior, or achievement

Children who suffer sexual abuse may

- Complain of pain or itching in the genital area
- Exhibit unusual odors or signs of trauma in the genital area
- Wear bloody, torn, or stained undergarments
- Create stories or drawings of an unusually sexual nature
- Exhibit unusually sophisticated knowledge of sexual behavior
- Have difficulty sitting or walking
- Talk about sexual involvement with an adult
- Try to run away from home
- Be extremely mature or seductive in dress and behavior
- Exhibit symptoms of sexually transmitted diseases
- Become pregnant

Source: Adapted from Texas State Teaching Association for Instruction and Professional Development, *The Abused Child Pamphlet* (Austin, TX: TSTA/NEA, 1984)

universal. That might explain in part why other surveys reveal that only half of the public supports school programs that directly promote specific values.[26] How do we bridge this chasm of teaching values without encouraging a narrow set of beliefs? In the following sections, we will discuss several approaches that schools use to provide an ethical dimension to their curriculum.

Moral Education: Programs That Teach Right from Wrong

During the American colonial experience, schools transmitted a common set of values, an approach called **traditional inculcation.** Back then (and in many places today) it was the Protestant ethic: diligence, hard work, punctuality, neatness, conformity, and respect for authority. These few individuals who received a college education during the eighteenth and nineteenth centuries received, above all, an experience in character development. The most important course in the college curriculum was moral philosophy, required of all students and often taught by the college president. Even those receiving a minimal education got a heavy dose of morality, perhaps illustrated best by McGuffey Readers, replete with tales and poems of moral elevation. The tremendous influx of immigrants in the early part of the twentieth century prompted a resurgence of this traditional approach in order to "meld" these new Americans by teaching core U.S. values.

During the social and political uncertainty of the 1960s and 1970s, a more analytical and individual approach to moral education became popular. This **individual analysis** method emphasized the decision-making process of students and avoided prescribing a fixed set of beliefs or values. Students were encouraged to consider the moral implications of past and present events and to formulate a set of values based on their analyses. The advocates of each of these approaches offer different perspectives on moral education. (See the accompanying balance sheet.)

ETHICS BALANCE SHEET   TWO APPROACHES TO MORAL EDUCATION

Traditional

Societies not only have the right to inculcate values, but it is their historical obligation to teach these values to younger generations in order to promote unity, cultural traditions, and national purpose.

Recent problems, such as alienation, teenage pregnancy, and suicide, are the result of schools not teaching traditional values. Most Americans want greater discipline, clear values, and character development to be taught and practiced in school.

Without effective moral development, human beings are likely to engage in selfish, self-serving activities. The sacrifice and community spirit necessary for the general good may be lost without the inculcation of a moral code.

We can all agree on a common code of values for our society. American values include tolerance, patriotism, justice, moderation, and parental respect, to name but a few. These represent commonly accepted virtues that are needed for any culture to survive and thrive.

Children are unable to make wise moral decisions and need adult guidance and supervision.

Analytical

We are at a new and more complex stage of human development, and the historical practices of the past are no longer appropriate for the complexities and individual development needed in contemporary society.

Inculcating traditional values is ineffective in eliminating these problems. Adolescent problems are not reduced by promoting values that are not critically understood and receive at best only a superficial commitment from students.

Individuals need to develop a code of behavior that they themselves form, with thought and personal commitment. Selfishness is not a natural state, and students who critically develop values will undoubtedly exhibit a moral code that reflects sensitivity to others.

Our pluralistic society makes the inculcation of a single set of values impossible. For example, we can now extend "life" for brain-dead patients through artificial means. Does "honor your parents" mean this is the wisest course? Other issues, such as abortion, also defy national consensus. We are beyond the era of a single value system applicable to all.

Children can be taught to make their own moral decisions and to abide by them.

Source: Adapted from "The School's Role in Developing Character," *Educational Leadership* 43, no. 4 (December 1985–January 1986).

Today, many school districts, in order to avoid controversy, simply avoid teaching about values or ethics. For schools that choose to confront this challenge, several paths are available. Four of the most widely known are (1) values clarification, (2) character education, (3) moral stages of development, and (4) comprehensive values education.

Values Clarification

The controversial, yet widely used, series of classroom activities called **values clarification** is designed to help students develop and eventually act on their values. For example, students might be asked to describe their preferences (select the ten things you most enjoy doing), analyze behavior (when did you last do each of these activities?), analyze reasons (what appeals to you about each of these activities?), and develop action plans (how can you schedule more time to do what you enjoy?). These strategies, developed by Louis Raths, Merrill Harmin, and Sidney Simon *(Values and Teaching),* are attractive to teachers, because they are easy to use, touch on issues usually omitted from the curriculum, and are engaging to students. Students begin to bring their private values into a public light, where they can be analyzed and evaluated. The developers believe that, when values are verbalized in public, and others respond to them, students are able to consider them more carefully, to select the finest ones, and eventually to act on them. In the free marketplace, the best ideas will emerge.

Critics charge that values clarification is itself valueless. In this approach, all values are treated equally, and there is no guarantee that good and constructive values will be promoted or that negative ones will be condemned. If, for example, a student decides that anti-Semitism or fascism is a preferred value, values clarification might do little to contradict this view. This "value neutral" stance is troubling to some and has led to the barring of values clarification in several school districts.

Character Education

Character education programs—currently used in some form by an estimated 20 percent of all public school districts[27]—assume that there are core attributes of a moral individual that children should be directly taught in school. While still a form of moral inculcation, character education programs are less didactic and more analytic than are previous approaches.[28] What values are promoted? Core values include trustworthiness, respect, responsibility, fairness, caring, and good citizenship, which are encouraged through the school culture, conduct codes, curriculum, and community service.[29] Younger students may be asked to find examples of these qualities in literature and history, while older students may consider these values through ethical reasoning exercises. School districts using character education report a drop in discipline problems and enhanced student responsibility. Some states (e.g., Maryland), as well as numerous school districts, have character education programs in place.

Not everyone is enamored with character education. Opponents view this approach as superficial, artificially forcing a diverse student population into a simplistic and narrow set of unexamined values that does not really alter behaviors. They point out that, when adults promote one set of values but do not always live up to it, it is the dissonance that becomes the lesson. The real challenge, according to these critics, is changing the behavior of those who influence children.[30]

Other critics believe that character education is little more than the old-fashioned "fix-the-kids" approach, a return to the past conservative, religious agenda that simply rewards students who do what adults desire. Who selects the values or the way the values are taught are issues at the heart of the concerns expressed by these critics. Although character education attempts to walk a middle ground, not all Americans are convinced that the values or the approach is appropriate.[31]

Moral Stages of Development

Based on the work of Jean Piaget, the psychologist who identified stages of intellectual development (see "The Education Hall of Fame" in Chapter 9), a schema proposed by **Lawrence Kohlberg** identifies **moral stages of development.** The earliest stages focus on simple rewards and punishments. Young children are taught "right" and "wrong" by learning to avoid physical punishment and to strive for rewards. Most adults function at a middle, or conventional, stage, in which they obey society's laws, even laws that may be unjust. At the highest level, individuals act on principles, such as civil rights or pacifism, that may violate conventional laws. Kohlberg believes that teachers can facilitate student growth to higher stages of morality.

Detractors express concern that traditional (what Kohlberg calls "conventional") values are attacked. Kohlberg pushes toward higher levels of moral development (like the ideals of Moses, Jesus, Buddha, and Mohammed, discussed earlier), principled beliefs that may run counter to current law. Other critics point out that Kohlberg's theory was developed on an all-male population and that females may go through different stages of moral reasoning. Harvard professor **Carol Gilligan,** for example, found that women and men react differently when responding to moral

IN THE NEWS . . . SCHOOLS CLOSED FOR HUNTING SEASON

The Fund for Animals, Inc. sent a letter to the West Virginia Board of Education protesting its policy that allows school systems to close on the first day of hunting season. *There is nothing educational or wholesome about turning the three R's into reading, 'riting, and reloading,* said animal rights activist Heidi P.

Source: *The American School Board Journal,* February 1998.

dilemmas. While males seem to strongly value those who follow the rules and laws, females value relationships and caring. No wonder that Kohlberg rated males as reaching a higher level of moral development than females, since the scales he developed were male-oriented. Finally, Kohlberg's stages are intellectually based. Some critics believe that behavior, not intellect, is the real measure of one's morality.

Comprehensive Values Education

Now that we have reviewed three approaches to teaching about values and ethics, it is worth noting that some teachers "mix and match," creating what might be considered a hybrid or fourth approach. Howard Kirschenbaum suggests that both values clarification and traditional inculcation have important lessons for children. His model, called **comprehensive values education** insists that traditional values, such as honesty, caring, and responsibility, should be taught and demonstrated directly. However, since other values are less straightforward, such as favoring or rejecting the death penalty, students should be taught the analytical skills that will help them make wise decisions. There is an appropriate place in the school curriculum for each approach, Kirschenbaum insists, and many teachers instinctively apply multiple approaches.[32] Figure 11.1 underscores the pressing need for effective ethical education.

Classrooms That Explore Ethical Issues

For many educators and parents, concerns about values are daily events, too important to be left solely to a specific program or curriculum. How should teachers handle matters of ethics that appear on a daily basis? Consider that as a teacher, you find

> A student complains that her Vietnamese culture is being demeaned by the Christian and Western classroom activities.

> A student is upset because his e-mail has been opened and read by classmates.

> Your best student, the one you just recommended for a special award, is looking at a crib sheet during an examination.

> A poor, awkward youngster is the object of sarcastic remarks from several students in your class.

Students' ethics at school.
A recent survey of 10,760 high school students and 10,069 middle school students found that many admit to lying to their teacher and cheating on an exam at least once in the past twelve months. The survey has a margin of error of three percentage points.

Source: *Education Week* November 4, 1998

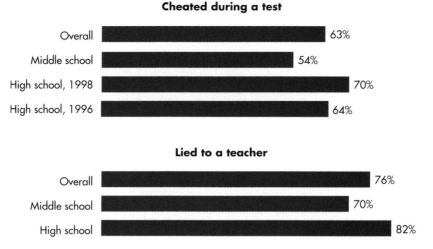

How are teachers to navigate this tricky moral minefield? Educators have offered several recommendations, summarized below:

The Setting

Climate. Classroom atmospheres differ enormously. It is helpful to create an environment that respects and encourages diverse points of view and that promotes the sharing of diverse opinions, by both the teachers and the students.

School and class rules. Requiring that students unquestioningly follow rules does not lead to democratic values. School and class rules need to be explained to students, and the reasons behind them understood. Safety and courtesy, for example, are common reasons for creating such rules. Many teachers go further and ask students to participate in formulating the rules they will live by.

Parents and community. Citizens and community leaders should participate with the school in developing mission statements and ethical codes of responsibility. One way to encourage such cooperation is to plan joint efforts that tie the family and civic organizations into school-sponsored programs. The key is to reinforce ethical lessons in the school, the home, and the community.

The Teacher

Model. Teachers need to demonstrate the ethical lessons they teach. Teacher behavior should reflect such values as tolerance, compassion, forgiveness, and open-mindedness. (Values are often *caught not taught*.)

Interpersonal skills. Teachers need effective communication skills to encourage students to share their concerns. A critical component of interpersonal skills is empathy—the ability to see problems from more than one point of view, including through the eyes of students.

Commitment. It takes determination and courage on the part of the teacher to confront ethical dilemmas, rather than to take the sometimes easier path of indifference or even inattention.

NATIONAL EDUCATION ASSOCIATION CODE OF ETHICS

Preamble

The educator, believing in the worth and dignity of each human being, recognizes the supreme importance of the pursuit of truth, devotion to excellence, and the nurturing of democratic principles. Essential to these goals is the protection of freedom to learn and to teach and the guarantee of equal educational opportunity for all. The educator accepts the responsibility to adhere to the highest ethical standards.

The educator recognizes the magnitude of the responsibility inherent in the teaching process. The desire for the respect and confidence of one's colleagues, of students, of parents, and of the members of the community provides the incentive to attain and maintain the highest possible degree of ethical conduct. The Code of Ethics of the Education Profession indicates the aspiration of all educators and provides standards by which to judge conduct. The remedies specified by the NEA and/or its affiliates for the violation of any provision of this Code shall be exclusive and no such provision shall be enforceable in any form other than one specifically designated by the NEA or its affiliates.

Principle I—Commitment to the Student

The educator strives to help each student realize his or her potential as a worthy and effective member of society. The educator therefore works to stimulate the spirit of inquiry, the acquisition of knowledge and understanding, and the thoughtful formulation of worthy goals.

In fulfillment of the obligation to the student, the educator—

1. Shall not unreasonably restrain the student from independent action in the pursuit of learning.
2. Shall not unreasonably deny the student access to varying points of view.
3. Shall not deliberately suppress or distort subject matter relevant to the student's progress.
4. Shall make reasonable effort to protect the student from conditions harmful to learning or to health and safety.
5. Shall not intentionally expose the student to embarrassment or disparagement.
6. Shall not on the basis of race, color, creed, sex, national origin, marital status, political or religious beliefs, family, social or cultural background, or sexual orientation, unfairly:
   a. Exclude any student from participation in any program;
   b. Deny benefits to any student;
   c. Grant any advantage to any student.
7. Shall not use professional relationships with students for private advantage.
8. Shall not disclose information about students obtained in the course of professional service, unless disclosure serves a compelling professional purpose or is required by law.

Principle II—Commitment to the Profession

The education profession is vested by the public with a trust and responsibility requiring the highest ideals of professional service.

In the belief that the quality of the services of the education profession directly influences the nation and its citizens, the educator shall exert every effort to raise professional standards, to promote a climate that encourages the exercise of professional judgment, to achieve conditions which attract persons worthy of the trust to careers in education, and to assist in preventing the practice of the profession by unqualified persons.

In fulfillment of the obligation to the profession the educator—

1. Shall not in an application for a professional position deliberately make a false statement or fail to disclose a material fact related to competency and qualifications.
2. Shall not misrepresent his/her professional qualifications.
3. Shall not assist entry into the profession of a person known to be unqualified in respect to character, education, or other relevant attribute.
4. Shall not knowingly make a false statement concerning the qualifications of a candidate for a professional position.
5. Shall not assist a noneducator in the unauthorized practice of teaching.
6. Shall not disclose information about colleagues obtained in the course of professional service unless disclosure serves a compelling professional purpose or is required by law.
7. Shall not knowingly make false or malicious statements about a colleague.
8. Shall not accept any gratuity, gift, or favor that might impair or appear to influence professional decisions or actions.

AMERICAN FEDERATION OF TEACHERS BILL OF RIGHTS

The teacher is entitled to a life of dignity equal to the high standard of service that is justly demanded of that profession. Therefore, we hold these truths to be self-evident:

I. Teachers have the right to think freely and to express themselves openly and without fear. This includes the right to hold views contrary to the majority.

II. They shall be entitled to the free exercise of their religion. No restraint shall be put upon them in the manner, time or place of their worship.

III. They shall have the right to take part in social, civil, and political affairs. They shall have the right, outside the classroom, to participate in political campaigns and to hold office. They may assemble peaceably and may petition any government agency, including their employers, for a redress of grievances. They shall have the same freedom in all things as other citizens.

IV. The right of teachers to live in places of their own choosing, to be free of restraints in their mode of living and the use of their leisure time shall not be abridged.

V. Teaching is a profession, the right to practice which is not subject to the surrender of other human rights. No one shall be deprived of professional status, or the right to practice it, or the practice thereof in any particular position, without due process of law.

VI. The right of teachers to be secure in their jobs, free from political influence or public clamor, shall be established by law. The right to teach after qualification in the manner prescribed by law is a property right, based upon the inalienable rights to life, liberty, and the pursuit of happiness.

VII. In all cases affecting the teacher's employment or professional status a full hearing by an impartial tribunal shall be afforded with the right to full judicial review. No teacher shall be deprived of employment or professional status but for specific causes established by the law having a clear relation to the competence or qualification to teach, proved by the weight of the evidence. In all such cases the teacher shall enjoy the right to a speedy and public trial, to be informed of the nature and cause of the accusation, to be confronted with the accusing witnesses, to subpoena witnesses and papers, and to the assistance of counsel. No teacher shall be called upon to answer any charge affecting his employment or professional status but upon probable cause, supported by oath or affirmation.

VIII. It shall be the duty of the employer to provide culturally adequate salaries, security in illness and adequate retirement income. The teacher has the right to such a salary as will: a) Afford a family standard of living comparable to that enjoyed by other professional people in the community; b) To make possible freely chosen professional study; c) Afford the opportunity for leisure and recreation common to our heritage.

IX. Teachers shall not be required under penalty of reduction of salary to pursue studies beyond those required to obtain professional status. After serving a reasonable probationary period a teacher shall be entitled to permanent tenure terminable only for just cause. They shall be free as in other professions in the use of their own time. They shall not be required to perform extracurricular work against their will or without added compensation.

X. To equip people for modern life requires the most advanced educational methods. Therefore, the teacher is entitled to good classrooms, adequate teaching materials, teachable class size and administrative protection and assistance in maintaining discipline.

XI. These rights are based upon the proposition that the culture of a people can rise only as its teachers improve. A teaching force accorded the highest possible professional dignity is the surest guarantee that blessings of liberty will be preserved. Therefore, the possession of these rights imposes the challenge to be worthy of their enjoyment.

XII. Since teachers must be free in order to teach freedom, the right to be members of organizations of their own choosing must be guaranteed. In all matters pertaining to their salaries and working conditions they shall be entitled to bargain collectively through representatives of their own choosing. They are entitled to have the schools administered by superintendents, boards or committees which function in a democratic manner.

Reflection skills. To unravel moral questions, teachers must know how to analyze a dilemma objectively and how to evaluate its essential components. Teachers with effective and deliberate reasoning skills are best suited for this challenge.

Personal opinions. Teachers should not promote or indoctrinate students with their personal points of view, nor should they shy away from showing students that they have strong beliefs. The key is to create a classroom in which individuals can freely agree or disagree, as they see fit.[33]

While laws direct us to what we can and cannot do, moral guidelines direct us in what we should and should not do. Professional associations have also suggested ethical guidelines for educators. (See the NEA and AFT codes of ethics.) Moral issues will continue to be a major concern in the years ahead, in many ways a measure of the quality of our culture. Indeed, even as our society grows in wealth and makes great scientific strides and technological breakthroughs, the final measure of our worth may not be our materialistic accomplishments but, rather, the way we treat each other.

Summary

1. As a teacher, it is important to be aware of your own legal rights and responsibilities, as well as those of your students.

2. When applying for a teaching position in your local county, you should be aware of your rights. Under Title IX of the Education Amendments and Title VII of the Civil Rights Act, you do not have to answer questions an interviewer may ask that are unrelated to the job requirements, and you are protected from words and behaviors that can be considered sexual harassment.

3. The general standard, resulting from court decisions, is that, if a teacher's behavior or personal life does not disrupt or interfere with teaching effectiveness, he or she cannot be suspended or fired because of it.

4. Generally, the courts hold that the teacher's right to academic freedom is not absolute, and each case depends on its own unique facts.

5. When determining whether a teacher has been negligent in a situation, the courts judge whether a reasonable person with similar training would act in the same way and whether the teacher could have foreseen the possibility of injury. A teacher may be liable for misfeasance, nonfeasance, or malfeasance.

6. As stated by the Supreme Court in *Pickering v. Board of Education,* teachers are protected under the First Amendment to exercise freedom of speech and to publicly express themselves, unless their statements are malicious, are intentionally inaccurate, disclose confidential material, or hamper teaching performance.

7. Teachers must be sure to comply with Public Law 94-553 when distributing copies of other people's works in the classroom, observing the three criteria of brevity, spontaneity, and cumulative effect.

8. Under the Buckley amendment (the Family Rights and Privacy Act), parents and guardians have the right to see their child's educational records. On reaching 18 years of age, the student is allowed to see the record, and he or she becomes responsible for providing permission for others to see it.

9. Under Title IX, students may not be discriminated against based on gender for awards, scholarships, or financial aid.

10. Students have constitutionally protected rights to due process before they can be disciplined or suspended from school. Although corporal punishment is rarely used, courts have upheld the school's authority to administer it as long as it is reasonable and not excessive.

11. In *Tinker v. Des Moines Independent Community School District,* students were successful in protecting their First Amendment right to freedom of speech. As long as students do not disrupt the operation of the school or deny other students the opportunity to learn, they have the right to freedom of speech within the schools.

12. Schools must be neutral with regard to religion. Thus, school prayer is not permitted under the doctrine of separation of church and state.

13. Students, like teachers, have the right to freedom of the press. However, student publications can be censored if they are an integral part of the school curriculum, such as part of a course, or if they are obscene, psychologically damaging, or disruptive.

14. Teachers today are potential targets of litigation. Sexual harassment and child abuse charges can short-circuit the careers of even innocent teachers. Taking appropriate precautions to avoid even the appearance of impropriety is advised.

15. Nearly 2 million cases of child abuse are reported each year, with perhaps as many or more cases going unreported. Teachers can be an important force for prevention if they learn to identify the warning signs and report their suspicions.

16. The teaching of ethics and values continues to receive a great deal of attention and concern. Today's schools use both traditional and more innovative approaches, including values clarification, character education, stages of moral development, and a comprehensive combination of all three. Whether part of a formal curriculum or not, what teachers do and say continually teaches students important lessons in morals and ethics. This chapter concluded with suggestions for teachers concerning the kinds of teacher skills and classroom climates that promote ethical behaviors in students.

Key Terms and People

www.mhhe.com/sadker

academic freedom
Buckley Amendment
character education
child abuse
comprehensive values
    education
corporal punishment
due process
educational malpractice
establishment clause

fair use
Carol Gilligan
in loco parentis
individual analysis
Lawrence Kohlberg
malfeasance
misfeasance
moral stages of
    development
nonfeasance

sexual harassment
Tinker case
Title IX of the Education
    Amendments (1972)
Title VII of the Civil Rights
    Act (1964)
traditional inculcation
values clarification

Discussion Questions and Activities

1. If you were to suggest a law to improve education, what would that law be? Would you make it federal, state, or local? Why?

2. How have the rights of students and teachers been altered by legal decisions involving schools?

3. What are some supporting and opposing arguments for the following? "Teaching is not a job; it is a special responsibility. Working with impressionable minds, teachers must be held accountable for all their behaviors that influence children, both in the classroom and outside the classroom."

4. Distinguish among malfeasance, misfeasance, and nonfeasance. Give an example of each.

5. What are the legal factors you should keep in mind if you are about to discipline a student?

6. Define and evaluate the concept of "educational malpractice."

7. What kinds of questions are employers prohibited from asking during an interview?

8. Outline the limits of academic freedom.

9. "The *Tinker* decision sent a strong message that students do not abandon their constitutional rights at the schoolhouse door." Do you agree or disagree with this statement? Support your position with specific examples.

10. The role of religion and prayer in schools has always been controversial, and teachers are advised to neither *encourage* nor *discourage* religious observances. As a teacher, what religious celebrations or practices might you encounter in your class? How would you respond to these issues while maintaining your neutrality?

11. In each of the following cases, indicate if there are grounds for dismissing a teacher:

    - Being identified as a homosexual
    - Publicly criticizing the school system
    - Hitting a student
    - Photocopying material without permission
    - Striking
    - Carrying the HIV virus
    - Sexually harassing a student

12. Construct an argument to support the principle that students and their property should not be searched without the students' consent.

13. "The Buckley amendment increased the access to, but decreased the value of, student records." Explain.

14. What are some of the physical indications of child abuse? What is the teacher's role in preventing such abuse and neglect?

15. "Moral education is not a new focus of the curriculum but a newly identified need." Why? What are the arguments for and against bringing moral issues into the classroom?

16. Which of the paths to moral education (values clarification, moral development, character education, or comprehensive values education) appeals to you most? Why?

17. Describe some steps you might explore to promote ethical student behavior in your classroom.

18. Review with an ethical eye the legal situations described in this chapter. How do ethical considerations reinforce (or weaken) the legal arguments?

Philosophy of Education

With Daniel Spiro, Lynette Long, and Elizabeth Ihle

Focus Questions

- How did Socrates, Plato, and Aristotle contribute to Western philosophy?
- How do metaphysics, epistemology, ethics, political philosophy, aesthetics, and logic affect education?
- What are the fundamental principles of essentialism, perennialism, progressivism, existentialism, and behaviorism?
- Who are the key educators associated with each philosophy?
- How are these five philosophies reflected in school practices?
- How would you describe your own philosophy of education?

Chapter Preview

Philosophy is the love of wisdom. For thousands of years, philosophers have been wrestling with many of the same questions: What is most real—the physical world or the realm of mind and spirit? What is the basis of human knowledge? What is the nature of the just society? These and other philosophical questions influence education. Educators must take stances on such questions before they can determine what and how students should be taught.

Since educators do not agree on the answers to these questions, different philosophies of education have emerged. Although there are similarities, there are also profound differences in the way leading educators define the purpose of education, the role of the teacher, the nature of the curriculum and assessment, and the method of instruction.

This chapter will introduce the foundation of Western educational philosophy with three ancient Greeks: Socrates, Plato, and Aristotle. It will then explore philosophical issues important to teachers. In addition, the chapter will discuss five major educational philosophies and will describe examples of each in practice. We encourage your attempt to resolve the ultimate questions of philosophy and challenge you to create a consistent position on education and schools.

What Is Your Philosophy of Education?

Each of us has a philosophy of education, a set of fundamental beliefs regarding how we think schools should be run. To discover your philosophy of education, decide whether you agree or disagree with each of the following statements about the nature of education. Use the following scale to express your response:

5 Agree strongly

4 Agree

3 Neutral

2 Disagree

1 Disagree strongly

———— 1. The school curriculum should be subject-centered. In particular, student learning should be centered around basic subjects, such as reading, writing, history, math, and science.

———— 2. The school curriculum should focus on the great thinkers of the past.

———— 3. Many students learn best by engaging in real-world activities, rather than by reading.

———— 4. Students should be permitted to determine their own curriculum.

———— 5. Material is taught effectively when it is broken down into small parts.

———— 6. A school curriculum should be shaped by a body of information that all students should know.

———— 7. Schools, above all, should develop students' abilities to think deeply, analytically, and creatively; this is more important than developing their social skills or providing them with a useful body of knowledge about our ever changing world.

———— 8. Schools should prepare students for analyzing and solving the types of problems they will face outside the classroom.

———— 9. Reality is determined by each individual's perceptions. There is no objective and universal reality.

———— 10. People are shaped much more by their environment than by their genetic disposition or the exercise of their free will.

———— 11. Students should not be promoted from one grade to the next until they have read and mastered certain key material.

———— 12. An effective education is not aimed at the immediate needs of the students or society.

———— 13. The curriculum should be built around the personal experiences and needs of the students.

_____ 14. Students who do not want to study much should not be required to do so.

_____ 15. Computer software that emphasizes repeated practice is an effective method of teaching information.

_____ 16. Academic rigor is an essential component of education.

_____ 17. All students, regardless of ability, should study more or less the same curriculum.

_____ 18. Art classes should focus primarily on individual expression and creativity.

_____ 19. Effective learning is unstructured, personal, and informal.

_____ 20. Students learn best through reinforcement.

_____ 21. Effective schools assign a substantial amount of homework.

_____ 22. Education should focus on the discussion of timeless questions, such as "What is beauty?" and "What is truth?"

_____ 23. Since students learn effectively through social interaction, schools should plan for substantial social interaction in their curricula.

_____ 24. The purpose of school is to help students understand themselves and find the meaning of their existence.

_____ 25. Frequent objective testing is the best way to determine what students know.

_____ 26. For the United States to be economically competitive in the world marketplace, schools must bolster their academic requirements in order to train more competent workers.

_____ 27. Students must be taught to appreciate learning primarily for its own sake, rather than because it will help them in their careers.

_____ 28. Schools must place more emphasis on teaching about diversity and multiculturalism.

_____ 29. Each person has free will to develop as he or she sees fit.

_____ 30. Reward students well for learning, and they will remember and be able to apply what they have learned, even if they were not led to understand why the information was worth knowing.

_____ 31. U.S. schools should attempt to instill traditional American values.

_____ 32. Teacher-guided discovery of profound truths is crucial for effective teaching.

_____ 33. Students should be active participants in the learning process.

_____ 34. There are no external standards of beauty. Beauty is what an individual decides it is.

_____ 35. We can place a lot of faith in our schools' and teachers' ability to determine which student behaviors are acceptable and which are not.

_____ 36. Schools must provide students with a firm grasp of basic facts regarding the books, people, and events that have shaped the nation's heritage.

_____ 37. Philosophy is ultimately as practical a subject to study as is computer technology.

_____ 38. Whether inside or outside the classroom, teachers must stress the relevance of what students are learning.

_____ 39. It is more important for a student to develop a positive self-concept than to learn specific subject matter.

_____ 40. Education is more effective when students are given frequent tests to determine what they have learned.

Now that you have responded to all forty items, write the number of your response to each statement in the following spaces. Add the numbers in each column to determine your attitudes toward key educational philosophies.

A **Essentialism**	B **Perennialism**	C **Progressivism**	D **Existentialism**	E **Behaviorism**
1. _____	2. _____	3. _____	4. _____	5. _____
6. _____	7. _____	8. _____	9. _____	10. _____
11. _____	12. _____	13. _____	14. _____	15. _____
16. _____	17. _____	18. _____	19. _____	20. _____
21. _____	22. _____	23. _____	24. _____	25. _____
26. _____	27. _____	28. _____	29. _____	30. _____
31. _____	32. _____	33. _____	34. _____	35. _____
36. _____	37. _____	38. _____	39. _____	40. _____
Scores				
_____	_____	_____	_____	_____

The scores in columns A through E, respectively, represent how much you agree or disagree with the beliefs of five major educational philosophies: essentialism, perennialism, progressivism, existentialism, and behaviorism. The higher your score, the more you agree with philosophers who represent that viewpoint. The highest possible score in any one area is 40, and the lowest possible score is 8. Scores in the mid- to high 30s indicate strong agreement, and scores below 20 indicate disagreement with the tenets of a particular philosophy. Compare your five scores. What is your highest? What is your lowest?

Now you have examined some of your basic beliefs about education, and you may even lay claim to a philosophical label. But what do these philosophical labels or terms mean? In this chapter, you will learn about all five of these educational philosophies, as well as the beliefs that underlie them. After you finish reading the chapter, you may want to take another look at this quiz to gain a better understanding of what you believe at this point in your education.

What Is Philosophy?

The root for the word **philosophy** is made up of two Greek words: *philo,* meaning "love," and *sophos,* meaning "wisdom." As lovers or seekers of wisdom, students of philosophy grapple with the issues of most fundamental significance to humankind.

Philosophy pervades all aspects of education, and this chapter highlights the philosophical issues that are most relevant to teachers. For example, consider the following philosophical question: Is knowledge best acquired through observing and analyzing nature scientifically, by developing reasoning skills, or by cultivating intuitive and emotional faculties? Depending on how teachers resolve that philosophical issue, they decide which capacities of their students to develop most fully.

The Three Legendary Figures of Classical Philosophy

Any truly great teacher is a practicing philosopher. Three teachers in particular—Socrates, Plato, and Aristotle—represent the apex of the Greek philosophical tradition, which is the birthplace of Western philosophy.

The name of **Socrates** is practically synonymous with wisdom and the philosophical life. Socrates (469–399 B.C.) was a teacher without a school. He walked about Athens, engaging people in provocative dialogues about questions of ultimate significance. Socrates is hailed as an exemplar of human virtue and piety whose goal was to help others find the truths that lie within their own minds. In that regard, he described himself as a "midwife." The **Socratic method** is the term given to Socrates' approach. By repeatedly questioning, disproving, and testing the thoughts of his pupils on such questions as the nature of "love" or "the good," he helped his students reach deeper, clearer ideas. Socrates was confident that he could help his pupils eventually discover invaluable guides to a virtuous life.

Socrates' unique approach to learning was not without danger. Although his method promoted intellectual insights in his students, it also challenged the conventional ideas and traditions of his time. As a result, Socrates offended many powerful people and was eventually charged with "corrupting" the youth of Athens. Even in this, Socrates provided a lesson for today's teachers: challenges to popular convention and tradition may lead to community opposition and sanctions. (Luckily, sanctions today are less severe than those meted out to Socrates, who was executed for his "impiety.")

We know about Socrates and his teachings through the writings of his disciples, one of whom was **Plato** (427–347 B.C.). After Socrates was put to death for alleged impiety, Plato became disillusioned with Athenian democracy and left the city for many years. Later, he returned to Athens and founded **The Academy,** considered by some to be the world's first university.

Plato's writing is renowned not only for its depth but also for its beauty and clarity. His most famous works were dialogues, conversations between two or more people, that present and critique various philosophical viewpoints. Plato's dialogues feature Socrates, questioning and challenging others and presenting his own philosophy.

AN EXAMPLE OF THE SOCRATIC METHOD IN ACTION

TEACHER: Today we will try to understand what we mean by the concepts of right and wrong. What are examples of conduct you consider wrong or immoral?

STUDENT: Lying is wrong.

TEACHER: But what if you were living in Germany around 1940 and you were harboring in your house a certain Mr. Cohen, who was wanted by the Nazis? If asked by a Nazi if you knew the whereabouts of that Mr. Cohen, wouldn't it be acceptable, even obligatory, to lie?

STUDENT: I suppose so.

TEACHER: So could you rephrase what you meant when you said that lying is wrong or immoral?

STUDENT: I think what I meant is that it is usually wrong to lie. But it is true that there are times when lying is acceptable, because the overall effects of the lie are good. Look at how much your "Mr. Cohen" was helped; the lie about where he was may have saved his life.

TEACHER: So you are saying that it is okay to lie, as long as the consequences of the lie are positive. But consider this hypothetical situation: I am a business tycoon who makes millions of dollars selling diamonds to investors. I sell only to very rich people who can afford to lose the money they invest in my diamonds. I tell my customers that my diamonds are worth $10,000 each, but they really are fakes, worth only $2,000 each. Rather than keeping the profits myself, I give all the money to the poor, helping them obtain the food and shelter they need to live. If you look at the obvious consequences of my business—the rich get slightly poorer and the needy are helped out immensely—you may conclude that my business has a generally positive effect on society. And, yet, because the business is based on fraud, I find it immoral. Do you agree?

STUDENT: Yes, I find it immoral. I suppose I was wrong in saying that whenever a lie has generally good results it is morally acceptable. In your diamond example, unlike the Nazi example, the lie was directed at innocent people and the harm done to them was significant. I want to change my earlier statement that a lie is acceptable whenever it has generally good results. What I want to say now is that you should never lie to innocent people if that would cause them significant harm.

As is typical of Socrates' dialogue, this one could go on indefinitely, because there is no simple, "correct" solution to the issues being discussed—the meaning of right and wrong and, more specifically, the contours of when a lie is morally acceptable. By asking questions, the teacher is trying to get the student to clarify and rethink his or her own ideas, to come eventually to a deep and clear understanding of philosophical concepts, such as right and wrong.

Plato held that a realm of eternally existing "ideas" or "forms" underlies the physical world. In Plato's philosophy, the human soul has three parts: intellect (reason), spirit (passion), and appetite (basic animal desires). He believed that these faculties interact to determine human behavior. Plato urged that the intellect, the highest faculty, be trained to control the other two.

Just as Plato was the student of Socrates, **Aristotle** (384–322 B.C.) studied under Plato. Aristotle entered Plato's Academy at age 18 and stayed for twenty years, until Plato died. In 342 B.C., Aristotle went to northern Greece and, for several years, tutored a young boy named Alexander, later known as Alexander the Great. After educating Alexander, Aristotle returned to Athens to set up his own school, the **Lyceum,** adjacent to Plato's Academy.

The depth and breadth of Aristotle's ideas were unsurpassed in ancient Western civilization. In addition to tackling philosophical questions, Aristotle wrote influential works on biology, physics, astronomy, mathematics, psychology, and literary criticism.

Aristotle placed more importance on the physical world than did Plato. Aristotle's teachings can, in fact, be regarded as a synthesis of Plato's belief in the universal, spiritual forms, and a scientist's belief that each animal, vegetable, and mineral we observe is undeniably real.

PLATO'S POLITICAL PHILOSOPHY AND THE "PARABLE OF THE CAVE"

Plato's political philosophy was set forth in his most well-known dialogue, the *Republic.* In that work, Plato showed himself to be one of the pioneers in envisioning the essential relationship between education and government. Plato's ideal, or "utopian," republic was anything but democratic. He envisioned a society with three classes of people: the common people, the warriors, and the rulers (or philosopher-kings). Only the last group, according to Plato, was entitled to political power.

The most famous passage of the *Republic* is known as the "Parable of the Cave." In that timeless passage, Plato compares the realm of human affairs as we know it to an underground cave. That cave is populated by prisoners who are tied down such that they can only see straight ahead of them. A light in the cave creates shadows on the cave wall,

and the prisoners stare intently at the shadows. Those who see the shadows most clearly and can best explain their movements are praised by their fellow prisoners. They, presumably, are the people who, in a nonideal society, rule over business and government. In an ideal society, on the other hand, the philosopher-kings must be educated to escape from the cave and head to the outside world, the world of sunlight. That world is the transcendent realm of "forms," or "ideas." While leaving the cave is painful at first, a life spent contemplating the world of forms is truly pleasant. However, concludes Plato, the philosopher-kings must eventually return to the cave (that is, participate in practical politics) for fifteen years in order to obtain the experience necessary to rule over society with wisdom.

WHY WE REMEMBER SOCRATES, PLATO, AND ARISTOTLE

- *Socrates.* His philosophical lifestyle; the Socratic method, in which students are provocatively questioned so that they can rethink what they believe; his noble death
- *Plato.* Discussions of philosophy through eloquent dialogues; the theory of "forms," or "ideas," that exist in an eternal, transcendent realm; a vision of utopia, where

an elite group of philosopher-kings rules over other members of society
- *Aristotle.* The breadth of his knowledge; the synthesis of Plato's belief in the eternal "forms" and a scientist's belief in the "real" world that we can see, touch, or smell; the theory of the Golden Mean (everything in moderation)

Aristotle is also renowned for his ethical and political theories. He wrote that the highest good for people is a virtuous life, fully governed by the faculty of reason, with which all other faculties are in harmony. Aristotle envisioned a properly functioning society as one that would give each person the role most appropriate to his or her abilities and inclinations. Aristotle promoted the doctrine of the **Golden Mean,** or the notion that virtue lies in a middle ground between two extremes. Courage, for example, is bordered on the one side by cowardice and on the other side by foolhardiness.

Many of the ideas first formulated by the ancient Greeks have long been integrated into Western culture and education. By now, these ideas may seem obvious, whereas they once were startling and profound.

Basic Philosophical Issues and Concepts

Philosophy has many subdivisions that are of particular significance to educators: metaphysics, epistemology, ethics, political philosophy, aesthetics, and logic. Your educational philosophy will be informed by your understanding of key terms, issues, and concepts in philosophy. (See Figure 12.1.)

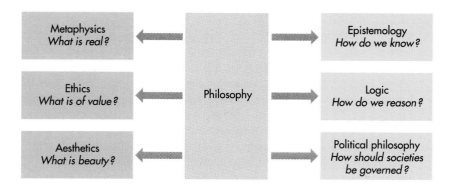

FIGURE 12.1

Branches of philosophy.

Metaphysics and Epistemology

Metaphysics and epistemology are closely related philosophical disciplines. **Metaphysics** deals with the nature of reality, its origin, and its structure. Metaphysicians ask, "What really is the nature of the world in which we live?" **Epistemology** examines the nature and origin of human knowledge. Epistemologists are interested in how we use our minds to distinguish valid from illusory paths to true knowledge. It may be easiest to remember the scope of these disciplines by considering that epistemology and metaphysics address, respectively, *how we know* (epistemology) *what we know* (metaphysics) about reality.

Is Reality Composed Solely of Matter?

One of the most basic metaphysical issues is whether anything exists other than the material realm that we experience with our senses. Many philosophers assert the existence only of the physical. Because this philosophy affirms fundamentally the existence of matter, it is called **materialism.** By emphasizing in their curriculum the study of nature through scientific observation, modern public schools clearly favor the interpretation that the physical (material) world is real and important. Other philosophers assert that the physical realm is but an illusion. They point out that matter is known only through the mind. This philosophy is called spiritualism or **idealism.** Educators responding to ideals might focus on the relationships students have with each other or with a more spiritual world. Still a third group of philosophers asserts that reality is composed of both materialism and idealism, body and mind, a belief associated with French philosopher René Descartes and called **Cartesian dualism.**

Is Reality Characterized by Change and Progress?

Metaphysicians question whether nature is constantly improving through time. The belief that progress is inevitable is widely held in the United States, particularly by those who champion the political and cultural reforms of recent centuries. On the other hand, some philosophers believe that change is cyclical; it swings widely from one side of center to the opposing side. Still others hold that change is illusory and that a foundation of timeless, static content underlies all reality.

Some teachers also believe in the inevitability of progress. They seek new approaches to teaching and new subjects to be taught, thereby "keeping up with the times." Other teachers less enamored with change de-emphasize current trends and technologies. They prefer to teach everlasting, timeless truths discovered by great thinkers, such as Plato and Aristotle. Finally, there are teachers who suggest that, with change such a constant, it is pointless to try to keep pace. They choose to ignore these cycles and to simply select the teaching methods they find most comfortable.

What Is the Basis of Our Knowledge?

Before you can decide how best to teach your students, it is important to consider how students learn. This is the underlying issue in both epistemology and education.

Empiricism holds that sensory experience (seeing, hearing, touching, and so on) is the source of knowledge. Empiricists assert that we experience the external world by sensory perception; then, through reflection, we conceptualize ideas that help us interpret that world. For example, because we have seen the sun rise every day, we can formulate the belief that it will rise again tomorrow.

The empiricist doctrine that knowledge is gained most reliably through scientific experimentation may be the most widely held belief in Western culture. People want to hear the latest research or be shown documentation that something is true. Teachers expect students to present evidence before drawing conclusions. Even children demand of one another, "Prove it."

Rationalism emphasizes the power of reason—in particular, logic—to derive true statements about the world, even when such realities are not detected by the senses. Rationalists point out that the field of mathematics has generated considerable knowledge that is not based on our senses. For example, we can reason that 7 cubed equals 343 without having to count 7 times 7 times 7 objects to verify our conclusion experientially.

The educational empiricist would support hands-on learning activities as the primary source for discovery and validation of information. Not surprisingly, rationalists encourage schools to place a greater emphasis on teaching about mathematics, as well as such nonempirical disciplines as philosophy and logic. As you might suspect, some philosophers oppose both rationalism and empiricism. They believe that our emotions and intuitions are our surest sources of truth. This natural, emotional developmental approach was set forth by Jean-Jacques Rousseau in his novel *Emile.* (For a biography of Jean-Jacques Rousseau, see "The Education Hall of Fame" in Chapter 9.) In Rousseau's book, Emile's passions and interests drive a child-centered curriculum. Shielded from societal corruption, the youngster can progress through natural and virtuous stages of development.

Ethics, Political Philosophy, and Aesthetics

As philosophers move from what "is" to what "ought to be," discussions often include ethics, political philosophy, and aesthetics. They confront openly and directly the issue of what we should value. Many of the questions that confront philosophers also challenge teachers and students. As you read about these three philosophical topics, consider how these questions emerge in the classroom.

Ethics is the study of what is "good" or "bad" in human behavior, thoughts, and feelings. It asks "What is the good life?" and "How should we treat each other?" (And it asks what schools should teach children about what is "good" and what is "bad.")

Political philosophy analyzes how past and present societies are arranged and governed and proposes ways to create better societies in the future. (How might schools engage in an objective evaluation of current governments, including our own?)

Aesthetics is concerned with the nature of beauty. It asks, "What is beauty? Is beauty solely in the eyes of the beholder? Or are some objects, people, and works (music, art, literature) objectively more beautiful than others?" (How can teachers help students understand how their personal experiences, peer group values, and cultural and racial history shape their standards of what is beautiful?)

Ethics, political philosophy, and aesthetics underlie much of the official school curriculum and have extensive influence in shaping the hidden curriculum. These approaches are a portion of a larger inquiry about what we value. One school of thought, **absolutism,** claims that values exist independently of any human being. Objective and universal, they exist for all. Whenever a universal value is identified, all people must follow it, or they are acting outside the boundaries of a virtuous life. The opposing school of thought is called **relativism.** It argues that values are determined by the interests, perceptions, and desires of each individual.

Logic

Logic is the branch of philosophy that deals with reasoning. It focuses on how to move from a set of assumptions to valid conclusions and examines the rules of inference that enable us to frame our propositions and arguments. While epistemology defines reasoning as one way to gain knowledge, logic defines the rules of reasoning.

Schools teach children to reason both deductively and inductively. When teaching **deductive reasoning,** teachers present their students with a general rule and then help them identify particular examples and applications of the rule. Inductive reasoning works in the opposite manner. When teaching **inductive reasoning,** teachers help their students draw tentative generalizations after having observed specific instances of a phenomenon.

A teacher who explains the commutative property of addition ($a + b = b + a$) and then provides the student with specific examples of this rule (such as $3 + 2 = 2 + 3$) is teaching deductive reasoning. Contrast this with a teacher who begins a lesson by stating a series of addition problems of the form $3 + 2 = 5$ and $2 + 3 = 5$, then asks, "What do you notice about these examples?" If students can draw a generalization about the commutative property of addition, they are reasoning inductively.

Philosophies of Education

[I]n modern times there are opposing views about the practice of education. There is no general agreement about what the young should learn either in relation to virtue or in relation to the best life; nor is it clear whether their education ought to be directed more towards the intellect than towards the character of the soul. . . . [A]nd it is not certain whether training should be directed at things useful in life, or at those conducive to virtue, or at nonessentials. . . . And there is no agreement as to what in fact does tend towards virtue. Men do not all prize most highly the same virtue, so naturally they differ also about the proper training for it.[1]

Although Aristotle wrote that passage more than 2,300 years ago, educators are still debating the issues he raised. Different approaches to resolving these and other fundamental issues have given rise to the quiz that opened this chapter and, more significantly, to the different schools of educational philosophy. We will examine five such schools of thought: essentialism, progressivism, perennialism, existentialism, and behaviorism. Each has many supporters in U.S. education today. Together, these five schools of thought do not exhaust the list of possible educational philosophies you may adopt, but they present strong frameworks from which you can develop your own educational philosophy.

PROFILES IN TEACHING: WILLIAM BAGLEY

William Bagley (1874–1946) popularized the concept of essentialism as an educational philosophy. He served as a professor at the University of Illinois and at Columbia University's Teachers' College. He was also president of the National Council on Education and an editor of two education-related journals. Bagley believed that the major role of the school is to produce a literate, intelligent electorate that will protect U.S. democracy. Bagley saw the school not as a vehicle for social change but as a stabilizing force in society, where cultural heritage is passed on from one generation to the next. Bagley argued against electives and stressed the value of thinking skills to help students apply their academic knowledge. A major critic of progressivism, he used his forum as editor of the *National Education Association Journal* to voice his concerns.

Essentialism

Essentialism is the traditional, or back-to-basics, approach to education that strives to instill students with the "essentials" of academic knowledge and character development. The term *essentialism* as an educational philosophy was originally popularized in the 1930s by U.S. educator **William Bagley** (1874–1946).[2] The philosophy has been the dominant approach to American education from the beginning of our history to current times. At several points in the twentieth century, essentialism was criticized as being too rigid to prepare students adequately for adult life, yet such events as the launching of *Sputnik* in 1957 and the 1983 *A Nation at Risk* brought essentialism back to center stage in America's schools.

Underlying Philosophical Basis

American essentialism is grounded in a conservative philosophy that accepts the traditional social, political, and economic structure of U.S. society. Essentialists contend that schools should not try to radically reshape society. Rather, they argue, schools should transmit the traditional moral values and intellectual knowledge that students need in order to become model citizens. Essentialists believe that teachers should instill respect for authority, perseverance, fidelity to duty, consideration for others, and practicality.

The Essentialist Classroom

Essentialists urge that the most essential or basic academic skills and knowledge be taught to all students. Traditional disciplines, such as math, natural science, history, foreign language, and literature, form the foundation of the essentialist curriculum. Essentialists frown on vocational, special interest, or other courses with "watered-down" academic content.

Elementary students receive instruction in such skills as writing, reading, measurement, and computing. Even when learning art and music, subjects most often associated with the development of creativity, students are required to master a body of information and basic techniques, gradually moving from less to more complex skills and detailed knowledge. Only by mastering the required material for their grade level are students promoted to the next higher grade.

Essentialist programs are academically rigorous. Essentialists maintain that classrooms should be oriented around the teacher, who ideally serves as an intellectual, moral role model for the students. The teachers or administrators decide what is most important for the students to learn and place little emphasis on student interests, particularly when such interests divert time and attention from the academic curriculum. Essentialist teachers rely on achievement test scores to evaluate progress.

In an essentialist classroom, students are taught to be "culturally literate"—that is, to be familiar with the people, events, ideas, and institutions that have shaped U.S. society. Essentialists hope that, when students leave school, they will possess not only basic skills and an extensive body of knowledge but also disciplined, practical minds capable of applying schoolhouse lessons in the real world.

Essentialism in Action: The Amidon School

Carl Hansen was superintendent of schools for the District of Columbia when he founded the Amidon Elementary School. Created in 1960, three years after the Soviet Union launched *Sputnik,* the Amidon School was an experiment in essentialist, back-to-basics education in an urban public school. Its goal was to provide a rigorous academic program that would prepare students for effective citizenship. The curriculum of the Amidon School was organized into the following traditional subjects: reading, writing, spelling, penmanship, speaking, grammar, math, science, U.S. history, geography, music, art, and health and physical education. Students received organized presentations of the facts and principles considered basic to each of these subjects. They were expected to learn the subject matter presented and to apply their knowledge to concrete situations. Promotion from one grade to the next hinged on successful student achievement.

Hansen presented the case for essentialist education in *The Amidon Elementary School: A Successful Demonstration in Basic Education.*[3] Hansen focused on achievement tests as a measure of a school's success. He presented statistics indicating that the Amidon School's test scores for the first group of students were substantially higher than the scores of other schools with comparably intelligent students. Hansen concluded from these test results that the instruction provided at Amidon was of superior quality.

The Amidon School did change. In the late 1960s, following community protests that the school was not responsive to the needs of all the children, the Hansen model was replaced with a more child-centered, less rigorous approach.

Progressivism

[W]e may, I think, discover certain common principles amid the variety of progressive schools now existing. To imposition from above is opposed expression and cultivation of individuality; to external discipline is opposed free activity; to learning from texts and teachers, learning through experience; to acquisition of isolated skills and techniques by drill is opposed acquisition of them as means of attaining ends which make direct vital appeal; to preparation for a more or less remote future is opposed making the most of the opportunities of present life; to statics and materials is opposed acquaintance with a changing world.[4]

John Dewey

Progressivism's respect for individuality, its high regard for science, and its receptivity to change harmonized well with the U.S. environment in which it was created. The person most responsible for the success of progressivism was **John Dewey** (1859–1952). Dewey entered the field of education as a liberal social reformer with a background in philosophy and psychology. In 1896, while a professor at the University of Chicago, Dewey founded the famous Laboratory School as a testing ground for his educational ideas. Dewey's writings and his work with the Laboratory School set the stage for the progressive education movement. (For a biography of John Dewey, see "The Education Hall of Fame" in Chapter 9.)

The progressivist movement stimulated schools to broaden their curricula, making education more relevant to the needs and interests of students. Its influence waned during the 1950s, particularly after the 1957 launching of *Sputnik* prompted schools to emphasize traditional instruction in math, science, foreign languages, and other defense-related subjects. In the social reform era of the 1960s and 1970s, many of Dewey's ideas enjoyed a renewed popularity. However, by the 1980s and 1990s, more traditional approaches dominated many of the nation's schools.

The Roots of Progressivism: John Dewey's Philosophy

Dewey regarded the physical universe as real and fundamental. He also claimed that the one constant truth about the universe is the existence of change. For Dewey, change was not an uncontrollable force; rather, it could be directed by human intelligence. He explained that, as we alter our relationship with our environment, we ourselves are made different by the experience.

Dewey not only believed in the existence of change but also welcomed it. He regarded the principles of democracy and freedom espoused in the United States as representing tremendous progress over the political ideas of earlier times. Nevertheless, Dewey found much that was wrong with U.S. society, and he had little affection for the traditional U.S. approach to education. He hoped that his school reforms would alter the American social fabric, making it a more democratic nation of free-thinking, intelligent citizens.

Dewey taught that people are social animals who learn well through active interplay with others and that our learning increases when we are engaged in activities that have meaning for us. Book learning, to Dewey, is no substitute for actually doing things. Fundamental to Dewey's epistemology is the notion that knowledge is acquired and expanded as we apply our previous experiences to solving new, meaningful problems. Education is a reconstruction of experience, an opportunity to apply previous experiences in new ways. Relying heavily on the scientific method, Dewey proposed a five-step method for solving problems: (1) become aware of the problem,

(2) define it, (3) propose various hypotheses to solve it, (4) examine the consequences of each hypothesis in light of previous experience, and (5) test the most likely solution.

Progressivism in the Schoolhouse

Believing that people learn best from what they consider most relevant to their lives, progressivists center the curriculum around the experiences, interests, and abilities of the students. Teachers plan lessons that arouse curiosity and push the students to a higher level of knowledge. In addition to reading textbooks, students must learn by doing. Often, students leave the classroom for field trips, during which they interact with nature or society. Teachers also stimulate students' interests through thought-provoking games. For example, modified forms of the board game Monopoly have been used to illustrate the principles of capitalism and socialism. Similarly, computer games and simulations allow students to analyze and tackle global challenges or local concerns without leaving their seats.

In a progressivist school, students are encouraged to interact with one another and to develop social virtues, such as cooperation and tolerance for different points of view. Also, teachers feel no compulsion to focus their students' attention on one discrete discipline at a time, and students may be responsible for learning lessons that integrate several subjects.

Progressivists emphasize in their curriculum the study of the natural and social sciences. Teachers expose students to many new scientific, technological, and social developments, reflecting the progressivist notion that progress and change are fundamental. Students are also exposed to a more diverse curriculum, which recognizes the accomplishments of women and people of color. In addition, in the classroom, students solve problems similar to those they will encounter outside of the schoolhouse; they learn to be authentic problem solvers.

Progressivists believe that education should be an enriching process of ongoing growth, not merely a preparation for adult lives. They also deny the essentialist belief that the study of traditional subject matter is appropriate for all students, regardless of interest and personal experience. By including instruction in advanced vocational technologies (formerly industrial and home arts), progressivists strive to make schooling both interesting and useful. Ideally, the home, workplace, and schoolhouse blend to generate a continuous, fulfilling learning experience in life. It is the progressivist dream that the dreary, seemingly irrelevant classroom exercises that so many adults recall from childhood will become only a thing of the past.

Progressivism in Action: The Laboratory School

Based on the view that educators, like scientists, need a place to test their ideas, Dewey's Laboratory School eventually became the most famous experimental school in the history of U.S. education, a place where thousands observed Dewey's innovations in school design, methods, and curriculum. Although the school remained under Dewey's control for only eight years and never enrolled more than 140 students (ages 3 to 13) in a single year, its influence was enormous.

Dewey designed his school with only one classroom but with several facilities for experiential learning: a laboratory, an art room, a woodworking shop, and a kitchen. Children were likely to make their own weights and measures in the laboratory, illustrate their own stories in the art room, build a boat in the shop, and learn chemistry in the kitchen. They were unlikely to learn through isolated exercises or drills, which, according to Dewey, the students consider irrelevant. Since Dewey believed that students learn well from social interaction, the school used many group methods, such as cooperative model making, field trips, role-playing, and dramatizations. Dewey maintained that group techniques make the students better citizens, developing, for example, their willingness to share responsibilities.

Children in the Laboratory School were not promoted from one "grade" to another after mastering certain material. Rather, they were grouped according to their individual interests and abilities. For all its child-centered orientation, however, the Laboratory School remained hierarchical in the sense that the students were never given a role comparable to that of the staff in determining the school's educational practices.

Perennialism

The great books of ancient and medieval as well as modern times are a repository of knowledge and wisdom, a tradition of culture which must initiate each generation.[5]

Mortimer Adler

Textbooks have probably done as much to degrade the American intelligence as any single force.[6]

Robert M. Hutchins

Espousing the notion that some ideas have lasted over centuries and are as relevant today as when they were first conceived, **perennialism** urges that these ideas should be the focus of education. According to perennialists, when students are immersed in the study of those profound and enduring ideas, they will appreciate learning for its own sake and will become true intellectuals.

The roots of perennialism lie in the philosophy of Plato and Aristotle, as well as that of St. Thomas Aquinas, the thirteenth-century Italian whose ideas continue to shape the nature of Catholic schools throughout the world. Perennialists are generally divided into two groups: (1) those who espouse the religious approach to education adopted by Aquinas and (2) those who follow the secular approach formulated in the twentieth-century United States by such individuals as **Robert Hutchins** and **Mortimer Adler.** We will concentrate on this second branch of perennialism. It strives above all to develop our capacity to reason, and it regards training in the humanities as central to the development of our rational powers.

Similarities to Essentialism

While Hutchins and Adler regard perennialism as a badly needed alternative to essentialism, the two philosophies have many similarities. Both aim to rigorously develop students' intellectual powers and moral qualities. Both advocate classrooms centered around teachers in order to accomplish these goals.

As with essentialism, perennialism accepts little flexibility in the curriculum. For example, in his *Paideia Proposal,* published in 1982, Mortimer Adler recommends a single elementary and secondary curriculum for all students, supplemented by years of preschooling in the case of the educationally disadvantaged. He would allow no curricular electives, except in the choice of a second language.

Differences from Essentialism

Unlike essentialism, perennialism is not rooted in any particular time or place. The distinctively American emphasis on the value of scientific experimentation to acquire knowledge is reflected in essentialism, but not in perennialism. While essentialism reflects the traditional U.S. view that the "real" world is the physical world we experience with our senses, perennialism is more open to the notion that universal spiritual

PROFILES IN TEACHING: ROBERT M. HUTCHINS

Robert M. Hutchins (1899–1979) was a primary spokesperson for the perennialist movement in U.S. education. In 1929, a year after he was appointed dean of the Yale Law School, he was named president of the University of Chicago. During the sixteen years he served as president of that university, Hutchins developed and implemented his philosophy of education. Stressing intellectual attainment and the need for a liberal education, he argued against the vocational emphasis in U.S. education. While at the University of Chicago, he also abolished the course credit system, since he was opposed to granting a degree based on the number of credits a student earned. Instead, his plan for undergraduates measured achievement by comprehensive examination. In addition, Hutchins abolished fraternities, football, and compulsory attendance and introduced the Great Books program into various levels of the University of Chicago curriculum. In the Great Books program, students read works by history's finest minds, including Plato, Newton, Rousseau, and Darwin but few books by women or non-Western authors.

forms are equally real. The study of philosophy is a crucial part of the perennialist curriculum. Perennialists regard essentialism, and its view that knowledge stems primarily from the empirical findings of scientists, as undermining our capacity to reason—to think deeply, analytically, flexibly, and imaginatively.

Perennialists teach about the processes by which scientific truths have been discovered. Perennialists emphasize, though, that students should not be taught information that may soon be obsolete or found to be incorrect because of future scientific and technological findings. They would not be as interested as the essentialists, for example, in teaching students how to use current computer technology.

Perennialists criticize the vast amount of factual information that essentialists traditionally have required students to absorb. Perennialists urge schools to spend more time teaching about concepts and explaining how these concepts are meaningful to students. Particularly at the high school and university levels, perennialists decry undue reliance on textbooks and lectures to communicate ideas, suggesting that a greater emphasis be placed on teacher-guided seminars and mutual-inquiry sessions. In addition, perennialists recommend that students learn directly from the **Great Books**—the creative works by history's finest thinkers and writers—which perennialists believe continue to be meaningful today.

Perennialists lament the change in universities over the centuries, from institutions where students (and teachers) pursued truth for its own sake to glorified training grounds for the students' careers.

Perennialism in Action: St. John's College

The best-known example of perennialist education today takes place at a private institution unaffiliated with any religion: St. John's College, founded in 1784 in Annapolis, Maryland. It adopted the Great Books as a core curriculum in 1937 and assigns readings in the fields of literature, philosophy and theology, history and the social sciences, mathematics and natural science, and music. Students write extensively and attend seminars twice weekly to discuss assigned readings. They also complete a number of laboratory experiences and tutorials in language, mathematics, and music, guided by the faculty, who are called *tutors*. Seniors take oral examinations at the beginning and end of their senior year and write a final essay that must be approved before they are allowed to graduate.

Although grades are given in order to facilitate admission to graduate programs, students receive their grades only on request and are expected to learn only for learning's sake. Since the St. John's experience thrives best in a small-group atmosphere, the college established a second campus in 1964 in Santa Fe, New Mexico, to handle additional enrollment.

Existentialism

Childhood is not adulthood; childhood is playing and no child ever gets enough play. The Summerhill theory is that when a child has played enough he will start to work and face difficulties, and I claim that this theory has been vindicated in our pupils' ability to do a good job even when it involves a lot of unpleasant work.[7]

A. S. Neill

Man is nothing else but what he makes of himself. Such is the first principle of existentialism.[8]

Jean-Paul Sartre

Existentialism as a Philosophical Term

Born in nineteenth-century Europe, **existentialism** is associated with such diverse thinkers as Søren Kierkegaard (1813–1855), a passionate Christian, and Friedrich Nietzsche (1844–1900), who wrote a book entitled *The Antichrist* and coined the phrase "God is dead." While existentialists passionately disagree with one another on some basic philosophical issues, they share a respect for individualism.

Jean-Paul Sartre's classic formulation of existentialism—"existence precedes essence"—means that there exists no universal, inborn human nature. We ourselves freely determine our essence—that is, our innermost nature. The "existence precedes essence" principle is fundamental to the existentialist movement in education.

Existentialism as an Educational Philosophy

Educational existentialism sprang from a strong rejection of the traditional, essentialist approach to education. (Hereafter in this chapter, *existentialism* will refer simply to the existentialist movement in education.) Existentialism rejects the existence of any source of objective, authoritative truth. Instead, individuals are responsible for determining for themselves what is true or false, right or wrong, beautiful or ugly.

In the existentialist classroom, subject matter takes second place to helping the students understand and appreciate themselves as unique individuals who accept complete responsibility for their thoughts, feelings, and actions. The teacher's role is to help students define their own essence by exposing them to various paths they

IN THE NEWS . . . REFLECTION

After a hectic school year, Kentucky High school graduate Juan C. avoided the beach graduation celebration and chose instead to spend the week in reflection at a Trappist monastery. The student explained: *We spend a lot of time nourishing our bodies, but we spend little time nourishing our souls.*

Source: *American School Board Journal,* September 1998.

may take in life and by creating an environment in which they can freely choose their way. Existentialism, more than other educational philosophies, affords students great latitude in their choice of subject matter.

To the extent that the staff, rather than the students, influences the curriculum, the humanities are commonly given tremendous emphasis. They are explored as a means of providing students with vicarious experiences that will help unleash their own creativity and self-expression. For example, existentialists focus on the actions of historical individuals, each of whom provides a possible model for the students' own behavior. Math and the natural sciences may be de-emphasized, presumably because their subject matter is considered less fruitful for self-awareness. Career education is regarded more as a means of teaching students about their potential than of teaching a livelihood. In art, existentialism encourages individual creativity and imagination more than it does the imitation of established models.

Existentialist methods focus on the individual. Learning is self-paced, is self-directed, and includes a great deal of individual contact with the teacher, who relates to each student openly and honestly. Although elements of existentialism occasionally appear in public schools, this philosophy has not enjoyed wide acceptance, but it can still be found in some private schools and alternative public schools.

Existentialism in Action: The Sudbury Valley School

After **A. S. Neill** established the Summerhill school in England in the early 1920s, a number of existentialist private schools were founded in the United States. One of those schools, which remains in operation today, is the Sudbury Valley school, established in 1968 in Framingham, Massachusetts.

Sudbury Valley operates on the principle that education should be founded on children's natural tendencies toward wanting to grow up, to be competent, to model older children and adults, and to fantasize. No fixed curriculum is set forth, and no activity takes place unless a student asks for it. Instead, the school offers a wide variety of educational options, including instruction in standard subjects in both group and tutorial formats; field trips to Boston, New York, and the nearby mountains and seacoast; and the use of facilities that include a laboratory, a woodworking shop, a computer room, a kitchen, a darkroom, an art room, and several music rooms. School governance is democratic, with each student and staff member having one vote. Parents participate, along with students and teachers, in deciding the school's budget, tuition rates, and questions of general policy.

PROFILES IN TEACHING: A. S. NEILL

A. S. Neill (1883–1973) was a famous existentialist educator and the founder of Summerhill, an English experimental school. Born in Scotland, he was such a poor student that he was the only one of eight children not to go to college. Instead, at age 14, he began work in a factory. Frustrated with that job, he then went to work for his father, who was a schoolmaster. In this way, Neill became a teacher and launched an influential career that culminated in the establishment of Summerhill, a school based on his belief in freedom and student government. Founded in 1924, Summerhill became the most famous model of existentialist philosophy.

Neill's attitude toward education stemmed from his own problems as a student and from his observations of the students he met and taught across the Scottish countryside. Many of those students were bored with school and wanted to learn only that information they saw as personally useful. According to Neill, the best treatment for these students was noninterference—allowing them to make decisions for themselves. Summerhill exemplified this philosophy. At Summerhill, the students governed the school and issued all punishments. The students even decided whether or not they wanted to attend class.

Today Summerhill is still in operation; however, according to a 1992 *Wall Street Journal* report, poor student attendance and discipline problems plague the school.

Sudbury Valley is fully accredited. It accepts anyone from 4-year-olds to adults and charges low tuition, so as not to exclude anyone. Evaluations or grades are given only on request. A high school diploma is awarded to those who complete relevant requirements, which mainly include the ability to be a responsible member of the community at large. The majority of Sudbury Valley's graduates have continued on to college.

Behaviorism

Give me a dozen healthy infants, well-formed, and my own specified world to bring them up in and I'll guarantee to take anyone at random and train him to become any type of specialist I might select—doctor, lawyer, artist, merchant-chief, and yes, even beggar-man and thief, regardless of his talents, penchants, tendencies, abilities, vocations, and race of his ancestors.[9]

John B. Watson

In stark contrast to existentialism, **behaviorism** is derived from the belief that free will is an illusion. According to a pure behaviorist, human beings are shaped entirely by their environment. Alter a person's environment, and you will alter his or her thoughts, feelings, and behavior. Provide positive reinforcement whenever students perform a desired behavior, and soon they will learn to perform the behavior on their own.

Behaviorism has its roots in the early 1900s in the work of Russian experimental psychologist Ivan Pavlov (1848–1936) and U.S. psychologist John B. Watson (1878–1958). Harvard professor **B. F. Skinner** (1904–1990) popularized behaviorism in the United States. Skinner developed the now-famous "Skinner box," which he used to train small animals by behavioral techniques, a controversial air crib for keeping babies in a climatically controlled environment, and programmed learning, a forerunner of today's educational software. (For a biography of B. F. Skinner, see "The Education Hall of Fame" in Chapter 9.)

Underlying Philosophical Basis of Behaviorism

Behaviorism asserts that the only reality is the physical world that we discern through careful, scientific observation. People and other animals are seen as complex combinations of matter that act only in response to internally or externally generated physical stimuli. We learn, for instance, to avoid overexposure to heat through the impulses of pain our nerves send to our brain. More complex learning, such as understanding the material in this chapter, is also determined by stimuli, such as the educational support you have received from your professor or parents and the comfort of the chair in which you sit when you read this chapter.

Human nature, according to behaviorism, is neither good nor bad but merely the product of one's environment. To a behaviorist, there is no such thing as free will or an autonomously acting person.

Skinner recommends that moral standards be derived from the scientific observation of human behavior. We should experiment and identify environments that best use human potential. In such environments, we would find the *correct* code that people ought to follow. That code would be much preferable to our present codes, which are derived from personal and group histories.

Behaviorists consider our sense of beauty environmentally formed. Have you ever wondered why something deemed beautiful by another culture appears ugly to you? Behaviorism argues that environment shapes your taste. A good example is the media's influence on your appreciation of clothing styles. Over a few months or years, the media may convince you to regard as beautiful a style you previously found unattractive.

Behaviorism in the Classroom

Behaviorism urges teachers to use a system of reinforcement to encourage desired behaviors, to connect learning with pleasure and reward. According to Skinner, behaviorism can enable students to learn material even if they do not fully understand why it will have value in their futures.

A **behavior modification** program usually begins by consistently giving the student an extrinsic reward (a smile, candy, a token, and so on) each time he or she performs a desired behavior. The extrinsic rewards are gradually lessened as the student acquires and masters the targeted behavior. In fact, by association, the desired behavior now produces its own reward (self-satisfaction). This process may take minutes, weeks, or years, depending on the complexity of the learning desired and on the past environment of the learner. Whatever time is needed, the key is moving the learner from extrinsic to intrinsic rewards.

After visiting his daughter's fourth-grade arithmetic class, Skinner developed **programmed learning,** which decades later provided the foundation for computer games and educational software. Programmed learning and interactive computer instruction organize learning into brief segments, elicit student responses, provide immediate feedback about the correctness of the student answers, and allow learners to proceed at their own pace. The next time you see the joy of a student oblivious to surroundings and intently focused on a computer screen, think of Skinner, whose learning principles have been brought to life by today's technology.

Despite Skinner's successes, criticism of behaviorism persists. Some decry the behaviorists disbelief in the autonomy of the individual. They also question whether any educator is qualified to exert the control over our youth that behaviorists demand. However, educators defend the use of behaviorism, claiming that such techniques are particularly helpful when working with technology, very young learners, or disruptive students.

Behaviorism in Action: Token Economies in Schools

Although many teachers use social reinforcers, such as smiles and nods, the behaviorist programs that have received the most attention are those using more tangible reinforcements.

Little Rock, Arkansas   A federal grant helped one inner-city school with a history of severe disciplinary problems and corporal punishment implement a positive reinforcement program in which teachers issued tokens (rewards) for both acceptable behavior and good academic work. During a special period each week, the students could exchange their tokens for tickets to variously priced activities. Students with insufficient tokens spent the time quietly reading or studying. During its first year, the program successfully eliminated corporal punishment but did not completely solve all disciplinary problems. Often, the most disruptive children were unable to earn enough tokens to benefit from the system.[10]

Gilman, Vermont   Billed as a "microeconomy" designed to teach students about real-life economics, the "thaler system" at a small middle school let students earn up to $8 weekly in thalers (tokens) during nonclass hours for working around the school, operating their own business, or working in their system's own bank, court system, recreation office, or redemption center. Thalers could be spent for extra cafeteria food, access to games, or special trips or at one of the student businesses. Twenty-five percent of students' incomes could also be used to buy items through a mail-order catalog. Rewards were not given by teachers, and the system was totally separate from the school's academic program. Both student and community responses were favorable, and the program eliminated almost all disciplinary problems. Although there is no proof that the thaler system was responsible, students' academic achievement climbed as well.[11]

The Five Philosophies Clash in the Real World

The school board of Bingham County has decided to establish a charter high school as a unique educational experience, an alternative to the county's other schools. The school board has commissioned a planning team, consisting of five teachers from Bingham County, to make recommendations about the proposed school's mission and curriculum. Listen as the five teachers try to come to agreement on the educational philosophy of the new charter school.

MARCUS WASHINGTON: Back to basics, back to basics! That's all I've heard since *A Nation at Risk* came out when I left college. We can't afford to waste time teaching our students *what* to think. We need to teach them *how* to think. Children must learn how to solve problems, not just math or history problems in a book—*real* problems. When I was in eighth grade, my class took a three-week trip around the midwestern states by train. Most of the semester was spent planning this trip. We worked together, researching different areas of the region and deciding where we wanted to go. We learned how to read train schedules and maps because we had to. We discovered we had to be organized and run meetings effectively. Math, history, geography, writing . . . all the subjects were involved. Talk about an integrated curriculum! We learned it by doing it. I still remember that trip and what went into it as a high point in my life. I want all students to have that kind of intense experience.

ALICIA BOAS: That sounds good, but you haven't gone far enough. I want our new school's focus to be on the students themselves. Our teachers should have training in facilitating and counseling. They need to learn how to listen effectively and guide students toward their personal goals. Most teachers wouldn't be suited for this school. They would be uncomfortable being so open to student views—especially if they don't agree with the kids. I'm also saying that we give every child (even the youngest or least able) a voice equal to the head of the school in governance and decision making. We would use our school and faculty resources to help students learn about themselves and find their own interests. Parents and teachers wouldn't dictate what students should learn or how they should learn it. Students must assume primary responsibility for their own learning. It's not enough to slowly reform education. We need to deconstruct it and change the whole structure.

JACKIE POLLACK: I can't believe what I'm hearing! We can't let students wander around the country, hoping they'll learn what's important, or sit around looking at the clouds until they feel interested in learning. We can't afford these luxuries anymore, and neither can the kids. We are competing in a global economy, against other nations whose students outscore ours on many standardized tests. Do you think they are going to sit still while our young people meander around, trying to find themselves or when the next train leaves, for that matter? The school we establish has to provide all students with factual knowledge and skills to apply that knowledge; this is what they need in a competitive world. I want a school with a solid curriculum and high academic standards—one that's willing to assign a lot more homework and demand a lot more student discipline. We've got to train students in the academic disciplines—English, math, history, geography, and science. Computer technology, too, since it's so important in our economy. We're crazy to let students decide for themselves what is "right" or "wrong"; we must instill in them the values that have made this a great country. We need a school that will develop leadership to carry on the traditions of democracy—you know, get with the program and join the workforce. Anything else is an irresponsible waste of tax dollars.

ROBIN MILLER: Jackie, you and I agree that schools must rigorously develop the intellectual powers of all students. But you want students to learn so they can become model citizens who are productive in a career. I'm interested in students who can pursue learning for its own sake. Given the existence of Plato's *Republic* and other fabulous books, I can't possibly understand why students learn mainly from textbooks. The resources today are drier than the Sahara. They break down knowledge into such little parts that students can hardly tell why the lessons they are learning are meaningful. The school I envision would focus its curriculum on the timeless ideas that underlie all academic disciplines. Students would learn largely from classic works of literature and art, and lessons would often be taught through Socratic dialogue. If I ask the right questions, their thinking and the right answers will follow.

CIS LERNER: I can't believe this. Knowledge has come a long way since the ancient Greeks, Robin. Experimental psychologists applying scientific methods have found that our nature isn't determined primarily by our genes or our "free," conscious choices. Rather, who we are is determined essentially by our environment via advertising, the media, and peer groups. We must learn to engineer this situation. As educators, we need an environment that rewards students for learning. Tasks must be broken down into small parts, and student learning should be monitored in order to see what objectives the students have mastered and what they need to repeat or relearn. Computer programs can be used to check the students and generate new methods of practice. Illiterate students are graduating from high school every day, and that's a waste of everyone's time. That would never happen in the school I'd contrive. Besides being carefully monitored, students would also be systematically reinforced for learning, as well as for good behavior. In my school, everything would be carefully designed and controlled. We know where we are going, and step-by-step it becomes a reality.

The discussion has just begun in what promises to become a long afternoon meeting, but chances are that none of these teachers will get precisely what he or she wants. Their goals and philosophies are too divergent (and too passionate) for easy consensus, and this planning team will either break up in frustration or reach a compromise.

If these five teachers manage to hammer out a philosophical blueprint for a new school, it is likely that the mission and curriculum will reflect **eclecticism**—that is, components of each philosophy that are consistent with one another and can be integrated.

Do you agree with the progressivism of Marcus Washington, the existentialism of Alicia Boas, the essentialism of Jackie Pollack, the perennialism of Robin Miller, or the behaviorism of Cis Lerner? (See Table 12.1 for a summary of the five philosophies.) Or are you beginning to develop a more eclectic approach, identifying components of each philosophy that are compatible and congruent with one another? It is important for you to reflect on and clarify your educational philosophy, because what you believe will tremendously shape how and what you teach.

Summary

1. Behind every school and every teacher is a set of related beliefs—a philosophy of education—that influences what and how students are taught. Philosophies of education are based on the way the schools and teachers resolve the various philosophical questions that have puzzled Western and Eastern thinkers since the time of the ancient Greeks.

2. Socrates, Plato, and Aristotle are the three most legendary ancient Greek philosophers. Socrates is hailed today as the personification of wisdom and the philosophical life. He gave rise to what is now called the Socratic method, in which the teacher repeatedly questions students to help them clarify their own deepest thoughts.

TABLE 12.1	FIVE PHILOSOPHIES OF EDUCATION

	Underlying Basis: Metaphysics	Underlying Basis: Epistemology	Focus of Curriculum	Sample Classroom Activity	Role of Teacher	Goals for Students	Educational Leaders
Essentialism	The physical world is the basis of reality.	We learn through reasoning, primarily empirical reasoning.	Core academic curriculum; students learn traditional academic subjects and such modern "basics" as computer science; students are taught to extol traditional American virtues.	Teacher instructs entire class by lecturing about "essential" information or by supervising the development of particular skills.	Model of academic and moral virtue; center of classroom	To become intelligent problem solvers, culturally literate individuals, and model citizens, educated to compete in the modern economic world	William Bagley
Progressivism	The physical world is the basis of reality; the world inevitably progresses over time.	We learn best from meaningful life experiences, social interaction, and scientific experimentation.	Flexible; integrated study of academic subjects around activities that reflect personal integrity, needs, and experiences of students; embraces concerns of women and people of color	Learning by doing—for example, students plan a field trip through Shenandoah National Park and Monticello, the home of Thomas Jefferson, in order to learn about history, geography, and natural sciences	Guide or director; must be creative in finding integrated learning activities that can be presented as meaningful to students	To become intelligent problem solvers, to enjoy learning, to live comfortably in the world while also helping reshape it	John Dewey
Perennialism	The realm of thought, of spirit, may be at least as real and substantial as the physical world; all human beings are by nature rational animals.	We learn through reasoning—particularly through creative, deep, and logical analysis.	Core, academic curriculum; students at higher levels read and analyze great works of literature; students learn timeless principles of science rather than technological and scientific information that may later become obsolete with new discoveries.	Socratic dialogue analyzing a philosophical issue or the meaning of a great work of literature	Scholarly role model; philosophically oriented, he or she helps students seek the truth for themselves.	To increase their intellectual powers and to appreciate learning for its own sake	Robert Hutchins, Mortimer Adler

(Table 12.1 continues on next page)

3. Plato, Socrates' pupil, crafted eloquent dialogues that present different philosophical positions on a number of profound questions. He believed that a realm of externally existing "ideas," or "forms," underlies the physical world.

4. Aristotle, Plato's pupil, was remarkable for the breadth as well as the depth of his knowledge. He provided a synthesis of Plato's belief in the universal, spiritual forms and a scientist's belief in the physical world we observe through our senses. He

	TABLE 12.1	FIVE PHILOSOPHIES OF EDUCATION *(concluded)*					
	Underlying Basis: Metaphysics	Underlying Basis: Epistemology	Focus of Curriculum	Sample Classroom Activity	Role of Teacher	Goals for Students	Educational Leaders
Existentialism	Reality is whatever each individual determines it to be; people shape their innermost nature in accordance with their free will.	Each individual determines how he or she learns best; important life decisions are made by engaging the emotional as well as the intellectual faculties.	Each student determines the pace and direction of his or her own learning.	Students choose their preferred medium—such as poetry, prose, or painting—and depict their own image of what is beautiful and ideal.	One who seeks to relate to each student honestly and directly and is skilled at creating a free, open, and stimulating environment	To accept personal responsibility for their own lives; to understand deeply and be at peace with one's own unique individuality	A. S. Neill
Behaviorism	The physical world is the basis of reality; human beings are primarily shaped by their environmental influences; free will does not exist.	Learning is a physiological response to stimuli; it is best induced through positive reinforcement for correct behavior.	Curriculum is determined by school staff rather than students; students learn organized bits of information and discrete skills.	Students engage in programmed learning.	Expert in conditioning the students; one who understands how to apply the techniques of behavioral engineering	To act and think in a manner congruent with the school's objectives	B. F. Skinner

taught that the virtuous life consists of controlling desires by reason and by the moderate path between extremes.

5. Philosophical questions include the following: Is reality composed solely of matter? Is it characterized by constant progress through time (*metaphysics*)? What is the basis of human knowledge (*epistemology*)? What is the nature of the good life (*ethics*)? The just society (*political philosophy*)? Beauty (*aesthetics*)? What are the principles behind human reasoning (*logic*)?

6. This chapter presents five educational philosophies: essentialism, progressivism, perennialism, existentialism, and behaviorism. Essentialism focuses on teaching whatever academic and moral knowledge is needed for children to become productive citizens. Essentialists urge that schools get back to the basics; they believe in a strong core curriculum and high academic standards.

7. Progressivism is based largely on the belief that lessons must seem relevant to the students in order for them to learn. Consequently, the curriculum of a progressivist school is built around the personal experiences, interests, and needs of the students.

8. Perennialism focuses on the universal truths that have withstood the test of time. Perennialists urge that students read the Great Books and develop their understanding of the philosophical concepts that underlie human knowledge.

9. Existentialism is derived from the belief in human free will. Students in existentialist schools are allowed to control their own education. They are encouraged to understand and appreciate their uniqueness and to assume responsibility for their actions.

10. Behaviorism is founded on the view that human beings are primarily the product of their environment and that children can become moral, intelligent people if they are rewarded for proper behavior. Behaviorists break down material into small lessons, test students after each lesson, and reward students for proper responses.

11. While essentialism is currently the most popular of these five educational philosophies, there also exist schools based primarily on each of the other four philosophies. Many schools do not ascribe to any one of these philosophies in a pure form; they are considered eclectic in approach.

12. You should continue to develop and reflect on your own philosophy of education; it will shape the kind of teacher you become.

Key Terms and People

absolutism
The Academy
Mortimer Adler
aesthetics
Aristotle
William Bagley
behavior modification
behaviorism
Cartesian dualism
deductive reasoning
John Dewey
eclecticism
empiricism
epistemology

essentialism
ethics
existentialism
Golden Mean
Great Books
Robert Hutchins
idealism
inductive reasoning
logic
Lyceum
materialism
metaphysics
A. S. Neill
Paideia Proposal

perennialism
philosophy
Plato
political philosophy
programmed learning
progressivism
rationalism
relativism
Jean-Paul Sartre
B. F. Skinner
Socrates
Socratic method

www.mhhe.com/sadker

Discussion Questions and Activities

1. Consider a teacher who had an impact on you and describe that teacher's philosophy of education.

2. Suppose that you are a student who must choose one of five schools to attend. Each reflects one of the five philosophies. Which would you choose and why? Which school would you choose to work in as a teacher? Why?

3. Interview a teacher who has been teaching for several years. Find out what that teacher's philosophy was when he or she started teaching and what it is today. Is there a difference? If so, try to find out why.

4. If you could meet a philosopher discussed in this chapter, who would it be and what questions would you ask? What answers might you anticipate?

5. Reread the five statements by the teachers of Bingham County. In what areas do you think these teachers could agree? In what areas are their philosophies distinct and different? What do you predict will be the result of their meeting?

6. Which of the statements by the five teachers of Bingham County do you agree with most? Are there elements of each teacher's philosophy that could combine to form your own philosophy of education?

7. How would you describe your own philosophy of education? Imagine you are a teacher. Create a 3-minute speech that you would give to parents on back-to-school night that outlines your philosophy of education and identifies how it would be evident in the classroom.

8. The key terms and people that end this chapter could be widely expanded by including Far Eastern and Middle Eastern philosophy. Consider the following additions: Buddhism, Christianity, Confucianism, Islam, Hinduism, Jain, Judaism, Mohammed, Shinto, Tao, Zen Buddhism. Research and briefly describe each of these. What has been (or might be) the impact of these religions, principles, and individuals on our present school philosophy?

inter-mission

Part 3 Foundations

Four more chapters have slipped by since your last Inter-mission. You are probably ready to stretch your teaching legs and re-examine your educational mission. Now is the right time to walk through the foundations of education.

Applications and Reflections

3:1 Self-Fulfilling Prophecy

Purpose: Someday, at the end of your career in education, you will no doubt recall your early hopes and dreams. Will you have realized your goals? Project yourself into the future, and imagine you have accomplished all that you set out to do. A future orientation can help you attain your goals.

Activity: Time flies: your own offspring have chosen to be teachers and they open *Teachers, Schools, and Society* (12th edition!) to "The History of American Education," "The Education Hall of Fame." And **you are there.** Why? Let's find out. Write yourself into The Education Hall of Fame by following the format in Chapter 9. Provide a graphic image, a statement of significant contribution, and about 250 words that detail your accomplishments in education. Be sure to include your subject-matter expertise in this essay as a major factor in your achievement.

Reflection: The activity should help you define your professional direction and goals. What actions might help you reach your long-time goals? What intermediate steps might you need to make in the future? Are there mentors and professional relationships that might help support your success? Keep this Education Hall of Fame entry in your portfolio. You could even seal and date it in an envelope to be opened when you teach your first class of students, receive your doctorate in education, are named U.S. Secretary of Education, or attend your retirement dinner.

3:2 Money Matters

Purpose: Most state offices of education work to equalize per-pupil expenditures. Still, children live with very different financial realities at home and at school. A family's income influences a student's physical, social, emotional, moral, and cognitive growth. To better understand and meet the needs of your learners, consider how economics has impacted you and your education.

Activity: Under each developmental area, list ways that your education was helped and/or hindered by money. Money is frequently a culturally taboo topic of conversation; therefore, you may want to keep this activity as a private journal entry or a draft chart you share selectively with a peer.

DEVELOPMENTAL AREAS AND SOCIOECONOMIC CLASS

Physical (such as size, shape, fitness, health, medical resources):

Social (such as autonomy, civility, relationships):

Emotional (such as expressiveness, empathy, motivation):

Moral (such as ethics, honesty, good will):

Cognitive (such as intellectual resources, academic services, inherent abilities):

Reflection: Consider how your childhood's financial security (or lack thereof) contributed to your educational reality. How was your growth and development distinguished by economic class? How might your life have been different if you were raised with a very different financial base?

3:3 Movie Classics

Purpose: The philosophies of education are captured not just in this section of the book but in classic films that portray the "good old days" of school. In those movies, you can see many diverse approaches to teaching. Watching will help you consider or reconsider your philosophical preferences.

Activity: As a preview, scan the major philosophies of education (essentialism, perennialism, progressivism, existentialism, behaviorism). Then, watch a classic movie. *Goodbye Mr. Chips, Up the Down Staircase, The Prime of Miss Jean Brodie, To Kill a Mockingbird, The Corn Is Green* and *Blackboard Jungle* are some masterpieces that have much to say about teaching. As you watch (with or without popcorn), attend to the various techniques the teachers use to meet the needs of the learners. Can you match the theories of philosophy to the cast of characters? Take notes and try to capture the indicators of educational philosophy that appear in the film.

Reflection: Pull your notes together and develop a statement of philosophy that represents the teacher or another important educator in the film. Limit yourself to about 200 words. (That's almost the number of words describing this activity.)

3:4 The Great Lecture Theory of Learning

Purpose: Most of us have attended, even been moved by, a great lecture, yet, when we learn about strategies for classroom instruction, the lecture is often relegated to the least effective method or, simply, "disparaged." Lecturing is not inherently evil. While it can be tiresome and boring, it can also be motivating, filled with information, clearly understood, and easily recalled. There are reasons that great lecturers are great, and, the sooner you figure out some of the reasons, the sooner you will be able to give terrific lectures yourself.

Activity: Check around the campus with friends and acquaintances to find out which professors give great lectures. Choose one and ask permission to attend a class. (Or, if necessary, check into television courses, videotapes from a distance learning course, or satellite seminar series.) Take notes, not on the specific information the speaker imparts, but on presentation and style. Ask some of the following questions about technique:

- What pulled you into the lecture? (a great story? a provocative question?)
- How did you know where the lecture was going? (Was the purpose or objective stated or implied?)
- How did the speaker use presentation or communication skills?

  Facial expressions?

  Gestures?

  Eye contact?

  Voice?

Movement?

Interaction with the "audience"?

Other skills?

- What technical aids or materials (videotapes, power point presentation) promoted your understanding and interest?
- Did the speaker use vivid examples, stories, metaphors, or role-play to enhance your comprehension?
- How might you assess the speaker's expertise in the lecture's content?

Reflection: All in all, was this lecturer worthy of his or her reputation? Why? How are *you* when it comes to public speaking? What's your comfort zone? Given what you know about yourself, which of the observed lecturer's strengths might be strengths of yours as well? Which might you want to add to your repertoire?

3:5 What You See and What You Get

INTASC PRINCIPLE 5
Motivation and Management

Purpose: The philosophy of a classroom can be seen, felt, and heard, yet future teachers sometimes have a difficult time "getting" it, even when examples of educational philosophy surround us. This activity will help you connect with specific clues that signal a teacher's philosophy.

Activity: As you attend classes, record observations on a chart similar to the one that follows. Gather at least three different observations.

INDICATORS OF EDUCATIONAL PHILOSOPHY

Course: _____

Room arrangement:

Teacher-student interactions:

Student-initiated actions:

Instructional grouping and organization (full class, individuals/groups, centers/stations):

(Box concludes on next page)

Instructional resources:

Other:

Reflection: What classroom indicators have you observed? What do these indicators suggest about the philosophy of your teachers, classes, program, or institution? What do your notes tell you about how faculty members manage instruction and motivate learning? Which elements do you want to include in your teaching? Which would you prefer to omit or avoid?

3:6 A Passion Play

Purpose: Teachers may be valued not only by how they teach students but also by how well they communicate clearly with faculty, administrators, parents, and members of the community. Refining and declaring your opinions will allow you to practice professional communication skills.

Activity: Ethical issues can inspire passion in teachers. Taking a strong stand on an ethical concern can, in fact, empower you in your work. Write a letter or e-mail that states your educational opinion and requests a course of action. Limiting yourself to 350 words will help you clarify your thoughts and make your point. Mix and match ideas from the following columns, use real-life situations, or invent your own details.

MIX AND MATCH LIST

Letter To

President of the United States
Newspaper editor (school or local)
Chief school officer
Teacher's union leadership
School district board
State board of education
College board of trustees
Your family
Family of a student or a peer
Faculty, friend, or foe
Mentor
Radio or television station
Internet site

Education Concern

Taxes
Technology
Laws
Elections
Safety
Violence
Curriculum (explicit, informal, hidden)
EMOs
Ethics
Lotteries
Inequalities
Vouchers
Textbooks

Don't even think about sending your letter or e-mail until you reread it, edit it, and reflect on it. (You might want to ask someone to read it and offer suggestions.) When it is *just right* (and especially if it has been drawn from an authentic circumstance), consider submitting it as a model of your advocacy. You may also want to save it in your portfolio as an indication of your current communication skills.

Reflection: What writing techniques and skills created a strong and concise statement? Were there research elements (perhaps from the text) that provided support for your opinion? How did your most recent copy change from your first draft? What did the rewriting, editing, and peer review teach you about your communication skills?

3:7 A Real In-Service Program

INTASC PRINCIPLE 7
Instructional Planning Skills

Purpose: Several districts and states, along with independent schools, are instituting a service obligation with high school graduation requirements. The intent is to instill a contributory ethic in students. While an ongoing service requirement may be one way to meet this principled goal, you, as a teacher can help by integrating this "service ethic" into your lessons.

Activity: Recall a lesson or unit you have seen. Brainstorm (alone or with others) how you might add a service component. Briefly outline the lesson or unit and then describe, in about 150 words, how you would integrate the service project or activity.

SELECTED SERVICE INTEGRATION IDEAS

Lesson	Sample Service Component
Language arts	Read with special population students, children, or seniors
Science	Assist with student health appraisal
Math	Be a homework helper, one on one, with a student
Social studies	Work on a student or teacher rights campaign
Technology	Volunteer to *wire* a school on Net Day
Physical education	Referee or supervise a children's sport event or recess
Health	Bring the Great American Smoke Out to a local school
Vocational and career	Review career materials, for bias, at a school job fair
Foreign language	Assist bilingual parents with school visits and conferences
Arts	Volunteer with children in theater, art, dance, or music

Reflection: This reflection might be better called a projection. Project yourself into the future, actually teaching your lesson and including your ethical service component. What goals do you hope to accomplish? Good lesson planning always carries with it the need to respond to unanticipated challenges. What might (and probably will) happen that causes you to monitor and adjust? What solutions might you propose?

3:8 Assessing the Assessor

INTASC PRINCIPLE 8
Assessment

Purpose: With all the attention being given to the performance of American students on national and local tests, it makes sense for you to explore the promise and problems of districtwide evaluation.

Activity: Invite a school district administrator with assessment responsibilities to your class or study group for one hour. (Create a class chat room on your department's web site if that is more viable). Prepare a series of questions regarding districtwide assessment. Ask your guest to describe the district's history and current evaluation procedures. Then, use the following questions (or your own) to expand your guest's commentary.

- What are the purposes behind these tests?
- What policies and procedures work effectively?
- What benefits have resulted from testing?
- What is the biggest problem you face?
- What role does the public (parents, media, chamber of commerce) play?
- Do special interest groups interfere, or do they support assessments?
- How do these tests affect the teacher?

Reflection: Assessment issues vary among states, districts, schools, courses, and teachers, and they seem to change often. What have you learned? What information surprised you? What do you still have on your "need to know" list?

3:9 Mag of the Month

INTASC PRINCIPLE 9
Reflection and Responsibility

Purpose: While the Internet represents ready sources of information, not all of the information on the Internet is of high quality. Professional journals and magazines often include the best writing in our field. Journal articles are submitted and reviewed by educational experts, selected for their high standards of excellence. To be a reflective and responsible teacher, you will need to keep current by reading one or more professional journals.

Activity: Pick a journal or an educational magazine that is new to you. Try one at your professor's suggestion or use sources listed in the endnotes of this text. Spend at least one hour studying the literature. Harvest a sense of what this journal offers by analyzing its intended audience, format, content, style, policy, and readability.

Reflection: If you were marketing this journal to your peers, what sales points would you include? What are its weaknesses? If you could read only one journal a month, would this be it? Why or why not?

3:10 Get on Board

INTASC PRINCIPLE 10
Relationships and Partnerships

Purpose: One seemingly distant group, the school board, influences every teaching day. As an elected agency of the community, school boards hold regular meetings, usually open to visitors. Because their norms and procedures vary, you have to see one to understand one. The purpose of this activity is to better understand how school boards function and how they might impact your life in the classroom.

Activity: Attend a school board meeting or watch one on television (many are broadcast by local cable networks). Imagine you are covering the meeting for your district's teacher association. Note what is going on. Try to grasp the formal curriculum (old and new business and procedures). Look also at the hidden curriculum, the cultural cues and the nonverbal signals, that tell you what else is going on. Write your notes into a column for your professional colleagues. Limit your final draft to a page.

Reflection: What were your personal and professional impressions of the meeting? What rituals and routines did you observe? How were your assumptions about school boards and meetings altered by your attendance? Were underlying politics evident? How were attendees treated? Did any of the school board's decisions directly impact district teachers? How? Based on your observation of the school board meeting, would you consider teaching in this district? Would you consider running for a school board position? Why or why not?

Portfolio Artifact Collections

3:P2 Charts of Change

INTASC PRINCIPLE 2
Human Development and Learning

Purpose: Talented teachers consider the growth and development of their students. Growth and development charts, from infancy through adulthood, can often be found in child development and psychology texts, journals, and Internet resources. Keeping a copy of selected charts in your portfolio collection will make the information accessible.

Activity: Collect at least three growth and development charts that display information about students. Look for height and weight scales across various racial and ethnic groups, gender differences in children's decision making, fitness at various ages, the use of free time by children and adolescents, homework recommendations for particular grade levels, and cognitive development. Be sure to note where you found each chart for later reference and updating.

3:P5 Philosophy Statement

INTASC PRINCIPLE 5
Motivation and Management

Purpose: This is the time to begin writing your philosophy of education statement. It will help promote your own philosophical clarity, give you a foundation for career development, and contribute to positive job interviews. Your statement should be stored in your portfolio, revised throughout your preservice program, and eventually submitted as part of a teaching application or presentation portfolio.

Activity: Your teacher education program may have specific criteria for the format, style, and content of your philosophy of education. In general, your draft statement would be one page long, written in the first person, accurate in representing who you are, and correct regarding spelling and grammar. We offer the following phrases as possible opening lines:

- I am convinced that teachers make a contribution to student achievement in specific ways. I intend to . . .
- Teachers are responsible for creating a learning environment that includes "the basics" of instruction. My version of "the basics" means . . .
- My core beliefs about education will be evident with students as I . . .
- Different students learn differently. I plan to meet the individual needs of my learners by . . .
- I have been inspired by meaningful educators. Their strengths will travel with me to the classroom when . . .
- I believe the goals of education are . . .

Your third Inter-mission is over. It's time for "Tomorrow."

Part Four

Tomorrow

Class Act

At this time of year, graduates may feel a little lost. We have been students for SO long, and now suddenly things are changing. At such time of transition, we need a larger purpose to guide us—why have we chosen these careers as educators? It certainly wasn't for the money! I would like to share some words that I have turned to for a sense of purpose.

Over thirty years ago, W.E.B. DuBois, the great African American writer and activist, said from his death bed; "One thing alone I charge you: As you live, believe in life! Always human beings will live and progress to greater, broader, and fuller life. The only possible death is to lose belief in this truth. . . ."

Despite all the injustice he experienced, DuBois died believing that the future will be ever brighter. In our line of work, it is not always easy to believe in progress. Apparently, DuBois never tried to get licensed at the New York City Board of Ed.! I have had many discussions with other students, wondering how to tackle problems such as glaring educational inequity based on race and class, negative or indifferent attitudes toward bilingual and special education, international disparities in the quality of education, and a general lack of respect in this country for the work that we do. What impact can I have as one individual educator? True, one person alone cannot change society. But each of us does have the power to change other people, and collectively we are an impressive force. For example, think of a teacher or family member who has passed on a legacy to you.

I am imagining two people up here with me: my mother's mother and my father's father. My grandmother, Mercy Oduro, was a West African woman who touched hundreds as a teacher and headmistress of an elementary school. It's a testament to her life's work that, although she died six years ago, I am still called "Teacher Mercy's granddaughter" when I go back to Ghana. To me, she has passed on a flair for celebration and an unshakeable belief in her students, and I will pass these on to my own students.

My American grandfather, William Steel, 83 years old, is a retired teacher, but STILL tutoring daily at his local school. His legacy is so strong that on his eightieth birthday he got letters from people he taught over fifty years ago, acknowledging his influence on them. To me, he has passed on a fantastic curiosity about the world and a playful sense of humor, and I will pass these on when I teach.

Imagine now that all the people we will reach ARE crowded in this room today—hundreds, thousands of them. In each of these people there is a piece of one of us, continuing the legacy of those who came before. Look around. Can you see the ocean of possibility flowing from us here today? Together, how can we NOT create DuBois' vision of greater, broader, and fuller life? Let me tell you, we are powerful: We are educators.

Melissa Steel
Teachers College Graduation
  Speech
Columbia University
May 1998

The Struggle for Educational Opportunity

Focus Questions

- What major developments have marked the educational history of Native Americans, Hispanics, African Americans, and Asian Americans/Pacific Islanders?
- What educational barriers and breakthroughs have girls and women experienced?
- How can teachers organize classrooms to recognize the needs of culturally diverse learners?
- How might educators respond to pressing social issues that place children at risk?

Chapter Preview

Have you ever felt the cold slap of rejection because of race, religion, color, sex, language, national origin, social class, sexual orientation, or physical or learning disability? Have you ever denied a family history that included divorce, suicide, or abuse? Frequently, the dominant culture has little tolerance for those who are in any way "different." As most of us know from personal experience, when you happen to be the one who is outside—the one who is deprived even briefly of the benefits, privileges, and status of the inside group—the feeling of being labeled "less worthy" can be more than painful.

Ideally, education should be for all children. In reality, education has repeatedly labeled, tracked, and excluded students who are in any way different. These children have met prejudicial treatment early, right at the schoolhouse door.

This chapter will review the major developments that have pried open the school door and have brought these once excluded learners into the educational mainstream. At times, breaking down the barriers of bias and discrimination has overwhelmed those who have struggled to cope with federal regulations and court decisions. Most have persisted.

Intersecting with racism and sexism, considerable economic and social problems engulf our children and our schools. The recent past has not been kind to children, who now make up the poorest segment of society. Their survival and educational achievements are threatened by poverty, changing family patterns, substance abuse, depression, and even suicide. We will identify strategies that help keep the school door open for these troubled students as well.

Student diversity continues to increase dramatically. Teachers, schools, and society must respond, so that both equity and excellence can be achieved and maintained.

Today's Students: Patterns of Diversity

IF THE DIVERSE CHARACTERISTICS OF TODAY'S CHILDREN WERE MERGED INTO YOUR CLASSROOM OF THIRTY STUDENTS . . .

18 would be white.

15 will live in a single-parent family at some point in childhood.

15 will never complete a single year of college.

10 were born to unmarried parents.

10 will be poor at some point in childhood.

10 are a year or more behind in school.

7 were born poor.

7 were born to a mother who did not graduate from high school.

7 live with only one parent.

6 would be Hispanic.

6 live in a family receiving food stamps.

6 are poor today.

5 would be African American.

5 have a foreign-born mother.

5 have no health insurance.

5 live with a working relative but are poor nonetheless.

4 were born to a teenage mother.

4 speak a language at home other than English.

3 will never graduate from high school.

3 live at less than half the poverty level.

2 have a disability.

2 have difficulty speaking English.

1 would be an Asian American.

1 might be Native American.

1 lives with neither parent.

Several might be biracial or bicultural.

And, for every 22 classrooms, 1 student will be killed by gunfire before age 20.

Source: Adapted from *The State of America's Children Yearbook 1998,* available from Children's Defense Fund Publications. Updated 9 July 1998; *America's Children: Key National Indicators of Well-Being,* 1998; *The Condition of Education,* 1997, Indicator 4; *Washington Post,* 29 December 1998.

Native Americans: The History of Miseducation

In the beginning, God gave to every people a cup of clay, and
from this cup they drank their life. They all dipped in the water, but
their cups were different. Our cup is broken now. It has passed away.

Digger Indian proverb

Over the centuries, the impact of white people on the tribal life of Native Americans has been one of conquest and the attempted and often successful destruction of tradition and culture.[1] The early attempt of whites to provide their own brand of education for Native Americans was carried out by church missionary societies. They operated schools for Native Americans, although the tribes themselves provided most of the resources for their own education. Many Native Americans responded enthusiastically to the white approach to their education—as long as this approach did not attempt to eradicate their cultures. The missionaries, however, often saw their goal as one of "civilizing" and Christianizing the tribes. They ignored or actively suppressed the languages of their pupils and tried to teach exclusively in English.[2]

Despite such adverse conditions, Native Americans achieved some extraordinary educational accomplishments. For example, in 1822, **Sequoyah** invented a Cherokee syllabary. This permitted the Cherokee language to be written; books were published in Cherokee; Cherokee schools became bilingual; and the Cherokee nation wrote, edited, and published the *Cherokee Phoenix,* a bilingual weekly newspaper. There have been many other Native American achievements in education,

Indian boarding schools were established to assimilate young Native Americans into the dominant European-American values: veneration of property, individual competition, European-style domesticity, toil, and European standards of dress.

accomplishments that rejected white attempts to deny tribal heritages and languages. However, as federal interventions became more systematic, the tribes' control over their own education diminished.

After the Civil War, the federal government, through the **Bureau of Indian Affairs (BIA),** dominated the education of Native Americans. Education became a tool of conquest, and the reservations saw more and more white superintendents, farm agents, teachers, inspectors, and missionaries. For example, the largest of the tribes, the Navajos, despite their years of resistance, were assigned to a reservation. The treaty with the Navajos promised that schools would be built to educate their children. In 1892, almost twenty years after the treaty was signed, only seventy-five students attended the one and only school on the reservation. This represented less than 0.5 percent of the Navajo population.

Many Native Americans refused to send their children to reservation schools. Arrest and kidnapping were common practices in forcing Native American children to attend. Rations were often withheld from parents as a means of compelling them to send their children to school.

After 1920, there was an increase in political and legal activity as Native Americans fought for tribal and educational rights. In two instances, Native Americans challenged the federal government for violating treaties, including failure to provide adequate education. The federal courts were not responsive. Greater gains at the state level were made, and in several court cases Native Americans won the right to attend public schools.[3]

Over half of the 2 million Native Americans in this country do not live on reservations, and their youngsters have become invisible children of color in urban centers. As the students have been desegregated across neighborhoods, they have lost their "critical mass," which is often associated with higher achievement.[4]

The recent decades have witnessed continued activity by Native Americans to win control of the reservations, including the schools. The tribes feel strongly that such control will enable them to maintain cultural identity, as well as to increase the academic achievement of their children. More than 85 percent of Indian children are educated in public schools. Most other Native youth are clustered in programs under the advisory of the Bureau of Indian Affairs or private schools.

Black Americans: The Struggle for a Chance to Learn

Much of the history of African American education in the United States has been one of denial. The first law prohibiting slaves the opportunity for education was passed in South Carolina in 1740. During the next hundred years, many states passed similar and even stronger compulsory-ignorance laws. For example, an 1823 Mississippi law prohibited six or more Negroes from gathering for educational purposes. In Louisiana, an 1830 law imposed a prison sentence on anyone caught teaching a slave to read or write. However, because education has always been integral to African Americans' struggle for equal opportunity, they risked the penalties of these laws and even the dangers of violence for a chance to learn. They formed clandestine schools throughout most large cities and towns of the South. Suzie King Taylor described what it was like to attend one of those secret schools in Savannah, Georgia:

> We went every day about nine o'clock with our books wrapped in paper to prevent the police or white persons from seeing them. We went in, one at a time, through the gate, into the yard to the L Kitchen which was the schoolroom.[5]

The Civil War brought an end to policies of compulsory ignorance and an affirmation of black people's belief in the power of education. Most of the schooling of African Americans immediately following the Civil War was carried out by philanthropic societies. These associations worked with the Freedmen's Bureau, a federal agency established to provide various services, including the establishment of schools. School staffs were usually a mixture of instructors from the North, blacks of Caribbean island heritage, and formerly enslaved literate blacks.

Many white Southerners responded to the education of blacks with fear and anger. Sometimes there was terrorism against black schools. In the end, however, politics replaced violence as the principal means of denying blacks equal educational opportunity. As conservatives began regaining political power, state after state passed laws that explicitly provided for segregated schools. With the 1896 **Plessy v. Ferguson** Supreme Court decision, segregation became a legally sanctioned part of the American way of life. In this landmark case, the Court developed the doctrine of **separate but equal** in relation to railroad travel, a doctrine that was immediately used to justify a legally segregated school system, which in many states lasted for more than half a century.

The racial discrimination of "separate but equal" was clearly visible in the different funding patterns for white and black schools. In 1907, Mississippi spent $5.02 for the education of each white child but only $1.10 for each black child. In 1924, the state paid more than $1 million to transport whites long distances to schools. No money was spent for blacks, and for them a daily walk of more than twelve miles was not out of the question. Attending schools without enough books, seats, space, equipment, or facilities taught African American children the harsh reality of "separate but unequal." In the South, a dual school system based on race was in existence. This was *de jure* **segregation**—that is, segregation by law or by official action.

The famous Tuskegee Normal School founded by Booker T. Washington became a national symbol for the educational aspirations of African Americans.

In the North, school assignments were based on both race and residence. *De facto* (unofficial) **segregation** occurred as the result of segregated residential patterns, patterns that were often prompted by discriminatory real estate practices. As housing patterns changed, attendance zones were often redrawn to ensure the separation of white and black children in schools. In schools that were not entirely segregated, black children were routinely placed in special classes or separate academic tracks, were counseled into low-status careers, and were barred from extracurricular activities. Whatever the obstacle, however, African Americans continued their struggle for access to quality education. As W.E.B. DuBois noted: "Probably never in the world have so many oppressed people tried in every possible way to educate themselves."[6]

Political gains by blacks followed their participation in World War II and the New Deal policies of Franklin Roosevelt. In May 1954, the Supreme Court handed down a ground-breaking decision. In the case of ***Brown v. Board of Education of Topeka*** (Kansas), the Court unanimously ruled that "in the field of public education the doctrine of 'separate but equal' has no place. Separate educational facilities are inherently unequal." In indicating how quickly the **desegregation** of Southern schools was to take place, the Court used the phrase "with all deliberate speed." In effect, the Court established a vague timetable, one without a deadline of any kind, so yet another generation of black children experienced segregated education. Ten years after *Brown,* almost 91 percent of all African American children in the South still attended all-black schools.

In schools that did achieve desegregation, extensive ability grouping or tracking resulted in a virtually all-white college preparatory track and a virtually all-black basic or remedial track. The educational rationale behind tracking was to provide remedial work, so that all students could eventually move to higher tracks. In practice, this rarely occurred.

In 1964, Congress moved boldly to eradicate racial segregation and discrimination in schools by passing the **Civil Rights Act,** including two titles of particular importance to schools. **Title IV** gave the U.S. Commissioner of Education the power to help desegregate and the U.S. Attorney General the power to initiate law suits to

Scenes like this one became commonplace all across America in the years following the landmark *Brown v. Board of Education of Topeka* decision in 1954 and the passage of the Civil Rights Act in 1964.

force school desegregation. **Title VI** prohibited the distribution of federal funds to schools with racially discriminatory programs of any kind. Together, these two titles produced more desegregation in their first four years than the Supreme Court's decision in *Brown* had produced during the preceding decade.

During the late 1960s and early 1970s, the courts became the primary battleground in the African American communities' fight for equal educational opportunity. The Supreme Court handed down a series of decisions indicating its impatience with the slow pace of desegregation. The Court also began attacking *de facto* segregation stemming from racially imbalanced neighborhoods. In Charlotte-Mecklenburg County, North Carolina, a U.S. district judge ordered extensive **busing** of pupils to achieve integration. In addition to busing, the courts later supported such devices as racial quotas and school pairing in attempts to eradicate school segregation.

Because initial desegregation activity was directed at Southern schools, by the 1970s they were among the most integrated in the country. The Court then turned its attention to the North and West, where *de facto* segregation continued.

In the 1980s and 1990s, a more conservative Supreme Court loosened federal influence on state and local institutions and retreated from civil rights initiatives, such as desegregation and affirmative action. In the 1996 ***Hopwood v. State of Texas*** law school admissions decision, a federal court eliminated racial set-asides as the path to student diversity, a decision that influenced admissions policies for other schools.[7]

In 1968, the Kerner Commission appointed by President Johnson issued a warning: "Our nation is moving toward two societies, one black, one white—separate and unequal." The commission charged that white society must assume responsibility for the black ghetto. "White institutions created it, white institutions maintain it, and white society condones it."[8]

During the 1970s, mandatory busing was a key desegregation tool, one that created turmoil and upset many parents. School districts began to experiment with other remedies more acceptable to school families. Typically, these procedures involved more freedom of choice and greater emphasis on improved instruction. Such remedies included magnet schools, choice plans, and voluntary metropolitan desegregation arrangements.

Controversy still surrounds school desegregation. Detractors question whether the process is worth all the effort, expense, and conflict. More than a quarter of a century after court-ordered busing took effect, school districts from Oklahoma to

Magnet schools offer students exceptional educational opportunities and attract culturally diverse students.

Delaware are taking their students off the buses entirely. Many parents, both black and white, have agreed with the courts: busing has not desegregated the nation's schools.

The more current concern is the resegregation of America's schools. With middle-class Americans fleeing cities and without school buses carrying children of color to suburban facilities, African American children remain in very segregated urban schools. (See Figure 13.1.)

The Kerner report's warning is relevant to this day. Consider the following:

- In 1997, close to 35 percent of Temporary Assistance to Needy Families (TANF) goes to African American families, a significantly higher percentage than any other racial or ethnic group.[9]
- African Americans have the lowest average Scholastic Assessment Test (SAT) verbal and math scores among the nation's major racial and ethnic groups.
- Special education classes continue to have a high percentage of black students, while enrollment in gifted and talented school programs remains low.
- Teenage pregnancies, alcohol and drug abuse, and dropout and school suspension rates among black students continue at high levels.[10]

While these statistics reflect patterns of educational and economic poverty among African American students, there has also been substantial academic progress. High school completion rates increased for African Americans from 74 percent in 1972 to nearly 86 percent in 1996.[11] This progress must be maintained and built upon, for, as noted child psychiatrist James Comer points out,

> Past and present policies which made it extremely difficult for black Americans to achieve at the level of their ability are like dropping the baton. And black America is not another team in competition with white America. Black Americans are part of America's team. If America keeps running without the baton, no matter how fast or how far, we're going to lose.[12]

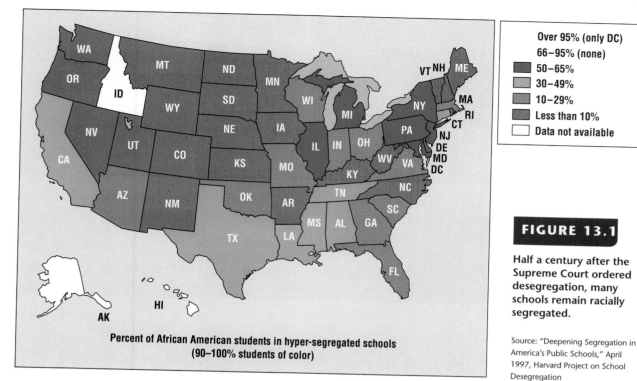

Percent of African American students in hyper-segregated schools (90–100% students of color)

Over 95% (only DC)
66–95% (none)
50–65%
30–49%
10–29%
Less than 10%
Data not available

FIGURE 13.1

Half a century after the Supreme Court ordered desegregation, many schools remain racially segregated.

Source: "Deepening Segregation in America's Public Schools," April 1997, Harvard Project on School Desegregation

Hispanics: Growing School Impact

More than 30 million Hispanics, also called Latinos, live in the United States, including Puerto Rico, up 70 percent since 1980. Over two-thirds of Hispanics living in the United States are U.S.-born citizens and constitute 10 percent of the nation's population. Because many Latinos immigrated to the United States to escape economic and political repression, not all of them entered the country legally. Consequently, their numbers may be underestimated. Ongoing legal and illegal immigration, together with high birth rates for young families in their childbearing years, have made Hispanics the youngest and fastest-growing *school-age* population in the United States. By the year 2030, Hispanic children will represent one-fourth of the total school-age population.[13]

Hispanics consist of several subgroups, which share some characteristics, such as language, but differ in others, such as race, location, age, income, and educational attainment. The three largest Hispanic subgroups are Mexican Americans, Puerto Ricans, and Cuban Americans. There is also significant representation from other Latin American and Caribbean countries, such as the Dominican Republic, El Salvador, Nicaragua, and Honduras.[14] (See Figure 13.2.) In contrast to these new immigrants, many from war-torn or hurricane-ravaged countries, there is also an "old" population of Mexican and Spanish descent living in the Southwest with a longer history on this continent than those who trace their ancestors to the New England colonies.

Although Latino children are the fastest-growing segment of the school population, their educational challenges are enormous. Consider the following:

- The poverty line, for a family of four, is about $16,000 annually. For twenty years, blacks had the highest number of families below the poverty line. But,

By 2030, Hispanic
children will comprise
one quarter of the total
school-age population.

FIGURE 13.2

U.S. Hispanic subgroups.

*Our Nation on the Fault Line:
Hispanic American Education*
President's Advisory Commission on
Educational Excellence for Hispanic
Students, September 1996

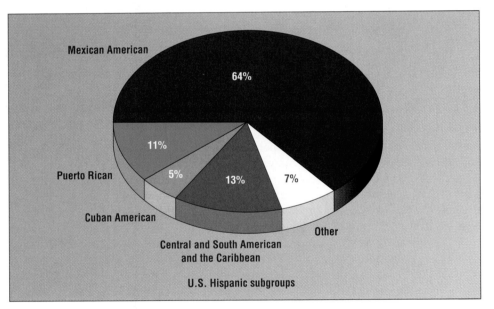

Mexican American 64%

Puerto Rican 11%

Cuban American 5%

13%

7%

Other

Central and South American
and the Caribbean

U.S. Hispanic subgroups

by the mid-1990s, close to 30 percent of all Hispanics fell below the line and
are now the largest segment living in poverty.[15] It is estimated that two out of
every five Latino children live in poverty.[16]

- By kindergarten, Hispanic children are less able than their white peers to
  identify colors, recognize letters, count to fifty, or write their first name.
- Latinos have the lowest high school completion rate of any ethnic group. The
  Latino dropout rate, at over 28 percent, is double that of African Americans
  and more than three times the rate for whites. Latinos also drop out of school
  earlier than other groups. One factor is their retention rate, with over 40
  percent of dropouts repeating more than one grade. The limited English
  proficiency of many Latinos also contributes to this high dropout rate.

- Hispanic high school graduates are substantially less likely to be enrolled in four-year institutions[17] or to get a graduate degree than are non-Latinos.[18]

Mexican Americans

At the end of the United States' war with Mexico (1846–1848), the Mexicans who decided to stay in the new U.S. territories were guaranteed full citizenship. By 1900, approximately 200,000 Mexican Americans were living in the Southwest, having built the cities of Los Angeles, San Diego, Tucson, Albuquerque, Dallas, and San Antonio. Then, as now, significant numbers migrated once or twice a year, exploited as a source of cheap labor in rural, agricultural communities. With constant transitions, children's learning suffered. One superintendent in Texas, reflecting deeply engrained prejudice, argued that education was actually dangerous for Mexican Americans:

> Most of our Mexicans are of the lower class. They transplant onions, harvest them, etc. The less they know about everything else, the better contented they are. You have doubtless heard that ignorance is bliss; it seems that it is so when one has to transplant onions. . . . If a man has very much sense or education, either, he is not going to stick to this kind of work. So you see it is up to the white population to keep the Mexican on his knees in an onion patch. . . . This does not mix well with education.[19]

The devices that were used to deny educational opportunity to Mexican Americans were similar to those imposed on African Americans. By 1920, a pattern of separate and unequal Mexican American schools had emerged throughout Texas and California. Not only were the facilities in these schools far inferior to those in white schools, but the school year was only half as long, because many of the children worked in the fields during the harvest seasons. Today, more than one in four public schools enroll migrant students, mostly Mexican Americans. The greatest numbers are in rural sections of California, Texas, and North Carolina.[20]

Mexican Americans in schools with Anglo classmates frequently suffer abuse and indignities. One youngster from Nueces County, Texas, remembers the insults and exclusion from his own childhood:

> I was the only Mexican in my high school, and well liked by the Americans. I used to go to picnics with them and drink water out of the same cups and pitchers. Then we came to the Alamo in our study of history, and then it was "gringo" and "greaser." They expelled me from the baseball nine and would not sit with me any more and told me to drink water out of my own cup.[21]

Puerto Ricans

During the nineteenth century, many of the Puerto Ricans in the United States were highly respected political exiles striving for the independence of their homeland. But all that changed in 1898, when Puerto Rico was acquired from Spain and became a territory of the United States. Citizenship, through the Jones Act in 1917, provided free movement between the continent and the island. Migration to the mainland peaked during the 1950s, with the majority of Puerto Ricans settling in New York City. By 1974, there were more than a quarter of a million Puerto Rican students in

In the late 1960s, Cesar Chavez led the fight of migrant Mexican American laborers to organize themselves into a union and to demand a more responsive education that included culture-free IQ tests, instruction in Spanish, smaller classes, and greater cultural representation in the curriculum.

the New York City public schools. Currently, while 3 million Puerto Ricans live within the fifty states, nearly 4 million live in Puerto Rico. The frequent passage between the island and the United States, as families search for a better economic life, makes schooling all the more difficult for Puerto Rican children.

Cuban Americans

Following the Castro-led revolution in the 1950s, Cuban immigration to the United States increased significantly. During the 1960s, Cubans who settled in the United States were primarily well-educated, professional, and middle- and upper-class. By 1980, 800,000 Cubans—10 percent of the population of Cuba—were living in the United States. For the most part, Cubans settled in Miami and other locations in southern Florida, but there are also sizable populations in New York, Philadelphia, Chicago, Milwaukee, and Indianapolis. Cubans, considered one of the most highly educated people in American immigration history, tend to be more prosperous and more conservative than most of the other Latino groups.[22]

During the 1980s, there was a major exodus of 125,000 immigrants from Cuba to the United States. Attention and concern were focused on the 4,000 "Marielitos," criminals Castro had released from Cuban jails. In this second immigration wave, there were many more black Cubans, who have not been accepted as readily into communities in the United States.

New Immigrants from Latin America

Since the 1960s, 34 percent of the nation's new immigrants, legal and illegal, have come from Latin America, mainly Mexico, El Salvador, Guatemala, and Nicaragua. For example, after the Sandinista revolution in the 1980s, 200,000 Nicaraguans fled to the United States. Half a million Salvadorans arrived in the 1980s; over half settled in Los Angeles, making it the second-largest Salvadoran city. These recent arrivals now augment the extensive diversity of Hispanic Americans.

Many of the Latin American immigrants survived war, torture, and terrorism in their homelands of El Salvador, Guatemala, and Nicaragua. Those children brought both physical and psychological scars into the schools of their new land. Mental health professionals noted that symptoms of trauma and stress plague many of these children, including depression, nightmares, insomnia, and guilt. In El Salvador, there were "countless situations where children were in the classroom and their teacher was killed." An education advocate from New York City counseled an 8-year-old girl who "saw her father put up against the wall and shot by government troops."[23] Psychological scars, poverty, and limited ability to speak English present enormous educational obstacles for generations of Latino immigrants.

Asian Americans and Pacific Islanders: The Magnitude of Diversity

As the largest and most culturally diverse group to legally enter our nation since the 1970s, Asian Americans and Pacific Islanders account for 9 million Americans, or approximately 4 percent of the population. Demographers predict that this figure will have increased several fold by the year 2050.[24] Asian Americans come from areas as diverse as China, India, and Vietnam. Pacific Islanders are from Guam, Samoa, Tonga, and countless other islands spread across an area larger than the North American continent.

As a group these Americans have attained a high degree of educational and economic success. Despite outstanding accomplishments, the statistics hide problems that many of the new immigrants from Southeast Asia and the Pacific Islands face. Cultural conflict, patterns of discrimination, and lower educational achievement are all concealed by the title "model minority." This section will describe the differing experiences of four of the largest Asian immigrant groups—Chinese, Filipinos, Asian Indians, and Japanese—as well as problems faced by refugees from Southeast Asia.[25]

Frequently, Asian Americans see education as a way to regain status that was lost when their families immigrated to the United States. Education is also viewed as a means of gaining acceptance in U.S. society. These two powerful motivators have driven many to succeed in school, giving rise to the stereotype of the **model minority.** However, as with many stereotypes, there is some truth and a good deal of misconception in this image:

- Asian Americans/Pacific Islanders have a college graduation rate of 42 percent. One year after graduation, they have the highest starting salary of any racial and ethnic group.[26]
- Typically, Asian Americans score approximately 50 points higher than the national average on the math portion of the SAT. Their combined verbal and math SAT scores rank them higher than whites, American Indians, Latinos, and blacks.[27]
- Although they are just 4 percent of the total population, Asian Americans have a much higher representation at prestigious universities, such as Harvard and Stanford.[28]

These successes also mask problems:

- Special services, including teachers and curriculum resources for limited English speakers, are typically more available in Spanish than the myriad of Asian languages.
- Only about 60 percent of Vietnamese and Samoan American students graduate from high school.
- Pacific Island and Southeast Asian Americans are greatly underrepresented at colleges and universities.[29]

Chinese Americans

When the Chinese first began immigrating to the West Coast in the 1850s, they were mostly young, unmarried men who left China, a country ravaged by famine and political turmoil, to seek their fortune in the "Golden Mountains" across the Pacific and then take their wealth back to their homeland. The California gold mines were largely depleted by the time they arrived, and, after the completion of the transcontinental railroad signaled a loss of jobs for Chinese laborers, many found that the hope of taking fortunes home to their families in China was an impossible dream.

By 1880, approximately 106,000 Chinese had immigrated to the United States, fueling a vicious reaction: "The Chinese must go." With the passage of the Immigration Act of 1882, along with a series of similar bills, further Chinese immigration was blocked. The Chinese already in this country responded to increasing physical violence by moving eastward and consolidating into ghettos called *Chinatowns*. Inhabited largely by male immigrants, these ghettos offered a grim and sometimes violent lifestyle, one with widespread prostitution and gambling. Chinatowns, vestiges of century-old ghettos, can still be found in many of America's cities.

In 1949, the institution of a Communist government in mainland China caused Congress to reverse more than a century of immigration quotas, naturalization, and antimiscengenation laws and grant refugee status to five thousand highly educated Chinese in the United States. Despite facing active prejudice and discrimination, Chinese Americans of today have achieved a higher median income and educational level than that of white Americans.

Filipino Americans

After the 1898 Spanish-American War, the United States acquired the Philippines. Filipinos, viewed as low-cost labor, were recruited to work in the fields of Hawaii and the U.S. mainland. Thousands left the poverty of their islands to seek economic security.

With a scarcity of women (in 1930, the male–female ratio was 143 to 1) and the mobility of their work on farms and as fieldhands, the Filipinos had difficulty establishing cohesive communities. Like other Asian immigrants, they came with the goal of taking their earnings back to their homeland; like other Asian immigrants, most found this an impossible dream.

By the 1920s Filipinos were immigrating in greater numbers, and fear of the "yellow peril" became pervasive. Riots erupted, especially in California, where most of the Filipinos had settled. Because of their unique legal status (the United States had annexed the Philippines in 1898), Filipinos were not excluded as aliens under the Immigration Act of 1924. However, the Tydings-McDuffie Act of 1934 was a victory for those who wanted the Filipinos excluded from the United States. Promising independence to the Philippines, this act limited immigration to the United States to fifty per year.

All that changed in 1965, when a new immigration act allowed a significant increase in Filipino immigration. Between 1970 and 1980, the Filipino population in the United States more than doubled. The earlier presence of the U.S. military in Manila generated an educated elite who spoke English, studied the American school curriculum, and moved to the United States with professional skills, seeking jobs commensurate with their training.[30] Concentrated in urban areas of the West Coast, Filipinos are the second-largest Asian American ethnic group in the United States.

Asian Indian Americans

Traders from India arrived in New England in the 1880s, bartering silks and spices. Intellectuals Henry David Thoreau, Ralph Waldo Emerson, and Walt Whitman *(Passage to India)* gravitated to the culture, religion, and philosophy of the Eastern purveyors. On the West Coast, Indians from Punjab migrated to escape British exploitation, which had forced farmers to raise commercial rather than food crops. With farming conditions in California similar to those in India, Punjabees became successful growers and landowners. They were destined to lose their lands, however, and even their leasing rights, under the California Alien Land Law, which recalled the ownership of land held by Indians and Japanese.

In addition to legal restrictions, Indian laborers were attacked by racist mobs in Bellingham, Washington, in 1907, triggering other riots and expulsions throughout the Pacific region. U.S. government support for British colonial rule in India became the rationale to further restrict Indian immigration. It was not until 1946 that a law allowing Indian naturalization and immigration was passed.

During the 1980s and 1990s, tens of thousands of Indians arrived in America. Most Indians are extremely well educated, and many are professionals. More than 85 percent have graduated from high school, over 65 percent have college degrees, and 43 percent have graduate or professional degrees. Their educational and income levels are the highest of any group in the United States, including other Asians.[31]

Japanese Americans

Only when the Japanese government legalized emigration in 1886 did the Japanese come to the United States in significant numbers. For example, in 1870, records show only fifty Japanese in the United States, but, by 1920, the number had increased to more than 110,000.

With the immigration of the Chinese halted by various exclusion acts, Japanese immigrants filled the need for cheap labor. Like the Chinese, the early Japanese immigrants were males who hoped to return to their homeland with fortunes they earned in the United States. For most, this remained an unfulfilled dream.

Few women were among the early Japanese immigrants. However, the practice of "picture brides," the arrangement of marriages by the exchange of photographs, established Japanese families in the United States. Many researchers suggest that the strong Japanese family structure, maintained in the early system of picture brides, is key to the achievement of Japanese Americans today.

Praised for their willingness to work when they first arrived in California, the Japanese began to make other farmers nervous with their great success in agriculture and truck farming. Anti-Japanese feelings became prevalent along the West Coast. Such slogans as "Japs must go" and warnings of a new "yellow peril" were frequent. In 1924, Congress passed an immigration bill that halted Japanese immigration to the United States.

After Japan's attack on Pearl Harbor on December 7, 1941, fear and prejudice about the "threat" from Japanese Americans were rampant. On February 19, 1942, President Franklin Roosevelt issued Executive Order No. 9006, which declared the West Coast a "military area" and established federal "relocation" camps. Approximately 110,000 Japanese, more than two-thirds of whom were U.S. citizens, were

Asian Americans and Pacific Islanders are the most culturally diverse group to enter the United States since the 1970s.

removed from their homes in the "military area" and were forced into ten **reloca-tion camps** in California, Idaho, Utah, Arizona, Wyoming, Colorado, and Arkansas. Located in geographically barren areas, guarded by soldiers and barbed wire, these internment camps made it very difficult for the Japanese people to keep their traditions and cultural heritage alive. Almost half a century later, the U.S. government officially acknowledged this wrong and offered a symbolic payment ($20,000 in reparations) to its victims.

Despite severe discrimination in the past, today's Japanese Americans enjoy both a high median family income and educational attainment. Their success is at least partially due to traditional values, a heritage some fear may be weakened by increasing assimilation.

Indochinese Americans

Before 1975, the United States saw only small numbers of immigrants from Indochina, the area in Southeast Asia including Vietnam, Laos, and Kampuchea/Cambodia. Their arrival in greater numbers was related directly to the end of the Vietnam War and resulting Communist rule.

The refugees came from all strata of society. Some were wealthy; others were poverty stricken. Some were widely traveled and sophisticated; others were farmers and fishing people who had never before left their small villages. Most came as part of a family, and almost half were under age 18 at the time of their arrival. Refugee camps were established to dispense food, clothing, medical assistance, and temporary housing, as well as to provide an introduction to U.S. culture and to the English language.

By December 1975, the last refugee camp had closed and the U.S. government had resettled large numbers of Indochinese across the nation without too high a concentration in any one location. This dispersal was well intentioned but often left the refugees feeling lonely and isolated. In fact, many moved from original areas of settlement to cities where large numbers of Asian Americans were already located.

A second wave of Indochinese refugees followed in the years after 1975. Cambodians and Laotians migrated to escape poverty, starvation, and political repression in their homelands. Many tried to escape in small fishing boats not meant for travel across rough ocean seas. Called *boat people* by the press, almost half of them, according to the estimates, died before they reached the shores of the United States.

Similar to war refugees from Latin America, these children brought memories of terrible tragedy to school. For example, a teacher in San Francisco was playing hangman during a language arts lesson. As the class was laughing and shouting out letters, she was shocked to see one child, a newcomer, in tears. The girl spoke so little English she could not explain the problem. Finally, another child translated. The game had triggered a traumatic memory. In Cambodia, the girl had watched the hanging of her father.[32]

Since 1975, more than 1.4 million Indochinese have resettled in the United States. More recent refugees are less affluent, less educated, and less healthy than those who came earlier. While some have prospered, others suffer from culture shock and depression over family left behind.

Women and Education: A History of Sexism

The peopling of America is a story of voluntary immigration and forced migration. The story of women's struggle for educational opportunity may be just as hard to uncover but equally important to reclaim.

For almost two centuries, girls were barred from America's schools.[33] Although a woman gave the first plot of ground for a free school in New England, female children were not allowed to attend the school. In 1687, the town council of Farmington, Connecticut, voted money for a school "where all children shall learn to read and write English." However, the council quickly qualified this statement by explaining that "all children" meant "all males." In fact, the education of America's girls was so limited that fewer than a third of the women in colonial America could even sign their names. For centuries, women fought to open the schoolhouse door.

In colonial America, secondary schools, called female seminaries, appealed to families financially able to educate their daughters beyond elementary school. In New York, Emma Hart Willard struggled to establish the Troy Female Seminary, while, in Massachusetts, Mary Lyon created Mount Holyoke, a seminary that eventually became a noted women's college. Religious observance was an important part of seminary life in institutions such as Mount Holyoke. Self-denial and strict discipline were considered important elements of molding devout wives and Christian mothers. By the 1850s, with help from Quakers, such as Harriet Beecher Stowe, Myrtilla Miner established the Miner Normal School for Colored Girls in the nation's capital, providing new educational opportunities for African American women. While these seminaries sometimes offered superior educations, they were also trapped in a paradox they could never fully resolve: they were educating girls for a world not ready to accept educated women. Seminaries sometimes went to extraordinary lengths to reconcile this conflict. Emma Willard's Troy Female Seminary was devoted to "professionalizing motherhood" (and who could not support motherhood?). But, en route to reshaping motherhood, seminaries reshaped teaching.

For the teaching profession, seminaries became the source of new ideas and new recruits. Seminary leaders, such as Emma Hart Willard and Catherine Beecher, wrote textbooks on how to teach and on how to teach more humanely than was the practice at the time. They denounced corporal punishment and promoted more cooperative educational practices. Since school was seen as an extension of the home and another arena for raising children, seminary graduates were allowed to become teachers—at least until they decided to marry. Over 80 percent of the graduates of Troy Female Seminary and Mount Holyoke became teachers. Female teachers were particularly attractive to school districts—not just because of their teaching effectiveness but also because they were typically paid one-third to one-half of the salary paid to male teachers.

By the end of the Civil War, a number of colleges and universities, especially tax-supported ones, were desperate for dollars. Institutions of higher learning experienced a serious student shortage due to Civil War casualties, and women became the source of much-needed tuition dollars.

Female funding did not buy on-campus equality. Women often faced separate courses and hostility from male students and professors. At state universities, male students would stamp their feet in protest when a woman entered a classroom.

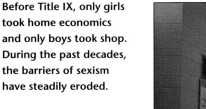

Before Title IX, only girls
took home economics
and only boys took shop.
During the past decades,
the barriers of sexism
have steadily eroded.

Although enforcement of the law remains sporadic, there is still cause for optimism. As teachers begin challenging **sex-role stereotyping** for girls who think that only boys can be doctors and for boys who hate poetry and ballet, they will be advancing gender equity and equality of opportunity for all our children.

In *Backlash,* Susan Faludi documents the negative impact on women resulting from the conservative political gains of the 1980s and 1990s. Most of the educational programs designed to assist girls and women have been eliminated. In certain areas, such as engineering, physics, chemistry, and computer science, few women can be found. In nursing, teaching, library science, and social work, few men can be found. A "glass wall" still keeps women from the most lucrative careers and keeps men from entering traditionally "female" jobs. Even in careers in which tremendous progress

Photos in Contrast

The Sports Gender Gap: Then & Now

Title IX, passed in 1972, requires comparable athletic experiences for females and males. What differences and similarities can you observe over time?

has been made, such as medicine and law, a second generation of bias persists. In both professions, women find themselves channeled into the least prestigious, least profitable areas.

CLASSROOM TIPS FOR NONSEXIST, NONRACIST TEACHING

Classroom Organization

- *Segregation.* Avoid segregated seating patterns or activities. Sometimes teachers segregate: "Let's have a spelling bee—boys against the girls!" Other times, students segregate themselves. Gender, race, or ethnic groups that are isolated alter the dynamics of the classroom and create barriers to effective communication among students, as well as obstacles to equitable teaching. If necessary, you will need to move students around to create a more integrated class. Knowledgeable teachers know there are times when children need to be in same language, gender, or similar clusters. If there are only two or three students of a certain group in a class, separating them can actually increase the sense of isolation. Diversity and good judgment are both important as teachers group and organize students.

- *Mobility.* Students sitting in the front row and middle seats receive the majority of the teacher's attention. This is because, the closer you get to students, the more likely you are to call on them. If you move around the room, you will get different students involved. By the way, students are mobile too. You may want to change their seats on a regular basis to disperse classroom participation more equally.

- *Cooperative education.* Collaboration, rather than individual competition, is a social norm for many groups, including African Americans, Native Americans, and females. When cooperation is less valued, research suggests, inequities emerge, especially when students choose their own partnerships. For instance, in cooperative learning groups, girls tend to assist both other girls and boys, while boys are more likely to help only other boys. Boys get help from everyone in the group, but girls must make do with less support. In addition, some students (usually boys) may dominate the group, while others (usually girls) are quiet. It is a good idea to monitor your groups, in order to intervene and stop these inequitable patterns.

- *Displays.* Check your bulletin boards, your displays, and your textbooks. Are women and other underrepresented groups evident? Should you find resources to supplement materials and create a more equitable classroom climate? Do you remember the phrase "If the walls could speak"? In a sense they do. What messages are the classroom walls and curriculum sending to your students?

Cultural Cues

- *Eye contact.* Teachers sometimes assume that children's nonverbal messages are identical to their own. But many factors can change the meaning of "eye" messages. A teacher's respectfully stated request to "Look at me when I am talking to you" anticipates a student will feel comfortable with the request. In fact, many Asian American, Pacific Islander, and Native American children lower their eyes as a sign of respect. For other children, lowered eyes is a sign of submission or shame, rather than respect. Consider the background of your students. Even silent eyes speak many languages.

- *Touching and personal space.* Our personal cultural history contributes to how "touchy" we are and how we reach out and touch others. Many Southeast Asians feel it is spiritually improper to be touched on the head. A similar touch, on an African American child's head, may be perceived as demeaning, rather than kind. Getting close or even "right up in someone's face" can be threatening,

A newly visible cadre of equity advocates decry the focus on females as they claim that the real victims of sexism are males. Males' lower grades, higher presence in special education, and problematic behavior are in need of a teacher's primary attention. For both boys and girls, gender bias continues to be documented in curricular materials, staffing patterns, and teaching behaviors. Given the powerful and painful history of sexism in U.S. schools, it is surprising that so many Americans are unaware of the past efforts to achieve gender equity or of the subtle (and not so subtle) barriers that still exist.[35]

Classroom Interaction

If asked whether they treat male and female students equally, most teachers would probably respond somewhat indignantly, "Of course, I do!" If observed closely, however, a good many differences can usually be detected. For example, many teachers expect boys to be active, aggressive, independent, and good in math and science. Conversely, they expect girls to be quiet, dependent, cooperative, and good in

or caring. Some teachers, worried that any touch may be misconstrued as sexual harassment, avoid touching students at all, yet we know that touch which supports learning can be a powerful and positive force.

Teachers need to be conscious and culturally sensitive when being near or touching students. Let students know you will respect their nonverbal comfort zones. In fact, many teachers "read the need" of a child, observing students' use of touch and space.

- *Teacher-family relationships.* Students, depending on their heritage, view teachers with varied degrees of attachment. Hispanics may include the teacher as an extension of family, with high expectations for contact and closeness. Asian Americans may seem more formal, or even distant, evidencing respect for adults and the teacher's role. Parents from certain cultural groups may see the teacher's job as independent of parental influence, so conferences or phone calls may appear unwanted or awkward. Wealthy parents may relate to teachers as subordinates, part of a hardworking staff that serves their child's interests. The teacher's goal is to expand relationship skills and relate effectively with diverse student families and cultures.

Interaction Strategies

- *Calling on and questioning students.* Do not rely on the "quickest hand in the West," which is usually attached to a male. Relying on the first hand raised will skew the pattern of classroom participation. Be aware that some students will feel intimidated anytime they are called on. Whether it is a lack of English language skill, a personal power strategy to shun the teacher's control or even a sign of respect, some students work to escape teacher

contact. Asking a teacher for help can suggest a lack of understanding and may be avoided by Asian American and Native American children.

Develop other strategies for student participation besides hand raising—for example, writing each student's name on a card and using the cards to select students. Or set an expectation for full participation, and then call on students who don't raise their hands. Instead of a few students "carrying" the class, all students will be pulled into the learning process.

- *Wait time 1.* Wait time can be a big help in promoting equitable participation. Giving yourself 3 to 5 seconds before you call on a student allows more time to deliberately and thoughtfully choose which student to call on. The extra wait time also allows you more time to develop an answer. Research indicates that many females, students of color, and limited English speakers particularly benefit from this strategy.
- *Wait time 2.* Give yourself more wait time *after* a student speaks, as well. Research shows that boys get more precise feedback than girls do. Waiting will give you the opportunity to think about the strengths and weaknesses of a student's answer, to be more specific in your reaction, and to provide all students with more specific feedback as well.

And by the way . . . these tips are not meant to be secret. Explain why you are working to include all students in class discussions. Students need to learn how important it is for them to participate effectively in school and beyond. With knowledge and practice, teachers and their students can expand multicultural understanding.

reading and the language arts. Such attitudes are in evidence when teachers consistently ask boys to do tasks that require physical activity or mechanical skills and girls to do those that are more sedentary, such as grading papers. These assignments inform students that different behaviors and skills are appropriate for male and female students.

Research tells us that teachers talk differently to female than to male students. Boys are reprimanded more often (one study shows that they receive eight to ten times as many control messages as girls do) and are punished more harshly. Not only do teachers punish boys more, but they also talk to them more, listen to them more, and give them more active teaching attention.

When teachers learn that in many classrooms boys get more than their fair share of questions, they often express disbelief. "This certainly doesn't apply to me" is a common reaction. "I direct questions to all of my students. I interact with them equally."

LEGAL LANDMARKS DISCRIMINATION IN THE SCHOOLS

During the past century, charges of discrimination on the basis of race, gender, ethnicity, and national origin have been lodged against schools. Following is a summary of landmark cases that have brought education to court.

Race

Plessy v. Ferguson, *163 U.S. 537 (1896)*

An 1890 Louisiana law required that railway passenger cars have "separate but equal" accommodations for the white and "colored" races. Plessy, an African American man, brought suit after being arrested for refusing to vacate a seat in the area for whites, and lost his case. The doctrine of "separate but equal" was born and held for fifty-eight years.

Brown v. Board of Education of Topeka, *347 U.S. 483 (1954)*

This case combined four cases from the states of Kansas, South Carolina, Virginia, and Delaware. In each instance, African American children were seeking permission to be admitted to the public schools in their community on a nonsegregated basis. The Supreme Court reversed its doctrine of "separate but equal" and concluded that, in the field of public education, separate educational facilities are inherently unequal. Even if the physical facilities and other tangible factors appear to be equal, race segregation has a negative psychological and educational impact.

Green v. County School Board, *391 U.S. 430 (1968)*

In 1965, the school board adopted a "freedom-of-choice" plan in order to continue receiving federal funds under federal guidelines. After three years of the freedom-of-choice program, the schools continued to be segregated. The courts found that, when a desegregation plan such as the freedom-of-choice is ineffective, it is the responsibility of the school board to establish a more effective plan.

Swann v. Charlotte-Mecklenburg Board of Education, *402 U.S. 1 (1971)*

Another ineffective local desegregation plan was overturned and the district courts given power and wide discretion to create a plan. Specifically, the court may (1) order teachers to be reassigned to achieve faculty desegregation, (2) rearrange plans for construction of schools that would aid in segregation, (3) impose flexible racial quotas in the beginning of the desegregation plan, and (4) rearrange school zones and require reasonable busing in order to achieve integration.

Hopwood v. State of Texas, *92 CA 563 (1994)*

This decision may be remembered as the case that killed affirmative action. The University of Texas Law School argued that substantial racial admissions preferences were necessary practices to ensure a diverse law school and compensate for a history of discrimination. The *Hopwood* case finding held that the school may not use race as a factor in admissions.

National Origin

Lau v. Nichols, *414 U.S. 563 (1974)*

Many students enrolled in the San Francisco school system spoke Chinese, and the school system did not provide them with any remedial instruction to learn English. Because the Chinese students were not provided with instruction in the English language, they were not able to participate successfully in the rest of the education program. Under Title VI of the Civil Rights Act of 1964, a school district that is receiving federal aid has an affirmative duty to provide special instruction for non-English-speaking students in order for them to receive an effective education. The *Lau* decision required school districts to attend to the needs of non-English-speaking students.

Sex

Grove City College v. Bell, *465 U.S. 555 (1984)*

Since the federal aid (grants at Grove City College) was given only through student assistance, the Supreme Court stated that the college was not bound to comply with Title IX regulations in areas other than financial aid. Title IX regulates only the specific programs that receive the federal aid, not the entire institution. Congress disagreed and passed a new law, the Civil Rights Restoration Act (1988), which ensured that any institution receiving federal funds could not discriminate in *any* of its programs, policies, or practices.

Source: This "Legal Landmarks" section was co-authored with Nancy Gorenberg, an attorney and graduate of the MAT Program at American University.

Of course, not all teachers interact more with boys. But, for most teachers, who are immersed in a dizzying number of interactions with students—as many as one thousand a day—it is impossible to track questioning patterns accurately. Frequently, when the teachers are shown videotapes or an objective tally of the number of questions directed at girls and boys, they are surprised at the disparities in interaction. Awareness and appropriate training can promote change to fair and effective instruction.

Our Children, Your Students

Today, children are the poorest group in our society, and current programs and policies are woefully inadequate to meet their growing needs. Stanford's Michael Kirst sums it up this way:

> Johnny can't read because he needs glasses and breakfast and encouragement from his absent father. Maria doesn't pay attention in class because she doesn't understand English very well and she's worried about her father's drinking and she's tired from trying to sleep in her car. Dick is flunking because he's frequently absent. His mother doesn't get him to school because she's depressed because she lost her job. She missed too much work because she was sick and could not afford medical care.[36]

As a teacher, you will be on the front line, working with youngsters who have been too long neglected. Depending on the school where you teach, you may be shocked and saddened by the condition in which the students come to school and by the way they behave. *The Condition of Teaching* (1988), reporting the results of the largest national survey of teachers ever conducted, found that teachers were deeply concerned about the physical and emotional well-being of their students. In describing school children, they use such phrases as "emotionally needy" and "starved for attention."

American children living in poor families are among the poorest in all industrial nations. Most parents of poor children work, but they don't earn enough to provide their families with basic necessities—adequate food, shelter, child care, and health care. Fifteen percent of youngsters age 10 to 18 have no health insurance coverage, while one out of three poor adolescents is not covered by Medicaid.[37] Children, with little voice and no votes, are among the first to lose services. When children are poor, they are more likely to drop out of school and be involved in violent crime, early sexual activity, and drugs. In short, poverty puts children at risk.

Children living today in the wealthiest American families are easily the most affluent in the world but they too may be plagued by stress, fast-paced lifestyles, new family structures, and predicaments rarely mentioned or even acknowledged just a few decades ago.

Family Patterns

Not too many years ago, the Andersons of *Father Knows Best* lived through weekly, if minor, crises on television; Dick and Jane lived trouble-free lives with their parents and pets in America's textbooks; and most real families contained a father, mother and three children confronting life's trials and tribulations as a family unit. But today's family bears little resemblance to these images. In fact, just over half of American "families" have no children under 18 at home, and one fourth of all households are people living alone.[38]

Leave It to Beaver may live in rerun land forever, but Beaver Cleaver resolves the bumps and bruises of childhood in a way that by today's standards appears half a step from a fairy tale. Only fifty years ago, a single-parent family meant one thing: a premature death. Out-of-wedlock children and pregnant, unmarried teenagers were hidden from the public's attention. Divorce was rare. Mothers stayed at home and fathers went to work.

Stay at home moms, working dads and two children populate television reruns like *Leave It to Beaver,* but no longer reflect most of today's families.

Beaver Cleaver's family structure now represents fewer than 6 percent of U.S. families. Generally, our families are getting smaller, older, and more diverse. While Americans still prefer marriage, the past twenty years have seen a doubling of unmarried heterosexual couples living together, from 2 to 4 million. Since live-in relationships generally last about eighteen months, the arrival and rearing of children mean less stability for everyone.[39] Approximately 13 million children—more than one in five—live in single-parent families. The divorced mom often struggles with a severe loss of income. Research shows that children from single-parent families are less likely to achieve and more than twice as likely to drop out of school.[40]

Wage Earners and Parenting

In 1960, 39 percent of married women with children between the ages of 6 and 17 worked outside the home; this number had increased to 74 percent by 1994. The rise in salaried employment for married women with children under 6 has been even more striking, jumping from 19 percent in 1960 to 62 percent in 1994.[41]

Even when both parents are wage earners, the mother typically continues to be responsible for most housekeeping and parenting chores. Unlike family roles of the past, parenting today is more likely to be a part-time rather than a full-time activity. Mothers, as well as fathers, often feel frustrated by inadequate child care facilities and arrangements. Studies show that the crucial issue for mothers is not whether they work in the salaried labor force or work as homemakers. Rather, a mother who feels satisfied, has adequate child care arrangements, and does not feel guilty about working or not working outside the home is more likely to have contented children.

For schools, wage-earning mothers represent a change from the past. Parent-teacher organizations find it more difficult to involve parents in school activities—such as attending general school meetings, parent teacher conferences, and school or class events and volunteering at the school. The school participation of mothers in two-parent families is similar to that of single-parents, male or female. The reservoir of volunteers for a variety of school functions has been greatly reduced, while the need for child care has increased significantly.[42] (As Figure 13.4 indicates, about two-thirds of America's families have both or only parents working outside the home.)

Divorce

Although today divorce is common (more than a million children experience divorce each year), it is hardly routine.[43] The underlying stress can increase a child's anguish. Children who have experienced divorce may exhibit a variety of problem behaviors. Symptoms from depression to aggression diminish school performance. Children often go through a classic mourning process similar to that experienced after a death in the family. However, most children are resilient and can rebound from the trauma of divorce, with 80 to 90 percent recovering in about a year. Teachers should give children the chance to express their feelings about divorce and let them know they are not alone in their experience.[44]

Rank	State	Percentage	Rank	State	Percentage
1	Iowa	83.2	26	South Carolina	68.1
2	North Dakota	83.0	27	Washington	67.5
3	South Dakota	79.4	28	Massachusetts	67.3
4	Vermont	79.0	29	Oregon	67.3
5	Nebraska	78.7	30	Michigan	67.2
6	Wisconsin	77.6	31	Georgia	66.9
7	Missouri	76.9	32	Ohio	66.9
8	Kansas	76.4	33	Illinois	66.6
9	Minnesota	76.1	34	Alabama	66.5
10	Connecticut	75.4	35	Florida	66.3
11	Maryland	73.8	36	Mississippi	65.9
12	Montana	73.7	37	Utah	65.0
13	Wyoming	72.7	38	Oklahoma	64.7
14	New Hampshire	72.6	39	New Jersey	64.7
15	Colorado	72.5	40	Pennsylvania	64.6
16	North Carolina	72.4	41	Delaware	63.6
17	Maine	72.2	42	Alaska	63.4
18	Hawaii	71.7	43	Texas	62.9
19	Indiana	71.6	44	Kentucky	61.4
20	Virginia	71.4	45	Louisiana	61.3
21	Nevada	70.0	46	District of Columbia	61.0
22	Idaho	69.8	47	Arizona	60.1
23	Arkansas	69.4	48	New York	59.4
24	Rhode Island	69.3	49	New Mexico	59.1
25	Tennessee	68.9	50	California	56.3
			51	West Virginia	54.6

FIGURE 13.4

Percentage of school-age children with both or only parent(s) working.

Source: 24-Month Average April 1996 through March 1998, based on the CPS, Bureau of Labor Statistics

National average: 66%

Stepfamilies, Interracial Marriages, and Alternative Families

One in six U.S. families is a stepfamily, and about one in three children lives in a stepfamily. **Stepfamilies** are created when divorced or widowed parents remarry, and most do. Stepfamilies consist of biological and legal relationships with stepparents, stepsiblings, multiple sets of grandparents, and what often becomes a confusing array of relatives from old and new relationships.

Other families are blended, not by remarriage, but through cross-cultural and racial unions. It was only in 1967 that the Supreme Court overruled antimiscegenation laws, which had banned **interracial marriage.** Interracial unions are a small yet rapidly growing portion of today's households.[45] The children of interracial marriages do not fit neatly into today's labels. Is the child of an African American and an Asian American to be categorized as African American, Asian American, "blended," or "other"?

Alternative families include family lifestyles other than a married male and female living with their children. Alternative families can consist of single moms or dads with children; biological parents who are not married; relatives or friends acting as child guardians; same-sex couples sharing parenting roles; non-married couples living as families; serial relationships with continually changing partners. Yet, the conventional family stereotype still permeates the school curriculum, and children in nontraditional families may feel discomfort about their "abnormal" lifestyle. Clearly, many educators have a way to go before they successfully integrate all family structures into school life.

The problems faced by latchkey children cannot be attributed to low socioeconomic or educational levels of the parents as is the case with many other student problems.

Latchkey Kids

Jennifer unlocked her door quickly, raced inside, and shut it loudly behind her. She fastened the lock, threw the bolt, dropped her books on the floor, and made her way to the kitchen for her usual snack. Within a few minutes Jennifer was ensconced on the sofa, the television on and her stuffed animals clutched firmly in her hand. She decided to do her homework later. Her parents would be home then, and she tried not to spend too much time thinking about being lonely. She turned her attention to the television, to spend the next few hours watching talk shows.

Jennifer is a latchkey kid. More than 3 million children between 5 and 13, like Jennifer, are left to care for themselves after school.[46] Lynette Long and Thomas Long coined the term **latchkey** (sometimes **self-care**) **kids** to describe these children, who carry a key on a rope or chain around their necks, a key to unlock their home door. Coming from single-parent homes or families with two working parents, they are products of new economic and social realities in the United States. With few extended family units (grandparents and other relatives living with or near parents) and a shortage of affordable, convenient, high-quality child care facilities, many children are simply left on their own.

Latchkey kids are found in all racial and socioeconomic groups, but most are white middle-class children. The more educated the parents, the more likely they are to have a latchkey child. Although the average latchkey child is left alone two and a half hours per day, a significant number are alone much longer, more than thirty-six hours per week.

Latchkey children may need special attention and resources, although not all latchkey children are at risk. Literally millions adjust to their situations, supervising themselves in terms of homework and other decisions. But, for some, problems do develop, and there are few educational or social agencies available to respond to these needs.

Hidden America: Homeless Families

Official government statistics, such as those of the Census, are unable to tabulate accurately the number of homeless in the United States. Estimates suggest that up to 2 million adults and 1 million children are homeless; others say the figures are even higher. Families with children are the fastest-growing segment of the homeless population.[47]

Not since the Great Depression of the 1930s have so many Americans been forced to exist without homes. While the income of poor Americans has stagnated or decreased, the cost of housing has skyrocketed. The U.S. Conference of Mayors revealed that, in most major cities, requests for subsidized housing have increased. Applicants currently wait approximately two years before they receive assistance. Approximately one in four requests for emergency shelter goes unmet in major cities.[48]

In Washington, D.C., a 3-year-old girl and her 5-year-old brother spend their nights with their mother, assigned to a cubicle in a school gym. The mother lost her job because of unreliable child care. Unable to meet her rent payments, she lost her apartment. Now the family is awakened at 5:30 a.m. in order to catch the 7:00 a.m. bus to a welfare hotel where breakfast is served. After breakfast, it is another bus ride to drop the 5-year-old off at a Head Start program, then back to the welfare hotel for lunch. Another bus takes them to pick up the boy from day care and then transports them to dinner back at the hotel. The final bus ride takes them to their cubicle in the gym. The 3-year-old misses her afternoon nap on a daily basis. The mother does not have the time or means to look for a job.

The cycle continues.[49]

Homelessness is not just an urban problem. According to the Housing Assistance Council, rural people account for almost one-quarter of those assigned to homeless shelters. America's homeless are urban and rural, and of every racial and ethnic background; it is truly a national problem.

The millions of children in the United States who spend part or all of their childhood without a home pose a significant concern for educators, going, as they do, from shelter to shelter, from school to school. Homeless children may be tested, counseled, assigned to a class, and then leave. They lack even rudimentary facilities for study. Many arrive at school hungry and tired. Some school districts require proof of residency or birth certificates, frequently denying education to the homeless. Add to this equation the drugs, crimes, violence, and prostitution sometimes found in shelters, and it is clear that these children are struggling uphill, against overwhelming odds, in order to get an education. Many give up.

Unfortunately, there has not been much of a national response. In 1987, Congress passed the **McKinney Homeless Assistance Act,** providing the homeless with emergency food services, adult literacy programs, job training, and other assistance. In 1990, the act was amended to underscore the importance of education and to facilitate the public school enrollment of homeless children. For example, the requirement of furnishing proof of immunization, a simple task for most families, was often enough to keep a homeless child out of school. The amended act reduced or eliminated many such barriers.[50] Despite this progress, funding remains inadequate to meet the educational needs of the nation's homeless children.

WHAT TEACHERS NEED TO KNOW ABOUT THE EDUCATION OF HOMELESS CHILDREN

- No one needs a permanent address to enroll a child in school.
- The child may remain at the same school he or she attended before becoming homeless or may enroll at the school serving the attendance area where he or she is receiving temporary shelter.
- The homeless child cannot be denied school enrollment just because school records or other enrollment documentation are not immediately available.
- The child has the right to participate in all extracurricular activities and all federal, state, or local programs for which the child is eligible, including food programs; before- and after-school care; vocational education; Title I; and other programs for gifted, talented, and disadvantaged learners.
- The child may have a right to transportation services to and from school.
- The child cannot be isolated or separated from the mainstream school environment solely due to homelessness.

Source: Adapted from the National Law Center on Homelessness & Poverty Fact Sheet: What You Should Know About the Education of Homeless Children (1998).

Children: At Promise or At Risk?

It was not too long ago that family life was captured by simplistic TV images, with problems easily solved in fewer than thirty, almost commercial free, minutes. The 1940s teacher was concerned about students talking out of turn, chewing gum, making noise, running in the halls, cutting in line, and violating dress codes. Half a century later, teachers' top student concerns reflect the devastating changes in the lives of their pupils: drug and alcohol abuse, pregnancy, suicide, rape, robbery, and assault.

Dropping Out

Lamar was finishing junior high school with resignation and despair. He had just managed to squeak through Beaton Junior High with poor grades and no understanding of how this frustrating experience would help him. He wasn't good at schoolwork and felt that the classes he had to sit through were a waste of time.

Lamar's father had left school after eighth grade to go to work. Although he did not make much money, he had a car and seemed to be getting along okay. Lamar's mother had left high school when she became pregnant and had never returned. Neither of Lamar's parents thought school was critical, although both wanted Lamar to finish. But Lamar's patience was wearing thin. He wanted to end these long, boring days, get a job, and get a car. He'd had enough of school.

Lamar is a good candidate to join the nation's dropouts. Students indicate that they drop out of school for a variety of reasons: poor grades, teenage pregnancy, "school was not for me," "school was too dangerous," "couldn't get along with teachers," "didn't get into the desired program," and "was expelled or suspended."[51] Although the United States has made progress toward universal education, we still fall short of that goal. In 1950, just over half of 25- to 29-year-olds completed high school. By the late 1990s the figure had jumped to 87 percent.[52]

STAY IN SCHOOL! DROPOUT PREVENTION

- *Intervene early.* Target special services to develop more positive school attitudes, more effective learning skills, and regular attendance patterns.
- *Identify and address the cause for dropping out.* Counseling and special services respond to personal and family needs, such as teenage pregnancy and parent-child conflicts. Remedial and tutorial services reduce academic obstacles.
- *Restructure school practices to reduce alienation.* Changes might include increasing student self-esteem and motivation; relating schoolwork to practical, useful skills; increasing personal contacts via smaller classes; and

encouraging businesses to have students work part-time and reserve employment openings for those who complete their education.

- *Offer alternative programs.* "Schools within a school" or "schools without walls," for example, usually include a smaller school and class size, informal instruction, field placement, a nontraditional curriculum, and more flexible rules and regulations. When operating in storefront facilities, they are sometimes termed "street academies." Homebound instruction provides schooling to students who are physically unable to attend.

Source: Adapted from S. F. Hamilton, *The Interaction of Family, Community, and Work in the Socialization of Youth* (Washington, DC: William T. Grant Foundation Commission on Youth and America's Future, 1988).

Today, roughly one out of every nine students does not graduate from high school. This represents not only a loss of human potential but also increased future costs in welfare, unemployment benefits, and potential criminal activity.

Sexuality and Teenage Pregnancy

Who can blame today's adolescents for being confused about society's view of sexuality? They hear "Just say no" yet are bombarded with sexually suggestive advertising for clothes, drinks, sports, and cars. The media are filled with sexuality, both real-life and made-for-TV stories, yet parents and teachers rarely talk with (or listen to) kids. This puts schools in a difficult position, likely to offend one group or another and trying to walk the fine line between teaching and preaching.

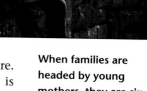

When families are headed by young mothers, they are six times as likely to be in poverty.

Preaching morality while teaching sex education can be a dangerous mixture. Research indicates that U.S. teenagers receive the message that premarital sex is wrong yet the use of contraception at first intercourse has risen from 48 percent to 78 percent since 1980. On average, secondary schools offer only 6½ hours a year of sex education. Less than 2 hours is spent on contraception and the prevention of sexually transmitted diseases.[53]

Where are students getting their sex education? Teens rely on peer networks to explain sexuality and relationships. As one young woman said, "When you're in sex education class, they just tell you what goes on inside your body. They don't tell you what goes *on*."[54]

At this point, we do not know enough about how to instruct and implement effective sex education programs, and statistics underscore our failings. We are in the midst of a teenage pregnancy epidemic unrivaled in any other industrialized nation. Students could benefit from a more effective sex education curriculum, one that is responsive to cultural and linguistic differences.

FACT SHEET ON ADOLESCENTS WHO HAVE BABIES

- Almost 1 million teenage women (11 percent) of those aged 15–19 become pregnant each year.
- One in five sexually active teen women becomes pregnant.
- Fifty percent of adolescents who have a baby become pregnant again within two years.
- Teenage mothers and their babies are more likely to suffer medical complications and have higher mortality rates than mothers over 20.

- Teen mothers are much more likely to come from low-income families (83 percent).
- About one-third of 15-year-old mothers have partners who are over 21.
- The children of adolescent mothers are at increased risk for being a teen parent themselves.

Source: Alan Guttmacher Institute, *Facts in Brief (1998); reports* from the National Center for Health Statistics; reports from the U.S. Bureau of the Census; Children's Defense Fund, *A Vision for America's Future* (Washington, DC: Children's Defense Fund, 1998); Fred M. Hechinger, *Fateful Choices: Healthy Youth for the 21st Century.* New York: Hill and Wang, 1992; Marianne E. Felice, M.D. Professor of Pediatrics & Psychiatry, Director of Adolescent Medicine, University of Maryland, Board of Directors, *Campaign for Our Children.* Facts, Figures and Statistics (Baltimore, MD).

The widespread publicity surrounding Ryan White, a young AIDS victim who led a courageous fight to open school doors to young AIDS patients, did much to relieve the ignorance that surrounds this deadly disease.

AIDS: HIV Comes to School

For many communities, decades of opposition to sex education were unceremoniously cast aside with the emergence of the medical nightmare AIDS. Sexually active children represent a major at-risk population for the disease, and sex education has become a prime weapon against the spread of the virus. In the early 1990s, the House Select Committee on Children, Youth, and Families estimated that forty thousand teens each year contract the HIV virus.[55] A decade of very public attention resulted in a decline in AIDS incidence and deaths in 1996. The largest diagnosed population with AIDS in 1997 were men who had sex with men. But, even in this group, AIDS incidence and death is on the decline. The greatest decline, 40 percent, is evident in younger children, following efforts to reduce perinatal transmission for pregnant HIV-infected women and their children.[56]

Throughout the early 1990s, AIDS-related sex education was an accepted part of some school programs, a controversial part of others, and something that was avoided in still other communities. To many, but not all Americans, the threat of this nearly always fatal disease was horrific enough to eliminate reservations concerning sex education programs in the schools.

Substance Abuse: Drinking, Drugs, and Smoking

"I know personally kids who drink whole bottles of liquor on the weekends by themselves."

"You won't see the drug culture here unless you know what to look for. You'll get a lot of parent and school denial, but the reputation of this school is 'cocaine heaven.'"

"On an average week, I gross over $2,000 dealing drugs at this school."

These statements from high school students add a personal dimension to official reports indicating that the United States has the highest rate of teenage drug use of any industrialized nation in the world. **Substance abuse** ranges from alcohol and chewing tobacco to cocaine, LSD, and heroin.

Alcohol abuse represents by far the most widespread form of substance abuse. One-third of all 1998 high school seniors reported being drunk in the preceding month.[57] Justice Department figures show that alcohol or drug use is associated with more unplanned pregnancies, more sexually transmitted diseases, and more HIV infection than is any other single factor.[58] The more teenagers drink, the more likely they are to be involved in violent crime, such as murder, rape, or robbery, either as victim or perpetrator.

Substance abusers suffer significant school problems. Marijuana users are twice as likely as nonusers to average Ds and Fs. A Philadelphia study showed that four out of five dropouts were regular drug users. Unfortunately, many parents and educators are unaware of the extent of the problem. In an Emory University study, although 3 percent of parents said that their children had used marijuana in the past month,

The United States has the highest rate of teenage drug use of any industrialized nation in the world.

28 percent of those children reported that they had actually taken the drug.[59] "It's normal denial and suburban American dream denial. This isn't supposed to happen here."[60]

Cigarette smoking provides a window on teen substance abuse. Consider the following:

- Teenagers who smoke are more likely to get poor grades, drink alcohol, get drunk, and try marijuana than are nonsmokers.
- Teens who smoke hang out with friends after school, while nonsmokers are more prone to be involved in school sports and activities.
- Almost a third of teens who smoke report doing no homework, compared with 8 percent of their nonsmoking peers.
- Perceptions on smoke-free campuses vary greatly. In middle schools, 83 percent of principals and 71 percent of teachers say their schools are smoke-free but only 45 percent of students see it that way. In high school, 67 percent of principals and 36 percent of teachers feel their buildings are smoke-free. Barely 14 percent of students agree.
- Although teens understand that smoking is bad for their health, nearly one-fourth admit they cannot quit because they are addicted.[61]

Youth Suicide

A closely knit New Jersey community across the Hudson River from Manhattan was viewed as a model town. The high school frequently won the state football championship, the police department won awards for its youth-assistance programs, and the town was known for the beauty of its parks and safety of its streets.

On an early Wednesday morning in March, the citizens of Bergenfield woke up to discover that four of their teenagers had locked themselves in a garage, turned on a car engine, and left a note requesting that they be buried together. The group suicide brought the total of teen suicides in Bergenfield to eight that year.

Suicide is a leading cause of death among Americans aged 15 to 24. In the next 24 hours, almost 1,500 teens will attempt suicide. At least 13 of them will succeed. Ten percent of teenage boys and 18 percent of teenage girls make at least one attempt to kill themselves.[62] Particularly at risk are girls who have been physically or sexually abused and adolescents struggling with their sexual orientation.

What should teachers look for? Depression often precedes suicide attempts. Manifestations include persistent sadness, boredom or low energy, loss of interests in favorite pastimes, irritability, physical complaints and illness, serious changes in sleeping and eating, and school avoidance or poor performance.[63] Impulsivity, which accounts for about one-fourth of all adolescent suicides, is particularly difficult for adults to deal with, since it may cause students to commit suicide in response to their first bout with depression. To date, teachers and parents have not done well in preventing youth depression and suicide.

Gays, Lesbians, and Bisexuals: Our Invisible Students

When I was 11, I started smoking dope, drinking alcohol, and snorting speed every day to make me feel better and forget I was gay. I would party with friends but get more and more depressed as the night would go on. They would always make anti-gay remarks and harass gay men while I would just stand there. Late at night after they went home, I would go down to the river and dive in—hoping I would hit my head on a rock and drown.[64]

STUDENT SEXUAL DIVERSITY GUIDELINES FOR TEACHERS

- Confront directly school incidents of antilesbian and antigay prejudice—harassment, labels, jokes, put-downs, and graffiti.
- Work to change personnel policies in order to protect students and staff from discrimination on the basis of sexual orientation.
- Provide support groups and other resources for gay, lesbian, and bisexual students and their families.
- Submit requests in order to improve both fiction and nonfiction library holdings on sexual diversity.
- Include gay, lesbian, and bisexual concerns in prevention programs (pregnancy, dropout, suicide).

If a student comes to you to discuss gay, lesbian, or bisexual concerns,

- Be aware that the student may be feeling grief and emotional pain.
- Use the terms the student uses. Say "homosexual" if that is the term used, or "gay," "lesbian," or "bisexual" if the student chooses these terms.
- Be aware of your own feelings. Avoid making negative judgments that may cause the student even more pain.
- Respect confidentiality.
- Let the student know you appreciate his or her trust.
- Remember that gay and bisexual male students are particularly in need of information concerning protection from AIDS.

Source: Adapted from *Affording Equal Opportunity to Gay and Lesbian Students Through Teaching and Counseling* (Washington, DC: National Education Association, 1992).

Fear and intolerance toward homosexuals, labeled **homophobia,** characterize the culture of secondary schools and cause depression and suicidal feelings. Some schools have a climate that is actively hostile: students and even faculty make jokes about "faggots," "dykes," "gays," and "queers," and antigay graffiti cover bathroom walls and school desks. At times, verbal abuse turns physical, as in the case of a black male student in Ohio who was dragged into a bathroom stall. There eight boys called him a faggot, bashed his head against a toilet, and threatened to kill him. As punishment, the eight boys were given demerits for the incident.[65]

Because homophobia is so prevalent and so virulent, most lesbian and gay students go into hiding and try to "pass" as "straight." Afraid to let other students, faculty, or even their families know, too many become painfully isolated.

The National Education Association (NEA) adopted a resolution advocating equal opportunity for students and staff regardless of sexual orientation and encouraging schools to provide counseling by trained personnel. It developed training materials and workshops on "Affording Equal Opportunity to Gay and Lesbian Students Through Teaching and Counseling." School districts have also responded. San Diego, Boston, and St. Paul have issued antiharassment measures and policies designed to protect homosexual students.[66] These are steps, but much more must be done.

Tension Point: Are Equity and Excellence Compatible?

When 6000 young people are killed every year with a gun, when 5000 young people commit suicide every year, when over a million young people run away from home every year, when almost half a million young people drop out of school every year, and when hundreds of thousands of young people get into drugs and alcohol and tobacco and just mess up their lives, can we truly say we are a child-centered society . . . ?

Richard Riley, U.S. Secretary of Education
Washington Post, 23 July 1998

While not denying the importance of meeting these pressing social needs, critics question whether this is a proper role for schools. If schools are dispensing social services, at what cost? Investing in cultural sensitivity and responding to social problems are resources not invested in raising school standards and student achievement.

Equity proponents counter that, without equity, without attending to these basic social needs, America can never be a truly great nation. Without equity and social justice, excellence becomes a hollow goal.

Are equity and excellence compatible? Should investments in equity be made, even at the possible cost of detracting resources from academic excellence? The basic question may be, Can education be excellent if it is not excellent for all?

Summary

1. For centuries, the impact of white people on Native Americans has been one of territorial conquest and attempts to diminish the Indian culture, often through schooling. Today, less than half of the 2 million Native Americans in this country live on reservations.

2. The education of African Americans during the colonial period was sometimes illegal, and, when schools were provided, they were inadequate and underfunded. The doctrine of "separate but equal" *(Plessy v. Ferguson)* legalized segregated schools, but, in 1954 *(Brown v. Board of Education of Topeka)*, "separate but equal" was declared unconstitutional. The Civil Rights Act of 1964 was passed in an effort to eliminate continuing discrimination and promote the desegregation of schools.

3. Desegregation still persists, thanks in part to racially segregated neighborhoods. African American children are often assigned to special education programs and tracked into less challenging academic areas. African American students have lower test scores and higher dropout rates than do white students.

4. There are more than 30 million Hispanics (or Latinos) living in the United States today. The nation's Latinos comprise several major groups, including Mexicans, Puerto Ricans, and Cubans. Hispanic immigration from Central America, including Nicaragua and El Salvador, is increasing. Students from poverty-stricken, war-torn countries must overcome psychological trauma, poverty, and language barriers to succeed in the United States. The Hispanic dropout statistics are even higher than those of African Americans.

5. Asian is a label assigned to several billion people from a score of nations. Asian Americans and Pacific Islanders, especially new immigrants from war-ravaged nations in Indochina, must overcome trauma and adjust to a new culture and language, not unlike many Hispanics. Other Asian Americans, such as the Chinese and Asian Indians, are stereotyped as model minorities, a label that often masks the impact of prejudice on these children.

6. Although females have been in North America as long as males, their struggle for equal educational opportunities continues. At first denied access to schools, once admitted they were often segregated into gender-restricted programs and careers. Today, researchers find subtle patterns of bias as teachers interact more frequently and more precisely with male students.

7. Title IX of the 1972 Educational Amendments Act prohibits sex discrimination in schools that receive federal financial assistance. Progress toward gender equity is evident by increased female participation in athletics and improved test scores in math and biology. Other areas, such as computer technology and vocational programs, remain gender segregated. Compliance with Title IX is erratic.

8. One in five U.S. children lives in poverty, a condition that frequently short-circuits their educational promise.

9. The traditional family unit of the past has undergone a radical transformation. Divorce, remarriage, wage earning, parenting, and alternative relationships have restructured the family and the home-school connection.

10. Latchkey children are those who are left home alone for a significant portion of the day. Many latchkey children are found in middle-class white homes with working parents. Psychologists do not share a universal view as to whether this is a harmful experience, but some express concern about possible trauma, poor nutrition, and safety problems.

11. The dramatic decrease in the amount of low-cost housing built and available during the 1980s and the rising cost of rent led to an increase in the need for public shelters and specific educational services for homeless children. Passage of the 1987 McKinney Homeless Assistance Act, amended in 1990, was intended to lessen the impact of this problem. This law protects the rights of children, who have no permanent address, to attend school and receive all necessary services and opportunities.

12. Today 86 percent of students complete high school. Poor students, urban students, and students of color are more likely to drop out than are others. Reasons for dropping out range from lack of motivation to teenage pregnancy. Schools continue to develop programs to retain students through high school graduation.

13. The mixed messages sent to students in our society have contributed to an alarmingly high rate of teenage pregnancy. More than one in eleven teenage girls become pregnant, and many are destined for an early end to their educational careers and poverty. Current school responses vary according to community norms. In some communities, sex education is a major emphasis; in others, it is minor or missing entirely.

14. Fear of AIDS has served as a catalyst for establishing sex education programs, in hopes of reducing this deadly disease. The courts, contending that AIDS is a disability, do not allow schools to discriminate against students or teachers with HIV.

15. Although substance abuse by teens has generally declined since the 1970s, reports in recent years suggest drug use (especially alcohol) may again be on the rise. Statistics on the extent of the problem are difficult to quantify and interpret, but, clearly, substance abuse has a devastating impact on the education and health of those involved.

16. Teen suicide, often the result of depression, is attempted by 10 percent of teenage boys and 18 percent of teenage girls. Although there are some warning signs, parents and teachers find it difficult to anticipate who will be involved in suicide attempts.

17. Gay, lesbian, and bisexual youth are more likely to commit suicide than are heterosexual youngsters. Schools need to do much more to address the needs of these often "invisible" students. Guidelines for teachers include directly confronting homophobia across the school culture.

18. An ongoing debate exists over whether equity and excellence in education are compatible. Some claim that efforts for equity drain resources from educational programs and subvert academic excellence. However, others claim that education cannot be excellent unless it is excellent for all.

Key Terms and People

www.mhhe.com/sadker

alternative families
Brown v. Board of Education of Topeka
Bureau of Indian Affairs (BIA)
busing
Civil Rights Act
de facto segregation
de jure segregation
desegregation

homophobia
Hopwood v. State of Texas
interracial marriage
latchkey (self-care) kids
McKinney Homeless Assistance Act
model minority
Plessy v. Ferguson
relocation camps

separate but equal
Sequoyah
sex discrimination
sex-role stereotyping
stepfamilies
substance abuse
Title IV
Title VI
Title IX

Discussion Questions and Activities

1. Select one of the groups discussed in this chapter for further reading and research. Analyze historical and contemporary educational developments that have affected this group, and discuss your findings with other members of your class.
2. Do research on a group not discussed in this chapter that faces discrimination. Discuss your findings with other members of your class.
3. Observe a classroom, noting how many times teachers call on girls and boys. Compare the amount of attention boys and girls get to their representation in the classroom. Do boys or girls get more than their fair share of teacher attention?
4. How do you react to the various issues raised in this chapter? On a separate sheet of paper complete the following sentences as honestly as you can. If you wish, share your responses with your classmates.

   • When I hear the stories about blatant racial discrimination in education, I . . .

   • I think the most important thing educators can do to achieve equal educational opportunity for all students is to . . .

   • If I were to teach in a school that in my opinion used culturally biased testing practices to track Spanish-speaking children into special education classes, I . . .

   • If a boy were to bring a favorite doll to "Show and Tell" in my first-grade classroom and the other kids laughed at him, I . . .

   • If there were no information about members of groups of color in the social studies book assigned for my class, I . . .

5. How do the following impact students?

   • Poverty

   • High divorce rates

   • Single-parent families

   • Alternative families

   • Wage-earning parents

6. What can schools do to address each of the issues discussed in question #5?
7. What are some of the major barriers limiting the education of homeless children?

8. Identify some of the typical programs used to prevent students from dropping out of school. What alternatives might you suggest?

9. Predict the hazards that a school might encounter if it were to implement a curriculum that includes sexuality, teenage pregnancy, and AIDS.

10. What can schools and society do to reduce teenage suicide?

11. For each of the following issues, identify at least one teacher intervention that is important for all students: latchkey kids; homelessness; dropouts; drug use; teenage pregnancy; carriers of HIV; gay and lesbian students.

12. Do you think equity and excellence in the field of education are compatible? Why or why not?

Technology in Education

Focus Questions

- Has technology changed schools?
- How does television affect children?
- Why is computer technology difficult to implement in schools?
- In what ways does global education refocus the curriculum?
- What are some of the educational uses of computers and the Internet?
- How are the teaching and learning roles redefined in the virtual high school?
- Does technology exacerbate racial, class, and gender divisions?

Chapter Preview

In an earlier time, before there were factories, there were "cottage industries." People manufactured products, not as a group of workers in a central place but individually, in their houses. Some believe that schools may be retracing these steps—in reverse. Today's factorylike schools may soon be replaced by children learning in their homes. "Cottage schools" may be created as technology brings the teacher, the curriculum, and the library onto our home computer screens. Rather than taking the yellow school bus to a large school building, tomorrow's students might travel to school on the Internet.

Then again, they may not. The dramatic changes predicted for the imminent technological revolution may never happen. In the end, tomorrow's schools may look remarkably similar to schools you attended as a child. The future, if nothing else, is unpredictable.

In this chapter, we will probe some of those possibilities. Whether or not it revolutionizes education, technology is likely to play a role in your classroom. This chapter explores how technology is currently modifying classroom life and how it may impact your teaching.

The Technology Revolution

In the twentieth century, education was forever changed. Human beings serving as teachers, the core of schooling for centuries if not millennia, were made technologically obsolete. The new invention was used at home and then in the more affluent schools. Eventually, all schools were connected. Slowly but surely, the classroom teacher was replaced. These new machines took students where they had never been before, did things no human could do, and shared an unlimited reservoir of information. Clearly, this technological breakthrough had the potential to teach more effectively at a far lower cost than human teachers. Predictions varied from the replacement of all teachers to the replacement of most teachers. Some even predicted the replacement of schools themselves.

Sound familiar? While today's computer revolution has sparked these sorts of predictions, the machine described above is not a computer. These predictions were made in the 1950s about television. The popular perception back then was that educational television would reshape the classroom. If predictions about classroom innovations were exaggerated, predictions about television's impact on America were not. Television has reshaped America's cultural landscape.

Many of today's homes have multiple television sets, tied into satellite dishes, antennae, and cables, pulling hundreds of stations into our lives for an average of six hours a day. Some families turn on television sets in the morning and turn them off in the evening, imitating the waking and sleeping of another family member. Television has reduced our time for sleep, social gatherings, leisure activities, and even conversations with each other. By the time the average student has reached 18 years of age, he or she will have attended eleven thousand hours of school—and watched fifteen thousand hours of television. To ignore the impact of this medium is to ignore a major educational influence on children.

Television is not only a force; it is also a target. Television has been blamed for an array of crises and behavior problems, from a lack of school discipline to student passivity, from a decline in standardized test scores to an increase in family tensions and violence. It is unlikely that television, or any single factor, is responsible for all of society's ills. On the other hand, television does present a bizarre and disturbing view of the world. By the time the average child reaches age 15, he or she will have seen thirteen thousand murders on television, and television violence can influence children. In one study, 9- and 10-year-olds were shown a violent episode of *The Untouchables* (a show about 1920s gangsters). A second group watched a nonviolent sports show. Both groups were then taken into a room with a box that had two buttons labeled "help" and "hurt." The children were told that pressing the "help" button would help a child in another room complete a game. Pushing the "hurt" button would hinder this effort. The children who watched the violent episode of *The Untouchables* pressed the "hurt" button 33 percent more often than the other children. Longitudinal data collected on television viewing and violence since 1960 present overwhelming evidence that higher levels of viewing violence on television correlate with increased aggressive behavior, in both children and adults.[1]

Television, our national storyteller, presents an image that is not only violent but distorted.[2] If television programs are to be believed, we are a nation destined for extinction. Less than 1 percent of television characters have children under 6. This is surprising, because, according to TV plot lines, caring for children is a snap. In almost half of the television families with young children, child care concerns are never

IN THE NEWS . . . JERRY! JERRY! JERRY!

Four sixth-grade girls attacked their teacher in a Brooklyn classroom after she refused to let them watch the *Jerry Springer Show.*

Source: *New York Daily News,* 30 May 1998.

mentioned, yet children are magically cared for anyway. Although two-thirds of the nation's mothers work for pay, only one-third of television's mothers do. America's population is 51 percent female, but not on television, where some calamity has evidently reduced females to less than 40 percent of the population.

Family life is not the only subject suitable for television "make-overs," as ethnicity and race are jumbled as well. In televisionland, Asian Americans are servants, villains, detectives, and karate experts. Native Americans are presented without tribal distinctions and are often characterized as lazy, alcoholic, and humorless. African American criminals are a mainstay of many police and adventure shows, offset by a growing number of African American police officers. Characters in children's after-school programs are overwhelmingly white. It is not surprising, therefore, that research indicates that television viewers have a garbled world view, overestimating the percentage of the world population that is white and wealthy and underestimating the number of Americans living in poverty.

A distorted world scene is only part of the cost paid by the television audience; unregulated viewing robs children of both play and study time while teaching some abhorrent attitudes and behaviors. According to studies in the 1990s by the American Psychological Association and by Stanford University, television increases prejudice, obesity, aggressive behavior, and even drinking. For high school students, each hour of daily television watching corresponds to a 9 percent greater risk of alcohol consumption during the following 18 months. If music videos are watched, the drinking risk rises 31 percent.[3]

Children are more susceptible to, less knowledgeable about, and more naive about the techniques and products promoted on television than are adults. Bombarded by twenty thousand TV commercials a year, children often have trouble distinguishing advertisements from the programs themselves.[4] A good part of television's advertising budget is aimed at children to promote the purchase of toys, cereals, candies, and fast food. Critics complain that the cereals, candies, and fast foods targeted at children are of low nutritional value. Others worry that consumerism is running amuck as children learn to want more and, later as adults, purchase more than they need.

Some believe that the case against television may be both too convenient and overstated. Researchers Daniel Anderson and Patricia Collins found that television's impact depends greatly on who is watching and their general viewing habits, and that many of the bad practices and negative behaviors promoted by television can be prevented by attentive adults.[5] According to the American Psychological Association, when teachers and parents regulate television viewing, children improve their vocabulary, cognitive, and social skills.[6]

IN THE NEWS . . . MR. ROGERS' 'HOOD

The longest running children's program on public television is Mister Rogers' Neighborhood, but pleasant Mr. Rogers is not happy.. He is suing a Texas-based chain of novelty stores for selling t-shirts that display him with his sweater, smile, and a silver handgun.

It's bad for the kids, said Rogers' attorney, who is asking the court to have the t-shirts destroyed.

Source: *Washington Post,* 29 December, 1998.

At its best, television can promote constructive values and teach useful skills and information. The Children's Television Workshop (CTW), for example, produces such programs as *Sesame Street* and *The Electric Company.* To capture children's attention and promote early learning skills, **educational television programming** uses brief, engaging episodes, a lesson learned from commercials. Research indicates that viewing *Sesame Street* increases children's verbal IQ test scores, creates more positive attitudes toward school, and promotes better performance in the first grade.[7] Children who watch *The Electric Company* improve reading test scores. *Mister Rogers' Neighborhood* viewers have greater persistence and more positive interpersonal relationships. While not everyone is a fan of these shows, research suggests that well-crafted television programs can result in greater educational achievement.

Television is now a part of school life as well. The new cable television stations, including A&E, C-Span, CNN, The History Channel, Bravo, The Learning Channel, and The Discovery Channel, join noncable Public Broadcasting to bring high-quality movies and plays, exciting biographies, historical re-enactments, and breaking news stories directly into the curriculum. Monthly television guides written specifically for teachers alert them to upcoming programs of special educational interest. The growing number of videotapes and videodiscs offers teachers a library of rich television resources. Advocates point out that television can be a valuable learning resource, a real asset to classroom instruction. Critics charge that watching television is an unproductive use of class time, an activity that at best should be used as an instructional supplement, to be viewed at home or in the school's media resource room.

Channel One takes the controversy over television in schools to another level. *Channel One* is piped into more than 12,000 high schools and junior high schools across the nation by Whittle Communications. Participating schools receive several tangible benefits: programming, television monitors, and a satellite dish are provided at no charge. When all are in place, students get to watch ten minutes of news each day. And the cost? The children must also watch two minutes of commercials with each newscast. Studies suggest that students who watch *Channel One* do slightly better on a current events test than do their nonviewing counterparts. Critics charge that such minimal benefit does not warrant taking away school time to sell things to kids. However, many students and teachers in *Channel One* schools report that they are satisfied with the program.[8]

Television is a persuasive and powerful medium, one that can be used to promote education or aggression, understanding or intolerance, community improvement or unhealthy products. As cable and satellite programming increases, so does television's capability to offer more programs to more people in more areas of the world than ever before.

The satellites and cables that have made television a global phenomenon have also provided the information highway for computers to travel. Like television half a century earlier, computers are today's technological wonder predicted to change schools forever. Television and computers are not unique in this regard. Consider the following soothsayers:

"The motion picture is destined to revolutionize our educational system, and . . . in a few years it will supplant largely, if not entirely, the use of textbooks."

Thomas Edison

"The time may come when a portable radio receiver will be as common in the classroom as is a blackboard."

William Levenson, director of Cleveland Public School's radio station

"With the help of teaching machines and programmed instruction, students can learn twice as much in the same time and with the same effort as in a standard classroom."

B.F. Skinner[9]

Computer technology is only the most recent milestone along a path that has witnessed many innovations, including the chalkboard. With the introduction of the chalkboard, teachers wondered, Could they learn to use this new chalk technology efficiently and how would this fresh innovation affect the curriculum? As is common with novel technologies, chalkboards first collected dust as they went unused in classrooms. Over time, instruction manuals and teacher training programs gave teachers the practical advice and confidence to move the chalkboard to center stage in the

Technological breakthroughs in satellite communications and increasing international trade suggest that global education will become a reality in the years ahead.

teaching-learning process. Similar histories surround duplicating machines, the overhead projector, videotapes, television, and foreign language labs. Technological change includes even the modest highlighter that you use to underline the scintillating sentences and important information in this text. But highlighters get little attention, while computers are all the rage.

It is helpful to remember that chalkboards, highlighters, and silicon chips are all part of ongoing technological change. Given the number of technological advances, it is reasonable to ask why today's schools look so remarkably similar to the schools of a century ago. Why has technology had such a modest impact on education? Will computers be the technological "breakthrough," the magic bullet that finally revolutionizes education? The next sections, while skillfully sidestepping this question, attempt to capture some of the excitement, controversy, and captivating applications surrounding computers in the classroom.

Wiring Up Schools, Charging Up Teachers

The arrival of computer technology offers a poignant reminder of how the classroom has isolated America's teachers. Before schools could join the computer revolution and be connected to the Internet, they needed to have what virtually every American home and business had for almost a century: phone lines. In short, while teachers had waited in vain for decades for phones to be installed in their classrooms, computers moved to the front of the line.

Bringing schools into the computer age has been expensive. Wiring schools has proved to be just one of many major costs: hardware and software purchases were at the center of school budget debates for most of the 1990s. This costly venture has been relatively successful. Although very few schools were "online" during the 1980s, according to the National Center for Education Statistics (NCES), approximately eight out of ten schools (although only a minority of classrooms) had connected to the Internet by the late 1990s. To alleviate the sizable costs required to bring computer technology to students, Congress passed the Telecommunications Reform Act (1996), establishing a discounted school cost, or **E-Rate** (education rate), for using the Internet. (See Figures 14.1 and 14.2.)

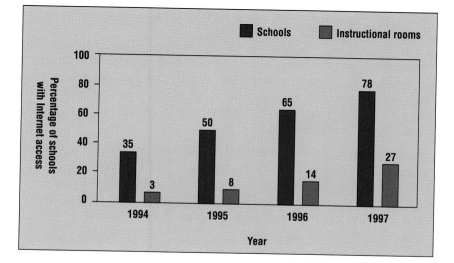

FIGURE 14.1

Wiring schools. The percentage of public schools and classrooms with access to the Internet has been rising quickly, according to surveys of a nationally representative sample of schools between 1994 and 1997.

Source: National Center for Education Statistics, U.S. Department of Education

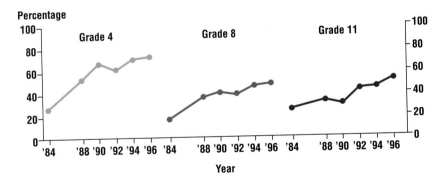

FIGURE 14.2

Percentage of students who reported using a computer at school at least once a week, by grade.

Source: NCES Condition of Education 1998

While wiring schools has been a monumental challenge, plugging in teachers has been no less daunting. While educational technology advocates encourage teachers to move from the "sage on the stage" to the "guide on the side," teachers have been slow to apply for cyber-citizenship. In fact, the reasons for investing time and energy in acquiring computer skills are not always persuasive.[10] Teachers can teach effectively, even inspirationally, without computers. Embarking on a computer journey compels teachers to acquire new classroom strategies and lessons. Years of experience developing valuable classroom methods and lessons may be lost or minimized. Computer equipment itself can create problems. Exciting lessons can be short-circuited when there are too few computers, or if they are not working. For teachers to learn computer skills requires literally hundreds of hours of training, yet tangible rewards for this investment of time and energy seem elusive. (Salary increases, for example, rarely follow technological mastery.) The irony of all this is that many students arrive at school knowing far more than their teachers. It is not surprising, therefore, that so many teachers decide to avoid technology, especially if they suffer from "technophobia."

Technophobia is the anxiety that renders all mechanical things foreign, alien, and frightening. Even answering machines and VCRs can cause technophobes concern and dismay, so imagine how intimidating computers can be. A survey done in the mid-1990s revealed that 55 percent of Americans indicated a fear of computers and a sign of technophobia; those reporting the highest levels of anxiety were over 45, an age group termed "digitally homeless, and needy."[11] Of the more than 100 million Americans who use computers at home, school, or work, 60 percent are 17 or younger.[12] This technologically induced age gap represents a divisive cultural wedge for educators and students.[13]

While some teachers work to overcome technophobia, others are technological pathfinders, taking to the new technology with skill and excitement. Still others adapt slowly, but they do eventually adapt. The different attitudes and skills that teachers bring to using computers can make schoolwide implementation of new technology a challenge. Let's see how these concerns emerge in a fictitious faculty meeting, as principal Whyerd greets his staff:

PRINCIPAL WHYERD: Welcome back, although maybe welcome forward would be a better greeting. It's our first time to be together as the faculty of Bill Gates Middle School. With the new name and our new building, we have really opened up the latest window [he waits for a little laughter] on technology in education. We have finished the computer lab; in every classroom, we have

IN THE NEWS . . . IS BARBIE SAFE?

Barbie's 1.5 billion dollar yearly sales are formidable, but her supremacy is being challenged by new software toys that are capturing an increasing share of the toy market. Lego Mindstorm, for example, allows children to build Lego structures by programming commands into a hand-held electronic nerve center. Although the directions indicate that it is intended for youngsters 12 and older, children half that age buy and enjoy it. Even very young children are bringing increasingly sophisticated technological skills to school.

Source: *Washington Post,* 15 December, 1998.

three online computers, video monitors, and telephone hookups, and we've hired a full-time technology resource instructor. Have you all met Pat Blizzard? Pat [Pat stands confidently], I suspect your college nickname, "Wizard," will be the one that sticks around here. Okay? We also got the grant for the video production lab with computer hookups for editing and enhancement, so the project based learning activities at the core of the social science program should really take off. Let's see . . . our Tech Task Force, eleven of you, from six departments, took advantage of the T3 (that's Teacher Tech Training) at the university. Anyone want to give us some quick feedback about those five days? Rafaela?

[As many eyes move to Rafaela Nueva, a few minds wander elsewhere]

MR. STONEWALL: [with a slight of eye roll] *Here we go again. If it's not one fad, it's another. I've been at this for years, and I can't fit one more thing on my plate. I don't have a computer at home, and I don't see why having one here is supposed to matter to me. Sure, if the kids want to use it, in their free time, to type—excuse me!—word process their papers, that's fine. But I am not about to waste another series of Saturdays on workshops that have nothing to do with my teaching style, my courses, and my students. My kids aren't sure which is bigger, our sun or our moon, but I suppose playing computer games will be more fun than learning.*

MS. HOPALONG: *Okay, okay, I've got it. We have all this new equipment and the kids probably know how to use it better than I do. At home my own kids taught me to do overheads for lessons and, now, if I don't get a handle on this Internet stuff, my students will be using the web for who knows what. My daughters just laughed when I asked, "Where exactly is the web?" (But I recognize that laugh. I'm not really sure they know.) When they hooked me into that chat room of teachers last night, it was weird but kind of fun. People were talking about tricks to learn students' names at the beginning of school. I got two good ideas that I'll try next week. Glad I learned how to type as a teenager. At least I could keep up with the conversation. Is that what they call it . . . conversation?*

MS. READDI: *This is so amazing. I'm student teaching and I'm totally nervous about the job. But these people are totally nervous about computers! The tech part is so easy! Even my college had what they've just purchased around here. I'll never forget my science methods course. We tested water samples from schools all over the country through a web site. Most of my profs were using PowerPoint presentations when I started as an undergrad. Our dorm rooms were online . . . we used to see how much of a paper we could write without going to the library. Taking that Ed Tech course junior year may have been my best move. The faculty here see me as a resource. My early graduation present, the laptop, is downloading class lists as I sit here. That reminds me, I owe Steve, Anna, and Carlos an e-mail.*

YOU'VE GOT MAIL

```
To: Steve@AU.edu, Anna@State.edu, Carlos@medtech.com
SUBJ: They appreciate me!
```

```
Here I am, a student teacher, and already I am getting
recognition—and a job. I have been invited to join the
school's technology committee. We have a budget, and we
are supposed to uppgrade hardware and select software
for the entire school.

I know what you are thinking, Anna (you being the big
computer geek). "Why is she an expert?" Well, at
college I am definitely not an expert. And, around you,
it is all I can do to avoid falling into a cyberspace
black hole, but, here, at this school, I am an expert.
They say the newest, youngest staff member usually
knows the most. That's me. Part-time, not licensed,
not even a graduate, but I am a local tech-expert.
Go figure!
```

MR. APPLETOSS: *So, this school's finally moving into the next century and it's a good thing. The kids have been ready for years. These kids need computer skills if they want to land almost any job. They're motivated, especially some of the at-risk students. I actually think they can learn more and learn better with some of these tools. Funny how so many of the teachers are spooked by computers. I've always liked technology. Being an AV guy gave me a step up. From the stage crew in elementary school to the "AV Squad" in middle school, I have always been at home with machines. For the past eight years, teachers have come to me to solve their computer problems. Heck, I had my first computer when they were called by names, not numbers . . . Taking that computer animation class this summer will be a real boost when I teach Advanced Production Arts in the spring. I'm glad I stayed. This could be a great year.*

MRS. GUDBRAKE: *I suspect it's going to be the same old, same old . . . but my kids lose, because they are the Title I pull-out crowd. Our rich kids, especially the boys, already have better equipment at home than we had in the "new" tech lab. They're using it for written reports, term papers, even college applications. They've got access, opportunity, skills, equipment, summer computer camps, and the computer club. Too many of my Title I students have never touched a mouse, except when they try to corner one at home. [Meanwhile, Ms. Nueva wraps up her remarks.]*

MRS. NUEVA: . . . tools for education, chalkboard, pencils and texts for everyone, calculators, and now computers touch different learners in different ways. Technology will be with our students long after they have left our classes. We really believe that how we incorporate computers into our curriculum could make this a wonderful year.

The Apple Classrooms of Tomorrow (ACOT) project yielded insight into the stages teachers go through when dealing with technology in their classrooms. Initially, most of the teachers who participated in the project experienced uncertainty and frustration. But, with support and training, they became more comfortable and incorporated computers into their classroom routines, using them as tools to support traditional methods of instruction. The key turning point came when the teachers were able to feel mastery over the technology and began to change instruction to suit the possibilities of the computers. One teacher, impressed by the potential of desktop publishing, simulated a newspaper company in her class. The students worked in groups, each with their own task, writing articles, producing artwork, laying out business graphs, and editing. Learning became more interactive as the teachers and students felt empowered to use technology together.

The final stage described was invention. At this phase, teachers began to revamp all their classroom practices. A teacher explained, "As you work into using the computer in the classroom, you start questioning everything you have done in the past and wonder how you can adapt it to the computer. Then, you start questioning the whole concept of what you originally did." Computer technology, according to these teachers, can be the gateway to a whole new process of learning and teaching.[14]

Computers in the Classroom

How can teachers use computers in the classroom? Computer applications have ranged from the mundane, such as the drill and practice of basic academic skills and assistance of teachers with administrative tasks, to the more exciting representation of real-world phenomena, online visits to events and places, the simulation of laboratory work, and the facilitation of student collaboration.[15] Educators continue to explore innovative computer applications. In some classrooms, personal computer tutors meet the unique learning needs of individual students. Voice-activated computers provide foreign language instruction, complemented by e-mails written to overseas penpals in their language. Some teachers have created the Hypertext Folklife Curriculum, where students research and record their various cultural backgrounds.[16] In other schools, teachers have organized information into databases, giving their students the equivalent of an electronic encyclopedia at their fingertips. Science classes have simulated dissections or other experiments too dangerous or difficult for a high school lab.[17] New applications seem to emerge on a daily basis.

Computer technology has a two-stage history. At first, computers (typically, Apple models) arrived in schools, and students and teachers experimented with educational software programs. A few years later, the Internet arrived, representing the second stage, extending the reach and power of computers. Teachers and students exploring Internet education have been termed **Internauts**, trailblazers on this new educational frontier.[18] Internauts tap into data sources far beyond the limits of their local libraries, and communication among students and teachers over great distances has been made commonplace. Discussion groups and e-mail are replacing schoolyard conversations and physical bulletin boards. The Internet not only redefines distance, but it also creates a different learning dynamic. Large-group interactions in class are

A COMPUTER PRIMER IN THE CLASSROOM

Teaching and the Internet

Ready or not, the Internet will probably be a part of your classroom. As school systems invest in the hardware and software required to join the global network, teachers wonder if the Internet will be as earthshaking as the media and political hype seem to indicate. Current trends suggest that the Internet will, indeed, have a significant impact on your life as a teacher. If you are new to the Internet or have never thought about its classroom applications, here is a primer you should find useful.

What Is the Internet?

The **Internet** is the name given to the network of computers all over the world that are linked not only to each other but to a massive amount of information on an endless array of topics contained on many of those computers. There are two types of computers on the Internet, servers and clients. A server computer "serves up" the information, which can come from a variety of sources, including libraries, museums, universities, and commercial businesses. A client computer is the "window" on this information. Client computers connect to the Internet and download the information from the server computers.

What Will I Need to Get Connected?

For teachers, the key is learning how to access, view, and use this information, to broaden the classroom to include the resources provided by museums, libraries, news sources, and media outlets. The easiest way to access the Internet is through the **World Wide Web** (WWW). In order to see the web, your computer needs an Internet connection, such as a modem, and web browser software. Browser software tells the computer how to find and display WWW pages. Web browser software is often provided free of charge, but net access is rarely free. If your school does not provide you with a connection, you can get your own account on a commercial Internet service or Internet service provider (ISP). Services usually charge by the hour for the amount of time users are connected. (Some states sponsor Internet access for teachers—check with your education program for information.) If you connect via a modem, adequate phone line support may be a problem, especially in older buildings. Sometimes businesses, universities, and service organizations help schools finance such connections. If you can't afford a high-speed connection that supports graphics, sound, and other more exotic features, you can still use many of the most powerful tools available on the web. One of the most common is e-mail.

E-mail

One of the first Internet features was electronic mail (e-mail for short). As the name suggests, **e-mail** is similar to traditional mail service (haughtily called "snail mail" by Internet users) but usually takes just seconds or minutes to be delivered. One of the most significant advantages of e-mail (and many other Internet tools) is that it is basically free. If you use a telephone and modem to connect to the Internet, you pay only the charge for a local telephone call that connects you to the Internet computer, even if you send a message across the country—or to the other side of the world. Once the message is sent, it travels free of charge. Another benefit is that, unlike your postal address, which is tied to a fixed location, on the Internet your address "follows you." No matter where you are in the world, as long as you can find a client computer and access the Internet, you can receive or send mail. How does this marvel work?

Like the traditional post office, e-mail is sent directly to a name and an address. But, unlike letters that are all delivered by the U.S. Postal Service, the Internet boasts many postal options, called servers. Servers can pick up and deliver e-mail, so one person can send and receive e-mail from many server addresses. One user composes a message on the terminal and hits a key, and the message is electronically delivered to a server computer a few feet, or a few thousand miles, away. You can send copies of your e-mail to many people, forward other mail, or edit documents sent via e-mail (the options continue to grow), all at the stroke of a key.

If you have an e-mail account, you also have an Internet address made up of two parts, a userid (pronounced "user-I-D") and a domain name. Your userid is the part of your address that is specific to you (think of it as the name and street address on a standard envelope). Many people construct an e-mail address by using all or part of their name and a predetermined, abbreviated reference to the sponsoring organization, if there is one. Your domain name indicates what part of the Internet your account is located in (think of it as the city and state lines of your snail mail address). Your userid and your domain name together, separated by an "@" sign, are your Internet address. For example, if the user Horace Mann has an e-mail account at Fictional University, his e-mail address might be "hmann@fictional.edu." The last three letters alert you to whether you are corresponding with an educational institution (edu), a commercial organization (com), a government body (gov), or an organization (org).

(Box continues on next page)

The World Wide Web

Whenever you see an address that starts with "www" or "http://" (they often appear on television or radio) you are seeing a location on the World Wide Web.

Perhaps the most educationally exciting use for the WWW is the opportunity it affords students to connect with other users around the world. Although the technology that makes homepages visible around the world is very complex, the programming language web authors use is relatively simple. Students can easily write their own homepages that connect the outside world with their classrooms. Examples of such projects include

- Students can create surveys that Internet users answer. Responses could come from users throughout the world, through a hyperlink connected to a class e-mail address.
- Students can collaborate with a class in another part of the country, or the world, to trade information about their lives, customs, and culture in a social studies project.
- An ESL class might create a homepage celebrating each of their respective cultures, including links to homepages in their own countries.
- A reading and writing class could build a creative writing homepage filled with student work. With the collaboration of another classroom linked to the web, students could run a virtual creative writing workshop.
- Math students and teachers could create a math-phobia homepage, featuring step-by-step approaches to solving problems for and by students, while reducing math anxiety.
- Foreign language students can converse with native speakers on other continents by e-mail or by using advanced Internet tools that allow for the transmission of video and sound through the computers. Conversely, your class can help others touch up on their English.
- Students can participate in an online science fair, presenting science projects using text and graphics.
- Electronic student publications—school yearbooks, newspapers, and literary magazines—can be made accessible to the rest of the world.
- Students interested in science can browse the pictures uploaded by NASA, along with resources from almost every major science or health organization.
- Students applying to colleges can browse the homepages set up by various colleges and universities.

You may have noticed from this list that many of these projects sound very much like projects you might already be doing or planning to do in your classroom without computers.

But, unlike the typical projects, the global scope of the network is what really sets it apart. The Internet is creating classrooms without walls and even without national boundaries.

Internet Sites for Educators

Are you looking for intriguing Internet addresses for use in schools? Everything from dissecting a frog to the latest professional articles can be found on this textbook's webpage at www.mhhe.com/sadker. World Wide Web information is presented on "homepages." These pages range from the Internal Revenue Service's page giving tips on how to fill out your tax return, to pages that contain albums of popular music, to files containing classic literature or paintings, to information on how to join some bizarre extremist groups. Many universities have homepages that feature course offerings, professor profiles, scholarly information, school calendars or access to libraries, documents, and other university resources. Everything from literary classics to pictures taken by NASA spacecraft are available. While the WWW contains a huge volume of information, there is no guarantee that all of it will be useful, or even accurate, or that educators will want to make it all available to students. The WWW makes critical reading and understanding of author motives more vital than ever.

To weave your way through the web, a useful place to start is with a webpage that includes a subject list—a set of topics from which users choose their area of interest. As you might expect, subject lists are found at webpages sponsored by libraries (Library of Congress), professional associations (National Council for the Social Studies), and news organizations (CNN). As the user chooses new categories of information, the lists become more and more detailed. A user seeking the web site of a particular school might choose "Education" from a list of general topics, then choose "K–12" from a list of topics within education, and finally choose the desired page from a list of school districts. Due to the hierarchical nature of subject lists, users may have to navigate through many levels of subdirectories before finding the desired topic.

Another popular information-finding tool is an Internet search. A special homepage, known as a "search engine," allows the user to type in "key words." Key words are the words the user hopes to find in a homepage. The words are sent to a computer that contains a database of most homepages available on the web. Search engines (e.g., Lycos, Hotbot) operate in different ways. Some search for the words in the title of a webpage, while others seek out special tags (called "meta tags"). Different approaches net different results. When the computer finds a homepage containing the words,

(Box concludes on next page)

it sends a message to the user, listing homepages of interest (and providing a link to those pages). Sometimes search engines report how well the query matches the finding (e.g., 92 percent), but matches are not always as on target as these percentages suggest. It is important to be as specific as possible with this type of searching. Otherwise, a teacher looking for lesson plans for a reading unit might get a list containing the homepage of the Reading, Pennsylvania, Chamber of Commerce. This is a good time to remind you that search engines are fueled by dollars. They sell advertising space to commercial interests in order to earn their profits. Do not be surprises to see advertising "banners" on your screen as you search.

Explore and enjoy!

Note: The section on teaching and the Internet was written by Paul Degnan, an MAT graduate, and was updated by Professor Sarah Irvine-Belson, a faculty member, both of the School of Education at American University.

Typically, computers have been used for drill and practice, simple programming, and educational games.

replaced by smaller electronic meetings. For shy or quiet students, whose learning style may be submerged and lost in large classroom discussions, the Internet offers a more personal, even intimate, way to learn. The same is true of students whose disabilities are invisible over the Internet.

By eliminating national barriers and geographic distance, the Internet is creating a "global village," although it is a village with an entrance fee, populated by people of means. If you were to design a curriculum for the international power of the Internet, what issues, concepts, and skills would you include? Perhaps you might teach conflict-resolution strategies, to avoid a cataclysmic nuclear war. Problem-solving strategies could be useful in tackling ecological issues, such as global warming, deforestation, and toxic waste disposal. Maybe your curriculum would promote cross-cultural knowledge and communication skills to increase tolerance and understanding of the cultural, ethnic, religious, and racial groups that share our planet. Educators investigating a world-based curriculum call their work **global education.**[19]

Author William Kniep suggests four domains for global inquiry:

1. *Human values.* The universal values shared by humanity, as well as the diverse values of various groups
2. *Global systems.* Emphasis on global systems and an interdependent world, including economy, ecology, politics, and technology
3. *Global issues and problems.* Worldwide concerns and challenges, including peace and security, environmental issues, and human rights
4. *Global history.* Including the evolution of universal and diverse human values, the history of global systems, and the roots of global problems.[20]

Schools around the country combine technology and global education. In Massachusetts, middle school students completed a unit on environmental science through a live teleconference with students from Karlsruhe, Germany. Computer and telecommunications technology enabled students from both countries to communicate with and learn from each other throughout the year and encouraged cross-cultural communication of all kinds.[21] In another Massachusetts school, in Foxboro, students reached out to their peers in Kindersley, Saskatchewan, and learned through direct computer discussion about the realities of life in that Canadian province.[22]

Global educators, like technology advocates, emphasize the need to "educate children for the world they are entering rather than the world they are leaving behind."[23] Following are some examples of educational technology, often with a global component, preparing students for tomorrow's world, and even redefining that world.

Virtual field trips. The National Zoo in Washington, DC, holds weekly virtual field trips for students all over the world. On Thursday afternoons, the zookeepers give a 15-minute presentation on African and Asian elephants, and students can pose questions via a "chat interface." This web camera (or web-cam, for short) allows anyone with access to the Internet to view people, places, and events live. In this case, the elephant cam is always on, and students anywhere in the world can see the elephant eat, sleep, bathe, and do all sort of elephant things. Students and even whole classrooms can join virtual expeditions and learn about continents and cultures by "traveling" across Africa, South America, the Eastern Mediterranean, and the United States, in a project called Globalearn. Similar virtual field trips take students to aquariums (Cabrillo High School Aquarium Cam) and to NASA's Shuttle Site to see live footage of the shuttle and space stations.

Distance learning. The old correspondence courses, dependent on the post office, and television shows that carried college credits (and were broadcast so early that they were known as the "Sunrise Semester") are early examples of distance learning, learning that takes place despite the physical separation of a teacher and a student. Historically, rural areas have depended on distance learning to meet their educational needs, but distance learning is also popular among home schooling families, those working unusual or unpredictable hours, commuters who would rather travel the Internet than the interstate, and individuals who simply like learning on their own time and in their own place. A "distance healing project" (funded by the George Lucas Foundation) enables hospitalized children around the world to interact with each other. In this project, critically and chronically ill children use video conferencing equipment (computers, cameras, and a connection to the Internet) to see and talk to each other. These personal connections offer a valuable tool in the treatment of everything from loneliness to cancer, enabling young patients to reduce some of their fears and frustrations.

Simulations. Simulations create an environment that replicates a real situation (e.g., an election, a cross-cultural meeting, a historical event) in order to gain a more realistic appreciation of the situation. Simulations were used by teachers before computers, but computers add a new level of realism and excitement. For example, Lego Mindstorms® is a software program that enables a student to use simple to advanced programming commands to create an interactive robotic structure, such as a car.

Laptops. The use of laptop computers in classrooms is a popular option, one that enables students to take computers home and create a second learning environment for themselves and their families. In several school districts, students and their parents have been given laptops and have attended training programs on their use. The goal of such efforts is to ensure parental support for the new technology, but some children complain that there is too much support. Parents are competing with their children to use the laptop in order to fill out applications, help them in their work, and explore the

Internet. The hope is that this parental interest will extend to attaining a General Equivalency Degree over the Internet, since many of the parents involved never completed high school.[24]

Integrated learning systems (ILS). ILS is educational software that enables students to improve their academic skills independently. For example, students at Metrotech High School in Phoenix, Arizona, go to class to prepare for careers in areas as disparate as auto mechanics and television production, but they use ILS outside of class to refine their math and reading skills. The software allows students to log onto the computer to have their levels of academic proficiency diagnosed and then offers an individually prescribed program designed to improve students' academic skills, all outside of class time.

Student authoring. Some teachers are building on students' technological strengths, encouraging them to demonstrate their skills by developing their own videos, stories, software, PowerPoint presentations, and games for school projects and portfolios. Student authoring can also become an important skill beyond the classroom. Plugged-In Enterprises (PIE) in east Palo Alto, California, is a center where people can walk in and use the computers for free. PIE is also a training hub where high school students with computer talent can refine their skills. Students become part of webpage design teams, working on projects as diverse as sports, ecology, and special events. Student authoring is a regular part of learning and earning at Plugged-In Enterprises.

Artificial intelligence. Artificial intelligence is an attempt to emulate the decision-making capabilities of the human mind. One such program, called Intelligent Essay Assessor, is a software package designed to grade students' essays.[25] Artificial intelligence remains one of the most controversial areas of computer technology.

Technology in special education. Federal legislation passed in the 1990s, including the Individuals with Disabilities Education Act (IDEA) and the Americans with Disabilities Act (ADA), encouraged the development and use of technology for students and educators with disabilities. Devices designed especially to help those with disabilities are called **assistive** or **adaptive technology.** Assistive technologies include wheelchairs, switches that respond to voice commands, and computer programs that read material for blind students. Students with visual motor problems, some students with learning disabilities, and students with difficulty controlling their arms can use voice-activated software to talk to the computer. Youngsters who find the traditional keyboard difficult use specialized touch screens to direct the computer's actions. Those with learning disabilities report that computers are useful for taking notes in class (especially when their handwriting is nearly illegible), and they benefit enormously from such tools as Spellcheck. These students are even able to organize their daily schedule with the help of a computer appointments book and an accompanying beeper. The list of adaptive technology devices promises to grow in the years ahead.[26]

Online curriculum. Today schools need to wait years for new scientific breakthroughs and other advances to slowly make their way into textbooks. The knowledge explosion has made traditional textbooks continually

WHY USE THE INTERNET?

Educator Cynthia S. Mutryn, of Maryland Public Television, offers several important functions of the Internet in the classroom:

- To enable students to work at their own pace
- To encourage quick access to information, research persistence, and academic engagement
- To explore nontraditional research sources
- To enhance communication skills and critical and analytical thinking

- To encourage team collaboration and improve socialization skills
- To investigate global issues
- To reach students with a variety of learning styles
- To enable teachers to research, communicate, and share ideas, resources, and information with, to collaborate with, to network with, and to support colleagues, parents, and curriculum area experts.

Source: Adapted from Cynthia S. Mutryn, Manager, Technology Professional Development Projects Maryland Public Television, Owings Mills, MD.

IN THE NEWS . . . COMPUTER TALES

Galena, Alaska has experienced a school population jump from 60 students to almost 2,000, even though no new families have moved to town. In the mid 1990s Galena was wired for a direct satellite uplink to the Internet, becoming a major stop on Alaska's information highway. Isolated families unable to reach a school building are home schooling through the Galena link. The school district also flies computers to families that have none, powering them up by local generators. An on-line Native American curriculum reflects the history and role of the state's native population. And historically isolated groups are now talking to each other through e-mail and chat rooms. Little Galena has moved from the state's 180th largest school district to 8th largest.

Campus News. What are the most wired colleges, the campuses where students enjoy the greatest access to computers, the Internet, and other technological advances? Perhaps not the ones you think. According to *Yahoo* magazine, the nation's ten most wired campuses are Dartmouth College, New Jersey Institute of Technology, Rensselaer Polytechnic, Carnegie Mellon, California Institute of Technology, Indiana University, University of Oregon, and Worcester Polytechnic Institute.

Source: *CyberTimes, New York Times on the Web,* 5 September 1997; *Yahoo Internet Life,* May 1998.

out-of-date. The Internet can help a school keep its curriculum current by providing almost instantaneous updates, electronic supplements to the printed curriculum. Because the publication process for textbooks and other print materials is so time-consuming, some believe that the Internet may eventually replace textbooks entirely.

The rate of technological innovation is so fast that, even as today's applications are being disseminated, newer ones are being tested. Will the next generation of computers continue the trend toward less expensive, smaller, yet more powerful machines, yielding pocket computers that outperform today's desktops? Will the next generation of computers converse with us, eliminating the need for keyboard skills and programming? Will we be able to print letters and papers by simply speaking, or will simply thinking our thoughts be enough to create computer commands? Will we still print papers, or will we be able to instruct our computer to transmit information, not only to other computers but also to people's minds? Will the next breakthrough be true artificial intelligence, computers that can counsel us on our professional and personal lives, becoming mechanical mentors? Or are these little more than fanciful illusions, examples of America's overconfidence in all things technological?

The Virtual High School

Picture this: you are a student in a very warm, comfortable, but small high school. You would love to take a course about Native Americans, but your small school does not offer such a course. The course cannot be found at the nearby community college either, and the nearest university is hundreds of miles away. Are you out of options? Not if you can enroll in the Virtual High School, where that course and many others are offered. To enroll, you need not travel hundreds of miles but simply sit down at the nearest computer.

Started in 1997 by the Concord Consortium and the Public Schools in Hudson, Massachusetts, the **Virtual High School (VHS)** is the first large-scale project to create Internet-based courses at the high school level and has grown from thirty participating high schools and several hundred students to scores of schools and thousands of students. As a result, a small town in Colorado can offer a physics course even after the physics teacher has left. In Amman, Jordan, students are able to enroll in a geometry course never before offered at their school. Because the classes are asynchronous (that is, students can join classroom activities at any time of the day or night), students from around the world can take the same course, regardless of time zones. Participating instructors have added more variety and spice to their teaching schedules, since they are now able to teach special topics and unique courses which they were unable to teach in their own high school. While not enough students were available to enroll in these courses in their small, home school, now the world was, if not their oyster, at least their classroom.

How does this Virtual High School work? VHS is basically a barter system, in which participating high schools contribute a teacher's time to develop and deliver one VHS netcourse. In return, the school is allowed to enroll twenty of its students in other netcourses offered by VHS. The courses offered do not compete with the regular offerings at each participating high school but are designed to augment local curricula. Each participating instructor receives training to become a VHS teacher, to learn how to teach on the Internet. Course offerings have included Bioethics Symposium; Earth 2525: A Time Traveler's Guide to Planet Earth; A Model United Nations Simulation Using the Internet; Business in the 21st Century; Folklore and Literature of Myth, Magic and Ritual; and Writing: From Inner Space to Cyberspace.

Some critics worry that the VHS isolates students, since each student works alone. But the students and the teachers report that just the opposite occurs. Courses are more personal and individualized than typical classes. Recounts one new recruit to the Virtual High School, "In just two weeks, I feel like I know my Virtual High School teacher better than I ever knew any of my face-to-face teachers."[27]

Rather than talk *about* VHS, let's take a tour of the school. The first of the following two accounts will take us through a student's day, while the second will allow us to see the school through a teacher's eyes. (If you want to visit and take this tour of the Virtual High School in cyberspace, visit our webpage for the URL.) Let's begin by joining one of the VHS students, Natalie.

Natalie is an eleventh-grader in a midsized suburban high school in California. When Natalie heard about the VHS project and read through the course catalog, she immediately asked her guidance counselor if she could take the philosophy class, "Eastern & Western Thought: A Comparison." Her school offers quite a few core courses, but it doesn't have the resources or enough student interest to offer a specialized course, such as Eastern & Western Thought. Natalie was excited about the idea of learning about the great thinkers of the East and the West, and she looked forward to conducting online research for the class. She also liked the idea of taking a class with students from around the country.

A DAY IN THE LIFE OF A STUDENT: NATALIE'S STORY

8:30 A.M., Computer Lab

Natalie goes to the computer lab during the period that has been set aside for VHS students. The twenty VHS students at her school are enrolled in thirteen different VHS courses this semester. She chats briefly with another student who is taking Eastern & Western Thought and with her friend who is taking Astronomy: Stars and the Cosmos, a class she thinks she might want to take next year. She then opens up an Internet browser, checks the homepage of the VHS web site for recent announcements, and logs into her netcourse with her personal user name and password.

Natalie begins reading the welcome page of her netcourse:

> . . . the only thing we require to be good philosophers is the faculty of wonder . . .
>
> from *Sophie's World* by Jostein Gaarder

On the welcome page of her course, Natalie sees a quote posted recently by her teacher and the words "Good Morning, Natalie!" Her teacher always places friendly messages, sayings, or announcements on the welcome page, and Natalie feels she's getting to know her teacher's personality well, even though they've never met in person. Natalie starts her VHS day by going to the Schedule module of her course and clicking on Week 8: "The Ideas of Gandhi." She reads all the documents posted by her teacher, including the assignment overviews, background information, and instructions and she double-checks the due dates, so she can gauge how to allot her time this week. Most of the assignments are due on a weekly basis, so Natalie and her classmates can work on their own schedules. Natalie's nineteen classmates this semester are physically located in twelve schools in eight states, from Washington to Massachusetts!

"Eastern & Western Thought: A Comparison" Schedule Module

Natalie's teacher has assigned three tasks for the week. First (to do some background research), students go to the

~Mahatma Gandhi~

LIVE SIMPLY THAT OTHERS MAY SIMPLY LIVE

Oct 2, 1869 to Jan 30, 1948

"Nonviolence is the greatest force at the disposal of mankind. It is mightier than the mightiest weapon of destruction devised by the ingenuity of man."

Mohandas K. Gandhi on nonviolence

"Gandhi was inevitable. If humanity is to progress, Gandhi is inescapable. He lived, thought and acted, inspired by the vision of humanity evolving toward a world of peace and harmony. We may ignore Gandhi at our own risk."
- Dr. Martin Luther King Jr.

A Brief History of Mohandas K. Gandhi

"Generations to come will scarce believe that such a one as this ever in flesh and blood walked upon this earth."

- Albert Einstein

Death Before Prayers January 30, 1948

"Gandhi murmured, "Hey, Rama (Oh, God)." A third shot rang out..."

Map of India

Vegetarian Resources

Gandhi's thoughts on diet and resources on vegetarianism

"For a bowl of water give a goodly meal;

For a kindly greeting bow thou down with zeal;

For a simple penny pay thou back with gold;

If thy life be rescued, life do not withhold.

Thus the words and actions of the wise regard;

Every little service tenfold they reward.

But the truly noble know all men as one,

And return with gladness good for evil done.

THE EXPERIMENTS BEGIN

This page designed and maintained in loving memory of Mohandas 'Mahatma' Gandhi who was not born a saint (as is the case in most humans) but grew gradually into the state of a 'realized being' through his study of the human condition. Good luck to us all.

leislie williams, author
leislie@engagedpage.com

please e-mail me if you can contribute anything to this page. Especially any letters he may have written.

Back to the Engaged Buddhist Dharma Page

http://www.engagedpage.com/gandhi.htm

FIGURE 14.3 MediaCenter area of the course to read a biographical sketch of Gandhi created and posted by the teacher. Then they are directed to several web sites to learn more about Gandhi's life and ideas. After completing this background research, the students will collaborate on creating a list of key elements of a nonviolent movement based on the principles of Gandhi. Each student will make at least one addition to the list in the CourseRoom discussion area, and then the students will discuss their combined list in a discussion thread started and moderated by the teacher. Finally, each student is to respond to three hypothetical scenarios posed by their teacher and determine what advice Gandhi might give, based on their readings and research. Students will post their recommendations in the CourseRoom, where they are expected to read and comment on each other's posted work.

For the next forty-five minutes, Natalie researches Gandhi's life on the web and discusses some of her findings with another student at her local high school, who is taking the same VHS course. She types some notes in a CourseRoom work document and makes the document private to herself (and her teacher). She'll use her notes later, when she creates her contribution to the class list of key points. As she does some research, she also adds notes to a list of ideas and web sites she is collecting to use later in deciding on the topic for her final project.

Natalie also takes some time to look at an essay draft she had submitted to her teacher for review last week. Her teacher has reviewed the work and her comments are shown in red. Natalie still has a week to incorporate her teacher's comments, revise her essay, and submit it for a grade.

During the class period, the VHS site coordinator comes and checks in briefly with each student. The site coordinator asks Natalie how she's doing. It has been a little while since Natalie last checked her progress, so she takes a few minutes to go to the Profiles database to look at her private portfolio. The portfolio lists all of the work she has done, along with grades and teacher's comments and a cumulative grade for the course. Natalie prints out a copy of her portfolio for her site coordinator.

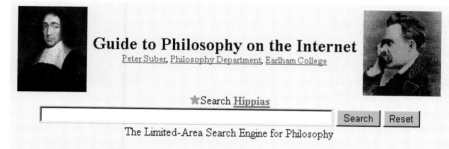

Guide to Philosophy on the Internet
Peter Suber, Philosophy Department, Earlham College

★Search Hippias

[ ] Search | Reset

The Limited-Area Search Engine for Philosophy

The Hippias search engine covers all the sites to which I link in this guide, plus many more, and only sites in philosophy. Unless you want to browse, then, you needn't wait for my entire page to load. Just run a Hippias search now.

Hippias was launched August 10, 1997. Please help spread the word. If you would like to link to Hippias, or include a Hippias search box at your site, see these details.

- This the **single-file edition** of the guide. It is large and loads slowly, but once loaded is easy to browse and search.
- The guide is also available in a multiple-file edition, whose sections load more quickly. Details.

Table of Contents

Guides	Philosophers	Topics	Associations
Journals	Teaching/Learning	Etexts	Bibliographies
Mailing Lists	Newsgroups	Projects	Preprints
Jobs	Dictionaries	Quotations	Miscellany
Hippias	Top	Bottom	About

These links will only work when the corresponding section of the file has loaded, which may take a while.

Welcome to my collection of online philosophy resources.

If you're stuck in a frame, click here to escape.

I've marked recommended sites with a red star ★. Generally the starred sites are those I've found especially helpful for shortening the search for what one wants, as opposed to outstanding sites in themselves for which one ought to search. One day I may rate both.

http://www.earlham.edu/~peters/philinks.htm

FIGURE 14.4

Natalie searches for Gandhi links on the "Guide to Philosophy on the Internet."

Source: Note that these pages and this entire tour is provided by the Virtual High School, and is available through their homepage on the Internet.

2:45 P.M. Study Hall

Natalie has free time during her last period of the day, so she gets a pass to go to the school library. She looks for books on Gandhi in the library and then accesses her VHS course from a computer there. She reads new discussion comments that have come in from other students during the day and posts a comment to an ongoing discussion from Week 6. Looking ahead to next week's assignments, Natalie sees that they will be asked to interview an "expert" on one of the philosophies they are studying in class. Natalie's teacher has posted the e-mail address and web site of a Buddhist believer who is willing to be interviewed but encourages the students to find someone in their local community to interview if they can. Natalie logs off and goes to ask the librarian if he knows anyone she can interview.

9:45 P.M. Home

VHS students are not required or expected to have a computer at home, but Natalie's family does have a computer with an Internet connection. This evening, Natalie uses the family computer to access VHS. She goes to the private Student Lounge and reads the most recent postings on a discussion thread some students have started about a recent movie. She writes a response to another student in Massachusetts, who is working on an article for the VHS newspaper. He's looking for students to interview via e-mail, and Natalie volunteers. The Massachusetts student mentions that there was a blizzard in his town today. Natalie can't believe that he spent the afternoon shoveling, as she sits writing back to him in 70-degree weather!

After she reads a few more messages in the discussion area, Natalie goes to next year's online course catalog, which has just been released. She has an appointment with the guidance counselor in two days, and she definitely wants to take VHS courses again next year. She sorts the catalog by level, and then by discipline; after skimming for a while, Natalie decides that Screenwriting Fundamentals is her first choice. She also thinks two science courses sound interesting: The Bioethics Symposium and Astronomy: Stars and the Cosmos. Her younger brother comes over and looks through the course descriptions with her; he is in eighth grade and is thinking of taking some VHS netcourses next year. She sorts through the catalog again and finds all the courses that are open to ninth-graders. (See Figure 14.5.)

Before shutting down the computer for the night, Natalie goes to the Virtual Cafe and posts a message to a classmate from North Carolina. They recently teamed on a project for

FIGURE 14.5

Natalie links to the
Course Catalog through
the VHS homepage.

Bringing Innovative Education to the World!

Hello Guest!
Announcements for
Wednesday, April 21:

Reminder:
Progress reports up-to-date
and in-danger-of-failing
notices due April 28, 1999.

VHS NetCourse in the
Spotlight
Are you looking for a biology
course not usually available to
H.S. students? Intro to
Ornithology, will introduce
you to the fascinating world of
birding. You'll learn how to
identify birds, compare
reports on local species, &
monitor trends in bird
populations.

Reminder:
Last day to make up 1st term
incompletes is April 21.

Campus Life
Yes, school can be cool! Check
out this fun stuff for Students,
Faculty, and Visitors!

Academics
Go straight to class, browse the
course catalog, or attend a demo
course.

About Us
What is it? Where is it? And
why it's cool to go to Virtual
High School!

Main Office
The office staff is happy to answer
questions, register students, tell
you how to join VHS and more.

Login

If you are a VHS student or faculty member be sure to log in to
take full advantage of the services available to you!

Much of the VHS site is available to all users. Some areas,
including the actual NetCourses are only available to VHS
students and Faculty (take a look at the site map for a quick look
at access levels for the site). If you are not a VHS student or
faculty member and would like to be, visit our Main Office for all
the information and forms that are needed to get you started.

Spotlight on Education:
Teachers looking for good
web sites on curriculum
frameworks and
assessments, including sample
questions and scoring rubrics,
please see
Cynthia Good's work.

This just in...
CD on adaptive technology
for students with disabilities
Details Available

Spotlight on Education:
Crisis in Kosovo: Web
Resources for Classroom
Lessons

This project is made possible in part by the U.S. Department of Education
under grant number R303A60571.

Spotlight on Education:
Check out "the laboratory that
never sleeps! The MAD
Scientist Network is a
collective cranium of scientists
providing answers to your
questions."
http://madsci.wustl.edu/

Hey, have you heard the
Buzz? Check out what VHS
students, teachers, faculty,
and staff are saying about
VHS!

http://vhs.concord.org/home.htm

the course, and now they have become e-mail buddies. She asks if he's read about their "interview an expert" assignment yet and if he has picked an expert. She also posts a message to the other students sharing the URL of an interesting web site she came across today when she was researching Gandhi's life.

A DAY IN THE LIFE OF A TEACHER: ANA'S STORY

Ana teaches in a small, rural school in Massachusetts. She started incorporating Internet research into her classes a couple of years ago but wondered how else she could use the Internet in her instruction. When her school was considering joining VHS, Ana applied to be one of the first VHS teachers. She enrolled in the Concord Consortium's graduate-level Teacher's Learning Conference (TLC), with about thirty other teachers from around the country, and began developing a netcourse, which she has delivered three times, to a total of sixty students in the VHS cooperative.

Part of what Ana loves about VHS is the way it has made her take a fresh look at her instructional methods after fifteen years of teaching. She has found that her evaluation is carrying over into her local classroom as well. She also loves being a "pioneer" and being connected to an intimate network of other teachers around the country.

8:00 A.M. Teachers' Lounge

Before her first local class of the day, Ana uses a free phone line in her school's teachers' lounge to check in on her VHS course. She plugs in her laptop, connects to the phone line, and opens her Internet browser. She logs onto the VHS site, goes to the VHS Faculty Lounge to check for any new announcements, and then accesses her class over the Internet. This semester, Ana has students from eight states and fourteen high schools in her class. She wants to see if any new work assignments or discussion comments have come in from students over the weekend. She loves seeing work come in from her students at all hours of the day, sometimes seven days a week. She assigns all work on a weekly basis, making it possible for all twenty students to contribute equally to the course, despite their varying schedules and time zones. After checking her course, Ana quickly peruses her e-mail to see if anyone has sent her a private message and then logs out to go teach her onsite classes.

2:15 P.M. Teachers' Lounge

Ana has finished her reduced load of onsite courses for the day and now switches gears to focus on her VHS course. Ana sets up her laptop and opens up Lotus Notes, so she can work on her course. Her students can access the class on any computer with an Internet browser, but she needs to use Lotus Notes software to make certain additions and changes to the course. Ana didn't know anything about using this software before she joined VHS, but the TLC professional development netcourse trained her to create and manage her course within Notes' LearningSpace environment.

The first thing she does is "replicate" her course locally; then she disconnects from the phone line. She can now work on her course offline. When she is done making all the necessary changes, she'll "replicate" back. This process allows her to work more quickly and efficiently, and she doesn't have to tie up a phone line.

Creating a New Team Profile in the CourseRoom

Ana fine-tunes next week's assignment, which she will unlock soon for students who want to get an early start. She uses the instructor's tools in the CourseRoom to create student teams. Next week, she will ask the students to pair up and start working on a long-term project. The assignment centers around gathering and comparing regional information, so she purposefully partners students from different states when she creates the new teams. After she creates teams, the students will be able to create work documents that can be accessed and edited only by the two members of each team and the teacher.

Creating a New Discussion Topic in the CourseRoom

Next, Ana creates a new discussion topic to go along with the team assignments. She creates a link from the Schedule document, which describes the assignment right to the new discussion thread where she wants students to post comments. Ana checks the CourseRoom for new discussion comments and work documents from her students. She reads the new student comments and posts some responses to facilitate a deeper group discussion. A few new work assignments have been posted by students, marked "submitted for grading." Ana reviews the documents and resaves them in the CourseRoom. Her students will be able to open their graded work privately to read Ana's edits and comments. After going through the work documents, she enters her comments and grades in the student's online portfolios, located in the Profiles database.

She is impressed with one student's work in particular, and
she sends an e-mail to the VHS staff, nominating the work
for possible inclusion in the VHS showcase. She is worried
about another student, who hasn't posted anything in a
week, so she creates a private message for him in the
CourseRoom and sends an e-mail to him and his site
coordinator, both marked "urgent."

The Portfolio View in the Profiles Database

Ana connects to the Internet again and replicates all her
changes back to the VHS server, so her students will see
them. She packs up her laptop and heads for home.

After dinner, Ana sets up the laptop on her desk at home.
The TLC instructors had asked her and some of the other TLC
graduates to act as mentors for the group of teachers
currently in TLC training. Ana has been assigned as the
"Buddy" to a group of three teachers whose netcourses will
be in a similar content area. The "newbies" in Ana's group
have been posting course outlines and sample assignments
for the netcourses they are developing. They are expected
to comment and offer suggestions on each other's work in
their small groups. The latest TLC assignment was for each
teacher to create a group activity for his or her
netcourse. Ana reads the three group activities created by
her group members, smiling at their creativity. She posts a
response to one of the activities, which she thinks is
especially strong. In the activity, the teacher asks his
students to do a hands-on experiment at home with their
family and then asks them to share their data with all the
students in the class by posting their results in the
CourseRoom. The activity then asks the students to compare
and contrast their findings with the rest of the class. Ana
writes some positive feedback to that assignment and tells
the group that, in her experience, assignments are most
successful when they balance work both on and off the
computer. Ana is having a lot of fun sharing her expertise
and experiences with this new group of teachers. It helps
her feel connected to the project and keeps her from
feeling isolated within her own course. Ana finishes and
then shuts down her computer for the night, the end of
another VHS day.

—LINKS: Interested in teaching a
course in VHS? You can read
"Information for Prospective VHS
Teachers" and the "VHS teacher
and course application" in the
"Want to Join?" section of the
Main Office. Check our webpage
for the address of the Virtual
High School.

Technology and Equity

While technology has many cheerleaders, not everyone gets to be a
player. Wealth, race, and class influence computer access, both at school
and at home.[28] While the vast majority of school districts across the country
have computers and are connected to the Internet, enormous differences persist.
Internet-connected, modern computers are far more plentiful in wealthy school

districts serving white students.[29] In the late 1990s, 84 percent of wealthier suburban schools enjoyed Internet access, while only 63 percent of schools with a high percentage of poor students were connected.[30] As wealth and poverty become more extreme, so do the differences. White children are three times more likely to have computers at home than are black or Hispanic children, and they are three times as likely to have those computers connected to the Internet. This early computer gap contributes to a later economic gap. African American men between the ages of 19 and 54 are the largest group not using computers. Their salaries average between $11,000 and $20,000. College-educated Asian American males represent the other end of the spectrum, the group most likely to use computers. Their salaries average about $75,000 a year.[31] (See Figure 14.6)

While race, class, and wealth create one technology gap, gender creates another. In the early years, girls are as interested in computers as boys are, but, as they grow older, girls develop technology alienation. Video games and software help fan the flames of female disaffection, since they are computer games marketed for stereotypical male interests, such as athletics and combat. (Particularly offensive software targets female characters for scorn, abuse, and even violence.) Schools contribute to sex-typing technology by placing computer courses in the math department. As one writer put it, "Women are not free to roam around computer-land. This field has a math and science image."[32] The maleness of technology is reinforced in literature, replete with the recurrent theme that technology was developed by men to serve their purposes. It is not surprising that female enrollment in technology courses drops as they progress through school. By the upper elementary school, as females' sex roles and sex identification strengthen, computer usage declines. Boys flock to video arcades, computer summer camps, high school technology electives, and after-school computer clubs. Males constitute over 80 percent of high school students taking advanced placement tests in computer science and a similar proportion of computer science majors at college. Female enrollment is higher than male enrollment only in clerical and data entry classes, reminders of the secretarial careers of the past.[33]

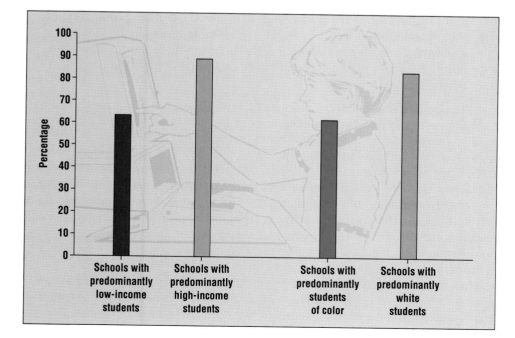

FIGURE 14.6

Percentage of public schools with Internet access by race and income level.

Source: National Center for Education Statistics. (1998). Internet Access in Public Schools. Washington, DC: U.S. Department of Education.

IN THE NEWS . . . CYBERGIRLS

Parkside Junior High School in Manchester, New Hampshire, offers an *Alternative Technology* course that is officially open to all, but attracts only girls. The course explores issues like eating disorders and career exploration, but investigates these topics through computers. With only girls in attendance, inhibitions are reduced. Learning together also eliminates that geek stereotype—the idea that if you are interested in computer science, you must not have a social life. The course is credited with an increase in female enrollments in computer science courses and an increase in the number of girls taking the computer science advanced placement exam.

Source: *Teachers Magazine on the Web,* March 1998.

It is little wonder that males enjoy greater access to and comfort with this new technology.

Is Computer Technology Worth the Effort?

To quote one educator, "If technology is the answer, what was the question?"[34] To evaluate the effectiveness of computers, we must first figure out what they are supposed to accomplish, and, according to University of California professor Henry Jay Becker, we have yet to identify clear goals for technology or to determine how to measure progress toward these goals.

> Traditional theory says that kids need to know discrete skills in computation or reading so that's what teachers teach. . . . But most of the people who are excited about technology in schools . . . care more about having kids do sophisticated writing or engage in complex reasoning or learn to figure out things like adults do. And we don't have great ways of measuring such outcomes.[35]

The bottom line is that the monumental investments in computer technology have not been matched by monumental gains in student achievement. In fact, researchers are divided on the academic benefits brought by computers. Some evidence shows that drill and practice done with a computer may help children develop basic skills. Computers are patient and diligent drill sergeants. Other studies indicate that students in classes with sizable numbers of computers do more writing than students in low-tech classrooms, but the research does not indicate whether more writing is better writing; for that to occur, teacher feedback it needed. Teachers report that some students, unmotivated by other instructional approaches, are excited when learning on the computer. Then again, not everything done on the computer is educationally germane. The most prevalent uses of computers by fourth- and eighth-graders, for example, are playing games and word processing.[36] Little evidence supports technology's effectiveness reflected in higher standardized test scores or a deepening student understanding of concepts and issues.

Although computers have little to show in the way of educational effectiveness, technology does have pizzazz. With or without research, support for technology in schools remains high. Most parents, school board members, and business leaders believe that computers offer essential workplace skills—an important, if nonacademic goal. The public also believes that computers and the Internet provide a window on the latest information, and somehow computers make education both more efficient and more enjoyable. In fact, the public has more confidence in computers than teachers do. (See Figures 14.7 and 14.8.)

Larry Cuban, Stanford University professor, writes that, when academic advances do not follow technological advances, we often blame teachers for not adequately embracing new technology. If teachers are not to blame, we place our criticism on the doorstep of an unresponsive school bureaucracy unable to manage change. If that does not work, then we explain failure in terms of insufficient resources, a public unwilling to fund costly technology. Rarely do Americans question the technology itself. He points out that we know little about using technology to enhance instruction, that the problem may not be teachers, administrators, or funding but, rather, America's unbridled faith in technology. Cuban believes that our technological expectations are unreasonably high.[37]

Teachers are caught in the middle. On the one hand, researchers can offer little in the way of strong evidence that computers significantly contribute to learning, yet public enthusiasm about technology is pushing schools and teachers into implementing computer education. What are educators to do?

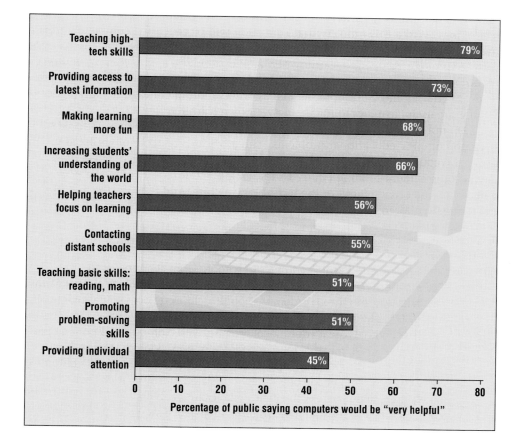

FIGURE 14.7

Public perceptions of computers in the classroom. Members of the public are more likely to say computers would be "very helpful" in promoting high-tech skills and making learning more fun than to say computers would increase academic learning.

Source: Milken Exchange on Education Technology, Second Annual Public Opinion Survey, 1998.

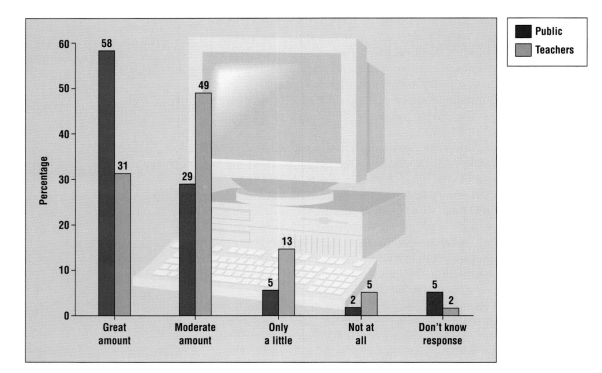

FIGURE 14.8

A difference of opinion. The public and teachers were asked "How much do you think computers have helped improve student learning?" Members of the public were nearly twice as likely to say "a great amount."

Source: MCI Nationwide Poll on Internet in Education, 1998.

It is helpful for teachers to maintain a sense of perspective when it comes to technology. While it is unlikely that education will be redefined completely in the near future, it is also clear that technology's influence is growing. Get comfortable with technology. Be open to learning new applications and approaches. Be willing to try out ideas. Consider technology mastery as part of your professional development. Relevant courses and workshops, as well as observation of colleagues applying technology, are useful avenues to increasing your own learning.

Do not lose your skepticism, however. Be wary of "magic bullets," simple solutions to complex educational problems. The advocates of technology have yet to prove the educational effectiveness of computers. Even if its effectiveness does one day become evident to all, inequity issues remain. Children of color, the poor, and females are too often left out of the technology picture. And they are the majority of the nation's children.

Summary

1. Technology has long been a part of life in schools. From chalkboards to duplicating machines to filmstrip projectors, a stream of technological innovations has made its way into the classroom. Although technology does influence schools, historically it has had only modest impact on education.

2. While television holds great educational promise, with high-quality programming such as *Sesame Street,* much of television fare is, at best, unproductive and, at worst, damaging. The world view presented through the TV lens is quite distorted, leaving viewers with an image of a society populated mostly by males, with few young children, and replete with ethnic and racial stereotypes.

3. Violence, racism, and sexism on television send negative messages to children. Advertising, often targeted at young viewers, adversely influences children's behavior, including their diets and spending habits.

4. While viewing television at home creates one set of questions, bringing television into the classroom raises other issues. How much television, and what kind of television, is worth class time? The growth of cable channels, such as C-Span, A&E, and The History Channel, offers new media learning opportunities. The growth of video libraries provides additional resources. The introduction of *Channel One,* a for-profit enterprise that brings current events and commercials into classrooms, raises questions about the role of commercial television in public schools.

5. The latest technological innovation in education has been computers and Internet access. But implementation has been expensive. The costs of computer hardware and software purchases and the expense of "wiring" schools for Internet access have eaten into school budgets.

6. Training teachers to use computers has also been challenging. While some teachers are able to adapt to the new technology, others resist, and some suffer from "technophobia," a fear of technology. Contrast teacher fears with the computer knowledge and skills many students bring to school, and a technological age gap is obvious.

7. There are numerous educational applications of computers and the Internet. Virtual field trips take students around the world, assistive technology helps special needs students succeed, simulations recreate events, personal tutors diagnose learning needs, and distance learning brings education directly into the home.

8. Global education investigates world issues that span national borders, including such issues as conflict reduction and ecology. Global education is a growing curricular phenomenon, thanks in part to the Internet.

9. The Virtual High School enables students from around the nation, and around the world, to register for courses not available in their local high schools. Through the use of the Internet, e-mail, and other technological tools, students in different geographic areas can enroll in the same class. The Virtual High School is an example of the potential of technology to alter the way students learn and the way teachers teach.

10. Technology has not been an equal educational resource. Inequity continues to be a major problem as race, gender, and economic status influence access to computers and the Internet. Wealthier Americans, especially Asian and white males, are the most likely to use computers in school, and the most likely to realize salary benefits from that involvement after graduation.

Key Terms and People

artificial intelligence
assistive (adaptive)
  technology
Channel One
distance learning
e-mail
E-Rate

educational television
  programming
global education
Integrated Learning Systems
Internauts
Internet
laptops

online curriculum
simulations
student authoring
technophobia
virtual field trips
Virtual High School (VHS)
World Wide Web

www.mhhe.com/sadker

Discussion Questions and Activities

1. Agree or disagree with each of the following:

   "Television viewing leads to misinformation."

   "Television viewing leads to unbridled capitalism, which often injures children."

"Television viewing is a wasted educational resource."

"Television viewing . . ." (You complete and support the sentence.)

2. How would you use television in your classroom? What rules might you establish for your students in relation to their viewing habits?
3. Will computer technology make a radical difference in America's schools? Support your position.
4. Why has technology not radically altered the way teachers teach and the way students learn? Can you envision a technological breakthrough that will revolutionize schools? Describe it.
5. Suggest six uses of the computer and the Internet in your classroom. Then identify six potential problems associated with computer and Internet use.
6. The Internet is filled with rich resources—and junk. Pornography topics are available on the Internet but are usually filtered out by schools. Other problems remain: political tracts couched as scholarship, hate information embedded in innocent-looking articles, inaccurate information presented as fact, and authors whose credentials are suspect. How would you prepare your students to handle the unreliable and unscholarly material found on the Internet?
7. Do you think it is important to include global education in the curriculum? Why or why not? What are some dangers inherent in a global education curriculum?
8. Describe the advantages and disadvantages of the Virtual High School. Would you like to teach a course in the Virtual High School? Why?
9. How can teachers work to overcome the restrictive role that class, gender, and race play in computer access?

Your First Classroom

Focus Questions

- What are the stages of teacher development?
- What resources do school districts provide for a teacher's first year in the classroom?
- How can schools create "learning communities"?
- What steps can new teachers take to increase the probability of working in a school of their choice?
- How are teachers recognized and rewarded?
- What role do teacher associations play in a teacher's professional life?
- What are the differences between the National Education Association and the American Federation of Teachers?

Chapter Preview

It looks so small: the distance between the student chairs and the teacher's desk. But traveling from a student's desk to a teacher's desk is an enormous journey. This final chapter is intended to prepare you for that transformation, from student to teacher.

New teachers are confronted with a plethora of issues: Will I be good at teaching? Will I be able to control my class? Should I join a teachers' association? How do I juggle the concerns of parents, students, administrators, and colleagues? Should I stay in teaching long term? If so, what are the routes to advancement?

Even before these considerations emerge, other decisions need to be made: Where to teach? How to win that ideal (at least satisfying) teaching position? This chapter provides you with some insights and practical advice about that influential first teaching year.

```
┌─────────────────────────────────────────────────────┐
│                    YOU'VE GOT MAIL                    │
├─────────────────────────────────────────────────────┤
│  TO: Anna@Macrocorp.org                               │
│  Carlos@peacecorps.org                                │
│  SUBJ: My First Teaching Job                          │
├─────────────────────────────────────────────────────┤
│  You asked me to report in when I landed my first     │
│  teaching job. I did it! I spent the weekend setting  │
│  up my classroom, meeting colleagues teaching in my   │
│  area, and sorting out the school calendar. And I     │
│  met Ms. Shertok, my mentor. She reminded me of some  │
│  forms I forgot to sign, gave me ideas for first-day  │
│  "ice breakers," and already set up a visit for next  │
│  week, so she can "observe" my class. (I already do   │
│  not like that word observe. I am REALLY nervous      │
│  about that.)                                         │
│                                                       │
│  Tomorrow I meet the kids. I hope they like me. I     │
│  hope I like them. I hope I can control them. And     │
│  tomorrow afternoon there is a union briefing. Busy.  │
│  Excited. Happy. Did I leave any emotions out? Oh,    │
│  yes, . . . scared to death!                          │
└─────────────────────────────────────────────────────┘
```

Stages of Teacher Development

Will I be able to manage this class? Can I get through the curriculum? Do I know my subject well enough? Will the other teachers like me? Will the administrators rehire me? Am I going to be a good teacher? Will I like this life in the classroom?

These are questions that first-year teachers ask. When you arrive in the classroom, the questions that occupy you are mostly about your ability, about visits by supervisors, and about control of the students. By the second year, teachers are more experienced (and confident), and they usually move beyond these questions, shifting the focus of their attention to student performance. For example, experienced teachers might spend time analyzing the needs of individual students, exploring a new curriculum strategy, and asking such questions as "How can I help this shy child?" and "Why is this student encountering learning problems?" If a colleague is achieving success using a new teaching strategy, an experienced teacher might observe, then adapt that strategy. As talented and experienced teachers mature, their interests and vision extend beyond their own classrooms. At this more advanced stage, they work to develop programs that could benefit large numbers of students. The chart in Figure 15.1 might be helpful in suggesting stages that teachers pass through as they become more skilled in their craft.[1]

Attempts to reform education and improve student achievement are dependent on our ability to move teachers through these developmental stages. Although earlier studies by James Coleman and others seem to call into question the educational impact of teachers, comprehensive studies in the 1990s found that teacher performance is critical. Every dollar spent to increase teacher qualifications (as measured by teacher test scores, number of graduate degrees, professional training, etc.) improves students' academic performance more than money invested in other areas. Although

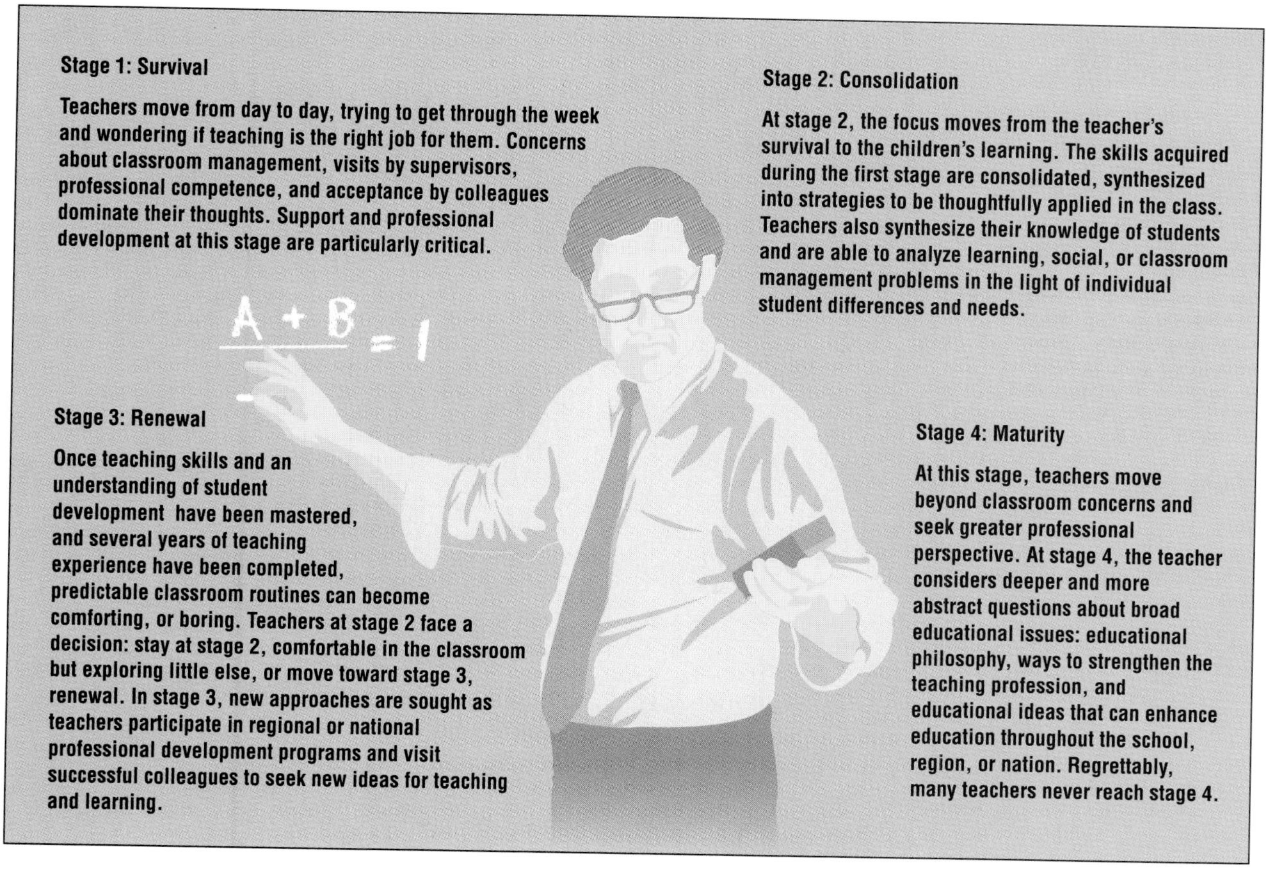

Stage 1: Survival

Teachers move from day to day, trying to get through the week and wondering if teaching is the right job for them. Concerns about classroom management, visits by supervisors, professional competence, and acceptance by colleagues dominate their thoughts. Support and professional development at this stage are particularly critical.

$$A + B = 1$$

Stage 2: Consolidation

At stage 2, the focus moves from the teacher's survival to the children's learning. The skills acquired during the first stage are consolidated, synthesized into strategies to be thoughtfully applied in the class. Teachers also synthesize their knowledge of students and are able to analyze learning, social, or classroom management problems in the light of individual student differences and needs.

Stage 3: Renewal

Once teaching skills and an understanding of student development have been mastered, and several years of teaching experience have been completed, predictable classroom routines can become comforting, or boring. Teachers at stage 2 face a decision: stay at stage 2, comfortable in the classroom but exploring little else, or move toward stage 3, renewal. In stage 3, new approaches are sought as teachers participate in regional or national professional development programs and visit successful colleagues to seek new ideas for teaching and learning.

Stage 4: Maturity

At this stage, teachers move beyond classroom concerns and seek greater professional perspective. At stage 4, the teacher considers deeper and more abstract questions about broad educational issues: educational philosophy, ways to strengthen the teaching profession, and educational ideas that can enhance education throughout the school, region, or nation. Regrettably, many teachers never reach stage 4.

FIGURE 15.1

Stages of teacher development.

Source: Based on the work of Lillian Katz.

teachers applaud efforts to reduce class size or provide schools with up-to-date computer technology, research reveals that teacher expertise is more important. In fact, *teacher qualifications and skills are among the MOST important factors in improving student performance.*[2] (See Figure 15.2.)

What do we mean by a qualified and skillful teacher? The most effective teachers not only demonstrate mastery of the subject they teach but also are adept in the methods of teaching and understand student development. Unfortunately many teachers receive little support, make little progress in their subject area or their teaching skills, and never grow to the more sophisticated levels of teaching. Some teachers struggle to master the initial survival level: approximately one-third of all new teachers leave teaching within the first five years.[3]

Will you like teaching, be good at it, and advance through these developmental stages? The answer may be determined by your "first impressions," your initial experiences as a teacher, and school districts know it. That is why a growing number of districts are investing resources to ensure that, when you step into your first classroom, you will not be alone.

Although graduation may be in your not too distant future (if it isn't already in the not too distant past), your best learning experiences may still lie ahead. While some teachers are "naturals," gifted classroom instructors from the first day they step foot in a classroom, most of us benefit from a support system that helps us refine our teaching skills. Ongoing support, in the form of professional development, is provided, not just for new teachers but for all teachers. States and school districts have

FIGURE 15.2

School resources and
student achievement:
size of increase in
student achievement
for every $500 spent on
four areas.

Source: Linda Darling-Hammond,
"Teachers and Teaching: Testing
Policy Hypothesis From a National
Commission Report," *Educational
Researcher,* 27, No 1, Jan–Feb 1998.

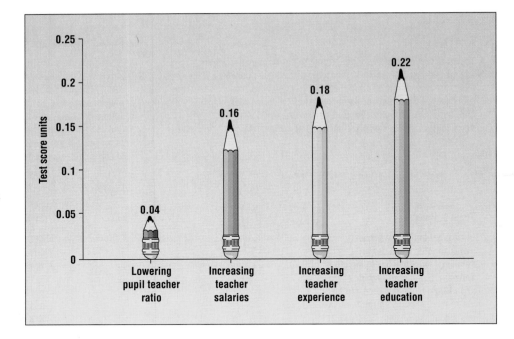

long required continuous graduate training and credits for teachers in order to maintain their licenses. In recent years, many school districts have gone further, creating and implementing induction programs for beginning teachers.

Your First Year: Induction into the Profession

Mentors

An **induction program** "provide(s) some systematic and sustained assistance to beginning teachers for at least one school year."[4] Induction programs promote a positive transition into the classroom by matching new teachers, called **intern teachers,** with an experienced instructor, sometimes called a consulting teacher or mentor. Mentors may be assigned by the school administration, or by the local teachers' association, or by a combination of the two. **Mentors** guide intern teachers through the school culture and norms, shedding light on the "official" and "hidden" school governments (which memos need a quick response, which do not; who keeps the key to the supply room; where the "best" VCRs are hidden). Mentors can offer information about curricular materials, as well as observe a class to offer insights into teaching skills. In the best of circumstances, they help new teachers become skilled professionals. On a personal level, mentors can be valuable confidants, providing a friendly ear and helpful advice through new, and sometimes difficult, times. They may be able to help new teachers work out scheduling problems or smooth out stressful communication with a student, parent, administrator, or colleague (no minor feat during a year filled with new faces).

If having a mentor sounds appealing, and you find yourself in a school district that does not provide official mentors, you can certainly try to recruit an unofficial mentor to guide you through that first year. You might want to ask colleagues or administrators about teachers known for creative lessons or effective management or who generally might lend a helpful hand to a rookie such as yourself.

In many programs, mentors provide more than friendly support; they have an official responsibility to assess new teachers and to file reports to school supervisors. A poor performance report from a mentor can result in a recommendation for extra training for an intern teacher, which could be absolutely wonderful in solving a persistent problem. If the problem is not resolved with additional resources and training, continuous negative classroom observations can lead to dismissal. Obviously, a mentor's evaluation responsibilities can inhibit open and effective communication, particularly if a new teacher is struggling and is concerned about being rehired.

Observation

Whether new teachers are assigned a mentor, find a mentor, or are mentorless, they are likely to have their classroom performance observed. It is not unusual for teachers to be observed three or four times in their first year and, in some districts, much more frequently. Observations come in two varieties: *diagnostic*, designed to help the teachers, and *evaluative*, intended to be used for employment decisions. Sometimes the same observation serves both purposes.

Observations may be conducted by your mentor, an administrator, or a veteran teacher. This last option, called **peer review,** has become popular in an increasing number of school districts, including Minneapolis, Cincinnati, and Columbus, Ohio.[5] These school districts, sometimes in cooperation with local teacher associations, identify their strongest teachers to evaluate and assist others, an approach that recognizes the movement toward greater teacher professionalism and autonomy. Whoever undertakes the evaluation, it is wise for beginning teachers to ask a mentor or colleague about which skills and qualities are particularly valued in these observations. Some teachers find it useful (if a bit disconcerting) to arrange to be videotaped, so they can develop strategies to improve their instruction.

What do observers look for during classroom observations of beginning teachers? An evaluation framework, used by the Toledo Public Schools, offers insight into the typical skills and attributes considered worth evaluating. (See Figures 15.3 and 15.4)

Official and informal observations are usually followed by a conference, in which the mentor or supervisor shares the high points and "not-as-high-as-we-would-like" points of your teaching. It is a good idea to take notes and carefully consider these comments. You may find some comments to be quite insightful, offering you wise counsel on how to improve. Other comments might be less appealing, even off the mark. Attend to all of them, for, in most cases, they are helpful. Your attitude and openness in these conferences is an indication of your willingness to analyze your teaching, consider changes, and explore additional professional development options that can help you refine your teaching skills.

Professional Development Programs

Many new teachers soon discover that their induction program includes professional development classes and activities. School systems sponsor an amazing variety of professional training options, for new and veteran teachers, both during the summer and throughout the school year. Through these programs, teachers might obtain an advanced degree, attend a summer institute to master new skills, satisfy state requirements for renewal of teacher licensure, work toward an endorsement or a license in a second teaching field, or earn a higher salary.

Most teacher pay schedules are connected to professional development. Sometimes salaries are linked to the number of hours invested in courses and training programs, so that a teacher who takes thirty graduate credits at a college or thirty

FIGURE 15.3

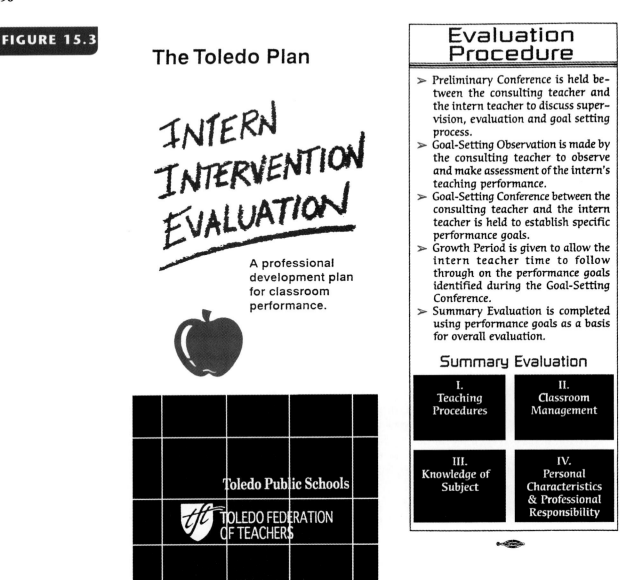

The Toledo Plan

INTERN INTERVENTION EVALUATION

A professional development plan for classroom performance.

Toledo Public Schools

tft TOLEDO FEDERATION OF TEACHERS

Evaluation Procedure

➤ Preliminary Conference is held between the consulting teacher and the intern teacher to discuss supervision, evaluation and goal setting process.
➤ Goal-Setting Observation is made by the consulting teacher to observe and make assessment of the intern's teaching performance.
➤ Goal-Setting Conference between the consulting teacher and the intern teacher is held to establish specific performance goals.
➤ Growth Period is given to allow the intern teacher time to follow through on the performance goals identified during the Goal-Setting Conference.
➤ Summary Evaluation is completed using performance goals as a basis for overall evaluation.

Summary Evaluation

I. Teaching Procedures	II. Classroom Management
III. Knowledge of Subject	IV. Personal Characteristics & Professional Responsibility

training hours offered by a school district would get a certain salary raise. In other districts, teacher performance is evaluated to determine salary increases. In these districts, the assumption is that effective professional development activities produce improved classroom performance, and it is that performance that determines salary increments.

School districts vary greatly in their approaches to professional training. Sometimes districts identify a topic (e.g., "student portfolio development" or "emotional intelligence"), invite in one or more speakers to organize a presentation on that topic, and require the whole faculty to participate. These professional development efforts are scheduled before, during, and at the end of the academic year, becoming a predictable part of the school calendar. Teachers call them **in-service** days, while students are more likely to consider them vacation days. Many have criticized these one-time programs as "dog and pony" shows, brief presentations given to a large group of educators that may lack long-term impact.

TEACHER SUMMARY EVALUATION REPORT

Name _____

College _____

School _____ Date _____

Grade or
Subject _____ Period of   Period of   Period of
                              Sept.-Dec. ☐   Jan.-March ☐   Apr.-Dec. ☐

Certification _____

Number of Observations and Time _____ Conference Time _____

Intern semester completed _____

**Check on March
and Dec Report**

☐ Outstanding
☐ Satisfactory
☐ Unsatisfactory
☐ Written comment only
☐ Irregular term
☐ Recommended for 2nd
    semester intern program

**Check on
March Report Only**

☐ Recommended for first
    one-year contract
☐ Recommended for a second
    one-year contract
☐ Recommended for initial
    four-year contract
☐ Recommended for third
    one-year contract
☐ Not recommended for
    reappointment

Contract Status

☐ First year contract
☐ Second year contract
☐ Four-year contract
☐ One-year contract
☐ Continuing contract
☐ Long-term substitute
    (60 or more days)

* OUTSTANDING: Performance shows exceptional professional qualities and growth.
   SATISFACTORY: Performance at expected and desired professional qualities and growth.
* UNSATISFACTORY: Performance shows serious weaknesses or deficiencies.
* For more complete definition refer to page 10 in the Toledo Plan.
* Unsatisfactory and/or outstandings must have a written supportive statement.

	Out-standing	Satis-factory	Unsatis-factory
I. TEACHING PROCEDURES			
A. Skill in planning			
B. Skill in assessment and evaluation			
C. Skill in making assignments			
D. Skill in developing good work-study habits			
E. Resourceful use of instructional material			
F. Skill in using motivating techniques			
G. Skill in questioning techniques			
H. Ability to recognize and provide for individual differences			
I. Oral and written communication skills			
J. Speech, articulation and voice quality			
II. CLASSROOM MANAGEMENT			
A. Effective classroom facilitation and control			
B. Effective interaction with pupils			
C. Efficient classroom routine			
D. Instructional leadership			
E. Is reasonable, fair and impartial in dealing with students			
III. KNOWLEDGE OF SUBJECT–ACADEMIC PREPARATION			
IV. PERSONAL CHARACTERISTICS AND PROFESSIONAL RESPONSIBILITY			
A. Shows a genuine interest in teaching			
B. Personal appearance			
C. Skill in adapting to change			
D. Adheres to accepted policies and procedures of Toledo Public Schools			
E. Accepts responsibility both inside and outside the classroom			
F. Has a cooperative approach toward parents and school personnel			
G. Is punctual and regular in attendance			

Evaluator's Signature _____   Teacher's Signature _____   Principal's Signature _____
     (when required)   (when required)

Evaluator's Position _____
                         Date of Conference _____

DIRECTIONS
1. Rate all categories, bold face and subcategories.
2. Attach all supporting documents that have been signed or initialed.

FIGURE 15.4

Intern assessment form.

Source: Toledo Public Schools

Other staff development strategies require more time and offer greater focus on a specific subject or skill area. Meetings and workshops over the course of a year to improve the science program and weekly sessions on relevant software are examples of this more in-depth approach. Recent research has underscored the value of teacher-designed programs, closely tied to practical classroom skills. Educational reformers suggest that the best **professional development** programs

- Connect directly to the teacher's work with students
- Link subject content with teaching skills
- Use a problem-solving approach
- Reflect research finding
- Are sustained and supported over time[6]

How can professional development programs incorporate these characteristics? One way is to ask teachers to prepare portfolios for board certification or merit review. Portfolio construction encourages teachers to develop insight and reflection about their instruction by creating tangible examples of their competence. Hopefully, over time, these examples will document their progress and development. Some school districts create a "teaching academy" that offers courses directly linked to particular teacher needs. Over the period of a semester, summer, or year, teachers might enroll in these courses to improve their questioning skills, create more equitable classroom participation, establish effective management strategies, or implement a new curriculum. Many programs tie course assignments to daily instructional activities, providing a useful link between professional development and real-world application.

Collaborative action research (CAR) also connects daily teaching responsibilities with professional growth, but in this case through the use of research. Typically, a group of teachers identifies a genuine problem in the school or classes, designs ways to address the problem, and then evaluates their success. If the teachers are concerned about the poor performance of girls in high school science courses, for example, they might decide to experiment with new methods to improve that performance. One teacher might try cooperative learning strategies in her science class, while a second teacher develops techniques to directly involve parents in their daughters' science work. A third teacher might initiate a new science curriculum designed to motivate female students. Each of these approaches would be evaluated and the most effective selected for use by all teachers. CAR encourages thoughtful, objective analysis of real teacher concerns.

Professional development takes many forms: graduate degree programs, collaborative action research projects, and teaching academies or inservice days. A quick glance at Figure 15.5 should convince you of the wide range of professional development programs. These descriptions are adapted from *Education Week*, a weekly newspaper and Internet publication that covers national education events, so they reflect realistic opportunities available to teachers.

Personalizing Schools

From a new teacher's perspective, what were once familiar school surroundings soon become strange. Teachers and students see school very differently. As a teacher, you will likely be shocked by the endless stream of paperwork that engulfs you, and you will struggle to learn the names of the students in your classes, as many as 150 classes or more at the secondary level. You will work even harder getting to know the people behind the names. Typically, you will have only three to five scheduled hours a week to prepare your lessons or coordinate with your colleagues. You will find little time to meet with individual students, much less their parents. Much of your professional

Professional Development
Once a Teacher, Always a Learner

FIGURE 15.5

These announcements provide a taste of the continuous learning opportunities available to educators.

*Adapted from: *Education Week on the Web* September 16, 1998

Aesthetic Realism Teaching Method Explains the True Purpose of Education: teachers and administrators, Aesthetic Realism Foundation, NYC

Hands-on Science workshop by the American Association for the Advancement of Science, K–6, Washington, DC

Adult Education **Always Traveling the Speed of Life,** Sacramento, CA

Teacher Training Sessions: **National Foundation for Teaching Entrpreneurship,** San Francisco, CA

Annual Conference for **Year-Round Education,** K–12 teachers, principals superintendents, board members, parents, Waikiki, HI

Geraldine R. Dodge Poetry Festival Foundation: student and teacher special events, Waterloo Village, NJ

Educational Theatre Association: **Lighting for Musicals,** Orlando, FL; **Disciplined-Based Theatre Education,** Austin, TX

Teachers' Symposium, American Montessori Society, Alburquerque, NM

Learning Disabilities: **Attention Deficit/Hyperactivity Disorder** teachers grades 1–6, NYC

Urban Education: Council of Urban Boards of Education and National School Boards of Education, Atlanta, GA

School Facilities Annual Conference, **Council of Educational Facilities Planners International** for K–12 adminstrators and planners, architects, construction program managers, manufacturers, and suppliers and government representatives, Vancouver, British Columbia, Canada

Making Sense of Looping: Non-Graded Primary and Multi-age Classrooms, Cleveland, OH

Reaching all Students: Assessment in a Standards-Based Environment, Worchester, MA

Shape of the Future of Techological Literacy by Opening Communication Lines Between Educators and Engineers, by the Institute of Electrical and Electronic Engineers, Baltimore, MD

The Nuts and Bolts of Operating a Local Teacher Organization by the National Association of Catholic School Teachers, Philadelphia, PA

Character Education Training and Information Conference, Baltimore, MD

Success, Standards, and Struggling Secondary Students: K–12 educators who work with at-risk youth, Renton, WA

National 1 Day Conference For Substitute Teachers, Petersburg, VA

Miles to Go, Promises to Keep in the New Millennium, National Black Child Development Institute, Chicago, IL

Raising Standards in Rural Education, National Rural Education Association, Fort Collins, CO

International Conference on Computers in Education, Beijing, China

Intergrating the Curriculum With Multiple Intelligences: The Balancing Act, Bloomington, IN

Council of School Attorneys' Advocacy Seminar and School Law Retreat, San Antonio, TX

Integrating the Arts with Literacy for teachers and administrators, Los Angeles, CA

day will be spent trying to manage students in a world of adult isolation.[7] This school organization is a century old, and new teachers, as well as experienced ones, find it both dehumanizing and inadequate.

It is not surprising, therefore, that educators are reconceptualizing schools in order to make them more responsive to the intellectual and emotional needs of both teachers and students. As you contemplate where you want to begin your teaching career, you may want to consider how school organization will affect your life in the classroom.

One major school reorganization effort is intended to nurture learning communities, an effort to create a more intimate and goal-oriented environment. When **learning communities** are established, students and teachers get to know each other both personally and intellectually as they develop shared academic goals and values. Reducing class size and lengthening school periods are two of several organizational changes that can reduce student alienation and build learning communities. As you explore that first teaching position, you may want to look for these and other changes intended to personalize school life:

- *Size.* As you consider where to teach, give some thought to the size of the schools on your list. The movement now is toward smaller schools and smaller classes to help teachers and students develop more meaningful relationships. What if the school is already bulging with thousands of students? One approach being used is to divide the school into smaller units, sometimes called "houses." Creating small schools within larger ones can help build intimacy and learning communities.

- *Looping.* Schools are also encouraging greater rapport and longer relationships by promoting teachers along with their class, a process called **looping.** It sounds a bit bizarre, but consider yourself an elementary school teacher who graduates to the next grade along with your students. This affords you extended time to know all students in depth, to diagnose and meet their learning needs, and to develop more meaningful communications with their parents and families. Time is not lost at the start of each school year as teachers and students get to "know one another" after the summer break. Looping offers students an increased sense of stability and community.

- *Block scheduling.* **Block scheduling** reduces the number of periods a day, while increasing the length of time allotted to each period. If you were to teach in a school with block scheduling, you might have 75 students on any given day or in a particular semester, instead of 150. The longer periods allow you to get to know these students better, while the students benefit from an uninterrupted period of in-depth academic study. Block scheduling is more efficient than traditional approaches, since less time is lost moving between classes, taking attendance, and refocusing the class on the task at hand.[8]

- *Strengthening teacher roles.* Another way to personalize schools is to build stronger student-adult relationships. In other nations, teachers assume a greater number of responsibilities; as a result, they work more intensively with each student. In Japan, Germany, Switzerland, and Sweden, for example, teachers serve as counselors as well as instructors and have a greater range of interactions with their students. To meet their expanded responsibilities, teachers are given additional time to confer with their colleagues and plan their lessons. There are fewer support staff and administrators in these countries, and greater emphasis is placed on the teacher-student connection. While teachers constitute 60 to 80 percent of the school staff in European and Asian countries, they represent only 43 percent of the education staff in the United States. In fact, in the United States, the number of administrators and nonteaching staff members has more than doubled over the past three decades. Reformers believe student performance will not improve unless we reverse this trend.[9] (See Figure 15.6 for an international comparison of staffing patterns.)

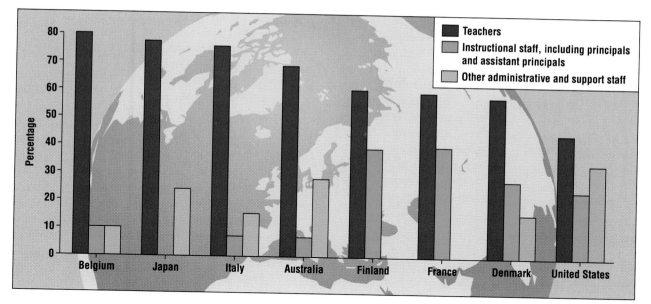

Finding That First Teaching Position

FIGURE 15.6

International comparisons of teacher staffing patterns.

Source: Organization for Economic Cooperation Development (OECD), Education at a Glance: OECD Indicators (Paris: OECD, 1995), Table p. 31, 176–77.

Is the idea of organizing schools to personalize education appealing to you? What matters most to you as you consider where to teach? Matching your values, interests, and skills with the right school is a useful way to narrow your search for that first teaching position. You may want to make a list of the issues that matter to you most. Here are some questions to consider:

What subject or grade level do I prefer? What kind of community and students do I want to serve? What part of the country appeals to me? Is there a particular school organization I like? What educational philosophy and school culture am I most comfortable with? How important to me are incentives for superior teaching? What salary and benefits am I seeking? Am I more interested in private or public school, or perhaps a charter or magnet school? Am I flexible and open to different options or pretty focused in my preferences?

Many of the activities in this book, including the Balance Sheets in the first chapter, the inventory of your educational philosophy in Chapter 12, and the Inter-missions, will help you answer these questions. Once you sort out your priorities and identify the schools that are right for you, the next task is to get that first job.

Résumés and Portfolios

Possibly the most crucial document in your job search is your **résumé.** A fundamental purpose of your résumé is to obtain a job interview, so it should herald your strengths and competencies. The résumé should include standard information that employers need to know (your name, address, telephone number), along with other information that you want them to know. Sometimes candidates choose to write an employment objective at the beginning of their résumé. If you like this approach, you could write an employment objective that reflects the kind of teaching position in which you are interested. A standard résumé indicates your formal educational background—your college and university, your major and your minor if you have one, and a description of your student teaching experience, as well as other relevant educational experiences. Teaching in a religious school, being a camp counselor, working in a day care center, being involved in a recreation program for the elderly—all can enhance a candidate's attractiveness to a potential employer. Even if there is no direct educational experience, other employment can be included. If you list professors, supervisors, and cooperating teachers as references, ask if they are comfortable with this role. This is not only a basic courtesy but also a way to measure their willingness to recommend you. (See Figure 15.7 for a sample résumé.)

Your résumé should be typed in a clear and readable format, so that a prospective employer can scan it quickly for pertinent information. The availability of various software templates should help you tailor your résumé. Be sure to proofread carefully. A typographical error, a spelling mistake, or missing punctuation will steer an otherwise promising résumé into the "reject" pile.

FIGURE 15.7

Sample résumé.

Casey Washington
5825 Tanglewood Drive
Bethesda, MD 20817
Home Phone (301) 555-2468
e-mail < cwash@amer.edu >

PERSONAL

Seeking a position as a social studies teacher at the middle school level. Extracurricular skills include soccer coaching and theater arts. Particularly interested in working with bi-lingual Spanish speakers.

EDUCATION

1999-2003	B.A. Education	American University, Washington, DC
		Major: American History Minor: Spanish
1999-1996	Walt Whitman High School, Bethesda, MD	

EMPLOYMENT

2003 *Student Teaching, Cozadd Middle School, Arlington, VA*
Team teaching program for grade six; integrated civics and student government cadre; self-contained Spanish exploratory; Faculty Tech Task Force

2001-2003 *Partners Project, Community Tutor*
Girls, Inc. Start Smart Instructor; Path to Math Latinas Group

OTHER EXPERIENCES

1999-2002 *Team Sports, Camp Wohelo, Waynesboro, PA*
Bunk counselor, sports and recreation program including skill development and leagues

2001-2002 *Guatemala Exchange Group*
Campus winter break soccer series in Guatemala City

CAMPUS ACTIVITIES

2000-present *Dormitory Resident Assistant Director, Beach Hall*
Organization and management; ad-hoc programs; counseling team

2000-2002 *Orientation Week Staff and Director*
Evening activities; harassment sessions facilitator; faculty dinner coordinator

SPECIAL HONORS and SKILLS

- Parent's Association Scholar-Athlete Achievement Award
- Spanish written and verbal fluency
- Technology skills, volunteer webmaster (The Advocates)

REFERENCES

Personal references are on file at American University and will be supplied upon request.

You may want to consider videotaping your teaching and collecting other samples of your work to supplement your résumé. This more comprehensive presentation is commonly known as a portfolio.

Think of a **portfolio** as a collection of materials that documents a teacher's strengths. While a résumé offers a snapshot, a portfolio, sometimes called a "presentation portfolio," can paint a rich picture of you as a teacher. Portfolios might include

Résumé

Videotape of teaching (perhaps in different situations to reflect a range of skills)

Sample lesson plans

Teaching journal with reflections and analysis of teaching skills

Supervisor's observations

Letter from parents, students, supervisors, and others

Examples of student work

Statement of your educational philosophy

National Teacher Exams or other relevant test reports

Many of the Inter-missions included in this book provide you with the means to begin your own portfolio. If the portfolio is effective, you may be called in for that all-important interview. By a stroke of good fortune, interviewing is our next topic.

Interviewing

Congratulations! Your résumé or presentation portfolio was so persuasive that a school system has called for an interview. At this stage, the school district is checking to see if someone who looks good on paper looks promising in real life as well. Some candidates who are résumé superstars become interview "also-rans." Conversely, some candidates who have only mediocre paper credentials come out of an interview with a job offer, because they know how to diagnose and respond to the interviewer's needs. An average interview usually lasts thirty minutes to an hour, and typically half of the teachers interviewed are hired after three or fewer interviews.[10] Therefore, it is essential to make your interview count.

The first thing that will strike an interviewer is appearance. Your prospective interviewer will be looking not only for appropriate professional attire, but also for such qualities as poise, enthusiasm, self-confidence, and an ability to think quickly and effectively on your feet. He or she will be listening as well as looking, so appropriate grammar, a well-developed vocabulary, and clear speech and diction are important. You should also be focused about your teaching philosophy and goals if you want to appear confident and purposeful in the interview. Having the proper reference materials on hand is another principle of good interviewing. Therefore, if you have developed a portfolio of teaching materials or other information that you are particularly proud of, you should take it to the interview. It cannot hurt to have it present, and it might help win the day.

Before interviewing with a school system, it is wise to find out as much as possible about both the particular school and the community. If you do not have friends in the community who can supply such information, you can try the local library or, better yet, stop by the school to talk with the students and others, scour the bulletin boards, and pick up available literature. Once you obtain information about a school or school system, you can begin matching your particular interests and skills with the school district's programs and needs.

As important as such preparatory work is, the most important way of learning what an interviewer is looking for is to listen. Sometimes interviewers state their needs openly, such as "We're looking for a teacher who is fluent in both Spanish and English." In other cases, interviewers merely imply their needs—for example, "Many of the children who attend our school are Hispanic." In this case, you have first to interpret the interviewer's remark and then to check your interpretation with a statement such as "Are you looking for someone who is fluent in both Spanish and English?" Or "Are you looking for someone who has had experience in working with Spanish-speaking children?"

Once you have a clear understanding of the opening, it is your task to show that you have the interests, skills, and experience that are required. To continue with the previous example, you would now show, if you could, that you speak Spanish and that you have worked with Spanish-speaking children. If you do not possess these qualifications, the only thing you can do is to express an interest in working with Latino students and, in the process, learning their language and culture.

It is important to be prepared for some of the questions an interviewer is likely to ask. Common interview topics include strengths, weaknesses, personal philosophy of teaching, future plans, employment history, teaching style, and classroom management. The same survey that uncovered these common topics also listed characteristics that interviewers look for: enthusiasm, warmth, caring, leadership skills, willingness to learn new things, and confidence.[11] You may also want to note what questions cannot legally be asked—for example, questions about your religion or marital or parental status. Such questions do not relate to your qualifications as a teacher. The Office for Civil Rights is one of several agencies that you can contact if you are victimized by such queries.

After interviewing, it is wise to send the interviewer a brief follow-up note, reminding her or him of how your qualifications meet the school system's needs. The interviewer may have talked with dozens of candidates, and under such circumstances it is easy to be forgotten in a sea of faces—your job is to make sure you stand out.

One word of caution: when a job offer comes your way, analyze the school system to make sure that you really want to teach there before signing on the dotted line. Try to find out

- If teachers in the district view it as a good place to work
- If there have been personnel problems recently and, if so, for what reasons
- What are the benefits and potential problems in the teachers' contract
- Typical class size
- What kind of support services are available
- If the school is adopting organizational changes to personalize the school climate.

Not all of these issues may be appropriate for discussion during an initial interview. However, once you have received an offer, you should find out the answers to these questions; if the answers do not please you, the job may not be right for you. It is unwise to accept a position with the notion that you will leave as soon as a better offer is made. That attitude can quickly lead to a job-hopping profile that may stigmatize

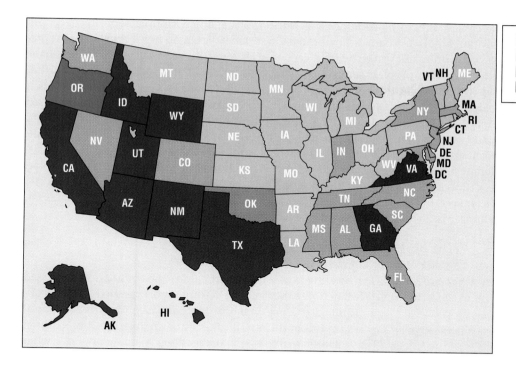

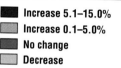

Increase 5.1–15.0%
Increase 0.1–5.0%
No change
Decrease

FIGURE 15.8

Where the students are. Percent change in students enrolled in public school, 1998–2008. As you consider where to teach, you may want to consider student enrollments.

Source: U.S. Dept. of Education, Nat'l Center for Education Statistics

you as someone who is either irresponsible or unable to work well with others. In short, do not simply jump at the first available job offer. If your credentials are good and you know how to market yourself, you will get other teaching offers.

Teacher Recognition

Project yourself into the future. You have worked hard in your school, and you are widely acclaimed as a terrific teacher (congratulations!). After some wonderful years in the classroom, you begin to think about what lies ahead. Having parents, students, and colleagues sing your praises is wonderful, but is there more than that? How are dedicated and excellent teachers recognized and rewarded? Without formal and meaningful recognition, frustration may well follow, a sentiment captured in the all-too-typical teacher comments, such as the following:

> How would I describe my teaching? Well, let me put it this way—I work hard. Free time is a thing of the past. My students are really important to me, and I'm willing to go the extra mile to give them feedback, organize field trips and projects, meet with them or their parents, and give them a stimulating classroom. In fact, most Saturdays I'm working on grades or new projects. And I think it pays off—my kids are blossoming! That's a great feeling. But sometimes I wonder if it's all worth it. Is anyone ever going to notice my hard work? Brad down the hall just comes in and does his job without a second thought, and his paycheck looks just like mine. It doesn't seem fair. Teachers who deserve it should be able to earn something more—more money, more respect.

This view is held by thousands of teachers struggling for professional recognition. Working hard in a demanding profession, teachers often do not feel valued or appreciated, and many leave the field each year as a result. National reform efforts have identified this problem and are working on solutions. Three possible solutions that we will discuss in this section are the National Board for Professional Teaching Standards, merit pay, and career ladders. The **National Board for Professional Teaching Standards (NBPTS)** is establishing higher standards for teaching and grants special certification to teachers who qualify. **Merit pay** is a plan to give additional financial compensation to teachers who demonstrate excellence, though different plans define *excellence* differently. **Career ladders** allow teachers to take on additional responsibilities along with their teaching as a way of advancing in the field. Each of these solutions has its drawbacks as well as its advantages. Nevertheless, all three influence how teachers are recognized.

The National Board for Professional Teaching Standards

In *A Nation Prepared: Teachers for the 21st Century,* the Carnegie Foundation addressed the need for improved teacher preparation. This reform report resulted in the establishment of a national board to evaluate and certify outstanding teachers. For the first time in history, the National Board for Professional Teaching Standards defines what every classroom teacher should know and do to be considered a true professional.

When the NBPTS was launched, former North Carolina governor James Hunt, Jr., proclaimed,

> For once in this country, we are working out standards for measuring excellence rather than minimum competency. The certification process has the potential to transform the current educational system, leverage current investment in teaching, and build a national consensus for increased support of schools.[12]

As alluded to earlier in this text, board certification goes beyond the standards to obtain a license to teach and identifies the qualifications needed for an advanced level of professional recognition. Imagine yourself with the responsibility of determining what skills and behaviors identify truly excellent teachers. How would you begin? The board has identified five general areas that serve as criteria for **board certification**:

Part of the drive to assess, train, and reward qualified teachers involves direct observation of classroom teaching performance.

- *Teachers are committed to students and their learning.* Board-certified teachers should know about research in the psychology of learning, exhibit positive expectations for student abilities, demonstrate equitable treatment of students, and effectively individualize instruction.
- *Teachers know the subjects they teach and how to teach those subjects to students.* Board-certified teachers are expected not only to have mastered their subject but also to have mastered strategies and techniques for conveying the subject to students.

- *Teachers are responsible for managing and monitoring student learning.* Board-certified teachers are competent in using motivational techniques, establishing appropriate class norms, and using a variety of techniques to measure student performance.
- *Teachers think systematically about their practice and learn from experience.* Board-certified teachers model what they teach and exemplify such traits as openness, curiosity, tolerance, and the ability to critically examine their own performance.
- *Teachers are members of learning communities.* This area includes such behaviors as collaborative work on curriculum and policy, staff training, innovations such as the looping and block scheduling previously discussed, and other efforts to improve the school and community.[13]

How could the NBPTS or others measure these areas? Far more than the traditional paper-and-pencil tests are required, and a variety of evaluation strategies are recommended:

- *Portfolios.* Teachers provide documentary evidence and examples of their performance, such as lesson plans, videotapes of teaching, and writing samples.
- *Observations.* Qualified observers view and assess teacher performance in the classroom.
- *Assessment centers.* At special centers located throughout the nation, teachers participate in simulations and interviews dealing with a variety of professional skills, such as lesson planning and textbook selection.
- *Written examination.* A comprehensive test assesses mastery of subject matter and knowledge of developments and research in education.[14]

Once the testing obstacle is resolved, the next question is, "What does board certification mean?" Clearly, just being recognized as exceptional is incredibly rewarding. There are literally millions of teachers, and to be among a selected few is a major boost. To add to this distinction, board certification has become a catalyst for rewarding superior teachers with salary increments and new job responsibilities. However, such tributes are not universal. When funds are in short supply or a school district's organizational structure is inflexible, board-certified teachers receive few tangible rewards or responsibilities for their excellence. There have been some instances of board-certified teachers becoming the object of jealously or derision from their colleagues. Fortunately, this is the exception rather than the rule.

As you enter the teaching profession, you will want to stay abreast of the activities concerning the national board and determine if you want to work toward board certification.

Merit Pay and Career Ladders

Merit pay plans attempt to make teaching more accountable, as well as more financially rewarding, by linking teacher performance and teacher salary. Many groups support this approach, including the National Science Board, the National Association of Secondary School Principals, the American Association of School Administrators, the National Association of Elementary School Principals, and the National Commission on Excellence in Education. But not all plans are acceptable to everyone, and the problem of bias and politics raises concerns, one reason that teacher associations are cautious.[15]

Why would merit pay raise teacher anxieties? Why are such plans controversial? Let's listen in on a faculty meeting to see what merit pay really involves for teachers.

Dr. Moore faced her staff and began, "You know our district has been given the go-ahead to develop a merit pay proposal. There are several different approaches. For example, Rochester, New York, awards merit pay for teachers who receive a second teaching license in reading; work in its professional development academy; accept teaching assignments in more challenging, low-achieving schools; or receive national board certification, so we have to decide how to implement our plan. To help us understand our options, I'd like to outline some of the different plans and then open the floor for your reactions." You watch intently as she lays a transparency on the overhead projector to illustrate the different plans. "Basically, there are four different types of merit pay:

> *"Merit pay based on student performance.* This rewards teachers whose students make gains on standardized tests. It implies that a good teacher will help students achieve in the content areas."

> *"Merit pay based on teacher performance.* Under this program, the district would develop criteria to measure your teaching effectiveness, and you would receive raises based on evaluations by outside observers."

> *"Merit pay based on individualized productivity plans.* Do you remember the personal goals each of you wrote for this school year? This plan would ask you to write more detailed goals for what you would like to accomplish this year. Once they are approved, you would receive financial bonuses based on how much you accomplish."

> *"Merit pay based on the teaching assignment.* With this plan, you could receive compensation according to how difficult or how much in demand your teaching position is. Our math, science, and special education teachers would probably receive the greatest bonuses if we were to adopt this plan."

You think this sounds very interesting. There seem to be mixed feelings among the teachers, however. You overhear a number of different opinions:

> "This sounds great! I can finally get that bonus I deserve for all my extra hours."

> "I wonder how this can work. After all, does the teacher with all the smart kids really deserve a raise if they do well on tests?"

> "I don't think I'd feel comfortable if other people found out I was getting merit pay. Teaching is supposed to mean working as a team, not competing for bonuses."

> "Only the people who are in good with the supervisors will get merit pay. How can that be fair?"

> "I think we need some sort of merit pay system in teaching that will give all of us something to work for."

Obviously, there are many ways to look at merit pay. Many teachers fear the competition or the methods for judging who deserves merit pay, while others are excited about the possibility of a higher salary. Nevertheless, a few merit pay programs have succeeded in pleasing their districts, and the rest of the country can learn from their experience. The Granite School District in Salt Lake City, Utah, developed both criteria for excellence in teaching and a comprehensive evaluation process. The district instituted an optional program, in which a bonus can be earned each year and

IN THE NEWS . . . MERIT PAY

Teachers in Robbinsdale, Minnesota, have an important project due every five years. That's when they assemble their portfolios documenting their teaching skills. Teachers who do well on their portfolio assignments will be paid an additional $15,000 each year for five years. That amounts to $75,000 above their regular salary. The performance pay replaces automatic salary increments.

Source: *Education Week on the Web,* February 1998.

in which in-service training and development are considered part of performance evaluation.[16] More experience is still needed to shape universally successful merit pay programs, but progress in individual school systems is being made.

Career Ladder Programs

Career ladder programs are another alternative to the teacher recognition dilemma. The career ladder is designed to create different levels for teachers by creating a "ladder" that one can climb to receive increased pay through increased work responsibility and status.[17] By the beginning of the 1990s, more than half the states had established a career ladder or an incentive program with state assistance in place. Some critics argue that career ladders have the same drawbacks as merit pay—a lack of clear standards or appropriate evaluation tools—but others claim that career ladders can be more effective because they are rooted in professionalism. The distinguishing characteristic of the career ladder is the increased responsibility given to the teacher. The Rochester, New York, *Career in Teaching* plan is a good example. Here, an outstanding teacher has the opportunity to become a "master" or "mentor teacher," write curricula, select textbooks, or plan staff development programs while continuing to teach in the classroom.[18] Thus, good teachers are not removed from the classroom, yet they receive an increase in responsibility and in salary.

All teacher recognition plans share the goal of making the teaching profession more attractive and more rewarding, whether through official certification, financial compensation, or increased professional responsibility. In what other ways might teachers be able to earn more respect or more money? As you enter the teaching profession, you will want to be aware of the kinds of incentives available in different school districts and consider which incentives appeal to you.

Teacher Associations: Where They Came From, Where They Are Going, and How They Can Affect You

In colonial times, teachers typically were meek and quiet public servants. In fact, some of them actually were servants, since they had obtained the money to pay for their passage to American by indenturing themselves. Their pitiful wages were equivalent to those of a farmhand. In order to survive, many teachers were forced to board with a different family each week.[19] (Can you

Often marked by acrimony and bitterness, strikes changed the traditional image of teachers as meek and passive public servants.

imagine eating dinner with a different student's family every week?) In 1874 in Massachusetts, male teachers were paid a monthly salary of $24.51. Women earned less than $8. This lowly status provided one motivation for teachers to organize.

In 1794, the Society of Associated Teachers of New York City became the first teacher association in this country. In 1857, this movement went national when the National Teachers' Association was formed, later to become the **National Education Association (NEA).** Half a century later, in 1916, the **American Federation of Teachers (AFT)** was created as a union of teachers affiliated with the American Federation of Labor. Through **collective bargaining** (that is, all the teachers in a school system bargaining as one group through a chosen representative), through organized actions (including strikes), and through public relations efforts, the NEA and the AFT succeeded in improving both the salaries and the working conditions of teachers, and they continue to influence teachers' professional lives. (See Figure 15.9)

In your first few years as a teacher, you will find yourself in a new environment and without the protection of tenure. Teacher associations, such as the NEA and the AFT, can help alleviate that sense of vulnerability by providing you with collegial support, opportunities for professional growth, and the security that one derives from participating in a large and influential group. Today, teaching is one of the most organized occupations in the nation. Nine out of ten teachers belong to either the NEA or AFT. Total NEA membership is 2.3 million, while the AFT membership approaches 1 million. Six out of ten teachers are represented by one or the other in collective bargaining. It is not too early for you to start thinking about whether you want to join a professional association and which one may best represent you.

Does the National Education Association Speak for You?

Mediumtown Education Association (MEA) Announces
A Reception and Business Meeting
Howard Jackson Hotel 8:00 P.M.
All New Faculty Members Invited

1794	The Society of Associated Teachers of New York City becomes the country's first teacher association.
1840–1861	Thirty state teacher associations form.
1857	The first National Teachers' Association is formed. In the late 1870s, this group merges with the National Association of School Superintendents and the American Normal School Association to become the National Education Association (NEA).
1902	A group of teachers from San Antonio, Texas, becomes the first to join a labor union, the American Federation of Labor (AFL).
1916	The American Federation of Teachers (AFT) is formed.
1920s	The AFT has more than 10,000 members.
1940s	More than 200,000 teachers belong to the NEA (up from about 7,000 in 1910). More than 30,000 teachers belong to the AFT.
1940s–1950s	More than 100 strike threats are carried out.
1960s–1970s	First the AFT and then the NEA take up militant tactics, including collective bargaining and strikes.
1980s–1990s	Teacher organizations are involved in political action and show growing concern for increased professionalism.

FIGURE 15.9

Milestones in the birth and growth of teacher associations.

You have been a teacher in Mediumtown for all of two weeks, and you know about five faces and three names of other faculty members. You decide the MEA meeting will be a good opportunity to find out about the MEA and to meet some of your colleagues at the same time.

Before you attend, you decide to do a little research on the MEA's parent organization, the National Education Association. You learn that, in the past, many people thought that the NEA was not aggressive enough in striving to better teachers' salaries and working conditions. You discover, for example, that the NEA refused to take a stand on segregated education until long after the Supreme Court's 1954 desegregation decision.

One of the reasons for the NEA's historical lack of power can be traced to its origin. When the forty-three founders of the NEA gathered in the mid-nineteenth century, they intended to form a broad organization that would encompass many different educational interests and groups. But, for many years, the NEA was dominated by school administrators, and its policies conflicted with the interests of most of its members, who were classroom teachers. By attempting to draw all educators under one great canopy, the NEA so diluted its focus that it became ineffective in representing its diverse interest groups.

During the 1960s and 1970s, the NEA became a stronger advocate of teachers' rights. During the 1980s and 1990s, the association moved more slowly, defining its position on various educational reform proposals.

Your research tells you that now the NEA is the largest professional and employee organization in the nation. It enrolls 2.3 million members, including elementary and secondary teachers, higher-education faculty, retired educators, and educational support personnel. Besides state-level associations, approximately thirteen thousand local associations are affiliated with the NEA. An organization that attracts that many people must have something to say, you think to yourself, so, promptly at 8:00 P.M., you settle into your chair at the Howard Jackson Hotel and give the NEA speaker your attention. He begins:

Professional organizations like NEA have not only made "teacher power" a reality, they have also contributed much to national educational policy.

The NEA has always worked for the best in education. We believe in high educational standards, increased funding from the federal government, and equal educational rights for all our students and for those who educate them. Our policies are determined by our membership through their delegates at the association's annual representative assembly. And the services we provide our members are effective and wide-ranging.

The speaker distributes a multicolor brochure outlining the association's programs and services. Even a cursory glance shows you that these are impressive. As you flip through the brochure, you see

- *Publishing.* All members receive a newspaper, *NEA Today;* leaders receive a newsletter, *NEA Now;* and NEA student members receive the annual *Tomorrow's Teachers;* and many visit the NEA web site.
- *Human and civil rights.* The NEA's Human and Civil Rights unit offers information and training on such topics as women's leadership, sexual harassment, child abuse protections, affirmative action, and academic freedom.
- *Educational innovation.* NEA's National Center for Innovation (NCI) creates and supports diverse reform projects. NCI promotes high-quality education, advances the profession, and provides professional development opportunities for association activists.
- *Legal services.* The Kate Frank/DuShane Legal Services Program offers legal assistance for NEA members in disputes with employers. The program provides counsel and pays legal expenses, such as court costs and filing fees. Through a professional liability insurance policy offered to members, the Educators Employment Liability (EEL) program protects members if they are sued by parents or children for negligence.
- *Membership and affiliates.* This division assists affiliates in leadership training, collective bargaining, grievance procedures, and other labor related projects. Teachers need relevant training if they are to negotiate effectively for the rights and benefits of their colleagues. Under this program area, the National Education Employee Fund provides interest-free loans to education personnel who are in financial trouble because of strike activity. The Uni-Serv program provides members with staff services at the local level, providing an NEA representative and funds to help local affiliates organize various staff development and other programs.

- *Government Relations.* The Government Relations unit organizes and trains NEA members to elect proeducation candidates to federal office and to promote legislation that supports education in general and teachers in particular.

You begin to read about some of the other special programs NEA provides, such as the Health Information Network, which brings health-related information into schools, when you are jolted to attention by a heated debate. You recognize the angry speaker as the chair of your school's English department:

> "I think we ought to pay less attention to political education and more attention to education."

The NEA orientation leader interrupts:

> "Let's not get into an argument on this one issue. NEA has been involved politically during the past few years. In our democracy, all citizens have the right—indeed, the obligation—to work to elect responsive officials. Thankfully, we live in a country that celebrates such political freedom.

> "But let's get away from politics. You're right, we need to discuss the education issues. From tuition tax credits to sex education, NEA isn't afraid to face the tough questions. And we put our money where our mouth is. We always keep in mind the old NEA motto, spoken by Horace Mann more than 100 years ago: 'Be ashamed to die before you have won some victory for humanity.'"

You are so impressed with the accomplishments and promise of the NEA and the local MEA that you are about to ask for an application form and write out a check for membership dues. Just then, a man who has been sitting quietly next to you leans over and says, "I belong to the MFT, the Mediumtown Federation of Teachers. It's the local affiliate of the AFT, the American Federation of Teachers. Don't sign anything until you've heard our side."

Does the American Federation of Teachers Speak for You?

The following week, you again bump into the quiet, unknown man who attended the MEA meeting. He introduces himself with "just call me Al" and invites you to attend the meeting of the MFT to be held at Union Hall on Friday. He is pretty persuasive, and, since you want to know about all of your options before you sign on any dotted line, you agree to go.

You enter the MFT meeting place and take your seat. As you glance around the room, you find yourself staring at the podium up front, George Meany's picture on one wall, and the American flag on the other. You get an immediate sense of the labor orientation of the AFT and of this local, the MFT. As the speaker begins her talk, your original impressions are confirmed:

> "When John Dewey became our first member back in 1916, he recognized that teachers need their own organization. Teachers are the backbone of the educational system, and we must speak for ourselves. That is why the AFT will continue to be exclusively of teachers, by teachers, and for teachers.

> "It was the AFT that backed school desegregation years before the 1954 Supreme Court decision that established the principle that separate is not equal. We ran freedom schools for Southern black students, and we have a strong record on academic freedom and civil rights.

TEACHER ASSOCIATION PROFILES   ALBERT SHANKER

In working-class Queens, New York, during the Great Depression, Albert Shanker's mother, a sewing machine operator, would talk with respect about America's professionals—the doctors, lawyers, and teachers. From his first $28-a-week job as an elementary school teacher in New York City to head of the nearly one-million-member American Federation of Teachers, building respect for teachers was always central to Shanker.

As a young teacher, Shanker joined the United Federation of Teachers (UFT), the AFT local for New York City. In 1959, he became a full-time organizer, a leader of several very successful teacher strikes, and in 1964 president of the UFT. In 1974, he became national president of the American Federation of Teachers, a position he held until his death in 1997. During his long presidency, he worked to make teaching a profession.

During his early years in education, however, the word *professional* had an unusual connotation for Shanker, one with negative overtones. It did not represent a standard of excellence but, rather, a threat to force teachers to behave in a servile manner and to obey rules, even those that went against their own judgment about good education: "Mr. Shanker, there are a couple of pieces of paper on the floor over there. It is very unsightly and very unprofessional."[a]

Shanker redefined the word *professional:*

> "A professional is a person who is an expert, and by view of that expertise is permitted to operate fairly independently, to make decisions, to exercise discretion, to be free of most direct supervision. No one stands over a surgeon at the operating table with direction to cut a little to the left or to the right. . . . If we are to achieve that professional status, we have to take a step beyond collective bargaining—not to abandon it, but to build

on it, develop new processes, new institutions, new procedures that will bring us what teachers want in addition to what we get from collective bargaining: status, dignity, a voice in professional matters, the compensation of a professional."[b]

[a]Albert Shanker, "The Making of a Profession," *American Education* 9, no. 3 (fall 1985): pp. 10–17, 46, 48.
[b]Shanker, "The Making of a Profession," pp. 10–17.

"It was the AFT that demanded and fought for the teacher's right to bargain collectively.

"It was the AFT leaders who went to jail to show the nation their determination that teachers would no longer stand for second-class status.

"It was the AFT that won New York City teachers their pay increases and other benefits.

"And, as part of the great labor movement, the AFL-CIO, the AFT continues to show the nation that through the power of the union the voice of America's teachers will be heard."

SANDRA FELDMAN

Another New Yorker, Sandra Feldman became president of the AFT after Shanker's death. In her youth, she was active in the Civil Rights movement of the 1960s. While trying to establish herself as a writer, she became a free-lance editor, and eventually came to the classroom in order to earn a better salary. After three years of elementary school teaching, she became a field representative for the UFT (United Federation of Teachers), the New York chapter of the AFT. Now, as the first woman leader of the AFT since 1930, Feldman has several items on her agenda, including improving urban schools and reducing class size. Feldman takes the reins of leadership during a period of intense criticism of the nation's schools. She has urged the AFT to take the lead in identifying and closing weak schools, and complains that too often, educational reform has been reduced to getting rid of *teachers* instead of *bad practices*. She has created a system which sidesteps seniority, a sacred union cow, in order to hire the most competent teachers for a school. She has gained a reputation as a hard working, progressive union leader. *"When you're representing teachers, you're representing people with master's degrees, people who have lots of strong opinions about things, and are very aware and conscious of issues. We have tremendous participation and active involvement in the union. You've got to meet their standards to be a leader."*

Source: Ann Bradley, "Contract for Change," *Teacher Magazine* (November-December 1997): pp. 38–41.

While you are reading literature handed out at the MFT meeting, you learn that the AFT, with under a million members and more than two thousand locals, is a good deal smaller than the NEA. The association began gaining impetus in the latter part of the 1950's. By 1961, the AFT had won the right to bargain for New York City teachers, and through collective bargaining and strikes it set precedents by obtaining raises and other benefits for them. As a result of successes in New York, AFT membership began to grow in labor-oriented urban areas where teachers were fed up with low salaries and poor working conditions and were willing to strike as a means of improving things. In Washington, DC, Boston, Cleveland, Chicago, and other cities, the AFT won elections and their right to represent teachers. Militancy was bringing the AFT both members and victories, although its successes were usually confined to urban centers. The AFT's image as a streetwise, scrappy union has shifted since the 1970s. In fact, through the ideas and activities of its long-time president, Albert Shanker, the AFT took a leadership role in education reform. Shanker supported national exams for students as well as national standards for teachers and was a pioneer in the creation of charter schools. The AFT also supports both induction programs that enable new teachers to work with master teachers and active recruitment of people of color into the teaching profession.[20]

BOB CHASE

For most of its existence, the NEA has been seen as a large, bureaucratic organization slow to change and quick to defend teachers, even bad teachers. Bob Chase recounts that when he was preparing a speech, half a year after becoming NEA President, he went against staff advice. His staff warned him not to use the phrase "bad teachers," because it would probably offend his membership. Instead, he was advised to say: "There are some teachers in our classroom who aren't doing a particularly good job." But Chase rejected their advice. He believes that there are bad teachers, and everyone knows that, and that he ought to say it. He concedes that some teachers are ineffective, and believes that their teaching needs to be improved, or they need to be removed. Bob Chase entitled his speech, "A New Approach to Teacher Unionism: It's Not Your Mother's NEA." Like his contemporary Sandra Feldman at the AFT, Chase has become the leader of a national teacher's organization at a time of educational upheaval. Rather than inhibit change, Chase and the NEA are working to become influential participants in the direction of that change.

In the 1996 Presidential campaign, Senator Robert Dole, the GOP presidential candidate, attacked the NEA as a liberal special interest group concerned only with power and protecting teachers, and not with quality education. While Shanker and the AFT were viewed by many politicians as more realistic in accepting change, the NEA was viewed as intransigent, and became a national target of conservative politicians. Dole said: *If education were a war, you'd be losing it. If it were a patient, it would be dying. When I am president, I will disregard your political power for the sake of the children, the schools, and the nation.* The NEA was cast as an obstacle to progress.

What Senator Dole's speech initiated was an intense self-evaluation of the NEA. As a result, the NEA has become a more active partner in the reform movement. After a hotly contested campaign, Chase won union endorsement for *peer review*, the idea that teachers should monitor their peers and insure quality teaching. Chase's advocacy for an AFT-NEA merger, however, was rejected.

Born in Wellfleet, Massachusetts, Bob Chase was one of five children living in a poor household where both parents worked as laborers. Although Chase was interested in becoming a Catholic priest, after two years in a seminary, he couldn't forget the words he had heard earlier: *Bobby, have you ever thought about becoming a teacher?* A high school English teacher, his favorite teacher, had spoken those words years earlier, but they resonated. Now Bob Chase finds himself the head of the largest teachers' organization, trying to reform the profession.

Source: David Hill, "In the Line of Fire," *Teacher Magazine* (November-December 1997): pp. 32–36.

Your materials point out that the AFT offers a wide array of services, including

- *The American Teacher,* a monthly newspaper; the *American Educator,* a quarterly professional journal; and *Action,* a weekly newsletter, and of course, a web page.
- Local workshops and national forums on such topics as teacher education, staff development, critical thinking, school finance, and other education reform issues.
- Political action in favor of the candidates who support public education.

A LOOK AT . . . A FIRST YEAR TEACHER

A Classroom Challenge I Just Had to Take
By Mathina Carkci

Mathina Carkci, who wrote about education as a reporter for suburban Maryland newspapers for three years, became a fourth-grade teacher at Bailey's Elementary School in Fairfax County.

The most surprising thing about being a teacher is how often I feel like a failure. I knew that teaching fourth grade would be hard, but I expected to be able to keep up with everything and to succeed. So it's disheartening, just two months into my first job, to feel the weight of things left undone, questionable decisions made and professional duties unmet.

My teacher friends say they used to feel the same way. Some admit they still do. My student-teaching supervisor sympathetically cautions that the first two years are so unlike the "real thing" that they don't count. The teacher across the hall reminds me to take baby steps. My mom, a university professor, promises it will get better. I'm too hard on myself, a former professor tells me; it takes time to grow into the teacher I want to be.

I take some comfort from the fact that friends who were in the same one-year master's certification program at the University of Maryland last year have found it hard from the word go. I called Natalie the evening of her first day, a week before I started.

"If you told me I didn't have to go tomorrow," she said, "I wouldn't."

I called Al on his second day. "After the kids left today, I shut the door and cried," he said.

My friends and family told me I'd be a great teacher. They said they imagined a group of children gazing up at me, accompanying me on exciting journeys that would fill their minds with wonder. "You're such a good person," my husband told me. "The kids are going to love you." It gave me the chills, the way good classical music does, to think of myself and my merry band of students, gallivanting through the curriculum.

So it's difficult to admit now how hard it is to be a first-year teacher: how every single day I feel as if I am drowning; how I spend 12 hours at school each day working and four hours at home worrying; how each evening as I leave school, I have to decide which of 100 equally important things I should leave undone; how I feel so far behind that I will never catch up until Christmas, when I have 10 days "off."

When I get to school, anywhere from an hour and a half to two hours before the kids, a list of tasks swims through my head, and, as the minutes tick away until 8:40 arrives, I run through my priorities. With any luck, I'll have put up the day's schedule, written the daily message to the students and created the math warm-up exercise the night before. I might

respond to kids' journals but change my mind when I realize the math lesson I had planned misses an important element. (Half my mind, all this time, is wondering what the best way is to teach kids to determine the volume of solid shapes.) I might walk to the copier, see the line of other teachers and decide instead to swing by the library to schedule a block of time for my students. Or I might run into the guidance counselor and discuss ways to help a student who's been misbehaving.

Then I notice a student's desk that seems to be exploding papers and books, and wonder how best to help the child get organized: Does she need me to go through the pile with her, paper by paper? (And when would I do that?) Or should I write her a note and carve out a chunk of the day for her to organize things herself? Or do I need to have a talk with the whole class about keeping things straight?

It isn't as if I wasn't well prepared or don't have support. My year-long internship, including 12 weeks of student teaching, gave me a taste of the challenges I'd face. A mentor at my school, Bailey's Elementary, meets with me regularly, and Fairfax County bends over backward to provide new teachers with help. Bailey's teems with kind, helpful colleagues. Volunteers, including my mom who comes in every Friday, offer assistance of all sorts. Short of having a personal assistant 12 hours a day, I don't think there's anything more anyone could do to ease my transition.

Idealistic grad school conversations about pedagogy and democracy in the classroom made me surer than ever that I was right to go into teaching, that here was where I would make my impact on a part of the world that mattered to me. The master's program helped me build a solid educational philosophy based on wanting children to discover for themselves how rewarding learning can be.

I never thought my career switch would be easy. I had covered education when I was a newspaper reporter, so I'd seen the kinds of tightropes that many teachers walk. But I wanted to do something more active than writing about them. As a teacher, I could be with students every day and show them in tangible ways that their ideas mattered.

I try to make this happen in the classroom, but as we all know, theory and practice don't always overlap. I spend more time thinking up ways to get students to hand in homework than I do thinking about how to help them to pursue their own questions, or promoting their curiosity. Despite having vowed not to use rewards and punishments as a method of controlling the class, I have found myself giving kids extra recess for walking quietly in line or sending them back to their seats if they seem disruptive. My interactions with kids are less positive than I once hoped they would be, and I say "No,"

(Box concludes on next page)

without explanation, far more often than I would like. Instead of designing creative, hands-on lessons in every subject, I sometimes teach straight from the book in science and social studies classes.

But, in the end, I don't think I'm really a failure. We have meetings, where my whole class tries to solve problems anyone puts on the agenda. I play with the kids at recess, which might make me seem more like another kid than like a teacher, but I think it also helps them to see me as someone worth following. I've managed to avoid being ruled by the lesson plan. The other day, two boys invented their own way of conducting a science project that involved analyzing rocks, and, when I realized their way was better, I encouraged the rest of the class to go with it instead of following the instructions.

I may not be on the same social studies textbook chapter as the other fourth-grade teachers, and I'll probably be late returning standardized tests to the assistant principal, but I think my kids know they're important to me. I see it in tiny, fleeting moments. I see it when a student says, "Mrs. Carkci, I wish you could come to my house for the weekend. That would be fun." I see it when a boy writes to me to ask if I will take him to the movies, or when a girl gives me a goofy smile after I've led the class down the hall taking giant, silly steps. I'm proud that a girl believes it is okay to ask "Why in America do people speak lots of languages, while in Vietnam, they only speak one language?" Or that a boy knows I will encourage him to pursue his question, "Who invented the planets?"

Once or twice, early on, I considered quitting. But no longer. I like helping my 21 students learn about the four regions of Virginia; I enjoy encouraging them to write and to use new paragraphs for new ideas; and I thrive on watching them become mathematical thinkers. Just the other day a student told me, out of the blue, that he'd noticed how the desks in our classroom were like intersecting lines. It was our geometry unit made real.

I can't imagine what it will be like in two years, when I have figured out a good response to tattling and when I have prepared a classroom set of spelling games. I don't love teaching yet, but I am beginning to catch glimpses of what it will be like when I do.

As you deliberate between the two groups, you cannot help but speculate about a merger of these two professional organizations, because a possible merger is constantly in the news. A merger of the NEA and AFT would form an incredibly powerful union of 3 million teachers. Such an organization could wield enormous national leverage, potentially gaining significant benefits for education in general and teachers in particular.

As you weigh the relative merits of the two organizations, and the impact of a future merger, you find yourself pondering some basic questions, including whether either of the associations makes sense for you to join. Some teachers are opposed to both, claiming that the NEA and AFT put the salaries of teachers above the needs of children. They argue that teacher associations have pitted administrators against teachers, and teachers against the public, creating needless hostility. And, perhaps worst of all, these critics charge that unions have too often protected incompetent teachers who should be removed from the classroom. Now you add a new question to ponder: are teacher associations really good for education?

Decision time may be closer than you think. Have you decided which, if either, to join? Does the NEA or the AFT speak for you?

Summary

1. Teachers make a difference. Studies underscore that, dollar for dollar, investments in teacher qualifications and training directly and substantially improve student achievement.

2. Teachers provided with sufficient support can move through a series of stages: survival, consolidation, renewal, and maturity. At each level, the teacher's influence becomes more powerful as the teacher's focus moves from personal concerns

(such as classroom management) to broader educational issues (school strategies that could enhance student learning).

3. School districts are implementing a variety of induction programs designed to assist first-year teachers. Mentors, or consulting teachers, work with intern teachers to help them succeed in their new position. These mentors provide both personal and professional support, as well as observe and evaluate new teachers' skills. Classroom observations of teachers are done not only by mentors but also by supervisors or colleagues. When other teachers do the observation, the approach is called peer review.

4. Professional development has become an integral part of a teacher's life, not just for new teachers but for all teachers. Effective professional development is directly related to a teacher's work, links subject content with teaching skills, uses problem solving, and is research-based and supported over time.

5. Educational reform advocates are reshaping schools to build learning communities, more intimate and personal educational climates. These changes include smaller size, looping to increase student-teacher connections, block scheduling for longer and more in-depth study, and broadening of the teacher's role.

6. Focused résumés, comprehensive portfolios, and effective interviewing skills are useful strategies available to new teachers seeking that first teaching position.

7. One of the reform recommendations established the National Board for Professional Teacher Standards is to identify and assess superior educators, who are identified as board-certified teachers. This is one of several efforts designed to increase the professional status of teaching.

8. Merit pay and career ladders are two other efforts aimed at professionalizing teaching. Merit pay offers teachers more money based on various criteria, including gains in student performance, typically measured by standardized tests; teacher performance, as measured by outside evaluators; individualized plans, in which teachers have a voice in setting their own goals; and the nature of the teaching assignment. Each of these approaches is controversial. Career ladders, on the other hand, offer teachers increases in salary based on their competence and advance teachers through increasing levels of job responsibility. Some argue that the problems of this approach mirror those of merit pay, while others insist that career ladder programs offer room for true professional development.

9. The National Education Association (NEA) is the largest professional and employee association in the nation. Formed during the second half of the 1800s, initially it was slow to work for the needs of its members. (In its early days, women were not even admitted.) During the 1960s and 1970s, the NEA became a stronger advocate of teachers' rights. In the 1980s and 1990s, it refined its position on a variety of educational reform proposals while exploring merger possibilities with the AFT.

10. When teachers' unions from the Midwest affiliated with the American Federation of Labor in 1916, the American Federation of Teachers (AFT) was formed. While significantly smaller than the NEA, the AFT has historically taken a more militant position, demonstrated by its early support of teacher strikes. Under the longtime leadership of Albert Shanker, the AFT changed its image from that of a scrappy union to that of an important force in education reform.

11. Today both the NEA and the AFT offer a range of services, including magazines, journals, and other professional communications; legal assistance; workshops and conferences; assistance in collective bargaining; and political activism.

Key Terms and People

www.mhhe.com/sadker

American Federation of
   Teachers (AFT)

block scheduling

board certification

career ladders

Bob Chase

collaborative action research
   (CAR)

collective bargaining

Sandra Feldman

induction program

in-service

intern teachers

learning communities

looping

mentors

merit pay

National Board for
   Professional Teaching
   Standards (NBPTS)

National Education
   Association (NEA)

peer review

portfolio

professional development

résumé

Albert Shanker

stages of teacher
   development

Discussion Questions and Activities

1. How might you redefine or modify any of the stages of teacher development? Can these stages be applied to other careers?

2. Visit a school and analyze the faculty in terms of the stages of development. What are the specific behaviors and skills that place a teacher at each of these stages?

3. Survey local school districts and analyze their first-year induction programs. What resources do they provide new teachers to assist them in making their transition into teaching successful? Will this affect your decision as to where to teach? You might want to research first-year teacher induction programs in the library, to get a sense of the range of resources offered to first-year teachers.

4. Interview one or more first-year teachers. What are their biggest challenges? Where do they go to seek support? What lessons can they offer you?

5. Interview a mentor, a veteran teacher who has worked with new teachers during the induction period. What advice does the mentor have for you to help your first year be a success? Are there steps you can take now to build toward a successful first year?

6. What do you look for in a mentor? What strategies can you use to recruit such a mentor in your first teaching job?

7. In order to get a sense of the breadth of professional opportunities available to you, add to the list started in this book. Construct a folder of professional service courses, workshops, and other opportunities available to teachers. To do this, you may want to contact local school districts, professional associations, the state department of education, and colleges and to review professional journals.

8. Develop some potential topics for a collaborative action research project. Consider undertaking this project as a research activity during your teaching education program.

9. What are the similarities and differences between the NEA and the AFT? Write to both organizations to find out more about them, or visit their web pages. Which do you think will best meet your needs as a teacher?

10. Interview some practicing teachers to determine their opinions of the NEA and the AFT. Interview retired teachers for their reactions. Summarize your findings.

11. In your own words, summarize the historical development of these professional associations. You might want to do a research paper on this topic to learn more. Interview teachers who have participated in strikes. What are their opinions? Interview citizens, both those with and those without children in school. What are their opinions about teacher strikes?

A Final Word

American Schools: Better Than We Think?

> Everyone is aware today that our educational system has been
> allowed to deteriorate. It has been going downhill for some years
> without anything really constructive having been done to arrest the
> decline, still less to reverse its course. We thus have a chronic crisis: an
> unsolved problem as grave as any that faces our country today. Unless this
> problem is dealt with promptly and effectively, the machinery that sustains
> our level of material prosperity and political power will begin to slow down.[1]

Does this sound familiar, as though you just read it in today's newspaper? Actually, this was written in the 1950s by Admiral Hyman Rickover, a frequent critic of U.S. schools. And that's the point that a growing number of educators are making: school bashing is nothing new; it is as American as apple pie, an old tradition that has reached a new peak in recent years. In fact, these educators believe that not only is the current crescendo of criticism old hat, but it is terribly misguided, because today's schools are doing as well as they ever have—maybe, just maybe, they are doing better.

Relatively low performance by U.S. students on international tests has frequently been cited as evidence that the nation's schools are in terrible shape. But school advocates point out that this is a classic case of misinterpreting test data. What the tests may reflect are cultural and curricular differences, not necessarily problems with our educational system. Consider the comparison between Japanese and U.S. middle school students on algebra tests. Japanese students score significantly higher, but most Japanese students take algebra a year or two earlier than U.S. students do. Comparing the algebra scores of those who have taken an algebra course with the scores of those who have not is hardly a fair comparison of educational systems. Moreover, most Japanese children attend private academies, called *Juku* schools, after regular school hours and on weekends. By 16 years of age, the typical Japanese student has attended at least two more years of classes than has a U.S. student, another reason international comparisons are misleading. In fact, because of the greater comparative effectiveness of U.S. colleges in relation to Japanese colleges, many of these differences evaporate on later tests. Perhaps there are two lessons here: (1) U.S. students should spend more time in school and (2) the Japanese need to improve the quality of their colleges.

Student selection also affects test scores. In the United States, the full range of students is included in test populations, strong and weak students, English-speaking and non-English-speaking students. In other countries, students who do not speak the dominant language are routinely excluded. In some nations, only a small percentage of the most talented students are selected or encouraged to continue their education and go on to high school. As one might imagine, this highly selective population does quite well on international tests. Comparing all of America's students with the best of another nation's is a biased comparison.

Cultural differences affect not only student selection but also test performance. Americans value a comprehensive education, one in which students are involved in a wide array of activities, from theater to sports to community service. The U.S. public typically values spontaneity, social responsibility, and a degree of independence in their children, values that are not assessed in international tests. Where the United States values the breadth of education, some other cultures more narrowly emphasize competitive testing. In a number of European and Asian countries, a student's entire future may hinge on a single critical test. In this "test-well-or-perish" mentality, only the few students who are successful "test takers" are allowed to go on to academic high schools and college, or to take international tests. Consider the way a South Korean teacher identifies the students selected for the International Assessment of Education Progress (IAEP).

> The math teacher . . . calls the names of the 13-year-olds in the room who have been selected as part of the IAEP sample. As each name is called, the student stands at attention at his or her desk until the list is complete. Then, to the supportive and encouraging applause of their colleagues, the chosen ones leave to [take the assessment test].[2]

U.S. students selected to take international exams do not engender cheers from their classmates and do not view such tests as a matter of national honor, as do the South Korean students. Quite the contrary, they are more likely to view such exams as a inconvenience. Too often, our culture belittles "intellectuals" and mocks gifted students.

A larger number of American test-takers are likely to be poor, another factor depressing U.S. test scores. About one in five children in the United States lives in poverty. The United States has by far the largest proportion of poor children, when compared with other developed nations participating in these exams. These students bring precious few resources to schools or to tests. Facing such problems as malnutrition, inadequate housing, and family instability, these poverty-stricken students would lower the average score of any nation. As if extensive poverty of families and their children were not enough of a handicap, school funding practices amplify the problem. Americans tolerate enormous inequities in school funding levels, and typically schools in the poorest neighborhoods struggle the most for adequate funding. Other nations distribute school funds more equitably, avoiding the extremes of wealth and poverty that characterize U.S. education. Funding inequities and high levels of poverty are factors few commentators mention when discussing the test scores of U.S. students.

Despite these obstacles, on several key tests the nation's students are doing quite well. For example, by the mid-1990s, American students had achieved the second highest average score among thirty-one nations on international comparisons of reading. On the National Assessment of Education Progress (NAEP), students had attained all-time high scores in seven of the nine areas, including reading, math, and science. The proportion of students scoring above 650 on the SAT mathematics tests had reached an all-time high. The number of students taking Advanced Placement (AP) tests soared from 98,000 in 1978 to 448,000 in 1994, a sign that far more students are in the race for advanced college standing. Improvements have been documented on the California Achievement Test, the Iowa Test of Basic Skills, and the Metropolitan Achievement Test, tests used across the nation to measure student learning. One of the most encouraging signs has been the performance of students of color, whose scores have risen dramatically. Among 17-year-old African American students, average reading scores on the NAEP tests rose two grade levels between 1971 and 1992.[3] Decades ago, many of these students probably would not have even been in school, much less taking tests. In 1940, the overall high school graduation rate in the United States was only 38 percent; by the early 1990s, it was approaching 90 percent. Other indicators reflect that students are not only staying in school longer but also are enrolling in more advanced math and science classes. It is evident that U.S. schools are teaching more students, that students are staying in school for longer periods of time, and that children are studying more challenging courses than ever before. Then why is there a national upheaval about education—why all the furor about our failing schools and why the demands for radical school reform? Educators have advanced a number of possible explanations:

- School bashing is simply a traditional U.S. pastime. Journalists and politicians have been critiquing schools since the nation began.
- Adults tend to romanticize what schools were like when they attended as children, for they always studied harder and learned more than their children do (and when they went to school, they had to walk through four feet of snow, uphill, in both directions!).
- Americans hold unrealistic expectations. They want schools to conquer all sorts of social and academic ills, from illiteracy to teenage pregnancy, and to accomplish everything from teaching advanced math to preventing AIDS. Since today's social problems of crime, violence, and poverty are growing, schools must be failing.
- If progress has been slower than desired, perhaps part of the reason is that the challenge is greater than ever before. Schools today work with tremendous numbers of poor students, non-English-speaking children, and special education students who just a few years ago would not be attending school as long or, in some cases, would not be attending school at all.
- In the 1990s, Americans expressed dissatisfaction with many institutions, from government bureaucracies to labor unions to journalists. The perception of schools has been colored by this general feeling of discontent.
- In *The Manufactured Crisis,* David Berliner and Bruce Biddle put much of the blame for the current criticism on neoconservative policies reinforced by conservative Republican Congresses elected through the mid-1990s. Their political agenda supporting private schools, business interests, and vouchers marked the beginning of a major assault on public education, on federal involvement in schools, and on equal education programs targeted at minority groups and women. The result has been a loss of confidence in the performance of public schools, an emphasis on alternative forms of education, and the rapid growth of "for-profit" educational companies.
- Along with a political change of climate, Berliner and Biddle also finger the press, which has been all too willing to publish negative stories about schools—stories based on questionable sources. From uncritically accepting the idea that campuses are characterized by "political correctness" gone to extremes to publishing selective test scores that reflect negatively on U.S. education, sloppy, biased reporting has damaged the public's perception of schools.

These are only some of the possible reasons underlying the current criticism of education, but they provide perspective. It is helpful to remember two points. First, criticism can be fruitful. If additional attention and even criticism help shape stronger schools, then the current furor will have at least some positive impact. Second, there are countless students in all parts of the country who work diligently every day and perform with excellence. The United States continues to produce leaders in fields as diverse as medicine and sports, business and entertainment. To a great extent, these success stories are also the stories of talented and dedicated teachers. Although their quiet daily contributions rarely reach the headlines, teachers do make a difference. You represent the next generation of teachers who will, no doubt, weather difficult times and sometimes adverse circumstances to touch the lives of students and to shape a better America.

inter-mission

Part 4 Tomorrow

Here we are, at your final Inter-mission. These last applications and reflections are intended to get you ready for—tomorrow.

Applications and Reflections

4:1 Add a Nontraditional Hero

INTASC PRINCIPLE 1
Knowledge of Subject Matter

Purpose: We know that students need inspiring figures—individuals who serve as role models and motivate students. Your subject matter expertise affords you knowledge of people who might motivate your future students. Although heroes come from all backgrounds, curricular materials do not always reflect diversity. The result is a "disconnect" between the growing diversity of America's students and the curriculum they study. You can tighten this connection by supplementing the curriculum. Can you add to the list of champions in their lives, especially nontraditional individuals (consider ethnicity, race, gender, age, class, lifestyle, and circumstances)? Identifying such heroes has the additional advantage of broadening your own scholarship.

Activity: In a subject area that you will be teaching, select a unique individual or hero who has *made a difference*. Create a billboard, poster, or computer graphic that captures the importance of this person. Make the language, content, and style relevant to the grade level you plan to teach, one that will attract and motivate your students.

Reflection: What has this activity taught you about nontraditional heroes? How might you make this assignment applicable to your classroom instruction? What criteria might you add to guarantee good selection of a nontraditional hero? What structure might produce informative research (questions to be covered, length and depth of coverage, assessment)? What format might you create for displaying your student's final products?

4:2 Getting to Know Whom?

INTASC PRINCIPLE 2
Knowledge of Human Development and Learning

Purpose: Chapter 13, "The Struggle for Educational Opportunity," exposed some of life's heritage and happenings that influence who we are. Many of us have grown up in relatively homogeneous environments, knowing individuals who have comparable backgrounds and cultures. Meaningful conversations about how race, nationality, substance abuse, and family crisis impacted our own education are rare when diverse backgrounds are missing, yet such conversation could add essence and texture to your understanding of students.

Activity: Partner with a classmate, campus colleague, or friend who seems to come from a different background than you. Use the issues mentioned in the chapter to conduct an interview that will uncover information, stories, and perhaps feelings. Concentrate on being a good and an active listener. Some opening thoughts might include

- How do you identify your race or ethnicity?
- How would you describe your family heritage?
- How would you describe your family structure and patterns of daily life?
- Do you have memories of bias and discrimination?
- Do you have recollections about friends who struggled with substance abuse (drinking, drugs, and smoking), depression and suicide, or sexuality and teen pregnancy?
- What other concerns have you experienced or witnessed that denied or impeded educational opportunity?
- How has diversity influenced your own education or your commitment to teach?

Reflection: How are you and your interviewee different? How are you similar? How might this anecdotal information add to your understanding of child and human development? What aspects of your partner's cognitive, social, and emotional growth paralleled your own schooling? All in all, what words might describe your conversation: *insightful, laborious, superficial, intimate?* What words do you think your partner might use as a description?

4:3 A Novel Read

Purpose: Great teachers have an incredible ability to care, really deeply, about children. Such teachers learn about their students, hold high expectations for them, and fully appreciate their diverse cultural perspectives and learning styles. One marvelous way to understand youngsters is to read literature about the challenges they face. The right books will not only inspire you, but also will expand your awareness of diverse learners.

Activity: Maybe this is an Inter-mission activity you will save for summer vacation or a beach-based holiday. Or let this be a change of pace from your textbooks and research papers. Your education faculty will probably have additions to this book list. Pick a book and dig into it:

Teacher, Sylvia Ashton-Warner

Warriors Don't Cry: A Searing Memoir of the Battle to Integrate Little Rock's Central High, Melba Patillo Beals

Mentors, Masters and Mrs. MacGregor: Stories of Teachers Making a Difference, Jane Bluestein (Editor)

Bury My Heart at Wounded Knee, Dee Brown

America Is in the Heart, Carlos Bulosan

Family Values: A Lesbian Mother's Fight for Her Son, Phyllis Burke

Black Ice, Lorene Cary

House on Mango Street, Sandra Cisneros

The Water Is Wide, Patrick Conroy

Reflections of a Rock Lobster: A Story About Growing Up Gay, Aaron Fricke

One Child, Torey Hayden

Goodbye, Mr. Chips, James Hilton

Up the Down Staircase, Bel Kaufman

Among Schoolchildren, Tracy Kidder

Amazing Grace, Jonathon Kozol

Coming of Age in Mississippi, Ann Moody

The Bluest Eye, Toni Morrison

900 Shows a Year, Stuart Palonsky

The Education of a WASP, Lois Stalvey

Tales Out of School: A Teacher's Account from the Front Lines of the American High School Today, Patrick Welsh (editor)

Native Son, Richard Wright

Reflection: What did you learn from reading this book? Did you "unlearn" or abandon any misconceptions after your reading? Can you identify implications for your classroom? Would you assign this book to your students or suggest it for a faculty book club?

4:4 Cybervision

Purpose: For over a century, researchers have observed and analyzed classrooms. Now, technology is giving us another reason to examine teachers and student achievement. As Chapter 14, "Technology in Education," pointed out, the monumental investments in computer technology have not been matched by monumental gains in student achievement. Observing technology in the classroom will help you determine your future investment as a teacher. What will your "cyber visitation" reveal in terms of technology's impact on instructional strategies?

Activity: Visit a high-tech educational site (a school with an established computer lab or a classroom that integrates technology). Take notes on what you see and hear. Focus on the teacher and the techniques that promote or inhibit learning.

Reflection: What do your notes reveal? Look for themes, concepts, and patterns. Given the teacher's instructional strategies (and your recall of Chapter 3, "Teacher Effectiveness"), what made the lesson successful? If you were going to coach the teacher, what skills might you suggest for his or her improvement? How will instructional strategies change as students huddle over isolated screens, work in global groups on the Internet, or e-mail homework from a holiday hideaway? What teaching techniques will look familiar? What new skills should be developed and practiced? What other questions and answers might you offer?

4:5 Class Comedy Club

INTASC PRINCIPLE 5
Motivation and Management

Purpose: Thank goodness! For all the crises in classrooms and children at risk, humor in the educational workplace survives and even thrives. Healthful humor (as opposed to targeted humor and sarcasm) can motivate students to participate and learn. Student humor, often unintentional, can be a major factor in keeping you happy and in the business of teaching. While you may never aspire to be a comic, sharing a funny teaching story will help you practice setting a positive and welcoming learning climate.

Activity: While there are books about kids who say and do the darnedest things, as well as e-mail and magazine features filled with funny stories, there is nothing like oral history and the stories of your peers to tickle a funny bone. Begin by freewriting answers to the following questions:

- The funniest teacher I recall from school . . .
- The funniest student happening was . . .
- It sure was funny in school when . . . and she/he/they really did (or didn't) get in trouble . . .

Practice and dramatically deliver your funny stories. Encourage your peers to help you embroider them with colorful commentary, body language, and well-timed punchlines. Is there any chance that your class will finish the course with a post-exam comedy club? If so, let your storytelling add to the performance.

Reflection: Are you ready for the stage? Even if you are not, what was the impact of hearing about the humorous escapades of students, teachers, and school life? What is your philosophy regarding the role of humor in education? How can you imagine using humor to motivate and manage students?

4:6 "Do It Yourself" Tech Balance Sheet

INTASC PRINCIPLE 6
Communication Skills

Purpose: You certainly have your own experience, as a student, with computer technology. Are you wired into everything or stonewalling yourself away from it all? We want you to take both sides of the technology debate and fully develop two points of view: pro and con. Researching and refining polarized opinions is a communication challenge!

Activity: Consider what you have read about and explored in educational technology and generate a balance sheet that both supports and refutes the place of technology in education. (For a model, consider any of the balance sheets scattered throughout the textbook that take contrasting views on timely educational topics.) Select a very specific theme, especially one that is related to your subject area or grade level. Generate a title that polarizes opinions such as the following suggestions:

- Word Processing—Helping or Hurting Writing Skills
- Computers in Kindergarten—Absolutely Not or For Sure
- Our Technology Dollars—Classes For the Arts or For Computers
- Computers—One per Classroom or One per Child

For a more challenging activity, cite research studies to support both positions.

Reflection: By constructing both sides of an issue, what did you learn about balance and fairness in communication? What side of the balance sheet are you on? Could a reader detect that from your end product? Did you find that your views changed as you worked to present each side convincingly?

4:7 Video View

INTASC PRINCIPLE 7
Instructional Planning Skills

Purpose: When the door between the hall and the classroom closes, the teacher is often the only adult in the room. Technological advances may open up tomorrow's classrooms, so that administrators, staff developers, mentor teachers, and even parents can observe your instruction through the magic of video. Can you imagine how being "on camera" might affect your teaching and students' learning? Try.

Activity: Write a 450- to 500-word essay about what's happening in your room, as if you were watching from the office video monitor. Remember, you are playing the role of teacher. Consider camera placement and room arrangement in your critique. Describe students who have starring or supporting roles. Detail the scene that is visible and suggest what might be happening off camera. Include an episode with a particular learner or lay out the entire lesson plan.

Reflection: What's happening in your room? Have you used the textbook's content to provide a firm and an informative foundation for your classroom? How do you feel about "seeing" yourself as the teacher in this video? This might be a worthwhile essay to retain in your portfolio, as it represents an overview of your classroom planning, philosophy, and accomplishments.

4:8 Pruning Your Portfolio

INTASC PRINCIPLE 8
Assessment

Purpose: Earlier Inter-mission activities, reflections, and artifacts helped you create a *working* portfolio. Now is the time to assess your portfolio and decide what is worth keeping or upgrading.

Activity: Consider, as a complete package, the quality of your *working* portfolio. Use the following rubric to chart the status of your collection. Score your portfolio according to how well it meets the criteria listed, on a scale of 1 to 5. Provide verbal or written evidence to support your position. Select a partner (or two) and set aside ten minutes to discuss and share your *working* portfolios and the assessment charts.

- Purposeful—with a structure that is sound, such as professional standards
- Selective—based on a specific purpose
- Diverse—representing a broad array of teaching talent beyond your transcript, student teacher critique, letters of recommendation, and philosophy statement
- Ongoing—relays learning incidents over time
- Reflective—both in process and product, should inspire thoughtfulness
- Collaborative—through conversations and interactions with others (peers, students, parents, professors, teachers, administrators, and others)

STATE OF THE PORTFOLIO

	Not at All				Very	Not Applicable
	1	2	3	4	5	

Item

Purposeful:

Selective:

Diverse:

Ongoing:

Reflective:

Collaborative:

Other: _____

Overall Appraisal:

Reflection: What did you learn about your portfolio, including its strengths and weaknesses at this point? What did your discussion with your partners teach you? What are the next steps in selecting and organizing the materials that will become your *presentation* portfolio?

4:9 Web Site of the Month

Purpose: Web sites and Internet sources may prove to be of extraordinary benefit to your professional growth. However, quality control does not exist on the Internet, so, to be a reflective and responsible practitioner, you must learn to evaluate Internet sources.

Activity: Select three educational web sites. (Links from our textbook site are certainly a good starting place.) Choose one that is relevant to a subject matter area; another that is interactive, featuring bulletin boards or opportunities to "chat" with colleagues; and a third that is monitored or sponsored by a professional organization such as the NEA or AFT.

Explore the sites by determining frequency of updates, investigating links, monitoring "conversations," and assessing quality of content and graphics. Print out sample pages from the three sites and share your results informally with classmates.

Reflection: What other criteria can you use to decide which web sites and Internet resources are reliable? Are there techniques and shortcuts to *surfing* educational sites? What addresses might offer lesson plans, emotional support for new teachers, factual materials for curriculum planning, and colleagues for an issue-based dialogue?

4:10 Do Drop In

INTASC PRINCIPLE 10
Relationships
and Partnerships

Purpose: Many youths are served by agencies and support services beyond schools. Particularly when poverty threatens to limit children's potential, these community programs fill an important role. Your teaching can be more effective if you understand the contributions of those who work with children outside of schools.

Activity: Visit a community youth service agency, such as a Head Start center or one of the Boys and Girls Clubs of America. Request a tour of the facilities and try to arrange for a youth member or leader to spend some time with you. Use your questioning and interviewing skills (honed to a fine edge in previous Inter-missions) to find out about the impact of the organization on children and adolescents. Observe overt and subtle interactions between staff and members—watch procedures and rituals carefully.

Reflection: How does this agency serve youths in ways that support their education and achievement? How do issues of race, ethnicity, language, and class intersect in this nonschool environment? Do the children behave differently during the informal program than they do in school? Would you consider getting involved with this organization? What might you gain from working or volunteering in this nonschool setting? What formal connections exist between the schools and this agency?

Portfolio Artifact Collections

4:P6 Newsworthy

INTASC PRINCIPLE 6
Communication Skills

Purpose: A brief and accurate declaration about you is an important introduction to your portfolio. As a template, you can use one of three formats sprinkled throughout the text: *Profiles in Teaching*, *Class Acts*, or an expanded *In the News* feature. These designs will set up a unique approach to describing you as a future teacher.

Activity: Write a brief personal statement (150 words) using one of the layouts, or create a design of your own. Whether your effort becomes the cover page to your presentation portfolio or an insert in your job application packet, this tight and compelling bio will be an invitation to read further.

4:P8 Letters, You'll Get Letters

Purpose: Trying to keep your portfolio up-to-date is a long-term investment of your time and energy, and keeping letters of recommendation current is challenging. Former faculty, mentors, and employers can be tough to track down. This activity will keep your artifact collection contemporary.

Activity: Request a letter of recommendation from individuals who know the caliber of your work as a student, an employee, or a youth leader. Volunteer to help by providing a résumé, key points, or even a rough draft. Useful information includes

- Critical details (name, classes you have taken, your final grade, any special products or papers you submitted)
- Your specific job interest
- Personal and professional attributes that make you a good candidate for a position

Be sure to provide any necessary forms and envelopes with the correct address and postage. Filing a copy with the placement office at your university career center is advantageous. If your writers are willing, encourage them to provide extra copies, either open or signed and sealed, for your portfolio. This should be an ongoing activity to keep your file up-to-date. A handwritten thank-you note is always a courteous final step.

Finale

Your Inter-missions are over. The activities, reflections, and artifact collection tasks applied the major themes found in *Teachers, Schools, and Society*. Your completed assignments have become the foundation of your *working* portfolio. It will take further refining, considerable course work, and many hours of practice teaching to produce your *presentation* portfolio. We wish you every success.

Appendix 1

Addresses for State Offices of Certification

ALABAMA
Teacher Education and Certification
State Department of Education
P.O. Box 302101
Montgomery, AL 36130-2101
334-242-9560
334-242-0498 (fax)

ALASKA
Department of Education
Teacher Education & Certification
801 West 10th Street, Suite 200
Juneau, AK 99801-1894
907-465-2831 or 2026

ARIZONA
Certification Unit-70016
P.O. Box 6490
Phoenix, AZ 85005-6490
602-542-4367

ARKANSAS
Teacher Education & Licensure
State Department of Education
4 State Capitol Mall
Little Rock, AR 72201-1071
501-682-4342

CALIFORNIA
Commission on Teacher Credentialing
Box 944270
Sacramento, CA 94244-2700
916-445-7254

COLORADO
Educator Licensing
State Dept. of Education
201 E. Colfax Avenue
Denver, CO 80203
303-866-6628

CONNECTICUT
Bureau of Certification and
  Teacher Preparation
State Dept. of Education
Box 2219
Hartford, CT 06145-2219
860-566-5201

DELAWARE
Teacher Certification
Dept. of Public Instruction
P.O. Box 1402
Dover, DE 19903
302-739-4686

DISTRICT OF COLUMBIA
Division of Teacher Services
825 North Capital Street, N.E.
6th Floor
Washington, DC 20002
202-442-5377

FLORIDA
Bureau of Teacher Certification
Florida Education Center
325 W. Gaines, Rm. 201
Tallahassee, FL 32399-0400
904-488-2317

GEORGIA
Professional Standards Commission
Certification Section
1454 Twin Towers East
Atlanta, GA 30334
404-657-9000

HAWAII
Office of Personnel Services
Teacher Recruitment Unit
P.O. Box 2360
Honolulu, HI 96804
808-586-3420
800-305-5104

IDAHO
Certification Division
State Dept. of Education
P.O. Box 83720
Boise, ID 83720-0027
208-332-6880

ILLINOIS
Illinois State Board of Education
Certification & Placement Section
100 N. First Street
Springfield, IL 62777-0001
217-782-4321

INDIANA
Indiana Professional Standards Board
Teacher Licensing
251 East Ohio Street, Suite 201
Indianapolis, IN 46204-2133
317-232-9010
317-232-9023 (fax)

IOWA
Board of Educational Examiners
Grimes State Office Building
Des Moines, IA 50319-0147
515-281-3245

KANSAS
Certification Section
Kansas State Dept. of Education
Kansas State Education Building
120 SE 10th Ave.
Topeka, KS 66612-1182
913-296-2288

KENTUCKY
Kentucky Dept. of Education
Division of Certification
1024 Capital Center Drive
Frankfort, KY 40601-1972
502-573-4606

LOUISIANA
Louisiana Dept. of Education
Teacher Certification, Room 700
P.O. Box 94064
Baton Rouge, LA 70804-9064
504-342-3490

MAINE
Division of Certification and
   Placement
Department of Education
State House Station 23
Augusta, ME 04333
207-287-5944

MARYLAND
Division of Certification 18100
State Dept. of Education
200 West Baltimore St.
Baltimore, MD 21201
410-767-0412

MASSACHUSETTS
Massachusetts Dept. of Education
Office of Teacher Certification
   and Credentialing
350 Main Street
Malden, MA 02148
617-388-3300

MICHIGAN
Office of Professional Preparation
   & Certification
Michigan Dept. of Education
P.O. Box 30008
Lansing, MI 48909
517-373-3310

MINNESOTA
Teacher Licensing
State Dept. of Children, Families
   and Learning
616 Capitol Square Building
St. Paul, MN 55101
612-296-2046
612-282-2403 (fax)

MISSISSIPPI
Teacher Certification
State Dept. of Education
Box 771
Jackson, MS 39205-0771
601-359-3483
601-359-2778 (fax)

MISSOURI
Teacher Certification
Dept. of Elementary and
   Secondary Education
P.O. Box 480
Jefferson City, MO 65102
573-751-3486

MONTANA
Teacher Certification
Office of Public Instruction
P.O. Box 202501
Helena, MT 59620-2501
406-444-3150

NEBRASKA
Teacher Certification
State Dept. of Education
301 Centennial Mall South
Box 94987
Lincoln, ME 68509-4987
800-371-4642

NEVADA
Licensure and Certification
Nevada Dept. of Education
700 East 5th St.
Carson City, NV 89701
702-687-3115

NEW HAMPSHIRE
Bureau of Credentialing
State Dept. of Education
101 Pleasant St.
Concord, NH 03301
603-271-2407
603-271-1953 (fax)

NEW JERSEY
Office of Licensing and Academic
   Credentials
CN 503
Trenton, NJ 08625-0503
609-292-2070

NEW MEXICO
Director
Professional Licensure Unit
Education Building
300 Don Gaspar
Santa Fe, NM 87501-2786
505-827-6587

NEW YORK
Office of Teaching
University of the State of New York
State Education Department
Albany, NY 12230
518-474-3901/2/3/4

Buffalo Board of Education
City Hall
65 Niagara Square
Buffalo, NY 14202
716-842-4646

NORTH CAROLINA
North Carolina Dept. of Public
   Instruction
Licensure Section
301 N. Wilmington Street
Raleigh, NC 27601-2825
919-733-4125
800-577-7994

NORTH DAKOTA
Education Standards and Practice Board
Teacher Certification
600 E. Boulevard Ave.
Bismarck, ND 58505-0440
701-328-2264

OHIO
Teacher Education & Certification
State Dept. of Education
65 South Front St., Rm. 1009
Columbus, OH 43215-4183
614-466-3593

OKLAHOMA
Professional Standards
State Dept. of Education
2500 N. Lincoln Blvd.
Rm. 211
Oklahoma City, OK 73105-4599
405-521-3337
405-522-1520 (fax)

OREGON
Teacher Standards and Practices
   Commission
Public Service Bldg.
255 Capitol Street, N.E.
Suite 105
Salem, OR 97310-1332
503-378-3586

PENNSYLVANIA
Bureau of Certification
Dept. of Education
333 Market Street
Harrisburg, PA 17126-0333
717-787-2967

RHODE ISLAND
Office of Teacher Certification
State Dept. of Education
Shepard Building
255 Westminster St.
Providence, RI 02903-3400
401-277-4600

SOUTH CAROLINA
Office of Teacher Education,
    Certification, & Evaluation
Teacher Licensure Section
1600 Gervais St.
Columbia, SC 29201
803-734-8466

SOUTH DAKOTA
Teacher Certification
Office of Policy and Accountability
700 Governors Drive
Pierre, SD 57501-2291
605-773-3553
605-773-6139 (fax)

TENNESSEE
Office of Teacher Licensing
State Dept. of Education
5th Floor, Andrew Johnson Tower
710 James Robertson Parkway
Nashville, TN 37243-0377
615-533-4885
615-532-7860 (fax)

TEXAS
State Board for Educator Certification
1001 Trinity
Austin, TX 78701
512-469-3001

UTAH
Certification and Personnel
    Development Section
State Board of Education
250 East 500 South Street
Salt Lake City, UT 84111
801-538-7740

VERMONT
Licensing Office
Dept. of Education
120 State Street
Montpelier, VT 05620-2501
802-828-2445
802-828-3140 (fax)

VIRGINIA
Office of Professional Licensure
Department of Education
P.O. Box 2120
Richmond, VA 23216-2120
804-225-2022

WASHINGTON
Office of Professional Education
State Board of Education
Old Capitol Building
P.O. Box 47206
Olympia, WA 98504-7206
206-753-6773

WEST VIRGINIA
State Dept. of Education
Building 6, Room 337
1900 Kanawha Blvd., East
Charleston, WV 25305-0330
800-982-2378

WISCONSIN
Teacher Education, Licensing and
    Placement
Box 7841
Madison, WI 53707-7841
608-266-1027

WYOMING
Professional Teaching Standards Board
2300 Capitol Avenue
Hathaway Building, 2nd Floor
Cheyenne, WY 82002
307-777-6248

Appendix 2

Information About the National Teacher Exam (Praxis Series)

The Praxis Series is an Educational Testing Service (ETS) program that provides tests and other services for states to use as part of their teacher licensure or certification process. Some colleges and universities use these assessments to qualify individuals for entry into teacher education programs.

The Praxis Series is the choice of thirty-five of the forty-three states that include tests as part of their teacher licensure process. You will take The Praxis Series if you want to teach public school in one of these thirty-five states or if you want to enter a teacher education program at a college or university that uses Praxis I: Academic Skills Assessments. Different states and institutions require different tests in the Praxis Series, so be sure you know which tests you need before you register.

The Praxis Series OnLine (www.ets.org) provides useful information about the test series, how these assessments are used, how to register to take the tests, and how to get your scores. This information is from the Praxis Series: Professional Assessments for Beginning Teachers, Registration Bulletin, available free from ETS or from your college or university. In addition, this online service lets you review and download specific teacher certification policies and test requirements in each state that uses the Praxis Series program. And you'll find information from "The Praxis Series Tests at a Glance" booklets.

The three categories of assessments in the Praxis Series correspond to the three milestones in teacher development.

Praxis I: Academic Skills Assessment. These assessments are designed to be taken early in the student's college career to measure reading, writing, and mathematics skills vital to all teacher candidates. The assessments are available in two formats, paper-based and computer-based. Both measure similar academic skills, but the computer-based tests (CBTs) are tailored to each candidate's performance. They also offer a wider range of question types, provide an immediate score in reading and math, and are available on demand throughout the year by appointment, eliminating the need to register in advance. The paper-based tests, called the PPST® or Pre-Professional Skills Tests, are given six times a year.

Praxis II: Subject Assessments. These assessments measure candidates' knowledge of the subjects they will teach, as well as how much they know about teaching that subject. More than 140 content tests are available. The tests are regularly updated, and several are available in each subject field, so a state can customize its program by selecting the assessments that best match its own licensure requirements. For added flexibility, each state can base its assessments on standard multiple-choice questions or incorporate new candidate-constructed-response modules. These performance-based items allow test-takers to demonstrate in-depth knowledge and reinforce the importance of writing in the teaching profession.

Praxis III: Classroom Performance Assessments. These assessments are used at the beginning teaching level to evaluate all aspects of a beginning teacher's classroom performance. Designed to assist in making licensure decisions, these comprehensive assessments are conducted in the classroom by trained local assessors who use a set of consistent, reliable, nationally validated criteria. Pathwise™, a companion product designed to be used in nonlicensing situations, is an in-class observation system created to guide preservice and inservice development activities for student and beginning teachers.

If you are planning to take one or more of these tests, you need a copy of "The Praxis Series: Professional Assessments for Beginning Teachers, Registration Bulletin." The bulletin is free and provides complete test information plus test registration instructions. It's available at your college or university, or you can request one by calling 1-609-771-7395. You can also review and download the Registration Bulletin and Tests at a Glance information instantly, from www.ets.org. The "Registration Bulletin" and "Tests at a Glance" information is in the form of downloadable PDF files in Adobe® Acrobat® format. (In order to view and print these files, you need information on downloading Acrobat Reader software and configuring your browser.)

If you prefer to order your own free copy of any of the "Tests at a Glance" booklets, check with your college or university or call ETS at 1-609-771-7395.

The states and territories listed below use the Praxis Series tests as part of their teacher certification process. You should check with each state to find out which tests are required, passing scores, and other information.

Alaska
Arizona
Arkansas
California
Connecticut
Delaware
District of Columbia
Florida
Georgia
Hawaii
Indiana
Kansas
Kentucky
Louisiana
Maine
Maryland
Minnesota
Mississippi

Missouri
Montana
Nebraska
Nevada
New Hampshire
New Jersey
New Mexico
New York
North Carolina
Ohio
Oklahoma
Oregon
Pennsylvania
Rhode Island
South Carolina
Tennessee
Texas
U.S. Virgin Islands
Virginia
West Virginia
Wisconsin

Appendix 3

A Summary of Selected Reports on Education Reform

Title	Source	Data
The Paideia Proposal (1982)	Mortimer Adler for the Paideia Group	Twenty-two members contributed to a philosophical analysis of educational needs.
A Nation at Risk: The Imperative for Educational Reform (1983)	The National Commission on Excellence in Education—U.S. Department of Education	Eighteen political and educational leaders commissioned papers and reviewed available materials, including national and international test scores.
American's Competitive Challenge: The Need for a Response (1983)	Business—Higher Education Forum	Sixteen representatives of business and higher education reviewed expert opinions and past surveys.
Action for Excellence: A Comprehensive Plan to Improve Our Nation's Schools (1983)	Task Force of the Education Commission of the States, chaired by Governor James Hunt	Forty-one governors, legislators, labor leaders, business leaders, and school board members collected data and interpreted results.
Academic Preparation for College: What Students Need to Know and Be Able to Do (1983)	Education Equality Project—The College Board	Two hundred high school and college teachers and college board members collected and interpreted test results.
Making the Grade (1983)	Twentieth-Century Fund Task Force on Federal Elementary and Secondary Education Policy	Eleven members of state, local, and higher education organizations reviewed research studies.
Educating Americans for the 21st Century: A Report to the American People and the National Science Board (1983)	National Science Board Commission on Pre-College Education in Mathematics, Science and Technology	Commission members and others reviewed a number of professional association, business, and other education programs.

Recommendations

The book urges a radical reorganization to focus on three areas: (1) the development of personal, mental, moral, and spiritual growth; (2) citizenship; and (3) basic skills. Teaching methods and subject areas would be revised, and there would be a core curriculum for all students from elementary through secondary education.

The report's powerful rhetoric, such as the "rising tide of mediocrity" and "a nation at risk," galvanized public attention regarding school reform. The report suggests that poor school performance threatens our nation's economic health. It emphasizes rigorous courses, a core curriculum, the recruiting of talented teachers, and a thorough assessment of student and teacher competence.

The report indicates that a major reason for U.S. economic problems and falling productivity is the inadequate education of the nation's workers, who need more schooling in mathematics, science, critical-thinking skills, and verbal expression.

The report urges state leadership to develop action plans for improving education, including more community involvement, additional funds, better preparation and pay for teachers, stronger curricular offerings, greater accountability, more effective principals, and better programs for poorly achieving students.

More rigorous preparation for college is called for, including better-trained teachers, more demanding elementary and secondary curricula, and higher expectations of students. Colleges should also provide remedial help for ill-prepared students and should work more closely with high schools in preparing students for college.

The report states that the criticism of U.S. schools is exaggerated and that schools are fundamentally doing their job. Suggestions for improvement include federal aid for schools, a clearer focus on educational quality, a continued commitment to educational equality, and support for local decision making.

Emphasizing a strong mathematics and science curriculum, the report highlights the need to attract individuals with these skills into teaching.

Title	Source	Data
The Good High School: Portraits of Character and Culture (1983)	Sara Lawrence Lightfoot	Field study of six private and public schools
High School: A Report on Secondary Education in America (1983)	The Carnegie Foundation for the Advancement of Teaching	Ernest Boyer chaired a national panel of educators and citizens, which reviewed past research and undertook field studies in public high schools.
A Place Called School (1983)	John Goodlad	Presents observations of and results of questionnaires administered in schools over an eight-year period
Horace's Compromise: The Dilemma of the American High School (1984)	Theodore Sizer	Interviews and observations in the fifteen schools in the report *A Study of High Schools*
The Shopping Mall High School (1985)	Arthur Powell, Eleanor Farrar, and David Cohen	One of three efforts in *A Study of High Schools,* this field analysis of fifteen schools used comprehensive interviews and classroom observation.
The Last Citadel (1986)	Robert Hempel	Four of the fifteen schools visited in *A Study of High Schools* were examined historically through oral histories, published and unpublished records, and historical files of a variety of educational institutions.
A Nation Prepared: Teachers for the 21st Century (1986)	Task Force on Teaching as a Profession, Carnegie Forum on Education and the Economy	Fourteen-member panel of educators, policy-makers, politicians, and others analyzed existing data.
Tomorrow's Teachers (Holmes Report, 1986)	Deans of selected teacher education colleges	Thirteen education deans and one college president formulate their professional and philosophical views.
Time for Results (1986)	National Governors Association	Lamar Alexander chaired the governor's task force that reviewed research and existing reports.
First Lessons (1986)	U.S. Department of Education	William Bennett and twenty-one other distinguished citizens summarize critical findings concerning more effective elementary education.

Recommendations

Although this is not technically a reform report, the author's observations of four public and two private high schools provide valuable insights into effective and ineffective school practices.

The report recommends a heavy emphasis on English (particularly writing) and a strong academic core for all students. It suggests elimination of the vocational track and advocates a five-year teacher education program.

This report recommends making the principal a manager and creating a "head teacher" to focus on instructional improvement. Goodlad also calls for grouping students in clusters rather than by grade level. The book highlights the need for a greater variety of teaching methods to deal with student diversity.

Dramatizing the difficult working conditions facing teachers, Sizer emphasizes the need to develop close teacher-student relationships, high student motivation, and a less fragmented curriculum.

To ensure effective reform, the authors recommend an informed public, involved parents, high expectations and outstanding teachers, and more time in study and preparation of lessons, as well as greater standards of professionalism for teachers.

Hempel offers a study of the alteration of the U.S. high school since the 1940s, noting that academic subjects have remained intact and schedules and routines are virtually unchanged. The book highlights the need to deal sensitively with multiple priorities and recommends that more emphasis be place on orderly thinking than on orderly discipline.

The report calls for the establishment of a National Board of Professional Teaching Standards to test and certify all teachers, as well as testing for and issuing an advanced teaching certificate. It recommends that all teachers take a five-year teacher education program, including four years of liberal arts and science.

Expressing their personal and professional views, these educators call for reforming teacher education by requiring that all teachers receive a bachelor's degree in an academic field and a master's degree in education. The report recommends greater recognition of teaching and improvement of teachers' working conditions.

The governors placed themselves on the cutting edge of school reform by producing numerous recommendations, including parental choice in school selection, career ladders, state takeovers of poorly performing school districts, programs to prevent students from dropping out, and emphasis on technology in teacher preparation.

The former secretary of education calls for elementary students to be taught a rigorous regime of reading and other basic skills, including foreign language and computer skills.

Title	Source	Data
James Madison High (1986)	U.S. Department of Education	William Bennett provides his ideas for a high school curriculum, based on research and practice in secondary schools.
Turning Points: Preparing American Youth for the 21st Century (1989)	Carnegie Foundation Task Force on Education of Young Adolescents	David Hornbeck chaired the eighteen-member task force of educators, government officials, and others who, through analysis of interviews and commission studies, collected relevant data.
America 2000: An Education Strategy (1991) **Goals 2000: Educate America Act (1994)**	President Bush and governors; continued and modified by the Clinton administration	Administration-led political effort to respond to educational needs cited in numerous reports, international test scores, etc.

Recommendations

The former secretary of education recommends a traditional high school curriculum with few electives; four years of literature; a senior research paper; three years of math, science, and social studies with a U.S. and Western focus; and emphasis on foreign language.

This is an unusual report in that it focuses on the junior high, or middle school, a period of significant physical, social, and psychological change for young adolescents. Recommendations include the creation of small learning communities within large schools, a core curriculum that is academically demanding, the elimination of tracking, the empowerment of teachers and principals by giving them more authority, the improvement of school-community-parent relationships, and the promotion of student self-esteem.

A political consensus identified a number of national goals: among others, a 90 percent or higher high school graduation rate, number one ranking for U.S. students in math and science, 100 percent adult literacy, parental involvement, and teacher development.

Appendix 4

Observation Manual

Many education courses now require or recommend field observation activities. This Appendix will help you sharpen and focus your field observation skills. Accurate data collection and thoughtful reflection about what you see can give you new insights into life in the classroom and the process of teaching.

General Observation Guidelines

While the field experience is an integral part of virtually all teacher preparation programs, the specific design and approach of school observation varies greatly. In some teacher education programs, the field experience is a component of the Introduction to Teaching Course or the Foundations of Education Course; in others, it is a separate course. In still others, it has become a continuous strand that links most, if not all, education courses.

Whatever approach your college or university provides, this experience, if used well, can offer rich insight into the real world of teaching and schools and can help answer your concerns and questions about teaching as a career. Unfortunately, poorly structured school visits quickly deteriorate into a vacuous waste of time. This Appendix, along with the Inter-missions, provide the structure and focus to ensure accurate observation and thoughtful reflection about the information you gather. But that is only half—perhaps less than half—of the formula needed for successful school observation. The other central ingredient is you. How you approach the experience, and what you do or do not do with the information you gather, ultimately will determine how well your field experience will work for you.

John Dewey, perhaps America's most famous educator, wrote extensively about *reflective thinking,* which he defined as avoiding "routine" and "impulsive" behaviors in favor of taking the time to give "serious consideration" to our actions. According to Dewey, the intelligent person thinks before he or she acts, and action becomes deliberate and intentional. If you want to glean knowledge and insight from your field experience, your observations must be careful, analytical, and deliberate. Once your observations have been made, you will need to consider carefully what you have seen before you formulate conclusions about life in schools.

Identifying Your Goals and Concerns

The reflective field experience structured in this Appendix and in the Inter-missions will encourage you not only to see what schools do but also to consider what they might do differently. Although each student approaches the field experience with a unique personal history and set of expectations, it is useful to think about and prioritize these perceptions and concerns before you begin. Take a minute and, on a separate sheet of paper or in your journal or notebook, write a brief list of your goals as you prepare for your field experience. In short, what information and insight do you want to get out of your field experience? After you have written down your goals, consider the following questions. Are your goals clear, or do you need to give them more thought? Are some of these goals more important than others? (You may want to rank them in order of priority.) Do your goals fall into one or two broad categories, or are they more diverse? This Appendix structures your field experiences into several categories: the setting, the teacher, the student, and the curriculum. Have you considered all these areas in your goals—or, like many beginning teachers, have you omitted one or more? Which areas have you omitted? Why? Since these are the key areas your field experience should emphasize, take a few moments before you arrive at your observation site and consider what you want to learn about the following components.

Setting. What is the socioeconomic status of the community? What are the community's values concerning education generally and the schools in particular? Are parents involved in the schools? What is the academic and social culture of the school? What is important in this community and in this school? How would you describe the physical environment of the community, the school, and the classroom? How are the classrooms organized to promote learning?

Teaching: Why do people enter teaching? What do they like about teaching? Why do people leave teaching? What are the responsibilities of teachers? How do you become an effective teacher? What successful teaching skills are used in this school? What needs to be improved? Do you like teaching? Are you good at it? How can you apply what you learn in your education courses to your own teaching?

Students. As you prepare for a teaching career, your concerns and interests are naturally focused on the teaching aspect of the classroom and whether you will like teaching and be good at it. But teaching does not exist in isolation; key to the context of teaching are the students. Who are the learners and what are their interests? What motivates students to learn? What are the barriers? How can work be individualized? How can discipline problems be handled? avoided? Which age group and which type of students do you prefer to work with?

Curriculum. Students spend approximately 90 percent of their academic time involved in reading textbooks and other curricular materials. Curricular issues that could be addressed in the field experience include the following: What is taught in your school? Is breadth or depth emphasized? Are students responsible for problem solving and critical thinking? Or are drill and rote memorization emphasized? Is adequate time provided for each subject? Is there bias in the curriculum? Which topics are emphasized? omitted? Is the curriculum interesting and motivating? What is the school's policy concerning a core curriculum? Has your college work prepared you to teach the curriculum? How might you present the curriculum differently?

This Appendix introduces each of these areas, providing you with a few sample activities. Working with your instructor and colleagues, you may want to develop and use other data collection activities as well.

Learning How to Observe

Students preparing to be teachers suffer from the handicap of too much familiarity with school. Consequently, they may block out valid and useful insights. Thousands of hours spent behind students' desks inure many to the subtle and not-so-subtle aspects of schooling in the United States. In order to become an effective teacher, you need to erase this past conditioning and reawaken yourself to the realities of school and classroom life. The development of observation skills will not only sensitize you to these realities but also will enable you to compare and contrast the effectiveness of the various instructional and management practices that teachers and administrators use in dealing with them.

I sat in class for days wondering what there was to observe. Teachers taught, reprimanded, rewarded while pupils sat at desks squirming, whispering, reading, writing, staring into space, as they had in my own grade school experience, in my practice teaching in a teacher training program, and in the two years of public school teaching I had done before World War II.[1]

So wrote George Spindler, the researcher who is credited with developing educational anthropology as a legitimate field of scholarship. His problem was one that faces any serious observer in an environment that is too familiar. Everything seems trivial and obvious. As Margaret Mead said, "If a fish were to become an anthropologist, the last thing that it would discover would be the water."[2]

Spindler became so frustrated with viewing the commonplace that he almost gave up his research. Education majors who are asked to observe in local elementary and secondary schools face similar problems. Because they find the environment as comfortable and everyday as a worn shoe, they often miss subtle incidents and the underlying significance of events.

Fortunately, Spindler did not give up school-based observations. He interviewed the target teacher he was observing, as well as supervisors and students. He collected autobiographical and psychological information from the teacher, analyzed the teacher's evaluations of his students, and conducted sociograms (i.e., recording popular and isolated students, as well as cliques) to determine students' attitudes toward one another. As a result of careful data collection, Spindler discovered that the target teacher, who at casual glance seemed to treat all students similarly, actually favored white middle- and upper-class students. The teacher was completely unaware of this differential treatment, but the students were readily able to identify the teacher's favorites. If the teacher had known how to observe subtle classroom dynamics, he would have been aware of this disparity. Without the skills of observation, interpretation, and reflection, the teacher remained ignorant of important elements of the classroom social structure.[3]

Classrooms and schools are complex intellectual, social, personal, and physical environments, where the average teacher has more than one thousand interactions a day, each with different levels and nuances of meaning. In this multifaceted, fast-paced, confusing culture called *school*, it is all too easy to miss much of what you think you "see." But, if you immerse yourself in this culture, observe and record your experiences systematically, then reflect on and interpret what you have seen, you can gain greater insight into how and why teachers and students behave the way they do.

There are many sources for collecting objective data. These include direct observation; document analysis of school mission statements, discipline codes, textbooks, student portfolios, and lesson plans; and interviews with key participants, such as teachers, students, administrators, and parents. Observation followed by reflection will provide crucial data about the realities, frustrations, and rewards of classroom life—information that will help you become a better teacher.

Observation Techniques

This Appendix provides you with a variety of *observation techniques* to collect information. You and your instructor may determine to use only a few of these methods—or all six.

Interviewing

Depending on the role they play in school, various participants may have different interpretations of and opinions about events. For example, a student's feelings about a pep rally may differ from those of the school principal. Interviews are an excellent method for bringing to light these different perspectives and points of view. Your interviewing protocol may consist of very specific questions ("How many years have you taught in this school?") or questions that are broad and open-ended ("How does this school differ from other elementary schools where you have taught?").

Asking questions that draw the subject out is a challenging skill to master. For example, during an interview you may ask, "Do you enjoy teaching?" If you get a simple "yes" or "no," you will need to ask follow-up, or probing, questions to get more detailed information. Assuring the interviewee that answers will be kept confidential may be helpful in obtaining frank and comprehensive responses.

Whenever possible, audio or video record or take notes during the interview, perhaps just jotting down key phrases if you do not have time to record complete sentences. Later you may find it difficult to remember exactly what the interviewee said, or you may inadvertently distort or rephrase what was said to fit your own preconceived notions of people and events. Although most of us like to think we are completely objective, our past experiences and our perspectives may interfere with clear vision.

Questionnaires

Interviews are a good strategy for gathering in-depth information, but time constraints will limit the number of people you can reach. Questionnaires provide the opportunity to gather information from a much larger sample of faculty, staff, or students. You will need to decide what you want to ask and how you want participants to respond. For example, you can ask an open-ended question:

> How would you describe the audiovisual equipment in this school? _____

Or you might want to structure your questions so that a particular type of response is generated:

> Audiovisual technology is used frequently.
> Agree Strongly   Agree   Disagree   Disagree Strongly

You will also need to decide whether you wish respondents to identify themselves or whether questionnaires should be anonymous. Although questionnaires are not stressed in the data collection activities in this manual, they are a good source of information. If you are interested in this method of data collection, discuss how to develop and distribute questionnaires with your course instructor.

Observation Data

A much-used technique for capturing, comparing, and analyzing human behavior of all kinds is the *structured observation system*. Community life, school activities, and classroom behaviors can be recorded and evaluated through a coherent set of questions or more sophisticated coding techniques. In fact, a number of these structured observation systems were originally designed for educational research, but they have now found their way into everyday school practice. These instruments measure everything from the kinds of questions teachers ask to the nature of peer-group interaction. One of the earlier and more influential observation instruments is the Flanders Interaction Analysis, which is summarized briefly in Figure 1.

Typically, standardized observation instruments are developed by researchers over an extended period of time, and sometimes observers require training, so that they can use these tools accurately and reliably. Several books listed at the end of this manual contain collections of different standardized observation instruments. Your instructor will indicate whether you should use any of these instruments during your observations and whether training is necessary for accurate and reliable data collection using these tools.

Document Analysis

By analyzing the documents, written records, and other classroom and school materials, you can gain important information about how the school works and what is emphasized. For example, does your school have a philosophy or mission statement in which goals are set forward? What policies govern staff and student behavior? Is there a disciplinary policy for students, and are they aware of it? What kinds of textbooks are used, and do teachers supplement texts with additional materials? What kind of report card or evaluation system is in use? What do newspapers and yearbooks tell you about the school's social system? The school's written records should provide an important complement to the data you collect from observing and interviewing.

Note Taking

Note taking, a technique borrowed from cultural anthropologists, is one of the most commonly used methods for gathering data. When you first begin observing and taking notes on what you see, you may try to record everything. But, in the hectic, multifaceted school and classroom environment, you will soon discover that it is impossible to capture accurately so many different stimuli at one time. You will need to narrow your focus and target specific aspects of the environment for your data collection and note-taking activities. For example, you may choose to focus on how the curriculum is developed or the nature of

Originally developed as a research tool, Flanders Interaction Analysis became a widely used coding system to analyze and improve teaching skills. This observation system was designed to categorize the type and quantity of verbal dialogue in the classroom and to plot the information on a matrix so that it could be analyzed. The result gave a picture of who was talking in a classroom and the kind of talking that was taking place.

As a result of research with his coding instrument, Flanders uncovered the **two-thirds rule:** About two-thirds of classroom time is devoted to talking. About two-thirds of this time the person talking is the teacher, and two-thirds of the teacher's talk is "direct" (that is, lecturing, giving directions, and controlling students). The two-thirds rule is actually three related two-thirds rules and serves to substantiate that, typically, teachers verbally dominate classrooms.

Some people feel that Flanders' work has underscored the fact that a teacher's verbal domination of the classroom conditions students to become passive and to be dependent on the teacher. It is claimed that this dependency has an adverse effect on student attitudes toward school and student performance in school. Interestingly, Flanders found that when teachers are trained in his observation technique and become aware of the importance of language in the classroom, their verbal monopoly decreases.

To use the Flanders Interaction Analysis, one codes the verbal interaction in 1 of 10 categories, plots the coded data onto a matrix, and analyzes the matrix. Following are the 10 categories in the Flanders Interaction Analysis Coding Instrument.

Summary of Categories for Interaction Analysis

Indirect Teacher Talk

1. *Accepts feeling*
   Acknowledges student-expressed emotions (feelings) in a nonthreatening manner
2. *Praises or encourages*
   Provides positive reinforcement of student contributions
3. *Accepts or uses ideas of students*
   Clarifies, develops, or refers to student contribution, often nonevaluatively
4. *Asks questions*
   Solicits information or opinion (not rhetorically)

Direct Teacher Talk

5. *Lectures*
   Presents information, opinion, or orientation; perhaps includes rhetorical questions
6. *Gives directions*
   Supplies direction or suggestion with which a student is expected to comply
7. *Criticizes or justifies authority*
   Offers negative evaluation of student contributions or places emphasis on teacher's authoritative position

Student Talk

8. *Student talk—response*
   Gives a response to the teacher's question, usually a predictable answer
9. *Student talk—initiation*
   Initiates a response that is unpredictable or creative in content
10. *Silence or confusion*
   Leaves periods of silence or inaudible verbalization lasting more than 3 seconds

FIGURE 1

Flanders Interaction Analysis: an early and influential coding system.

leadership exerted by the principal. You may target your activities to record the frequency and quality of teacher questions or the way discipline is handled in the school. In order to select the most important information, you will need to go into the environment with a series of *focusing questions*.

Several focusing questions are included in the data collection activities in the next section, or you may wish to work with your peers and instructor on developing your own focusing questions. These will guide your observations and interviews and help you organize the field notes you record.

It is wise to keep your notes in a looseleaf notebook (such as the one you may have already begun using to record your observation goals and priorities). This gives you the advantage of being able to move and shift your notes around into different organizational formats. As you spend more time in field observation and collect increasing amounts of data, this ability to reorganize notes without losing them will be extremely helpful.

Sometimes it is impossible to take notes during observations and interviews. There may not be time, or you may sense that the interviewee will "clam up" if you whip out your notepad and pencil. In cases such as these, you will need to summarize your notes later. Whether you take notes during observations and interviews or make summary observations, you should record when and where each data collection activity took place. The more detailed dialogue and clearly defined images you include in your notes, the more useful they will be. Thorough and complete notes, filled with anecdotes and details, are called "rich data" and will help you reach the most insightful interpretations of events and behavior.

Logs and Journals

Many teacher education programs require or recommend that you maintain a log or journal during your field experiences. Some programs specify a particular format, while others allow a more open-ended approach. In either case, the log or journal is intended to help you document and reflect on your observations. As you write your account, you will be giving thought both to the field experience and to its impact on you. Over time, you will detect growth and possibly significant change in what you believe about teaching and schools. When your field experiences are completed, you will have a written account of your activities and changing views during this formative period of your professional preparation.

In your log, you should also describe incidents observed or activities participated in as objectively as possible. This log should be kept on a daily basis, because time erases memories and feelings. Each day, your log should include one or two events that are particularly meaningful to you. An event may be significant because it impresses you (for example, a terrific teaching technique), because it is

educationally important (such as a successful strategy for classroom management), because it disturbs you (for example, a poorly executed activity or a negative interaction you have), or because it challenges or confirms your beliefs and ideas. These events, whether positive or negative, should be selected and described because they are critical incidents for learning. The descriptions should be objective and detailed. Later you should set time aside, mull them over, and interpret what you learned. This part of the log is akin to a professional diary. If you have trouble analyzing any of these significant events, your instructor or other students may be able to assist. Identifying what events are most significant to you is a key step both in keeping a journal and in developing a reflective and professional approach to teaching. If your field experience does not have a specific log or journal format, here is one you may find useful:

Sample Log Format

Location: _____ Name: _____
Date: _____
Time: Activities:

_____   _____
_____   _____
_____   _____
_____   _____
_____   _____
_____   _____
_____   _____
_____   _____
_____   _____
_____   _____

Significant event: _____

Description:

Analysis:

Other significant events, if appropriate:

In the log, as well as in your observation activities, it is useful to distinguish between description and judgment. It is also helpful to recognize some basic rules for observing. The next two sections focus on these issues.

Becoming Accepted as an Observer

A principal once told a story of an observer who became so involved in a teacher's lesson that he was soon raising his hand, responding to the teacher's questions, inserting personal anecdotes, and monopolizing classroom interaction. By the end of the class, the observer and the teacher were engaged in an animated dialogue, and the students had become passive onlookers. The observer had completely disrupted the classroom activities he was there to study. Such a complete role reversal is uncommon, but the following guidelines are offered as an antidote to the potentially disruptive effect posed by any classroom observer.

As an observer, you can generally avoid such direct verbal involvement as was described, but the more subtle challenge is to avoid nonverbal intrusion. What do you do when children engage you in nonverbal conversation consisting only of eye contact and facial expressions? Do you smile back, wink, and establish an unspoken kinship? Or, for fear of disturbing the class routine, do you ignore the students and possibly alienate them?

Although hard-and-fast rules are difficult to come by, it is clear that your presence in the classroom is not intended either to win friends and influence people or to alienate others. You must learn to accept students' nonverbal messages yet avoid prolonging these interactions. Ignoring all eye contact can be just as disruptive as encouraging such contact can be. With experience, you will be able to accept these subtle forms of communication without amplifying them. In this way, you can demonstrate that, although you are not insensitive to the interest and curiosity of students, your purpose in the classroom is to observe, not to alter, classroom life.

A primary goal is to observe the most and intrude the least. For most observations, this means positioning yourself as inconspicuously as possible, where you are behind the students but have a clear view of the teacher. It is also useful to conduct some observations from the side of the room, so that you can see the children's faces and nonverbal cues. The expressions, comments, and activities of the students will give valuable insights into student-teacher relationships and the nature of classroom life. In some cases, you may have to change your location while a lesson is in progress (for example, moving among various groups of students to observe their activities). Whatever your location, it is important to avoid coming between people who wish to communicate.

To some extent, our society consists of a series of minisocieties, each with its values and rules of order. Schools are examples of such minisocieties, with each level (elementary, secondary, college) having its own unique set of norms. As an observer in schools, you will be judged by students and staff alike on the basis of their norms, not on the basis of those you have become accustomed to in

college. You will probably be expected to dress rather formally, to arrive early or notify the school if you will be late, and to conform to the school's rules and regulations. Your college supervisor will probably inform you of the prevailing norms.

Confidentiality of Records

As you observe and collect data, you must make certain that your actions do not invade the privacy of or in any other way harm those you are observing. Most schools require anonymity in your observations and confidentiality in the data you collect. Individual teachers, students, and others should not risk inconvenience, embarrassment, or harm as a result of your field experience.

Each school has its own norms and rules regarding what observers can and cannot do. Some require a signed release from school officials and/or from students (informed consent), while others are less formal. You should share your observation plan and data-gathering activities with your instructor to make certain that you are following the appropriate procedures. Your cooperating teacher and/or the principal in the school where you will be observing may also need to be informed. In cases where permission is not granted, you will need to find another setting.

All data that you collect should remain absolutely confidential. The importance of this point cannot be stressed too much. You may wish to use code names or numbers for people you describe, and you should never discuss observations with any members of the school community. For example, if you tell teachers some information you have learned about students, you run the risk of losing trust and credibility and possibly harming a member of the school community. Your records should be stored away from the field school, in a location that is both safe and private. In this way you can ensure that the confidentiality of your subjects will be protected.

Distinguishing Between Description and Interpretation

As you collect data, your information should be recorded—at least initially—in a descriptive rather than a judgmental manner. As a student, your observations about school were probably casual, resulting in the formation of opinions, such as Teacher A is "interesting," School B is "the pits," or geometry is "hard." These interpretations, although colorful and useful, are personal and would have been likely to evoke disagreement from some of your fellow students.

A better approach for an observer is to gather descriptive data regarding an aspect of school or classroom life, interpret the data, and, when appropriate, form conclusions and judgments. Rather than saying that Teacher A is "good" (an interpretation), you might count the number of questions Teacher A asks, the amount of time Teacher A spends helping students, or even the number of advanced degrees Teacher A holds. All these findings provide objective, descriptive data. Although some of your descriptive data may not be useful, other notes may be crucial to your final interpretations and insights.

Data collection activities presented in this manual frequently ask you to record descriptive details and, after reflection, to interpret the information. The following examples will help you distinguish between description and interpretation:

> *Description:*   The teacher asked twenty-three questions in seven minutes.
> *Interpretation:* The teacher asked too many questions.
> *Description:*   The teacher scolded Henry ten times during the morning.
> *Interpretation:* The teacher picked on Henry.
> *Description:*   The student yawned twice and spent eight minutes looking out the window.
> *Interpretation:* The student was bored.
> *Description:*   The building was constructed in 1940.
> *Interpretation:* The building is old.
> *Description:*   This school consists of 121 elementary school classrooms.
> *Interpretation:* The school is too big.
> *Description:*   Twenty-five out of twenty-seven students volunteered answers during math class.
> *Interpretation:* The students are interested in math.

This ability to separate fact from opinion is a crucial skill that can prevent you from jumping to erroneous conclusions. Most of us like to think that "seeing is believing," but sometimes "believing may be seeing." In other words, each of us brings to any observation a set of biases and perspectives through which events may be distorted. The way to guard against reaching inaccurate interpretations is first to make a careful record of what you see. Judgmental comments can also be made, but they should be kept separate from your descriptive observations. Some observers insert interpretations and questions into their records, but they separate them from their descriptive notes with parentheses.

Interpreting the Data

After you have collected your data, you will need to interpret and make sense of a vast amount of information. To do this, it will be helpful to look for words, patterns, phrases, and topics that keep recurring in your records. If competency testing is being used in your school, for example, you may find that the teachers talk about these exit exams in many classes and spend a great deal of time preparing students for them. After analyzing your notes from patterns, you may reach the conclusion that competency testing is exerting too great an influence on what is taught. As you form impressions and interpretations, it is a good idea to check these with participants in the environment. For example, you might ask the teachers, "I have noticed that your students will take competency exams this year. What

influences do you think these exams have in the school?" You can also check your interpretations by searching for instances of contrary behavior. In this hypothetical situation, you have found that many teachers spend a great deal of time teaching for the competency tests. However, it is also important to look for counter instances, teachers who devote little time or attention to the competency tests. If you find several teachers in this category, your initial impressions may not be accurate. After all your notes have been recorded and analyzed, the final product is often an ethnographic report or case study. How insightful your report is will depend on the richness of detail in your notes and how thoughtfully you have interpreted the data. Typically, an ethnographic report comprises two sections: (1) a descriptive summary of the data you observed and (2) an interpretation or evaluation section that sets forth your conclusions. Your instructor can help you determine the particular form your final report should take.

Data Collection Activities: The Setting

No student or teacher functions in isolation. As you think about your future life in the classroom, you must also consider the general community, the school building, and even the physical environment of the classroom. Students arrive at school after years of being taught the unofficial curriculum of parents, friends, and neighbors; their previously learned values and skills can help or hinder their efforts in the classroom. Understanding community attitudes and actions can be pivotal to enhancing your teaching effectiveness, as well as the classroom performance of your students. The physical qualities of the school building and the quantity and quality of classroom resources also will shape your life in the classroom.

Sample Activity 1: Local Newspaper   Most communities have a local newspaper or are covered in a section of a large-circulation newspaper that focuses on community affairs. If your school library or the public library carries back issues of these publications, read those for the past several months. In addition, keep up with local news coverage for that community. From your analysis of the news stories, editorials, advertisements, and letters to the editor, how would you answer the following?

Guidelines: Local Newspaper

What are the major community concerns?
What are the school's major projects? Are there any school-community partnerships to accomplish education-related goals?
Which aspect of school life receives the most coverage (athletics, academics, cultural activities, and so on)?
How does the community react to standardized test scores, financial needs, new facilities, and other educational concerns?

Sample Activity 2: Unobtrusive Measures *Unobtrusive measurement* is a way of assessing a situation without altering it.[4] For example, if you ask students what they think of a school, they may guard their comments and share only part of their real feelings. They do not know you or what you might do with the information. Just by asking such questions, you decrease the accuracy of the information you receive. Obtrusive methods, such as asking questions directly, frequently contaminate the findings.

As a student, you probably experience a similar phenomenon when you take exams. Before answering the questions, you may consider the attitudes and values of the teacher and tailor your responses accordingly. You may try to answer the questions not only correctly but also in a way that pleases the teacher. Have you ever changed the response you gave in order to fit your teacher's expectations? This strategy may improve your grade, but it denies the teacher an accurate insight into your attitudes and perspective.

One famous experiment in unobtrusive measures attempted to determine which exhibit in a museum was attracting the most visitors. An obtrusive measure (direct questioning) had previously indicated that a prestigious work of art was the most popular. However, an examination of the wear and tear on the floors, of the number of fingerprints on the protective glass, and of other unobtrusive data indicated that an incubator with hatching chickens was the most frequently visited exhibit. This contradiction between verbal and nonverbal responses was probably the result of the patrons' belief that visiting a work of art was more intellectually appropriate than watching chickens hatch. In short, the obtrusive interview technique distorted the responses and was, therefore, less effective than was the unobtrusive measure (that is, assessing the amount of dirt and the wear and tear on carpets and windows).

As these examples illustrate, unobtrusive measures are intentionally indirect in order to avoid contaminating the evidence. In the data collection activity that follows, you will be using unobtrusive procedures. Answer each question with descriptive data. Then think about the information you have gathered and consider what interpretations or judgments to make.

Guidelines: Unobtrusive Measures

Record the graffiti written on walls, desks, and, especially, in bathrooms.
Examine the exhibits and bulletin boards to determine if they are student-made, teacher-made, or commercially produced. Do they appear to have been there a long time, or do they seem to be changed regularly? As the students pass by, do they stop and look at them?
Ask the librarian if you may look at information about books that were checked out during the past two weeks. How many were checked out, and what were they about? Examine some books. Are they in good condition? Are they badly worn? defaced?

Check the lunchroom after lunch has been served. Are the trash cans filled with normal debris—or uneaten lunches?
Examine the floors for wear and tear. What floor spaces in the school and in the classrooms seem to be most worn? What is located in these areas? What areas of the school seem to be getting the least traffic? What is located in these areas?
Visit the main office and keep a tally of the conversations held by the school secretary. Who is scheduled to meet with the principal? How many of these visitors are students? faculty? parents? others? Whom does the principal visit? How often does he or she leave the office to interact with teachers and students?

Data Collection Activities: The Teacher

As you approach your field experience, your primary concerns may be focused on teaching. Will you like it? Will you be good at it? Will the teacher you work with be helpful? What, precisely, is "good teaching"? During your teacher education program, and even during your initial years as a teacher, you will, in all likelihood, continue to focus on questions relating to teachers and teaching.

Many of these activities rely on a similar data collection approach and the use of a class seating chart. The research on teacher effectiveness discusses the importance of active student interaction in promoting learning and positive attitudes toward school. Unfortunately, teachers do not distribute their attention evenly; rather, they ask many questions of some students and none of others. Teachers may direct questions more to children of one gender or race than to those of another. Attention, questions, and praise may be distributed on the basis of which students the teacher likes, or even on the basis of where the students happen to be seated in the classroom. One very common form of bias is for teachers to direct most of their questions to the better students, because their replies are more likely to be on target and, therefore, satisfying. Both the quantity and quality of teacher attention have an impact on student achievement.

In the following activity, you will need to construct a seating chart. (Perhaps the teacher has one that you can use.) But, unlike the teacher's, your chart should include the name, gender, and, when possible, race or ethnicity of each student. (A sample seating chart is provided in Figure 2.)

To begin, on your seating chart you will record with whom the teacher interacts in the classroom. There are two types of teacher-student interactions to be recorded: (1) those that depend on voluntary responses offered by the students and (2) those that are involuntary. Voluntary student responses occur when students

- Raise their hands to respond
- Call out an answer

Teacher's name _____ Date _____

Observer's name _____ Time begin _____

Time end _____

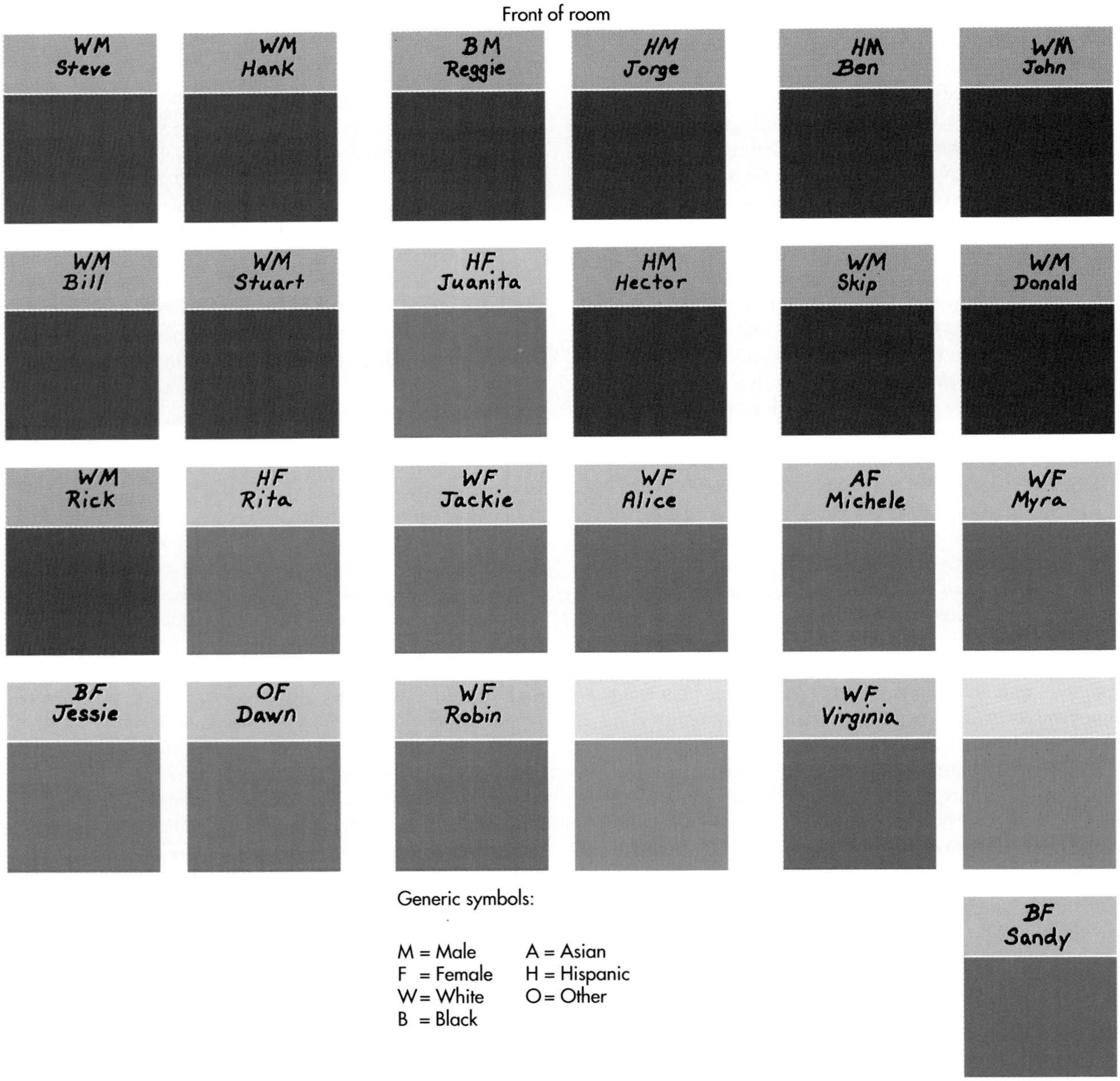

Front of room

WM Steve	WM Hank		BM Reggie	HM Jorge		HM Ben	WM John

WM Bill	WM Stuart		HF Juanita	HM Hector		WM Skip	WM Donald

WM Rick	HF Rita		WF Jackie	WF Alice		AF Michele	WF Myra

BF Jessie	OF Dawn		WF Robin			WF Virginia	

Generic symbols:

M = Male   A = Asian
F = Female   H = Hispanic
W = White   O = Other
B = Black

BF Sandy

FIGURE 2

Sample seating chart 1.

- Voluntarily respond to the teacher through any established classroom procedure

Involuntary student responses occur when the teacher initiates or requests a response from a student who has not expressed any desire to communicate. The student, in this case, has not raised a hand, called out an answer, or in any other way indicated an interest in answering. It is because of the teacher's initiative and desire that the student is expected to respond.

Each time a teacher elicits a response, the observer records a *V* or an *N* for that student directly on the classroom seating chart. *V*, representing a volunteer, indicates that the teacher is investing time in a student who is volunteering to respond. *N*, representing a nonvolunteer, indicates that the teacher is intentionally soliciting a response from a nonvolunteering student. (Note: a student calling out or in any other way responding who is not recognized by the teacher does not receive a code. The teacher has ignored this volunteer and not invested any time in this student.)

Figure 3 is a sample classroom dialogue, demonstrating how this coding system works. This description of classroom interaction is coded on the sample seating chart in Figure 4.

Once the observation data have been collected, several activities and levels of analysis are possible. Analyses such as those that follow provide important insights into the distribution of teacher attention.

Sample Activity 1: Classroom Geography   Simply examining the pattern of teacher questions directly from the seating chart provides you with an immediate, visual impression of the areas in the classroom that receive a great deal of interaction, as well as the areas that are interaction-poor. Some students may be involved in no interaction at all; others may take part in a number of interactions. Some students may only have one or two *N*s, while others may have a great number of *V*s. You may want to circle the areas of the classroom that are rich with teacher attention, as well as those areas that are interaction-poor.

Sample Activity 2: Detecting Racial Bias   Although educators as a group are firmly committed to educational equality, subtle and often unintentional biases can emerge.[5] Teachers often unknowingly give more attention to students of one race than to those of another, or give different kinds of attention to one group than they give to another. Detecting these subtle biases is a matter of recording data on your seating chart. It is best to record several sessions of classroom interaction in order to obtain an accurate measure

	Dialogue	Action	Code
Teacher:	"Who can answer question number three?"	Hank raises hand.	
Teacher:	"Hank."		Mark *V* for Hank.
Hank:	"Twenty-two."		
Teacher:	"No. That's not correct. Maria?"	Maria not volunteering.	Mark *N* for Maria.
Maria:	"Twenty."		
Teacher:	"Correct."		
Steve:	"I thought the answer was 18."	Steve calling out.	
Teacher:	"Let's look at the next question."		No mark. Steve was not recognized.
Teacher:	"Rita?"	Rita not volunteering.	Mark *N* for Rita.
Rita:	(no response)		
Teacher:	"Apply the formula, Rita."	Rita still not volunteering.	Mark *N* for Rita.
Rita:	"Oh, I see. Is it seven?"		
Teacher:	"Good. That's it. Why is it seven, Rita?"	Rita not volunteering.	Mark *N* for Rita.
Rita:	"You add the two sides."		
Teacher:	"Terrific."		

FIGURE 3

Sample classroom dialogue.

Teacher's name _____   Date _____
Observer's name _____   Time begin _____
                                                              Time end _____

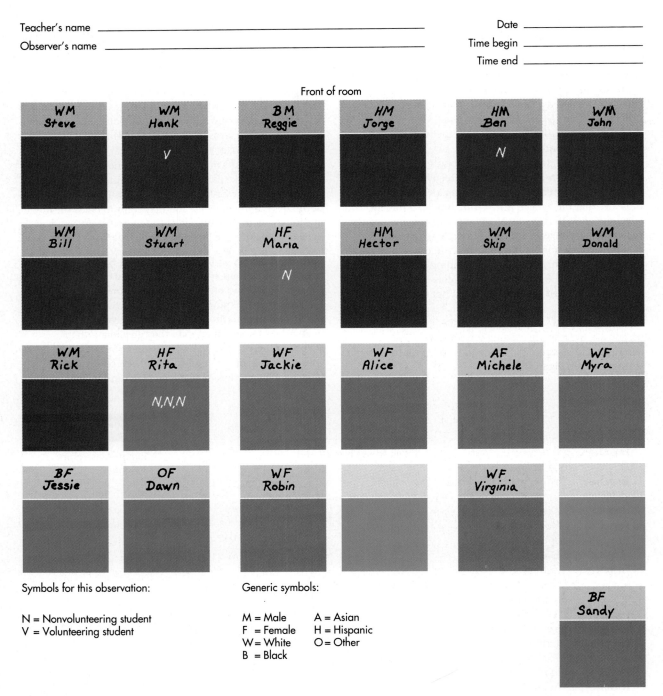

Front of room

WM Steve	WM Hank *V*	BM Reggie	HM Jorge	HM Ben *N*	WM John
WM Bill	WM Stuart	HF Maria *N*	HM Hector	WM Skip	WM Donald
WM Rick	HF Rita *N,N,N*	WF Jackie	WF Alice	AF Michele	WF Myra
BF Jessie	OF Dawn	WF Robin		WF Virginia	

BF Sandy

Symbols for this observation:

N = Nonvolunteering student
V = Volunteering student

Generic symbols:

M = Male   A = Asian
F = Female   H = Hispanic
W = White   O = Other
B = Black

FIGURE 4

Sample seating chart 2.

of potential racial or ethnic bias. The procedure then becomes one of simple mathematics. First, identify the expected number of interactions or questions (that is, a fair share) for each group. If, for instance, a class consists of 40 percent students of color, then a fair share would mean that students of color receive 40 percent of the teacher's questions. If the students of color receive fewer than 40 percent, they are not getting their fair share. For the second step, determine the actual number of interactions that each group receives. Finally, compare the figures. Here is how you would do the computations:

Sample Classroom Data

Class attendance   5 students of color

                        10 white students

                        15 total students in the class

Teacher questions   15 to students of color

                        45 to white students

                        60 total interactions

Step 1

Determine expected or fair share of questions, by race/ethnicity:

$$\text{Students of color fair share} = \frac{\text{students of color attendance}}{\text{total attendance}} = \frac{5}{15} = 33\%$$

$$\text{White fair share} = \frac{\text{white attendance}}{\text{total attendance}} = \frac{10}{15} = 67\%$$

Step 2

Determine actual share of interactions, by race/ethnicity:

Percentage students of color interactions = number of interactions with students of color ÷ total interactions

$$\frac{\text{Students of color interactions}}{\text{Total interactions}} = \frac{15}{60} = 25\%$$

Percentage white interactions = number of interactions with white ÷ total interactions

$$\frac{\text{White interactions}}{\text{Total interactions}} = \frac{45}{60} = 75\%$$

Step 3

Determine the difference between expected (or fair share) and actual distribution of interactions:

Students of color actual share = 25%

Students of color fair share   = 33%

    Difference   = −8%   (8% fewer interactions than a fair share)

White actual share   = 75%

White fair share   = 67%

    Difference   = +8%   (8% more interactions than a fair share)

Students of color received approximately 8 percent fewer questions than would be their fair share, or the amount that would be expected based on their representation in the class. White students received approximately 8 percent more than their fair share, or the amount that would be expected, based on their attendance in class. Subtle bias exists in this sample classroom interaction.

Sample Activity 3: Questioning Level   John Dewey was one of many noted educators who believed that questioning is central not only to education but to the process of thinking itself. Unfortunately, research indicates that most teachers do not use effective questioning techniques. Not only is the distribution of questions often inequitable, but teachers rarely use challenging classroom questions. Instead, they tend to rely on lower-order, or memory, questions. This observation activity focuses on the problem of too much emphasis on lower-order questions.

Lower-order questions are those that deal with the memorization and recall of factual information. The student is not required to manipulate (that is, apply, analyze, synthesize, or evaluate) information. There is nothing inherently wrong with asking memory questions, such as "When did the American Revolution begin?" or "Identify one poem written by Robert Frost." However, a heavy reliance on such questions reduces the opportunity for students to develop higher-order thinking..

Conversely, higher-order questions are those that require students to apply, analyze, synthesize, or evaluate information. They encourage students to think creatively. When a teacher asks, "What is your opinion of this poem by Robert Frost, and what evidence can you cite to support your opinion?" that teacher is asking a higher-order question. Only 10 percent of most teachers' questions fall into this higher-order category.

To help you distinguish between lower-order (memory) questions and higher-order (thought) questions, here are some examples of each:

Lower-Order Questions

- Who founded abstract art?
- Name three Romantic authors.
- Whose signatures appear on the Declaration of Independence?
- In what year did the war begin?
- Who wrote your text?

Higher-Order Questions

- What conclusions can you reach concerning the images Shakespeare uses to portray death?
- What forces motivated Romantic authors?
- Why did no females or African Americans sign the Declaration of Independence?
- Was this a good idea? Why or why not?
- What does this poem mean to you?

• What would you say in a letter to the president of the United States?

To record lower-order and higher-order questioning, use the following procedure. When a lower-order question is asked, record an *L* on your seating chart. When a higher-order question is asked, record an *H* on the seating chart. The sample coding form in Figure 5 illustrates the use of this approach. Each student who is asked a question receives an *H* or an *L* (to denote higher- and lower-order questions). On Sample Seating Chart 3 in Figure 5, recording a hypothetical classroom discussion, the preponderance of lower-order questions is evident, as well as several patterns of bias. Can you detect some of these patterns? Take a minute to analyze the teacher's level and distribution of questions and jot down any problems you detect. Then compare your analysis to the one that follows.

Problems Reflected on Sample Seating Chart 3, Figure 5:

• Preponderance of lower-order questions
• More questions asked to males
• More questions asked to white students than students of color
• Left side of the room and back of the room ignored

Try this in a classroom that you are observing. After constructing a seating chart, choose a 20- or 30-minute segment of teacher-student interaction. Record the number of higher-order and lower-order questions asked of each student in the class by noting *H*s and *L*s, as called for, on your seating chart. Then analyze the questioning pattern, using the following questions as a guide.

Guidelines: Questioning Level and Race/Ethnicity and Gender Bias

How many questions were asked? What was the average number of questions per minute (total questions divided by minutes observed)? What was the ratio of lower- to higher-order questions? What were the areas of the class that received a greater number of higher-order questions? Do you detect any patterns of racial, ethnic, or gender bias in the distribution of questions in general and of higher-order questions in particular?

Data Collection Activities: The Students

Although the students in any school constitute the reason for everything else—the building, the curriculum, the teachers—their interests are sometimes overlooked. You can learn a great deal about the school milieu, the community, and the kind of teaching students prefer by including an analysis of learners in your field experience. This section focuses on students and the social system in which they live and learn.

It is easy to lose sight of the fact that schools are created and maintained by the larger society for the express purpose of socializing its young into the roles of the prevailing culture.[6] To the casual observer, this socializing function is not apparent. The school seems to be an isolated and self-contained subculture accountable to no one. Data on the school and classroom social system will show the links between school and society with great clarity, and you will be able to interpret their significance.

Since most of us are so accustomed to the norms, values, and beliefs that constitute our culture, we have difficulty detecting their influence all about us. We are much more alert to things that are new and different. Consequently, the data collection activities in this section are designed to help you perceive with fresh meaning and significance, events that are so routine that you may no longer even see them.

To gain new insights from the commonplace, researcher Seymour Saranson recommends that you take the perspective of a visitor from outer space, who will be more alert to both blatant and subtle patterns of the school as a social system.[7] For example, an important aspect of our schools, but one not usually thought about, is that they must provide custody and control of youngsters for a major part of the work week. Housing a large group of children and adolescents in a small space for many hours a day has a major impact on the classroom social system. "Only in school do thirty or more people spend several hours a day literally side by side. Once we leave the classroom, we seldom again are required to have contact with so many people for so long a time."[8] In these crowded conditions, students and teachers often clash, because their purposes may be vastly different. The teacher is there to socialize the young and to help them learn. Grade school students are often in class to play and have fun, whereas adolescents' goals may involve developing social and even intimate relationships.

In the densely populated classroom, the teacher functions as a supply sergeant (giving out paper, books, and so on), as a timekeeper (determining how long the class will spend on given activities), and as a gatekeeper to class discussion (deciding who will talk and for how long).[9] While the teacher is busy filling all these roles, students are left to wait and do nothing. They stand in lines, they sit with their hands raised, and they wait for other students to finish so that they can go on to other activities. Sitting still and remaining silent are denials of their natural instincts.

Frustrated by this densely populated and artificial situation, students often rebel, pitting their own group power against the authority of the teacher. Sometimes this power struggle is subtle, with the sizing up and testing of the teacher its only visible signs (for example, by not handing in homework on time or cajoling to get an assignment lessened or postponed). At other times, the power struggle erupts to the surface of the social system as students openly flout or

Teacher's name _____

Observer's name _____

Date _____

Time begin _____

Time end _____

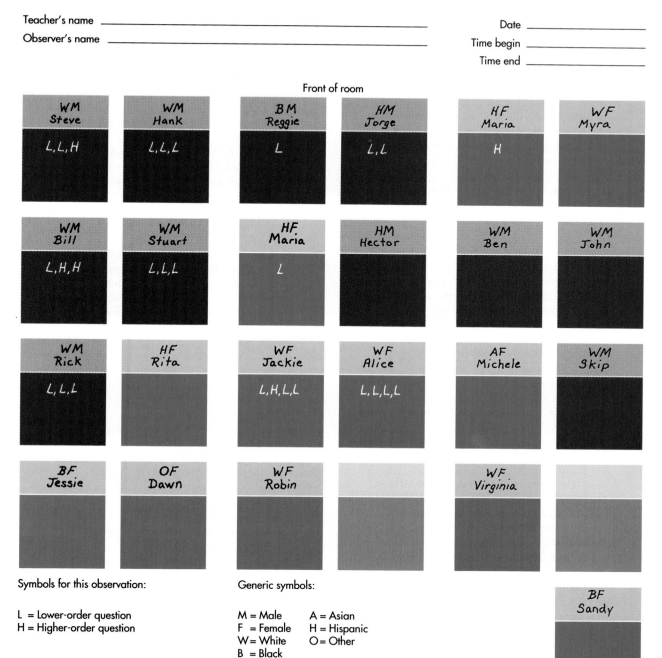

Front of room

WM Steve L,L,H	**WM** Hank L,L,L	**BM** Reggie L	**HM** Jorge L,L	**HF** Maria H	**WF** Myra
WM Bill L,H,H	**WM** Stuart L,L,L	**HF** Maria L	**HM** Hector	**WM** Ben	**WM** John
WM Rick L,L,L	**HF** Rita	**WF** Jackie L,H,L,L	**WF** Alice L,L,L,L	**AF** Michele	**WM** Skip
BF Jessie	**OF** Dawn	**WF** Robin		**WF** Virginia	**BF** Sandy

Symbols for this observation:

L = Lower-order question
H = Higher-order question

Generic symbols:

M = Male   A = Asian
F = Female   H = Hispanic
W = White   O = Other
B = Black

FIGURE 5

Sample seating chart 3.

disregard adult authority. Observing these overt signs of the power struggle is easy. Picking up the subtle rituals and patterns of the social system that underlie these disruptions is a more challenging task.

Sample Activity 1: Student Groups   Social status is a powerful force in school, and groups and cliques are often officially or unofficially labeled. The race/ethnicity, gender, national origin, social class, or ability level of a group's members may affect how it is labeled. The following activity focuses on the treatment of these special groups. Some of these data can be collected through observation; in other cases, information can best be gathered through interviews. Answer as many of the following as you can to glean insight into the special world of students.

Guidelines: Student Groups

Do students form groups, or cliques, based on such characteristics as race/ethnicity, gender, religion, national origin, achievement level, or social class?
Do these groups occupy ("hang out" around) certain school areas? Do they sit together in class?
What are the values and priorities of such groups? How do they differ from other social groups?
Do school displays and classroom bulletin boards reflect all groups (females, students of color or with disabilities, and so on) or mainly white males? Do these displays promote stereotypic or nonstereotypic perceptions?
Do students from these different groups actively and equitably participate in classroom interaction? in extracurricular activities?
How does the school reflect community values in its treatment of females, students of color or with disabilities, and so on? How does the school environment differ from that of the community?
What special education needs are represented by exceptional children in the school? If physically disabled children are present, are there physical barriers within the school that restrict their access to facilities?
To what degree are students with special needs mainstreamed? To what degree are they provided with segregated special education?
Are students in the school "tracked"? If so, what generalizations can you make about the students in each track?
What provisions are made for students whose native language is not English? How does this affect their adjustment to the school?

Sample Activity 2: Teachers' Views of Students   Try to talk to three or four teachers to assess their perceptions of the students who attend the school. The following teacher interview questions will enable you to learn about each

teacher's perception of the students' social system, as well as the norms and rules they establish for classroom management.

Guidelines: Teachers' Views of Students

What are your classroom norms and rules for appropriate behavior?
What are the penalties for students who violate the rules?
What was the worst discipline problem you have ever had to handle?
What advice would you give a new teacher about classroom management?
How many cliques are there in your classroom? Are there isolates, students who do not seem to belong to any social group?
Is there race/ethnic or class segregation in work or play groups? Who does the segregating? Are there any penalties for students who try to integrate these groups?
How are the needs of special education students met? What is done to meet the needs of the gifted?
What social or interpersonal aspects of the class have given you the greatest pleasure during the past year? the greatest problem?

Data Collection Activities: The Curriculum

In the midst of a worldwide knowledge explosion, it has become impossible to teach or learn all the information and skills now known. Moreover, every year more and more knowledge becomes available. Clearly, decisions need to be made about what to teach and what to learn. Although states and local school districts are pivotal in shaping the curriculum you will be teaching, you have some decisions to make as well. You need to consider your own ability in the subject or subjects you are to teach. Do you need to take additional academic courses to improve your own preparation? Once assigned a curriculum, how do you decide what to emphasize? What are the most important things for your students to learn?

The nature and direction of the school curriculum are explored in several chapters in this text, but it is useful for you to consider these and other curricular issues during your field experience. The activities in this section will start you on a career-long investigation of what you should teach and what is worth knowing.

Sample Activity 1: People and Experiences   Take a moment to think about how your individual experiences have led to your unique outlook on the curriculum. Next to the people and experiences listed below, indicate which have influenced your view of subject matter and the curriculum. (Note at least three people and three experiences and indicate how each has influenced your view.)

People
Family: _____
Relatives: _____
Teachers: _____
Friends: _____
Others: _____

Events
Trips: _____
Volunteer work: _____
Salaried employment: _____
Personal successes: _____
Personal failures: _____
Other: _____

Your personal life experiences, in conjunction with your school classes, have shaped and directed your view of subject matter and the curriculum. Your background also contributes to your philosophy of teaching and learning. Examine your answers to the last two activities and complete the following statement:

> I believe that some of the most important reasons to study my subject (or, if in elementary school, the subjects at my grade level) include _____
> _____.

Sample Activity 2: Textbook Analysis   Review a textbook used in your school. In your analysis, look carefully at narrative and pictures. The following questions should guide your textbook review.

Guidelines: Textbook Analysis

How recent is the textbook edition? What is the copyright date?
How would you characterize the quality of the writing? Is it stilted and dull or rich and interesting? Give examples to support your point of view.

Is the textbook guilty of "mentioning"—providing facts and figures without adequate context and explanation? Give examples to support your point of view.
Does the text include an adequate representation of males and females from many diverse groups? Count the number of males, females, and their group membership in order to reach your conclusions.
What kind of supplementary materials accompany the textbook? Is there a workbook, a teacher's manual, or other supplementary materials? Do these supplementary materials treat the teacher as a professional—or are the directions so specific that the teacher becomes little more than a technician?

Reflection: Looking Back on Your Field Observations

Your field experience is an exciting part of your professional preparation, bridging all your past experiences as a student with your future career as a teacher. After you have completed the field experience, you may find it particularly useful to consider what you have learned and how you have grown from this experience. The sample activities discussed in this Appendix, and many of the Inter-mission activities included in the textbook, only touch on the hundreds of techniques that have been developed to analyze school life. This myriad of observation instruments attests to the importance of understanding the complex world of the school. The activities in this manual provide you with opportunities for experience and reflection. These forge a critical link between your current role as a student and your future role as a professional in the field of education. The more expert you become in observing and reflecting on school life, the more insight and understanding you will gain about the nature and challenges of teaching.

Glossary

A

ability grouping The assignment of pupils to homogeneous groups according to intellectual ability or level for instructional purposes.

academic freedom The opportunity for teachers and students to learn, teach, study, research, and question without censorship, coercion, or external political and other restrictive influences.

academic learning time The time a student is actively engaged with the subject matter and experiencing a high success rate.

academies The private or semipublic secondary schools in the United States from 1830 through 1870 that stressed practical subjects.

accelerated program The more rapid promotion of gifted students through school.

accountability Holding schools and teachers responsible for student performance.

accreditation Certifying an education program or a school that has met professional standards of an outside agency.

achievement tests Examinations of the knowledge and skills acquired, usually as a result of specific instruction.

adult education Courses and programs offered to high school graduates by colleges, business, industry, and governmental and private organizations that lead to academic degrees, occupational preparation, and the like.

advanced placement Courses and programs in which younger students can earn college credit.

aesthetics The branch of philosophy that examines the nature of beauty and judgments about it.

affective domain The area of learning that involves attitudes, values, and emotions.

affirmative action A plan by which personnel policies and hiring practices reflect positive steps in the recruiting and hiring of women and people of color.

allocated time The amount of time a school or an individual teacher schedules for a subject.

alternative families Family units that differ from the traditional image; examples include foster care children, single parents, central role of grandparents, and gay couples.

alternative school A private or public school that provides religious, academic, or other alternatives to the regular public school.

American Federation of Teachers (AFT) A national organization of teachers that is primarily concerned with improving educational conditions and protecting teachers' rights.

assistive (adaptive) technology Devices that help the disabled to perform and learn more effectively, from voice-activated keyboards and mechanical wheelchairs to laptops for class note taking and personal scheduling.

authentic assessment A type of evaluation that represents actual performance, encourages students to reflect on their own work, and is integrated into the student's whole learning process. Such tests usually require that students synthesize knowledge from different areas and use that knowledge actively.

B

back to basics During the 1980s, a revival of the back-to-basics movement evolved out of concern for declining test scores in math, science, reading, and other areas. Although there is not a precise definition of back to basics, many consider it to include increased emphasis on reading, writing, and arithmetic, fewer electives, and more rigorous grading.

behavioral objective A specific statement of what a learner must accomplish in order to demonstrate mastery.

behaviorism A psychological theory that interprets human behavior in terms of stimuli-response.

behavior modification A strategy to alter behavior in a desired direction through the use of rewards.

bilingual education Educational programs in which students of limited or no English-speaking ability attend classes taught in English, as well as in their native language. There is great variability in these programs in terms of goals, instructional opportunity, and balance between English and a student's native language.

block grants Federal dollars provided to the states, with limited federal restrictions, for educational aid and program funding.

block scheduling Arrangement that expands the time per class meeting (with fewer classes per day) so lessons can provide greater depth.

board certification Recognition of advanced teaching competence, awarded to teachers who demonstrate high levels of knowledge, commitment, and professionalism through a competitive review process administered by the National Board for Professional Teaching Standards.

board of education Constituted at the state and local levels, this agency is responsible for formulating educational policy. Members are sometimes appointed but, more frequently, are elected at the local level.

busing A method for remedying segregation by transporting students to schools that have been racially or ethnically unbalanced. Before busing and desegregation were linked, busing was not a controversial issue, and, in fact, the vast majority of students riding school buses are not involved in desegregation programs.

C

canon The collection of literature and other works that typically reflects a white, Euro-centered view of the world.

career education (vocational education) A program to teach elementary and secondary students about the world of work by integrating career awareness and exploration across the school curriculum.

career ladder A system designed to create different status levels for teachers by developing steps one can climb to receive increased pay through increased responsibility or experience.

Carnegie unit A credit awarded to a student for successfully completing a high school course. It is used in determining graduation requirements and college admissions.

categorical grant Financial aid to local school districts from state or federal agencies for specific purposes.

certification State government evaluation and approval that results in an applicant's being provided with a license to teach.

character education A model comprised of various strategies that promote a defined set of core values to students.

charter school A group of teachers, parents, and even businesses may petition a local school board, or state government, to form a charter school which is exempt from many state and local regulations. Designed to promote creative new schools, the charter represents legal permission to try new approaches to educate students. First charter legislation was passed in Minnesota in 1991.

chief state school officer The executive head of a state department of education. The chief state school officer is responsible for carrying out the mandates of the state board of education and enforcing educational laws and regulations. This position is also referred to as *state superintendent.*

child abuse Physical, sexual, or emotional violation of a child's health and well-being.

child advocacy movement A movement dedicated to defining and protecting the rights of children. Child advocates recognize that children are not yet ready to assume all the rights and privileges of adults, but they are firmly committed to expanding the rights currently enjoyed by children and to no longer treating children as objects or as of the property of others.

child-centered instruction (individual instruction) Teaching that is designed to meet the interests and needs of individual students.

classroom climate The physical, emotional, and aesthetic characteristics, as well as the learning resources, of a school classroom.

cognitive domain The area of learning that involves knowledge, information, and intellectual skills.

Coleman report A study commissioned by President Johnson (1964) to analyze the factors that influence the academic achievement of students. One of the major findings of James Coleman's report was that schools in general have relatively little impact on learning. Family and peers were found to have more impact on a child's education than the school itself did.

collaborative action research Connects teaching and professional growth through the use of research relevant to classroom responsibilities.

collective bargaining A negotiating procedure between employer and employees for resolving disagreements on salaries, work schedules, and other conditions of employment. In collective bargaining, all teachers in a school system bargain as one group through chosen representatives.

Comer model James Comer of Yale has created and disseminated a program that incorporates a team of educational and mental health professionals to assist children at risk by working with their parents and attending to social, educational, and psychological needs.

Committee of Ten In 1892, the National Education Association formed the committee, influenced by college presidents, to reform the nation's high schools. The result was an academically oriented curriculum geared for colleges, and the creation of the Carnegie unit as a measure of progress through the high school curriculum.

common school A public, tax-supported school. First established in Massachusetts, the school's purpose was to create a common basis of knowledge for children. It usually refers to a public elementary school.

community schools Schools connected with a local community to provide for the educational needs of that community.

compensatory education Educational experiences and opportunities designed to overcome or compensate difficulties associated with a student's disadvantaged background.

competency The ability to perform a particular skill or to demonstrate a specified level of knowledge.

competency-based teacher education (CBTE) A teacher preparation approach in which knowledge and skills requisite for successful teaching performance are specified and teacher candidates are held responsible for mastering these competencies. It is also referred to as *performance-based teacher education (PBTE)*.

comprehensive high school A public secondary school that offers a variety of curricula, including vocational, academic, and general education programs.

compulsory attendance A state law requiring that children and adolescents attend school until reaching a specified age.

computer-assisted instruction (CAI) Individualized instruction between a student and programmed instructional material stored in a computer.

computer-managed instruction (CMI) A recordkeeping procedure for tracking student performance using a computer.

conditional teacher's license Sometimes called an emergency license, a substandard license that is issued on a temporary basis to meet a pressing need.

consolidation The trend toward combining small or rural school districts into larger ones.

cooperative learning In classrooms using cooperative learning, student work on activities in small groups, and they receive rewards based on the overall group performance.

core curriculum A central body of knowledge that schools require all students to study.

corporal punishment Disciplining students through physical punishment by a school employee.

cultural literacy Student knowledge of the people, places, events, and concepts central to knowledge of the standard literate culture.

cultural pluralism Acceptance and encouragement of cultural diversity.

curriculum (formal, explicit) Planned content of instruction that enables the school to meet its aims.

curriculum development The processes of assessing needs, formulating objectives, and developing instructional opportunities and evaluation.

D

dame schools Primary schools in colonial and other early periods in which students were taught by untrained women in the women's own homes.

day care centers Facilities charged with caring for children. The quality of care varies dramatically and may range from well-planned educational programs to little more than custodial supervision.

decentralization The trend of dividing large school districts into smaller and, it is hoped, more responsive units.

deductive reasoning Working from a general rule to identify particular examples and applications to that rule.

de facto segregation The segregation of racial or other groups resulting from circumstances, such as housing patterns, rather than from official policy or law.

de jure segregation The segregation of racial or other groups on the basis of law, policy, or a practice designed to accomplish such separation.

Department of Education (ED) U.S. cabinet-level department in charge of federal educational policy and the promotion of programs to carry out policies.

descriptive data Information that provides an objective depiction of various aspects of school or classroom life.

desegregation The process of correcting past practices of racial or other illegal segregation.

direct teaching A model of instruction in which the teacher is a strong leader who structures the classroom and sequences subject matter to reflect a clear academic focus. This model emphasizes the importance of a structured lesson in which presentation of new information is followed by student practice and teacher feedback.

disability (handicap) A learning or physical condition, a behavior, or an emotional problem that impedes education. Educators now prefer to speak of "students with disabilities," not "handicapped students," emphasizing the person, not the disability.

distance learning Courses, programs, and training provided to students over long distances through television, the Internet, and other technologies.

dual-track system The European traditional practice of separate primary schools for most children and secondary schools for the upper class.

due process The procedural requirements that must be followed in such areas as student and teacher discipline and placement in special education programs. Due process exists to safeguard individuals from arbitrary, capricious, or unreasonable policies, practices, or actions. The essential elements of due process are (1) a notice of the charge or actions to be taken, (2) the opportunity to be heard, (3) and the right to a defense that reflects the particular circumstances and nature of the case.

E

early childhood education Learning undertaken by young children in the home, in nursery schools, and in kindergartens.

eclecticism In this text, the drawing on of elements from several educational philosophies or methods.

Edison Project An educational company that contracts with local school districts, promising to improve student achievement while making a profit in the process.

educable child A mentally retarded child who is capable of achieving only a limited basic learning and usually must be instructed in a special class.

educational malpractice A new experimental line of litigation similar to the concept of medical malpractice. Educational malpractice is concerned with assessing liability for students who graduate from school without fundamental skills. Unlike medical malpractice, many courts have rejected the notion that schools or educators be held liable for this problem.

educational park A large, campuslike facility often including many grade levels and several schools and often surrounded by a variety of cultural resources.

educational television programming Television programs that promote learning.

educational vouchers Flat grants or payments representing the cost of educating a student at a school. Awarded to the parent or child to enable free choice of a school—public or private—the voucher payment is made to the school that accepts the child.

Eight-Year Study Educator Ralph Tyler's study in the 1930s that indicated the effectiveness of progressive education.

elementary school An educational institution for children in grades 1 through 6 or 8, often including kindergarten.

emergency certificate A substandard certificate that recognizes teachers who have not met all the requirements for certification. It is issued on a temporary basis to meet the needs of communities that do not have certified teachers available.

EMO (Educational Maintenance Organization) The term is borrowed from Health Maintenance Organizations (HMOs) and refers to the growing number of profit-driven companies in the business of public education.

emotional intelligence (EQ) Personality characteristics, such as persistence, can be measured as part of a new human dimension referred to as EQ. Some believe that EQ scores may be better predictors of future success than IQ scores.

empiricism The philosophy that maintains that sensory experiences, such as seeing, hearing, and touching, are the ultimate sources of all human knowledge. Empiricists believe that we experience the external world by sensory perception; then, through reflection, we conceptualize ideas that help us interpret the world.

enculturation The process of acquiring a culture; a child's acquisition of the cultural heritage through both formal and informal educational means.

endorsement Having a license extended through additional work to include a second teaching field.

engaged time The part of time that a teacher schedules for a subject in which the students are actively involved with academic subject matter. Listening to a lecture, participating in a class discussion, and working on math problems all constitute engaged time.

English grammar school The demand for a more practical education in eighteenth-century America led to the creation of these private schools that taught commerce, navigation, engineering, and other vocational skills.

environmental education The study and analysis of the conditions and causes of pollution, overpopulation, and waste of natural resources, and of the ways to preserve Earth's intricate ecology.

epistemology The branch of philosophy that examines the nature of knowledge and learning.

equal educational opportunity Refers to giving every student the educational opportunity to develop fully whatever talents, interests, and abilities he or she may have, without regard to race, color, national origin, sex, disability, or economic status.

equity Educational policy and practice that are just, fair, and free from bias and discrimination.

essentialism An educational philosophy that emphasizes basic skills of reading, writing, mathematics, science, history, geography, and language.

establishment clause A section of the First Amendment of the U.S. Constitution that says that Congress shall make no law respecting the establishment of religion. This clause prohibits nonparochial schools from teaching religion.

ethics The branch of philosophy that examines questions of right and wrong, good and bad.

ethnic group A group of people with a distinctive culture and history.

evaluation Assessment of learning and instruction.

exceptional learners Students who require special education and related services in order to realize their full potential. Categories of exceptionality include retarded, gifted, learning disabled, emotionally disturbed, and physically disabled.

existentialism A philosophy that emphasizes the ability of an individual to determine the course and nature of his or her life and the importance of personal decision making.

expulsion Dismissal of a student from school for a lengthy period, ranging from one semester to permanently.

extracurriculum The part of school life that comprises activities, such as sports, academic and social clubs, band, chorus, orchestra, and theater. Many educators think that the extracurriculum develops important skills and values, including leadership, teamwork, creativity, and diligence.

F

fair use A legal principle allowing limited use of copyrighted materials. Teachers must observe three criteria: brevity, spontaneity, and cumulative effect.

Five Factor Theory School effectiveness research emphasizes five factors, including effective leadership, monitoring student progress, safety, a clear vision, and high expectations.

Flanders Interaction Analysis An instrument developed by Ned Flanders for categorizing student and teacher verbal behavior. It is used to interpret the nature of classroom verbal interaction.

flexible scheduling A technique for organizing time more effectively in order to meet the needs of instruction by dividing the school day into smaller time modules that can be combined to fit a task.

foundation program Program for distribution of state funds designed to guarantee a specified minimum level of educational support for each child.

Franklin Academy A colonial high school founded by Benjamin Franklin that accepted females as students and promoted a less classical, more practical curriculum.

Full Service School These schools provide a network of social services from nutrition and health care to parental education and transportation, all designed to support the comprehensive educational needs of children.

future shock Term coined by Alvin Toffler. It refers to the extraordinarily accelerated rate of change and the disorientation of those unable to adapt to rapidly altered norms, institutions, and values.

futurism The activity of forecasting and planning for future developments.

G

gender bias (sex bias) The degree to which an individual's beliefs and behavior are prejudiced on the basis of sex.

gifted learner There is great variance in definitions and categorizations of the "gifted." The term is most frequently applied to those with exceptional intellectual ability, but it may also refer to learners with outstanding ability in athletics, leadership, music, creativity, and so forth.

global education Because economics, politics, scientific innovation, and societal developments in different countries have an enormous impact on children in the United States, the goals of

global education include increased knowledge about the peoples of the world, resolution of global problems, increased fluency in foreign languages, and the development of more tolerant attitudes toward other cultures and peoples.

H

Head Start Federally funded pre-elementary school program to provide learning opportunities for disadvantaged students.

heterogeneous grouping A group or class consisting of students who show normal variation in ability or performance. It differs from homogeneous grouping, in which criteria, such as grades or scores on standardized tests, are used to group students similar in ability or achievement.

hidden (implicit) curriculum What students learn, other than academic content, from what they do or are expected to do in school; incidental learnings.

hidden government The unofficial power structure within a school. It cannot be identified by the official title, position, or functions of individuals. For example, it reflects the potential influence of a school secretary or custodian.

higher-order questions Questions that require students to go beyond memory in formulating a response. These questions require students to analyze, synthesize, evaluate, and so on.

home schooling A growing trend (but a longtime practice) of parents educating their children at home, for religious or philosophical reasons.

homogeneous grouping The classification of pupils for the purpose of forming instructional groups having a relatively high degree of intellectual similarity.

hornbook A single sheet of parchment containing the Lord's Prayer and letters of the alphabet. It was protected by a thin sheath from the flattened horn of a cow and fastened to a wooden board—hence, the name. It was used during the colonial era in primary schools.

humanistic education A curriculum that stresses personal student growth; self-actualizing, moral, and esthetic issues are explored.

I

idealism A doctrine holding that knowledge is derived from ideas and emphasizing moral and spiritual reality as a preeminent source of explanation.

independent school A nonpublic school unaffiliated with any church or other agency.

individualized education program (IEP) The mechanism through which a disabled child's special needs are identified, objectives and services are described, and evaluation is designed.

individualized instruction Curriculum content and instructional materials, media, and activities designed for individual learning. The pace, interests, and abilities of the learner determine the curriculum.

Individuals with Disabilities in Education Act (IDEA) Federal law passed in 1990, which extends full education services and provisions to people identified with disabilities.

induction A formal program assisting new teachers to successfully adjust to their role in the classroom.

inductive reasoning Drawing generalizations based on the observation of specific examples.

infrastructure A substructure of underlying foundation; especially, the basic installations and facilities on which the continuance and growth of a community depend.

in loco parentis Latin term meaning "in place of the parents"; that is, a teacher or

school administrator assumes the duties and responsibilities of the parents during the hours the child attends school.

instruction The process of implementing a curriculum.

integrated curriculum (interdisciplinary curriculum) Subject matter from two or more areas combined into thematic units (i.e., literature and history resources to study civil rights laws).

integration The process of developing positive interracial contacts and improving the performance of low-achieving students of color.

interest centers Usually associated with an open classroom, such centers provide independent student activities related to a specific subject.

J

junior high school A two- or three-year school between elementary and high school for students in their early adolescent years, commonly grades 7 and 8 or 7 through 9.

K

kindergarten A preschool, early childhood educational environment first designed by Froebel in the mid-nineteenth century.

L

labeling Categorizing or classifying students for the purposes of educational placement. One unfortunate consequence may be that of stigmatizing students and inhibiting them from reaching their full potential.

laboratory schools Schools often associated with a teacher preparation institution for practice teaching, demonstration, research, or innovation.

land grant colleges State colleges or universities offering

agricultural and mechanical curricula, funded originally by the Morrill Act of 1862.

latchkey (self-care) kids A term used to describe children who go home after school to an empty house; their parents or guardians are usually working and not home.

Latin grammar school A classical secondary school with a Latin and Greek curriculum preparing students for college.

learning communities The creation of more personal collaboration between teachers and students to promote similar academic goals and values.

learning disability An educationally significant language and/or learning deficit.

least restrictive environment The program best suited to meeting a disabled student's special needs without segregating the student from the regular educational program.

license Official approval of a government agency for an individual to perform certain work, such as a teacher's license granted by a state.

limited English proficiency (LEP) A student who has a limited ability to understand, speak, or read English and who has a native language other than English.

logic The branch of philosophy that deals with reasoning. Logic defines the rules of reasoning, focuses on how to move from one set of assumptions to valid conclusions, and examines the rules of inference that enable us to frame our propositions and arguments.

looping The practice of strengthening teacher-student connections by "promoting" teachers along with their students, so that multiple-year connections are established.

lower-order questions Questions that require the retrieval of memorized information and do not require more complex intellectual processes.

M

magnet school A specialized school open to all students in a district on a competitive or lottery basis. It provides a method of drawing children away from segregated neighborhood schools while affording unique educational specialties, such as science, math, and the performing arts.

mainstreaming The inclusion of special education students in the regular education program. The nature and extent of this inclusion should be based on meeting the special needs of the child.

malfeasance Deliberately acting improperly and causing harm to someone.

mastery learning An educational practice in which an individual demonstrates mastery of one task before moving on to the next.

McGuffey Reader For almost 100 years, this reading series promoted moral and patriotic messages and set the practice of reading levels leading toward graded elementary schools.

mentor A guide or an adviser, and a component of some first-year school induction programs designed to assist new teachers.

merit pay A salary system that periodically evaluates teacher performance and uses these evaluations in determining salary.

metacognition Self-awareness of our thinking process as we perform various tasks and operations. For example, when students articulate how they think about academic tasks, it enhances their thinking and enables teachers to target assistance and remediation.

metaphysics The area of philosophy that examines the nature of reality.

microteaching A clinical approach to teacher training in which the teacher candidate teaches a small group of students for a brief time while concentrating on a specific teaching skill.

middle schools Two- to four-year schools of the middle grades, commonly grades 5 through 8, between elementary school and high school.

minimum competency tests Exit-level tests designed to ascertain whether students have achieved basic levels of performance in such areas as reading, writing, and computation. Some states require that a secondary student pass a minimum competency test in order to receive a high school diploma.

misfeasance Failure to act in a proper manner to prevent harm.

moral stages Promoted by Lawrence Kohlberg as a model of moral development in which individuals progress from simple moral concerns, such as avoiding punishment, to more sophisticated ethical beliefs and actions.

multicultural education Educational policies and practices that not only recognize but also affirm human differences and similarities associated with gender, race, ethnicity, nationality, disability, and class.

multiple intelligences A theory developed by Howard Gardner to expand the concept of human intelligence to include such areas as logical-mathematical, linguistic, bodily-kinesthetic, musical, spatial, interpersonal, and intrapersonal.

N

National Assessment of Educational Progress (NAEP) Program to ascertain the effectiveness of U.S. schools and student achievement.

National Association of State Directors of Teacher Education and Certification (NASDTEC) An organization, comprising participating state departments of education, that evaluates teacher education programs in higher education.

National Board for Professional Teaching Standards (NBPTS) A professional organization charged with establishing voluntary standards for recognizing superior teachers as "board certified."

National Council for the Accreditation of Teacher Education (NCATE) An organization that evaluates teacher education programs in many colleges and universities. Programs approved by the NCATE have assured approval of applications for teacher certification in over half the states.

National Education Association (NEA) The largest organization of educators, the NEA is concerned with the overall improvement of education and of the conditions of educators. It is organized at the national, state, and local levels.

New England Primer One of the first textbooks in colonial America, teaching reading and moral messages.

nonfeasance Failure to exercise appropriate responsibility that results in someone's being harmed.

nongraded school A school organization in which grade levels are eliminated for two or more years.

nonverbal communication The act of transmitting and/or receiving messages through means not having to do with oral or written language, such as eye contact, facial expressions, and body language.

normal school A two-year teacher education institution popular in the nineteenth century, many of which were expanded to become today's state colleges and universities.

norm-referenced tests Tests that compare individual students with others in a designated norm group.

O

objective The purpose of a lesson expressed in a statement.

objective-referenced tests Tests that measure whether students have mastered a designated body of knowledge rather than how they compare with other students in a norm group.

observation techniques Structured methods for observing various aspects of school or classroom activities.

open classroom Based on the British model, it refers not only to an informal classroom environment but also to a philosophy of education. Students pursue individual interests with the guidance and support of the teacher; interest centers are created to promote this individualized instruction. Students may also have a significant influence in determining the nature and sequence of the curriculum. It is sometimes referred to as *open education*.

open enrollment The practice of permitting students to attend the school of their choice within their school system. It is sometimes associated with magnet schools and desegregation efforts.

open-space school A school building without interior walls. Although it may be designed to promote the concept of the open classroom, the open-space school is an architectural concept rather than an educational one.

outcome based education (OBE) An educational approach that emphasizes setting learning outcomes and assessing student progress toward attaining those goals, rather than focusing on curricular topics.

P

paraprofessional A lay person who serves as an aide, assisting the teacher in the classroom.

parochial school An institution operated and controlled by a religious denomination.

peace studies The study and analysis of the conditions of and need for peace, the causes of war, and the mechanisms for the nonviolent resolution of conflict. It is also referred to as *peace education*.

pedagogical cycle A system of teacher-student interaction that includes four steps: structure—teacher introduces the topic; question—teacher asks questions; respond—student answers or tries to answer questions; and react—teacher reacts to student's answers and provides feedback.

pedagogy The science of teaching.

peer review The practice of having colleagues observe and assess teaching, as opposed to administrators.

perennialism The philosophy that emphasizes rationality as the major purpose of education. It asserts that the essential truths are recurring and universally true; it stresses Great Books.

permanent license Although there is some variation from state to state, a permanent license is issued after a candidate has completed all the requirements for full recognition as a teacher. Requirements may include a specified number of courses beyond the bachelor's degree or a specified number of years of teaching.

phonics An approach to reading instruction that emphasizes decoding words by sounding out letters and combinations of letters (as contrasted with the whole language approach).

political philosophy An approach to analyzing how past and present societies are arranged and governed and how better societies may be created in the future.

portfolio Compilations of student work (such as papers, projects, videotapes) assembled to demonstrate student progress, creativity, and competence. Often advocated as a more comprehensive assessment than test scores.

Praxis series of tests Developed by ETS to assess teachers' competence in various areas: reading, writing, math, professional and subject area knowledge. Praxis test requirements differ among states. (Appendix 2)

primary school A separately organized and administered elementary school for students in the lower elementary grades, usually grades 1 through 3, and sometimes including preprimary years.

private school A school controlled by an individual or agency other than the government, usually supported by other than public funds.

privatization The movement toward increased private sector, for-profit involvement in the management of public agencies, including schools.

probationary teaching period A specified period of time in which a newly hired teacher must demonstrate teaching competence. This period is usually three years for public school teachers and six years for college professors. Generally, on satisfactory completion of the probationary period, a teacher is granted tenure.

progressive education An educational philosophy emphasizing democracy, student needs, practical activities, and school-community relationships.

project-based instruction An approach that builds a curriculum around intriguing real-life problems and asks students to work cooperatively to develop and demonstrate their solutions.

provisional license Also referred to as a *probationary license*, a provisional license is frequently issued to beginning teachers. It may mean that a person has completed most, but not all, of the state requirements for permanent licensure. Or it may mean that the state requires several years of teaching experience before it will qualify the teacher for full certification.

R

racial discrimination Actions that limit or deny a person or group any privileges, roles, or rewards on the basis of race.

racism Attitudes, beliefs, and behavior based on the notion that one race is superior to other races.

rationalism The philosophy that emphasizes the power of reason and the principles of logic to derive statements about the world. Rationalists encourage schools to emphasize teaching mathematics, because mathematics involves reason and logic.

readability formulas Formulas that use objective, quantitative measures to determine the reading level of textbooks.

reciprocity States recognize and honor another state's actions, such as recognizing a teacher's license in one state as valid in another.

reconstructionism Also called social reconstructionism, this is a view of education as a way to improve the quality of life, to reduce the chances of conflict, and to create a more humane world.

reflective teaching Predicated on a broad and in-depth understanding of what is happening in the classroom, reflective teaching promotes thoughtful consideration and dialogue about classroom events.

revenue sharing The distribution of federal money to state and local governments to use as they decide.

Robin Hood Laws As a result of court actions, many states are redistributing revenue from wealthier to poorer communities to equalize educational funding, a process not unlike the efforts of the hero of Sherwood Forest.

romantic critics Critics such as Paul Goodman, Herbert Kohl, and John Holt who believed that schools were stifling the cognitive and affective development of children. Individual critics stressed different problems or solutions, but they all agreed that schools were producing alienated, uncreative, and unfulfilled students.

S

sabbatical A leave usually granted with full or partial pay after a teacher has taught for a specified period of time (for example, six years). Typically, it is to encourage research and professional development. While common at the university level, it is rare for K–12 teachers.

school-based management The recent trend in education reform that stresses decision making on the school level. In the past, school policies were set by the state and the districts. Now there is a trend toward, individual schools' making their own decisions and policies.

school bonds A method of financing a substantial, one-time education expenditure, such as a new school building. School bonds are typically brought before the public to be approved or disapproved, for they usually require a tax increase.

school financing Refers to the ways in which monies are raised and allocated to schools. The methods differ widely from state to state, and many challenges are being made in courts today because of the unequal distribution of funds within a state or among states.

school infrastructure The basic facilities and structures that underpin a school plant, such as plumbing, sewage, heat, electricity, roof, masonry, and carpentry.

school superintendent The chief administrator of a school system, responsible for implementing and enforcing the school board's policies, rules, and regulations, as well as state and federal requirements. The superintendent is directly responsible to the school board and is the formal representative of the school community to outside individuals and agencies.

schools without walls An alternative education program that involves the total community as a learning resource.

secular humanism The belief that people can live ethically without faith in a supernatural or supreme being. Some critics have alleged that secular humanism is a form of religion and that publishers are promoting secular humanism in their books.

separate but equal A legal doctrine that holds that equality of treatment is accorded when the races are provided substantially equal facilities, even though those facilities are separate. This doctrine was ruled unconstitutional in regard to race.

service credit By volunteering in a variety of community settings, from nursing homes to child care facilities, students are encouraged to develop a sense of community and meet what is now a high school graduation requirement in some states.

sex discrimination Any action that limits or denies a person or group of persons opportunities, privileges, roles, or rewards on the basis of sex.

sexism The collection of attitudes, beliefs, and behavior that results from the assumption that one sex is superior to the other.

sex-role stereotyping Attributing behavior, abilities, interests, values, and roles to a person or group of persons on the basis of sex. This process ignores individual differences.

sexual harassment Unwanted, repeated, and unreturned sexual words, behaviors, or gestures prohibited by federal and some state laws.

simulation A role-playing technique in which students take part in re-created life-like situations.

sociogram A diagram that is constructed to record social interactions, such as which children interact frequently and which are isolates.

Socratic method An educational strategy attributed to Socrates by which a teacher encourages a student's discovery of truth by questions.

special education Programs and instruction for children with physical, mental, emotional, or learning disabilities or gifted students who need special educational services in order to achieve at their ability level.

special license A nonteaching license that is designed for specialized educational careers, such as counseling, library science, and administration.

state adoption The process by which members of a textbook adoption committee review and select the books used throughout a state. Advocates of this process say that it results in a common statewide curriculum that unites educators on similar issues and makes school life easier for students who move within the state. Critics charge that it gives too much influence to large states and results in a "dumbed down" curriculum.

state board of education The state education agency that regulates policies necessary to implement legislative acts related to education.

state department of education An agency that operates under the direction of the state board of education, accrediting schools, certifying teachers, appropriating state school funds, and so on.

stepfamilies These relationships are created when divorced or widowed parents remarry, creating a whole set of new relationships, including stepchildren, stepgrandparents, and stepparents.

street academies Alternative schools designed to bring dropouts and potential dropouts, often inner-city youths, back into the educational mainstream.

superintendent of schools The executive officer of the local school district.

T

taxonomy A classification system of organizing information and translating aims into instructional objectives.

teacher centers Sites to provide training to improve teaching skills, inform teachers of current educational research, and develop new curricular programs.

teacher flexibility Adapting a variety of skills, abilities, characteristics, and approaches, according to the demands of each situation and the needs of each student.

tenure A system of employment in which teachers, having served a probationary period, acquire an expectancy of continued employment. The majority of states have tenure laws.

Tesseract Formerly Educational Alternatives, this private company works in the public school sector, attempting to improve school efficiency and student achievement, while making a profit.

textbook adoption states States, most often those in the South and West, that have a formal process for assessing, choosing, and approving textbooks for school use.

tracking The method of placing students according to their ability level in homogeneous classes or learning experiences. Once a student is placed, it may be very difficult to move up from one track to another. The placements may reflect racism or sexism.

transitional bilingual education Teaching students in their primary language until they can learn in English.

tuition tax credits Tax reductions for parents or guardians of children attending public or private schools.

U

unobtrusive measurement A method of observing a situation without altering it.

V

values clarification A model, comprising various strategies, that encourages students to express and clarify their values on different topics.

virtual field trip Visiting distant sites and events via the computer and the Internet.

vouchers A voucher is like a coupon, and it represents money targeted for schools. In a voucher system, parents use educational vouchers to "shop" for a school. Schools receive part or all of their per-pupil funding from these vouchers. In theory, good schools would thrive and poor ones would close for lack of students.

W

wait time The amount of time a teacher waits for a student's response after a question is asked and the amount of time following a student's response before the teacher reacts.

whole language approach Teaching reading through an integration of language arts skills and knowledge, with a heavy emphasis on literature (as contrasted with a phonics approach).

women's studies Originally created during the 1970s to study the history, literature, psychology, and experiences of women, topics typically missing from the traditional curriculum.

Z

zero reject The principle that no child with disabilities may be denied a free and appropriate public education.

Notes

Chapter One

1. Quoted in Myron Brenton, *What's Happened to Teacher?* (New York: Coward, McCann, & Geoghegan, 1970), p. 24.
2. Quoted in Ann Lieberman and Lynn Miller, *Teachers, Their World and Their Work* (Alexandria, VA: Association for Supervision and Curriculum Development, 1984), p. 45.
3. Ibid., p. 22.
4. Ibid., p. 47.
5. Ibid.
6. William Lyon Phelps, quoted in Oliver Ikenberry, *American Education Foundations* (Columbus, OH: Merrill, 1974), p. 389.
7. Quoted in Brenton. *What's Happened to Teacher?* p. 164.
8. Quoted in Haim Ginott, *Teacher and Child* (New York: Macmillan, 1972), p. 305.
9. Ibid., p. 315.
10. Quoted in Brenton, *What's Happened to Teacher?* p. 97.
11. Ibid., p. 96.
12. Ibid., p. 94.
13. Louis Harris and Associates, *The Metropolitan Life Survey of the American Teacher 1996* (New York: Metropolitan Life Insurance Company, 1996).
14. Robert Howsam et al., *Educating a Profession,* Report on the Bicentennial Commission of Education for Profession of Teaching (Washington, DC: American Association of Colleges for Teacher Education, 1976), pp. 6–7.
15. Ibid., pp. 8–9.
16. Ellen Hogan Steele, "Reflections on a School Strike II," *Phi Delta Kappan,* 57, no. 9 (May 1976) pp. 590–92.
17. Patricia Dombart, "The Vision of a Professional Insider: A Practitioner's View," *Educational Leadership* 43, no. 3 (November 1985): pp. 71–73.
18. *Teachers' Working Conditions: Findings from* The Condition of Education 1996 (Washington, DC: National Center for Educational Research and Improvement, 1996), p. 12; See also NEA surveys, such as *The Conditions and Resources of Teaching;* quote taken from "Are You Treated Like a Professional? Or a Tall Child?" *NEA Today,* December 1988, p. 4.
19. Ron Brandt, "On Teacher Empowerment: A Conversation with Ann Lieberman," *Educational Leadership* 46, no. 8 (May 1989): pp. 23–24.
20. Linda Darling-Hammond, "Who Will Speak for the Children?: How 'Teach for America' Hurts Urban Schools and Students," *Phi Delta Kappan* 76, no. 1 (September 1994): pp. 21–34.
21. Linda Darling-Hammond, "The Futures of Teaching," *Educational Leadership* 46, no. 3 (November 1988): p. 6.
22. *Tomorrow's Teachers: A Report of the Holmes Group* (East Lansing, MI: Holmes Group, 1986).
23. Carnegie Forum on Education and the Economy, Task Force on Teaching as a Profession, *A Nation Prepared: Teachers for the Twenty-First Century* (New York: Forum, 1986).
24. John Goodlad, "A Study of the Education of Educators: One Year Later," *Phi Delta Kappan* 73, no. 4 (December 1991): pp. 311–16.
25. "Clinton Teacher Board Proposal Marks Milestone." *Education Week on the Web,* 1997; "Board Certification: Here at Last!" *American Teacher* 79 (March 1995): p. 3; Ann Bradley, "National Board Announces First Teacher Certificates." *Education Week,* 11 January 1995, p. 9.
26. Anne Meek, "America's Teachers: Much to Celebrate," *Educational Leadership* 55, no. 5 (February 1998): pp. 12–16; National Education Association, *Status of the American Public School Teacher,* 1995–96, (Washington, DC: NEA, 1997).
27. *Different Drummers: How Teachers of Teachers View Public Education* (New York, NY: Public Agenda, 1997).
28. Carol Langdon, "The Fourth Phi Delta Kappa Poll of Teachers' Attitudes Toward the Public Schools," *Phi Delta Kappan* 79, no. 3 (November 1997): pp. 212–20; for other public reaction to education issues, follow the annual Kappan report on the Gallup Poll, such as Lowell C. Rose, Alee M. Gallup, and Stanley M. Elam, "The 29th Annual Phi Delta Kappa/Gallup Poll of the Public's Attitudes Toward Schools," *Phi Delta Kappan,* 79, no. 1 (September 1997): pp. 41–56.

Chapter Two

1. National Center for Education Statistics, *Projections of Education Statistics to 2008* (Washington, DC: U.S. Department of Education, 1998).

2. R. R. Henke, S. P. Choy, X. Chen, S Geis, and M. Alt, *America's Teachers: Profiles of a Profession, 1993–1994* (Washington, DC: U.S. Department of Education, 1997).

3. *Eighteenth Annual Report to Congress on the Implementation of the Individuals with Disabilities Education Act* (Washington, DC: U.S. Department of Education, 1996).

4. Anne Meek, "America's Teachers: Much to Celebrate," *Educational Leadership* 55, no. 5 (February 1998): pp. 12–13.

5. Louis Harris and Associates, *The Metropolitan Life Survey of the American Teacher, 1984–1995: Old Problems, New Challenges* (New York: Louis Harris and Associates, 1995): p. 15.

6. *Teachers' Working Conditions, Findings from* The Condition of Education 1998 (Washington, DC: U.S. Department of Education, 1998).

7. *Public and Private Schools: How Do They Differ? Findings from* The Condition of Education 1997 (Washington, DC: U.S. Department of Education, 1997).

8. Joseph Cronin, "State Regulations of Teacher Preparation," in Lee Shulman and Gary Sykes (eds.), *Handbook of Teaching and Policy* (New York: Longman, 1983), p. 174.

9. C. Emily Feistritzer and David T. Chester, *Alternative Teacher Certification: A State by State Analysis* (Washington, DC: National Center for Education Information, 1996), p. 4; C. Emily Feistritzer, *Alternative Teacher Certification: A State by State Analysis* (Washington, DC: National Center for Education Information, 1990).

10. Feistritzer and Chester, *Alternative Teacher Certification,* p. 5.

11. Jessica Sandman, "Study Finds Alternative Teachers Less Qualified, but Meeting Needs," *Education Week on the Web,* 10 September 1997.

12. Brenda Freeman and Ann Schopen, "Quality Reform in Teacher Education: A Brief Look at the Admissions Testing Movement," *Contemporary Education* 62, no. 4 (summer 1991): p. 279.

13. Thomas Toch, *In the Name of Excellence* (New York: Oxford University Press, 1991), p. 164.

14. Freeman and Schopen, "Quality Reform in Teacher Education," p. 280.

15. Findings from *The Condition of Education 1998* (Washington, DC: U.S. Department of Education, 1998).

16. Kerry White, "In a Push for Accountability, Tenure Becomes a Target," *Education Week on the Web,* 25 June 1997.

17. "Principals Losing Tenure," *Teacher Magazine on the Web,* April 1998.

18. Special thanks to Diana Coleman, Kevin Dwyer, Phyllis Lerner, and Kathryn McNerney for their assistance in preparing this section.

Chapter Three

1. Among the resources on teacher effectiveness that you may want to read are the *Journal of Teacher Education, Handbook of Research on Teaching,* and *The Review of Research in Education.*

2. N. Filby Fisher, E. Marleave, L. Cahen, M. Dishaw, M. Moore, and D. Berliner, *Teaching Behaviors, Academic Learning Time, and Student Achievement: Final Report of Beginning Teacher Evaluation Study* (San Francisco: Far West Laboratory, 1978).

3. John Goodlad, *A Place Called School* (New York: McGraw-Hill, 1984).

4. Herbert Walberg, Richard Niemiec, and Wayne Frederick, "Productive Curriculum Time," *The Peabody Journal of Education,* 69, no. 3 (1994): pp. 86–100; Steve Nelson, *Instructional Time as a Factor in Increasing Student Achievement* (Portland, OR: Northwest Regional Lab, 1990); David Berliner, "The Half-Full Glass: A Review of Research on Teaching," in P. Hosferd (ed.), *Using What We Know About Teaching* (Alexandria, VA: Association for Supervision and Curriculum Development, 1984).

5. C. M. Evertson, E. T. Emmer, B. S. Clements, J. P. Sanford, and M. E. Worsham, *Classroom Management for Elementary Teachers* (Englewood Cliffs, NJ: Prentice-Hall, 1984). See also Carolyn Evertson and Alene Harris, "What We Know About Managing Classrooms," *Educational Leadership* 49, no. 7 (April 1992): pp. 74–78.

6. Robert Slavin, "Classroom Management and Discipline," in *Educational Psychology: Theory into Practice* (Englewood Cliffs, NJ: Prentice-Hall, 1986).

7. E. T. Emmer, C. M. Evertson, J. P. Sanford, B. S. Clements, and M. E. Worsham, *Classroom Management for Secondary Teachers* (Englewood Cliffs, NJ: Prentice-Hall, 1984).

8. Jacob Kounin, *Discipline and Group Management in Classrooms* (New York: Holt, Rinehart & Winston, 1970).

9. Jere E. Brophy, "Classroom Organization and Management," *The Elementary School Journal* 83, no. 4 (1983): pp. 265–85.

10. Marilyn E. Gootman, *The Caring Teacher's Guide to Discipline: Helping Young Students Learn Self-Control, Responsibility, and Respect* (Thousand Oaks, CA: Corwin Press, 1997).

11. David Berliner, "What Do We Know About Well-Managed Classrooms? Putting Research to Work," *Instructor* 94, no. 6 (February 1985): p. 15.

12. Arno Bellack, *The Language of the Classroom* (New York: Teachers College Press, 1966).

13. Several of the sections on the pedagogical cycle are adopted from Myra and David Sadker, *Principal Effectiveness—Pupil Achievement (PEPA) Training Manual* (Washington, DC: American University, 1986).

14. Donald Cruickshank "Applying Research on Teacher Clarity," *Journal of Teacher Education* 36 (1985): pp. 44–48.

15. Robert Slavin, "The Lesson," in *Educational Psychology: Theory into Practice.*

16. John Dewey, *How We Think,* rev. ed. (Boston: D. C. Heath, 1933), p. 266.

17. Myra Sadker and David Sadker, "Sexism in the Schoolroom of the 80s," *Psychology Today* 19 (March 1985): pp. 54–57.

18. Benjamin Bloom (ed.), *Taxonomy of Educational Objectives, Handbook I: Cognitive Domain* (New York: David McKay, 1956).

19. Myra Sadker and David Sadker, "Questioning Skills" in James Cooper (ed.), *Classroom Teaching Skills,* 6th ed. (Boston: Houghton Mifflin, 1999); Trevor Kerry, "Classroom Questions in England," *Questioning Exchange* 1, no. 1, (1987): p. 33; Arthur C. Grassier and Natalie K. Person, "Question Asking During Tutoring," *American Educational Research Journal,* 31 (1994): pp. 104–37; William S. Carlsen, "Questioning in Classrooms: A Sociolinguistic Perspective," *Review of Educational Research,* 61, (1991): pp. 157–78; Meredith D. Gall, "Synthesis of Research on Teacher's Questioning," *Educational Leadership* 42, (1984): pp. 40–47; David Berliner, "The Half-Full Glass: A Review of Research on Teaching"; In Philip L. Hosford (ed.) *Using What We Know About Teaching* (Alexandria, VA: Association for Supervision and Curriculum Development, 1984): pp. 51–84; L. M. Barden, "Effective Questions and the Ever-Elusive Higher-Order Question," *American Biology Teacher,* 57, no. 7 (1995): pp. 423–26; Meredith D. Gall and T. Rhody, "Review of Research on Questioning Techniques," in William W. Wilen (ed.), *Questions, Questioning Techniques, and Effective Teaching* (Washington, DC: National Education Association, 1987), pp. 23–48; G. Brown and R. Edmondson, "Asking Questions," in E. C. Wragg (ed.), *Classroom Teaching Skills* (New York: Nichols, 1984), pp. 97–119; William W. Wilen and Ambrose A. Clegg, "Effective Questions and Questioning: A Research Review," *Theory and Research in Social Education,* 14, (1986): pp. 153–61.

20. Sadker and Sadker, "Questioning Skills."

21. Mary Budd Rowe, "Wait Time: Slowing Down May Be a Way of Speeding Up!" *Journal of Teacher Education* 37 (January/February 1986): pp. 43–50; Mary Budd Rowe, "Science, Silence, and Sanctions," *Science and Children,* 34 (September 1996): pp. 35–37; Jim B. Mansfield,

"The Effects of Wait-time on Issues of Gender Equity, Academic Achievement, and Attitude Toward a Course," *Teacher Education and Practice,* 12, no. 1 (spring–summer 1996): pp. 86–93.

22. Myra Sadker, David Sadker, and Susan Klein, "The Issue of Gender in Elementary and Secondary Education," *Review of Research in Education* 17 (1991): pp. 269–334.

23. Goodlad, *A Place Called School.*

24. Jere E. Brophy, "Teacher Praise: A Functional Analysis," *Review of Educational Research* 51 (1981): pp. 5–32.

25. Gary Davis and Margaret Thomas, *Effective Schools and Effective Teachers* (Boston: Allyn & Bacon, 1989).

26. Bruce R. Joyce and Emily F. Calhoun, *Learning Experiences: The Role of Instructional Theory and Research* (Alexandria, VA: Association for Curriculum and Supervision, 1996); Barak Rosenshine, "Synthesis of Research on Explicit Teaching," *Educational Leadership* 43, no. 4 (May 1986): pp. 60–69. See also Davis and Thomas, *Effective Schools and Effective Teachers.*

27. David Johnson, Roger Johnson, Edythe Johnson Holubee, and Patricia Roy, *Circles of Learning: Cooperation in the Classroom* (Alexandria, VA: Association of Supervision and Curriculum Development, 1984); Robert Slavin, "Research on Cooperative Learning: Consensus and Controversy," *Educational Leadership* 47, no. 4 (December 1989/January 1990): pp. 52–54.

28. Robert E. Slavin, "Cooperative Learning in Middle and Secondary Schools," *Clearinghouse* 69, no. 4 (March–April 1996): pp. 200–204; Robert E. Slavin, "Cooperative Learning," *Review of Educational Research* 50 (summer 1980): pp. 315–42. See also Robert Slavin, *Cooperative Learning: Student Teams* (Washington, DC: National Education Association, 1987).

29. Robert E. Slavin, *Cooperative Learning: Theory, Research, and Practice* (Boston: Allyn & Bacon, 1995); Roger Johnson and David Johnson, "Student Interaction: Ignored but Powerful." *Journal of Teacher Education* 36 (July–August 1985): p. 24. See also Robert Slavin, "Synthesis of Research on Cooperative Learning," *Educational Leadership* 48, no. 5 (February 1991): pp. 71–82; Susan Ellis and Susan Whalen, "Keys to Cooperative Learning," *Instructor* 101, no. 6 (February 1992): pp. 34–37.

30. David Meichenbaum and Andrew Biemiller, *Nurturing. Independent Learners: Helping Students Take Charge of Their Learning* (Cambridge, MA: Brookline Books, 1998); Joan S. Hyman and S. Alan Cohen, "Learning for Mastery: Ten Conclusions After 15 Years and 3000 Schools," *Educational Leadership* 36 (November 1979): pp. 104–9.

31. Glenn Hymel, "Harnessing the Mastery Learning Literature: Past Efforts, Current Status, and Future Directions," Paper presented at the annual meeting of the American Educational Research Association, Boston, MA, 1990; Thomas Guskey and Sally Gates, "Synthesis of Research on the Effects of Mastery Learning in Elementary and Secondary Classrooms," *Educational Leadership* 43 (May 1986): pp. 73–80.

32. Mark A. Baron and Floyd Boschee, "Dispelling the Myths Surrounding OBE," *Phi Delta Kappan* 77, no. 8 (April 1996): pp. 574–76; Spence Rogers and Bonnie Dana, *Outcome-Based Education: Concerns and Responses* (Bloomington, IN: Phi Delta Kappa Educational Foundation, 1995); William Spady and Kit Marshall, "Beyond Traditional Outcome-Based Education," *Educational Leadership* 49, no. 2 (October 1991): pp. 67–72.

33. Richard Arends, "Project Based Instruction," in *Classroom Instruction and Management* (New York: McGraw-Hill, 1997).

34. Gaea Leinhardt, "What Research on Learning Tells Us About Teaching," *Educational Leadership* 49, no. 7 (April 1992): pp. 20–25.

35. Jere Brophy, "Probing the Subtleties of Subject-Matter Teaching," *Educational Leadership* 49, no. 7 (April 1992): pp. 4–8.

36. Leinhardt, "What Research on Learning Tells Us About Teaching," pp. 20–25.

37. Richard Prawat, "From Individual Differences to Learning Communities—Our Changing Focus," *Educational Leadership* 49, no. 7 (April 1992): pp. 9–13.

38. Joellen Killion and Guy Todnem, "A Process for Personal Theory Building," *Educational Leadership* 48, no. 6 (March 1991): pp. 14–16.

39. Bud Wellington, "The Promise of Reflective Practice," *Educational Leadership* 48, no. 6 (March 1991): pp. 4–5.

Chapter Four

1. *Do We Still Need Public Schools?* (Washington, DC: Center on National Educational Policy and Phi Delta Kappa, 1996), p. 14; Maxine Schwartz Seller, "Immigrants in the Schools—Again: Historical and Contemporary Perspectives on the Education of Post 1965 Immigrants in the United States," *Educational Foundations* 3, no. 1 (spring 1989): pp. 53–75.

2. Kenneth Dunn and Rita Dunn, "Dispelling Outmoded Beliefs About Student Learning," *Educational Leadership* 45, no. 7 (March 1987): pp. 55–63.

3. James Keefe, *Learning Style Theory and Practice* (Reston, VA: National Association of Secondary School Principals, 1987).

4. Dunn and Dunn, "Dispelling Outmoded Beliefs About Student Learning"; see also G. Price, "Which Learning Style Elements Are Stable and Which Tend to Change?" *Learning Styles Network Newsletter* 4, no. 2

(1980): pp. 38–40; J. Vitrostko, *An Analysis of the Relationship Among Academic Achievement in Mathematics and Reading, Assigned Instructional Schedules and the Learning Style Time Preferences of Third-, Fourth-, Fifth-, and Sixth-Grade Students,* unpublished doctoral dissertation, St. John's University, Jamaica, New York, 1983.

5. Howard Gardner and Thomas Hatch, "Multiple Intelligences Go to School: Educational Implications of the Theory of Multiple Intelligences," *Educational Researcher* 18, no. 8 (November 1989): p. 5.

6. Kathy Checkley, "The First Seven . . . and the Eighth: A Conversation with Howard Gardner," *Educational Leadership* 55, no. 1 (September 1997): pp. 8–13; Howard Gardner, "Beyond the I.Q.: Education and Human Development," *Harvard Educational Review* 57, no. 2 (spring 1987): pp. 187–93.

7. Thomas Armstrong, "Multiple Intelligences: Seven Ways to Approach Curriculum," *Educational Leadership* 52 (November 1994): pp. 26–28.

8. Howard Gardner, "Reflections on Multiple Intelligences: Myths and Messages," *Phi Delta Kappan* 77, no. 3 (November 1995): pp. 200–209; Veronica Borruso Emig, "A Multiple Intelligence Inventory," *Educational Leadership* 55, no. 1 (September 1997): pp. 47–50.

9. Thomas R. Hoerr, "How the New City School Applies the Multiple Intelligences," *Educational Leadership* 52 (November 1994): pp. 29–33.

10. Nancy Gibbs, "The E.Q. Factor," *Time* 146, no. 14 (2 October 1995): pp. 60–68.

11. Ibid. See also Kevin R. Kelly and Sidney M. Moon, "Personal and Social Talents," *Phi Delta Kappan* 79, No. 10 (June 1998): pp. 743–46.

12. Daniel Goleman, "Emotional Intelligence: Why It Can Matter More Than IQ," *Learning* (May/June 1996): pp. 49–50.

13. The demographic information in the following section is based on the following: William Branigin, "Nearly 1 in 10 in U.S. Is Foreign Born, Census Says," *Washington Post,* 9 April 1997, p. A18; Jessica I. Sandham, "Graduates Growing More Diverse, Study Finds," *Education Week on the Web,* 1 April 1998; *Statistical Abstract of the United States, 1997* (Washington, DC: U.S. Department of Commerce, Bureau of the Census, 1996); *Youth Indicators* (Washington, DC: National Center for Education Statistics, Department of Education, 1996).

14. James Banks, "Multicultural Education: Characteristics and Goals," in James A. Banks and Cherry A. McGee Banks (eds.), *Multicultural Education: Issues and Perspectives* (Boston: Allyn & Bacon, 1997), pp. 3–31.

15. Carol Gilligan, *In a Different Voice: Psychological Theory and Women's Development* (Cambridge, MA: Harvard University Press, 1982). See also Mary Field Belenky,

Blythe McVicker Clinchy, Nancy Rule Goldberger, and Jill Mattuck Tarule, *Women's Ways of Knowing: The Development of Self, Voice, and Mind* (New York: Basic Books, 1986).

16. Geneva Gay, "Achieving Educational Equality Through Curriculum Desegregation," *Phi Delta Kappan* 72, no. 1 (September 1990): pp. 56–62.

17. Peter Schmidt, "New Survey Discerns Deep Divisions Among U.S. Youths on Race Relations," *Education Week,* 25 March 1992, p. 5.

18. James Banks, "Approaches to Multicultural Curriculum Reform," in Banks and Banks, *Multicultural Education,* pp. 229–50.

19. S. D. McLemore and H. D. Romo, *Racial and Ethnic Relations in America* (Boston: Allyn & Bacon, 1998): John O'Neil, "Why Are the Black Kids Sitting Together?" *Educational Leadership* 55, no. 5 (December 1997/January 1998): pp. 12–17; Robert Slavin, "Research on Cooperative Learning: Consensus and Controversy," *Educational Leadership* 47, no. 4 (December 1989/January 1990): pp. 52–54.

20. Slavin, "Research on Cooperative Learning"; McLemore and Romo, *Racial and Ethnic Relations in America;* see also James C. Hendrix, "Cooperative Learning: Building a Democratic Community," *Clearinghouse* 69, no. 6 (July–August 1996): pp. 333–36.

21. Susan Ellis and Susan Whalen, "Keys to Cooperative Learning," *Instructor* 101, no. 6 (February 1992): pp. 34–37.

22. James Crawford, ed., *Language Loyalties: A Source Book on the Official English Controversy* (Chicago: University of Chicago Press, 1992); see also Jonathon Zimmerman, "A Babel of Tongues," *U.S. News & World Report,* 24 November 1997, p. 39.

23. Diane Ravitch, "Politicization and the Schools: The Case of Bilingual Education," in *Taking Sides,* James W. Noll (ed.) (Guilford, CT: Dushkin, 1997), pp. 232–40.

24. Harold Hodgkinson, quoted in *Education Week,* 14 May 1986, pp. 14–40.

25. D. Hugo Lopez and Merle T. Mora, "Bilingual Education and the Labor Market Earnings Among Hispanics: Evidence Using High School and Beyond," *READ Perspectives* (Amherst, MA: Institute for Research in English Acquisition and Development), 1998.

26. Jorge Amselle, "Adios, Bilingual Ed," *Policy Review* no. 86, November 1997 (Washington, DC: Heritage Foundation), pp. 52–55.

27. Rene Sanchez and William Booth, "California Rejection: A Big Blow to Bilingualism: Decisive Vote Could Set Pace for Rest of Nation," *Washington Post,* 4 June 1998, p. A16; Peter Baker, "Education Dept Faults Anti-Bilingual Measure," *Washington Post,* 28 April 1998, p. A3.

28. James Crawford, *Hold Your Tongue: Bilingualism and the Politics of "English Only"* (New York: Addison-Wesley, 1992), pp. 111–12.

29. Gary A. Cziko, "The Evaluation of Bilingual Education: From Necessity and Probability to Possibility," *Educational Researcher* 21, no. 2 (March 1992): p. 24; J. David Ramirez, "Executive Summary," *Bilingual Research Journal* 16 (winter, spring, 1992): pp. 1–245.

30. Rosalie Pedalino Porter. New York City Study. *READ Perspectives* 12 (2), 1995, quoted in Robert F. McNergney and Joanne M. Herbert, *Foundations of Education* (Needham Heights, MA: Allyn & Bacon, 1998): p. 311.

31. Peter Schmidt, "Three Types of Bilingual Education Effective, E.D. Study Concludes," *Education Week,* 20 February 1991, pp. 1, 23.

32. Wayne Thomas and Virginia Collier, "Two Languages Are Better Than One," *Educational Leadership* 55, no. 4 (December 1997/January 1998): pp. 23–26; Craig Donegan, "Debate over Bilingualism," *Congressional Quarterly Researcher* 6 no. 3 (19 January 1996): pp. 51–59; Stephen Krashen, "Why Bilingual Education?" *ERIC Clearinghouse* (ED403101) (Washington, DC: OERI, U.S. Dept of Education, 1997).

33. These categories build on the ones described by William Heward and Rodney A. Cavanaugh, "Educational Equality for Students with Disabilities," in James Banks and Cherry Banks (eds.), *Multicultural Education* (Boston: Allyn & Bacon, 1997), pp. 301–33; as well as William Heward and Michael Orlansky, "Educational Equality for Exceptional Students," in James Banks and Cherry Banks (eds.), *Multicultural Education* (Boston, Allyn & Bacon, 1989), pp. 231–50.

34. Findings from the *Condition of Education 1998* (Washington, DC: U.S. Department of Education, 1998) updated the original figures of Heward and Orlansky, "Educational Equality for Exceptional Students.".

35. Susan DeFord, "Inclusive Classrooms," *Washington Post Magazine,* 8 February 1998, p. 8.

36. Helen Keller, *The Story of My Life* (Garden City, NY: Doubleday, 1902), pp. 34–37.

37. Letter from Anne Sullivan, quoted in Keller, *The Story of My Life,* p. 257.

38. Marie Killilea, *Karen* (New York: Dell, 1952) p. 171.

39. Ed Martin, quoted in "PL 94-142," *Instructor* 87, no. 9 (1978): p. 63.

40. Michael D. Simpson, "Rights Watch: Who's Paying for Special ED?" *NEA Today* 15, no. 9 (May 1997): p. 20.

41. *Eighteenth Annual Report to Congress on the Implementation of the Individuals with Disabilities Education Act* (Washington, DC: U.S. Department of Education, 1996); see also Martha McCarthy, "Severely

Disabled Children: Who Pays?" *Phi Delta Kappan* 73, no. 1 (September 1991): pp. 66–71.

42. Steven Muir and Jerry Hutton, "Regular Education Initiative: Impact on Service to Handicapped Students," *The Journal of the Association of Teacher Educators* 11, no. 3 (fall 1989): pp. 7–11. See also "Mainstreaming," *Harvard Education Letter* (January/February 1990): p. 7; Madeleine Will, *Educating Students with Learning Problems: A Shared Responsibility* (Washington, DC: U.S. Department of Education, 1986).

43. Quoted in David Milofsky, "Schooling the Kid No One Wants," *New York Times Magazine*, 2 January 1977, pp. 24–29.

44. The anecdotes and many of the quotations in this section were cited in Gene I. Maeroff, "The Unfavored Gifted Few," *New York Times Magazine*, 21 August 1977, reprinted in Celeste Toriero (ed.), *Readings in Education 78/79* (Guilford, CT: Dushkin, 1978).

45. Joseph S. Renzulli and C. H. Smith, "Two Approaches to Identification of Gifted Students," *Exceptional Children* 43 (1977).

46. Robert Sternberg, "Giftedness According to the Triarchic Theory of Human Intelligence," in Nicholas Congelo and Gary Davis (eds.), *Handbook of Gifted Education* (Boston: Allyn & Bacon, 1991).

47. John F. Feldhusen, "Programs for the Gifted Few or Talent Development for the Many?" *Phi Delta Kappan* 79, no. 10 (June 1998): pp. 735–38.

48. Judy Galbraith, "Gifted Youth and Self-Concept," *Gifted Education* 15, no. 2 (May 1989): pp. 15–17.

49. Ibid., p. 16.

50. Robert Morris, "Educating Gifted for the 1990s," *Gifted Education* 15, no. 2 (May 1989): pp. 50–52; for more information about gender bias, see *Gender Gaps: Where Schools Still Fail Our Children* (Washington, DC: American Association of University Women Educational Foundation, 1998).

51. Joyce Van Tassel-Baska, "Curricular Approaches for Gifted Learners," *Gifted Education* 15, no. 2 (May 1989): pp. 19–34.

52. John Feldhusen, "Synthesis of Research on Gifted Youth," *Educational Leadership* 46, no. 6 (March 1989): pp. 6–11.

53. Lisa Leff, "Gifted, Talented, and Under Siege," *Washington Post Educational Review*, 5 April 1992, p. 14.

54. Quoted in Galbraith, "Gifted Youth and Self-Concept," p. 17.

Chapter Five

1. James Shaver and William Strong, *Facing Value Decisions: Rationale Building for Teachers* (Belmont, CA: Wadsworth, 1976).

2. Ernest L. Boyer, *High School: A Report on Secondary Education in America* (New York: Harper & Row, 1983), pp. 209–10.

3. Bill Bigelow, "The Human Lives Behind the Labels: The Global Sweatshop, Nike, and the Race to the Bottom," *Phi Delta Kappan* 79, no. 2 (October 1997): pp. 112–19.

4. Paulo Freire, *The Pedagogy of the Oppressed* (New York: Herder & Herder, 1970).

5. John Goodlad, *A Place Called School* (New York: McGraw-Hill, 1984), pp. 35–39.

6. Arthur Eugene Bestor, *Educational Wastelands: The Retreat from Learning in Our Public Schools* (Urbana: University of Illinois Press, 1953), p. 75.

7. Boyer, *High School*, p. 5.

8. National Commission on Excellence in Education, *A Nation at Risk: The Imperative for Educational Reform* (Washington, DC: U.S. Government Printing Office, 1983), p. 1.

9. David Hill, "Fixing the System from the Top Down," *Teacher Magazine*, (September/October 1989): pp. 50–55.

10. David L. Clark and Terry A. Astuto, "Reconstructing Reform: Challenges to Popular Perceptions About Teachers and Students," *Phi Delta Kappan* 75, no. 7 (March 1994): pp. 512–20.

11. Donald C. Ohlrich, "Education Reforms: Mistakes, Misconceptions, Miscues," *Phi Delta Kappan* 170, no. 7 (March 1989): pp. 512–17.

12. Clinton Boutwell, "People Without People," *Phi Delta Kappan* 79, no. 2 (October 1997): pp. 104–11.

13. Joy Dryfoos, "Full Service Schools," *Educational Leadership* 53, no. 7 (April 1996): pp. 18–23.

14. *America 2000: An Education Strategy* (Washington, DC: U.S. Department of Education, 1991); see also Julie Miller, "Clinton, in Attacking Bush's Policies, Pledges 'Real Education Reform' Plan," *Education Week*, 17 May 1992, p. 17; Richard W. Riley, "Reflections on Goals 2000," *Teachers College Record* 96, no. 3 (Spring 1995): pp. 380–88.

15. Henry J. Perkinson, *The Imperfect Panacea: American Faith in Education* (New York: McGraw-Hill, 1995), p. 191.

16. Debra Viadero, "Students Learn More in Magnets Than Other, Study Finds," *Education Week*, 6 March 1996, p. 6; Caroline Hendrie, "Magnets Value in Desegregating Schools Is Found to Be Limited," *Education Week on the Web* (13 November 1996); "Research Notes," *Education Week on the Web* (16 September 1998).

17. A. S. Byrk, Valerie Lee, and P. B. Holland, *Catholic Schools and the Common Good* (London: Harvard University Press, 1993).

18. John E. Koppich, "Considering Nontraditional Alternatives: Charters, Private Contracts, and

Vouchers," *The Future of Children* 7, no. 3 (winter 1997): pp. 96–111; Joseph P. Viteritti, "Stacking the Deck for the Poor: The New Politics of Schools Choice," *The Brookings Review* 14, no. 3 (summer 1996): pp. 10–13.

19. Alex Molnar, "Charter Schools: The Smiling Face of Disinvestment," *Educational Leadership* 54, no. 2 (October 1996): pp. 9–15.

20. Joe Nathan, "Heat and Light in the Charter School Movement," *Phi Delta Kappan* 79, no.7 (March 1998): pp. 499–505.

21. Bruno V. Manno, Chester E. Finn, Louann A. Bierlein, and Gregg Vanurek, "How Charter Schools Are Different: Lessons and Implications from a National Study," *Phi Delta Kappan* 79, no. 7 (March 1998): pp. 489–98.

22. Molnar, "Charter Schools," p. 10.

23. Joel Spring, *American Education* (New York: McGraw-Hill, 1996), pp. 184–85.

24. Peggy Farber, "The Edison Project Scores—and Stumbles—in Boston," *Phi Delta Kappan* 79, no. 7 (March 1998): pp. 506–11; Rene Sanchez, "Edison School Project Growing Slowly," *Washington Post,* 22 August 1997, p. A3; Kevin Fedarko, "Starting from Scratch," *Time,* 27 October 1997, pp. 82–85; Jay Mathews, "For Profit School Firm Offers Teachers Stock," *Washington Post,* 22 October 1998, pp. C-1, C-6.

25. Mike Hoffman, "Upstarts: Staking Out a Share of Public-School Gold," *Inc* (June 1998): pp. 25–27.

26. Mark Walsh, "Question[s?] About Finances Put Edison Project at Crossroad," *Education Week,* 3 August 1994, pp. 18–19; Walter Farrell, Jr., James Johnson, Cloyzelle Jones, and Marty Sapp, "Will Privatizing Schools Really Help Inner-City Students of Color?" *Educational Leadership* 52, no. 1 (September 1994): pp. 72–75.

27. Michael Winerip, "Schools for Sale," *New York Times Magazine,* 14 June 1998, pp. 42–49, 80, 86, 88–89; Mark Walsh, "Business," *Education Week on the Web,* 4 March 1998.

28. Mark Walsh, "Disney Holds Up School as Model for Next Century," *Education Week,* 22 June 1994, pp. 1, 16.

29. Spring, *American Education,* pp. 185–86.

30. Alex Molnar interviewed in "Giving Kids the Business, an Interview with Alex Molnar," *The Education Industry: The Corporate Takeover of Public Schools,* http://www.corpwatch.org/feature/education/; see also Alex Molnar, *Giving Kids the Business: The Commercialization of America's Schools* (Boulder, CO: Westview Press, 1996).

31. Pedro Noguerar, "More Democracy Not Less: Confronting the Challenge of Privatization in Public Education," *Journal of Negro Education* 623, no. 2 (1994): p. 238.

32. Bruce Fuller, "Is School Choice Working?" *Educational Leadership* 54, no. 2 (October 1996): pp. 37–40; Lorna Jimerson, "Hidden Consequences of School Choice: Impact on Programs, Finances, and Accountability," paper presented at the American Educational Research Association annual meeting, San Diego, CA; Steven Glazerman, "School Quality and Social Stratification: The Determinants and Consequences of Parental Choice," paper presented at the American Educational Research Association annual meeting, San Diego, CA; Edd Doerr, "The Empty Promise of School Vouchers," *USA Today Magazine,* 125, no. 2622 (New York: Society for the Advancement of Education). March 1997, pp. 89–90.

33. "Live and Learn," *Harper's Bazaar,* (September 1994), pp. 268–70.

34. Patricia Lines, "Educating a Minority: How Families, Policymakers, and Public Educators View Home Schooling," *Journal of Early Education and Family Review* 5, no. 3 (January/February 1998): pp. 25–28; Patricia Lines, "Home Schooling," *Eric Digest* 95 (1995): pp. 1–3; J. Natale, "Home, but Not Alone," *The American School Board Journal* 182, no. 7: pp. 34–36; Home School Legal Defense Association, *Answers to Commonly Asked Questions About Home Schooling, 1996,* available from Home School Legal Defense Association, P.O. Box 159, Paeonian Springs, VA 22129.

35. M. Mayberry, "Characteristics and Attitudes of Families Who Home School," *Education and Urban Society* 21 (1988): pp. 32–41; M. Mayberry, "Home-based Education in the United States: Demographics, Motivations, and Educational Implications," *Educational Review* 41, no. 2 (1989): pp. 171–80.

36. J. A. Van Galen, "Schooling in Private: A Study of Home Education," doctoral dissertation, University of North Carolina, Chapel Hill, 1986.

37. Nancy Gibbs, *Time,* 31 October 1994, pp. 62–63.

38. "Home-Taught Students Miss School Activities," *Washington Post,* 26 November 1995, pp. B-1, B-5; Chris Jeub, "Why Parents Choose Home Schooling," *Educational Leadership* 52, no. 1 (September 1994): pp. 50–52.

39. Darwin L. Webb, "Homeschools and Interscholastic Sports: Denying Participation Violates United States Constitutional Due Process and Equal Protection Rights," *Journal of Law and Education* 26, no. 3 (July 1997): pp. 123–32; Gary Knowles, James A. Muchmore, and Holly W. Spaulding, "Home Education as an Alternative, to Institutionalized Education," *The Education Forum* 58 (spring 1994): pp. 238–43.

40. Barbara Kantrowitz and Pat Wingert, "Learning at Home: Does It Pass the Test?" *Newsweek,* 5 October 1998, pp. 64–71; "Charter 'Profit': Will Michigan Heap

Money on an Electronic Charter School?" *The American School Board Journal* 181, no. 9 (September 1994): pp. 27–28; "The Dawn of Home Schooling," *Newsweek,* 10 October 1994, p. 67.

Chapter Six

1. Philip W. Jackson, *Life in Classrooms* (New York: Holt, Rinehart & Winston, 1968).

2. Ibid.

3. Manuel Justiz, "It's Time to Make Every Minute Count," *Phi Delta Kappan* 65, no. 7 (March 1984): pp. 483–85; see also Herbert Walberg, "Families as Partners in Educational Productivity," *Phi Delta Kappan* 65, no. 6 (February 1984): pp. 397–400.

4. John Goodlad, *A Place Called School* (New York: McGraw-Hill, 1984).

5. Quoted in Ernest L. Boyer, *High School* (New York: Harper & Row, 1983); C. Fisher, N. Filby, E. Marliave, L. Cohen, M. Dishaw, J. Moore, and D. Berliner, *Teacher Behaviors, Academic Learning Time, and Student Achievement,* Final Report of Phase III-B, Beginning Teacher Evaluation Study (San Francisco: Far West Laboratory for Educational Research and Development, 1978).

6. G. Madaus et al., *School Effectiveness: A Reassessment of the Evidence* (New York: McGraw-Hill, 1980).

7. Jackson, *Life in Classrooms.*

8. Ned Flanders, "Intent, Action, and Feedback: A Preparation for Teaching," *Journal of Teacher Education* 14, no. 3 (September 1963): pp. 251–60.

9. Arno Bellack, *The Language of the Classroom* (New York: Teachers College Press, 1965).

10. Goodlad, *A Place Called School.*

11. Romiett Stevens, "The Question as a Measure of Classroom Practice," in *Teachers College Contributions to Education* (New York: Teachers College Press, 1912).

12. Myra Sadker and David Sadker, "Questioning Skills," in James Cooper (ed.), *Classroom Teaching Skills* (Boston: Houghton Mifflin, 1998).

13. W. D. Floyd, *An Analysis of the Oral Questioning Activity in Selected Colorado Primary Classrooms.* Unpublished doctoral dissertation, Colorado State College, 1960.

14. Mary Budd Rowe, "Wait Time: Slowing Down May Be a Way of Speeding Up!" *Journal of Teacher Education* 37 (1986): pp. 43–50.

15. Talcott Parsons, "The School as a Social System: Some of Its Functions in Society," in Robert Havinghurst and Bernice Neugarten, (eds.), *Society and Education* (Boston: Allyn & Bacon, 1967), pp. 191–214.

16. Robert Lynd and Helen Lynd, *Middletown: A Study in American Culture* (New York: Harcourt Brace Jovanovich, 1929).

17. W. Lloyd Warner, Robert Havinghurst, and Martin Loeb, *Who Shall Be Educated?* (New York: Harper & Row, 1944).

18. August Hollingshead, *Elmtown's Youth* (New York: Wiley, 1949).

19. Robert Havinghurst et al., *Growing Up in River City* (New York: Wiley, 1962).

20. Ernest L. Boyer, *High Schools: A Report on Secondary Education in America* (New York: Harper & Row, 1983).

21. Shirl Gilbert and Geneva Gay, "Improving the Success in School of Poor Black Children," *Phi Delta Kappan* 67, no. 2 (October 1985): pp. 133–38.

22. Ray Rist, "Student Social Class and Teacher Expectations. The Self-Fulfilling Prophecy of Ghetto Education," *Harvard Education Review* 40, no. 3 (1970): pp. 411–51.

23. Jeannie Oakes and Martin Lipton, "Detracking Schools: Early Lessons from the Field," *Phi Delta Kappan* 73, no. 6 (February 1992): pp. 448–54.

24. Quoted in "Tracking," *Education Week on the Web,* 14 October 1998; see also Susan Allan, "Ability Grouping Research Reviews: What Do They Say About Grouping and the Gifted?" *Educational Leadership* 48, no. 6 (March 1991): pp. 60–65; Adam Gamoran, "Alternative Use of Ability Grouping in Secondary Schools: Can We Bring High-Quality Instruction to Low-Ability Classes?" *American Journal of Education* 102 (1993): pp. 1–22; Robert E. Slavin, "Achievement Effects of Ability Grouping in Secondary Schools: A Best-Evidence Synthesis," *Review of Educational Research* 60 (1990): pp. 471–99.

25. Quoted from a student letter in the *Arlingtonian,* 13 May 1993.

26. Quoted in Raphaela Best, *We've All Got Scars* (Bloomington: Indiana University Press, 1983), p. 9.

27. Ibid., p. 10.

28. Ibid., p. 162.

29. Steven Sher, "Some Kids Are Nobody's Best Friend," *Today's Education,* 71, no. 1. February/March 1982: pp. 23–29.

30. "Unpopular Children," *The Harvard Education Letter,* Harvard Graduate School of Education in association with Harvard University Press, January/February 1989, pp. 1–3. See also Lisa Wolcott, "Relationships: The Fourth 'R,'" *Teacher* (April 1991): pp. 26–27.

31. Zappa, Coleman, Friedenberg, Vonnegut, and Ford are quoted in Ralph Keyes, *Is There Life After High School?* (Boston: Little, Brown, 1976).

32. James Coleman, *The Adolescent Society* (New York: Free Press, 1961).

33. Goodlad, *A Place Called School.*

34. Quoted in Boyer, *High School,* p. 202.

35. Ibid., p. 206.

36. Sara Lawrence Lightfoot, *The Good High School* (New York: Basic Books, 1983).

37. David Owen, *High School* (New York: Viking Press, 1981).

38. Keyes, *Is There Life After High School?*

39. Lloyd Temme, quoted in Keyes, *Is There Life After High School?*

40. Mel Brooks and Dustin Hoffman are quoted in Keyes, *Is There Life After High School?*

41. Quoted in Boyer, *High School.*

42. *The Metropolitan Life Survey of the American Teacher, 1984–1995: Old Problems, New Challenges* (New York: Louis Harris and Associates, 1995).

43. Quoted in Ernest L. Boyer, "What Teachers Say About Children in America," *Educational Leadership* 46, no. 8 (May 1989): p. 73.

44. Ibid.

45. Ibid., p. 74.

46. Frances Ianni, "Providing a Structure for Adolescent Development," *Phi Delta Kappan* 70, no. 9 (May 1989): p. 677.

47. Patrick Welsh, *Tales Out of School* (New York: Viking, 1986), pp. 41–42.

48. Urie Bronfenbrenner, "Alienation and the Four Worlds of Childhood," *Phi Delta Kappan* 67, no. 6 (February 1986): pp. 430–35.

49. Lightfoot, *The Good High School.*

50. Quoted in Ianni, "Providing a Structure for Adolescent Development," p. 680.

51. Grace Pung Guthrie and Larry Guthrie, "Streamlining Interagency Collaboration for Youth At Risk," *Educational Leadership* 49, no. 1 (September 1991): pp. 17–22.

52. Alfie Kohn, "Caring Kids: The Role of Schools," *Phi Delta Kappan* 72, no. 7 (March 1991): pp. 496–506.

53. Carnegie Council on Adolescent Development, *Turning Points: Preparing American Youth for the 21st Century,* excerpted in "The American Adolescent: Facing a Vortex of New Risks," *Education Week,* 21 June 1989, p. 22.

54. Ibid.

55. George Weber, *Inner-City Children Can Be Taught to Read: Four Successful Schools* (Washington, DC: D.C. Council for Basic Books, 1971).

56. Ronald Edmonds, "Some Schools Work and More Can," *Social Policy* 9 (1979): pp. 28–32.

57. Barbara Taylor and Daniel Levine, "Effective Schools Projects and School-Based Management," *Phi Delta Kappan* 72, no. 5 (January 1991): pp. 394–97. See also Herman Meyers, "Roots, Trees, and the Forest: An Effective Schools Development Sequence." Paper delivered at the American Educational Research Association, San Francisco, April 1992.

58. Lightfoot, *The Good High School.*

59. Ibid., p. 67.

60. David Clark, Linda Lotto, and Mary McCarthy, "Factors Associated with Success in Urban Elementary Schools," *Phi Delta Kappan* 61, no. 7 (March 1980): pp. 467–70. See also David Gordon, "The Symbolic Dimension of Administration for Effective Schools."

61. Quoted in Boyer, *High School,* p. 221.

62. William Rutherford, "School Principals as Effective Leaders," *Phi Delta Kappan* 67, no. 1 (September 1985): pp. 31–34. See also R. McClure, "Stages and Phases of School-Based Renewal Efforts." Paper presented at the annual meeting of the American Educational Research Association, New Orleans, 1988.

63. Mary Hatwood Futrell, "An Educators Opinion, Reform Demands Restructured Schools," *Washington Post,* 6 April 1986, p. c5.

64. Lowell C. Rose and Alec M. Gallup, "The 30h Annual Gallup Poll of the Public's Attitudes Toward the Public Schools," *Phi Delta Kappan* 80, no. 1 (September 1998): pp. 41–56.

65. *Update: Indicators of School Crime and Safety, 1998* (Washington, DC: National Center for Educational Statistics, U.S. Department of Education, October 1998).

66. *Safe Schools, NEA Action Sheet* (Washington, DC: NEA, January 1996).

67. Kevin Dwyer, D. Osher, and C. Warger, *Early Warning, Timely Response: A Guide for Safe Schools* (Washington, DC: U.S. Department of Education, August 1998).

68. Lightfoot, *The Good High School.*

69. Wilbur Brookover, Laurence Beamer, Helen Efthim, Douglas Hathaway, Lawrence Lezotte, Stephen Miller, Joseph Passalacqua, and Louis Tornatzky, *Creating Effective Schools* (Holmes Beach, FL: Learning Publications, 1982).

70. Herbert Walberg, Rosanne Paschal, and Thomas Weinstein, "Homework's Powerful Effects on Learning," *Educational Leadership* 42 (1985): pp. 76–79.

71. Robert Rosenthal and Lenore Jacobson, *Pygmalion in the Classroom* (New York: Holt, Rinehart & Winston, 1968).

72. Patrick Proctor, "Teacher Expectations: A Model for School Improvement," *Elementary School Journal* (March 1984): pp. 469–81; William Wayson, "The Politics of Violence in Schools: Double Speak and Disruptions in Public Confidence," *Phi Delta Kappan* 67, no. 2 (October 1985): pp. 127–32.

73. Larry Cuban, "Effective Schools: A Friendly but Cautionary Note," *Phi Delta Kappan* 64, no. 10 (June 1983): pp. 695–96; Daniel Levine, "Creating Effective Schools: Findings and Implications from Research and Practice," *Phi Delta Kappan* 72, no. 5 (January 1991): pp. 389–93.

74. Rebecca Jones, "What Works: Researchers Tell What Schools Must Do to Improve Student Achievement," *The American School Board Journal* 185, no. 4 (April 1998): pp. 28–32, 33; Mary Anne Raywid, "Synthesis of Research: Small Schools: A Reform That Works,"

Educational Leadership (December 1997/January 1998): pp. 34–39.

75. Edward A. Wynne, "Looking at Schools," *Phi Delta Kappan* 62, no. 5 (January 1981): pp. 377–81.

Chapter Seven

1. Hilda Taba, *Curriculum Development: Theory and Practice* (New York: Harcourt Brace Jovanovich, 1962).

2. John Goodlad, *A Place Called School* (New York: McGraw-Hill, 1984).

3. National Center for Education Statistics, *The Condition of Education 1995*. Indicator 43, Extracurricular Activities. Washington, DC; Feminist Majority Foundation, *Empowering Women in Sports* Washington, DC, 1995.

4. Allyce Holland and Thomas Andre, "Participation in Extracurricular Activities in Secondary School: What Is Known, What Needs to Be Known," *Review of Educational Research* 57, no. 4 (winter 1987): pp. 437–66.

5. National Center for Education Statistics, *Trends Among High School Seniors, 1972–1992* (Washington, DC: U.S. Department of Education, 1995); American Association of University Women, *Gender Gaps: Where Schools Still Fail Our Children*, Washington, DC, 1998.

6. B. Bradford Brown, "The Vital Agenda for Research on Extracurricular Influences: A Reply to Holland and Andre," *Review of Educational Research* 58, no. 1 (spring 1988): pp. 107–11.

7. National Association of Secondary School Principals, *The Mood of American Youth* (Reston, VA: National Association of Secondary School Principals, 1984).

8. Data from *High School and Beyond* reported in "Extracurricular Activity Participants Outperform Other Students," *OERI Bulletin* (September 1986): p. 2.

9. Stephen Hamilton, "Synthesis of Research on the Social Side of Schooling," *Educational Leadership* 40, no. 5 (February 1983): pp. 65–72.

10. National Center for Education Statistics, *The Condition of Education 1998*. Indicator 21, International Comparisons of Adult Literacy. US Department of Education, Washington, DC.

11. Carla Haymesfeld, "Filling the Hole in Whole Language," *Educational Leadership* 46, no. 6 (March 1989): pp. 65–68. James Collins, "How Johnny Should Read," *Time*, 27 October 1997, pp. 78–81.

12. Ibid; James Collins, "How Johnny Should Read," *Time*, 27 October 1997, pp. 78–81.

13. Mary Jordan, "Snapshot of Student Writing Finds Care Absent," *Washington Post*, 17 April 1992, p. A-3.

14. Sandra Stotsky, "Whose Literature? American's!" *Educational Leadership* 49, no. 4 (December 1991/January 1992): pp. 53–56.

15. David Barton, "Classic Debate!" *Sacramento Bee*, 3 April 1998, p. SC-1.

16. Philip Cohen, "Challenging History: The Past Remains a Battleground for Schools," *Association for Supervision and Curriculum Development Curriculum Update* (winter 1995): p. 2.

17. Ernest L. Boyer, "Civic Education for Responsible Citizens," *Educational Leadership* 48, no. 3 (November 1990): pp. 5–7.

18. John Fonte and Andre Ryerson (eds.), *Education for America's Role in World Affairs* (Lanham, MD: University Press of America, 1994), p. 44.

19. Diane Ravitch and Chester Finn, Jr., *What Do Our 17-Year-Olds Know?* (New York: Harper & Row, 1987).

20. Jennifer Lee, "Helping Teachers Get on Top of the World," *Washington Post*, 15 August 1988, p. C-3.

21. David J. Hoff, "Math Council Again Mulling Its Standards," *Education Week on the Web*, 4 November 1998.

22. Eugene Owen (comp.), *Trends in Academic Progress* (Washington, DC: National Center for Educational Statistics, 1991); National Center for Education Statistics, *National Center for Educational Progress: 1996 Trends in Academic Progress* (Washington, DC: U.S. Department of Education, August 1997).

23. Ethan Bronner, "U.S. Trails the World in Math and Science," *New York Times*, 25 February 1998), p. 10.

24. Peter West, "'Common Core' High-School Math Curriculum Offered," *Education Week*, 8 April 1992, p. 8.

25. Annette Licitra, "Kids Start Strong in Science but Few Show Advanced Skills," *Education Daily*, 26 March 1992, p. 1; see also Owen (comp.), *Trends in Academic Progress*.

26. Steve Olson, "Science FRICTION." *Education Week on the Web*, 30 September 1998.

27. American Association for the Advancement of Science (AAAS), *Blueprints of Reform*, (Washington, DC, June 1998).

28. Steve Olson, "Science FRICTION."

29. Hugh McIntosh, "What Should Students Know? How Should Teachers Teach?" *National Research Council News Report* 43, no. 1 (winter 1993): pp. 2–6; Project 2061 (American Association for the Advancement of Sciences), *Benchmarks for Science Literacy* (New York: Oxford University Press, 1993).

30. Sara Melendy, "A Nation of Monolinguals, a Multilingual World," *NEA Today* (January 1989): pp. 70–74.

31. Education Vital Signs, "Common Measures," *American School Board Journal Supplement* (December 1997).

32. Richard W. Riley, "Education First: Building America's Future," *Fifth Annual State of America Education*, 17 February 1998.

33. National Center for Education Statistics, *The Condition of Education 1998. Indicator 3 and 4, Student Computer*

Use and the Internet in Public and Private Schools. US Department of Education, Washington, DC.

34. Barb Albert, "Study Says Computer Use Raises Test Scores," *Indianapolis Star,* 4 October 1998, p. B-1.

35. Debra Viadero, "38-Member Panel Adopts 81 Standards for the Arts," *Education Week,* 9 February 1994, p. 5.

36. Jane Bonbright, "Special Report: National Assessment of Educational Progress in the Arts," *JOPERD* 69, no. 8 (October 1998): pp. 28–33.

37. William Bennett, *American Education: Making It Work* (Washington, DC: U.S. Department of Education, 1988).

38. Scott O. Roberts, "Fit Kids," *American Health* 11 (September 1992): pp. 70–73.

39. National Association for Sport and Physical Education, *Shape of the Nation Report* (Reston, VA: National Association for Sport and Physical Education, 1997).

40. Ibid.

41. "Issues: Should physical education classes return to teaching males and females separately?" *JOPERD* 70, no. 1 (January 1999): pp. 11–13.

42. *Gender Gaps: Where Schools Still Fail Our Children* (Washington, DC: Commission by the American Association of University Women, 1998).

43. Compendium of Resolutions: Health Instruction and Curriculum, *American School Health Association.* McRel (1997) Kent, OH: (1998).

44. Richard W. Riley and Donna E. Shalala, "Joint Statement of the Secretaries of Education and Health and Human Services," *Journal of School Health* 64, no. 4 (7 April 1994): p. 136.

45. John G. Wirt, "A New Federal Law on Vocational Education: Will Reform Follow?" *Phi Delta Kappan* 72, no. 6 (February 1991): pp. 425–33.

46. Louis Raths, Selma Wasserman, Arthur Jones, and Arnold Rothstein, *Teaching for Thinking: Theory and Application* (Columbus, OH: Merrill, 1966.) See also Selma Wasserman, "Teaching for Thinking: Louis E. Raths Revisited," *Phi Delta Kappan* 68, no. 6 (February 1987): pp. 460–66.

47. Summaries of these approaches are found in Barbara Presseisen, *Thinking Skills: Research and Practice* (Washington, DC: National Education Association, 1986). See also R. Feuerstein, *Instrumental Enrichment An Intervention Program for Cognitive Modifiability* (Baltimore: University Park Press, 1980); A. H. Schoenfeld, "Measures of Problem-Solving Instruction," *Journal for Research in Mathematics Education* 13 (1962); E. de Bono, "The Cognitive Research Trust (CORT) Thinking Program," in W. Maxwell (ed.), *Thinking: The Expanding Frontier* (Hillsdale, NJ: Erlbaum, 1983); Joseph Hester, *Teaching for Thinking: A Program for School Improvement Through Teaching Critical Thinking Across the Curriculum*

(Durham, NC: Carolina Academic Press, 1994), pp. 1–23.

48. Robert J. Marzano, Ronald Brandt, Carolyn Hughes, Beau Fly Jones, Barbara Presseisen, Stuart Rarkin, and Charles Suhor, *Dimensions of Thinking* (Alexandria, VA: Association for Supervision and Curriculum Development, 1988).

49. Robert J. Marzano, *A Different Kind of Classroom: Teaching with Dimensions of Learning* (Alexandria, VA: Association for Supervision and Curriculum Development, 1992).

50. Jerome Bruner, *The Process of Education* (Cambridge, MA: Harvard University Press, 1960).

51. Donald Irish, "Death Education: Preparation for Living," in Betty Green and Donald Irish (eds.), *Death Education: Preparation for Living* (Cambridge, MA: Schenkman, 1971), pp. 45–68.

52. Ben Brodinsky, "Back to the Basics: The Movement and Its Meaning," *Phi Delta Kappan* 58, no. 7 (March 1977): pp. 522–27.

53. George Gallup, "Gallup Poll of the Public's Attitudes Toward the Public Schools," *Phi Delta Kappan* 64, no. 1 (September 1982): p. 39.

54. Philip Cusick, *The Egalitarian Ideal and the American High School* (New York: Longman, 1983).

55. Sara Lawrence Lightfoot, *The Good High School* (New York: Basic Books, 1983).

56. Ernest L. Boyer, *High School: A Report on Secondary Education in America,* The Carnegie Foundation for the Advancement of Teaching (New York: Harper & Row, 1983).

57. Goodlad, *A Place Called School,* p. 298.

58. Theodore Sizer, *Horace's Compromise: The Dilemma of the American High School* (Boston: Houghton Mifflin, 1984), p. 89.

59. Mortimer Adler, "The Paideia Proposal," *The Rotarian,* September 1982.

60. E. D. Hirsch, Jr., *Cultural Literacy* (Boston: Houghton Mifflin, 1987).

61. E. D. Hirsch, Jr., "Cultural Literacy: Let's Get Specific," *NEA Today,* January 1988, p. 18.

62. D. N. Perkins, "Educating for Insight," *Educational Leadership* 49, no. 2 (October 1991): pp. 4–18.

63. Robert Slavin, "PET and the Pendulum: Faddism in Education and How to Stop It," *Phi Delta Kappan* 70, no. 6 (June 1989): p. 752.

Chapter Eight

1. Liz Leyden, "Story Hour Didn't Have a Happy Ending," *Washington Post,* 3 December 1998, p. 3.

2. L. Adler, *Curriculum Challenges in California: Third statewide survey of challenges to curriculum materials and services* (Fullerton: California State University, (ERIC Document Reproduction Service No. 375 475), 1993).

3. Myra Sadker and David Sadker, *Now upon a Time: A Contemporary View of Children's Literature* (New York: Harper & Row, 1977).

4. *Attacks on the Freedom to Learn,* People for the American Way, 1995–1996 report.

5. Ibid.

6. Ibid.

7. Kathleen Kennedy Manzo, "Despite Flap, Seattle to Keep Grant for Books About Homosexuality," *Education Week on the Web,* 28 May 1997, pp. 1–2.

8. Paul Barry, "Interview: A Talk with A. Bartlett Giamatti," *College Review Board* (spring 1982): p. 48.

9. National Commission on Teaching and America's Future, *What Matters Most: Teaching for America's Future* (New York: National Commission on Teaching and America's Future, 1996).

10. John Elson, "History, the Sequel," *Time,* 7 November 1994, p. 53; see also Von Wiener, "History Lesson," *The New Republic,* 2 January 1995, pp. 9–11.

11. Joel Spring, *American Education* (New York: McGraw-Hill, 1996), pp. 237–41.

12. Lyn Nell Hancock with Nina Archer Biddle, "Red, White—and Blue," *Newsweek,* 7 November 1994, p. 54.

13. Christopher T. Cross, "The Standards Wars: Some Lessons Learned," *Education Week on the Web,* 21 October 1998, pp. 1–4.

14. Jack Nelson, Kenneth Carlson, and Stuart Palonsky, *Critical Issues in Education* (New York: McGraw-Hill, 1996), pp. 241–61.

15. Harriet Tyson Bernstein, *A Conspiracy of Good Intentions: America's Textbook Fiasco* (Washington, DC: The Council for Basic Education, 1988), p. 2.

16. Rodger Farr and Michael Tulley, "Do Adoption Committees Perpetuate Mediocre Textbooks?" *Phi Delta Kappan* 66, no. 7 (March 1985): pp. 467–71.

17. Bonnie Ambruster, Jean Osborn, and Alice Davison, "Readability Formulas May Be Dangerous to Your Textbooks," *Educational Leadership* 42, no. 7 (April 1985): pp. 18–20.

18. Susan Ohanian, "Ruffles and Flourishes," *Atlantic Monthly,* September 1987, pp. 20–22.

19. Quoted in Bernstein, *A Conspiracy of Good Intentions,* p. 19.

20. Quoted in David Elliott, Kathleen Carter Nagel, and Arthur Woodward, "Do Textbooks Belong in Elementary School Studies?" *Educational Leadership* 42, no. 7 (April 1985): pp. 22–25.

21. Jean Osborn, Beau Fly Jones, and Marcy Stein, "The Case for Improving Textbooks," *Educational Leadership* 42, no. 7 (April 1985): pp. 9–16; see also Michael Apple, "Regulating the Text: The Social Historical Roots of State Control." Paper delivered at the American Educational Research Association, San Francisco, April 1992.

22. Connie Muther, "What Every Textbook Evaluator Should Know," *Educational Leadership* 42, no. 7 (April 1985): p. 48.

23. The forms of bias were developed by Myra Sadker and David Sadker for Title IX equity workshops.

24. Bernstein, *A Conspiracy of Good Intentions,* pp. 35–36.

25. Quoted in Edward B. Jenkinson, "The Significance of the Decision in 'Scopes II,'" *Phi Delta Kappan* 68, no. 6 (February 1987): p. 446.

26. Frances Goodrich and Albert Hackett, *The Diary of Anne Frank. In Great Waves Breaking,* Bernard J. Weiss (ed.) (New York: Holt, Rinehart & Winston, 1983), p. 387.

27. Transcript of proceedings in *Mozert,* 14 July 1986, p. 24, as quoted in Jenkinson, *Scopes II.*

28. Robert Marzano and David Arredondo, *Tactics for Thinking—Teacher's Manual* (Alexandria, VA: Association for Supervision and Curriculum Development, 1986), p. 11; quoted in Edward Jenkinson, "The New Age of Schoolbook Protest," *Phi Delta Kappan* 10, no. 1 (September 1988): p. 66.

29. Thomas McDaniel, "On Trial: The Right to Think," *Educational Leadership* 49, no. 4 (December 1991/January 1992): p. 85.

30. Perry Glanzer, "Religion in Public Schools," *Phi Delta Kappan* 80, no. 3 (October 1998): p. 220.

31. Debra Viadero, "Christian Movement Seen Trying to Influence Schools," *Education Week,* 15 April 1992, p. 8.

32. Anthony Podesta, "For Full Discussion of Religion in the Schools," *Wall Street Journal,* 12 November 1986, p. 32. See also Perry Glanzer, "Religion in Public Schools: In Search of Fairness," *Phi Delta Kappan* 80, no. 3 (November 1998): pp. 219–22.

33. Ellen Goodman, "Denying Diversity," *Washington Post,* 11 November 1986, p. A-21.

34. Quoted in Lynne Cheney, *Humanities in America: A Report to the President, Congress and the American People* (Washington, DC: National Endowment for the Humanities, 1988), p. 17.

35. Quoted in William Bennett, *American Education: Making It Work* (Washington, DC: U.S. Department of Education, 1988).

36. Allan Bloom, *The Closing of the American Mind* (New York: Simon & Schuster, 1987), p. 63.

37. E. D. Hirsch, Jr., *What Your First Grader Needs to Know,* and *What Your Second Grader Needs to Know* (New York: Doubleday, 1991).

38. E. D. Hirsch, Jr., "The Core Knowledge Curriculum—What's Behind Its Success," *Educational Leadership* 50, no. 8 (May 1993): pp. 23–30.

39. James Banks, "Multicultural Education: For Freedom's Sake," *Educational Leadership* 49, no. 4 (December 1991/January 1992): pp. 32–36.

40. Marge Scherer, "School Snapshot: Focus on African-American Culture," *Educational Leadership* 49, no. 4 (December 1991/January 1992): pp. 17–21.

41. Arthur Schlesinger, *The Disuniting of America* (New York: Norton, 1992).

42. Fiske, Edward B. *Smart Schools, Smart Kids: Why Do Some Schools Work?* (New York: Simon & Schuster, 1991), p. 122.

43. Carin Rubenstein, "Surviving the Dreaded Kindergarten Exam," *Working Mother,* August 1989, p. 76.

44. Ibid., p. 75.

45. Joel Spring, *Conflict of Interests: The Politics of American Education* (New York: Longman, 1988), pp. 139–43.

46. Vito Perrone, "On Standardized Testing," *Childhood Education* 67, no. 3 (spring 1991): pp. 132–42.

47. Fiske, *Smart Schools, Smart Kids*, p. 117.

48. "Recent SAT Questions," *Fair Test Examiner* 3, no. 3 (summer 1989): p. 4.

49. Grant Wiggins, "Teaching to the (Authentic) Test," *Educational Leadership* 46, no. 7 (April 1989): pp. 41–47. See also Rieneke Zessoules and Howard Gardner, "Authentic Assessment: Beyond the Buzzword and into the Classroom," in Vito Perrone (ed.), *Expanding Student Assessment* (Alexandria, VA: Association for Supervision and Curriculum Development, 1991).

50. Gene I. Maeroff, "Assessing Alternative Assessment," *Phi Delta Kappan* 73, no. 4 (December 1991): pp. 272–81.

51. Theodore Sizer, *Horace's School: Redesigning the American High School* (New York: Houghton Mifflin, 1992).

52. Michael Apple, "Curriculum in the Year 2000: Tensions and Possibilities," *Phi Delta Kappan* 64, no. 5 (January 1983): p. 323.

53. Abner Peddiwell (Harold Benjamin), *The Saber-Tooth Curriculum* (New York: McGraw-Hill, 1939).

54. Rebecca Jones, "What Works: Researchers Tell What Schools Must Do to Improve Student Achievement," *The American School Board Journal* 185, no. 4 (April 1998): pp. 32–33.

55. Eliot Eisner, "Should America Have a National Curriculum?" *Educational Leadership* 49, no. 4 (October 1991): pp. 76–81.

56. Michael Apple, "Curriculum in the Year 2000: Tensions and Possibilities," *Phi Delta Kappan* 64, no. 5 (January 1983): p. 323.

Chapter Nine

1. Sheldon Cohen, *A History of Colonial Education, 1607–1776* (New York: Wiley, 1974).

2. Nathaniel Shurtlett, ed., *Records of the Governor and Company of the Massachusetts Bay in New England, II* (Boston: Order of the Legislature, 1853); see also H. Warren Button and Eugene F. Provenzo, Jr., *History of Education and Culture in America* (Englewood Cliffs, NJ: Prentice-Hall, 1983).

3. James Hendricks, "Be Still and Know! Quaker Silence and Dissenting Educational Ideals, 1740–1812," *Journal of the Midwest History of Education Society,* Annual Proceedings, 1975; R. Freeman Butts and Lawrence A. Cremin, *A History of Education in American Culture* (New York: Holt, 1953).

4. Lawrence A. Cremin, *American Education: The Colonial Experience, 1607–1783* (New York: Harper & Row, 1970); see also Button and Provenzo, *History of Education and Culture in America.*

5. James C. Klotter, "The Black South and White Appalachia," *Journal of American History* (March 1980): pp. 832–49.

6. John H. Best, *Benjamin Franklin on Education* (New York: Teachers College Press, 1962).

7. Jonathon Messerli, *Horace Mann: A Biography* (New York: Alfred A. Knopf, 1972); Steven Tozer, Paul Violas, and Guy Senese, *School and Society* (Boston: McGraw-Hill, 1998).

8. Lawrence Cremin, *The Transformation of the School: Progressivism in American Education, 1876–1957* (New York: Alfred A. Knopf, 1961).

9. Edward A. Krug, *The Shaping of the American High School, 1880–1920, I* (New York: Harper & Row, 1964); see also John D. Pulliam, *History of Education in America,* 4th ed. (Columbus, OH: Merrill, 1987); Joel Spring, *The American School, 1642–1985* (New York: Longman, 1986).

10. National Education Association, *Report of the Committee on Secondary School Studies* (Washington, DC: U.S. Government Printing Office, 1893).

11. Gerald Grant, *The World We Created at Hamilton High* (Cambridge, MA: Harvard University Press, 1988).

12. Special thanks to Kate Volker for developing the Crandall and Ashton-Warner biographies.

Chapter Ten

1. U.S. Department of Education, *Disparities in Public School District Spending 1989–90* (Washington, DC: U.S. Department of Education, February 1995), p. 56.

2. Barry Siegel, "Parents Get a Lesson in Equality," *Los Angeles Times* (Washington edition), 13 April 1992, pp. A-1, A-18–A-19.

3. L. Harp, "Momentum for Challenges to Finance Systems Still Seen Strong," *Education Week,* 27 September 1993, pp. 1, 26.

4. William N. Evans, Sheila F. Murray, and Robert M. Schwab, "Schoolhouses, Courthouses, and Statehouses After Serrano," *Journal of Policy Analysis and Management* 16, no. 1 (winter 1997): pp. 10–31; Indira A. R. Lakshmanan, "New Jersey Schools Offer Omen

for Massachusetts," *Boston Sunday Globe,* 20 June 1993, p. 1.

5. W. E. Thro, "The Third Wave: The Impact of the Montana, Kentucky and Texas Decisions on the Future of Public School Finance Reform Litigation," *Journal of Law and Education* 119, no. 2 (spring 1990): pp. 219–50; Robert F. McNergney and Joanne M. Herbert, *Foundations of Education: The Challenge of Professional Practice* (Boston: Allyn & Bacon, 1995), pp. 475–78; Chris Pipho, "Stateline: The Scent of the Future," *Phi Delta Kappan* 76 (September 1994): pp. 10–11.

6. Thomas Toch, "Separate but Not Equal," *Agenda* 1 (spring 1991): pp. 15–17.

7. Peter Keating, "How to Keep Your State and Local Taxes Down," *Money* 24, no. 1 (January 1995): pp. 86–92.

8. Bill Norris, "Losing Ticket in Lotteries," *Times Educational Supplement,* 19 March 1993, p. 17.

9. Joetta L. Sack, "Priorities Emerging for ESEA Reauthorization," *Education Week on the Web,* 30 September 1998; Anne C. Lewis, "Washington Report: House Democrats Criticize (in Unison) the Education Block Grant: Republicans Sing a Different Tune," *Phi Delta Kappan* 65, no. 6 (February 1984): pp. 379–80.

10. Jay Mathews, "More Public Schools Using Private Dollars," *Washington Post,* 28 August 1995, pp. A-1, A-8.

11. Anne Lewis, "Washington Seen: Buildings in Disrepair," *Education Digest* 60, no. 8 (April 1995): p. 71; Jacques Steinberg and John Sullivan, "In Disrepair for Years, Many Schools Pose a Risk," *New York Times,* 2 February 1998, p. A-21.

12. Chester Finn, "Reinventing Local Control," in Patricia First and Herbert Walberg (eds.), *School Boards: Changing Local Control* (Berkeley: McCutchan, 1992); Emily Feistritzer, "A Profile of School Board Presidents," in *School Boards: Changing Local Control;* Neal Pierce, "School Boards Get Failing Grades, in Both the Cities and the Suburbs," *Philadelphia Inquirer,* 27 April 1992, p. 11; Mary Jordan, "School Boards Need Overhaul, Educators Say," *Washington Post,* 5 April 1992, p. A-51.

13. Thomas Shannon, "Local Control and 'Organizations,' " in *School Boards: Changing Local Control;* Jacqueline Danzberger and Michael Usdan, "Strengthening a Grass-Roots American Institution: The School Board," in *School Boards: Changing Local Control;* Arthur Blumberg and Phyllis Blumberg, *The School Superintendent: Living with Conflict* (New York: Teachers College Press, 1985).

14. James G. Cibula, "Two Eras of Urban Schooling: The Decline of Law and Order and the Emergence of New Organizational Forms," *Education and Urban Society* 29, no. 3 (May 1997): pp. 317–41.

15. Quoted in "Building Better Business Alliances," *Instructor* (winter 1986): (special issue), p. 21; see also Brian Dumaine, "Making Education Work," *Fortune,* spring 1990 (special issue): pp. 12–22.

16. Mark Walsh, "Businesses' Enthusiasm for Reform Seen Flagging," *Education Week,* 14 June 1995, p. 11; see also Joseph F. Coates, Jennifer Jarratt, and John B. Mahaffie, "Future Work," *The Futurist* 25, no. 3 (May/June 1991): pp. 9–19; for a more sinister view of the motivations of some businesspeople, see Cinton E. Boutwell, "Profits Without People," *Phi Delta Kappan* 79, no. 2 (October 1997): pp. 104–11.

17. Joseph F. Coates, Jennifer Jarratt, and John B. Mahaffie, "Future Work," *The Futurist* 25, no. 3 (May/June 1991): pp. 9–19.

18. Quoted in Herbert J. Walberg, "Families as Partners in Educational Productivity," *Phi Delta Kappan* 65, no. 6 (February 1984): p. 397.

19. Lee Dye, "Blame the Federal Grant System for America's Ph.D. Glut," *Los Angeles Times,* 29 March 1995: p. D-4.

20. Debra Viadero, "Studies Chart Big Boost in Course Taking," *Education Week,* September 30, 1995: pp. 1, 16; Stanley Aronowitz and William DiFazio, *The Jobless Future* (Minneapolis: University of Minnesota Press, 1994): pp. 325–27; Dean Baker and Lawrence Mishel, "Profits Up, Wages Down," Economic Policy Institute, Washington, D.C., 1995: p. 5.

21. Cinton E. Boutwell, "Profits Without People," *Phi Delta Kappan,* 79, no. 2, October 1997: pp. 104–11.

22. "Big Blue's White Elephant Sale," *Business Week,* February 20, 1994: p. 36.

23. Cinton E. Boutwell, "Profits Without People," op. cit. p. 109.

24. Charles Russo, "The Legal Status of School Boards in the Intergovernmental System," in *School Boards: Changing Local Control.*

25. Arthur Blumberg and Phyllis Blumberg, *The School Superintendent: Living with Conflict* (New York: Teachers College Press, 1985), p. 67.

26. Maria Newman, "These Days, Uneasy Lies the Head That Runs the Suburban School System," *New York Times,* 12 May 1998, p. A-21.

27. Joanna Richardson, "Contracts Put Superintendents to Performance Test," *Education Week,* 14 September 1994, pp. 1, 12.

28. William H. Roe and Thelbert L. Drake, *The Principalship,* 2nd ed. (New York: Macmillan, 1980); J. Lloyd Trump, *A School for Everyone* (Reston, VA: National Association of Secondary School Principals, 1977).

29. Roger G. Barker and Paul V. Gump, *Big School, Small School* (Stanford, CA: Stanford University Press, 1964).

30. Jonathan P. Sher and Rachel B. Tompkins, *Economy, Efficiency and Equality: The Myths of Rural School and District Consolidation* (Washington, DC: National Institute of Education, U.S. Department of Health, Education and Welfare, 1976).

31. *The Metropolitan Life Survey of the American Teacher 1998,* "Building Family-School Partnerships: Views of Students and Teachers" (New York: Louis Harris and Associates, 1998); Mary Jordan, "Pupils Give Their Parents 'D' for School Involvement," *Washington Post,* 12 May 1992, p. A-3.

32. Robert Leitman, Katherine Binns, and Ann Duffett, *The Metropolitan Life Survey of the American Teacher, 1984–1995* (New York: Louis Harris and Associates, 1995), p. 60.

33. Jeremy Finn, "Parental Engagement That Makes a Difference," *Educational Leadership* 55, no. 8 (May 1998): pp. 20–24.

34. Thomas Hatch, "How Community Action Contributes to Achievement," *Educational Leadership* 55, no. 8 (May 1998): pp. 16–19; Ron Lewis and John Morris, "Communities for Children," *Educational Leadership* 55, no. 8 (May 1998): pp. 34–36; Frank E. Nardine and Robert D. Morris, "Parent Involvement in the States," *Phi Delta Kappan* 72, no. 5 (January 1991): p. 365; Meg Sommerfeld, "National Commitment to Parent Role in School Sought," *Education Week,* 15 April 1992, p. 1. See also Don Davies, "Schools Reaching Out: Family, School, and Community Partnerships for Student Success," *Phi Delta Kappan* 72, no. 5 (January 1991).

35. See Marianne Perie and David Baker, *Job Satisfaction Among America's Teachers: Effects of Workplace Conditions, Background Characteristics, and Teacher Compensation* (Washington, DC: National Center for Education Statistics, U.S. Department of Health, Education and Welfare, August 1997), pp. 41–42; Terry Stimson and Richard Appelbaum, "Empowering Teachers: Do Principals Have the Power?" *Phi Delta Kappan* 70, no. 4 (December 1988): pp. 313–16. See also Sarah Caldwell and Fred Wood, "School-Based Improvement—Are We Ready?" *Educational Leadership* 46, no. 2 (October 1988): pp. 50–53. See also John Lane and Edgar Epps (eds.), *Restructuring the Schools: Problems and Prospects* (Berkeley: McCutchan, 1992).

36. Ann Bradley and Lynn Olson, "The Balance of Power: Shifting the Lines of Authority in an Effort to Improve Schools," *Education Week,* 24 February 1993, p. 10.

37. Fern Shen, "New Strategy for School Management," *Washington Post,* 17 February 1998, pp. B-1, B-7.

38. Ann Bradley and Lynn Olson, "The Balance of Power."

Chapter Eleven

1. Julius Menacker and Ernest Pascarella, "How Aware Are Educators of Supreme Court Decisions That Affect Them?" *Phi Delta Kappan* 64, no. 6 (February 1983): pp. 424–26.

2. Louis Fischer and David Schimmel, *The Civil Rights of Teachers* (New York: Harper & Row, 1973).

3. The legal situations and interpretations included in this text are adapted from a variety of sources, including Myra Sadker and David Sadker, *Sex Equity Handbook for Schools* (New York: Longman, 1982); Fischer and Schimmel, *The Civil Rights of Teachers,* and *Your Legal Rights and Responsibilities: A Guide for Public School Students* (Washington, DC: U.S. Department of Health, Education and Welfare, n.d.).

4. Sadker and Sadker, *Sex Equity Handbook for Schools.*

5. *Gebsner v. Lago Vista Independent School District* (118 S. Ct. 1989, 1998); Richard Carelli, "Top Court Says Sexually Harassed Students May Sue Schools," Associated Press, 26 February 1992; Greg Henderson, "Court Says Compensatory Damages Available Under Title IX," UPI, 26 February 1992.

6. *Thompson v. Southwest School District,* 483 F. Supp. 1170 (W.D.M.W. 1980). See also *Board of Trustees v. Stubblefield,* 94 Cal. Rptr. 318, 321 [1971]; *Morrison v. State Board of Education,* 461 P. 2d 375 [1969]; *Pettit v. State Board of Education,* 513 P. 2d 889 [Cal. 1973]; *Blodgett v. Board of Trustees, Tamalpais Union High School District,* 97 Cal. Rptr. 406 (1970); Fernand Dutile, *Sex, Schools and the Law* (Springfield, OH: Charles C. Thomas, 1986).

7. *Kingsville Independent School District v. Cooper,* 611 F. 2d 1109 (5th Cir. 1980); *Parducci v. Rutland,* 316 F. Supp. 352 (M.D. Ala. 1979); *Brubaker v. Board of Education, School District 149, Cook County, Illinois,* 502 F. 2d 973 (7th Cir. 1974). See also Martha McCarthy and Nelda Cambron, *Public School Law: Teachers' and Students' Rights* (Boston: Allyn & Bacon, 1981).

8. *Pickering v. Board of Education of Township High School District 205, Will County,* 391 U.S. 563 (1968); *Givhan v. Western Line Consolidated School District,* 439 U.S. 410 (1979). See also Robert Monks and Ernest Proulx, *Legal Basis for Teachers* (Bloomington, IN: Phi Delta Kappa Educational Foundation, 1986).

9. *Basic Books v. Kinko's Graphics Corp.,* 758 F. Supp. 1522 (S.D.N.Y.1991); Miriam R. Krasno, "Copyright and You," *Update,* winter 1983; Thomas J. Flygare, "Photocopying and Videotaping for Educational Purposes: The Doctrine of Fair Use," *Phi Delta Kappan* 65, no. 8 (April 1984).

10. 115 ILCS 5/13 (1993 State Bar Edition); Ind. Code Ann 20-7.5-1-14 (West 1995); Nev. Rev. State 288.260 (1995); Leroy Peterson, Richard A. Rossmiller, and Marlin M. Volz, *The Law and Public School Operation,* 2nd ed. (New York: Harper & Row, 1978), pp. 132–34. See also Michael La Morte, *School Law: Cases and Concepts* (Englewood Cliffs, NJ: Prentice-Hall, 1987).

11. E. Gordon Gee and David J. Sperry, *Education Law and the Public Schools: A Compendium* (Boston: Allyn & Bacon, 1978). See also Louis Fischer, David Schimmel, and Cynthia Kelly, *Teachers and the Law* (New York: Longman, 1999).

12. Sadker and Sadker, *Sex Equity Handbook for Schools*. See also Fernand Dutile, *Sex, Schools and the Law* (Springfield, OH: Charles C. Thomas, 1986).

13. *Goss v. Lopez,* 419 U.S. 565 (1975); *Wood v. Strickland,* 420 U.S. 308 (1975); *Ingraham v. Wright,* 430 U.S. 651 (1977).

14. *Tinker v. Des Moines Independent Community School District,* 393 U.S. 503 (1969).

15. *Bethel School District No. 403 v. Fraser,* 478 U.S. 675 (1986).

16. Benjamin Sendor, "Guidance on Graduation Prayer," *The American School Board Journal* (April 1997): pp. 17–18; Benjamin Sendor, "When May School Clubs Meet?" *The American School Board Journal* (August 1997): pp. 14–15; Ralph D. Mawdsley, "Religion in the Schools: Walking a Fine Legal Line," *School Business Affairs* 63, no. 5 (May 1997): pp. 5–10; *Engel v. Vitale,* 370 U.S. 421 (1962); *School District of Abington Township v. Schempp and Murray v. Curlett,* 373 U.S. 203 (1963).

17. *Bellnier v. Lund,* 438 F. Supp. 47 (N.Y. 1977); *Doe v. Renfrou,* 635 F.2d 582 (7th Cir. 1980), *cert. denied,* 101 S.Ct. 3015 (1981).

18. *Hazelwood School District v. Kuhlmeier,* 108 S.Ct. 562 (1988); *Shanley v. Northeast Independent School District,* 462 F.2d 960 (5th Cir. 1972); *Gambino v. Fairfax County School Board,* 564 F.2d 157 (4th Cir. 1977).

19. Louis Fischer, David Schimmel, and Cynthia Kelly, *Teachers and the Law* (New York: Longman, 1999).

20. Ibid., p. 473; for privacy issues on the Internet, see Jeffrey T. Sultanik, "Legal Rights in Cyberspace," *School Business Affairs* 63, no. 5 (May 1997): pp. 25–33.

21. "U.S. Supreme Court Decision on Teacher-Student Sexual Harassment Changing Legal Landscape," *Educator's Guide to Controlling Sexual Harassment* 5, no.12 (September 1998): pp. 1, 3, 4–5; Joel Spring, *American Education* (New York: McGraw-Hill, 1996), p. 276.

22. Millicent Lawson, "False Accusations Turn Dream into Nightmare in Chicago," *Education Week,* 2 August 1994, p. 16; Louis Harris and Associates Poll, *Hostile Hallways* (Washington, DC: American Association of University Women, 1993).

23. Fred Hechinger, *Fateful Choices: Healthy Youth for the 21st Century* (New York: Carnegie Council on Adolescent Development, 1992).

24. Jan English and Anthony Papalia, "The Responsibility of Educators in Cases of Child Abuse and Neglect," *Chronicle Guidance* (January 1988): pp. 88–89.

25. P. E. Quinn, *Cry Out!* (Nashville, TN: Abingdon Press, 1984).

26. Louis Harris and Associates, *The Metropolitan Life Survey of the American Teacher, Part III Students Voice Their Opinions on: Learning About Values and Principles in School* (New York: Louis Harris and Associates, 1996); Stephen Bates, "A Textbook of Virtues," *New York Times,* 8 January 1995, education supplement, p. EL-161.

27. Philip Cohen, "The Content of Their Character: Educators Find New Ways to Tackle Values and Morality," *Association for Supervision and Curriculum Development Curriculum Update,* spring 1995, p. 1.

28. Bates, "A Textbook of Virtues.".

29. James Leming, "In Search of Effective Character Education," *Educational Leadership* 51, no. 3 (November 1993): pp. 63–70.

30. Thomas J. Lasley, "The Missing Ingredient in Character Education," *Phi Delta Kappan* 78, no. 8 (April 1997): pp. 654–55.

31. Alfie Kohn, "How Not to Teach Values," *Phi Delta Kappan* 78, no. 8 (April 1997): pp. 428–37.

32. Howard Kirschenbaum, "A Comprehensive Model for Values Education and Moral Education," *Phi Delta Kappan* 73, no. 10 (June 1992): pp. 771–76.

33. Diane Berreth and Sheldon Berman, "The Moral Dimensions of Schools," *Educational Leadership* 54, no. 8 (May 1997): pp. 24–27; Merrill Harmin, "Value Clarity, High Morality: Let's Go for Both," *Educational Leadership* 45, no. 8 (May 1988): pp. 24–31; Kenneth R. Howe, "A Conceptual Basis for Ethics in Teacher Education," *Journal of Teacher Education* 37 (May/June 1986): p. 6; Karl Hostetler, *Ethical Judgment in Teaching* (Boston: Allyn & Bacon, 1997).

Chapter Twelve
1. Aristotle, *Politics,* trans. and intro. by T. A. Sinclair (Middlesex, England: Penguin, 1978).

2. William Bagley, "The Case for Essentialism in Education," *National Education Association Journal* 30, no. 7 (1941): pp. 202–20.

3. Carl Hansen, *The Amidon Elementary School: A Successful Demonstration in Basic Education* (Englewood Cliffs, NJ: Prentice-Hall, 1962).

4. John Dewey, *Experience and Education* (New York: Macmillan, 1963).

5. Mortimer Adler, *Reforming Education* (Boulder, CO: Westview Press, 1977), pp. 84–85.

6. Robert M. Hutchins, *The Higher Learning in America* (New Haven, CT: Yale University Press, 1962), p. 78.

7. A. S. Neill, *Freedom—Not License* (New York: Hart, 1966).

8. Jean-Paul Sartre, *Existentialism,* trans. by Bernard Frechtman (New York: Philosophical Library, 1947), p. 13.

9. John B. Watson, *Behaviorism* (New York: Norton, 1924), p. 82.

10. Richard Elardo, "Behavior Modification in an Elementary School," *Phi Delta Kappan* 59, no. 5 (January 1978): pp. 334–38.

11. Richard Bumstead, "The Thaler System: A Slice of Life Curriculum," *Phi Delta Kappan* 59, no. 10 (June 1978): pp. 659–64.

Chapter Thirteen

1. Much of the earlier educational history discussion of Native Americans, African Americans, and Latinos is based on Meyer Weinberg, *A Chance to Learn: A History of Race and Education in the United States* (New York: Cambridge University Press, 1977).

2. Robert S. Catterill, *The Southern Indians: The Story of the Civilized Tribes Before Removal* (1954; reprinted, Norman: University of Oklahoma Press, 1966).

3. William Denmert, "Indian Education: Where and Whither?" *Education Digest* 42 (December 1976). See also Ron Holt, "Fighting for Equality: Breaking with the Past," *NEA Today*, March 1989, pp. 10–11; NEA Ethnic Report, *Focus on American Indian/Alaska Natives*, October 1991.

4. Lee Little Soldier, "Is There an 'Indian' in Your Classroom?" *Phi Delta Kappan*, 78, no. 8 (April 1997): pp. 650–53.

5. Susie King Taylor, *Reminiscences of My Life in Camp with the 33rd U.S. Colored Troop Late First S. C. Volunteers* (1902; reprinted, New York: Amo Press, 1968).

6. W. E. B. Du Bois, "The United States and the Negro," *Freedomways* (1971), quoted in Weinberg, *A Chance to Learn*.

7. Louis Fischer, David Schimmel, and Cynthia Kelly, *Teachers and the Law* (New York: Addison Wesley Longman, 1999), p. 352.

8. National Advisory Commission on Civil Disorders, *Report of the National Advisory Commission on Civil Disorders* (Washington, DC: U.S. Government Printing Office, 1968), p. 369. See also Andrew Hacker, *Two Nations Black and White, Separate, Hostie, Unequal* (New York: Charles Scribner's, 1992).

9. Administration for Children and Families, *Race of TANF Parents* (Washington, DC: U.S. Department of Health and Human Services: 1997).

10. Daniel Levine and Robert Havighurst, *Society and Education* (Boston: Allyn & Bacon, 1989). See also James Banks and Cherry McGee Banks, eds., *Multicultural Education* (Boston: Allyn & Bacon, 1989); NEA Ethnic Report, *Focus on Blacks*, February 1992.

11. The Condition of Education, *Education Attainment* Indicator 22, (Washington, DC: National Center for Education Statistics, 1996).

12. James Comer, "All Our Children," *School Safety*, winter 1989, p. 19.

13. Census, Population Project of the United States 1993–2050, CPS Report No. P25-1105, 1993.

14. President's Advisory Commission on Educational Excellence for Hispanic Americans, *Our Nation on the Fault Line: Hispanic American Education* (Washington, DC: President's Advisory Commission on Educational Excellence for Hispanic Americans, 1996).

15. Current Population Survey, *Poverty Rate: Below the Poverty Line by Race and Ethnicity* (Washington, DC: U.S. Census Bureau, March 1997).

16. The Annie E. Casey Foundation, *Kids Count Data Book* (Washington, DC: Center for the Study of Social Policy, 1992).

17. NEA Ethnic Report, *Focus on Hispanics*, December 1991 and December 1995.

18. President's Advisory Commission on Educational Excellence for Hispanic Americans, *Our Nation on the Fault Line: Hispanic American Education*.

19. Quoted in *A Chance to Learn*.

20. Office of Migrant Education, State Migrant Education Program Directors Common Core of Data file, *Enrolling Migrant Children*, 1997.

21. Quoted in Paul S. Taylor, *An American-Mexican Frontier Nueces County, Texas* (1934; reprinted, New York: Russell & Russell, 1971).

22. President's Advisory Commission on Educational Excellence for Hispanic Americans, *Our Nation on the Fault Line: Hispanic American Education*.

23. Joan First, "Immigrant Students in U.S. Public Schools," *Phi Delta Kappan* 70, no. 3 (November 1988): p. 206.

24. Federal Interagency Forum on Child and Family Statistics, *America's Children: Key National Indicators of Well-Being* (Washington, DC: Federal Interagency Forum on Child and Family Statistics, 1997).

25. Much of the information on the history of Asian Americans is adapted from James Banks, *Teaching Ethnic Studies* (Boston: Allyn & Bacon 1986).

26. U.S. Department of Education, National Center for Education Statistics, Recent College Graduates Surveys (1977–90) and 1993 Baccalaureate and Beyond Longitudinal Study, First Follow-up (B&B:93/94); *The Condition of Education 1996*, Supplemental Table 35-1; U.S. Bureau of the Census, Statistical Abstract of the United States (1998).

27. The College Board Online, Table 3: *Ten-year Trends in Average SAT Scores by Racial/Ethnic Groups*, Educational Testing Service, 1998.

28. NEA Ethnic Report, *Focus on Asian/Pacific Islanders*, May 1992. See also Daniel Goleman, "Probing School Success of Asian-Americans," *New York Times*, 11 September 1990, pp. C-1, C-10.

29. NEA Ethnic Report, *Focus on Asian/Pacific Islanders.* See also Rosalind Y. Mau, "Barriers to Higher Education for Asian/Pacific-American Females," The Urban Review 22, no. 3 (September 1990): 183–97. Stacey J. Lee, "Beyond the Model-Minority Stereotype: Voices of High- and Low-Achieving Asian American Students," *Multicultural Education 96/97* (Guilford, CT: Dushkin, 1996).

30. Fred Cordova, *Filipinos: Forgotten Asian-Americans* (Dubuque, IA: Kendall/Hunt, 1983), pp. 9–57.

31. Arthur W. Helweg and Usha M. Helweg, *An Asian Success Story—East Indians in America* (Philadelphia, PA: University of Pennsylvania Press, 1990). See also Srirajasekhar Bobby Koritala, "A Historical Perspective of Americans of Asian India Origin, 1790–1997," http://www.tiac.net/users/koritala/india/history.htm.

32. Laurie Olsen, "Crossing the Schoolhouse Border: Immigrant Children in California," *Phi Delta Kappan* 70, no. 3 (November 1988): p. 213.

33. Myra Sadker and David Sadker, "Sexism in the Classroom of the 80s," *Psychology Today,* March 1986. See also Myra Sadker, David Sadker, and Susan Klein, "The Issue of Gender in Elementary and Secondary Education," in Gerald Grant, ed., *Review of Research in Education* (Washington, DC: American Educational Research Association, 1991), pp. 269–334; American Association of University Women, *How Schools Shortchange Girls* (Washington, DC: American Association of University Women, 1992). See also Myra Sadker and David Sadker, *Failing at Fairness: How Our Schools Cheat Girls* (New York: Touchstone Press, 1995).

34. M. Carey Thomas, "Present Tendencies in Women's Education," *Education Review* 25 (1908): pp. 64–85. Quoted in David Tyack and Elisabeth Hansot, *Learning Together: A History of Coeducation in American Schools* (New Haven: Yale University Press, 1990), p. 68.

35. Adapted from "Through the Back Door: The History of Women's Education" and "Higher Education: Colder by Degrees," Myra Sadker and David Sadker, *Failing at Fairness: How Our Schools Cheat Girls.*

36. Quoted in John O'Neil, "A Generation Adrift?" *Educational Leadership* 49, no. 2 (September 1991): pp. 4–10.

37. Fred Hechinger, *Fateful Choices: Healthy Youth for the 21st Century* (New York: Carnegie Council on Adolescent Development, 1992), p. 2.

38. Barbara Vobejda, "Social Trends Show Signs of Slowing," *Washington Post,* 11 November 1996.

39. Pat Wingert, "I do, I do—Maybe," *Newsweek,* 2 November 1998.

40. Eitzen, "Problem Students"; David Francis, "New Figures Show Wider Gap Between Rich and Poor," *Christian Science Monitor,* 21 April 1995 pp. 1, 8.

41. U.S. Department of Education, *Youth Indicators 1991: Trends in the Well-Being of American Youth* (Washington, DC: U.S. Department of Education, 1991); U.S. Department of Labor, Bureau of Labor Statistics, unpublished data, 1996.

42. Jerry Adler, "Tomorrow's Child," *Newsweek,* 2 November 1998.

43. The Annie E. Casey Foundation, *Kids Count Data Book* (Washington, DC: Center for the Study of Social Policy, 1992).

44. Candy Carlile, "Children of Divorce," *Childhood Education* 64, no. 4 (1991): pp. 232–34.

45. Michael A. Fletcher, "Interracial Marriages Eroding Barriers," *Washington Post,* 29 December 1998, p. A-1.

46. Eitzen, "Problem Students."

47. Laura DeKoven Waxman and Lilia M. Reyes, *A Status Report on Hunger and Homelessness in America's Cities: 1990* (Washington, DC: U.S. Conference of Mayors, December 1990); George E. Pawlas, "Homeless Students at the School Door," *Educational Leadership* 51 (May 1994): p. 79–82.

48. Rick Fantasia and Maurice Isserman, *Homelessness: A Sourcebook* (New York: Facts on File, 1994), pp. 113–14.

49. This anecdote is based on information in Children's Defense Fund, *A Vision for America's Future,* pp. 27–36. Washington, DC, 1989.

50. Fantasia and Isserman, *Homelessness.*

51. Samuel Peng, "High School Dropouts: Descriptive Information from High School and Beyond," *Bulletin,* National Center for Education Statistics, November 1983.

52. U.S. Department of Education, *Youth Indicators 1996: Trends in the Well-Being of American Youth* (Washington, DC: National Center for Education Statistics, 1996).

53. Alan Guttmacher Institute, *Facts in Brief: Teenage Sexual and Reproductive Behavior* (New York: Alan Guttmacher Institute, 1991).

54. Jamie Victoria Ward and Jill McLean Taylor, "Sexuality Education in a Multicultural Society," *Educational Leadership* 49, no. 1 (September 1991): pp. 62–64.

55. House Select Committee on Children, Youth, and Families, *A Decade of Denial: Teens and AIDS in America* (Washington, DC: U.S. Government Printing Office, 1992).

56. Centers for Disease Control and Prevention, "The HIV/AIDS Epidemic in the United States 1997–1998: Highlights from the Reports," *National Center for HIV, STD and TB Prevention* (Rockville, MD: Centers for Disease Control and Prevention, 1998).

57. Roberto Suro, "Study Finds Decline in Teen Substance Abuse," *Washington Post,* 19 December 1998, p. A-3.

58. Paul Taylor, "Surgeon General Links Teen Drinking to Crime, Injuries, Unsafe Sex," *Washington Post,* 14 April 1992, p. A-1.

59. *Education Update* 9, no. 4 (fall 1986).

60. DeNeen Brown, "Fairfax Teenagers" LSD Arrests Send Parents a 'Wake-Up Call,'" *Washington Post,* 27 April 1992, p. B-1.

61. National Center on Addiction and Substance Abuse, *Teens Who Smoke Cigarettes Much Likelier to Try Pot* (New York: Columbia University Press, 1998).

62. John O'Neil, "A Generation Adrift?" See also Sidney Barish, "Responding to Adolescent Suicide: A Multi-Faceted Plan," *NASSP Bulletin* 75, no. 538 (November 1991): pp. 98–103.

63. Jeanne Wright, "Treating the Depressed Child" *Washington Post,* 2 December 1996, p. C-5.

64. Quoted in Paul Gibson, "Gay Male and Lesbian Youth Suicide," in Marcia Feinleib, ed., *Report of the Secretary's Task Force on Youth Suicide* (Washington, DC: U.S. Department of Health and Human Services, January 1989), pp. 3-110–3-142. See also James Sears, "Helping Students Understand and Accept Sexual Diversity," *Educational Leadership* 49, no. 1 (September 1991): pp. 54–56.

65. Jesse Green, "This School Is Out," *New York Times Magazine,* October 13, 1991, pp. 32–36, 59, 68.

66. Jessica Portner, "Districts Adopting Policies to Protect Gay Students' Rights," *Education Week,* 5 October 1994, p. 8.

Chapter Fourteen

1. Jeffrey Mortimer, "How TV Violence Hits Kids," *Education Digest* 60, no. 2 (October 1994): pp. 16–19.

2. *Balancing Acts: Work/Family Issues on Primetime TV Shows,* (Washington, DC: The National Partnership for Women and Families, 1998); Jack Levin, "Mapping Social Geography," *Bostonia* (March/April 1989): pp. 64–65.

3. "Study Links TV, Music to Teen Drinking," *USA Today* on the web, 2 November 1998; Annette Licitra, "Psychologists Spell Out Dangers of Unregulated TV Watching," *Education Daily,* 26 February 1992.

4. Richard P. Adler, "Children's Television Advertising: History of the Issue," in Edward Palmer and Aimee Dorr, eds., *Children and the Faces of Television.* (New York: Academic Press, 1980), pp. 46–47.

5. Daniel Anderson and Patricia Collins, *The Impact on Children's Education: Television's Influence on Cognitive Development* (Washington, DC: U.S. Department of Education, April 1988).

6. Licitra, "Psychologists Spell Out Dangers."

7. Bruce Watkins, Althea Huston-Stein, and John Wright, "Effects of Planned Television Programming," in Edward Palmer and Aimee Dorr, eds., *Children and the Faces of Television* (New York: Academic Press, 1980), pp. 46–49.

8. Susan Herzog, "Selling Out Kids: Commercialism in Public Schools," *Our Children* 23, no. 3 (November 1997): pp. 6–10; Jason Vaughn, "Big Business and the Blackboard: A Winning Combination for the Classroom," *Journal of Law and Education,* 26, no. 2 (April 1997): pp. 35–46; David Streitfeld, "Low Marks for Channel One," *Washington Post,* 2 May 1992, p. C-5; Drew Tiene, "Channel One," *International Journal of Instructional Media* 21, no. 3 (1994): pp. 181–89; Drew Tiene, "Teens React to Channel One," *Tech Trends* 39 (April/May 1994): pp. 17–20.

9. Todd Oppenheimer, "The Computer Delusion," *The Atlantic Monthly,* (July 1997): pp. 45–48, 50–56, 61–62.

10. Sara Dexter and Ron Anderson, "Teachers' Views of the Influence of Computers on Changes in Their Instructional Practice," Paper presented at the American Educational Research Association, April 1998; Bob Hoffman, "Integrating Technology into Schools," *NAASP Bulletin* (January 1997): pp. 51–55.

11. Lyn Nell Hancock, Patricia Wingert, D. Rosenberg, and A. Samuels, "The Haves and the Have-Nots," *Newsweek,* 27 February 1995, p. 53.

12. M. Marriott and T. T. Gegax, "Putting Your Best Foot Forward: Technophobia: How Unwired Luddites Can Mother Invention, *Newsweek,* 25 February 1995. See also Bernard Whitley, "Gender Differences in Computer-Related Attitudes and Behaviors: A Meta Analysis," *Computers in Human Behavior* 13, no. 1 (1997): pp. 1–22.

13. Maria Mouzes, "How Women Learn to Use Computers: Overcoming Negative Attitudes Toward Computers During the Learning Process," Doctoral dissertation, Texas A & M University, August 1995, p. 4.

14. David C. Dwyer, Cathy Ringstaff, and Judy H. Sandholtz, "Changes in Teachers' Beliefs and Practices in Technology-Rich Classrooms," *Educational Leadership* 48, no. 8 (May 1991): pp. 45–52.

15. Dorothy Frayer, "Educational Uses of Technology," American Association of Higher Education Information Technology Conference, Colleges of Worcester Consortium, Fitchburg, MA, April 1997; R. B. Kozma and J. Johnson, "The Technological Revolution Comes to the Classroom," *Change,* 23, no. 1 (1991): pp. 10–23.

16. Lisa Wolcott, Debra Ladestro, and Sharon Williams, "Something for Everyone," *Teacher* 2, no. 4 (January 1991): pp. 40–43.

17. Jeff Meade, "Tuning In, Logging On," *Teacher* 2, no. 4 (January 1991): pp. 30–31.

18. Carla Schutte, "Going Global," *Electronic School,* February 1995, pp. A39–A40; Elaine K. Bailey and Morton Cotlar, "Teaching via the Internet," *Communication Education* 43 (April 1994): pp. 184–93; Carol S. Holzberg, "Technology in Special Education," *Technology and Learning* 14 (7 April 1994): pp. 18–21.

19. Barbara Benham Tye and Kenneth Tye, *Global Education: A Study of School Change* (Albany: State University of New York Press, 1992) pp. 1–13.

20. Andrew F. Smith, "A Brief History of Pre-collegiate Global and International Studies Education," in John Fonte and Andre Ryerson, Eds. *Education for America's Role in World Affairs* (New York: University Press of America, 1994), p. 15.

21. Jane McLane, "From Seattle to Novosibirsk: A 1st Grade Exchange," *Educational Leadership* 48, no. 7 (April 1991): pp. 58–60; John LeBaron and Rebecca Warshawsky, "Satellite Teleconferencing Between Massachusetts and Germany," *Educational Leadership* 48, no. 7 (April 1991): pp. 61–64; Meg Little Warren, "Educating for Global Citizenship Through Children's Art," *Educational Leadership* 48, no. 7 (April 1991): pp. 53–57.

22. Bruce Watson, "The Wired Classroom: American Education Goes On-Line," *Phi Delta Kappan* 72, no. 2 (October l990): pp. 109–12.

23. William Kniep, "Global Education as School Reform," *Educational Leadership* 47, no. 1 (September 1989): p. 45.

24. Jackie Gottfried and Melissa G. McFeely, "Learning All Over the Place: Integrating Laptop Computers into the Classroom," *Learning and Leading with Technology* 25, no.4 (December/January, 1998): pp. 6–11; *Washington Post,* 20 December 1998, pp. A-18–19.

25. Peter W. Foltz, Darrel Laham, Thomas K. Landauer, "Automated Essay Scoring: Applications to Educational Technology." Paper presented at the ED-Media/ED-Telecom '99, World Conference on Educational Multimedia/Hypermedia & Educational Telecommunications, Seattle, WA, 19–24 June 1999.

26. Charles A. MacArthur, "Using Technology to Enhance the Writing Processes of Students with Learning Disabilities," *Journal of Learning Disabilities* 29, no. 4 (1996): pp. 344–54; Debra K. Bauder, "Assistive Technology: Learning Devices for Special Needs Students," *Media & Methods* 32, no. 3 (1996): pp. 16, 18.

27. Mary Anne Mather, "Virtual Schooling: Going the Distance—Any Distance—to School," *Technology and Learning,* 1 April 1998; Mary Lord, "On Line Students E-mail Music to a Teacher's Ears," *U.S. News on Line,* 28 December 1998; Sandy Kleffman, "Internet Creates a National Classroom," *The Atlanta Journal-The Atlanta Constitution,* 27 July 1997.

28. Ibid.; American Association of University Women, *Gender Gaps: Where School Still Fails Our Children* (Washington, DC: American Association of University Women, 1998); Emily Nye, "Computers and Gender: Noticing What Perpetuates Inequality," *English Journal* 80, no. 3 (March 1991): pp. 94–95. See also John Lipkin and David Sadker, "Sex Bias in Mathematics,

Computer Science and Technology: Report Card 3" (Washington, DC: Mid-Atlantic Center for Sex Equity, American University, 1984); Thomas Gilman, "Changes in Public Education: A Technological Perspective," series no. 1 (Eugene, OR: ERIC Clearinghouse on Educational Management, 1989).

29. Pamela Mendels, "Study Finds Big Gap in Schools," *New York Times on the Web,* 31 May 1997.

30. Pamela Mendels, "Study Shows Disparity in Schools' Internet Access," *New York Times on the Web,* 11 March 1998.

31. Royce T. Hall, "Blacks, Hispanics, Still Behind Whites in Level of PC Ownership," *The Wall Street Journal on the Web,* 3 August 1998; Hancock, Wingert, Rosenberg, and Samuels, "The Haves and the Have-Nots," pp. 50–53; Richard Wolf, "Computers Should Be Made Available to Children of Low-Income Families," *USA Today,* 18 September 1997.

32. A. Game and R. Pringle, *Gender at Work* (Boston: Allen & Unwin, 1983), p. 83.

33. American Association of University Women, *Gender Gaps: Where Schools Still Fail Our Children* (Washington, DC: American Association of University Women, 1998).

34. V. Robinson, "Methodology and Research-Practice Gap," *Educational Researcher* 27, no. 1 (1998): pp. 17–26.

35. J. Salpeter, "Taking Stock: What's the Research Saying?" *Technology and Learning* 18, no. 9 (1998); Mark Windschitl, "The WWW and Classroom Research: What Path Should We Take?" *Educational Researcher* 27, no. 1 (January/February 1998): pp. 28–32.

36. Patricia F. Campbell and S. S. Schwartz, "Microcomputers in the Preschool: Children, Parents, and Teachers," in Campbell & Greta G. Fein, eds., *Young Children and Microcomputers* (Englewood Cliffs, NJ: Prentice-Hall, 1986), pp. 37–44.

37. Andrew Trotter, "A Question of Effectiveness," *Education Week on the Web,* 1 October, 1998; Larry Cuban, *Teachers and Machines: The Classroom Use of Technology Since 1920* (New York: Teachers College Press, 1986).

Chapter Fifteen

1. Lilian Katz, "The Development of Preschool Teachers," *The Elementary School* Journal 73, no. 1 (October 1972): pp. 50–54.

2. Linda Darling-Hammond, "Teachers and Teaching: Testing Policy Hypothesis from a National Commission Report," *Educational Researcher* 27, no. 1 (January/February 1998): pp. 5–15; "Teachers Are the Key," *Reading Today* 14, no. 4 (February/March 1997): pp. 3–4.

3. National Center for Educational Statistics, *Characteristics of Stayers, Movers, and Leavers: Results from the Teacher Followup Survey, 1994–1995* (Washington, DC: U.S. Department of Education, 1997); David W. Grissmer and Sheila Natarj Kirby, *Teacher Attrition: The Uphill Climb to Staff the Nation's Schools* (Santa Monica, CA: RAND Corporation, 1987); Gus Haggertrom, Linda Darling-Hammond, and David W. Grissmer, *Teacher Attrition: The Uphill Climb to Staff the Nation's Schools* (Santa Monica, CA: RAND Corporation, 1988).

4. L. Huling-Austin, "Research on Learning to Teach: Implications for Teacher Induction and Mentoring," *Journal of Teacher Education* 43, no. 3 (May/June 1992): pp. 173–78.

5. Ellen Nakashima, "Montgomery Teachers May Face Peer Review," *Washington Post,* 2 January 1999, pp. B-1, B-6.

6. Judith W. Little, "Teachers' Professional Development in a Climate of Educational Reform," *Educational Evaluation and Policy Analysis* 15 (1993): pp. 129–51; Linda Darling-Hammond and Milbrey W. McLaughlin, "Policies That Support Professional Development in an Era of Reform," in Milbrey W. McLaughlin and Ida Oberman, eds., *Teaching and Learning: New Policies, New Practices* (New York: Teachers College Press, 1996), pp. 208–18.

7. National Education Association, *Status of the American Public School Teacher, 1995–1996* (Washington, DC: National Education Association, 1997).

8. J. Allen and Kimberley A. Gaskey, "Steps for Improving Climate in Scheduling," *Phi Delta Kappan* 79, no. 2 (October 1997): pp. 158–61; Daniel L. Burke, "Multi-Year Teacher/Student Relationships Are a Long-Overdue Arrangement," *Phi Delta Kappan* 77, no. 5 (January 1996): pp. 360–61; "Looping-Discovering the Benefits of Multiyear Teaching," *Education Update* 40, no. 2 (March 1998): pp. 1, 3–4.

9. Organization for Economic Cooperation and Development (OECD), *Education at a Glance, OECD Indicators* (Paris: OECD, 1995): pp. 176–77.

10. Maria Mihalik, "Thirty Minutes to Sell Yourself," *Teacher,* April 1991, p. 32d.

11. Ibid., p. 32e.

12. Quoted in "Forging a Profession," *Teacher* (September/October 1989): pp. 12, 16.

13. "National Certification Picks Up Steam," *American Teacher* 76, no. 6 (May/June 1992): p. 3.

14. Lee S. Schulman, "A Union of Insufficiencies: Strategies for Teacher Assessment in a Period of Educational Reform," *Educational Leadership* 46, no. 3 (November 1988): pp. 36–39.

15. Briant Farnsworth, Jerry Debenham, and Gerald Smith, "Designing and Implementing a Successful Merit Pay Program for Teachers," *Phi Delta Kappan* 73, no. 4 (December 1991): pp. 320–25.

16. Ibid.

17. *Is "Paying for Performance" Changing Schools?* The SREB Career Ladder Clearinghouse Report 1988 (Atlanta: Southern Regional Education Board), p. 8.

18. Adam Urbanski, "The Rochester Contract: A Status Report," *Educational Leadership* 46, no. 3 (November 1988): pp. 48–52.

19. Much of the information in this section was drawn from Marshall O. Donley, Jr.'s excellent article "The American School Teacher: From Obedient Servant to Militant Professional," *Phi Delta Kappan* 58, no. 1 (September 1976): pp. 112–17.

20. Albert Shanker, "Where We Stand: Is It Time for National Standards and Exams?" *American Teacher* 76, no. 6 (May/June 1992): p. 5.

A Final Word

1. David C. Berliner and Bruce J. Biddle, *The Manufactured Crisis* (Reading, MA: Addison-Wesley, 1995), p. 146. See also Richard Rothstein, *The Way We Were? The Myths and Realities of America's Student Achievement* (Washington, DC: Century Fund, 1998).

2. Lapointe quoted in Gerald W. Bracey, "The Second Bracey Report on the Condition of Public Education," *Phi Delta Kappan* (October 1992): pp. 104–17, cited in Berliner and Biddle, *The Manufactured Crisis,* p. 54.

3. Gerald W. Bracey, "U.S. Students: Better Than Ever," *Washington Post,* 22 December 1995, p. A-9; Robert J. Samuelson, "Three Cheers for Schools," *Newsweek,* 4 December 1995, p. 61. See also Berliner and Biddle, *The Manufactured Crisis,* pp. 13–64.

Appendix Four

1. George Spindler, *Doing the Ethnography of Schooling: Educational Anthropology in Action* (New York: Holt, Rinehart & Winston, 1982), p. 24.

2. Quoted in Spindler, *Doing the Ethnography of Schooling,* p. 24.

3. Marilyn Cohn, Robert Kottkamp, and Eugene Provanzo, Jr., *To Be a Teacher: Cases, Concepts, Observation Guides* (New York: Random House, 1987).

4. Eugene J. Webb, Donald Campbell, Richard Schwartz, and Lee Sechrest, *Unobtrusive Measures* (Skokie, IL: Rand McNally, 1966).

5. Hugh B. Price, "Multiculturalism: Myths and Realities," *Phi Delta Kappan* 74, no. 3 (November 1992): pp. 208–13.

6. Joseph Grannis, "The School as a Model of Society," *Harvard Graduate School of Education Association Bulletin* 21 (1967). See also Jules Henry, *Culture Against Man* (New York: Random House, 1963); Seymour Sarason, *The Culture of the School and the Problem of Change* (Boston: Allyn & Bacon, 1971); George D.

Spindler, ed., *Education and Culture: Anthropological Approaches* (New York: Holt, Rinehart & Winston, 1963); Talcott Parsons, "The School as a Social System: Some of Its Functions in American Society," in Robert J. Havighurst, Bernice L. Neugarten, and Jacqueline M. Falk, eds., *Society and Education* (Boston: Allyn & Bacon, 1967).

7. Sarason, *The Culture of the School and the Problem of Change.*

8. Philip Jackson, *Life in Classrooms* (New York: Holt, Rinehart & Winston, 1968).

9. Jackson, *Life in Classrooms.*

Photo Credits

Index